The Bloomsbury Companion to the Philosophy of Sport

The *Bloomsbury Companions* series is a major series of single volume companions to key research fields in the humanities aimed at postgraduate students, scholars and libraries. Each companion offers a comprehensive reference resource giving an overview of key topics, research areas, new directions and a manageable guide to beginning or developing research in the field. A distinctive feature of the series is that each companion provides practical guidance on advanced study and research in the field, including research methods and subject-specific resources.

Titles currently available in the series:

Aesthetics, edited by Anna Christina Ribeiro
Continental Philosophy, edited by John Mullarkey and Beth Lord
Epistemology, edited by Andrew Cullison
Ethics, edited by Christian Miller
Existentialism, edited by Jack Reynolds, Felicity Joseph and Ashley Woodward
Hegel, edited by Allegra de Laurentiis and Jeffrey Edwards
Hobbes, edited by S.A. Lloyd
Hume, edited by Alan Bailey and Dan O'Brien
Kant, edited by Gary Banham, Dennis Schulting and Nigel Hems
Leibniz, edited by Brendan Look
Locke, edited by S.-J. Savonious-Wroth, Paul Schuurman and Jonathan Walmsley
Metaphysics, edited by Robert W. Barnard and Neil A. Manson
Philosophical Logic, edited by Leon Horston and Richard Pettigrew
Philosophy of Language, edited by Manuel Garcia-Carpintero and Max Kolbel
Philosophy of Mind, edited by James Garvey
Philosophy of Science, edited by Steven French and Juha Saatsi
Plato, edited by Gerald A. Press
Pragmatism, edited by Sami Pihlström
Spinoza, edited by Wiep van Bunge

Forthcoming:

Aristotle, edited by Claudia Baracchi
Heidegger, edited by Francois Raffoul and Eric Sean Nelson
Political Philosophy, edited by Andrew Fiala and Matt Matravers
Socrates, edited by John Bussanich and Nicholas D. Smith

The Bloomsbury Companion to the Philosophy of Sport

Cesar R. Torres

B L O O M S B U R Y
LONDON · OXFORD · NEW YORK · NEW DELHI · SYDNEY

Bloomsbury Sport
An imprint of Bloomsbury Publishing Plc

50 Bedford Square   1385 Broadway
London   New York
WC1B 3DP   NY 10018
UK   USA

www.bloomsbury.com

BLOOMSBURY and the Diana logo are trademarks of Bloomsbury Publishing Plc

First published 2014

British Library Cataloguing-in-Publication Data
A catalogue record for this book is available from the British Library.

Library of Congress Cataloguing-in-Publication data has been applied for.

ISBN: HB: 978-1-4081-8257-4
        PB: 978-1-4729-2408-7

        ePDF: 978-1-4081-8258-1
        ePub: 978-1-4729-0539-0

2 4 6 8 10 9 7 5 3 1

Typeset in 9.5 on 12 Palatino by Saxon Graphics Ltd, Derby
Printed and bound in Great Britain by CPI Group (UK) Ltd, Croydon CR0 4YY

Acknowledgements
Cover photograph © Shutterstock
Inside photographs © The College at Brockport,
State University of New York Archives

To find out more about our authors and books visit www.bloomsbury.com.
Here you will find extracts, author interviews, details of forthcoming events
and the option to sign up for our newsletters.

Contents

Contributors

Diana Abad, Dortmund University
Jan Boxill, The University of North Carolina at Chapel Hill
Gunnar Breivik, Norwegian School of Sport Sciences
W.M. Brown, Trinity College
Daniel G. Campos, Brooklyn College, City University of New York
Chad Carlson, Eastern Illinois University
Lamartine P. DaCosta, Universidade Gama Filho
Mark Dyreson, Penn State University
Tim L. Elcombe, Wilfrid Laurier University
Warren P. Fraleigh, The College at Brockport, State University of New York
Francisco Javier López Frías, University of Valencia
Jeff Fry, Ball State University
Koyo Fukasawa, Tsukuba University
John Gleaves, California State University Fullerton
Peter F. Hager, The College at Brockport, State University of New York
Mark Hamilton, Ashland University
Alun Hardman, Cardiff Metropolitan University
Dennis Hemphill, Victoria University
Douglas Hochstetler, Penn State University Lehigh Valley
Peter M. Hopsicker, Penn State Altoona
Leslie A. Howe, University of Saskatchewan
Jesús Ilundáin-Agurruza, Lindfield College
Ivo Jirásek, Palacky University
Carwyn Jones, Cardiff School Metropolitan University
Scott Kretchmar, Penn State University
Sigmund Loland, Norwegian School of Sport Sciences
David Lunt, Southern Utah University
Irena Martínková, Charles University
Douglas W. McLaughlin, California State University Northridge
Vegard Fusche Moe, University College, Norway
William J. Morgan, University of Southern California
Stephen Mumford, The University of Nottingham and Norwegian University of
    Life Sciences
Claudia Pawlenka, Düsseldorf University
Adam G. Pfleegor, Mississippi State University
Simon Robinson, Leeds Metropolitan University
Danny Rosenberg, Brock University

J.S. Russell, Langara College
Emily Ryall, University of Gloucestershire
Pam R. Sailors, Missouri State University
Stephen E. Schmid, University of Wisconsin–Rock County
Angela J. Schneider, Western University
Robert L. Simon, Hamilton College
Mizuho Takemura, Waseda University
Sarah Teetzel, University of Manitoba
Cesar R. Torres, The College at Brockport, State University of New York
José Luis Pérez, Universitat Pompeu Fabra Trivino
Gregg Twietmeyer, Marshall University
Charlene Weaving, St. Francis Xavier University
Ron Welters, Radboud University Nijmegen

Introduction

Cesar R. Torres

The cultural significance of athletic activity is as multifold as the variety of forms athletic activity has taken across human cultures and historical periods. Much the same goes for philosophical activity, which, more often than not, directs its attention to culturally relevant phenomena. Yet, philosophical analyses of athletic activity were relatively sparse in most of human history. Although a number of distinguished philosophers, including Plato, Socrates, Marcus Tullius Cicero, Desiderius Erasmus, Thomas Hobbes and Friedrich Nietzsche, among others, used athletic contests as examples or metaphors to illustrate broader issues or points, such contests did not occupy a prominent and sustained role in these philosophers' inquiries. The advent of modern sports in the mid 19th century as well as the precipitous process of ludic diffusion and adaptation that ensued revitalized philosophical interest in athletic activity. With notable exceptions, until the mid 20th century, philosophical analyses of sport, at least in North America, were dominated by educational concerns and generated by an array of educators within the philosophy of education. Over time, philosophers and educators started to reflect on sport on its own terms instead of primarily as a means to achieve and further educational ends.

By the late 1960s, the philosophy of sport had emerged as an independent field of study, still practised by many physical educators but increasingly recognized and pursued by philosophers. In short, the philosophy of sport became a bona fide subject of philosophical inquiry in its own right. This, of course, did not mean the immediate embracing in philosophic circles of sport as a phenomenon worthy of scrutiny, but rather that sport was planted in the philosophic landscape and that philosophers started to take notice of it.

The publication, in 1969, of Paul Weiss' book *Sport: A Philosophic Inquiry* is generally acknowledged as a major development in this process. By then, Weiss, who in his academic life held positions at Bryn Mawr College, Yale University, Fordham University and the Catholic University of America, was a renowned philosopher and had founded *The Review of Metaphysics* and The Metaphysical Society of America. John Silber, a colleague from Boston University, wrote of Weiss that 'No one will forget his enlargement of the field of philosophy ... by his landmark examination of sports'.[1] Indeed, for Silber, Weiss 'was the first philosopher to recognize that sports ... were also worthy of the most careful and sustained philosophical examination'.[2] Even if Silber's laudatory remarks are slightly exaggerated, Weiss, as William J. Morgan has argued, was 'the more important influence here, given his high acclaim in the philosophic community'.[3]

That a philosopher of Weiss' calibre 'considered sport a topic worthy of his time and talents was not lost on his colleagues',[4] both in philosophy and education.

Weiss' book was followed in 1972 by three symposiums exclusively and explicitly dedicated to the philosophy of sport, the first of their kind. Two of these symposiums, the ones organized in February and October, were hosted at the State University of New York at Brockport, my current home institution, under the leadership of Warren P. Fraleigh, then Dean of the Faculty of Physical Education and Recreation, and with the support of the Center for Philosophic Exchange, directed by Howard E. Kiefer, who was then also Dean of the Faculty of the Humanities.[5] While Fraleigh recollected that participants in the February symposium 'discussed the possibilities of an organization',[6] the prospect of such a philosophy of sport organization matured towards the end of the year. According to Scott Kretchmar, who at the time was a faculty member at Brockport, Weiss and Fraleigh agreed during the interdisciplinary scientific congress held in Munich, Germany on the eve of the 1972 Olympic Games 'to form a steering committee for the formation of a scholarly society, a group that included two philosophers (Weiss and Richard Zaner) and two physical educators (Fraleigh and Ellen Gerber)'.[7] Weiss and Fraleigh 'determined that the recommendations of this group would be discussed at the ethics symposium later that fall in Brockport'.[8] The October symposium 'reflected the growing interest by physical education specialists in the philosophical problems arising from sport and by philosophers in sport as an area of human activity' and concluded 'with a discussion of forming a Philosophic Society for the Study of Sport'.[9] Kretchmar summarized the relevance of this symposium, which 'According to most sources ... was a fine success', for the future discipline in a letter to Kiefer. He wrote that:

> [...] this symposium coupled with our efforts last year, has provoked considerable interdisciplinary activity among philosophers, theologians and physical educators who share the common thematic interest of body-sport. As you may know, Paul Weiss is chairing the first session for the Philosophic Society for the Study of Sport at the APA meetings in Boston this Christmas. This society can be seen as a rather direct outgrowth of our activities here at Brockport. Thus, the Center for Philosophic Exchange not only helped in significantly adding to the body of knowledge in the philosophy of sport but also allowed for the laying of a foundation which will provoke further contributions of high quality.[10]

The events at Brockport in 1972, 'the ramifications of which', explained Kretchmar, 'far transcend the walls'[11] of his institution, led to the formal creation in December of that year of the Philosophic Society for the Study of Sport (PSSS) during the annual conference of the Eastern Division of the American Philosophical Association. Weiss was elected first president of the newly created society and Fraleigh its president-elect. The PSSS conducted its first full annual meeting in November of 1973 in Brockport and in 1974 published the first issue of the *Journal of the Philosophy of Sport*.[12] Both the annual meetings of the PSSS, which in 1999 changed

SYMPOSIUM ON THE PHILOSOPHY OF SPORT

SPONSORED BY:

The Department of Physical Education

The Center for Philosophical Exchange

The Department of Philosophy

STATE UNIVERSITY COLLEGE at BROCKPORT, NEW YORK

February 10, 11, 12, 1972
Thursday - Saturday

Front cover of the brochure of the *Symposium on the Philosophy of Sport* hosted at the State University of New York at Brockport on 10–12th February 1972. Courtesy of The College at Brockport, State University of New York Archives its name to the International Association for the Philosophy of Sport (IAPS) to reflect the increasing global nature of its membership, and the *Journal of the Philosophy of Sport* have served, since that time, as unique platforms to present, debate and disseminate philosophic analyses of sport.

In the preface of his book, Weiss asserted that while researching relevant literature he found himself:

> [...] in an endless desert through much of which, I am sorry to say, I had to make my way without compass or guide. I had to proceed alone, and try to think through the entire enterprise afresh. Some protection and guidance was, fortunately, provided by previous reflection on the nature of man, the aims of education, and the thrust of a number of activities and disciplines which seemed to have some relevance to sport.[13]

Considering that Weiss acknowledged finding some 'protection and guidance' in the scholarly production on education, it is somewhat puzzling that he described the literature on sport at large as an 'endless desert'. After all, in the 80 years or so before the publication of his book, educators had amassed a robust literature on the role of human movement, including sport, in education. In addition, for instance, the work of Johan Huizinga and Roger Caillois on play and games was widely available. More importantly, James W. Keating, a philosopher at DePaul University, had already published a series of articles that fell within what would soon become the philosophy of sport,[14] and Bernard Suits, a philosopher at the University of Waterloo, had already published his original account of games, soon to become a landmark study in the discipline.[15] Of course, there were other professionals reflecting on sport philosophically and publishing their work.[16] While admittedly the disciplinary literary landscape was not, to continue with Weiss' ecological metaphor, lush and tropical, neither was it an endless desert. The institutionalization of the philosophy of sport in the early 1970s invigorated and diversified the literary production in the philosophy of sport.

Philosophers, Morgan has argued, are notorious for their tendency 'to fret more about the nature, scope and aim of their intellectual craft, about what precisely it is that they do, than other intellectual workers in the vineyard'.[17] Consequently, 'their resultant conceptions of philosophy usually end up contested rather than accepted'.[18] There is no doubt that defining philosophy, and so the philosophy of sport, not to mention agreeing to any given definition, is a daunting task. Yet this challenge does not mean that the core preoccupations of philosophers, and in this case philosophers of sport, are essentially contested. The historical development of the discipline proves useful in this regard. Weiss proclaimed that his book 'makes but a beginning in a new enterprise, the examination of sport in terms of principles which are to be at once revelatory of the nature of sport and pertinent to other fields – indeed, to the whole of things and knowledge'.[19] Five years later, in 1974, Robert G. Osterhoudt, the first editor of the *Journal of the Philosophy of Sport*, wrote in the introduction to the journal's inaugural issue that the philosophy of sport was committed 'to the presentation of genuinely philosophical examinations, or reflective authentic examinations of the nature and significance of sport … [and] systematic discussions of issues peculiar to sport until they are reduced to matters of a distinctly philosophic order'.[20] More than four decades after Weiss' and Osterhoudt's initial demarcations of the discipline, Mike McNamee conceived it as being:

> […] concerned with the conceptual analysis and interrogation of key ideas and issues of sports and related practices. At its most general level, it is concerned with articulating the nature and purposes of sport. The philosophy of sport not only gathers insights from the various fields of philosophy as they open up our appreciation of sports practices and institutions, but also generates substantive and comprehensive views of sport itself. The philosophy of sport is never fixed: its methods require of practitioners an inherently self-critical conception of intellectual activity, one that is continuously challenging its own preconceptions and guiding principles both as to the nature and purposes of philosophy and of sports.[21]

McNamee's approach is more encompassing than those of sport philosophy's early practitioners and includes practices such as coaching, health promotion, sport journalism, exercise science and, not surprisingly, education, along with other cognate intellectual areas 'insofar as they challenge and critically inform our understanding of sports'.[22] The difference in scope should not obscure what appears to be common to these approaches – namely, that the philosophy of sport is primarily concerned with exploring the nature of sport (and related practices), how it functions, what its significance is and how it fits with other spheres of human experience. Evidently, even if it is implausible to have complete accord over the definition of the philosophy of sport, it does not seem to be equally implausible to strongly agree over the sort of issues and questions with which philosophers of sport are primarily engaged. I agree, and have written elsewhere, that core issues and questions can be identified, including inquiring what role sport should play in a satisfactory life, what it means to live sport satisfactorily and what type of satisfaction emerges from a life dedicated to sport.[23]

While the sorts of issues and questions philosophers of sport primarily engage with can be divided along the lines of the major branches of philosophic inquiry, which surely convey a sense of what the discipline is all about, they all fundamentally lead to the interrogation and analysis of what sport means and how it contributes to a good or meaningful life.[24] This is in the spirit of Weiss' and Osterhoudt's initial proposals for the philosophy of sport, although one has to read beyond their seemingly positivist appeal to principles to examine sport and the reduction of its issues to a distinct philosophic order. After all, Weiss hoped that his book would 'make evident how one might profitably approach any activity that is widely practiced and observed, but insufficiently understood'.[25] Along the same lines, Osterhoudt maintained that the philosophy of sport 'reveals what sport fundamentally is and what it is ultimately for'.[26] It is not a stretch, given their writings on sport, to claim that Weiss and Osterhoudt were flexible and pluralistic regarding the philosophic exploration of sport.

Center for Philosophic Exchange

STATE UNIVERSITY COLLEGE AT BROCKPORT

Announces a free public address in the general area of
the Philosophy of sport by Heffer Professor of Philosophy

PAUL WEISS

Catholic University of America

on

RECORDS AND THE MAN

With a response by

Associate Professor of Philosophy

RICHARD SCHACHT

University of Illinois

THURSDAY, FEBRUARY 10, 1972
8:00 P.M., EDWARDS HALL - ROOM 103 (GOLD)

FOR FURTHER INFORMATION CONTACT
HOWARD E. KIEFER CENTER DIRECTOR

Flyer of the "major address," as the opening paper was described in its programme, of the *Symposium on the Philosophy of Sport* held on the evening of 10th February 1972. Courtesy of The College at Brockport, State University of New York Archives

Be that as it may, the institutionalization of the philosophy of sport clearly established the goal and scope of the discipline and, at the same time, established a programme for its development. As can be seen, the contours of the discipline have been enlarged, both thematically and methodologically, but its goal has remained fairly stable, although it has been sharpened and now reflects the discipline's currently more variegated concerns. More than four decades of sport philosophy have spawned a significant volume of literature. Undoubtedly, the discipline has left behind the days when the literature on sport could be described, as Weiss exaggeratingly did, as leaving 'a place for only an occasional idea, and this is usually borrowed and rather frayed'.[27] As this companion clearly attests, nowadays the volume and, perhaps more importantly, the quality of the sport philosophy literature are remarkable. Equally remarkable is that the brunt of such an accomplished corpus of literature was developed in the relatively short period that covers the early 1970s to the present. In my judgement, there is no doubt that, following the call of those who established the discipline, philosophers of sport have made enormous strides in, paraphrasing Osterhoudt, refining our philosophical understanding of and sensitivity for sport.[28] The readers, hopefully with the assistance of this companion, can evaluate for themselves the extent to which this is the case.

Thus, this companion, by providing an overview of the advances in the philosophical understanding of sport (and related practices), serves as a measure of the development of the philosophy of sport but it also constitutes an expression of the discipline's state of the art. It could be said that this companion reflects the identity of the philosophy of sport and the process by which such an identity came to be. While collectively the contributions included here trace the philosophy of sport's genealogy as well as its present contours, they also speculate about potential disciplinary future directions.

This companion has several parts. Part I includes an essay surveying and critically analysing the historical development of philosophic ideas about sport, from antiquity to the dawn of the 21st century. It reflects on key stages and events, figures, major publications and theoretical developments in the discipline. Part II is on research methodology. The three essays in this part discuss the theoretical foundations, application, issues and characteristic challenges of the research methodologies typically implemented in the discipline. Part III includes 12 essays that address vital issues at the forefront of key research areas in the philosophy of sport. These essays expertly cover chartered terrain but also survey future issues and lines of inquiry. Rather than reflecting the traditional divisions of philosophy, these essays are organized around prominent, relevant and recurring themes in the philosophy of sport literature. In this sense, many of the essays knit several of these divisions together to have ample analyses of the themes at hand. This is followed by Part IV, which features four essays venturing into pressing topics that are currently shaping, and probably will continue shaping, the disciplinary landscape. Included in this section is an essay on the relatively recent development of the philosophy of sport around the world. Disciplinary development in the non-English speaking world will undoubtedly affect the future of the philosophy of sport in positive ways.

Next is Part V, which encompasses key terms and concepts that are central to understanding the historical development and state of the art of the discipline. These key terms and concepts could be seen as extended and detailed dictionary entries. Part VI comprises two essays. The first outlines the resources available to students, instructors and researchers in the philosophy of sport, including bibliographic and electronic resources, associations and journals. The second provides information on career opportunities, professional development (i.e. conferences, grants and awards) and examples of syllabuses for academic courses on the philosophy of sport. Closing the companion is Part VII, an annotated bibliography of notable breadth and depth that covers the evolution of the philosophy of sport literature. It should be noted that all contributions in this companion were specially commissioned and previously unpublished.

Any work of this kind has limitations. One limitation of this companion is that it deals with the philosophy of sport as it developed in the English-speaking world. A plausible explanation for this is that the discipline emerged and flourished in North Atlantic academic circles, where English is the lingua franca. Nevertheless, it is a limitation and to alleviate it, this companion includes, as indicated above, an essay devoted to the philosophy of sport around the world. There are now vibrant and expanding communities of teachers and scholars dedicated to the philosophy of sport in different corners of the world whose work should be recognized and welcomed. I am hopeful that the exchanges among these groups will increase in the future. It is also worth mentioning that this companion includes, based on institutional affiliations, professionals from 11 countries representing four of the world's continents. This multiplicity of voices, which in many cases comes from professionals, including myself, whose native language is not English, enriches the texture of this companion by diversifying the views, interest and perspectives it presents. Female sport philosophers constitute almost 23 per cent of the 49 contributors to this companion. While this representation is better than the most reliable statistics regarding the percentage of female philosophers in the faculty ranks in the United States (16.6 per cent), it shows that female philosophers interested in the study of sport and other related subject matters still face significant obstacles in academic philosophy. Hence, one of the challenges sport philosophy has for the future is to continue fostering a welcoming, nurturing and inclusive climate for women and other minority groups.[29]

Even though this companion is a rather large volume, I nevertheless had to make difficult choices about its scope and content. Its size does not mean, or even imply, the inclusion of everything that is of interest. I am sure I have left out themes, developments and bibliographic references that some colleagues might deem highly relevant to the philosophy of sport. My best reply is that the 22 essays, 19 entries introducing key terms and concepts, and the annotated bibliography included are central to charting and understanding the historical development of the discipline as well as its state at the present time along with potential future directions. I suspect that whatever questions might arise regarding the omissions in this companion, these questions would not preclude my colleagues from agreeing as much on its intent as on the relevance of its nature,

In the early afternoon of 11th February 1972, the *Symposium on the Philosophy of Sport* organized a "one-hour unrehearsed television tape on matters related to the previous evening's papers."* The participants in the session were, from left to right, Paul Weiss (The Catholic University of America), Richard Schacht (University of Illinois), and Warren P. Fraleigh and Joseph Gilbert (State University of New York at Brockport). Courtesy of The College at Brockport, State University of New York Archives

---

* Howard E. Kiefer to Richard Schacht, October 27, 1971, "Center for Philosophic Exchange/International Year. Correspondence and Papers. RG 18/10/5," The College at Brockport, State University of New York Archives.

scope and inclusions. Large as it is, and with the limitations made explicit here, this companion does present a reasonably comprehensive, updated and authoritative guide to a relatively young but sophisticated and exciting discipline. My hope is that this book will prove beneficial not only to established scholars in the philosophy of sport and the field of study known as sport studies but also to graduate and advanced undergraduate students in these domains. Administrators in international sport federations, professional and amateur sport organizations, sport advocacy groups and governmental and non-governmental institutions related to sport might also find it useful.

I would like to conclude this introduction by briefly musing about the future of the philosophy of sport. To do so, we need first to briefly touch upon the past. In 1988, William J. Morgan and Klaus V. Meier wrote, somewhat enthusiastically, that since the institutionalization of the discipline, 'particularly in the last decade, a significant and increasingly sophisticated corpus of literature on the philosophy of sport has emerged'.[30] Seven years later, these two philosophers acknowledged important changes in the literature. Metaphysical and aesthetic investigations of sport were increasingly sharing the philosophical stage with ethical analyses of sport. In spite of this growing movement, Morgan and Meier thought that 'the stature of the philosophy of sport as an academic subject [had] improved only slightly in the intervening years'.[31] Two years later, in 1997, pondering over its tribulations, Kretchmar declared that 'a final verdict regarding the disciplinary movement in sport philosophy is still difficult to reach',[32] but he admitted that there were signs suggesting that philosophy might be returning to the *agora*, where educated people make philosophic progress using less technical jargon on issues of deep human concern, including sport and other forms of human movement.[33] Three years later, Morgan was also encouraged and provided 'an upbeat prognosis of its [the philosophy of sport] future'.[34] Morgan based his prognosis on a revival of the American pragmatist tradition in philosophy at large and a deepening of moral studies in the philosophy of sport (and related practices). The good augur was that these developments would temper the dominance of analytic philosophy and its concomitant emphasis on scholasticism, positivist approaches and narrow technical issues that demand research methods paralleling science. Furthermore, these developments would promote the flourishing of disciplines such as the philosophy of sport, and interests within them that have been, so far, relatively neglected, because such developments rest on the belief that 'the central aim of philosophy is to apply critical intelligence to the resolution of social problems'.[35] Indisputably, sport is a social practice of tremendous appeal. It is equally indisputable that, given the excesses and quandaries that plague it, sport demands our philosophical attention. Therefore, the developments mentioned by Morgan would further undercut the dismissive regard for sport in the academy. Such dismissal has been deplored by Drew Hyland, among many others, 'as entirely unjustified'.[36]

What, then, is the future of the philosophy of sport? Disciplinary developments in the last 15 years or so seem to confirm Kretchmar's and Morgan's moderate optimism. On the one hand, the literature keeps expanding, demonstrating vitality through a plurality of interests, research methodologies and philosophical traditions and histories as well as vibrant disputes in both theoretical and applied issues. In 2007, a second journal, *Sport, Ethics and Philosophy*, was added to the discipline while a third journal, *Fair Play. Revista de Filosofía, Ética y Derecho del Deporte*, which accepts submissions in five languages, was added in 2013. In addition, a number of philosophy and sport studies journals keep publishing sport philosophy research articles. Consistent with this growth, the IAPS annual conferences are very well attended and, at least since 2011, have included over 110 papers each year, a marked improvement from a decade ago. Especially encouraging is the number of graduate students in attendance. Moreover, it is clear that the composition of IAPS is more international than ever. For instance, based on institutional affiliations, there were 21 countries represented at the 2013 annual conference and membership levels of IAPS are rapidly approaching an all-time high. Finally, it is worth reiterating that there are now several national and regional sport philosophy associations around the world and an increasing body of literature is being produced in different languages. The translation project recently launched by IAPS is meant to direct the attention of anglophone sport philosophers to excellent work by colleagues whose primary language of publication is not English.

There is much to be optimistic about with regard to the future of the philosophy of sport. However, there remain areas in which improvement is desirable. First, sport philosophy courses have declined or disappeared from many undergraduate curricula in kinesiology programmes. The fact that the American Kinesiology Association has identified 'Cultural, Historical and Philosophical Dimensions of Physical Activity' as one of 'four fundamental areas that should be included in the core of all undergraduate Kinesiology programs'[37] might help reverse this unfortunate trend. Anecdotal evidence suggests that sport philosophers are finding less resistance in academic circles, both in kinesiology and philosophy departments. In fact, they might now be more welcomed and valued than ever before for what they bring to the understanding of sport (and related practices).

A second concern focuses on the fact that there are still very few graduate programmes in the philosophy of sport. This is a serious issue for which no easy remedy exits. Perhaps the growing number of scholars engaged in the philosophy of sport coupled with the developments described above will eventually lead to an increased production of new scholars and the introduction of more graduate programmes in the discipline.

A third area of concern relates to the philosophy of sport's relationship with education. Sometime in the 1960s, the philosophy of sport cut ties with educational concerns to develop, as Osterhoudt put it in 1974, 'a progressively greater association with philosophy proper … and to take its rightful place besides the other so-termed departmental philosophies'.[38] There were undoubtedly benefits in this move, but there were also drawbacks, one of which was the distancing of many educators by what they considered an esoteric turn driven by the influence of analytic philosophy in the nascent philosophy of sport. The discipline, it should be remembered, was institutionalized by both philosophers and educators. Perhaps recent developments in the discipline described by Morgan will also lead to renewed collaborations between these two groups. One way or the other, the future of the philosophy of sport belongs to its practitioners. To my knowledge, the best way to keep expanding and legitimizing the discipline is to maintain a high level of productivity and engage politically at different levels in order to let academic colleagues and society at large know why the philosophic study of sport (and related practices) is a worthwhile endeavour, especially in current times.

Pondering the past and future of the philosophy of sport, Fraleigh wrote in 1983 that 'Scholarly Societies, like rivers, flow quietly and deeply and, over time, but in forceful ways, make their impact on the human landscape'.[39] The discipline, much as he predicted and hoped for 30 years ago, continued to 'jes' keep rollin' along' and is healthier, stronger and more vibrant than ever before.[40] In light of this auspicious present, but keeping in mind the very real challenges and opportunities looming on the horizon, we should keep expanding the work of this scholarly community and enjoy the fruits of such work. This will hopefully lead, as Fraleigh put it, the achievement of 'a more complete understanding of sport' and its place in a good and meaningful life.[41]

I would like to close by enthusiastically thanking the contributors to this companion. It has been a pleasure to work with them. Their dedication to the philosophy of sport is admirable as was their patience with my questions and requests. Their contributions and the fruitful exchanges they prompted helped me understand the discipline better. I am also grateful to Kirsty Schaper and Sarah Cole, Senior Commissioning Editor and Editor for Sport and Fitness at Bloomsbury. That a publishing company of Bloomsbury's stature was interested in the philosophy of sport is another sign of the discipline's stature. This companion is part of Bloomsbury Companions, a series of single volume companions to different fields in the humanities. Kirsty and Sarah have been, at all times, diligent, courteous and efficient. I am especially grateful to my wife, María Fernanda Astiz, who has been tremendously tolerant and supportive during the time in which this companion was conceived and materialized beyond what one could realistically expect. This companion is dedicated to Warren P. Fraleigh; the philosophy of sport is greatly indebted to his vision and leadership. This companion is also dedicated to Scott Kretchmar, who, since my years as a graduate student at the Pennsylvania State University, has mentored, advised and inspired me. For these reasons, I am deeply thankful.

Batavia, New York
November, 2013

Notes

1   John Silber, 'In Memoriam: Paul Weiss (1901–2002)', *The Review of Metaphysics* 56 (2002): 253.
2   Ibid.
3   William J. Morgan, 'The Philosophy of Sport: A Historical and Conceptual Overview and a Conjecture Regarding Its Future', in *Handbook of Sport Studies*, eds. Jay Coakley and Eric Dunning (London: SAGE, 2000), 205.
4   Ibid.

5   Today, the institution is known as The College at Brockport, State University of New York. The February and October events were called 'Symposium on the Philosophy of Sport' and 'Symposium on Sport and Ethics', respectively. The third event, called 'First Canadian Symposium on the Philosophy of Sport and Physical Activity', was organized in Windsor, Ontario in May. See Robert G. Osterhoudt, 'Preface', in *The Philosophy of Sport. A Collection of Essays*, ed., Robert G. Osterhoudt (Springfield, IL: Charles C. Thomas, 1973), ix-xi; and idem, *The Philosophy of Sport. An Overview* (Champaign, IL: Stipes, 1991), 19–20.

6   Warren P. Fraleigh, 'Philosophic Society for the Study of Sport 1972–1983', *Journal of the Philosophy of Sport* 10 (1984): 4. See also 'Sport Philosophy Meeting at College 10, 11, 12, Feb. to Feature Dr Paul Weiss', *Brockport News* (Brockport, NY), 4 February, 1972, 3.

7   Scott Kretchmar, 'Philosophy of Sport', in *The History of Exercise and Sport Science*, eds., John D. Massengale and Richard A. Swanson (Champaign, IL: Human Kinetics, 1997), 191. Fraleigh wrote that the steering committee was formed after the October symposium. See Fraleigh, 'Philosophic Society for the Study of Sport 1972–1983', 5. The interdisciplinary scientific congress was called 'Sport in the Modern World – Chances and Problems'. See Kay Schiller and Christopher Young, *The 1972 Munich Olympics and the Making of Modern Germany* (Berkeley and Los Angeles: University of California Press, 2010), 143–4; and Henry Kamm, 'Arts to Rival Athletics at Olympics', *The New York Times*, 4 August, 1972, 12.

8   Kretchmar, 'Philosophy of Sport', 191.

9   'Third Brockport Symposium Discusses Sport and Ethics', *The Stylus* (Brockport, NY), 31 October, 1972, 15.

10   Scott Kretchmar to Howard Kiefer, 9 November, 1972, 'Center for Philosophic Exchange/International Year. Correspondence and Papers. RG 18/10/5', The College at Brockport, State University of New York Archives. In his letter, Kretchmar wrote the date as 9/11/72. Given the letter's content, I believe this is an error and he actually meant 11/9/1972.

11   Ibid.

12   See Osterhoudt, 'Preface'; and idem, *The Philosophy of Sport. An Overview*, 20. Warren P. Fraleigh has recently reflected on the beginnings of IAPS; see his article 'IAPS – Past to Future', *Journal of the Philosophy of Sport* 39 (2012): 1–10.

13   Paul Weiss, *Sport: A Philosophic Inquiry* (Carbondale, IL: Southern Illinois Press, 1969), vii-viii.

14   See the following articles by James Keating: 'Winning in Sport and Athletics', *Thought* 38 (1963): 201–10; 'Sportsmanship as a Moral Category', *Ethics* 75 (1964): 25–35; 'Athletics and the Pursuit of Excellence', *Education* 85 (1965): 428–31; and 'The Heart of the Problem of Amateur Athletics', *The Journal of General Education* 16 (1965): 261–72.

15   See his article 'What Is a Game?', *Philosophy of Science* 34 (1967): 148–56.

16   See, for example, Aurel Kolnai, 'Games and Aims', *Proceedings of the Aristotelian Society* 66 (1965–1966): 103–28; John W. Loy, 'The Nature of Sport: A Definitional Effort', *Quest* 10 (1968): 1–15 and Earle F. Zeigler, *Problems in the History and Philosophy of Physical Education and Sport* (Englewood Cliffs, NJ: Prentice-Hall, 1968). A very early, perhaps premature, example is H. Graves, 'A Philosophy of Sport', *The Contemporary Review* 78 (1900): 877–93.

17   Morgan, 'The Philosophy of Sport: A Historical and Conceptual Overview and a Conjecture Regarding Its Future', 206.

18   Ibid.

19   Weiss, *Sport: A Philosophic Inquiry*, viii.

20   Robert G. Osterhoudt, 'Introduction', *Journal of the Philosophy of Sport* 1 (1974): 2.

21 Mike McNamee, 'Sport Philosophy', in *Directory of Sport Sciences*, 6th ed., eds. Herbert Haag, Kari Keskinen and Margaret Talbot (n.p.: International Council of Sport Science and Physical Education, 2013), 101. In 2008, Leon Culbertson, Mike McNamee and Emily Ryall defined the philosophy of sport in the same terms. See their *Resource Guide to the Philosophy of Sport and Ethics of Sport* (Hospitality, Leisure, Sport and Tourism Network, Oxford: 2008), 1.

22 Mike McNamee, 'Sport, Ethics and Philosophy; Context, History, Prospects', *Sport, Ethics and Philosophy* 1 (2007): 4.

23 Cesar R. Torres, *Gol de media cancha. Conversaciones para disfrutar el deporte plenamente* (Buenos Aires: Miño y Dávila, 2011), 17.

24 For a discussion of the major questions and issues that sport philosophers address and how they relate to the major branches of philosophic inquiry, see Morgan 'The Philosophy of Sport: A Historical and Conceptual Overview and a Conjecture Regarding Its Future', 205–9; and idem, 'Philosophy and Physical Education', in *The Handbook of Physical Education*, eds. David Kirk, Doune Macdonald and Mary O'Sullivan (London: Sage, 2006), 99–106.

25 Weiss, *Sport: A Philosophic Inquiry*, ix.

26 Osterhoudt, *The Philosophy of Sport. An Overview*, 21.

27 Weiss, *Sport: A Philosophic Inquiry*, vii.

28 Osterhoudt, 'Introduction', 1.

29 See Sally Haslanger, 'Women in Philosophy? Do the Math', *The Stone. Opinionator. Exclusive Online Commentary from The Times. New York Times*, 2 September, 2013 <http://opinionator.blogs.nytimes.com/2013/09/0 2/women-in-philosophy-do-the-math/?_r=0> (accessed 27 October, 2013).

30 William J. Morgan and Klaus V. Meier, 'Preface', in *Philosophic Inquiry in Sport*, eds., William J. Morgan and Klaus V. Meier (Champaign, IL: Human Kinetics, 1988), ix.

31 William J. Morgan and Klaus V. Meier, 'Preface', in *Philosophic Inquiry in Sport*, 2nd ed., eds., William J. Morgan and Klaus V. Meier (Champaign, IL: Human Kinetics, 1995), vii.

32 Kretchmar, 'Philosophy of Sport', 196.

33 Ibid., 197–8.

34 Morgan, 'The Philosophy of Sport: A Historical and Conceptual Overview and a Conjecture Regarding Its Future', 209.

35 Morgan, 'Philosophy and Physical Education', 106.

36 Drew Hyland, *Philosophy of Sport* (New York: Paragon, 1990), xiii.

37 American Kinesiology Association, 'The Undergraduate Core in Kinesiology', circa 2009 <http://www.american kinesiology.org/the-undergraduate-core-in-kinesiology> (accessed 27 October, 2013).

38 Osterhoudt, 'Introduction', 1.

39 Fraleigh, 'Philosophic Society for the Study of Sport 1972–1983', 7.

40 Ibid.

41 Ibid., 3.

Part I

History and Development

2 A History of Philosophic Ideas about Sport

David Lunt and Mark Dyreson

Philosophers have since antiquity pondered the role of sporting practices in relation to the human condition. A systematic philosophy of sport, however, has developed only since the middle of the 20th century. While activities that can be broadly defined as sport and philosophy can be found in all human cultures and time periods, modern scholars have mainly charted the history of ideas about athletics in Western civilization. This history of the philosophy of sport thus begins, as do most surveys, with Ancient Greece.

The Ancient Greeks

Athletics, sport and competition played an important role in the society and culture of Ancient Greece. Although scholars have investigated the possibility of athletic activity among the Bronze Age cultures of the Minoans and Mycenaeans, the lack of written sources precludes modern understanding of the ideals, values or even rules of these activities. With the development of alphabetic writing and the emergence of literary culture during Greece's Archaic period (beginning around 800 BCE), the attitudes towards competition, athletics and sport become accessible to modern scholars. From the works of Homer, attributed to the 8th century BCE, to the institution of the great Panhellenic contests, on through the Classical, Hellenistic and Roman periods, and into the Common Era, the prevalence of athletics and athletic culture is unmistakable.

Athletic contests served many purposes for the Ancient Greeks. Among other things, they provided an important vehicle to seek and to demonstrate excellence and virtue (*arete*), to construct identity in comparison with non-Greek peoples, and to inculcate their youth with appropriate civic and educational values.

Agon, Arete and Athla

In the 19th century, Jacob Burckhardt characterized Greece's Archaic Age as 'The Agonal Age'. The *agon*, or competitive spirit, summarized by Burckhardt with the Homeric line as the desire 'to always be the first and to outdo all others', was unique to Greeks among ancient peoples.[1] Although later scholars have downplayed the uniqueness of this characteristic to the Greeks, none have denied its importance in Greek culture and society. Whether attributable to the dynamics of a 'shame-culture' or to a thirst for honours, the 'agonistic spirit' of the Ancient Greeks caused them to compete in war, sport, politics, art, music and nearly every aspect of society.[2]

The athletic contest, or *agon*, represented an important proving ground for competitors to vie for victory and its attendant *arete*. Athletic contests were cultural, social and religious events, to be taken seriously, as the term *agon*, or 'struggle', implies (the English word 'agony' is a derivative). The Greek verb 'to play' (*paizein*) was never used in relation to athletics. Games were not 'played'. They were struggled.[3]

The goal of the agonistic struggles of ancient Greek culture was *arete*, an ancient Greek word that English speakers usually translate to 'virtue', but which also encompasses much more. As Heather Reid noted, *arete* includes 'particular virtues such as courage, self-discipline, fairness and wisdom' while Stephen Miller added 'skill, prowess, pride, excellence, valour and nobility'.[4] The pursuit and glorification of *arete* represented the largest unifying theme in ancient Greek athletics.

Another important component of the contests is the *athla*. Translated as 'prizes', an *athlete*, then, is one who competes for a prize. Lucrative prizes and rewards awaited those who claimed victory in the prestigious Crown Games of Ancient Greece, as well as a wide array of regional and localized contests. Despite modern assumptions (since discredited and discarded) about the idealized amateurism of the Ancient Greeks, a successful athlete could have earned a comfortable or even luxurious lifestyle through athletic victories. Whether or not such success brought abundant *arete*, however, was a topic of debate among the Ancient Greeks.

Athletics in Epic

The epics of Homer, part of a larger epic cycle of poems relating ancient Greek myths, played an integral role in crystalising and disseminating the cultural norms, ethics, values and ideals of the Ancient Greeks to future generations. Furthermore, the stories of Homer, like athletic competitions, were Panhellenic in nature, providing a cultural touchstone for all Greeks.

In Homer's epic poem the *Iliad*, the great hero Achilles offers prizes to his fellow Greeks in athletic contests after the funeral of his dear friend Patroclus. Homer's vivid account relates the competition and outcome of each event, including a chariot race, boxing, wrestling, a foot race, a throwing contest, spear thrusting and archery. These contests provide a forum for Homer's heroes to demonstrate their *arete*. Unsurprisingly, with the exception of Achilles, who acts as sponsor and declines to compete, the most accomplished of the *Iliad*'s heroes play the largest role in the athletic competitions. Thus, the pre-eminent Greek heroes display the greatest amount of *arete* through their athletic achievements.[5]

In the *Odyssey*, athletic competition reveals the *arete* of Odysseus during his long journey back to Ithaca when he competes with the Phaeacians. Odysseus impresses his hosts with a mighty throw of the discus. This immediately establishes him as an accomplished athlete and a powerful presence. King Alcinous quickly recognizes Odysseus' abilities and compliments him for his *arete*.[6] Here, as in the *Iliad*, the greatest athlete possesses the greatest amount of *arete*.

Nowhere was the opportunity to demonstrate athletic *arete* greater than at the famed festival to Zeus at Olympia. Held in the summertime once every four years, this celebration, along with the other 'Crown Game' festivals to Apollo at Delphi, to Zeus at Nemea and to Poseidon at Isthmia, carried with it enormous prestige for both competitors and winners. Traditionally dated to 776 BCE (although modern scholarship consistently pushes for a later date[7]), these athletic contests represented an integral part of an elaborate series of rituals, including procession, sacrifice and offerings. The religious connections of these Panhellenic festivals were central to their importance.

Arete, Aristocracy and Authority

Much of ancient Greek history describes the social strife suffered in individual city states, or *poleis*, as aristocratic elements and the occasional tyrant sought to consolidate power over the general citizen bodies. As the word itself suggests, *aristocracy* to the Ancient Greeks meant 'rule by the *aristoi*', or 'the best'. The *aristoi* were identifiable by their abundance of *arete*, and possession of *arete*, or virtue, in the minds of aristocracy indicated an individual's right to political and social authority. Aristocrats and tyrants capitalized on their athletic *arete* to justify their political power.[8] On the other hand, scholars have argued that the rules of athletic competition, perhaps paradoxically, also reinforced the rule of law among the Greeks. There existed a certain inherent equality among competitors in their contests of speed and strength and the 'absolute standards' of the competitions constituted a 'basic isonomia' or 'equal rights' among the competitors. Despite any inherent advantages of birth and wealth, those athletes who stepped into the stadium competed literally on a level playing field and enjoyed a basic equality with the other competitors.[9] In all of these circumstances, the connections between political authority and athletic competition relied on the possession and display of *arete*.

Gymnasium Culture and Athletics as Identity

Participation in athletics among the Ancient Greeks served as a marker of identity, with athletics helping to designate the superiority of the Greeks to the so-called barbarian 'other'. Herodotus related an anecdote where the invading Persian king Xerxes inquired about these Greeks who had recently killed so many of his soldiers at the Battle of Thermopylae in 480 BCE. When told of the Greek Olympic Games, and that the only tangible prize was a crown of olive branches, Xerxes expressed disbelief, exclaiming his surprise that the Greeks contended not for money, but for *arete*.[10] Although this is almost certainly a fictitious anecdote, the story would have resonated with Herodotus' Greek audience, and indicates the role of athletics in constructing Hellenic identity in comparison with the foreign Persians.[11] Similarly, Lucian, a writer during the 2nd century CE, composed an entire dialogue using athletics to reinforce the same dichotomy between Greeks and barbarians, emphasizing the merits of Greek-style athletic training.[12]

By the Hellenistic period (323–31 BCE), any Greek city-state of note maintained a gymnasium for its citizens. Athletic culture in the gymnasium centred on instruction and training, rather than competition. It was here that young Greek men learned techniques for sport, but also philosophy, literature, rhetoric and other intellectual pursuits. Indeed, many gymnasiums featured libraries, and both Plato and Aristotle attached their philosophical schools to gymnasiums at Athens in the 4th century BCE.[13] Heather Reid has emphasized the importance of gymnasium settings for the Socratic dialogues, drawing clear comparisons between the struggle of athletic competitors and the verbal wrangling of Socratic debates. Both activities, she noted, aimed at cultivating *arete*, whether training the body or training the mind.[14]

The Philosophers and Athletics

Despite these popular approvals, Greek intellectuals sometimes criticized the richness of athletic rewards and urged others to seek *arete* through philosophical rather than athletic avenues. The contributions of Ancient Greece's most influential philosophers, Plato and Aristotle (and Socrates through the writings of Plato), embraced athletic training and competition as a useful tool for educating ideal citizens, provided it acted as a component of a balanced curriculum. Rather than criticizing the athletic culture of the Ancient Greeks, these opinions condemned imbalance and excess.

In the 4th century BCE, the orator Isocrates marvelled that athletes should receive public honours when they contributed little to the common good. He began his *Panegyricus* address, delivered at Olympia and intended for all Greeks to hear, with a pronouncement that a single man aspiring to good (i.e. himself) might have a greater impact on others than all the athletes at the games.[15] Another anecdote relates the visit to the Isthmian Games of the 4th century BCE philosopher Diogenes of Sinope, founder of the Cynic movement of philosophy. Known for his dog-like shamelessness (the word 'cynic' is derived from the ancient Greek word for 'dog') in rejecting human convention, custom and traditional morality, Diogenes was famous for sleeping in the open and relieving himself in public. At the Isthmian Games, Diogenes declared his own struggles against thirst, hunger, physical pain and cold to be nobler than the contests of the athletes. The sprigs of pine or olive on offer to competitors were trivial tokens to Diogenes, who declared his own intention was to win 'happiness and *arete* throughout all his life'.[16] Like Isocrates, Diogenes considered his own endeavours superior to those of the competing athletes as both he and the athletes pursued the same goal of *arete*.

A fragment from the philosopher Xenophanes, who lived in the 6th century BCE, decried the honours and glory bestowed on athletes, claiming that a good athlete does not make a city well governed, nor does athletic victory enrich the city. Indeed, Xenophanes contended that he himself was more worthy of prizes and recognition than athletes, and that his 'wisdom' was 'better than the strength of men and of horses'.[17] Similarly, a section from a fragmentary play of Euripides criticized the race of athletes as the worst of the evils afflicting Greece since their skills are useless in war and statecraft. An immoderate athlete was 'a slave to his jaw and overcome by his belly'.[18] Such excessive behaviour contradicted the balanced and moderate lifestyle idealized by the Greek philosophers. These philosophers condemned excess, not athletics, and considered athletics an important component of a complete education.[19]

Ancient Greeks considered athletics to be an integral part of every basic education. Aristotle suggested four areas of education: reading and writing, athletics, music and drawing. An educated Greek would necessarily pursue athletic endeavours in order to formulate a well-balanced body and mind. An education balanced between physical and mental training would imbue the youth with some combination of higher knowledge, useful skills and *arete*.[20]

Plato expressed similar disapproval of an unbalanced education in *The Republic*. In the dialogue, the character of Socrates conveniently divides education into two components, those of training the mind (music) and training the body (gymnastics). Socrates contends that an unbalanced education will produce unbalanced people. Those who focus only on gymnastics will turn out harsh and savage, while the man who only pursues music finds himself softened and useless. The balanced training of mind and body was only a secondary benefit to the greater achievement: the more important benefit comes to the soul, with gymnastics and music together instilling a love of wisdom and high-spirited passion into their practitioners.[21]

Athletics at Rome

The Roman relationship with exercise and physical activity for recreational purposes seems to have consistently maintained pragmatism of purpose. In contrast with the Ancient Greeks, Roman sport focused exclusively on preparing young men for war. Although there is evidence for recreational ball games and the like, regimented athletics at Rome sought to infuse the Roman values of military ability.

Plutarch wrote that in the 3rd century BCE, Cato the Elder educated his own son in athletics, including javelin, fighting in armour, horsemanship, boxing and swimming. The military component of athletic competition is clear in the Roman foundation myth told by Virgil in his epic poem the *Aeneid*. During his journey from Troy to Italy, the hero Aeneas, the ancestor of the Roman people, holds funeral games for his father, Anchises. Virgil, who wrote during the last half of the 1st century BCE, devotes the fifth book of the *Aeneid* to describing these contests of speed and strength with a Roman emphasis on practicality. The contests suggest the importance of military training and preparation. In addition to running and boxing, the men compete in a ship race, archery and cavalry drills. A promised javelin event never happens, but the importance of training for military proficiency is clear.[22]

Like the gymnasiums of the Greeks, the culture of the Roman baths featured a wide array of recreational activities, among them athletic endeavours.[23] However, Romans turned a wary and scornful eye to the nudity of the Greek athletes. According to the historian Livy, the first observance of Greek athletics at Rome occurred during games sponsored by Marcus Fulvius Nobilior in 187 BCE.[24] Less popular than the chariot races, the stage plays and the gladiatorial exhibitions of the Roman games (*ludi*) and spectacles, Greek-style athletic contests at Rome generally featured athletes who maintained some type of covering. Several ancient authors related that upstanding Romans avoided showing themselves naked to other men.[25] In the 1st century CE, when the Emperor Nero founded a festival intended to rival the Crown Games of the

Greeks, the historian Tacitus noted that some Romans criticized the importation of Greek customs, worrying that they fostered luxury and sloth, and lamenting that these foreign influences would turn Roman youth to laziness, depravity and gymnasiums.[26]

Staged as part of great and elaborate spectacles, the athletic components of the Roman *ludi* usually featured athletes as hired entertainers rather than as free competitors striving for *arete* and *kleos*. As Aristotle noted in *Politics*, a person undertaking an action for himself, his friends or for *arete* is deemed free, while one who undertakes action for another (i.e. for pay) is thought menial and servile.[27] Although Aristotle was not a Roman, his point holds well for understanding the Roman treatment of athletes. Like the play-actors, gladiators or chariot drivers, those who competed in the *ludi* worked for the sponsoring agents, and as such did not enjoy the same status as their counterparts in Greece. Indeed, sober Romans dismissed the fanaticism surrounding the *ludi*. Marcus Tullius Cicero, the great Roman statesman of the 1st century BCE, advocated generosity over lavishness, and scorned the expense of the Roman *ludi* as wasted money for the amusement of 'children, foolish women, slaves and free persons who resemble slaves'.[28]

With the emergence and spread of Christianity throughout the Roman Empire, athletics remained an important cultural touchstone, although the importance of the great festivals waned as relics from a pagan past. New Testament writings frequently alluded to athletic imagery in the metaphorical sense of training to win the prize of salvation through Jesus, and Augustine referred to the apostle Paul as 'the athlete of Christ'.[29] In the vision attributed to Perpetua, a 3rd-century woman sentenced to die as a Christian martyr, she transforms into a (male) athlete who, stripped and oiled, fights and defeats an opponent in a metaphor for struggling against and overcoming the devil.[30]

In the 5th century CE, Augustine maintained Christianity's use of athletic vocabulary and imagery while eschewing the barbarity of the arena, the obscenity of the theatre and the nudity of Greek-style athletics. Despite these moral injunctions against the culture of spectacle, Augustine does not condemn the corporeal nature of humankind. It is the soul that inclines men towards sin, not the physical nature of the mortal body.[31] This debate about the relationship between body, soul and sin roiled through late antiquity and early medieval Europe, leading to diverse doctrines on the corporeality of Jesus, asceticism and practices of self-mortification. While games, sports and athletic endeavours continued uninterrupted among recreational pursuits, medieval Christianity emphasized the subjugation of the physical and the elevation of the spiritual.

In *The Song of Roland*, a medieval French poem set during the 9th-century reign of Charlemagne, pride and sin overcome the physically powerful characters while the weak prevail with divine aid. Betrayal and pride bring about the death of the great hero Roland. Because of his piety, the weak and humble Pinabel, Roland's apparent successor, is able to defeat the treacherous Ganelon in a trial by physical combat. The renouncement of the physical and the exaltation of the spiritual continued to influence much of Christian thought, including sport and games, throughout the Middle Ages. Despite Thomas Aquinas' 13th-century assertion that happiness results from both the body and the soul, Aquinas' approval of 'a well-ordered body' offers scant evidence for an argument supporting physical education or sport.[32] It is not until the Renaissance of classical ideals during the early modern era that a discussion of the values of sport and athletics re-emerged in Europe.

From Antiquity to Modernity – Renaissance Schoolmasters and Protestant Utilitarians

Historians date the emergence of modernity, a term derived from the Latin word *modo* that meant 'just now', to the 15th, 16th and 17th centuries when a new consciousness developed that perceived contemporary worlds as more enlightened and progressive than those of previous epochs. Significantly, this new historical consciousness emerged in an era in which Western civilization expanded and thrived, conquering and colonizing other civilizations and becoming the dominant global form of culture. Modernity both expanded and Westernized ideas about the role of sport in human cultures. Modernity also pluralized Western thought, as a series of roughly contemporaneous transformations in habits of mind, the Renaissance, the Reformation and the Scientific Revolution, laid the foundation for new ways of apprehending the world and new ideas about the role of sport and physical education in human endeavour.[33]

The preference for the 'modern' over older traditions did not mean, however, that most thinkers entirely jettisoned ancient ideas. The Renaissance, in particular, looked back to antiquity for inspiration and authority even as it lurched toward a modern future. The re-emergence of these debates revealed the power of antiquity in shaping the modern West. Even after more than a millennium had elapsed, early modern thinkers continued to look to the systematic rationalism of Ancient Greece to build their ideas about how sport could cultivate human excellence, train citizens to serve the state and improve the complex interactions of minds and bodies.[34] Indeed, the fragmented, mythologized and sometimes misunderstood models of Greek athletic traditions that moderns inherited and to which they regularly returned provided inspiration for the construction of modern pan-national athletic spectacles such as the revived Olympics as well as inspiring the modern ideology of amateurism – a paradoxically radical misreading of Greek ideas that nevertheless claimed an ancient lineage.[35] Western inheritances of Greek ideas undergirded an evolving series of philosophies that promoted sport as essential to a complete and useful education. Paying homage to their (often limited) understanding of Grecian ideals of *arete*, for several centuries educational theorists in emerging modern nations proposed systems of gymnastics for nurturing a modern citizenry and dubbed the buildings where modernized versions of the quest for individual and corporate excellence took place as gymnasiums.

Visions of Greek gymnastics and gymnasiums captivated Renaissance thinkers committed to cultivating modern versions of *arete*. In 15th- and 16th-century Italian city states, Renaissance pedagogues interested in creating an elite cadre of leaders preached the necessity of training the body as well as the mind. Italian schoolmasters such as Petrus Paulus Vergerius, Guarino da Verona, Vittorino da Feltre, Leone Batista Alberti, Mapheus Vegius and Aeneas Sylvius Piccolomini (who became Pope Pius II) produced treatises promoting the necessity of martial training in swordplay, archery and firearms combined with rigorous physical training in horsemanship, swimming, hunting and outdoor skills for educating Renaissance 'princes'. Physical training balanced princely inculcation into the liberal arts – an updating of the classic commandment that the harmonic balance of 'music' and 'gymnastics' inspired manly excellence – like the patriarchal Greeks, Renaissance educators focused almost entirely on the preparation for manhood.[36] In addition to useful martial sports, the Italian theorists promoted games that nurtured grace and sociability. The most famous educational tome produced during this period, Baldasare Castiglione's classic *The Book of the Courtier* (1528), included not only exercises that familiarized this elite class with weaponry and warfare, but also commanded 'princes' to play tennis in order to develop lithe coordination and learn noble traditions.[37]

Translated into Spanish, French, English and other languages of the European vulgate, *The Courtier* became a template for Renaissance apostles of neo-*arete* throughout the West. In England, Thomas Elyot's *Boke Named the Governour* (1531) devoted several chapters to physical education. Roger Ascham, a tutor to Elizabeth I, promoted a variety of sports and games to nurture the development of princely 'gentlemen'. As the system of elite schools such as Eton emerged, designed to educate an English ruling class, Renaissance revivals of Greek athletics pervaded these academies, laying a foundation for future notions that sport played an essential role in modern education.[38]

As Renaissance schoolmasters built a philosophical justification for sport and other forms of physical education into early modern school systems, a religious revolution, the Protestant Reformation, reshaped the foundations of Western civilization. A complex and sometimes chaotic and contradictory rejection of the theologies and institutions of the Catholic Church, the Reformation transformed the social, political and intellectual traditions as well as the religious practices of the West. Protestant reformers had far less interest in the Renaissance project of excavating Greco-Roman worldviews. They generally turned for authority not to the classics but to biblical scripture.[39] Ironically, many Protestants eventually arrived at similar destinations as their Renaissance counterparts on the issue of the role of sport in the education of good citizens for the modern cosmos – in spite of their aversion to the reliance of their scholarly opponents on rereading ancient paeans to *arete*.

Practical concerns rather than devotion to ancient models nurtured Protestant visions of sound minds. The Protestant command that individual believers and not an ecclesiastical leadership held ultimate authority for the interpretation of scripture meant in practice a broad support of mass education among denominations and sects for whom literacy was a primary article of faith. Protestant reformers developed their own educational philosophies, and many came to the conclusion that sport served useful purposes in tempering sound Christian bodies that could nurture sound Christian minds. The founding father of the Reformation, Martin Luther, endorsed sporting exercises as a critical component for the education of common folk. The English poet and firebrand John Milton advocated sport as a necessity for training Christian soldiers to advance the Protestant cause in Europe's wars of religion.[40]

Curiously, in spite of glowing endorsements of 'suitable' recreations as fundamental agents in the education of 'Saints', generations of scholars have labelled Protestant reformers as rabidly anti-sport and fundamentally opposed to indulgence in physicality in any form. Touting pious platitudes about 'idle hands' as the 'devil's playground' as evidence of sport-hating 'frowning Puritans', historians have created a caricature of Protestant ideas about leisure and recreation.[41] Certainly many Protestants manifested a deeply puritanical streak and detested the sport-filled festival culture that early modern Europe inherited from traditional medieval Catholicism. Protestant theologians sometimes dismissed sport as wasteful and wicked frivolity. Indeed, Desiderius Erasmus, the Dutch Renaissance humanist and theologian whom some Catholics indicted for introducing ideas that sparked the Reformation, once declared: 'We are not concerned with developing athletes, but scholars and men competent to affairs, for whom we desire adequate constitution indeed, but not the physique of Milo.'[42]

The vitriol of Protestant condemnations of play on the Christian Sabbath and the fervour with which they opposed what they perceived as the licentious worldliness of the sporting, gambling and drinking bacchanals of medieval tradition have overwhelmed some academic assessments of the complex views of the role of leisure that developed during the Reformation. In fact, Protestant reformers, far from the sport-hating puritans of stereotype, endorsed a variety of athletic endeavours as long as they were undertaken to make people better workers, better citizens, better soldiers and better Christians. Protestants inverted the medieval Thomistic tradition that placed leisure rather than labour at the centre of existence and took a very modern attitude toward sport and the body. Most Protestants endorsed those pastimes and recreations that regulated human lives, refreshed individuals for godly service, and re-energized 'Saints' in their faith journeys. Even the hyper-puritanical French theologian Jean Calvin, who created an influential Protestant theocracy at Geneva in the 16th century, admitted that some recreations played a useful role in his vision of a godly commonwealth. Calvin and his followers were the most extreme Protestants in dismissing most of the sporting practices of traditional Europe as impediments to their designs, but even they recognized a role for sport in their sketches of religious utopias and in the schools they built to train the 'Saints' to construct 'cities on hills'.[43] In fact, the Protestant focus on the body as a useful mechanism would eventually spawn a scientific mania for sculpting flesh and blood 'Milos' through modern pharmacology and hyper-rational training methods.[44]

Sport and Physical Education in the Age of Empiricism
Both Renaissance humanists and Protestant reformers made room in their visions of education for sports and games that trained bodies as well as minds. The pedagogical scholars who emerged during the same historical epoch from the third wellspring of modernity, the scientific revolution, joined the consensus

that united their Renaissance and Reformation brethren on these matters. The Renaissance and Reformation contributed to an intellectual ferment that gave rise to the modern scientific worldview. In spite of the radical dualism of René Descartes and some of his fellow scientific philosophers in separating, via logical gymnastics, the mind completely from the body, the growing faith in empiricism as the most reliable human guide to real knowledge of the workings of the cosmos guaranteed that sport and other physical activities that trained the senses to 'read' the world would play an indispensable role in the educational theorizing of early modern scientists.[45]

In England, educational theorists and scientific philosophers such as Richard Mulcaster, John Comenius and Francis Bacon argued that since human reason began in the body's sensory organs, physical training represented a crucial step in the acquisition of knowledge. The English empiricist John Locke in his enormously influential *Essay Concerning Human Understanding* promoted the idea that physical education preceded all other education. Locke posited that humans came into the world as 'blank slates' and were then configured by the sensory data gathered from the surrounding environment, though he did add that human minds were innately 'fitted' to receive environmental data and shape it into meaningful concepts.[46]

Locke's epistemological environmental psychology proved enormously influential in the centuries that followed, forming one of the foundations on which the Enlightenment of the 17th and 18th centuries rested. In Lockean terms, good bodies that provided accurate sensory data were essential to humanness. Thus educational systems needed to train bodies as well as minds, Locke concluded. The prophets of modern incarnations of *arete* had been arguing precisely that position since the dawn of modernity. Locke put a scientific stamp of approval on that fundamental premise. In addition, good 'environments', in both physical and social terms, produced good citizens, and bad environments had the converse impact on the human condition. Thus habits that nurtured virtue, including sporting habits, held the power to guarantee human progress, a foundational belief of the Enlightenment in particular, and modern Western thought in general. Locke's epistemology prepared the groundwork for the development of the idea that sport and physical education have a great deal to contribute to the creation of progressive modern societies.

The Revolutionary Training of Bodies and Minds: Gymnastics at the Service of the State

In Europe, the Genevan philosopher Jean-Jacques Rousseau radicalized Locke's empirical systems. In his 1762 tome *Emile: Or On Education*, Rousseau insisted that all traditional systems for training minds and bodies were hopelessly muddled by falsified human conventions. The West needed a fundamental educational reorientation in which the training of youngsters began with an abandonment of the schoolhouse and a swift return to nature, the wellspring of any accurate sensory knowledge about reality. Beneath Rousseau's radical posturing, however, rested a hard-core devotion to neo-*arete* and to classical admonitions of the harmonic connection of bodies and minds. 'Thus his body and his mind are exercised together,' Rousseau asserted. 'Acting always according to his own thought and not someone else's, he continually unites two operations: the more he makes himself strong and robust, the more he becomes sensible and judicious,' Rousseau insisted. 'This is the way one day to have what are believed incompatible and what are united in almost all great men: strength of body and strength of soul; a wise man's reason and an athlete's vigour.'[47]

In his political writings Rousseau promoted the notion that the reason of wise men and the vigour of athletes found their fullest expression in the 'social contracts' that suffused modern nations, energizing the collective 'general will' of their states. Rousseau's vision of systematic physical education as scientific fuel for making modern citizens found its most ardent and ironic embrace not in his native Geneva, nor in France where he spent most of his adult life, nor in the other emerging republics of the 18th century and 19th century, but in the discordant states of Germany. A coterie of German educators and nationalists known as the *Turners*, in deference to their creation of a meticulous routine of gymnastic exercises known as *Turnen*, proselytized that their physical training customs could build the collective physical and psychic will to lead the German people in a war of national liberation to evict Napoleon's French armies of occupation from their homeland and unite their discordant polities into a new German nation. Indeed, when the German principalities launched a successful uprising against Napoleon, *Turners* served as the shock troops in the campaign.[48]

The *Turners* married physical education to modern nationhood, making gymnastics an essential element in the forging of a vigorous citizenry and a robust state. Ironically, the *Turners*, as the historian Allen Guttmann has insightfully noted, ranked as the most important resistance group in combating the rise of modern sport into every nook and cranny of modern life. German gymnastics resembled modern sport in certain ways. The *Turners* created a system of vigorous physical culture that promoted secularism, equality, rationalization and bureaucratization but they adamantly opposed the competitive and record-seeking aspects of sport in pursuit of a more collective approach to educating the body. They were not anti-moderns who resisted the emergence of sport on the grounds that it represented the triumph of modernity, but a very modern movement that preferred collectivist physical education to the individualistic tendencies inherent in competitive sport.[49]

The *Turner* movement spread from Germany to a few other nations. Systems of Danish and Swedish gymnastics soon appeared. German immigrants planted *Turnverein* in Germanic migrant colonies around the world, including in the United States. But the vigorous opposition to modern sport that the *Turners* embodied had little long-term impact on the modern globe.[50] Most modern cultures, and in particular those cultures that comprised the Anglo-American world, discovered in sport rather than systematic programmes of collective gymnastics the nation-making promises that Enlightenment thinkers such as Rousseau had ladled on to the inculcation of physical culture. From the age of revolutions that marked the end of the 18th century and the beginning of the 19th century through the continuing economic, social and political transformations of the early 21st century, sport has become one of the primary vehicles for nurturing the patriotic chauvinism that animates contemporary nation states.[51]

Modern Sport and Neo-*Arete*

That the marrow of modern citizenship – the very essence of modern manhood and womanhood – is born in the competitive scrums of sporting competitions has become a hoary global truism. This ideologically charged and thoroughly updated version of *arete* flowered first in Great Britain and the other nations of the English-speaking world and has, since the early 20th century, saturated global markets.[52] Growing numbers of philosophers speculated about the importance of sport in the education of children and youth. Soon, a few minds began to build philosophies of sport itself. By the end of the 20th century the subject had become a topic, albeit at times a controversial one, that fell under the systematic gaze of both professional philosophers and dilettantes.[53]

The ideology of sport as a character-building exercise developed in its initial form in the work of popularizers rather than philosophers. The 1857 publication of a widely read English novel, *Tom Brown's Schooldays*, by the British muscular Christian Thomas Hughes, marks the first wave in the Anglo-American universe of a flood tide of devotionals testifying to the fundamental importance of sport as a character-building exercise.[54] Professional philosophers got into the act a few decades later. The American pragmatists, led by William James, used sporting analogies and examples. In his famous meditation on the 'Moral Equivalent of War', James argued that vigorous physical and mental challenges were essential in the modern development of moral beings.[55] Although he did not specifically mention sporting activities in that particular essay, many read James's assertion that ethical progress required a devotion to strenuous activity as a call to use sport as a tool to shape modern societies.[56] The idea that sport provided a moral equivalent of war with few of the downsides of combat, producing the character-shaping sacrifice of individual self-interest to the greater purposes of the collective good without the destructive 'side effects' of actual warfare, became an article of faith among Anglo-American educators who prescribed large doses of sporting activities in their modern pedagogies. Another pragmatist, John Dewey, theorizing about why traditional schools could not produce the qualities necessary for progressive citizenship, drew directly from this ever-deepening fount: 'Upon the playground, in game and sport, social organization takes place spontaneously and inevitably,' Dewey argued. 'There is something to do, some activity to be carried on, requiring natural divisions of labour, selection of leaders and followers, mutual cooperation and emulation,' he continued. 'In the schoolroom the motive and the cement of social organization are alike wanting,' Dewey lamented.[57] To reform the school, Dewey and his many followers asserted, required the importation of sport into the educational experience in order to produce the healthy social organization necessary for building a progressive civilization.

Dewey's followers reshaped education, including physical education, in the United States and had a tremendous impact on school reform in other nations.[58] Under the spell of Dewey and like-minded promoters of the notion that sport could build a better society, a pioneering group of American pedagogical thinkers articulated a vision of a 'new physical education'. Though their philosophic training was limited and their philosophic inquires were sometimes shallow and muddled, the new physical educators laid the foundation for a critical philosophy of physical activity to develop.[59]

Beyond a Sporting Pedagogy: Play, Games and Sport as the Focus of Philosophical Inquiry

By the mid-20th century, as the new physical education promised a new form of *arete* for a modern millennium, sport had become such an enormous cultural force that an eclectic group of thinkers began to subject it to the philosophical gaze as a thing-in-itself and not simply as an element in the educational development of human organisms. By that time the revived Olympic Games had become one of the world's most popular spectacles, the World Cup football tournament had engaged a multitude of nations and sport had evolved into a ubiquitous global habit.[60]

In 1938, the Dutch historian and cultural theorist Johan Huizinga published the first philosophical treatise in which sport, contests and play served as the central subject for critical reflection. Perhaps the fact that his father was a physiologist in part explains Huizinga's attraction to the subject, but whatever the reasons for his interest, *Homo Ludens* offered an extended analysis of the role of play, games and sport in shaping human cultures. Drawing from ancient Greek thought as well as modern history and philosophy, Huizinga concludes that the 'play element' provides an essential ingredient in the creation and recreation of cultures. Structured forms of play such as games and sports, in particular, provide the mechanisms on which civilizations are built and evolve. Throughout the volume Huizinga periodically worried that modern hyper-rationalism and instrumentalism were eroding the 'play element' in contemporary cultures and threatened the very core of civilization.[61]

Huizinga's extended excavation of the meaning of play, games and sport inspired other intellectuals to tackle the topic. The German neo-Thomist Josef Pieper took Huizinga's anti-modern tendencies to their logical conclusion in a 1948 essay entitled 'Leisure, The Basis of Culture'. Pieper contended that modern societies through their conviction that work served as the primary purpose of human life and their devotion to an arid utilitarianism that eroded classical notions of the good life had lost contact with the central reality of human existence. Pieper asserted that only a rediscovery of classical notions of leisure and play, complete with the sacred connotations they implied, could re-enchant the modern cosmos. 'Culture depends for its very existence upon leisure,' Pieper insisted, an idea that echoed Huizinga's conception of the role of the play element in the evolution of cultures.[62] A decade later the French sociologist Roger Caillois produced *Man, Play, and Games*, a treatise that built on Huizinga's theories and definitions and contended that human societies were structured around game forms and play behaviours. Caillois reintroduced classical terminology such as *arete* and *agon* into the philosophical lexicon.[63]

Considerations of play elements soon spilled over into other domains. In his landmark 1963 work *Beyond a Boundary*, C.L.R. James, the West Indian historian, independence advocate and civil rights activist offered, not only examinations of the nature and structure of sport and its role in the production of culture but a political philosophy of sport as an instrument to combat colonial and racial oppression.[64] The American anthropologist Clifford Geertz, approaching play, games and sports from a somewhat different angle, proposed in his influential 1972 essay 'Deep Play: Notes on a Balinese Cockfight' that sporting activities were not mere amusements but culture-making practices and that they could be read as 'texts' to help unravel the nature of human societies.[65] In 1978, the historian Allen Guttmann's provocative book *From Ritual to Record* sought not only to provide a chronology for sport but also to manufacture a metaphysical scheme to define the evolution of sporting practices from traditional to modern forms.[66] That same year, the philosopher Bernard Suits published *The Grasshopper: Games, Life, and Utopia*, a volume that many contemporary philosophers consider the starting point for any serious metaphysical attempt to define sport.[67]

From multiple domains of the social sciences, history, sociology, anthropology and politics, interest in the philosophy of sport blossomed in the aftermath of Huizinga's *Homo Ludens*. Huizinga and his followers from Pieper to Suits warned readers that not all activities that were popularly labelled 'sport' qualified as beneficent culture-building exercises. Indeed, critics warned that in particular the sort of high-performance, international-level sport that developed throughout the 20th century could manifest all the negative properties of 'total work' that Huizinga and Pieper decried as anathema to a real 'play element' or a true understanding of leisure. Totalizing sport could transform players into joyless robots performing for overstimulated fans, driven to ever-higher levels of achievement by the amoral mechanisms of instrumentalist sport science. Sport could, in political realms, reinforce totalitarianism and repression. Games and contests could erect as well as erase racial and gender barriers. Nevertheless, this eclectic menagerie of thinkers who took play, games and sport seriously held out the vision that these activities could enhance the good life, promote the commonweal and provide insights into the riddles of the human condition. Their work provided a robust set of ideas on which a new generation of scholars would soon construct a vibrant field in the philosophy of sport.

Building a Professional Domain

The formal organization of the philosophy of sport commenced in the 1970s, as similar scholarly guilds appeared in related fields devoted to research in the history, sociology and anthropology of sport.[68] In 1972, the Philosophic Society for the Study of Sport (PSSS) held its inaugural meeting. Soon thereafter, the North American-based society launched the *Journal of the Philosophy of Sport*, which began publishing regular issues in 1974. As in other domains in the study of human movement, scholars with training and professional positions in both traditional philosophy and a variety of permutations of physical education led the crusades to establish these fortresses of inquiry, giving the new coalition an interdisciplinary and cross-disciplinary strength rare in academic organizations, but at the same time failing to provide the PSSS with a haven in a well-established discipline within modern higher education. The PSSS quickly became a global society attracting scholars from numerous nations and holding annual meetings in Europe, Asia and Australia as well as in North America. In 1999, to reflect the expanding globalization of its membership, the PSSS became the International Association for the Philosophy of Sports (IAPS).[69] Sport philosophy societies also sprang up in several other parts of the world.[70]

The creation of a scholarly cabal energized the field and produced an enormous increase of new publications and new methodologies. The connections developed within the society to mainstream philosophy moved the field away from the polyglot approach that had characterized studies by an earlier generation of academics who had been enmeshed in debates within the philosophy of education and engendered a new intellectual climate in which the standards and canons of professional philosophy became the baseline template. That shift also sparked a change in the scope and focus of the problems that sport philosophers tackled. A long tradition of concerns about the role of sport and games in education unravelled as inquiries turned from specific pedagogical concerns to the broader horizons of the role of movement in multiple aspects of the human experience.[71]

In the nearly half-century since the early 1970s emergence of the philosophy of sport as a self-defined sub-discipline, the field has evolved in curiously paradoxical dimensions. On the one hand, the philosophy of sport has produced an enduring, well-respected and thriving academic journal (the *Journal of the Philosophy of Sport*), as well as several more recent competitors.[72] The sheer volume of quality philosophical publications in the field has increased exponentially. PSSS and IAPS over the course of nearly five decades have maintained a dedicated core of philosophers who continue to push the boundaries of the field. Conversely, until the mid-1990s, much of that volume had been produced by a relatively small cadre of philosophers. Their work has still not found a formal home or even consistent hospitality in mainstream departments of philosophy, albeit they are increasingly welcoming work in this area. Ominously, the number of courses and faculty positions in the philosophy of sport, games and movement, even in pedagogically inclined physical education departments, has declined even as the production of scholarship has blossomed. This pattern is not unique to sport philosophy but also characterizes many of the other humanities and social sciences of sport such as sport history, sport sociology and sport anthropology.[73]

In the early 21st century, the philosophy of sport remains in this paradoxical terrain. A handful of graduate programmes turn out a small number of new philosophers who keep the domain alive, but new professional niches or sustained growth remain elusive commodities. In the power centres of the academy and in funding agencies the assumption that reductionist science rather than philosophical inquiry provides the ultimate answers to the riddles of how movement shapes human experience and endeavours remains intact. Concurrently, a broad public interest in the philosophic meaning of human movement resists extinction with a hardy fortitude, as evidenced by the mass-market success of biologist and ultramarathon runner Bernd Heinrich's *Why We Run: A Natural History*, a meditation by a scientist that contains as many philosophical as physiological insights into the meaning of movement for the human species.[74]

Scott Kretchmar, one of the world's leading philosophers of sport, hopes that this unsteady location his field currently inhabits will soon yield to a new shift. Kretchmar notes several trends, including an increasing scepticism among both intellectuals and the public that science can answer all questions and solve all problems in regard to the role of movement in human existence and a return of academic philosophy from the rarefied confines of narrow technical inquiry to a more populist concern with exploring common human problems in an accessible vernacular. These trends embolden Kretchmar to envision a new, 'post-disciplinary' direction in philosophy of sport that 'would not be as serious or pretentious, nor would it be as interested in meeting external disciplinary criteria for success. It would be more interdisciplinary, more flexible, more interested in sport and other forms of human movement, still rigorous but more fun-loving.'[75]

Kretchmar's optimism comes at a moment when, following the playful spirit of Huizinga, new philosophies of sport explore its metaphysical dimensions, probe its ethical complexities and examine its social and political functions. As the less-than-a-century-old tradition of making sport a principal subject of the philosophical gaze reveals, this contemporary domain is remarkably interdisciplinary and increasingly rigorous.[76] Whether or not it will be 'fun-loving' remains to be seen.

Still, other notable philosophers of sport share Kretchmar's spirit of optimism about the future of the field if not necessarily his emphasis on interdisciplinarity. Before the end of the 20th century, notes William J. Morgan, '[i]n the main ... most philosophers simply ignored sport, convinced that it was too marginal an undertaking to warrant philosophic attention'. Morgan sees a dramatic change in the contemporary moment as the confluence of a sports-obsessed global culture and the revival of pragmatic notions of philosophy as an instrument to solve human social problems have combined to make critical inquiry about sport into a potential vibrant tool for exploring ethical behaviour, gender identity, pharmaceutical enhancement and a variety of other dimensions related to the quest to define human values.[77] Heather L. Reid stresses the globalization of sporting cultures and the philosophical dilemmas they inevitably engender as a signal that a robust international philosophy of sport will soon emerge.[78]

The history of the philosophy of sport reveals both continuity and change. For much of Western history sporting practices have been linked to education, excellence and the production of human virtue. When philosophers turned their gaze on to human movement, they mainly did so in the context of larger examinations of how to ensure that education produced virtuous outcomes and how to create challenges that summoned displays of excellence. In some ways, ancient Greek notions of the role of sport in these processes seem remarkably familiar to modern conceptions. Conversely, modern explorations of sport have frequently focused on its connection to play, a concept alien to classic Greek notions of athletic endeavours. The agonistic contests counselled by the original Greek ideas about sport did not normally invoke the concept of fun. Still, in both their conceptions of sport and philosophy the Greeks posited endeavours that freed people, if only temporarily, from the mundane experiences of daily life.

Notes

1   Jacob Burckhardt, *The Greeks and Greek Civilization*, ed., Oswyn Murray, trans. Sheila Stern (New York: St. Martin's Press, 1998), 160–184. The quotation, which is a translation of Homer, *Iliad* 6.208, is on page 164.

2   Anthony E. Raubitschek, 'The Agonistic Spirit in Greek Culture', *The Ancient World*, 7 (1983): 3–7. The application of a shame culture (as opposed to a guilt culture) in Archaic Greece stems from the views of E.R. Dodds, *The Greeks and the Irrational* (Berkeley: University of California Press, 1951), 17–18. Raubitschek rejected Dodds' view and argued that a love of honours motivated Archaic Greeks, including athletes, more than a fear of shame.

3   David C. Young, *The Olympic Myth of Greek Amateur Athletics* (Chicago: Ares Publishers, 1984), 171.

4   Heather L. Reid, *Athletics and Philosophy in the Ancient World: Contest of Virtue* (New York: Routledge, 2011), 2. Stephen G. Miller, *Arete: Greek Sports from Ancient Sources* (Berkeley: University of California Press, 1991), vii.

5   Homer, *Iliad* 23.272–897.

6   Homer, *Odyssey* 8.100–245.

7   Most recently (and compellingly) by Paul Christesen, 'Whence 776? The Origin of the Date for the First Olympiad' in *Sport in the Cultures of the Ancient World: New Perspectives*, ed., Zinon Papakonstantinou (London: Routledge, 2010), 13–34. Christesen supports a date around 700 BCE.

8   E.g. the Olympic victor Cylon's attempted coup at Athens in 632 BCE, and Alcibiades' contention that his victories at Olympia qualified him to lead the Athenians' invasion of Sicily in 415 BCE.

9   Reid, *Athletics and Philosophy in the Ancient World: Contest of Virtue*, 34–37. See also Stephen G. Miller, 'Naked Democracy' in *Polis and Politics: Studies in Ancient Greek History*, ed., Thomas Heine Nielsen, Lene Rubistein and Permille Flensted-Jensen (Copenhagen: Museum Tusculanum Press, 2000), 278.

10 Herodotus 8.26.

11 Truesdell S. Brown, 'Herodotus' View on Athletics', *The Ancient World* 7 (1983): 28.

12 Lucian, *Anarchasis, passim*, but especially 15 and 30.

13 In his *Description of Greece*, the 2nd century periegete Pausanias scoffed at Panopeus' claims to be a city since it had no state buildings, no theatre, no marketplace and no gymnasium (Pausanias 10.4.1). For discussion of ancient Greek gymnasium culture, see Olga Tzachou-Alexandri, 'The Gymnasium: An Institution for Athletics and Education' in *Mind and Body: Athletic Contests in Ancient Greece* (Athens: Ministry of Culture, The National Hellenic Committee, 1989), 31–40. Stephen L. Glass, 'The Greek Gymnasium: Some Problems' in *The Archaeology of the Olympics*, ed., Wendy Raschke (Madison: University of Wisconsin Press, 1988), 155–173.

14 Reid, *Athletics and Philosophy in the Ancient World: Contest of Virtue*, 43–55, especially 53.

15 Isocrates, *Panegyricus* 1–2.

16 Dio Chrysostom related the story in *Oration* 8. The quotation is found at Dio Chrysostom, *Orationes* 8.15.

17 Xenophanes, fragment §2 (Diehl) = Athenaus *Deipnosophistae* X 414a. Martin L. West, *Iambi et Elegi Graeci ante Aleandrum Cantati* (Oxford: Oxford University Press), 2:186–7.

18 Euripides, fragment §282 in Augustus Nauck's *Tragicorum Graecorum Fragmenta* (Leipzig: Teubner, 1889), 441 = Athenaeus, *Deipnosophistae* X 413c–d. For a treatment of these fragments from Euripides and Xenophanes, as well as an example from the trial of Socrates, see John P. Harris, 'Revenge of the Nerds: Xenophanes, Euripides, and Socrates vs. Olympic Victors', *American Journal of Philology* 130 (2009): 157–94.

19 In a similar sentiment, the historian Xenophon reported that the philosopher Socrates disapproved of overeating followed by rigorous exercise, preferring moderate amounts of both as being good for the soul. Xenophon, *Memorabilia* 1.2.4.

20 Aristotle, *Politics* (book 8) 1337a–39a. Tellingly, Aristotle here digresses into a discussion of work versus play not in the context of athletic training, but with respect to the inclusion of music into the educational programme. Music, for Aristotle, approached leisure, relaxation and pleasure, and so was only intermittently included in the areas of education. At 1337a Aristotle admits that there is some uncertainty about which of the three categories (higher knowledge, useful skills, *arete*) should be the principal goal in education, or even how to define them fully.

21 Plato, *The Republic* (book 3) 410a–12a. In addition to the modern meaning of the word, Plato's term 'music' can be understood literally as referring to the arts inspired by the Muses, such as literature, poetry and dance.

22 Virgil, *Aeneid* 5.109–608. The games are interrupted by the scheming goddess Juno.

23 Garrett Fagan's *Bathing in Public in the Roman World* (Ann Arbor: University of Michigan Press, 1999) is the seminal treatment of Roman bathing culture. For a discussion of Greek gymnasiums in Roman baths, see Hazel Dodge, 'Amusing the Masses: Buildings for Entertainment and Leisure in the Roman World' in *Life, Death and Entertainment in the Roman Empire*, eds., D.S. Potter and D.J. Mattingly (Ann Arbor: University of Michigan Press, 1999), 243–55.

24 Livy 39.22.

25 Notably, Plutarch, *Cato Maior* 20; Cicero, *Tusculanae Disputationes* 4.33.70 (who was in turn quoting the earlier poet Ennius); Dionysius of Halicarnassus 7.72.2. See Nigel Crowther, 'Nudity and Morality: Athletics in Italy', *The Classical Journal* 76 (1980–1981): 119–123 for sources and commentary.

26 Tacitus, *Annales* 14.20.

27 Aristotle, *Politics* (book 8) 1337b.

28 Cicero, *de Officiis* 2.55–57. Cicero here quotes from the writings of an earlier Greek philosopher named Theophrastus. However, Cicero disagreed with Theophrastus' conclusion, which praised the staging of games as an enjoyable benefit of possessing great riches.

29 E.g. 1 Corinthians 9.24–26; Philippians 3.13–14; Hebrews 12.1; 2 Timothy 4.6–8. See also 'Athlete of Christ' at Augustine, *City of God* 14.9.

30 *The Passion of the Holy Martyrs Perpetua and Felicitas* 3.2. The author of this treatise is unknown, although most of Perpetua's account is written in the first person, implying authorship by Perpetua herself. The first edition of the manuscript was edited by Petrus Possinus at Rome in 1663.

31 Augustine, *City of God* 14.3. Augustine's criticism of theatrical displays and his condemnation of gladiatorial contests (and how Augustine himself was swept up in the fervour) are found in *City of God* 4.26 and *Confessions* 6.7, respectively. The shame of nudity, albeit in the Garden of Eden, not an athletic context is found in: *City of God* 14.17.

32 Thomas Aquinas, *Summa Theologica*, First Part of the Second Part, Question 4, Article 6. The Latin reads: *bona disposito corporis*.

33   Merry E. Wiesner, *Early Modern Europe, 1450–1789* (Cambridge: Cambridge University Press, 2006).

34   Anthony Levi, *Renaissance and Reformation: The Intellectual Genesis* (New Haven, CT: Yale University Press, 2002).

35   Young, *The Olympic Myth of Greek Amateur Athletics*; and Donald G. Kyle, *Sport and Spectacle in the Ancient World* (Malden, MA: Blackwell, 2007).

36   John McClelland, *Body and Mind: Sport in Europe from the Roman Empire to the Renaissance* (London: Routledge, 2007).

37   Baldasare Castiglione, *The Courtier*, trans. George Anthony Bull (New York: Penguin, 1976; orig. 1528).

38   William J. Baker, *Sports in the Western World*, rev. ed. (Urbana: University of Illinois Press, 1988) and Allen Guttmann, *Sport: The First Five Millennia* (Amherst: University of Massachusetts Press, 2004).

39   Euan Cameron, *The European Reformation* (New York: Oxford University Press, 1991).

40   Gregory M. Colón Semenza, *Sport, Politics, and Literature in the English Renaissance* (Newark: University of Delaware Press, 2003).

41   See, for instance, the chapter on 'Frowning Puritans', in Baker, *Sports in the Western World*, 72–84. For more complex views of Puritan attitudes see 'Puritans at Play', in Allen Guttmann, *A Whole New Ballgame: An Interpretation of American Sports* (Chapel Hill: University of North Carolina Press, 1988), 23–34; and Nancy Struna, *People of Prowess: Sport, Labor, and Leisure in Early Anglo-America* (Urbana: University of Illinois Press, 1997). Baker offers a much more complex view of Puritan visions in William J. Baker, *Playing with God: Religion and Modern Sport* (Cambridge, MA: Harvard University Press, 2007).

42   *Desiderius Erasmus Concerning the Aim and Method of Education*, trans. and ed. by William Woodward Harrison (Cambridge, MA: Cambridge University Press, 1904), 202. Milo of Croton was an exceptionally successful Greek wrestler from the 6th century BCE who won six times at Olympia and six times at the Pythian Games.

43   David Curtis Steinmetz, *Calvin in Context* (New York: Oxford University Press, 1995).

44   For a provocative introduction to these trends see John M. Hoberman, *Mortal Engines: The Science of Performance and the Dehumanization of Sport* (New York: Free Press, 1992); John M. Hoberman, *Testosterone Dreams: Rejuvenation, Aphrodisia, Doping* (Berkeley: University of California Press, 2005).

45   Ernst Cassirer, *The Philosophy of the Enlightenment* (Princeton, N.J.: Princeton University Press, 1951).

46   John Locke, *An Essay Concerning Human Understanding*, additional editing by R.S. Woolhouse (New York: Penguin, 1997; orig. 1692).

47   Jean-Jacques Rousseau, *Emile, Or On Education*, trans. by Allan Bloom (New York: Basic Books, 1979; orig. 1762), 119.

48   Gertrud Pfister, ed., *Gymnastics, a Transatlantic Movement: From Europe to America* (London: Routledge, 2011); and Annette R. Hofmann, ed., *Turnen and Sport: Transatlantic Transfers* (New York: Waxmann, 2004).

49   Guttmann, *Sport: The First Five Millennia*, 273–84.

50   Ibid.

51   For a provocative introduction to this topic see John M. Hoberman, *Sport and Political Ideology* (Austin: University of Texas Press, 1984).

52   For rich histories of this process see J.A. Mangan, *Athleticism in the Victorian and Edwardian Public School: The Emergence and Consolidation of an Educational Ideology* (Cambridge: Cambridge University Press, 1981); and J.A. Mangan, *The Games Ethic and Imperialism: Aspects of the Diffusion of an Ideal* (New York: Viking, 1986).

53   And in one famous case, Howard Slusher was involved in both camps as both a philosopher and a 'super-agent' for professional athletes. For his philosophical side,

see Howard S. Slusher, *Man, Sport, and Existence: A Critical Analysis* (Philadelphia: Lea & Febiger, 1967).

54 Thomas Hughes, *Tom Brown's Schooldays* (New York: Oxford University Press, 1999; orig. 1857).

55 William James, *The Moral Equivalent of War* (New York: American Association for International Conciliation, 1910). For an example of a philosophical treatise in which James directly employs sporting ideas see William James, 'The Energies of Men', in *Essays on Faith and Morals*, ed., Ralph Barton Perry (New York: Longmans, Green, 1943), 216–37.

56 Mark Dyreson, 'Nature by Design: American Ideas about Sport, Energy, Evolution and Republics', *Journal of Sport History* 26 (1999): 447–70.

57 John Dewey, *The School and Society* (Chicago: University of Chicago Press, 1900), 28.

58 Rosa del Carmen Bruno-Jofré and Jürgen Schriewer, eds., *The Global Reception of John Dewey's Thought: Multiple Refractions through Time and Space* (New York: Routledge, 2012); and Molly Cochran, ed., *The Cambridge Companion to Dewey* (Cambridge: Cambridge University Press, 2010).

59 Scott Kretchmar, 'Philosophy of Sport', in *The History of Exercise and Sport Science*, John D. Massengale and Richard A. Swanson, eds. (Champaign, IL: Human Kinetics, 1997), 181–8.

60 Allen Guttmann, *The Olympics: A History of the Modern Games* (Urbana, IL: University of Illinois Press, 1992); Bill Murray, *The World's Game: A History of Soccer* (Urbana, IL: University of Illinois Press, 1996); and Barbara Keys, *Globalizing Sport: National Rivalry and International Community in the 1930s* (Cambridge, MA: Harvard University Press, 2006).

61 Johan Huizinga, *Homo Ludens: A Study of the Play-Element in Culture* (Boston: Beacon, 1955; orig. 1938).

62 Josef Pieper, *Leisure: The Basis of Culture* (San Francisco: Ignatius Press, 2009; orig. 1948). Quotation is from page 15.

63 Roger Caillois, *Man, Play, and Games* (New York: Free Press, 1961; orig. 1958).

64 C.L.R. James, *Beyond a Boundary* (Durham, NC: Duke University Press, 1999; orig. 1963).

65 Clifford Geertz, 'Deep Play: Notes on the Balinese Cockfight', *Daedalus* 101 (1972): 1–37.

66 Allen Guttmann, *From Ritual to Record: The Nature of Modern Sports* (New York: Columbia University Press, 1978).

67 Bernard Suits, *The Grasshopper. Games, Life, and Utopia* (Toronto: University of Toronto Press, 1978).

68 Kretchmar, 'Philosophy of Sport', 181–202. See, also, the chapters in the same volume by Nancy Struna, 'Sport History', 143–80 and George H. Sage, 'Sport Sociology,' 109–42. See also the website for IAPS at <http://iaps.net/>

69 Ibid.

70 There are currently several scholarly academies around the world devoted to the philosophy of sport. In addition to these societies, the philosophy of sport has developed in many other areas of the world. See the essay by Peter M. Hopsicker and Ivo Jirásek in this volume for details.

71 Kretchmar, 'Philosophy of Sport', 181–202.

72 The BPSA publishes *Sport, Ethics and Philosophy*. See the essay by Peter M. Hopsicker and Ivo Jirásek for details of these journals.

73 One of the founders of PSSS, IAPS and the contemporary field, Scott Kretchmar laments that 'almost 50 per cent of all the scholarly journal literature during this period was produced by only ten authors'. Kretchmar also ruefully observes that philosophy course requirements in physical education pedagogy departments have

evaporated over the same time period and that those remaining are frequently taught by instructors untrained and uninterested in the subject. Kretchmar, 'Philosophy of Sport', 195–6.

74 Bernd Heinrich, *Why We Run: A Natural History* (New York: Ecco, 2002).

75 Kretchmar, 'Philosophy of Sport', 198.

76 For evidence of both rigour and interdisciplinarity peruse the following recent monographs that collectively testify to the current vibrancy of the field. William J. Morgan, *Why Sports Morally Matter* (London: Routledge, 2006); Paul Christesen, *Sport and Democracy in the Ancient and Modern Worlds* (New York: Cambridge University Press, 2012); Robert L. Simon, *Fair Play: Sports, Values, and Society*, 3rd ed. (Boulder, CO: Westview Press, 2010); Andy Miah, *Genetically Modified Athletes: Biomedical Ethics, Gene Doping and Sport* (London: Routledge, 2004); Verner Møller, *The Ethics of Doping and Anti-Doping: Redeeming the Soul of Sport?* (London: Routledge, 2010) and Dave Zirin, *Game Over: How Politics has turned the Sports World Upside Down* (New York: New Press, 2013).

77 William J. Morgan, 'The Philosophy of Sport: A Historical and Conceptual Overview and a Conjecture Regarding its Future', in *The Handbook of Sport Studies*, eds., Jay Coakely and Eric Dunning (Thousand Oaks, CA: Sage, 2002), 204–12.

78 Heather L. Reid, *Introduction to the Philosophy of Sport* (Lanham, MD: Rowman and Littlefield, 2012), 199–204.

Part II

Research Methodology

3 The Philosophy of Sport and Analytic Philosophy

Scott Kretchmar

In this essay, I will attempt to distinguish analytic from continental philosophy (hereafter AP and CP, respectively), examine three exemplary contributions to the sport philosophy literature that emerged from the analytic tradition, underline strengths and weaknesses of this sport literature and discuss potential reconciliations between AP and CP. These possibilities range from minimal compatibility to more aggressive relationships of complementation and interpenetration.

The AP-CP distinction emerged in the early 20th century. Philosophers like Bertrand Russell, Donald Davidson, Gottlob Frege and Willard Quine were associated with AP, while individuals like Edmund Husserl, Martin Heidegger, Maurice Merleau-Ponty, Jacques Derrida and Hans-Georg Gadamer were identified with CP. Other well-known philosophers like Alasdair MacIntyre, John Searle and Charles Taylor appear to have been influenced by both traditions.

In the philosophy of sport, similar identifications can be made. Nicholas Dixon, Warren P. Fraleigh, Sigmund Loland, J.S. Russell, Robert L. Simon, Bernard Suits and Cesar R. Torres would serve as examples of analytic sport philosophers while Gunnar Breivik, Andrew Edgar, Ivo Jirásek, Lev Kreft, Irena Martínková, Vegard Moe, Jim Parry and Maxine Sheets-Johnstone are associated with continental thinking. Scott Kretchmar, Mike McNamee, William J. Morgan and many others show influences of both.

Some see the AP-CP divide as clear and significant. Others do not. All would have to agree, however, that a variety of characteristics have been suggested for distinguishing one from the other, perhaps some more useful than others. The identification of the origins of one school of thought with a geographic location (the European continent) is an obvious possibility. But this is less than satisfactory, for not all continental philosophers came from that part of the world, nor were all analytic philosophers located elsewhere. Even more importantly, geographic locations per se tell us nothing of philosophic commitments or tendencies. The same would hold true for basing the distinction on philosophic lineage traced to key figures in each tradition – for AP, an individual like Bertrand Russell and for CP, Husserl. That strategy merely pushes the issue back to questions about differences between these individuals.

Perhaps more to the point are suggestions about diverse styles. AC is said to be clear, careful, precise, modelled after mathematics, based squarely on logic and argument. CP, by way of contrast, is more literary and suggestive than precise. It has a tendency to rely more on rhetoric than argumentation.

Some draw lines of demarcation on content more than style. AP concerns itself with isolated issues, identifiable puzzles and tidy problems abstracted from their context. It is less impressed with so-called non-rational issues related to culture, embodiment and history. It often looks for 'in principle' distinctions rather than nuanced differences or ambiguous contrasts. It is impressed with the precision of science and, in some ways, models itself after systematic approaches that aim at solvable problems under high evidentiary requirements. Some even argue that analytic philosophers operate under a Kuhnian paradigm that reflects the values and procedures of science.[1] This may be what accounts for the existence of AP's sub-specializations (e.g. metaphysics, axiology, epistemology), the predominance of article-length publications and a vision focused on making systematic progress on solvable problems.

The continental tradition is more taken with political and social issues. Thus, it is typically concerned with a variety of 'givens', including cultural antecedents and historical conditions. It is often hostile to science in general and reductionist theories in particular. It carries more modest epistemological expectations and aims more frequently at clarifications and pointed suggestions than solutions. It has no specialized sub-disciplines and continental philosophers usually publish their seminal research in books rather than narrowly focused articles.

Both traditions continue to be alive and well, and both are well represented in the literature. However, in the philosophy of sport, the analytic tradition has been the more visible brand of thinking. McNamee agrees: 'In the West (and therefore in the *Journal of the Philosophy of Sport*), there has been a tendency for one philosophical tradition to dominate: analytical philosophy.'[2] According to some, this is also the case in the parent discipline. 'Most mainstream philosophers of today,' David Edmonds and John Eidinow argued, 'are operating with the framework that [Bertrand Russell] established.'[3]

With these rough and ready distinctions in hand, and with the realization that some philosophers do not fit neatly into the AP and CP categories, we can move ahead to examine samples of the 'dominant tradition'. We will look at an analysis by Suits on the nature of games, a work by Dixon on the ethics of running up the score and discussions by Russell, Simon, Morgan and Dixon on how we best come to understand the nature of sport.

Metaphysics: Games vs Performances

Much early work in the philosophy of sport was related to what might be called the identification of the players on the field. Many of our predecessors asked what sport is and how it differs from play, work, games, dance, exercise, art and other activities that feature intentional movement. As soon as these definitional issues were raised, participants divided themselves between those who thought such projects worthwhile (they sided with folks like Bertrand Russell) and those who did not (these individuals sided with Ludwig Wittgenstein and frequently cited his notion of 'family resemblances' when arguing against various forms of definitional essentialism).[4]

Bernard Suits was the most visible sport philosopher among those who took on the analytic task of distinguishing different movement forms.[5] When Wittgenstein recommended that philosophers 'look and see' if there are any common characteristics in games rather than assume or stipulate such features, Suits called it 'excellent advice'.[6] But how Suits looked and the things he saw were very different to what Wittgenstein had in mind when he uttered those words.

Suits' analysis of games provides a textbook example of the kind of careful, systematic, logic-based thinking that characterizes much analytic work. I've outlined some of the principal steps taken by Suits below:

1. Games seem very different from work. In work we try to do things efficiently. Trying to hit a golf ball into a distant, small hole using unwieldy sticks is very inefficient. (After all, one could carry the ball to the hole and drop it in!) Perhaps, then, games, in contrast to work, are characterized by doing things inefficiently.
2. But rules prevent a player from carrying the ball to the hole. Carrying the ball to the hole is not possible and thus cannot (in golf) be considered more efficient. In point of fact, given the rules of golf and the limitations they impose, golfers (just like those in work settings) try to be as efficient as possible. Thus, inefficiency does not distinguish games from work.
3. Yet there seems to be a kind of non-ultimacy in games because they are pastimes. Those who play games like golf do not *really* need to get golf balls into the designated holes. Perhaps, then, one is playing a game precisely to the extent to which one realizes this fact. But this does not seem to work because one can imagine game players who take their games too seriously – even more seriously than their work obligations. While we may be morally outraged by such behaviour, the outrage is only understandable because their excessive behaviour occurred in a *game*! Thus, non-ultimacy of game ends does not distinguish games from work.
4. It could be that games are non-ultimate, but this feature attaches to the means by which games are played, not their ends. Means for solving problems are intentionally non-ultimate. In other words, game players choose to put unnecessary hurdles in their way, whereas in work this would be utterly illogical. Non-ultimacy of means, therefore, seems to be a distinguishing and thus also a necessary feature of games.
5. But this feature is not sufficient either because there are other activities (e.g. those in which we choose to follow limitations imposed by ethics) that put hurdles in our way. But it makes no sense to suggest that the acceptance of ethical constraints places us in a game. Telling the truth, even though this behaviour sometimes puts extra hurdles in our way, does not turn us into game players.
6. If games are not grounded in the acceptance of limitations per se, they must be characterized by a certain species of limitation. Perhaps the attitude or stance required for the adoption of limitations or hurdles is crucial. In games, players seem to accept the hurdles just so they can create and enjoy solving the resultant problem. In ethics, of course, we do not do this. Thus, a lusory attitude is required for participating in the 'unnecessary' problems that constitute games. This, then, is a second necessary feature of game playing.

Suits continues with further distinctions and with a defence against a variety of attacks on his definition. But we can see from this analysis the kind of almost surgical thinking in which Suits was involved. First, he isolated what he saw as a solvable problem – identifying the necessary and sufficient conditions for games. Then, he attempted to bracket off context – embodiment, history, politics, gender and so on. He worked like a scientist in testing hypotheses, rejecting ones that did not pan out and then looking for alternatives. He identified clean, logical edges between games, on the one hand, and work, frivolous play and ethical behaviour on the other. His descriptions have a great deal of intuitive appeal. That is, they tell us something about an activity that is a lot like work (it is an exercise in efficient problem solving), but is very different from work too (it is an exercise in 'unnecessary' but 'just right' problem solving). The result was the following, pithy definition:

> To play a game is to attempt to achieve a specific state of affairs (prelusory goal), using only means permitted by rules (lusory means), where the rules prohibit use of more efficient in favour of less efficient means (constitutive rules), and where the rules are accepted just because they make possible such activity (lusory attitude) … [Or to put it more briefly] playing a game is the voluntary attempt to overcome unnecessary obstacles.[7]

As successful as Suits was, dangers lurk in any attempt to produce such definitions. If one lives by the analytic sword in what is arguably a complex and messy world, one may die by it too. Ironically, it was Suits himself who began to question the validity of the neat lines of demarcation he originally proposed.[8] He reversed his position on the kinds of activities that are games by claiming that sports like diving and gymnastics (he called them performances) did not qualify. Why? Because they had no lusory goal, and the existence of a lusory goal was one of his four necessary conditions for something to be a game.

In Suits' world, games had two important ends – prelusory and lusory goals. Prelusory goals are states of affairs or conditions – like crossing a finishing line – that one can achieve without being in the game. Lusory goals are those accomplishments that are specific to the game challenge in question – like crossing the finish while following all game rules.

Suits claimed he could not identify a lusory goal in activities like diving because there was no artificial problem present and thus no accomplishment related to falling into the water, becoming submerged and so on. Anybody could do that, he said.

Critics argued that while this is true, it is not a disqualifying factor. Suits was wrong in eliminating performances because, among other things, he was not aware of the multiplicity of ends that exist in games. In other words, the game phenomenon is more complex than the one he described, and he was a victim of his overly simplistic distinctions. In fact, most critics argued that Suits had it right in the first place.

Had Suits' analytic sword been sharper or wielded more effectively, he might have seen that his simple dichotomy of prelusory and lusory goals was not sufficient. Here are some of the different things that might be meant by the end or ends of a game:

1. The end as termination of testing, of having no more opportunities to show one's mettle (literally, the end of the game).
2. The end as termination of contesting, of having no more opportunities to show one's relative mettle (literally, the end of the contest).
3. The end as the purpose of the game non-competitively – specifically to show how well one can do in the test (the overall artificial challenge of the game, what the game is about).
4. The end as the purpose of the game competitively – specifically to show superiority over one or more opponents or teams of opponents (the way the game problem is to be shared and how superiority will be determined).
5. The end as the metaphysical requirement of reaching the end of testing and contesting by following the constitutive rules of games (the claim that one cannot play or win a game unless one follows its constitutive rules).
6. The end as the practical requirement of reaching the end of testing and contesting even without following all game rules, e.g. by cheating, umpiring error or other deviation from game requirements (the everyday fact that many athletes and teams reach this end even though [all] game rules have not been honoured).

Such complexity is not fatal to analytic philosophers. In fact, it is the very food on which they regularly dine. It could be argued that the fault here is not so much that Suits was analytic, but that he was insufficiently so. More and better distinctions, more careful discernment, would have allowed him to fully cash out his otherwise helpful analysis. Opponents, however, would argue that there are degrees of unwarranted optimism in such beliefs. We can pursue this question and others by examining a second example of analytic thinking, this one in the realm of ethics.

Ethics: Running Up the Score is Morally Acceptable vs Not Acceptable

Dixon is another successful analytic sport philosopher. Like Suits, he would typically isolate a problem, remove it from its historical, cultural and political context, and systematically set about the task of solving it. The problem he selected was one that has drawn attention from many sport ethicists. Is it right to run up the score on an overmatched opponent? Or more precisely, under what conditions might it be right to run up the score on a far weaker competitor? Most codes of sportsmanship suggest that concern for an overmatched opponent is warranted and that any number of steps might be taken to avoid or lessen potential harms that accompany one-sided contests. Dixon argued that these common ethical recommendations were wrong, or at least mostly so.

Dixon's analysis of running up the score provides another textbook example of careful, logical, sequential thinking about a discrete problem.[9] I've outlined some of the steps he took below:

1. Competitive games involve the quest for victory. But victory can be understood in two distinct ways – as rank order or degree of separation.
2. If rank order was all that mattered, there would be nothing more to play for after victory was secured. But this is not the case.
3. Athletes and spectators well understand that there is more to play for even after victory is assured – namely, a display of excellence, full knowledge of relative ability, the excitement that comes with great performances and the setting of new records, to name only a few.
4. Thus, continued efforts in lopsided contests make sense if such additional goods are to be pursued – including efforts that result in 'running up the score'.
5. But the pursuit of such additional goods may still not be ethical if it harms others – specifically if it humiliates or demeans one's opponent.
6. However, a lopsided defeat does not necessarily do this. It does not diminish or humiliate the opponent in any strong sense – that is, as a person rather than an athlete.
7. Strong humiliation and shame are warranted for only two reasons – first, for moral faults like cheating or giving up and second, for non-moral faults like displaying gross stupidity or incompetence. But losing by wide margins requires neither fault, particularly for those who play hard to the end of the game.
8. Likewise, no evil intent is required by the superior performer who is merely trying to play as well as possible.
9. In addition, both performers (runaway winners and losers) can keep emotional highs and lows in check by not overemphasizing the importance of sport. While losing by a wide margin in sport may be a cause for disappointment, it should not generate embarrassment or shame.
10. Disappointment is not a serious harm. Thus, there is nothing wrong with continuing to pursue excellence, knowledge and other goods even in lopsided contests.

As was the case with Suits' descriptions, Dixon's analysis has received considerable attention and support. By clarifying sporting purpose on the one hand (it has to do with knowledge and excellence, for instance, not just rank ordering and victory) and by noting the kinds of behaviour that merit shame on the other (he noted failings of character, for instance), he cleared the way for a new or revised understanding of sportsmanship. The precision of the argument and the clarity of the evidence were designed to solve a long-standing problem.

Dixon was also very careful to identify disqualifying conditions ... just as a scientist might do in claiming that his causal relationships work in certain temperatures or chemical environments but not others. For instance, Dixon noted that running up the score would not be appropriate with children. Nor would it be defensible if the superior player was mean-spirited or otherwise intended to embarrass the opponent. It would probably not be the sportsmanlike thing to do in a friendly game between neighbours or in a recreational setting. One by one, Dixon identified the conditions in which his thesis would not hold and those in which it would.

However, some have raised questions about Dixon's argument,[10] and these concerns are related to his analytic methodology. First, the tendency to dichotomize may cause us to overlook either differences by degree or multiple distinctions that require more than simple bifurcation. Dixon's division of the performer's qualities to those that belong to an athlete, on the one hand, and those that belong to the person, on the other, is a case in point. Some would argue that this is too neat and tidy and that a person may be defined, at least in part, by his or her athletic history and ability. Thus, to fail badly as a skier, for instance, is to fail badly, period – not just as an athlete.

There are also complexities here that may be overlooked in the analytic attempt to keep things straight and uncomplicated. Risks of humiliation, for instance, might be greater in interactive games, like American football, tennis and soccer, where part of the sporting test is provided by the opponent. This is so because a vastly superior opponent influences the sporting test and, in fact, can make it so difficult that the overmatched individual or team actually displays gross incompetence and stupidity. On the other hand, in closed games, like bowling or archery, where the testing difficulty is more or less fixed, there is less danger of such humiliation taking place.

Similarly, in physical contact sports, like ice hockey and wrestling, the chances of humiliation once again might be greater than in, say, tennis or golf. In those games, one merely plays a game and records a score. But in activities like wrestling and American football, a defeat is not merely recorded on the scoreboard. The loser in a lopsided contest is also likely to be physically beaten and defeated, if not also injured. Such messy details often do not neatly fit into analytic schema. But they nevertheless may be important in understanding the roots of common tenets of sportsmanship.

At the end of the day, Dixon's sharp analytic sword has forced readers to consider new possibilities for sport ethics. Running up the score may not be as universally inappropriate as some ethics codes have suggested it is. But then again, there may be more wisdom to that long-honoured recommendation than Dixon's analytic conclusions might have us believe.

Epistemology: Realism vs Relativism

A more modern debate has taken place on the issue of something called 'broad internalism'. One version of this discussion involved six articles and four authors.[11] Three of the articles appeared in the *Journal of the Philosophy of Sport* in a special issue entitled 'Symposium on Sport and Moral Realism'. The authors involved in this dispute are Dixon, Russell, Simon and Morgan. The dispute is related to which of three versions of the nature or value of sport is most compelling: the internalist-formalist account (a game is the product of its rules), the externalist or conventionalist interpretation (a game is defined by the likes and dislikes of the community at any given time and place) or the broad internalist or interpretivist claim (a game has core purposes and excellences that can be discerned by those who know the game in question). The fight is not over which of the three positions is more defensible. In fact, all four writers identify themselves as broad internalists of one stripe or another. Rather the fight is over the warrant or evidence that can be provided for defending any interpretivist account of sport.

In typical analytic fashion, the battle is framed in dichotomous terms. Either realism or relativism is the preferred epistemology. One has to be right and the other wrong. Russell, Dixon and Simon line up on the side of realism; Morgan is the lone relativist. Here is the gist of the argument:

1. Russell argues that rules are never sufficient, if only because players and officials always have to interpret them and because unexpected events not covered by the rules transpire. Thus, games necessarily transcend their rules. This requires that we interpret the correctness of some behaviours that are not clearly allowed or prohibited. This presents no unusual problems because, as rational agents, we can understand what games are about and thus make interpretations that are in line with a game's purposes and values. Simon, in a later article, fundamentally agrees with Russell.

2. Dixon suggests that Russell's and Simon's positions are reasonable ones, but such interpretivist thinking is compatible with both relativism and realism. It could be relativistic because interpretations might merely reflect the perspective or biases of the person making the interpretation. Or it could be realistic if the interpretation is based on principles and these principles reflect 'the way the world really is'.[12] Dixon suggests that broad internalism is more compatible with realism than relativism because it speaks to objective standards for good games – that is, once again, to 'the way the world really is'. Some interpretations of baseball, for instance, are not valid, and solid reasons could be given for their insufficiencies.

3. Simon agrees with Dixon. But he issues a few words of caution about how difficult it is to see reality clearly. He calls his more cautious approach 'justificatory realism'. The search for truth about the purpose and values of baseball is a lengthy, historical process. Additional impartial thinkers may well be needed to get it right ... or at least nearly right. But in the end, he comes down on the side of realism. 'Discourse, on the realist view, might originate in a particular social and historical context ... but it is based on principles and can lead to conclusions that purport to be something more than a more historical consensus.'[13]

4. Russell also agrees with Dixon that realism is the right choice, but Russell adds additional words of caution. He argues for a position referred to as 'Cornell realism', a view that attempts to show the compatibility of realism with the scientific world of atoms, chemical reactions and mechanical regularity. Intangibles like moral principles or the purposes of baseball, in this view, are real but they supervene on the natural world of atomic waves and particles. While Russell admits that the principles and values of a game like baseball cannot be analytically deduced, he notes that this is also true of some biological principles like homeostasis. This biological rule cannot be deduced from the principles of, say, physics and chemistry. But principles of homeostasis are nevertheless real and true. Russell concludes: 'Realism,

including moral realism, in sport should be the standing view until we are given clearly sufficient reasons to reject it.'[14]

5. Morgan rejects the thinking of all three, though he focuses on Dixon's defence of realism. He says that Dixon's faith in a-historical and a-contextual powers of reason is misplaced. Bias from socialization and other factors is unavoidable. Thus relativism is true. Morgan wrote: 'The fact that [Dixon's version of a game like baseball] resonates with us modern-day commentators and observers of sports suggests that it, too, is a product not of any objective conception of the world but of a reflective effort much closer to home.'[15]

This debate serves to display many of the products of analytic philosophy. It provides sharp contrasts, relatively clean lines between options and clear arguments for distinct positions. It presents what appears to be a manageable, solvable problem. It aims for the precision of mathematics. Two plus two is four … or it is not. If you are a broad internalist it clearly follows that you would also be a realist … or it does not.

Both sides present forceful arguments. On the side of realism: some interpretations of baseball might be ludicrous. And certainly, baseball is a game that is more about physical skill than, say, skills in reading or writing. And baseball is clearly a contest where both sides try to outdo one another. Many human activities are not like this. They are not competitive. These reflections make it clear that it is something real we are talking about.

On the side of relativism: we wonder if it really is possible to view something from no perspective whatsoever. Does that even make sense? If it doesn't, how would we ever know that our perspective was the right one or provided the whole picture? Certain interpretations, even those that depict baseball as physical competition, may be based more on local taste than objective truth. In another culture that honours chance or luck rather than skill, for instance, the characterization of baseball and its values might be different. Umpires, for example, might be encouraged to make decisions that highlight chance events rather than skilful performances.

The reader of this analytic argument has a clear choice. Either Russell, Dixon and Simon are right and realism is the best foundation for broad internalism, or Morgan is right and broad internalism is just another brand of relativism. But one might ask if there needs to be a third choice.[16] And this question brings us back to the sufficiency of analytic thinking and its potential relationship to CP and, possibly too, other brands of thinking.

Future of the Analytic-Continental Divide

Relationships between analytic and continental thinking are difficult to analyse for many reasons, not the least of which is the difficulty in seeing any clear differences between them. Nevertheless, we may be able to identify possibilities for reconciling their diverse tendencies as described previously in this essay. Consistent with analytic thrusts toward precision and clarity, I will try to identify three distinct kinds of relationship – those of complementation, facilitation and diffusion.

Complementation suggests that the world is both simple and complex, clear and hazy, composed of independent parts and composed of homogenized wholes whose parts have no independence whatsoever. If the world is indeed put together this way, some philosophic problems invite analytic treatment while others would be better served by a continental approach. For those inclined toward analytic analyses, they might note that some things do, in fact, come in twos, threes and fours and thus can be accurately and helpfully described that way. In addition, even where the world is not quite so cleanly arranged, there can be educational and other pragmatic reasons for emphasizing simplicity. Lessons on ethical rights and wrongs or dangerous and safe behaviour for children might be more effective if portrayed in terms of black and white than messy and less pedagogically powerful shades of grey. Complementary approaches, those that include both AP and CP work, in short, would produce a more complete picture of reality than either one could generate alone.

Facilitation can be effected when AP is used heuristically. That is, even in cases where the world is not amenable to mathematical treatment, extremes in any messy admixture can be identified in order to clarify issues, to see distinctions in more dramatic terms. Suits may have done precisely this when he argued for the importance of game playing in utopia. In other words, he used utopia as a heuristic device to make a point about the logic of games and their utility, not as a reality that should be taken literally. He facilitated our thinking about the relationship between solving game problems and relief from boredom by conjuring up an extreme utopian reality where, by definition, there are no (natural) problems.

The most radical denouement between analytic and continental traditions would be one in which they both disappear. This is what I have called, paradoxically, the diffusion relationship. It is paradoxical because relationships exist only where two or more elements stand in some kind of juxtaposition to one another. In diffusion, both sides forfeit some of their distinctiveness to the other … something we see, for instance, in homogenized milk where the skimmed milk and cream are still there but they have been transformed and no longer operate independently. One conclusion here might be that the historic analytic-continental divide was and is a mistake, an illusion. Philosophers, in other words, deluded themselves into thinking that science and art, maths and literature, order and chaos, predictability and unpredictability, the view from nowhere and the view from somewhere are indeed independent alternatives. They may actually be complementary pairs, as quantum mechanics, Zen Buddhism and others have suggested.[17] Diffusion, admixture and gradations – as well as a deeper appreciation of the role of measurement in affecting what we see – would then render the analytic-continental distinction uninteresting or at least less important.

Notes

1   Neil Levy, 'Analytic and Continental Philosophy: Explaining the Differences', *Metaphilosophy* 34 (2003): 284–304.

2   Mike McNamee, 'Editorial: Sport, Ethics and Philosophy: Context History, Prospect', *Sport, Ethics and Philosophy* 1 (2007): 1–6.

3   David Edmonds and John Eidinow, *Wittgenstein's Poker: The Story of A Ten-Minute Argument Between Two Great Philosophers* (New York: Harper Collins, 2001).

4   A fascinating book that details some of the battles that took place between analytic philosophers and their opponents is *Wittgenstein's Poker: The Story of A Ten-Minute Argument Between Two Great Philosophers* by David Edmonds and John Eidinow (New York: Harper Collins, 2001). Bertrand Russell and Karl Popper defended the view that philosophy aims at solving genuine problems and that language presents no inherent difficulties in carrying out such investigations. Wittgenstein, on the other hand, argued that philosophers are more properly engaged in wrestling with puzzles associated with the uses of language. He denied that the world had an essential nature that could be discovered.

5   Suits analysed sport in 'The Elements of Sport', in *The Philosophy of Sport. A Collection of Essays*, ed. Robert Osterhoudt (Springfield, IL: Charles C. Thomas, 1973), 48–64, play in 'Words on Play', *Journal of the Philosophy of Sport* 4 (1977): 117–31, and games in *The Grasshopper: Games, Life, and Utopia* (Peterborough, ON: Broadview Press, 2005). He argued that these are three distinct things or kinds of behaviour. The phenomenon of work also played a central role in his definitional efforts related to sport, play and games.

6   Suits, *The Grasshopper: Games, Life, and Utopia*, 22.

7   Ibid., 54–5.

8   Bernard Suits, 'The Trick of the Disappearing Goal,' *Journal of the Philosophy of Sport* 16 (1989): 1–12.

9   Nicholas Dixon, 'On Sportsmanship and "Running Up the Score"', *Journal of the Philosophy of Sport* 19 (1992): 1–14.

10   See, e.g. Alun Hardman, Luanne Fox, Doug McLaughlin and Kurt Zimmerman, 'On Sportsmanship and "Running Up the Score": Issues of Incompetence and Humiliation', *Journal of the Philosophy of Sport* 23 (1996): 58–69.

11   The four authors and six articles include the following: Nicholas Dixon, 'Canadian Figure Skaters, French Judges, and Realism in Sport', *Journal of the Philosophy of Sport* 30 (2003): 103–16; William J. Morgan, 'Moral Antirealism, Internalism, and Sport', *Journal of the Philosophy of Sport* 31 (2004): 61–83; J.S. Russell, 'Are Rules All an Umpire Has to Work With?', *Journal of the Philosophy of Sport* 26 (1999): 27–49 and 'Moral Realism in Sport', *Journal of the Philosophy of Sport* 31 (2004): 142–60; and Robert L. Simon, 'Internalism and Internal Value in Sport', *Journal of the Philosophy of Sport* 27 (2000): 1–16 and 'From Ethnocentrism to Realism: Can Discourse Ethics Bridge the Gap?', *Journal of the Philosophy of Sport* 31 (2004): 122–41.

12   Dixon, 'Canadian Figure Skaters, French Judges, and Realism in Sport', 110.

13   Simon, 'From Ethnocentrism to Realism: Can Discourse Ethics Bridge the Gap?' 138.

14   Russell, 'Moral Realism in Sport', 158.

15   Morgan, 'Moral Antirealism, Internalism, and Sport', 169.

16   Scott Kretchmar, 'Dualisms, Dichotomies and Dead Ends: Limitations of Analytic Thinking about Sport', *Sport, Ethics and Philosophy* 1 (2007): 266–80.

17   See, e.g. Scott Kelso and David Engstrom, *The Complementary Nature* (Cambridge, MA: MIT Press, 2006).

4 The Philosophy of Sport and Continental Philosophy

Vegard Fusche Moe

In this essay, the relationship between the philosophy of sport and continental philosophy (CP) will be taken up. The aim of the essay is to describe and discuss how the philosophy of sport has taken up concepts and issues from CP in order to expand the breadth and depth of its discourses on sport. In particular, I will attempt to throw light on the following two questions: what is continental sport philosophy (CSP) and why should we be engaged in it?

First, a short introduction to the term CSP will be provided. Then three problems that seem typical to the tradition of CSP will be described. The problems are related to the understanding of human movement or skilled motor behaviour in sport. In particular, the intentionality, context and embodied nature of skilled behaviour will be discussed by looking at relevant work published in sport philosophy.[1] This is intended to echo the progress of three major figures and conceptualizations in CP, that is, Edmund Husserl's phenomenology of intentionality, Martin Heidegger's existential description of being-in-the-world and Maurice Merleau-Ponty's perceptive body-subject.[2]

Continental Sport Philosophy (CSP)

The term CSP combines two components of philosophical activity: continental philosophy and sport philosophy. It is typically used to describe work where either CP is the direct source of analyses within the philosophy of sport or where ideas from the philosophy of sport are related to or inspired by philosophers in or elements from the continental tradition of philosophy.

CP emerged in the European continent with the publications of Immanuel Kant around 200 years ago and has led to a number of philosophical movements (i.e. German idealism, phenomenology, existential philosophy, Hegelianism and anti-Hegelianism, hermeneutics, Marxism and the Frankfurt School, structuralism, postmodernism and feminism).[3] As it is indicated in the distinct philosophical movements, there is not a single unifying theme in CP. Thus, entries in companions and handbooks as well as introductory texts are often organized in terms of prominent philosophers within this tradition instead of in themes.[4] However, there are certain characteristics of CP that are often recognized by philosophers.

CP is often distinguished from analytic philosophy (AP). Both John Searle and Mike McNamee emphasize, respectively, that AP is the dominant position in philosophy in general and sport philosophy in particular.[5] Searle finds AP to be so central that other philosophical traditions 'feel it necessary to define their position in relation to analytic philosophy'.[6] When the distinction between AP and CP is made, differences in geography and content, method or style are usually presented and discussed.

The geographical difference is that CP refers to mainland Europe, whereas AP refers to the Anglo-American world, mainly Britain and North America. But this distinction is very limited if not inaccurate. Both CP and AP emerged out of the same philosophical tradition as the work of Kant, Bernard Bolzano and Franz Brentano.[7] All three were from the European continent. Furthermore, there are quite a few philosophers living in mainland Europe who are mostly concerned with AP, as there are a number of philosophers in North American universities who are mainly concerned with CP. So, in the modern world, geography indicates little about philosophical preferences.

Regarding differences in content, method or style, AP has mostly been occupied with linguistic and logical analysis. Its language has thus been precision and clarity. AP has shared the problem-oriented and empirical-scientific outlook of the natural sciences, that is, its focus is to search for knowledge and truth in a rationalistic framework where a problem becomes divided and reduced into its smaller parts, analysed and explained in terms of logic or by the laws of nature.[8]

On the other hand, CP has been concerned with understanding what appears to be meaningful for a person in the sense that it has tried to comprehend life as it is lived from the first person point of view. The following questions exemplify this main concern. What kind of experiences does a person have? What is the structure of these experiences? How are experiences influenced by history and context? What are the underlying conditions making it possible for a person to act in meaningful ways in a given situation?

There are a number of philosophers from CP who have attempted to answer these and related questions by means of describing the variety and richness of human experience and action as completely and accurately as possible.[9] Furthermore, CP has endeavoured to perform these descriptions from a presuppositionless point of view, that is, from a perspective that tries to overcome or puts in brackets the assumptions inherited from the Cartesian tradition. In this sense, CP also represents a critique of the empirical-scientific worldview. So, instead of emphasizing the natural-scientific theories and laws and the empirical truths that are derived from these, CP has emphasized the conditions that make possible such a theoretical outlook. Husserl called these conditions the lifeworld, whereas Heidegger called them our pre-understanding of being or simply being-in-the-world.[10] According to the continental tradition, this understanding is the primary one. In other words, we arrive at theories and empirical truths on the basis of the world we live in and of which we have a pre-understanding. One of the main projects of the continental tradition has thus been to comprehend this pre-understanding, which underlies and sustains all of our actions and experiences. Furthermore, CP has also been more concerned with syntheses and gestalts than with the analysis and the division of a problem into its smaller parts.[11]

In earlier times, the contrast and the battles between CP and AP were loud and clear,[12] but today there are a number of philosophers inside and outside of sport that combine the research methods prevalent in both CP and AP,[13] and that is the basis on which this essay has been written. It seems there are interesting points of contact between the two traditions that can motivate further research in sport.

Before going on, some parameters of the essay should be made explicit. The work that will be taken up here has been inspired by and carried out within the tenets of phenomenology and existentialism. This is because most of the sport philosophy work that emanates from CSP is done within these two philosophical movements.[14] In addition, the work that will be analysed is either directly inspired by or related to philosophers that clearly fall under CP, such as Husserl, Heidegger and Merleau-Ponty as well as some of their successors. Some of the central concepts from the continental tradition will be taken up and I will show how sport philosophers such as Scott Kretchmar, Gunnar Breivik, Klaus V. Meier and others have used them to understand bodily movement and skills in sport.

Intentionality

One of the basic concerns of sport research is to understand skilled motor behaviour. Over the years several distinct models and conceptualizations, which account for the process of skill acquisition, have emerged. This background has allowed for a picture that will be called *the standard analysis* of skill acquisition.[15]

In general, the standard analysis describes skill acquisition as a process that goes from a conscious to an unconscious control of performance. When we start to learn a new skill we often fumble and tumble and try to sort out what needs to be done in order to perform adequately. Thus, at the beginning of a learning process, the athlete is consciously thinking things over in an overly controlled, slow and deliberate way. Furthermore, the athlete tries to move in accordance with the content of what she or he thinks is correct. When the athlete has got the main control on the skill, his or her movement patterns become more consistent as errors are eliminated. Finally, the learner may reach the level of automaticity where skills are performed fast and in an effortless way.[16] At this stage, the performance is often rendered unconscious.[17] Barbara Montero defines *the principle of automaticity* in relation to skill learning as follows: 'When all is going well, expert performance significantly involves neither self-reflective thinking, nor planning, nor predicting, nor deliberation, nor mental effort.'[18] Hence, the standard analysis and the principle of automaticity argue that the best performance of athletes never comes when they are thinking about it.[19] In other words, the expert simply acts in an automatic and unconscious way. But the standard analysis may leave us with at least a couple of problems.

The first problem is related to the distinction between conscious and unconscious processes and the theoretical framework from which this conceptualization has emanated. It has been common practice to relate this distinction to the relationship between controlled and automated information processing.[20] As a consequence, a wealth of knowledge about the information processes of the brain or mind has emerged, but the downside has been that the mind's relational character to the outside world has been underestimated or overlooked. We can then take into consideration what has been called a representationalist view of the mind[21] or what Robert Sokolowski describes as the 'egocentric predicament' where our 'consciousness is taken to be like a bubble or an enclosed cabinet; the mind comes in a box'.[22]

The second problem is about how athletes respond to the demands of specific situations. If the best performances in sport are captured by the principle of automaticity, that is, movements that are performed without thinking, planning, prediction, deliberation and mental effort, how can the best athletes respond in a flexible way to changing circumstances? Evidently, the very best athletes have the capacity to respond in a flexible way to immediate changes in a situation. Does this not require thinking, deliberation, or at least a minor degree of mental effort?

In order to throw light on the two questions above, I will discuss a classic essay in CSP, namely Kretchmar's '"Distancing": An Essay on Abstract Thinking in Sport Performances'. Here Kretchmar takes up a research method of the continental tradition – to describe consciousness as it is lived during performance. His emphasis is on the first person point of view, paying close attention to the phenomenon in question by describing it as thoroughly as possible. He also draws on the work of continental thinkers such as Merleau-Ponty, Hannah Arendt and Martin Buber.

The term 'distancing' is used by Kretchmar to describe our relation to the world. To be at a distance is to have a perspective on the surroundings. Thus, my perspective is different from yours. Consequently, distancing has the characteristics of a subjective point of view. There are different forms of distancing and Kretchmar distinguishes between a minimal and maximal distance between us and the world. A reflex movement is used to illuminate a minimal distance. When, for example, the light in a room dims, one's pupils dilate. This is not something one does. It is just something that happens. In this sense, the distance between me and the world is minimal or close to nothing.

On the other hand, 'conscious, intentional adaptation'[23] is characteristic of maximal distancing. It describes more fully human behaviour. Intentional distancing is Kretchmar's word for it. We are now following in the footsteps of continental thinkers such as Brentano and his student, Husserl. They underlined that the basic feature of consciousness is its intentionality, that is, consciousness is always of or directed at something. Thus, consciousness is object-directed. It provides us with an understanding of the world.

Husserl introduced strange words to account for the intentional experience. He distinguished between *noesis* and *noema*. It is *noesis* that specifies what kind of intentional experience a person is in (e.g. whether a person perceives, believes, remembers, etc.), whereas *noema* determines the object of our intentional experience (that is, the content of what a person perceives, believes or remembers).[24] Kretchmar appeals to this theoretical framework when he describes maximal distancing:

Objects of consciousness, under the mode of maximal distancing, become themes proper that can be 'seen' in limitless ways through any number of different intentional acts. Human consciousness displays a nimbleness of adjustment by intending various objects first, perhaps, through acts of judgement, then through acts of valuation, then acts of doubt, and so on – each time uncovering different aspects of the objects in question, each time opening up possibilities for new or different acts which would be consistent with the themes intended.

'Maximal distancing' seems to be a good metaphor to describe this type of thinking. To have such diversity of access to the objects of consciousness is to be at an 'intentional distance' from them.[25]

Intentional distancing captures an essential feature of skilled motor behaviour in sport, that is, its intentional, object-directed nature. The point I would like to make here is that descriptions of intentional distancing in sport seem to bring us away from the egocentric predicament and into 'the publicness of mind'.[26] This latter view emphasizes the relational character of the mind. Human beings are object-directed in a fundamental sense. Arguably, it is the concept of intentionality that opens the path for us to think precisely in this direction. Thus, intentional distancing introduces an alternative route to understanding the directed and varied nature of skilled behaviour in sport compared to the Cartesian connotations of the conscious-unconscious distinction. Hence, CSP may provide an interesting alternative to the standard analysis of skilled behaviour in sport.

Let us return to the second problem above. What characterizes the intentional behaviour of the highly skilled athlete in sport? By going back to the principle of automaticity, it seems as if highly skilled behaviour in sport could be understood based on the model of a reflex movement because thinking during performance seems to be ruled out. This seems to be precisely Paul Fitts' and Michael Posner's solution. They argue that 'there is a good deal of similarity between highly practiced skills and reflexes. Both seem to run off without much verbalization or conscious content.'[27] Kretchmar also underscores this point when he stresses that sport might be a poor place to look for intentional distancing because 'athletes rely on a variety of reflex actions. There is not time to think things over; the response must "be there", and it must be automatic!'[28]

However, Kretchmar's main argument is that there is nothing incompatible between automatic, effortless action in sport and intentional distancing, but one must, however, be able to describe the kind of distance and abstract attitude skilled athletes achieve while perfecting or performing skills in sport. By comparing the beginner to the advanced athlete, Kretchmar emphasizes that 'not all performers enjoy the same richness and variety of theme. Here those athletes who think more powerfully and, generally, those players who are more skilled have an insightful access to their world which cannot be fully appreciated or understood by others who lack such capability.'[29]

So what characterizes powerful performance, or thinking, in sport? The answer can be seen in the phenomenon of intentional distancing, a phenomenon that is described through four experiential features. First, the really good athletes perceive multiple invitations to act. They are more open to the opportunities called forth by the situation and their acquired skills enable them to sense more subtle variations in play than the beginner, who must often pay specific attention to his or her own movements. Second, once a particular invitation to act is taken up by the skilled athlete, she or he can modify it on its way to completion in a flexible manner. Thus, 'as skill increases, junctures for change and modification are encountered more frequently'.[30] Third, skilled athletes are inventive. They see new meanings, movement patterns and opportunities as the game is played. Finally, skilled athletes have stamina. They make effort-filled actions look effortless. Behind highly skilled performance in sport there are thousands of hours of deliberate practice.[31] Thus, highly skilled athletes in sport are motivated and resilient. As Kretchmar describes it, 'The athlete has to *give* himself to the contest, become committed to the game, fully live the activity, if he desires to understand some things about himself and his sport world which are most difficult to grasp.'[32]

Consequently, the phenomenon of intentional distancing may provide us with an answer to the second problem as well. As Kretchmar concludes, 'If *distancing* is a significant activity of mankind, then it may be proper, if not long overdue, to praise some athletes for their brand of thinking.'[33]

By the phenomenon of intentional distancing, Kretchmar applied a classical CP concept and initiated a debate about the role thinking and consciousness play in the performance of skilled behaviour that is very much alive in current sport philosophy.[34] Moreover, examples of skilled motor behaviour in sport have been applied to test and demonstrate the validity of conceptual frameworks in both CP and AP.[35] Thus, if the above connections are plausible the collaboration between CP and CSP seems mutually productive.

Context

In the previous section, I reviewed how the concept of intentionality provides us with the tools we needed to study our relational structure to objects in the world. In this section, I shall discuss the context of skilled behaviour in sport.

There is already a much-applied definition of the context of sport emanating from the emphasis of analytic sport philosophy (ASP) on necessary and sufficient conditions. Bernard Suits defined sport in terms of a game's constitutive rules.[36] This definition tells us that a game's constitutive rules define what is legitimate and illegitimate to do in a game, and furthermore, in order for something to be a game of sport the activity must be about the execution of physical skills.

An alternative exposition of the sport context is found in Heidegger's existential phenomenology and his description of being-in-the-world. Heidegger's main concern was to understand the meaning of being.[37] This query has also interested continental sport philosophers from Howard Slusher's and Eleanor Metheny's early work on the meaning on human movement to Paul Standish's, Vegard Fusche Moe's, Irena Martínková's and Gunnar Breivik's recent applications of Heidegger's framework to explore authenticity, movement, skilled behaviour and risk sports.[38] In what follows we will look into how Heidegger's description of being-in-the-world has prompted current discourses on skilled behaviour in

CSP[39] with Hubert Dreyfus' interpretation of being-in-the-world lurking in the background.[40]

Heidegger was concerned with the meaning of being and described how the human way of being revealed itself and how the things we encounter are revealed through our way of dealing with them. His basic approach was that our understanding of being must be seen as a unitary phenomenon, that is, as being-in-the-world. While the Cartesian tradition has emphasized that the human being is a subject contemplating objects, the hyphens and the unity of the structure being-in-the-world emphasize that the human being is closely interwoven with its environment.[41]

To avoid any Cartesian connotations, Heidegger even renamed the way we refer to human beings with the term *Dasein*, which literally means 'there-being', (German: *da* – there; *sein* –being). As *Dasein* we are always there, situated, with an understanding of our own way of being in a context that matters to us. In other words, as *Dasein* we are always thrown into situations with which we have a pre-understanding or with which we have a basic familiarity. Our way of being-in a situation is thus a way of being involved or engaged in one's surroundings. It is different from how an object, such as a piece of chalk, for example, is contained in its box, because as human beings we care about our own way of being-in a situation.[42] Furthermore, this is first and foremost not a theoretical worked-out understanding, but rather a practical pre-understanding that enables us to act meaningfully and adequately relative to the context we are in. To illustrate this insight, Breivik uses a quote from Charles Taylor that takes us directly into the world of sport:

> We can draw a neat line between my *picture* of an object and an object, but not between my *dealing* with the object and that object. It may make sense to ask us to focus on what we *believe* about something, say a football, even in the absence of that thing; but when it comes to *playing* football, the corresponding suggestion would be absurd. The actions involved in the game can't be done without the object; they include the object. Take it away and we have something quite different – people miming a game on the stage, perhaps.[43]

Taylor's point is that there is something essentially different between handling an object in a practical way and observing or analysing the object. We are dealing with the ball because it has a function. The athlete uses it to get something done. In a similar way a carpenter uses a hammer to get a job done, for example drive in a nail in order to secure a plank, the footballer kicks the ball in order to pass it, to score a goal and so on. Heidegger expands this description by showing that our daily and practical concerns eventually cohere with the overall projects we are engaged in. Let us illustrate this with an example from football.

An athlete plays football *in* a stadium, *with* a ball, *in order to* create a breakthrough, as a step *towards* scoring a goal, *for the sake of* being a professional or good footballer.[44] The example illustrates that the activity is deeply anchored in a relational structure, which makes up that meaningful whole, which circles in the overall project of being a professional or good football player. It is this structural whole that makes up the world according to Heidegger and that merges into *Dasein* in the sense that *Dasein* inhabits the world in an engaged way.

The example above illustrates that all human activity is contextual in the sense that it takes place in a practical context (a 'where-in') with an item of equipment (a 'with-which') that refers to other items of equipment through its function to get something done (an 'in-order-to'). Moreover, the function of equipment is organized according to a 'towards-which'. This purpose is further organized in terms of an end point, a 'for-the-sake-of-which', which ensures that the whole activity makes sense.[45] This end point is the long-term sense that the footballer makes of being a professional footballer in a similar sense to being a father, a carpenter and so on. According to Dreyfus, these end points should not be understood in terms of discrete goals the subject has in mind, rather each end-point is 'a self-interpretation that informs and orders all my activities'.[46]

Consequently, things show up as meaningful to us because they make sense within a practical and holistic context. Heidegger called these things ready-to-hand. They invite us to behave, to move or to dance, so to speak, in a certain way. For example, one may feel the pull of the situation, being drawn towards the objects around in order to handle them skilfully. Similarly, one may feel the objects around oneself as becoming a natural part of one's skilful movements.

But, as we all have experienced, the world of sport is not so openly available to us all the time. We often see that a football player fumbles and stumbles and thus stops to think and reflect in the middle of a game. Even the very best athletes have choked under the pressure of the situation and begun to stare at their own movements or the objects around them. In these situations the relational character above is 'lit up', as Heidegger says.[47] We become aware of what once was useful in a new way and we are back to Taylor's distinction above – the distinction between my way of dealing with the object and my picture of the object. When this happens the athlete no longer encounters things as available or ready-to-hand, but as present-at-hand. Now, objects get isolated from their context and we can stare at them and describe their properties. The ball is no longer useful, but it can be described in terms of its weight, size and so on.[48]

The general point of the application of Heidegger's phenomenology to describe the context of sporting behaviour is that we dwell in the world in the sense that we always have a familiarity with it.[49] This familiarity is equivalent to our understanding of being – what has been described as being-in-the-world. Hence, the phenomenon of world reveals that which is meaningful and relevant to do in a context and, moreover, this coheres with how *Dasein* inhabits a world. In this sense, CSP may provide us with an alternative account of how different sport worlds invite athletes to behave in different ways.

Body

One of the intractable problems of sport research is to understand the body. The problem of embodiment has been a standard part of the philosophical discourses on sport.[50] In one of the early contributions to the philosophy of sport, Klaus V. Meier tracks the Cartesian roots of the view of the body and shows how and why an existential phenomenological approach to the body provides us with an alternative to its Cartesian version.[51]

Descartes emphasized the Platonic-Christian distinction between mind and body. Under this approach, human beings are divided into two parts: *res cogitans* and *res extensa*. The essence of mind or consciousness is thinking – an activity that is immediately or directly accessible to us. It is through the conscious mind that one suddenly realizes, as Descartes did after a serious doubt, 'I think, therefore I am'. Descartes emphasized that the mind cannot be divided into parts and be subject to the laws of nature. With our conscious minds we are free to choose what kind of life we want to lead and what kind of athletes we should become. It expresses our free will from a subjective, first person point of view.

The body, however, is extended in time and space. It can be described in terms of its three dimensions similar to the way we describe and analyse a book, table or rock. It can thus be divided into its constituent parts and become parts of scientific inquiry.

The picture above expresses Descartes' substance dualism. Its main problem has been to explain how two distinct substances can interact. The naive solution at Descartes' time was that the interaction took part in the pineal gland. Currently, the mind-body problem is revealed through the neuroscientific study of consciousness – that is, the study of how we can grasp the subjective and experiential features of consciousness in terms of its underlying neurophysiology without reducing the experiential qualities that are uniquely tied to the first person point of view.[52]

The impact of Descartes in sport research has been enormous. It has, for instance, led to a division between those who focus on the mental side of sporting activities and those who pay attention to the brute facts of the body. Sport psychologists exemplify the former position. They emphasize how mental techniques can increase success in competitive and stressful sport contests. On the other hand, biomechanists have revealed how bodily techniques in sport can be determined by the laws of nature. Both of these approaches have one thing in common. They view the body as an objective entity that is either subordinate to thought or to the laws of nature. Existential phenomenology, however, provides us with an alternative view of the body.[53]

With Heidegger we have already seen that we are first of all active and engaged agents in the world. The precondition for this engaged style of being is found in our bodies – what Merleau-Ponty described as the lived, phenomenal body or simply the body-subject.[54]

The fact that the body is subjective has to do with our experiences and our perspectives of the world. I see with my eyes, hear with my ears, feel with my skin and so on. All this is ingrained in my body and thus part of me as an embodied creature. There is no distinction between who I am and my body, because I am my body and it is through my embodiment that I perceive the world.[55] When I participate in an activity such as football, I will always experience this activity from a particular point of view, that is, from my view of the playing field, which is determined by how I move around and alter my embodied perspective of the field.[56]

We can now relate this discussion about the body to the discussion of intentionality. As we saw with Kretchmar's discussions of intentional distancing, it is not only the mind that illuminates powerful thinking in sport. Our powerful way of thinking in sport is also illuminated through the body in movement. Following Merleau-Ponty's phenomenology, we can make a distinction between the body as a background phenomenon and as a specific motor-intentional activity.[57]

First of all, the body is the background for us having a world. As Merleau-Ponty describes it, 'one's own body is ... always tacitly understood, in the figure-background structure'.[58] This is due to our body schemas, which enable us to act in a dynamic and shifting world. The fact that the body schemas consist of this dynamic ability means, according to Merleau-Ponty, 'that my body appears to me as an attitude directed towards a certain existing or possible task. And indeed its spatiality is not, like that of external objects or like that of 'spatial sensations', a *spatiality of position*, but a *spatiality of situation*.'[59] Here we see that Merelau-Ponty's approach echoes that of Heidegger's. Our way of being engaged in a world is first and foremost an engaged body-in-the-world.[60]

Furthermore, the embodied basis of our being shows itself in particular intentional actions as well. Merleau-Ponty describes this as motor intentionality. Through the phenomenon of motor intentionality Merleau-Ponty draws our attention to an embodied understanding that cannot be fully explained by the model of a reflex movement or by the model of a thought-out movement governed by a conscious will. As he describes it, through motor intentionality 'we are brought to the recognition of something between movement as a third person process and thought as a representation of movement – something which is an anticipation of, or arrival at, the objective and is ensured by the body itself as a motor power, a "motor project" (*bewegungsentwurf*), a "motor intentionality"'.[61] Hence, motor intentionality provides us with an embodied understanding of the world that is ingrained in our skilful and directed way of dealing with objects in the surroundings.

Now, towards the end of this essay, let us go into the descriptive character of CSP in order to get a better grip of our embodied and motor-intentional way of understanding the surroundings. Let us imagine the situation of catching or grasping a ball in the midst of a game of European handball or basketball. This is an activity that most of us are able to perform in a competent and unreflective way. How can we describe this activity?

First, when someone throws you a ball and it is coming towards you, we can see that your arm will reach out to grasp the ball and it is in this sense that we can say that you have a bodily directedness – a motor-intentional understanding – of the object. We have to do this, as Merleau-Ponty has shown, with 'knowledge in the hands, which is forthcoming only when bodily effort is made and cannot be formulated in detachment of that effort'.[62]

Second, this understanding is very precise and finely grained in the sense that the arm goes up in precisely one particular way – it reaches 'the appropriate position'. Furthermore, this understanding is also highly context-sensitive.[63] You grasp the ball at a certain place, at a certain time and in a certain way. That is, if the conditions of the situation had been different, your arm movement would have been performed differently, as instantiated, for example, by being a little more extended, a little more to the left, and so on.

Third, our activity of grasping the ball is also a gestalt movement where one aspect, the arm movement, is projected as a figure on its background, in this case, the body schema. Another way of saying this is that motor-intentional activities provide us with a holistic and thus irreducible understanding of tasks.

Fourth, the motor-intentional activity of grasping the object is normative because upon its completion you will have a sense of success or failure, that is, are you able to grasp the ball successfully or not? Fifth, this normative function of one's motor-intentional activity is constantly ongoing in a direct and immediate way. There is no opportunity to turn it off. It is just *there*, underlying every movement in an enabling and constraining way.

Finally, if the description above is plausible, perhaps motor-intentional activity is a kind of understanding that is hard or even impossible to conceptualize adequately in the mind of the performer. Perhaps it is rather, as Sean Kelly describes it, an activity that 'gives us a relation to, or a bodily understanding of, the world that goes beyond the subject's capacity to characterize it. Motor intentionality is transcendent in precisely this sense.'[64]

If the descriptions above are adequate, the descriptive character of CP and CSP may provide us with the tools that we need in order to get a more comprehensive understanding of the way we perceive, act and understand through our intentional bodies in sport.

This essay started by establishing a few differences between AP and CP. It has been my attempt to follow up some of these differences by introducing each of its three sections with a traditional understanding of the topic in question and then provide an alternative interpretation by means of elements from CSP. My intention has been to demonstrate that CP in general and CSP in particular may provide a genuine alternative to a traditional way of understanding thinking and agency, context and the body in sport. Our alternatives have been illuminated through intentionality or intentional distancing, being-in-the-world or being-in-sport, and the body-subject, embodiment or motor intentionality.

If I should venture to see a little ahead, I am optimistic about the future of CSP. There is an increasing number of publications within this tradition[65] and it is becoming more common to see philosophers both inside and outside the sport context interested and updated on insights from the continental tradition. The significance of the body in movement to our existence is a case in point that characterizes today's discourses of sport and many other areas. It is my belief that we will see even more productive work in the coming years on the bodily basis of our existence, and I expect that quite a lot of this work will be related to or directly influenced by CP or CSP.[66]

Notes

1   The main source on intentionality will be Scott Kretchmar, '"Distancing": An Essay on Abstract Thinking in Sport Performances', *Journal of the Philosophy of Sport* 19 (1982): 6–18. The main source on context will be Gunnar Breivik, 'Skillful Coping in

Everyday Life and in Sport: A Critical Examination of the Views of Heidegger and Dreyfus', *Journal of the Philosophy of Sport* 34 (2007), 2: 116–34. The main source on embodiment will be Klaus V. Meier, 'Cartesian and Phenomenological Anthropology: The Radical Shift and its Meaning for Sport', *Journal of the Philosophy of Sport* 2 (1975): 51–73 and Klaus V. Meier, 'Embodiment, Sport, and Meaning', in *Philosophic Inquiry in Sport*, 2nd ed, eds., William J. Morgan and Klaus V. Meier (Champaign, IL: Human Kinetics, 1995), 89–95.

2   Edmund Husserl, *Ideas Pertaining to a Pure Phenomenology and to a Phenomenological Philosophy, First Book*, trans. F. Kersten (The Hague: Kluwer, 1983); Martin Heidgger, *Being and Time*, trans. J. Macquarrie and E. Robinson (New York: Harper & Row, 1962); and Maurice Merleau-Ponty, *Phenomenology of Perception*, trans. C. Smith (London: Routledge Classics, 2002).

3   Simon Critchley, *Continental Philosophy: A Very Short Introduction* (Oxford: Oxford University Press, 2001), 13.

4   Simon Critchley, 'What is Continental Philosophy', in *A Companion to Continental Philosophy*, eds., Simon Critchley and William R. Schroeder (Malden, MA: Blackwell, 1999), 1; and Robert C. Solomon and David Sherman, eds., *The Blackwell Guide to Continental Philosophy* (Oxford: Blackwell Publishing, 2003).

5   John R. Searle, 'Contemporary Philosophy in the United States', in *The Blackwell Companion to Philosophy*, 2nd ed., eds., Nicholas Bunnin and E.P. Tsui-James (Malden, MA: Blackwell, 2003), 1–22; and Mike McNamee, 'Editorial: Sport, Ethics and Philosophy: Context, History, Prospect', *Sport, Ethics and Philosophy* 1 (2007): 1–6.

6   Searle, 'Contemporary Philosophy in the United States', 1.

7   Critchley, 'What is Continental Philosophy', 3.

8   Ibid., 8-13; and Searle, 'Contemporary Philosophy in the United States'.

9   To seek for a 'complete and accurate understanding' is a locution that is used to determine the goal of phenomenology. See Sean Kelly, 'Grasping at Straws: Motor intentionality and the Cognitive Science of Skilled Behavior', in *Heidegger, Coping, and Cognitive Science: Essays in Honor of Hubert L. Dreyfus*, vol. 2, eds., Mark Wrathall and Jeff Malpas (Cambridge, MA: MIT Press, 2000), 162.

10 See Dermot Moran, *Introduction to Phenomenology* (London: Routledge, 2000).

11 Critchley, *Continental Philosophy: A Very Short Introduction*, 34–7.

12 Ibid.

13 For example, Scott Kretchmar, 'Dualisms, Dichotomies and Dead Ends: Limitations of Analytic Thinking about Sport', *Sport, Ethics and Philosophy* 1 (2007): 266-280; Gunnar Breivik, 'Zombie-Like or Superconscious? A Phenomenological and Conceptual Analysis of Consciousness in Elite Sport', *Journal of the Philosophy of Sport* 40 (2013): 85–106; C.G. Prado, ed., *A House Divided: Comparing Analytic and Continental Philosophy* (New York: Humanity Books, 2003); and Sean D. Kelly, 'Closing the Gap: Phenomenology and Logical Analysis', *The Harvard Review of Philosophy* 12 (2005): 4–24.

14 Arno Müller, 'From Phenomenology to Existentialism – Philosophical Approaches Towards Sport', *Sport, Ethics and Philosophy* 5 (2011): 202–16.

15 Hubert L. Dreyfus and Stuart E. Dreyfus, *Mind over Machine: The Power of Human Intuition and Expertise in the Era of the Computer* (New York: Free Press, 1986); and Paul M. Fitts and M.I. Posner, *Human Performance* (London: Prentice-Hall, 1973).

16 Fitts and Posner, *Human Performance*, 11–15.

17 See, for example, John F. Kihlstrom, 'The Cognitive Unconscious', *Science* 237 (1987): 1447; Bernard J. Baars, *A Cognitive Theory of Consciousness* (Cambridge: Cambridge University Press, 1998), 73; and Drew A. Hyland, *Philosophy of Sport* (New York: Paragon, 1990), 80.

18   Barbara Montero, 'A Dancer Reflects', in *Mind, Reason, and Being-in-the-World: The McDowell-Dreyfus Debate*, ed., Joseph K. Schear (London: Routledge, 2013), 304.

19   Timothy W. Gallwey, *The Inner Game of Tennis*, rev. ed. (New York: Random House, 1974), 7.

20   A.M. Williams, K. Davids and J.G. Williams, *Visual Perception and Action in Sport* (London: E & FN Spon, 1999), 43.

21   Charles Taylor, 'Overcoming Epistemology', in Charles Taylor, *Philosophical arguments* (Cambridge, MA: Harvard University Press, 1995), 1–19.

22   Robert Sokolowski, *Introduction to Phenomenology* (Cambridge, UK: Cambridge University Press, 2000), 9.

23   Kretchmar, '"Distancing": An Essay on Abstract Thinking in Sport Performances', 8.

24   David Cerbone, *Understanding Phenomenology* (Chesham, UK: Acumen), 30.

25   Kretchmar, '"Distancing": An Essay on Abstract Thinking in Sport Performances', 8–9.

26   Sokolowski, *Introduction to Phenomenology*, chap. 1.

27   Fitts and Posner, *Human Performance*, 15.

28   Kretchmar, '"Distancing": An Essay on Abstract Thinking in Sport Performances', 9.

29   Ibid., 9.

30   Ibid., 12.

31   K.A. Ericsson, 'The Influence of Experience and Deliberate Practice on the Development of Superior Expert Performance', in *The Cambridge Handbook of Expertise and Expert Performance*, eds. K.A. Ericsson, N. Charness, R.R. Hoffman and P.J. Feltovich (Cambridge: Cambridge University Press, 2006), 683–703.

32   Kretchmar, '"Distancing": An Essay on Abstract Thinking in Sport Performances', 17.

33   Ibid., 17.

34   See, for example, Breivik, 'Zombie-Like or Superconscious? A Phenomenological and Conceptual Analysis of Consciousness in Elite Sport'.

35   See, for example, Hubert L. Dreyfus, 'Intelligence Without Representation – Merleau-Ponty's Critique of Mental Representation', *Phenomenology and the Cognitive Sciences* 1 (2002): 367–83; and John R. Searle, *Intentionality: An Essay in the Philosophy of Mind* (Cambridge, MA: Cambridge University Press, 1983), 150–3.

36   Bernard Suits, 'The Elements of Sport', in *Philosophic Inquiry in Sport*, eds., William J. Morgan and Klaus V. Meier (Champaign, IL: Human Kinetics, 1988). See also Part 1 'The Nature of Play, Sport, and Games' in William J. Morgan and Klaus V. Meier, 2nd ed, eds. *Philosophic Inquiry in Sport* (Champaign, IL: Human Kinetics, 1995).

37   Heidegger, *Being and Time*.

38   Howard S. Slusher, *Man, Sport and Existence: A Critical Analysis* (Philadelphia: Lea & Febiger, 1967); Eleanor Metheny, *Movement and Meaning* (New York: McGraw-Hill, 1968); Paul Standish, 'In the Zone: Heidegger and Sport', in *Ethics and Sport*, eds., M.J. McNamee and S.J. Parry (London: E & FN Spon, 1998), 256–69; Vegard Fusche Moe, 'Understanding Intentional Movement in Sport: A Philosophical Inquiry into Skilled Motor Behavior' (PhD diss., Norwegian School of Sport Sciences, 2007); Irena Martínková, 'Anthropos as Kinanthropos: Heidegger and Patočka on Human Movement', *Sport, Ethics and Philosophy* 5 (2011): 217–30; Breivik, 'Skillful Coping in Everyday Life and in Sport: A Critical Examination of the Views of Heidegger and Dreyfus', and Gunnar Breivik, 'Being-in-the-void: A Heideggerian Analysis of Skydiving', *Journal of the Philosophy of Sport* 37 (2010): 29–46.

39   Breivik, 'Skillful Coping in Everyday Life and in Sport: A Critical Examination of the Views of Heidegger and Dreyfus'.

40   Hubert L. Dreyfus, *Being-in-the-world: A Commentary on Heidgger's Being and Time, Division 1* (New Baskerville: MIT Press, 1991).

41   Ibid.

42 Ibid., 40–5.
43 Charles Taylor, 'Overcoming Epistemology', 12. See also Breivik, 'Skillful Coping in Everyday Life and in Sport: A Critical Examination of the Views of Heidegger and Dreyfus', 118.
44 This example is modified from a similar one in Dreyfus, *Being-in-the-world: A Commentary on Heidgger's Being and Time, Division 1*, 92.
45 Ibid.
46 Ibid., 95.
47 Heidegger, *Being and Time*, 105–7.
48 For a discussion of how things ready-to-hand switch over to present-at-hand in sporting contexts, see Breivik, 'Skillful Coping in Everyday Life and in Sport: A Critical Examination of the Views of Heidegger and Dreyfus', 119–21.
49 For an extended account of dwelling, see Dreyfus, *Being-in-the-world*, 16-23.
50 See Part II 'Embodiment and Sport' in William J. Morgan and Klaus V. Meier, 2nd ed, eds. *Philosophic Inquiry in Sport* (Champaign, IL: Human Kinetics, 1995); Lynne Belaif, 'Meanings of the Body', *Journal of the Philosophy of Sport* 4 (1977): 50–67; John O'Neill, 'The Spectacle of the Body', *Journal of the Philosophy of Sport* 1 (1974): 110–22; and David Morris, 'Touching Intelligence', *Journal of the Philosophy of Sport* 29 (2002): 149–62.
51 Meier, 'Cartesian and Phenomenological Anthropology: The Radical Shift and its Meaning for Sport' and idem, 'Embodiment, Sport, and Meaning'.
52 For an exposition of this problem in analytic philosophy of mind, see Jens E. Birch, 'In the Synaptic Cleft: Caught in the Gap between Neurotransmitter Release and Conscious Experience in Sport' (PhD diss., Norwegian School of Sport Sciences, 2010).
53 For a discussion of a biomechanical and phenomenological view of the body in the study of sport technique, see Sigmund Loland, 'The Mechanics and Meaning of Alpine Skiing: Methodological and Epistemological Notes on the Study of Sport Technique', *Journal of the Philosophy of Sport* 14 (1992): 55–77.
54 Merleau-Ponty, *Phenomenology of Perception*.
55 Ibid.
56 John Hughson and David Inglis, 'Inside the Beautiful Game: Towards a Merleau-Pontian Phenomenology of Soccer Play', *Journal of the Philosophy of Sport* 14 (2002): 1–15.
57 See, for example, Taylor Carman, *Merleau-Ponty* (London: Routledge, 2008), 102–19.
58 Merleau-Ponty, *Phenomenology of Perception*, 115.
59 Ibid., 114–15.
60 Ibid., 162–70.
61 Ibid., 126–7.
62 Ibid., 166.
63 For a phenomenological description of the body's finely grained and context-sensitive understanding, see Sean D. Kelly, 'Merleau-Ponty on the Body', *Ratio (new series)* 15 (2002): 386–91.
64 Sean D. Kelly, 'Edmund Husserl and phenomenology', in *The Blackwell guide to continental philosophy*, eds. Robert C. Solomon and David Sherman (Malden, MA: Blackwell, 2003), 135.
65 See, for example, Irena Martínková and Jim Parry, eds., 'Special Issue: An Introduction to the Phenomenological Study of Sport', *Sport, Ethics and Philosophy* 5 (2011): 185–358.
66 Thanks to Cesar R. Torres and Gunnar Breivik for their constructive comments.

5 The Philosophy of Sport, Eastern Philosophy and Pragmatism

Jesús Ilundáin-Agurruza, Koyo Fukasawa and Mizuho Takemura

Two scenarios set the stage:

1. *In* Zen and the Art of Archery, *Eugene Herrigel recounts his five long years of struggle, self-doubt and failure before finally letting the arrow release itself.[1] In Kyudo, the way of archery, arrows hitting the target are secondary to process and proper form.*
2. *In the 1970s and 1980s the Soviet Union and German Democratic Republic implemented state-supported doping programmes. Coupled to unparalleled scientific training methods, this turned athletes into lab specimens, leading to unprecedented Olympic and world medals and records.*

These two scenarios diametrically illustrate central issues in contemporary sport philosophy concerning process and results, the aim(s) of sport, the nature of and relation between body and mind and the role of community. They also frame this chapter's driving question: How do Eastern philosophy and pragmatism contribute uniquely to sport philosophy? Aligned with the first scenario, they rethink sport's aims and nature in opposition to today's focus on performance, health and revenues. Highlighting similarities and differences, the ensuing presents their unique methodologies and philosophical contributions.

A thorough overview of Eastern philosophy and pragmatism in a single chapter is unfeasible. Eastern philosophy spans the millenary branches of India, China, Japan and other distinctive traditions, e.g. Korea's Chandogyo. Pragmatism, more circumscribed, remains highly fertile. We focus on East Asian philosophy, primarily Japanese philosophy and pragmatist classical figures because:[2] being chronologically last among the three millenary traditions, Japanese philosophy's comprehensively integrative development affords a more efficient presentation of Hindu, Buddhist, Daoist and Confucian tenets; as for pragmatism, its founding fathers – Charles Peirce, William James and John Dewey – are closest to sport philosophy's concerns. But also because interlacing their methodology and theory allows expedient application to signature topics that readily connect with sport philosophy.

Section 1 contextualizes matters. Sections 2 to 5 discuss respectively: pure experience, body-mind, community and contemporary issues with two applications – martial arts and Western sports, and doping and genetic technology.

1. Theoretical and Historical Background

Several facts justify coupling Eastern philosophy and American pragmatism. One, their temperamental affinity – to echo James, philosophy is largely a matter of temperament:[3] they share a determined attitude, eclectic philosophical appetite and eminent optimism. Two, a focus on practicality and the resultant flexibility: Indians are remarkably analytic and empirically oriented, the Chinese are markedly practical in life and their philosophies seek harmony (most evident in Confucianism), the Japanese display great openness and adaptive mien, while pragmatists embrace a 'whatever works best' attitude. However, they prioritize this optimism and practicality differently. Pragmatism is more concerned and theoretically begins with metaphysics and epistemology, the East centres on and starts from ethics and aesthetics.[4] This impinges on methodological matters – a methodology is a way of doing things. Pragmatism has a penchant for the scientific method. Peirce's seminal article 'The Fixation of Belief' first defends this, discussing how belief assuages the itch doubt causes, which we fix by a number of methods: tenacity, authority, a priori intuition and the scientific method.[5] With theoretically significant differences, James, Dewey and most pragmatists embrace various versions of the scientific method in a perennial quest after absolute truth. This is connected to their empiricism, for which experience vets truths about the world, and naturalism, which finds explanations for reality in the natural world, not a transcendental realm. In contrast, Japanese philosophy favours intuitive reflection marked by phenomenological and experiential analysis of pure experience over rational discourse. This divergence noted, both see experience as vital for understanding reality.

India's philosophical contributions begin with Hinduism, particularly the Upanishads. Buddhism, paralleling Christianity and Judaism, arises as an alternative within an orthodox Hindu context. It keeps certain tenets: *samsara*, the wheel of reincarnation where we are reborn as higher or lower life forms millions of times before reaching release (key to viewing life as ephemeral and equanimity in accepting death), and *karma*, the moral law of cause and effect. But it rejects the caste system, belief in *Atman* or self, and, discarding *Brahman* as ultimate reality, stresses this world's illusion. Buddhism also transforms the Hindu idea of *moksha*, blissful liberation from *samsara,* into *nirvana* or cessation once we reach Buddhahood. Siddhartha Gautama's focus is practical ethics, thus the first Buddha bypasses metaphysical ponderings. However, subsequent divisions among followers result in complex ontological disputations.

In East Asian philosophy, the main religious and philosophical systems issue forth from China's Daoism, Confucianism both native to the Middle Kingdom, and Chan Buddhism. Purportedly Bodhidharma brings Dhyana Buddhism from India in the 6th century CE, its stern character being dulcified into Chan Buddhism. Eventually, Buddhism splits into two schools that keep the basic doctrines of the four noble truths and the eightfold path: Theravada centres on personal release and enlightenment and Mahayana focuses on compassion for all beings. The latter becomes more influential in East Asia. Chinese Buddhism and culture trickle into Japan around the 7th century CE, coexisting with native Shinto. Japanese Buddhism progressively diversifies among others into Nichiren, Tendai, Pure Land and Zen. Nishida Kitaro,[6] Japan's pre-eminent 20th-century philosopher and the first to combine Western philosophy and methodology with native mores of thinking, and the Kyoto School (established by Nishida) incorporate Zen Buddhism, particularly intuitive pre-reflection – related to Zen's direct revelation, *satori* – and the idea of praxis-based inquiry.

Pragmatism is idiosyncratic in Western philosophy. An old system of thought for new ways of thinking, as James's subtitle to his work *Pragmatism* avers, it opposes mainstream views on all major philosophical areas. Its roots sink deeply in history, but it is in America that said method is systematically adopted.[7] Agreement being scant on whether it is mainly a method,[8] stance, attitude or even therapy,[9] what matters is that it *does* work as a method to settle metaphysical disputes. James memorably illustrates this with the example of the squirrel's tree trunk circling.[10] Indeed, a methodological norm of practical conduct guides pragmatists regardless of other differences. Since epistemology is less prominent below, the following approximates sport and pragmatism in relation to truth. Peirce starts the pragmatic business with 'How to Make Our Ideas Clear'.[11] He seeks to ground meaning via his pragmatic maxim, a simple criterion that can be paraphrased as 'meaning is fixed by the habits it produces'. James (mis) appropriates this, widening Peirce's narrower scope, making it a matter of practical consequences. For his part, Dewey emphasizes not the ability to settle dispute, as James does, but the methodological advantage of overcoming quandaries, broadening pragmatism into a philosophical system.[12]

These approaches fruitfully connect with sport. Eastern views are qualitatively attentive to experience itself, and pragmatism demands action to find out the merit and meaning of ideas because truth lies in practical consequences. As James asks, 'what concrete difference will its being true make in any one's actual life?'[13] Sport affords rich, varied opportunities to test said concrete differences. As Richard Lally explains regarding Dewey, the truths of sport are public, experimental and shared.[14] Through sport we find *lived* experiential truths – of life-changing consequences – which pragmatism seeks and East Asian philosophy cultivates.

2. Pure Experience

This is the keystone to James's radical empiricism, the zenith of his mature views. Methodologically, James uses a thick phenomenology to *concretely* explore experience's structure. This largely empirical project centres on human bodily interactions with the environment – the world alive for us – in mutually influential relationship. Jamesian pure experience is raw, pre-conceptual: 'it is plain, unqualified activity or existence, a simple *that*' on which we act.[15] To exemplify he tells readers to arrest themselves 'in the act of reading this article now. *Now* this is a pure experience, a phenomenon, or datum, a mere *that* or content of fact. *"Reading" simply is, is there.*[16] Elsewhere he clarifies, 'within this full experience, concrete and undivided, such as it is, a given, the objective physical world and the interior and personal world of each of us meet and fuse the way lines fuse at their intersection', a subject/object unity Nishida further refines.[17]

John Kaag shows the relevance of this for sport when discussing his rowing experience: 'According to James, "the world of concrete personal experiences … is multitudinous beyond imagination, tangled, muddy, painful and perplexed," and just like the first painful day of practice, is inseparable from a more cohesive understanding or athletic mastery.'[18] Continuity permeates pure experience,[19] which we divide and categorize conceptually but itself does not split into discrete elements. James details, 'the nucleus of every man's experience, the sense of his own body, is, it is true, an absolutely continuous perception; and equally continuous is his perception […] of a material environment of that body, changing by gradual transition when the body moves.'[20] Mark Johnson details the radical implications of this: 'every thought implicates a certain bodily awareness […] in all thinking, we are in some degree aware,' which is predicated on James's fulsome experience.[21] Concepts are useful but not irreducibly primitive (James staunchly defends non-conceptual thought). Kaag, quoting James, explains that we are to 'drop them [concepts] when they hinder understanding; and take reality *bodily* and integrally up into philosophy in exactly the perceptual shape in which it comes'.[22] Sport, remaining close to pure experience, permits the seasoned rower to disappear in a 'willingness to be as nothing'.[23]

James profoundly influences Nishida, who seeks to bring together East and West and bridge the fact/value-is/ought gap. Nishida explains that 'by *pure* I am referring to the state of experience just as it is without the least addition of deliberative discrimination',[24] that 'has no meaning whatsoever; it is simply a present consciousness of the facts as they are'.[25] This direct experience unites subject and object, knowing and object.[26] This unity, not its kind, makes the experience pure.[27] A dynamic, *acting intuition* unifies it,[28] amalgamating knowledge, emotion and volition.[29] Pure experience is continuous for him also. Trying to overcome psychologistic description for philosophical explanation, as he explains on a re-edition of his maiden work,[30] he makes of *mu* (無), nothingness, the primary concept. Developing a logic of place or *topos*, absolute nothingness negates the self or 'I' as both empirical and transcendental self, making of it, as Thomas Kasulis points out, an action – Nishida's acting intuition.[31] Thus, Nishida and James view the self as a function.[32] This establishes a dialectical unity of contradictories or identity of opposites where the subject/object, mind/body and other dichotomies disappear as such. That is, as our self dissolves we become integrated as pure experience with reality while reality also identifies with us. Importantly, in the resulting unity we push further the limits of pure experience through practice. This abstract system has quite practical applications.

Nishida states, 'when inspiration arises in a painter and the brush moves spontaneously, a unifying reality is operating behind this complex activity.'[33]

This applies to all disciplined behaviour. Therein, 'in the mutual forgetting of the self and the object, the object does not move the self and the self does not move the object', and we find 'simply one world, one scene'.[34] In martial arts, when a fighter effortlessly and reflectively unaware flips an opponent, heretofore opponents become integrated, both bodies moving together *as one* movement. Their opposition becomes a contradictory unity of opposites, their selves negated into an unselfconsciousness that is very aware of the felt experience, 'for they are development and completion of a single thing'.[35] They become nothing, filled by a pure, ineffable experience that the Japanese call *taiken* (体験), living experience, in contrast to the subsequent reflective remembrance and articulation they name *keiken* (経験), experience. Following Nishida, in sport we inhabit the action itself.[36]

There is a crucial difference in James's and Nishida's congruent views. James writes, 'only new born babes, or men in semi-coma from sleep, drugs, illnesses or blows, may be assumed to have an experience pure in the literal sense of a *that* which is not yet any definite *what*.'[37] He professes that mystical experience might extend our experience,[38] and distinguishes the experiencing from our ability to articulate it.[39] But ultimately, Jamesian pure experience is a *limit* experience. For Nishida, pure experience is both origin and terminus: we begin with and must cultivate, through bodily practice, a return to it (crucial for sport philosophy). This endeavour is normative: actualizing pure experience through lived praxis becomes the basis for Nishida's mature analysis of art, morality and religion.[40] Here, training and discipline are vital to nurture self-negation in lifelong practice (tied to Buddhism's *sen-nichi shugyo* (千日修行) – 1000 days of practice to refine oneself). In short, while James descriptively analyses pure experience, Nishida normatively resides in it.

Sport *is* a lived practice, should we listen intently to its kinaesthetic and kinetic dynamics. Sport specific, these open worlds of pure sensation. As we mature in sport, we are engaged in a continuous process where unity with reality is achieved. Yet, when trying to reach greater depths this gives rise to conflict. Then we become conscious again until we achieve unity anew in a spiral of perpetual perfection.[41] For James and Nishida, 'body both precedes and shapes thought', even if only the latter pursues the potential of engaging it as part of a lived practice.[42] This leads to the body-mind relation.

3. Body-Mind

Auspiciously, the term 'body-mind' refers to Dewey's coinage, meant to bypass prevalent Western ontology, and to the conventional translation for the Japanese *shinshin* (心身), an integrated body-mind. The dualistic ontology of Orthodox Western views faces the hard problem of consciousness: how to scientifically explain subjective phenomena, *qualia*. It is usually addressed by dualist or materialist theories. In epistemology, rationality reigns, excluding emotion and intuition from mainstream philosophical and scientific discourse. Japanese thought and pragmatism (especially Dewey and James), breaking ranks, both endorse holism.

In Japanese Buddhism, *shinshin* becomes explicit philosophically early on: Kukai (774–835 CE), the Shingon school founder, writes, 'one becomes a Buddha in and through this very body,'[43] Dogen (1200–1253 CE), Soto Zen's nominal 'patriarch', emphasizes the body to capture the meaning of cultivation,[44] rooting practice in the seated meditation he calls 'just sitting' (*shikan taza* (只管打坐).[45] Whereas in the West mind and body are static concepts, in Japan the body-mind is dynamic and pliable to cultivation. Yuasa Yasuo, a reference point in contemporary Japanese philosophy of the body, builds on Nishida, Kukai, Dogen and Watsuji Tetsuro.

Yuasa develops an integrative view of performance where different people's body-mind is in more or less advanced states of synchrony and levels of proficiency. This accords with people having different sporting, martial and artistic abilities. The highest level, *shinshin ichinyo* (心身一如), oneness of body-mind, seeks spontaneity through discipline and results in superior execution for Yuasa.[46] In China, this self-cultivation is achieved through *wuwei* (無為), effortless action, which paradoxically takes place spontaneously.[47] In Japan, *shugyo* (修行) denotes such self-cultivation that, if originally applied to the Buddhist practice of *senichi shugyo*, eventually extends to the arts, e.g. *sado* (茶道), the way of tea, *No* theatre (能) and martial arts. This self-cultivation is particularized, being different when engaging samurai, Buddhist monks or athletes. Action refinement is undertaken not seeking specific results (tasty tea or a bull's eye), but a state of no-mind, *mushin* (無心). Then we act unperturbed and unfettered, as Buddhist Monk Takuan Soho explained to legendary samurai Yagyu Munenori.[48]

Pure action, Yuasa's term,[49] may lead to better performance, but the goal is self-realization or awareness. This agrees with Nishida,[50] for whom the body is key.[51] Training, *keiko* (稽古), is necessary for all, gifted and average, but not sufficient. However, those less talented may still approximate the former's experience.[52] Pure action and experience are fundamental, but reflection remains cardinal. Thus *Shugyo* is *thoroughly* educational, and diverges from Western high-performance sport or the instrumental use of sports as a means toward health alone. In summary, the East seeks a holistic development of persons and their abilities. Pragmatism smiles on this.

Dewey, as an empirical naturalist, theorizes the 'body-mind' to counter dualist and materialist tendencies because they reify dynamic processes to solve the very problem they create. The body-mind is psycho-physical, not merely mental or material, and 'simply designates what actually takes place when a living body is implicated in situations of discourse, communication and participation'.[53] This works because the continuity of thought, perception and feeling is rooted in the body.[54] Agreeing with James, Dewey stresses the role of quality. Experience has an aesthetic quality all its own.[55] It also implies a consummation, as it is 'a whole and carries with it its own individualizing quality and self-sufficiency'.[56] Indeed, Dewey's complex conception of experience as fulfilled, holistic, complete, continuous and unified dovetails with James and Nishida. Closer than James to the Eastern ideal, he emphasizes development as continuous body-mind-centred skill refinement. For Dewey, self-cultivation means 'the development of the individual's personality to its fullest potential and energies'.[57] Instead of specific instructions, he describes catalytic conditions that do not lead us by the hand (agreeable to Japanese *do* as pedagogical ways of life).[58] Pragmatism's philosophy of self-cultivation readily applies to sport.

Sports, genuinely engaging discipline and cultivation, imply an exquisite attunement to the body that coheres with Dewey and James. For Dewey, revealing, fulsome experience is tied to suffering – unavoidable in sport – which begs for justificatory explanation.[59] Lally applies Dewey's interest in human self-cultivation to endurance sports: faith in the experimental method, risk and will power coalesce into present moments that define our character and make the world other than it is; thus they become *an* experience.[60] Yet, this cultivating process does not happen at the purely individual level; it needs a community.

4. Community

Adamant individualism characterizes Western socio-political culture. There are two main philosophic camps, liberalism and communitarianism. The former stresses a liberal agenda where individuals' autonomy to freely live their lives is central, the main task of government being fair access to liberty and economic means.[61] The latter emphasizes the role of community as an egalitarian locus for common flourishing and favours particularism – culturally idiosyncratic values – rather than a universal justice standard.[62]

Dewey, astride this divide, sees the goal of self-cultivation as personal flourishing within the context of a democratic society. He prizes individuals' cultivation and, agreeing with Plato, sees them happiest when engaged in activities for which they are naturally talented,[63] yet argues that we measure a social form of life's worth by 'the extent in which the interests of a group are shared by all its members, and the fullness and freedom with which it interacts with other groups'.[64] Among forms of communitarian organization, a democratic society fulfils this best because democracy stands out for its devotion to education and the realization of a social form of life. The biggest challenge to Western liberal democracy comes from East Asia's endorsement of community over individual;[65] there, theorists have managed to point to 'particular non-liberal practices and institutions that may be appropriate for the contemporary world'.[66]

In the East, a family-centred harmonious community is paramount. Confucianism, its influence still palpable, is the clearest exponent of this collectivist spirit. Confucius (Kongzi, 551–479 BCE) aims at developing a harmonious society rooted in a government that rules through virtue and moral example instead of punishment and force.[67] Like Dewey, he believes humans are capable of perfecting themselves and esteems best cooperative communal associations that share a body of knowledge and values. Education is the *exclusive* means to human self-realization.[68] Three key virtues are central to enact this harmonious society: kindness, justice and propriety. Exclusively patriarchal, men who actualize this are *Chunzi* (perfect gentlemen). Arguably, a salient problem is Confucianism's endorsement of patriarchal values, which subjugate women.[69] Alternatively, Buddhists emphasize compassion.

Tetsuro Watsuji, Japan's foremost 20th-century ethicist, builds his ethics on a Confucian and Buddhist legacy while incorporating Western thought, which, as Robert Carter explains, he criticizes for its out-of-touch individualism.[70] The centrepiece is his notion of 'in-betweenness of human beings', *ningen* in the Japanese vernacular (originally *jinkan* in Buddhism (人間)), both use the same *kanji*). He writes, 'the locus of ethical problems lies not in the consciousness of the isolated individual, but precisely in the in-betweenness of person and person.'[71] For Watsuji, a human being (versus an animal) must be a dialectical unity between individual and member of society.[72] We are defined *in* our relations with others. This takes place through a subjective spatiality, the essential characteristic of human beings, which arises from 'the manner in which multiple subjects are related to one another'.[73] Sport dynamics beautifully exemplify this dialectic: athletes, positions and plays are defined in relation to teammates *and* competitors.

In summary, in Western philosophy a community is an invariable object in contraposition to a subject. As an abstraction, it aggregates various functions. In pragmatism, it is a variable and developable existence that values harmony within a community where people actively participate in creating a better state. In Japanese philosophy, a community is a concrete element that connects with self-identity: there is no self and object/community split, rather people's very existence *is* a community where they remarkably tend to pursue solidarity.

A pragmatically inspired sport philosophy can ease several tensions. The freedom-versus-community conflict is palliated by a communitarian view of sports. Sportspersons must freely create within the restrictions set by the sport's constitutive rules as upheld by the community of players. In sports, a player's personal freedom issues from the dialectical relation with his or her own teammates (when applicable) in response to the opponents' tactics who, mirroring the process, create a self-replicating system. Relatedly, Daniel G. Campos revealingly applies Peirce's notion of personality as a coordination of ideas to a football club, which builds community by being endowed with a personality constituted by its members' sympathy and feelings of allegiance.[74] Hence, club and individual members, instead of competing with each other, embrace one another. The tension between cooperation and competition is effectively approached with an East-West comparative analysis where egolessness and benevolence encourage a collaborative model of competition. Additionally, Joan Forry's examination of movement's specificity and acquired meanings in relation to gender and sports appositely argues for an increased feminist awareness that, through habit change, can counterbalance Confucian patriarchal tendencies from within popular sporting practices.[75] Last, such cross-culturally applied ethics may alleviate the deeper theoretical tension between Eastern communitarian and Western liberal values, e.g. through an educational commitment that promotes development of individuals and community, or by increasing sporting opportunities within a framework of solidarity.

5. Contemporary Sport Philosophy: Two Applications[76]

Martial Arts and Sports

Both engage our physical skills, sometimes being kinetically analogous, e.g. Olympic archery and *kyudo* (弓道), shooting arrows at a target. But, as the opening scenarios show, there is a marked contrast between contemporary high-performance sport and traditional martial arts. We concentrate on two specific activities (the analysis extends to martial arts and sports generally): *kendo* (剣道), because it remains truer to its roots than many other martial arts, and football, given its worldwide popularity and inception when modern sport was institutionalized. To begin polemically: *kendo* focuses on process whereas football revolves around goals.

When Japan enters the peaceful Tokugawa era (1600–1868 CE) *Kenjutsu's* (剣術) sword warrior skills become *Kendo*, the way of the sword. The new ethos swaps violence for peace, lethality for a philosophical ethos, steel katana for bamboo *shinai* (竹刀) and seeks self-cultivation through formalized movement. It becomes less about winning than about the meaning behind our performance. Shinobu Abe attests of his *kendo* practice, 'whether winning or losing, I try to consider soon afterward the cause and process of victory and defeat.'[77] *Kendo*, steeped in Buddhist tenets, aligns with the body-mind and Nishida's views: *kendokas* (剣道家) must become egoless, and abiding in nothingness and pure experience, act spontaneously and without deliberation. This originates in samurai reliance on Zen to learn self-forgetfulness in order to lose concern for life. While necessary, an accurate hit is not sufficient; it is the process that matters. Judges award *ippon* (一本), the win, for the manner in which the attack is conducted. *Zanshin* (残心), a continuation of the attack with readiness to fight again even after a successful *ippon*, must also be demonstrated after a hit. Rulings and referees are *never* challenged, another way in which the fighter must remain egoless (like samurai accepting death).

Traditional martial arts training methods develop technique via *sennichi shugyo*: *kendokas* perform countless yet mindful repetitions of the same cuts and parries. When students get stuck in their development, the *sensei* (先生) does not give the answer but indirectly shows the way to self-realization. This invariably frustrating process is the way to *lived* truths. Herrigel's Japanese colleague tells him, 'you had to suffer shipwreck through your own efforts before you were ready to seize the lifebelt he [sensei Awa] threw you.'[78] Education predicated on a holistic and integrative body-mind permeates this. In short, *kendo* develops into an exercise in self-reflection and cultivation. In this paradigm, the activity (martial art, sport, game) must be engaged non-instrumentally.

Football is keen on results, on the scoring of goals. When sport becomes high performance, it splits its participants psychologically and physiologically, and drastically transforms tactics, technology and training methods. Dramatic changes in formations and strategies attest to this: the game evolves from all players converging on the ball via 3-4-3, 2-5-3 and other complex systems. As a thoroughly reductive model, quantified data – VO2 Max, Watt output, goals, assists – defines athletes and their performances. An overemphasis on results has inherent hazards: sport becomes an instrument, often subservient to questionable ends (money, fame, etc.). Instrumentalization also makes cheating, game fixing and drug use more likely, since ends justify means. Challenging, even assaulting referees, is just another feature of the game. Ultimately, wins matter not skill, character or how the game is played. There are notable exceptions, but this is the prevalent globalization-enforced paradigm on which media, institutional and governmental programmes and parents model themselves.

Counterbalancing this tendency, philosophers like Douglas Hochstetler mount a pragmatic defence of process-oriented sport. He writes, 'if we have enjoyed or found meaning in the process, we are more likely to feel at peace with the outcome – regardless of the result.'[79] Congruently with Abe, if we learn to face struggle when athletically pursuing excellence, particularly when we fall short, *then* we find uncommon insight.[80] To return to the football pitch, Jesús Ilundáin-Agurruza looks at the game as an outsider with a Zen beginner's mind: defending the intrinsic worth of the game through a Jamesian analysis, football flourishes when *all* involved – players, fans, officials, managers – learn to enjoy its unique internal goods (the art of the dribble) more than the thrill of the goal.[81] Cesar R. Torres, affably conversing with readers, enhances sport via broad internalism while echoing pragmatist themes: he revalorizes the know-how of 'physical' skills contra strict theoretical knowledge with James, incorporates a Deweyan sense of engaged communitarian instrumentalism and praises Thoreau's walking ruminations as meditative practice that, like Eastern ways, leads to insight.[82] To close, we can pragmatically bring East and West closer, mediating between the process and result entente: means and process should prevail, with ends and results included *as* part of the very process.

Doping and Technology in Sport

The bane of contemporary sports is found inside a syringe. Doping, a technology that pushes human limits thereby complicating notions of fair play, health and the ends of sport, is closely tied to developing new technologies, e.g. genetic modification. There are two camps. One favours autonomy, the right of self-determination, above all other values. Its liberal agenda largely condones doping and favours a trans-human future for us. The other embraces communitarian values and opposes doping and genetic modifications.

Japanese philosophy and American pragmatism conflict with permissive attitudes towards doping. First, concerning bodily autonomy, the key issue is ownership of the body. 'Ownership of the body' means that 'one's self is possessed by itself'. Generally speaking, the owner cannot logically be the owned concurrently. However, this becomes possible if we regard bodies as objects separate from minds and thinking: 'my mind owns my body'. Thus, mind-body dualism characterizes a theory accepting doping on the basis of autonomy. Contrariwise, Dewey overcomes such dualism by specifically valuing mind-body harmony. This differs from the approach where bodies are considered as means without restrictions. His democratic framework may entail certain permissiveness based on agreed-upon mores, but his understanding of the body limits this. Yuasa advocates mind-body integration, i.e. a body being synchronously object and subject. This approach rejects ownership of the body as unchecked entitlement for self-disposition. Second, doping makes the artificial constraints of sport less of a limitation. Consequently, it affords quicker or otherwise impossible gains, goes against sport's internal goods, and, emphasizing results, largely circumvents the process. Third, the concept of community proves noteworthy. Here, pragmatism boldly advocates a flexible platform to handle performance enhancement in nuanced ways that adjudicate between acceptable and impermissible methods. In contrast, Japanese philosophy opposes practices that bring disharmony to the community – doping egregiously doing so. However, both stress that athletes, supporting staff and fans commit to sporting activities as members of a community, and that *all* are responsible for its continued flourishing.

The novelty of genetic modification of reproductive cells means less available extant strategies. Pragmatism, which finds in this a source for human amelioration, may endorse pro-transhumanist views, pace Claudio M. Tamburrini[83] and Andy Miah,[84] so long as the enhancement does not devolve into a dualistic agenda that ignores psycho-physical unity or undercuts democratically embraced communitarian values. Those wary of any Promethean gifts research laboratories may gift us with – Mike McNamee[85] or Heather Reid[86] – urge pragmatists to distinguish between instrumentally questionable enhancement and legitimate self-cultivation. Traditional Japanese Shinto views mistrust modern Western medicine's hyper-technological focus. Shinto's reverence for *kami* (神) (ancestral, divine spirits inhabiting natural features) and belief in a sacred 'of itself' or soul for humans mean an appreciation of spiritual forces and traditional Chinese and Japanese holistic medicine. Belief in *kami* led to the justification of infanticide and a eugenic agenda at times, however, as Jan Swyngedouw points out, congruency with the belief of 'the sacredness of this "of itself" quality of the individual is far from any form of genetic manipulation based on the pretext of enhancing human nature and its potential'.[87] Taking a cue from Japanese modern views on bioethics (centred on brain death and organ transplantation) permits hypothesizing a rejection of transhumanism. Some critics (most Japanese embrace modern medical methods) argue that mechanistic-based views objectify the body as a locus of exchangeable parts: the Japanese feel a personal connection with the body of the deceased, believing that a human's personality resides in the entire body.[88] Besides, as Hayashi Yoshihiro points out, they are suspicious of views where wider relations to others are ignored for the sake of the individual alone and critical of utilitarian tendencies.[89] Extrapolation from this suggests that transhumanism will remain contentious.

We have considered how Eastern philosophy and pragmatism contribute, independently and jointly, to sport philosophy. Characterized by a flexible, optimistic character that pays close attention to experience itself, they are ideally suited to inquire into the kinesthetic corporeal matters central to sport, games, martial arts and movement. While they differ regarding methods or punctual thematic interests, they share many and important similarities in terms of philosophical temperament that, supplementing other methodologies, bring novel perspectives and profitable ways to understand sport's philosophical quandaries.

Notes

1   Eugen Herrigel, *Zen and the Art of Archery*, trans. R.F.C. Hull (New York: Vintage, 1999).
2   Generalizing for the sake of expediency and brevity, we acknowledge the many divergent views and suggest consulting Wing-Tsit Chan, *A Sourcebook in Chinese Philosophy* (Princeton, NJ: Princeton University Press, 1963); James W. Heisig, Thomas Kasulis and John Maraldo, eds., *Japanese Philosophy: A Sourcebook* (Honolulu: University of Hawaii Press, 2011); and Sarvepalli Radhakrishnan and Charles A. Moore, eds., *A Sourcebook in Indian Philosophy* (Princeton, NJ: Princeton University Press, 1989). With regard to pragmatism, see Richard Lally, Douglas Anderson and John Kaag, eds., *Pragmatism and the Philosophy of Sport* (London: Lexington Books, 2012).
3   William James, 'Pragmatism', in *Pragmatism and Other Writings* (London: Penguin, 2000), 5–132; 8.
4   This is a matter of emphasis; both traditions pursue inquiries in all main branches of philosophy.
5   Charles S. Peirce, 'The Fixation of Belief', in *Philosophical Writings of Peirce* (New York: Dover Publications, 1955), 5–22.
6   We follow Japanese mores, mentioning first family name then first name.
7   Cornelis De Waal, *On Pragmatism* (Belmont, CA: Wadsworth, 2005), 1–5.
8   Ibid., 4.
9   Robert Talisse and Scott Aikin, *Pragmatism: A Guide for the Perplexed* (London and New York: Continuum, 2008), 4.
10 James, 'Pragmatism', 24–5.
11 Charles S. Peirce, 'How to Make Our Ideas Clear', in *Philosophical Writings of Peirce* (New York: Dover Publications, 1955), 23–41.
12 Talisse and Aikin, *Pragmatism: A Guide for the Perplexed*, 9–25.
13 James, 'Pragmatism', 88.
14 Lally, 'Introduction', in *Pragmatism and the Philosophy of Sport*, 3.
15 William James, 'Does "Consciousness" Exist?' in *The Works of William James: Essays in Radical Empiricism* (Cambridge, MA and London: Harvard University Press, 1976), 3–19; 13.
16 William James, 'The Place of Affectional Facts', in *The Works of William James: Essays in Radical Empiricism*, 69–77; 73. James's emphasis.
17 William James, 'La Notion de Conscience', in *The Works of William James: Essays in Radical Empiricism*, 105–17, 115. Our translation.
18 John Kaag, 'Paddling in the Stream of Consciousness', in *Pragmatism and the Philosophy of Sport*, 47–61; 48.
19 William James, 'A World of Pure Experience', in *Pragmatism and Other Writings*, 316–9.
20 Ibid., 325.
21 Mark Johnson, *The Meaning of the Body: Aesthetics of Human Understanding* (Chicago: University of Chicago Press, 2007), 94.
22 Kaag, 'Paddling in the Stream of Consciousness', 55. Our emphasis.
23 Ibid., 59.
24 Kitaro Nishida, *An Inquiry into the Good*, trans. M. Abe and C. Ives (New Haven and London: Yale University Press, 1990), 3.
25 Ibid., 4.
26 Ibid.

27 Ibid., 7.
28 Ibid., 32.
29 Ibid., 39.
30 Ibid., xxxiii.
31 Robert Carter, *The Nothingness Beyond God: An Introduction to the Philosophy of Nishida Kitaro* (St. Paul, MN: Paragon House, 1997), xvi.
32 Ibid., 3.
33 Nishida, *An Inquiry into the Good*, 32.
34 Ibid.
35 Carter, *The Nothingness Beyond God: An Introduction to the Philosophy of Nishida Kitaro*, 32.
36 Shinobu Abe, 'Modern Sports and the Eastern Tradition of Physical Culture: Emphasizing Nishida's Theory of the Body', *Journal of the Philosophy of Sport* 14 (1987): 47.
37 William James, 'The Thing and its Relations', in *The Works of William James: Essays in Radical Empiricism*, 45–59; 46.
38 Carter, *The Nothingness Beyond God: An Introduction to the Philosophy of Nishida Kitaro*, 7. See William James, *The Varieties of Religious Experience: a Study in Human Nature* (New York: The Modern Library, 2000).
39 Carter, *The Nothingness Beyond God: An Introduction to the Philosophy of Nishida Kitaro*, 9.
40 Joel Krueger, 'William James and Kitaro Nishida on Consciousness and Embodiment', *William James Studies* 1 (2007): 1–16; 6.
41 Nishida, *An Inquiry into the Good*, 75.
42 Krueger, 'William James and Kitaro Nishida on Consciousness and Embodiment', 2.
43 Thomas Kasulis, Roger Ames and Wimal Dissanayake, eds., *Self as Body in Asian Theory and Practice* (Albany: State University of New York Press, 1993), 307.
44 Yasuo Yuasa, *The Body: Toward an Eastern Mind-Body Theory*, trans. S. Nagatomo and T. Kasulis (Albany: State University of New York Press, 1987), 119.
45 Shigenori Nagatomo, *Attunement Through the Body* (Albany: State University of New York Press, 1992), 79.
46 Yuasa, *The Body: Toward an Eastern Mind-Body Theory*, 200.
47 Edward Slingerland, *Effortless Action: Wu-wei as Conceptual Metaphor and Spiritual Ideal in China* (Oxford: Oxford University Press, 2003).
48 Soho Takuan, *The Unfettered Mind*, trans. W. Wilson (Tokyo: Kodansha, 1986), 19–44.
49 Yuasa, *The Body: Toward an Eastern Mind-Body Theory*, 200.
50 Carter, *The Nothingness Beyond God: An Introduction to the Philosophy of Nishida Kitaro*, 114.
51 Abe, 'Modern Sports and the Eastern Tradition of Physical Culture: Emphasizing Nishida's Theory of the Body', 45; Carter, *The Nothingness Beyond God: An Introduction to the Philosophy of Nishida Kitaro*, 108; 192 n. 24.
52 Yuasa, *The Body: Toward an Eastern Mind-Body Theory*, 200.
53 John Dewey, *Experience and Nature* (London: Allen and Unwin, 1929), 217.
54 Johnson, *The Meaning of the Body: Aesthetics of Human Understanding*, 122.
55 John Dewey, *Art as Experience* (New York: Perigee Books, 1980), 38.
56 Ibid, 35.
57 Richard Lally, 'Deweyan Pragmatism and Self-Cultivation', in *Pragmatism and the Philosophy of Sport*, 175–198; 175.
58 Ibid., 175.
59 Dewey, *Art as Experience*, 41.
60 Lally, 'Deweyan Pragmatism and Self-Cultivation', 189–90.
61 John Rawls, *A Theory of Justice* (Cambridge, MA: Harvard University Press, 1971).

62   See Alasdair MacIntyre, *After Virtue: a Study in Moral Virtue*, 2nd ed. (Notre Dame, IN: University of Notre Dame, 1984); and Michael Walzer, *Spheres of Justice* (Oxford: Blackwell, 1983).

63   John Dewey, *Democracy and Education: An Introduction to the Philosophy of Education* (New York: Macmillan Company, 1916), 105.

64   Ibid., 115.

65   Daniel Bell, 'Communitarianism', in *The Stanford Encyclopedia of Philosophy* (Spring 2012 edition), ed., Edward N. Zalta <http://plato.stanford.edu/archives/spr2012/entries/communitarianism/>

66   Ibid., 10.

67   Confucius, *The Analects*, trans. D.C. Lau (London: Penguin Books, 1979), 63. See 2.3.

68   John A.Tucker, 'Confucian Traditions: Overview', in *Japanese Philosophy: A Sourcebook*, 296.

69   Bell, 'Communitarianism', 32.

70   Tetsuro Watsuji, *Watsuji Tetsuro's Rinrigaku: Ethics in Japan*, trans. Y. Seisaku and R. Carter (Albany: State University of New York, 1996), 329.

71   Ibid., 10.

72   Ibid., 14–15.

73   Ibid., 157.

74   Daniel Campos, 'Peircean Reflections on the Personality of a *Fútbol Club*', in *Pragmatism and the Philosophy of Sport*, 33–45.

75   Joan Forry, 'Towards a Somatic Sport Feminism', in *Pragmatism and the Philosophy of Sport*, 125–53.

76   See Takayuki Hata and Masami Sekine's 'Philosophy of Sport and Physical Education in Japan: its History, Characteristics, and Prospects'; and Leo Hsu's 'An Overview of Sport Philosophy in Chinese-Speaking Regions', *Journal of the Philosophy of Sport* 37 (2010): 215–24 and 237–52 respectively.

77   Shinobu Abe, 'Zen and Sport', *Journal of the Philosophy of Sport* 8 (1986): 45–8; 47.

78   Herrigel, *Zen and the Art of Archery*, 23.

79   Douglas Hochstetler, 'Process and the Sport Experience', in *Pragmatism and the Philosophy of Sport*, 17–31; 20.

80   Ibid., 24.

81   Jesús Ilundáin-Agurruza, 'Goles Trascendentales', in *¿La pelota no dobla? Reflexiones filosóficas en torno al fútbol*, eds., Cesar R. Torres and Daniel Campos (Buenos Aires: Libros del Zorzal, 2006), 25–57. For a summary and critical evaluation in English, see Daniel Campos, 'On the Value and Meaning of Football: Recent Philosophical Perspectives in Latin America', *Journal of the Philosophy of Sport* 37 (2010): 69–87.

82   Cesar R. Torres, *Gol de media cancha. Conversaciones para disfrutar del deporte plenamente* (Buenos Aires: Miño y Dávila Editores, 2011).

83   Claudio M. Tamburrini and Tännsjö Torbjörn, *Genetic Technology and Sport: Ethical Questions* (New York: Routledge, 2005).

84   Andy Miah, *Genetically Modified Athletes: Biomedical Ethics, Gene Doping and Sport* (London: Routledge, 2004).

85   Mike McNamee, *Sports, Virtues and Vices: Morality Plays* (London: Routledge, 2008).

86   Heather Reid, *Introduction to the Philosophy of Sport* (Lanham, MD: Rowman and Littlefield, 2012).

87   Jan Swyngedouw, 'Ueda Kenji', in *Japanese Philosophy: A Sourcebook*, 543–9.

88   Hayashi Yoshihiro, 'Bioethics: Overview', in *Japanese Philosophy: A Sourcebook*, 1236; 1238.

89   Ibid., 1238–42.

Part III

Current Research and Key Issues

6 Theories of Sport

Robert L. Simon

What is a theory of sport and why do we need one? There are different theories about the best strategy for countering a zone defence in basketball, how best to train swimmers, or how best to swing a golf club. But a theory of sport seems to be a different thing altogether. Indeed, are we begging the question by assuming there is such a thing as 'sport' rather than a variety of sports that differ from one another often in significant ways? Perhaps what counts as sport changes from culture to culture or by historical context.[1]

In what follows, I will explore the nature and value of theories of sport by breaking down the inquiry into the following topics: What is a theory of sport? What purposes does a theory of sport serve? What are the most plausible theories of sport? Which if any is best or most justifiable?

Theories of Sport

Surely all of us would agree that basketball, football, baseball and rugby are sports and that watching television, sleeping and going up an escalator at a shopping mall are not sports. But what about mountain climbing, running a marathon, downhill skiing, recreational fishing and chess, sometimes called the sport of kings?

One function of a theory of sport is to help us make distinctions between activities that are sports from those that aren't, even if the distinction is not always a sharp one. Distinguishing sports from other related activities is important, not only because of the intellectual issue of whether we can even make such a distinction – perhaps the concept 'sport' is too vague to admit of useful analysis or that sports have nothing in common that defines them – but also for theoretical and normative reasons. For example, if we are to explain why sports are so fascinating to millions or people around the globe, we need to distinguish them from other activities, such as walking for exercise, that also may be important for reasons of health but that differ from sports in very significant respects.

Thus, there is a normative or evaluative function served by theories of sport; to the extent that they help us identify salient features of sport, they provide material we can use to morally assess sport as well. For example, the importance we assign to winning in athletic contests may be at least in part a function of what we believe are the values sports should promote.

This suggests that a theory of sport is a body of principles, some of which may be quite abstract, that helps us to identify sports and distinguish them from other activities, but that also provide an assessment of the value of sport and a normative framework for examining ethical issues that may arise in sport, especially in athletic competition.

Theories of sport, then, should serve at least the following functions. First, they should offer a characterization of sport that helps us to distinguish sports from other activities, even if we cannot always do so due to complex borderline cases. Second, they should explain the features of sport that make it of significant interest to people around the globe, not only participants but spectators as well. Third, they should explain the value (or disvalue if they are critical of sport and sporting practices) of sport and provide the resources for the moral evaluation of sport, perhaps especially competitive athletics, and the ethical issues that arise in particular sporting contexts.

Functional Approaches to Sport

Some theoretical approaches to sport attempt to characterize it by its social function. For example, sport may be viewed as a social mechanism for discharging aggression harmlessly, for producing social cohesion among what otherwise would be a mere aggregate of individuals (think of 'Red Sox Nation'), or for distracting masses of people from serious problems that exist on the world stage. These functions can be morally assessed both positively and negatively; thus, the members of Red Sox Nation can be viewed negatively as narrow partisans who value their team whether it is right or wrong or as a community that has developed ties of solidarity thus breaking away from the atomistic individualism and consequent loneliness that critics say characterize much of the modern state.[2] These approaches are *externalist* in the sense that they characterize sport and perhaps assess its value by its connections to social functions that can and do exist independently of sport and are intelligible entirely apart from it. Thus, religion might promote social cohesion. Moreover, rivalries in sport may be as likely to produce division as unity.

Functionalist theories, at least in their cruder forms, are open to serious criticism. Thus, the claim that participation in sports has the function of helping athletes (and fans) to discharge aggression may seem to fit contact sports such as American football and rugby, but has more difficulty explaining the nature and impact of sports such as curling, rowing, figure skating, gymnastics, archery and golf with their code of respect for and courtesy towards opponents. More importantly, these theories don't explain why people choose to discharge aggression through sport, if that indeed is what happens, rather than, say, through mere exercise such as hitting a punchbag. Moreover, even if sport does produce social cohesion, functionalist theories do not explain the passionate attachment of so many people to it (imagine a player or fan saying, for example, 'I love baseball so much because of its broad effect on producing social cohesion') or provide the basis for moral assessment of issues that arise in sport, such as the ethics of doping or even whether cohesion is always something we should value.

Contrary to functionalism, or other externalist approaches, internalists argue that sport involves a set of principles and values inherent in and perhaps conceptually tied to sporting activities and practices. On the internalist view, we can best understand and evaluate sport by attending to its internal features or characteristics rather than its connection to broader social practices, institutions or values.[3] Internalists, then, take sport seriously as an activity that is of interest and value over and above whatever social function it may also serve.

Internalist Theories of Sport

Formalism

An influential internalist approach to sport is often called 'formalism'. Formalism probably derives its inspiration from the work of Bernard Suits, who in his book *The Grasshopper: Games, Life, and Utopia* challenged the suggestion made by the great 20th-century philosopher Ludwig Wittgenstein that if we would just 'look and see', we would find that there is nothing in common to all games.[4] This suggestion was part of Wittgenstein's challenge to the Platonic ideal that philosophers should look for the form or essence of concepts such as 'beauty', 'truth' and 'knowledge'. In particular, Wittgenstein advanced the very influential notion that games might resemble each other in the same way members of families might resemble each other; the members might not share one common characteristic, but there might be overlapping sets of characteristics that some of the members shared with some others uniting all in a network of overlapping similarities and differences. Thus, on Wittgenstein's account, Monopoly, chess, Ring around the Rosie and baseball are all games but do not necessarily have one or more common properties that make them games. The concept of game is a 'family resemblance concept' with no one characteristic or set of characteristics that are necessary and sufficient for being a game.

In response to this, Suits argued that there are common features of games. Since he also plausibly suggested that all sports are games, games of physical skill, his analysis, even if open to some criticism, sheds much light on the nature of sports and provides the basis for formalistic analysis of sports.

In particular, Suits argued that games were characterized by four elements known as the prelusory goal, constitutive rules that prohibited the most efficient means for achieving the prelusory goal, the lusory goal and the lusory attitude (or accepting the constitutive rules just in order to make the activity possible). Thus, the prelusory goal of basketball might be putting a ball through a raised hoop, but doing that only counts as scoring a basket in basketball if the constitutive rules are followed (thus putting the ball through the hoop by climbing a ladder and dropping it through is not a move in basketball). The limitation on allowable means of achieving the prelusory goal is accepted just in order to make the game possible. Thus, other activities, for example taking the college entry exam, may be governed by rules, even constitutive rules, but these normally are not accepted just to make the activity of test taking possible. Basketball is a game by Suits' account, but taking the college entry exam is not.

The role of constitutive rules here is important. Their function is to create obstacles to attaining the prelusory goal by defining what are permissible and what are impermissible moves allowed within the game. Constitutive rules characterize how the game may be played and how it may be won. Golf, for example, involves putting a ball in a hole, ordinarily an easily achieved goal, but, as has often been noted, not when it must be accomplished with what Winston Churchill called 'implements ill designed for the purpose'. Hence, Suits' pithy abbreviated definition of games: 'the voluntary attempt to overcome unnecessary obstacles'.[5]

Suits' definition clearly is insightful, although it remains debatable whether it is entirely successful or open to counterexample or whether all sports fall under the heading of games.[6] Luckily, we need not delve into all those controversies here. Instead, let's focus on the central role Suits' account assigns to constitutive rules and the theory of formalism that arises from it.

Remember that constitutive rules define what counts as permissible moves within a game, as well as what constitutes winning.[7] Rules of skill, rules that suggest strategies for good play, such as 'in baseball, hit behind the runner so the runner can advance to scoring position', characterize strategies for competitive success, but do not identify what counts as a play within the game. Constitutive rules, it can be argued, *define* the game and are central to the theoretical approach to sport known as *formalism*.

Formalism is a theory of sport (or more accurately a family of closely related positions) that identifies sports with practices or activities governed by constitutive rules that, following Suits' suggestions, create obstacles to achieving the lusory goal of the game. What counts as a rule is determined by the formal or in some cases informal rulebook governing the sport in question. What distinguishes different sports from one another are the different sets of constitutive rules that apply. Formalism in sport closely resembles formalism in legal theory, which identifies a legal system with a set of rules derivable from a supreme rule, which in the sophisticated version developed by the British theorist H.L.A. Hart is called the Rule of Recognition.[8]

Although it is not entirely clear what normative implications can be derived from formalism, it is plausible to think that respect for the rules is paramount and cheating is a cardinal sin. In fact, formalism leads to what might be called the incompatibility thesis: the idea that cheats cannot actually win games since they are not actually playing the game (as they violate the rules that define it). In this view the good sport is one who respects and plays by the rules; generosity towards opponents over and above playing by the rules, is not required (although it may be encouraged), except perhaps in non-competitive contexts where a sport is played just for exercise or in an informal friendly context.[9]

Formalism is important because it builds on Suits' analysis by emphasizing the key role of constitutive rules in sport and the importance of fair play, understood as playing by the rules. However, it has been exposed to such extensive criticism that it is doubtful if many (or even any) contemporary theorists of sport endorse it, at least in the admittedly thin form sketched out in this section.

Conventionalism: A Criticism of Formalism

Formalism, or the model of rules as it is sometimes called when applied to law, is open to a number of significant criticisms. Two in particular have been especially influential. The first is that formalism ignores the social or conventional aspects of sport and hence is too abstract. The second is that formalism is inadequate as a resource for the moral evaluation of sport.

Consider what is now a common occurrence in football. Team A is on the attack, in possession of the ball, when a player on the defending team, Team B, sprains his ankle and falls to the ground in pain. Following a well-known practice, a player on Team A kicks the ball out of play, so the injured opponent can be treated, even though this deprives Team A of the advantage. When play is restarted Team B will take the throw-in and one of their players will intentionally return the ball to Team A, restoring as much as possible the state of affairs before the injury. In other words, Team B ensures that Team A is not disadvantaged for its act of sportsmanship.

This type of incident is not covered by any formal rule of the game. The rulebook does not require such behaviour or even encourage it. Rather, both teams are following a social convention that is accepted by footballers: the convention is part of the game but is not a formal rule. (In fact, this practice unfortunately is threatened by the act of 'flopping', where a defender pretends to be injured in order to stop play and deprive the attacking team of any strategic advantage they may have gained.)

The idea that sport is to be understood in terms of often tacit conventions as well as formal rules is often called *conventionalism*. According to an influential account of conventionalism, the 'ethos of the game', or common social understandings, is as crucial to understanding sports as rules.[10]

Conventionalists also suggest, contrary to the incompatibility thesis, that actual games are almost never played strictly according to the rules. Indeed, although formalists may argue that those who intentionally violate the rules aren't really playing the game, common understandings of sport suggest otherwise. For example, two golfers who agree before teeing off to allow a mulligan off the first tee (a chance to rehit if the first drive is inadequate) surely are still playing golf even if mulligans are prohibited by the rules. Similarly, a major league pitcher who throws an illegal spitball during a game may be cheating, but surely is still playing baseball and not some other game.

Second, others, including myself, have argued that the version of formalism sketched so far does not provide a good basis for the ethical evaluation of sports and behaviour within them.[11] That is, there is far more to the ethics of sport than is captured by the idea of adherence to the rules. For example, it does not tell us whether a change to the rules is better or worse for the sport, or what the ethical ramifications of such a rule change might be. Thus, a proposed rule change allowing head-to-head contact in American football might make the game more entertaining to some fans who love to watch devastating 'hits', but may be bad for the game, leading to injuries to star players whom the fans want to see perform, and more importantly may be ethically indefensible due to the seriousness of the head injuries that might follow.

Moreover, sportsmanship surely involves more than adherence to the rules. For example, the convention in football discussed above, where one team refuses to take advantage of an injured opponent, surely has much to be said for it ethically whether or not it is required by the rules. Similarly, while not required by the rules, regular-season opponents who help each other improve through common workouts in off-season sports camps or informal practice sessions are not required by any rules to assist one another, but their behaviour, as we will see in the section on broad internalism, should certainly be encouraged.

If these criticisms are sound, formalism as described so far is at best incomplete as a theory of sport. But do formalists have a satisfactory reply? If not, is conventionalism the best available theory of sport?

Criticisms of Conventionalism

Conventionalists suggest that each sport is best understood as a combination of rules and conventions; that they cannot be properly characterized or understood without appreciating the significance of the ethos of the game. While their approach is insightful and does establish the importance of understanding the culture surrounding sports, it is doubtful if conventionalism is any more satisfactory than the minimal version of formalism we have considered in providing an ethical basis for the moral evaluation of sport.

Before turning to ethical questions, however, consider not just how conventionalists might distinguish particular sports from each other, presumably by pointing to different combinations of rules and conventions, but whether they distinguish conventions peculiar to sport from those associated with non-sporting activities.

Of course, unlike many formalists, who might insist that all sports are games of physical skill and then appeal to Suits' account of games, conventionalists might agree with Wittgenstein and say there are no essential characteristics that distinguish conventions associated with sport from other kinds of conventions. Or they might acknowledge that constitutive rules are more fundamental than conventions and characterize sport much as the formalists do. Thus, they might amend the formalist account in a conventionalist direction by characterizing sports as games of physical skill in which constitutive rules create obstacles to achieving a lusory goal, the pursuit of which is governed by conventions as well as rules.

While conventionalism adds the importance of social context to formalism, we need to ask if social conventions or customary practices have moral force when we consider ethical issues in sport.

What are the ethical implications of conventionalism? One view is that conventionalism suggests that in making ethical decisions in sport, we support both the rules and the conventions applying to the sport in the context of the social environment in which they hold. Thus, practitioners and observers of sport who hold this view should simply follow the dominant social practices surrounding sport in their culture.

Surely this cannot be correct. Conventions are not ethical just because they are followed. Thus, if conventionalism as so far understood is correct, if football had an existing convention that allowed players to deliberately try to hurt injured opposing players while they were lying on the ground in pain, surely that would not make it right. This version of conventionalism is committed to an extreme kind of ultra-conservative relativism that encourages us to follow (rather than try to change) existing practices regardless of their content. Any proposed change, again regardless of content, would be wrong in this view since it would oppose existing conventions and practices. Because it is so accepting of the status quo, let us call this version of conventionalism uncritical conventionalism. (We will discuss a more critical version of conventionalism in another section of this essay.)

Perhaps at this point, conventionalists might offer an externalist version of their theory. In this version, conventions in sports are acceptable only if they do not violate moral requirements derived from outside sports, for example, from religion or from moral theories such as utilitarianism or Kantian deontology. However, this suggests that sport has no moral resources of its own to offer, and thus may prematurely reject internalist approaches to sports ethics.

Of course, athletes have no special dispensation to violate fundamental moral norms such as prohibitions against murder or stealing. However, it is also true that some actions are allowed in sports, such as tackling in football or body checking in ice hockey, that might constitute criminal acts if performed against random strangers outside the context of athletic competition. Presumably, such actions are legitimized in sport, at least in part, because the contestants have freely agreed to play by constitutive rules that allow such actions.

More importantly, there are ethical dilemmas that arise in sports on which a better understanding of the evaluational character of sport might shed much light. Such an internal morality, while not necessarily unique to sport, might at the very least help us apply broad and abstract moral principles in specific sporting contexts. For example, should a team accept a victory that it did not earn (it was outplayed by the opposition) and that resulted from a series of clearly and obviously bad calls by officials?[12] Should winning be the only or even the major goal of athletic competition? Do we owe more to opponents than just following the rules? What important values, if any, does athletic competition promote and what other values, if any, might it undermine? Let us consider how a different internalist approach might provide a rational framework for approaching such issues.

Broad Internalism: An Interpretivist Approach

Imagine a painting showing the following elements.[13] In the foreground is a farmer pushing an apparently antiquated plough high on a cliff overlooking a blue-green sea. An ancient longship powered by rows of oars (perhaps manned by slaves) cuts through the sea under a blazing sun. Birds circle overhead. In the background, a pair of feet are visible just above the surface of the water.

Clearly, it would be a misinterpretation of the painting to call it *Rush Hour Traffic in Manhattan*. Other titles such as *Swimming in Indiana in 1942* don't make sense of the farmer, the ship or the blue-green sea. Students of the classics might recognize the painting, given even my poor description of it, as Pieter Brueghel's *The Fall of Icarus*. Remember, in the Greek myth, Icarus and his father Daedalus escaped from prison on Crete by building wings of wax. Although warned, in the legend, not to fly too high because the heat of the sun would melt the wings,

Icarus gets carried away and does fly too close to the sun with disastrous results (the feet are his as he disappears beneath the waves forever).

Interpreting the painting as showing the fall of Icarus enables us to make sense of all the elements in it, unlike the other interpretations mentioned above. It provides the best available interpretation by explaining why each element of the painting is there; thus the ship sailing by and the farmer who looks only at the ground show the human trait of indifference to great achievement. Moreover, it also adds ethical and aesthetic depth to our understanding of the painting by bringing out both its celebration of greatness and the arguably sinful disregard of it.

As legal scholar and philosopher Ronald Dworkin has maintained, such an interpretative approach can also explain what might justify a judicial decision in a hard legal case. In Dworkin's view, when judges need to figure out what often vague and abstract constitutional requirements, such as not depriving anyone of 'equal protection of the law', mean and how they may be applied to hard cases, judges need to support their decisions by a similar interpretive process. For example, they need to advance an account or theory of equal protection that makes the best sense of salient legal precedents, coheres best with other bodies of the law and makes the best moral sense of equal protection. Dworkin's approach, often called interpretivism, suggests that in addition to legal rules, judges also need to rely on various *principles* for interpreting and applying the rules, which often must be weighed against one another in order to come up with the best interpretation of the law.[14]

J.S. Russell has provided an excellent example of how such intepretivism might apply to sport.[15] In an 1887 American Association baseball game between Louisville and Brooklyn, a Louisville player, Reddy Mack, who had just scored, jostled the Brooklyn catcher, interfering with his play and thereby allowing a Louisville teammate to score as well. Mack may have reasoned that since the rules only prohibited interference with a fielder by a base-runner, and since he ceased to be a base-runner when he scored, his action did not constitute interference under the rules. However, the umpire, Wesley Curry, called Mack out for interfering with the catcher. Did he make the right call?

Russell argues that the call was correct since any other decision would have risked turning baseball into a series of brawls. He explains that such a decision is warranted by an important principle that underlies competitive sports such as baseball, namely that 'rules should be interpreted in a manner that the excellences embodied in achieving the lusory goal of the game are not undermined but are maintained and fostered.'[16] Here, Russell is applying an overall theory of baseball that identifies skills such as catching, running, hitting and throwing as the primary skills tested during baseball games. Interference with fielders undermines baseball as a test of such skills and so the interference rule should be applied to runners after they have scored as well as while they are on the bases. Interference also makes baseball an uglier game, taking away from the beauty of crisp fielding and brilliant defence suggesting, as Cesar R. Torres has reminded us, that aesthetic criteria as well as ethical standards play a role in determining how a sport and its rules are best to be interpreted and understood.[17] Thus, the account of just which skills are basic to baseball can be justified by its fit with the rules, with baseball practice, and because it makes baseball a better game in a variety of ways (including morally and aesthetically) if interference is understood in the way suggested.

A number of other writers, including Nicholas Dixon, Angela Schneider and Robert Butcher, Cesar R. Torres and Peter Hager along with J.S. Russell, have developed interpretive approaches to sport. In a paper in which I tried to distinguish this approach from narrow versions of formalism, I called it *broad internalism* because it was wider in scope than narrow formalism (since it focuses on principles as well as rules) and is internalist since one of its major goals is to resolve normative issues in sport by developing theories that make the best sense of their internal features (such as which skills are basic or fundamental to the sport).[18]

In the next section, we will examine a theory of sport based on the broad internalist or interpretivist approach and then conclude by examining a major criticism of broad internalism developed by a proponent of a revised form of conventionalism, William J. Morgan.

Mutualism: The Mutual Quest for Excellence

Critics have attacked competition in athletics on a variety of grounds. For example, they have argued it creates a kind of elitist nationalism – our team against the world – that promotes an overemphasis on winning and consequent degradation of the opponent. Opponents are seen not as persons but as mere obstacles to success, a viewpoint that encourages disrespect and even enmity towards them. Winners are glorified and those who do not win are regarded as failures or 'losers'. Results become the most important thing and the value of the process of learning to compete is lost. More broadly, competition in this view teaches us to be selfish or partisan.

Many broad internalists would argue that this picture of competitive sport, while perhaps sometimes descriptively accurate, is normatively inadequate because it does not fit key features of competitive sport. It may be descriptively accurate in some contexts because some coaches and athletes sometimes do regard opponents as mere obstacles, stress winning above all else, and see competition in sport as a zero-sum game.

However, if we look at key features of competitive athletics, another account may be ethically superior to the critical view we have just sketched out. As we have seen, philosophers such as Bernard Suits have suggested that the constitutive rules of sport create challenges to securing goals that would otherwise be much easier to achieve. Scoring a goal according to the rules of football is much more difficult and more challenging than merely placing a ball within a goal. An account of sport that fits this feature of artificial obstacles created by the rules regards sports as games of physical (and related mental or strategic) skill designed to challenge the participants. A well-designed sport is one where the challenges require complex skills for success, the use of various strategies and the need to make good decisions in various game situations. A major goal of participating, then, is to achieve excellence in meeting the challenge.

Although it is true that sports have winners and losers, and that winning the game is the lusory goal, it does not follow that competition in athletics is a zero-sum game or that opponents must be regarded as mere obstacles to one's own success. Rather, opponents are necessary to create the challenge in the first place. In this view, athletic competition is at least partially cooperative; each participant consents to create a challenge for the opponent so that each can try to meet the challenge of the sport in pursuit of excellence. Athletic competition, then, should be (and sometimes is) what I have called a mutual quest for excellence.[19]

While mutualists recognize that winning often is the major criterion for success in meeting the challenge, they tend to question whether winning is always the primary or most important element of success. For one thing, as Dixon has pointed out, winning can be due to factors irrelevant to athletic excellence including bad calls by officials and vastly inferior opponents.[20] Should a team take pride in playing badly but still beating a much weaker opponent? Such a game is not only aesthetically deficient – it might be called 'an ugly win' – but also does not provide strong grounds for claims of just desserts since the superior team did not come near to playing to its potential. Conversely, couldn't a losing team take a lot of pride in taking a much better opponent to the absolute limit – for playing 'beautifully' and earning respect and praise?

Mutualists point out that opponents can each gain something from contests regardless of who wins and loses. In the mutualist view, competitive sport is an educational activity; both sides can learn from competing and develop better strategies, techniques or learn to make better decisions in competition as the result of post-game analysis. In this view, rather than being obstacles, let alone enemies, opponents are cooperating with each other by providing a challenge so that each side can learn and grow as a result of the challenge each provides to the other. While only one side can win, each side can learn from competing (often the losers learn more than the winners by profiting from their mistakes), and so sports are not zero-sum games but mutually beneficial activities. Our competitors are not obstacles or enemies, but facilitators in a mutual quest for excellence.

We now have what might be called a two-level theory of sport that provides an ethically defensible account of athletic competition and a model we can use to morally evaluate actual athletic practice. At one level, we have the broad internalist or interpretivist approach to understanding sport, characterizing it and justifying certain sorts of claims about it based on the criteria of fit and normative acceptability. Mutualists claim their approach fits or explains key features of sport, such as the challenges created by the constitutive rules. On a normative level, we have an account of athletic competition, mutualism or the mutual quest for excellence that arguably is ethically defensible and gives us guidelines for how competition should be understood and conducted.

Moreover, this approach allows us to characterize sports and distinguish at least paradigmatic cases of sports from other activities in a broader manner than provided by narrow versions of formalism. Roughly, sports are games of physical skill that have the features identified by Suits but (as Suits himself might not have denied) are also regulated by principles presupposed by the idea of unnecessary obstacles that constitute challenges.

Furthermore, broad internalism grounds an ethical defence of competitive sport by presenting it in its best light, namely, the mutualist approach. Broad internalism and the mutualist account of athletic competition should be exposed to critical inquiry; to the extent, however, that they survive extended examination, they may well constitute a justified theory of competitive sport.

A Conventionalist Critique of Broad Internalism

The broad internalist or interpretivist approach to sport sketched out above can be criticized on a variety of grounds. For example, mutualism can and has been criticized on the grounds that winning requires special skills that are hard to master and so should be given significantly more weight than mutualists such as myself have acknowledged.[21] However, in the space remaining, I will focus on a recent defence of conventionalism, and consequent critique of broad internalism, developed by William J. Morgan that raises fundamental questions about justification, not only in sport but more generally as well. Morgan's critique can be divided into two separate lines of argument, a defence of what might be called 'critical conventionalism' and a critique of what he takes to be the ahistorical or transcendent and realist implications of broad internalism, at least when it is interpreted in an overly rationalistic direction.[22]

Conventionalism was criticized above as ethically deficient. Just because a convention exists as part of a social practice does not mean it is ethically defensible. Morgan acknowledges that this criticism applies to one kind of convention, what he calls 'coordinating conventions', but argues that the critics have failed to recognize a second sort of convention to which the criticism does not apply. Coordinating conventions, as the name implies, allow people to coordinate their actions and engage in socially cooperative behaviour. For example, a convention of playground basketball in much of the United States is that the players do not call trivial fouls on their opponents but that hard fouls – especially dangerous ones – should be called and indeed avoided by the players themselves. However, an alternative convention might have been in force to the effect that no fouls, no matter how hard or dangerous, should be called in playground or 'pickup' games. The criticism against conventionalism is that it does not contain the theoretical resources to allow us to decide which convention is morally better.

However, there is a second kind of convention, Morgan argues, that avoids this criticism. Morgan calls them 'deep conventions'. According to Morgan, 'deep conventions play a central role in determining the point and purpose of athletic undertakings in certain contexts, in particular communities, at specific times. In other words, their main function is the normative ... one of establishing the worth and value of sport.'[23] These deep conventions allow conventionalists to be critical of existing practices if they conclude that the surface or coordinating conventions that are prevalent in actual practice violate or undermine the deep conventions of a particular sporting community.

An example cited by Morgan is the difference between the professional ideal of sport in the contemporary United States and the ideal dominant at least among the upper class in late 19th-century and early 20th-century England and the

United States. In the latter view, allegedly alien to modern competitive athletics, sport is a gentlemanly activity that would be spoiled by such ungentlemanly behaviour as having paid coaches or engaging in intense supervised training. Even the need to rely on officials to make calls would undermine this ethos of the game since no true gentleman would try to take advantage of the rules or cheat.

To paraphrase Morgan in a way I hope he would find sympathetic, these two paradigms of sport each provide a framework within which we can reason about the purpose, value and ethics of sport. The deep conventions of each paradigm determine what counts as a reason. Thus, under the professional paradigm, a basketball coach might be criticized for not being good at 'working' referees, but on the earlier paradigm failing to work referees would be a virtue, not a weakness.

Thus, deep conventionalism, as I will call it, allows for critical reflection within specific sporting practices. However, it does not allow for adjudication across paradigms. As Morgan maintains, such disputes between advocates of different paradigms is 'at best rival disputants talking past one another rather than profitably to one another'.[24] Thus, deep conventionalism can allow for critical discourse within a specific historical, cultural or social context but rejects what Morgan regards as the sin of going transcendental, or occupying a 'view from nowhere' in the attempt to reach a universal theory of sport justifiable to every rational person.

Deep conventionalists would probably resist calling their approach a theory of sport, since they might maintain that even what counts as a sport may differ (if only subtly) from context to context. Similarly, what makes sport valuable and what counts as a defensible ethical resolution to ethical issues in sport is relative to specific social-historical frameworks. Thus, different theories of sport might apply in different times and places.

According to the deep conventionalist argument, broad internalists have been too quick to reject conventionalism, because they ignore deep conventions and are too quick to go transcendent in appealing to abstract intepretations of sport that they allegedly accept because of the reasons in their favour, since they fail to see that what counts as a reason ultimately depends on socio-historical contexts. What can a broad internalist say in reply?

A Broad Internalist Response to Deep Conventionalism

In what follows, I will suggest two lines of argument broad internalists can develop in reply to Morgan's critique. Although I speak for myself, my suggestions are, I believe, compatible with the position of other interpretivists such as Russell and Dixon.[25]

First, broad internalists should ask if the deep conventions cited by Morgan are substantially different from the principles cited by broad internalists, such as Russell's principle that rules should be interpreted so as to protect and foster the primary skills and challenges of a sport. Like principles, deep conventions are not formal rules of a sport, often need to be weighed against one another and present a normative conception of how sports should be understood and carried out. Deep conventions, like principles but unlike surface or coordinating conventions, have ethical force. Like principles, deep conventions provide an interpretation that seeks to present sport in its morally best light.

Given that deep conventions so closely resemble principles (or are principles), does deep conventionalism even differ significantly from broad internalism? Morgan surely would reply that conventions, unlike principles, are wedded to particular historical contexts and so are contextual in a way principles are not. Principles allegedly are abstract and ahistorical and emerge from a process of reflection that transcends the particular social and historical circumstances from which it starts – a shift towards an impossible to achieve a 'view from nowhere'.

However, broad internalism, at least as I understand it, need not be committed to such an ahistorical or transcendent approach. As I have suggested elsewhere, we can start from discourse in a particular historical context with the goal that continued discussion among interlocutors with diverse viewpoints might promote a consensus among advocates who were at one time in disagreement. Thus, discussion starts in a particular historical context but can transcend it and work towards universality. The discussion always takes place in a historical context. However, if a consensus reached through rational discourse survives extended criticism from significantly differing perspectives over an extended period of time, that surely gives us good (although not infallible) reason to believe the theory of sport in question is in fact truly warranted or justified. I have called this position 'justificatory realism' since it holds that in such circumstances we have good grounds for thinking we agree on a theory because there truly is compelling evidence in its favour rather than thinking there is compelling evidence in its favour only because we already accept it.[26]

This suggests that debate between proponents of different paradigms of sport need not be incommensurable in the way deep conventionalists such as Morgan suggest. Although the point needs further development than can be given here, it surely is plausible to think that proponents of the amateur or gentlemanly paradigm can understand the importance of the pursuit of excellence and learning about oneself and others through the crucible of competition. On the other hand, proponents of the modern or professional model surely can understand the idea of competitors as facilitators rather than enemies or obstacles and the importance of respecting the deepest values of the game.

Two examples illustrate this point. After losing the 2013 PGA Sony Open in spite of firing a wonderful 63 in the last round, Tim Clark said in a post-round interview, 'I gave it all I had, and he [Russell Henley] just played phenomenal … He just never seemed to put a foot wrong, and when he did, he made those par putts … When a guy plays that well and beats you, you just have to be happy for them.' Similarly, after the University of Michigan's men's basketball team had their 2013 undefeated streak snapped 56-53, their point guard, whose last-second shot for a tie rimmed out of the basket, said in an interview, 'I enjoyed playing against one of the best defenders in the country (Aaron Craft) and learned from it.'[27] Incidents such as these, and many others, suggest that even at many of the highest levels of sport, we don't deal with pure or isolated paradigms but, just as interpretivism suggests, seek to balance competing principles from different sources into the overall best theory of sport.

Theories of sport, then, should provide us with a characterization that helps us to identify sports, that explains why they arouse such interest and passionate attachment and contains normative resources for the ethical and aesthetic assessment of athletic competition and the moral issues that arise within them. Our discussion suggests that narrow versions of formalism and conventionalism do less well at such tasks, particularly the task of ethical and aesthetic assessment, than what we have called broad internalism (interpretivism), which I have argued supports a mutualist approach to competitive success. Deep or critical conventionalism, however, also claims our allegiance as a worthy theory of sport. While broad internalists, as indicated, have important replies to criticisms arising from deep conventionalism, further debate as to the scope and nature of the best theory is sure to continue and can only advance our understanding of sports and the values that underlie them.

Notes

1 Although this issue will not be fully discussed here, we will examine the claim that paradigms of sport differ from context to context in our examination of deep conventionalism.

2 For discussion, see Nicholas Dixon, 'The Ethics of Supporting Sports Teams', *Journal of Applied Philosophy* 18 (2001): 149–58.

3 This does not mean, as we will see, that internalists are committed to the existence of a code of values or ethics unique to sport and independent of other ethical approaches, but rather only to the claim that there are values that need to be presupposed if we are to make the best sense of sporting practice, particularly athletic competition.

4 Bernard Suits, *The Grasshopper: Games, Life, and Utopia* (Peterborough, ON: Broadview Press, 2005) with a new introduction by Thomas Hurka. Suits' book was originally published by the University of Toronto Press and first appeared in 1978.

5 Suits, *The Grasshopper: Games, Life, and Utopia*, 55.

6 Suits himself discusses many possible counterexamples and objections in his book.

7 Restorative rules, which I would classify as a kind of constitutive rule, define what should be done in case of rule violations. For example, foul shots are awarded in basketball as compensation for disallowed forms of physical contact and time in the penalty box serves a similar function for rule violations in ice hockey.

8 See H.L.A. Hart, *The Concept of Law* (New York: Oxford University Press, 1997) for his account of law as what he calls the union of primary and secondary rules. The Rule of Recognition is a secondary rule. Secondary rules allow for identification, modification and change, and adjudication of the primary rules, such as the rules of criminal law.

9 James Keating distinguished between sports a recreational activity governed by the norm of generosity towards opponents, and competitive athletics, governed by competitiveness and adherence to the rules, in his 'Sportsmanship as a Moral Category', *Ethics* 75 (1964): 25–35. The discussion of broad internalism later in this paper suggests that Keating's distinction is inadequate, since some broad principles of ethical competition apply to sporting practice across the board.

10 For an influential account of conventionalism, see Fred D'Agostino, 'The Ethos of Games', in *Philosophic Inquiry in Sport*, 2nd ed, ed., William J. Morgan and Klaus V. Meier (Champaign, IL: Human Kinetics, 1995), 42–9.

11 See, for example, my similar criticism of formalism in *Fair Play: The Ethics of Sport*, 3rd ed. (Boulder, CO: Westview Press, 2010), 46–8.

12 J.S. Russell argues for a duty of coaches to try to correct obviously bad calls in favour of their team in his essay 'Coaching and Undeserved Competitive Success', in *The Ethics of Coaching Sports: Moral, Social and Legal Issues,* ed., Robert L. Simon (Boulder, CO: Westview Press, 2013), 103–20.

13 I first heard this example when it was employed by Arthur Danto in a lecture on aesthetics in an exact place or time I can't remember but any error in drawing out its implications is my responsibility alone.

14 See, for example, Dworkin's essay 'Hard Cases' in his *Taking Rights Seriously* (Cambridge: Harvard University Press, 1977).

15 J.S. Russell, 'Are Rules All an Umpire Has to Work With?', *Journal of the Philosophy of Sport* 36 (1999): 27–49.

16 Ibid., 35.

17 Cesar R. Torres, 'Furthering Interpretivism's Integrity: Bringing Together Ethics and Aesthetics', *Journal of the Philosophy of Sport* 39 (2012): 299–319.

18 Robert L. Simon, 'Internalism and Internal Values of Sport', *Journal of the Philosophy of Sport* 27 (2000): 1–16.

19 In his contribution to this volume, J.S. Russell argues that sport often does not live up to this mutualist ideal and that sport has internal features that can and too often do promote unethical behaviour.

20 Nicholas Dixon, 'On Winning and Athletic Superiority', *Journal of the Philosophy of Sport* 26 (1999): 10–26.

21 For example, see Scott Kretchmar, 'Competition, Redemption, and Hope', *Journal of the Philosophy of Sport* 39 (2012): 101–16 as well as Scott Kretchmar and Tim L. Elcombe, 'In Defense of Competition and Winning: Revisiting Athletic Tests and Contests', in *Ethics in Sport,* 2nd ed, ed. William J. Morgan (Champaign, IL: Human Kinetics, 2007), 181–94.

22 For recent statements of this position, see William J. Morgan, 'Broad Internalism, Deep Conventions, Moral Entrepeneurs, and Sport', *Journal of the Philosophy of Sport* 39 (2012): 65–100; and idem 'Interpretivism, Conventionalism and the Ethical Coach', in *The Ethics of Coaching Sports: Moral, Social and Legal Issues,* ed., Robert L. Simon (Boulder, CO: Westview Press, 2013), 61–77.

23 Morgan, 'Broad Internalism, Deep Conventions, Moral Entrepeneurs', 72.

24 See ibid., 71.

25 I am especially indebted to discussions with Russell and the opportunity to read an unpublished paper of his on deep conventionalism. I also criticize Morgan's critical or deep conventionalism, although on somewhat different grounds, in my paper 'Internalism' to appear in Mike McNamee and William J. Morgan, eds., *Routledge Handbook of the Philosophy of Sport,* forthcoming.

26 I have developed this view in my paper 'From Ethnocentrism to Realism: Does Discourse Ethics Bridge the Gap?', *Journal of the Philosophy of Sport* 31 (2004): 122–41.

27 The quotation from Tim Clark's interview can be found at 'Russell Henley, in His First PGA Event as a Rookie, Delivers Record Performance', *FoxNews.com,* 14 February, 2013 <http://www.foxnews.com/sports/2013/01/14/russell-henley-in-his-first-pga-event-as-rookie-delivers-record-performance/#ixzz2R1U280cx> (accessed 15 March, 2013). I believe I heard Michigan's Trey Burke's comments in a live interview but he expresses almost identical views in Nick Baumgardner, 'Michigan's Trey Burke Says He Loves Playing Against Aaron Craft, but the Game Can't Be 1-on-1', *MLive.com,* 5 February, 2013 <http://www.mlive.com/wolverines/index.ssf/2013/02/michigans_trey_burke_says_he_l.html?utm_source=feedburner&utm_medium=feed&utm_campaign=Feed%3A+annarbor-sports+%28Ann+Arbor+News+Sports+-+MLive.com%29> (accessed 15 March, 2013).

7 Fairness and Justice in Sport

Sigmund Loland

Questions of fairness and justice cause heated debates in sport and seem to touch upon some of its core values. Was the competition fair? Did the football team deserve the goal? Did the best competitor win? Are the rules against doping just? Should women to a larger extent be allowed to compete with men? Should athletes with prosthetic limbs be eligible in competitions with able-bodied athletes? Should inequalities in financial, scientific and technological resources between competitors in elite sport be eliminated or at least compensated for?

In this chapter, I will examine more closely the ideals of fairness and justice in sport. My discussions are limited to competitive sport or sporting games. First, I will provide a brief review of the relevant literature in the field. Second, I shall propose a critical interpretation of fairness and justice ideals and present a specific theory of sport fairness and justice. In the discussions, I will provide a series of examples of how fairness and justice are, and can be, implemented in sport practice. In the third and final part, I shall examine in more detail the possibilities and limitations of the theory in a discussion of two topical issues in sport: rule violations and the use of performance-enhancing biotechnologies.

Issues of fairness and justice are standard topics in the philosophical literature of sport and have been addressed by many authors in a variety of books, book chapters and articles. I will mention a few of what I see as the most important works. Peter McIntosh's *Fair Play: Ethics in Sport and Education*[1] is a modern classic. McIntosh presents a historical review of interpretations of fair play and discusses social-psychological and educational studies touching upon fair play. The philosophical part of the book comes across as eclectic but has provided important inspiration to later work. Among the first extensive and systematic philosophical volumes on the ethics of sport competition is Warren P. Fraleigh's *Right Actions in Sport: Ethics for Contestants*.[2] Fraleigh develops a normative system of action guides expressing more or less explicitly interpretations of fairness and justice. The analysis of rule violations and fouls (especially of the 'good' or the 'tactical' foul) has made a particular impact in the literature. Robert L. Simon's *Fair Play: Sport, Values, and Society* and the revised edition *Fair Play: The Ethics of Sport*[3] is a case-oriented text written on the basic normative premise of sport as 'a mutual quest for excellence through physical challenge'. Simon's work and definition of sport are widely cited and used both in education and research. A fourth volume is my own *Fair Play in Sport: A Moral Norm System*.[4] The book presents a systematic theory of the ideal of fair play. A particular ambition is to present a detailed theory of sport fairness and justice relevant to the world of modern, competitive sport.

Fairness and justice have also been discussed in a series of articles and book chapters addressing issues such as cheating, drugs in sport, gender and equality issues, the problem of 'running up the score' and one-sided contests, and the distribution of advantage and penalties in competitions. The more important works are collected in edited volumes such as in William J. Morgan and Klaus V. Meier's *Philosophical Inquiry in Sport*,[5] in Jan Boxill's *Sports Ethics: An Anthology*[6] and in Morgan's *Ethics in Sport*.[7]

My aim here is to provide a more systematic and critical overview of the fairness and justice ideals actually at stake, and if, and possibly how, they are interrelated. More specifically, in what follows, and based on my previous work on fair play, I will outline a theory of fairness and justice in sport.

Fairness in Sport

In his seminal book *A Theory of Justice*, John Rawls presents a theory of justice as fairness.[8] The theory represents a revitalization of classic social contract theory with a neo-Kantian foundation. Fairness is understood both in terms of an individual obligation on rule adherence arising when participants take part voluntarily in rule-governed practices, and as a guiding norm securing impartiality in the process of determining the principles of a just society. My analysis is to a large extent inspired by this conceptualization. Let me first discuss fairness as an individual obligation on rule adherence.

In terms of social logic, sport competitions can be seen as social practices with the institutionalized goal of measuring, comparing and ranking participants according to performance of athletic skills.[9] The performances in question are more or less clearly defined in a set of rules. Following John Searle's well-known distinction, the rules that define performances in a particular sport are constitutive to the sport in question and define its distinguishing criterion: athletic performance.[10] These are the constitutive rules of the sport. The constitutive rules of football include the proscription of touching the ball with the hands as well as definitions of how to score goals and win. In sports such as gymnastics and diving, constitutive rules define certain ideal movement patterns and how points are to be awarded to measure, compare and rank gymnasts performances. Constitutive rules really 'make up' a sport.

Against this background, it can be said that the individual obligation of fairness or rule adherence is a requirement for a sport to be realized at all. If participants break the rules, the practice ceases to exist. However, as Fred D'Agostino has observed, this does not mean that all sport participants have to adhere to the rules all the time.[11] In real life, very few sporting games are practised without any rule violations. But to be realized in a meaningful way, a majority of participants must be adhering to the rules. This illuminates the core justification of the ideal of individual fairness. Rule breakers both in sport and in life usually have an intention of reaching an exclusive advantage compared to rule-adhering participants. They depend upon the rule adherence of others. Typically, rule breakers are 'free-riders' and enjoy the benefits of a practice without doing their fair share. This is, according to Rawls, the commonly held intuitive justification of the individual obligation of fairness.

A further distinction needs to be made. Not all rule violations in sport are necessarily matters of unfairness and moral blame. In contradiction to the purely intellectual game of chess with its completely transparent moves of chess pieces, most sporting games involve extensive bodily movement that are not always easy to control fully. Unintentional rule violations, such as body contact in basketball or stepping over the line in long jumping, seem almost unavoidable. If performed in a non-intentional way, there seems to be no moral blame involved. Moreover, some intentional rule violations such as certain kinds of in-fights in boxing or violations leading to the 9-metre throw in European handball, seem to be more or less an accepted part of the respective sports and are not considered unfair. In D'Agostino's concept of an 'ethos' of a game, the constitutive rules provide a framework to be interpreted by the practice community. The commonly accepted interpretation of the rules makes up the ethos of the sport.

Tentatively, the individual obligation of sporting fairness, then, can be rephrased as follows: *Keep the socially agreed-upon interpretation of the constitutive rules (the ethos) of the sport in which you take part!*

The fairness obligation does not arise unconditionally. Rawls lists two conditions: that participants are voluntarily engaged, and that the rule system and ethos in question are just. In sport, the first condition seems to be met most of the time. To most athletes, sport is a voluntary activity in the sense of athletes having the option of not taking part if they so choose. Sport competitors are seen as moral agents with freedom of choice and with responsibility for their choices.

The second condition on justice is a more complex one. A set of sporting rules or a sport's ethos is not necessarily ethically defensible and just. In professional cycling there may have been a common agreement to accept banned doping substances. In European handball the level of accepted violence may have developed far beyond what is defined in the rules. In some synchronized swimming settings men are defined as ineligible for competition. Is the obligation of fairness still met under such circumstances? The acceptance of doping or violence, or the exclusion of competitors based on biological sex, raises justice issues that need to be further explored.

Justice in Sport

Simplistically speaking, questions of justice usually arise in the context of the distribution of goods and burdens. To be ethically relevant, the discussion should deal with significant goods and burdens concerning, for instance, life and death, health, quality of life, self-realization, wealth and power. If not matters of life and death, sport seems to provide significant values of many kinds to many people. Engagement in sport opens possibilities for strong experiential values. If practised in constructive ways, sport is reported to have the potential of contributing to self-realization, quality of life and a sense of community. What are the criteria of constructive sport practice? How can the potential values of sport be distributed in just ways? What are the relevant principles of sport justice?

By looking systematically and critically at the organizing principles that seem to underlie rule structures of sports, I will outline a scheme of justice that I hold to be characteristic of these practices.[12] I will put flesh on this analytic bone with a series of examples of how justice can be implemented in practice (and how injustice can be eliminated or compensated for).

An Analytic Scheme

In book V of his *Nicomachean Ethics,* Aristotle suggests a starting point to discuss justice in terms of three norms:[13]

- Equal cases ought to be treated equally
- Unequal cases can be treated unequally
- Unequal treatment ought to stand in a reasonable relationship to the actual inequalities between parties

These are formal norms and may indicate several distributive schemes in practice. Assume that certain goods, such as a sum of money, are to be distributed between a certain number of persons. This can be done on the basis of an egalitarian norm: everyone receives the same amount; a meritocratic norm: the parties are rewarded according to performance on the basis of an objective standard, or according to effort, to various kinds of need, social standing, statutory rights; or combinations of the above norms.[14]

In his work on local justice, Jon Elster has shown how various practices and institutions combine distributive norms in a variety of ways.[15] In most societies, social welfare is distributed according to need, whereas taxation can be estimated according to income (progressive taxation), or the use and consumption of certain goods or products (direct taxation). A physical education teacher gives her marks on the basis of both effort and standardized performance measurements, whereas sport competitors are rewarded based on merit according to performance alone.

Even distributive norms are ideal norms, however, and must be implemented in practice by various kinds of procedures. Rawls distinguishes between three different procedures.[16] Perfect procedural justice fully realizes the ideal distributive norm. Equal distribution of 100 euros among four persons means 25 euros for each. In real life, situations with equal distribution of quantifiable goods are rare. As in the case of the physical education teacher, distribution is based on a combination of norms and there is no possibility of exact quantification. The point is to find the least imperfect procedures, i.e. the procedures that seem to coincide most closely with the distributive norms in question. A third category is pure procedural justice. Pure procedures are defined by the absence of a distributive norm. The procedure in itself guarantees a just result. The standard example is the lottery. Imagine a lottery with one prize. If 100 persons hold one lottery ticket each, each individual has a 1:100 chance of winning, and the distribution has 100 possible just outcomes.

The relationship between formal justice, distributive justice and procedural procedures is illustrated in figure 1.

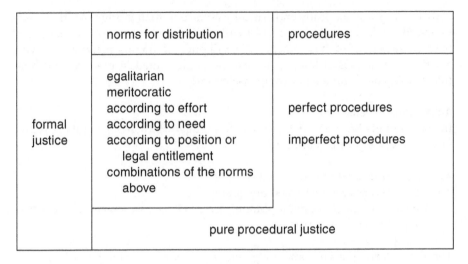

	norms for distribution	procedures

formal justice	egalitarian
	meritocratic
	according to effort
	according to need
	according to position or
	    legal entitlement
	combinations of the norms
	    above
		perfect procedures
		
		imperfect procedures

	pure procedural justice	

Figure 1   Overview of norms and procedures of justice

Equal Opportunity to Perform

The first part of the formal justice norm prescribes that equal cases ought to be treated equally. The institutional goal of sports competitions is to measure, compare and rank participants according to athletic performance as defined in the relevant constitutive rules. In this sense, the focus in sport is not on equality but on various kinds of inequalities among persons. The predominant distributive norm is meritocratic. To be able to evaluate meaningfully inequalities in performance in reliable and valid ways, other non-relevant kinds of inequalities have to be eliminated or at least compensated for. In other words: *All competitors should be given an equal opportunity to perform!*

At first sight, competitive sport seems just in this respect. In a marathon race, all competitors run the exact same distance of 42.195 kilometres and are timed in identical ways. Points in tennis and goals in football are awarded according to identical rules for all players and teams. Javelin throwers are given the same number of attempts and throw standardized javelins.

On second thoughts, however, it appears that we deal with imperfect procedures. Non-relevant inequalities are not always eliminated. There are at least three challenges in this respect. One challenge is associated with inequalities in external conditions. This is primarily relevant in outdoor sports. A sudden gust of wind can give a long-jumper the necessary centimetres to win. A strong headwind can spoil the race for a downhill skier. Consequently, rules have been established for the effects of wind in athletics and downhill skiing. Inequalities in external conditions are considered non-relevant inequalities and should be eliminated. But, at least in outdoor sports, this is impossible. Compensation of various kinds is the only possibility. Even here we deal with imperfect procedural justice.

Another challenge to the equality norm is related to rule violations. A rule violation may give some competitors an advantage on the basis of irrelevant criteria. If so, this will be a violation of the norm of equal opportunity. The aim is, then, to eliminate or compensate for an unjust advantage. Sport has more or less refined procedures for such instances. For example, the distinction between non-intentional and intentional rule violations is found in most rule systems.[17] A footballer is unfortunate, unintentionally tackles too late and 'takes the man rather than the ball'. By awarding a free-kick, an attempt is made to restore the initial situation. In the case of intentional violations, such as deliberately striking an opponent, restoring the initial situation is not sufficient. Players 'sabotage' the game. To balance rule violations and penalties, rule breakers are given warnings and in grave instances they are expelled from the game. The rule of thumb in the ethos of most sport seems to be that advantages arising due to non-intentional and intentional rule violations are eliminated or compensated for as far as possible.

A third challenge at high levels of performance is system inequality, or inequality in the financial, scientific and technological resources backing competitors. More than 30 years ago, Kalevi Heinilä described the increasing totalization process in elite sport.[18] Due to extensive possibilities for pay-offs in terms of profit and prestige, total systems of economic, technological, scientific and human resources are engaged in the quest for victory. One consequence seems to be that athletes' and teams' responsibility for their own performance is reduced. Developments in the last decade have proved this a fertile hypothesis.[19] For instance, in international club football, the best clubs in England, Germany, Italy and Spain form an almost unbeatable group by virtue of their superior resources and access to star players. This situation seems to run counter to the ideal norm of equal opportunity to perform. In current competitive sport there seems to be no real consensus for the need to compensate for system inequalities. Perhaps this is an emerging ethos in elite sport. For instance, by looking at medal statistics from the Olympic Games there is little doubt that elite sport reflects general inequalities in society at large. Such a development is highly debatable, in particular if elite sport has an ambition of serving as an ideal of equal opportunity.

Relevant Inequality: Athletic Performance

Discussions of equality point towards what can be considered the relevant inequality in sport competitions. Equal opportunity is a precondition for being able to measure, compare and rank athletic performances in reliable and valid ways. The true focus of competitive sport is a particular kind of human inequality: athletic performance. The second part of the formal justice norm opens for unequal treatment. As primarily a meritocratic system, competitive sport is clear on this point: *Inequalities in athletic performance ought to lead to unequal treatment among competitors.*

'Athletic performance' is defined in the constitutive rules and in the commonly accepted ethos of the sport in question. These rules and this ethos define a sport and provide its distinguishing criteria. Is it possible, however, to articulate more general ideas of what athletic performances are all about? By looking at the constitutive rules and the ethos of different sports, it could be asked if there are more general insights here in terms of what sport is all about.

Like any other human phenotype, sport performances are complex products of a large number of genetic and non-genetic factors. An analytical distinction can be drawn between an individual's genetic make-up, which in its pure form exists only at the moment of conception, and subsequent forms of influence that develop in interaction between genetic and environmental factors.[20] A person's genetic make-up is often called 'talent'. Talent is developed in a long chain of both intentional and non-intentional as well as controlled and uncontrollable interactions with the environment, ranging from the first interaction between a fertilized ovum and the mother's womb, via basic nourishment and care during infancy, subsequent general socio-psychological and sociocultural influence, sport-specific influence in the form of training and access to facilities, equipment and expertise, and even to situations and events on the day of performance and during performance. Some of these interactions are controlled by the athlete and are matters of intention and possible individual merit; others are matters of external control, and of chance and luck.

So far, the discussion of equality has dealt with rule violations, external conditions and resources. What are acceptable and unacceptable inequalities when it comes to the development of performance? How, more precisely, is athletic performance to be defined? In this essay I can only sketch some tentative lines.

Chance processes in 'the natural lottery' resulting in inequalities of talent is a matter of pure procedural justice and not unjust in itself. But unequal treatment based on such inequalities *alone* may appear unreasonable. In most ethical traditions there seems to be consensus on a general ideal, often referred to as a fair opportunity norm:[21] *Inequalities that individuals cannot influence or control in any significant way, and for which they therefore cannot be held responsible, should be eliminated or compensated for!*

To a large extent, in democratic societies, distribution of basic goods and burdens is built upon this principle. For example, physical and mental disabilities or other unfortunate conditions in life are compensated for by financial support and integrative efforts in work and leisure. The norm is relevant in sport as well. One example is the classification of athletes. Athletes are classified according to sex, age and sometimes body size. A lightweight boxer is not matched with a heavyweight as the outcome is usually determined based on inequality in body size. Similarly, female sprinters do not compete with male runners. The commonly accepted reason seems to be that there are significant inequalities in genetic predispositions for strength and speed to the advantage of men. Boxing fights between unequal parties and mixed-gender races among elite sprinters are considered unfair. In other words, sports compensate for uncontrollable inequalities where these are assumed to have a significant impact on performance.

This does not mean that sport is optimal in this respect. Classification is just as much a product of historical and social conditions and does not always involve a systematic fairness approach. For instance, why do men and women compete separately in shooting and sailing? Why are there no height classes in volleyball and weight classes in shot putting, where body size is of decisive importance to performance?[22] To improve justice in sport, a possible reclassification could involve eliminating sex classification in some sports where biological sex does not exert a significant and systematic impact on performance (in shooting, for instance) and replace sex classes with a classification according to body size (height and/or weight) in sports where these inequalities exert a significant and systematic impact on performance (in sailing classes where weight is important, for instance).

Let me conclude the discussion on relevant inequality in sport and point to a more general interpretation. We can assert that an underlying normative understanding is the idea of athletic performance as a product of the development of natural talent primarily by own efforts for which athletes and teams can be claimed responsible, and also admired. Sport at its best, to rephrase Thomas Murray, is about the virtuous development of natural talent towards human excellence.[23] I will return to this point below in the discussion of performance-enhancing biotechnologies.

Advantage and Unequal Treatment

The third part of formal justice prescribes a reasonable relationship between relevant inequality and unequal treatment. In the sport context, this can be rephrased as follows: *Actual inequalities in performance ought to stand in a reasonable relationship to inequalities in the distribution of competitive advantage!*

What procedures are used to realize the norm in practice? In the discussion of equality of opportunity I considered unfair advantages due to rule violations and how penalties are designed to eliminate or compensate for unfair advantages. In this context I shall take a closer look at unequal treatment due to relevant inequalities in performance.

Generally speaking, in competitive sports there are two different types of performance measurement. In some sports, performance is measured in exact physical-mathematical terms. For example, in the 100-metre-sprint, or in javelin throwing and weightlifting, competitors are ranked according to seconds, metres and kilograms. In other sports, other units are used that are defined in their constitutive rules. In tennis, advantages are given in the form of points, games and sets. Basketball players compete for points, football and handball players compete for goals. These can be called sport-specific advantages. In some sports, the two kinds of performance measurement are combined. In ski jumping, performances are evaluated in terms of the length of the jump (in metres) and a sport-specific scale of aesthetic points.

In competitions with physical-mathematical performance measurement, the relationship between performance and distribution of advantage is seemingly ideal. On closer examination, however, a problem arises. Modern high-tech measuring equipment is too fine-grained perhaps. Victories of one hundredth of a second in the 100-metre-sprint or of one-tenth of a second in the 50-kilometre cross-country skiing race are hardly under the full control of the competitors. Non-meritocratic elements such as luck can be decisive. Paradoxically, the quest for perfect meritocratic procedures increases the significance of non-meritocratic elements.[24]

In sports with sport-specific advantages the picture is even more unclear. Poor performance can actually sometimes lead to an advantage. A technically miserable hit on the tennis court may end up as a winning shot when the ball hits the net and falls down on the opponent's side. A good performance, for instance a brilliant technical and tactical return, may touch the net as well but fall down on the wrong side and lead to the loss of a point.

Nicholas Rescher distinguishes between pure chance, which by definition cannot be predicted or influenced such as in a lottery, and luck, which seems to be beyond the control of the affected person, but which in principle can be controlled if we possess sufficient knowledge and skill.[25] A good football player aims well and hits the post on the inside rather than on the outside, and scores. Good tennis players rarely misjudge the ball and ensure enough height over the net. Usually, the best tennis player and the best football team win. Golfer Lee Trevino is said to have expressed the idea like this: 'The more I practise, the luckier I get!'

To sum up, sport is a meritocratic practice in which there should be a reasonable relationship between actual performance and advantage awarded. In most sports, however, there seems to be embedded in the rules and in practice the acceptance of non-meritocratic elements of chance and luck. As long as all participants know of and voluntarily accept such elements, and as long as the non-meritocratic elements do not exert significant and systematic impact on competitive outcomes, they represent no ethical challenge and can be included in a local scheme of justice in sport.

The Varieties of Cheating in Sport[26]

Above I have outlined what I take to be the basic principles of a theory of fairness and justice in sport. During the discussion I have used a series of practical examples. In what follows, I will explore the possibilities and limitations of this theory by discussing in more detail two topical issues in sport ethics: cheating and the use of performance-enhancing biotechnologies.

Intentional and Unintentional Violation

A theory of fairness and justice in sport should allow for sharp and analytic differentiations between different kinds of rule violations and related penalties. A departure point can be the basic distinction mentioned above and drawn in most rule systems between intentional and unintentional violations.[27] A handball player may stumble and fall and kick the ball with his foot, or a tennis player may lose her balance and step over the line in her service. Both actions imply a violation of constitutive rules. However, none of them are intentional in kind. The players do not violate rules on purpose.

How can this be dealt with from the perspective of fairness and justice? Usually, unintentional violations are considered the result of bad luck and/or lack of skill, and do not imply attributing moral blame or accusations of unfairness to the rule breaker. Unintentional rule violations may still cause an imbalance in a competition. The handball player may gain possession of the ball after the accidental kick, while the tennis player is able to get closer to the net and hit a more efficient service. In most rule systems, unintentional violations are dealt with by eliminating, or at least compensating for, potential advantages due to the violation. This is done by reconstructing, as far as possible, the situation as it existed immediately before the violation. The opposing handball team is given the ball at the location where it was accidentally kicked, while the tennis player's service is disallowed and, if this was the first of two attempts, she has to serve again. Fairness and justice are restored as far as practically possible.

The more challenging rule violations from a moral point of view are those that are committed intentionally. In contradistinction to the case of unintentional violations, eliminating or compensating for advantages due to intentional violations does not seem to be sufficient. In some rule systems intentional rule violations are referred to as 'sabotage of the game'. This has a background in the idea of fairness. When free and equal moral agents voluntarily engage in a rule-governed practice, an individual obligation to fairness arises. Rule violators benefit from others' rule conformity without doing their fair share.

In most instances, therefore, such violations lead to additional penalties such as warnings and, in grave instances, expulsion from the competition. A footballer who trips an opponent violently and with risk of harm is given the red card. A tennis player who protests loudly against all decisions of the umpire is given a warning and, if the complaining continues, expelled from the game.

Intentional rule violations come in many forms. The most common is referred to as cheating. Ernest Cashmore defines cheating as 'to act fraudulently, to deceive, swindle or flout rules designed to maintain conditions of fairness'.[28] Typically, cheating includes deceit. A footballer's handball might be an intentional attempt to break the rules without getting caught and thus to secure an advantage with means that are not available to rule-abiding competitors. Other examples could be the tennis player who, in a self-refereed match, intentionally makes false calls on her opponent's good shots without her opponent realizing it, or the basketball player who, in a concealed manner, deliberately obstructs his opponent by holding on to his shirt without being caught and penalized.

A subcategory of cheating involving deceit is commonly referred to as 'simulation', or 'play-acting'. A handball or football player fakes a foul, falls and writhes as if in pain. The intent is to get a free-throw or -kick or a penalty. The player who fakes the foul may also have the intention of getting an opposing player who is (incorrectly) held responsible for the foul warned or even expelled from the game. Usually, play-acting thus involves multiple deceits. The aim of the rule breaker may be not only to get away with an exclusive advantage, but also to create a situation in which an innocent competitor is falsely accused and penalized.

A final main category of intentional rule violations is the so-called tactical or professional foul. Interestingly, in this case deceit plays no part and the tactical foul is usually not called cheating. Tactical rule violations imply breaking the rules and – this is the key difference from cheating – openly accepting the penalty that comes with it. The logic of the situation is that the rule breaker or the team benefits from the violation on a longer-term basis, and that the advantage gained is considered greater than the disadvantage associated with the penalty. Examples include the footballer who, to prevent a quick counter-attack from the opposing team and to gain time, deliberately concedes a free-kick, or the ice hockey player who ruthlessly tackles the other team's key player again and again to 'eliminate' from the game 'the brain' of the team. These are situations in which the penalties may appear too lenient and therefore do not seem to fit the crime. More than with single and multiple deceits, tactical fouls are controversial violations in terms of moral blame. Some accept such fouls as parts of the ethos of a sport, whereas others do not.

How are we to deal with this diversity of intentional violations from the perspectives of fairness and justice? How can unfair inequality (unfair advantage) be eliminated or compensated for by unequal treatment (penalties)? Traditional cheating involves deceit and is a paradigmatic case of unfairness. It is a clear example of lack of respect for opponents and can be considered a sabotage of the competition. It thus justifies not only the restoration of the game to the situation, as it existed prior to the cheating, but also the imposition of additional penalties on the cheat. A footballer being tripped in a good scoring position gets the chance again with opponents 10 yards away, which most of the time is overcompensation for the disadvantage caused by the violation. A tennis player may lose points or even games as a penalty for severe rule violations. The penalty is not only a restoration of fairness and justice, but is supposed to deter from and prevent cheating.

Play-acting can be considered an even more problematic rule violation, as it not only implies an intentional violation to get an exclusive advantage but also, very often, an attempt to impose a penalty upon the innocent. From a fairness point of view, this is a particularly destructive and degrading form of violation as it expresses very clearly disrespect for other competitors. Sometimes competitors actually express joy over their rivals' unfair misfortune. The penalties are usually even more severe.

Tactical fouls represent a more difficult case. In elite professional football, for instance, such fouls seem to a large extent to be part of the established ethos. If becoming a part of the ethos of a sport, problems of fairness and justice may seem to be solved. All participants have access to professional fouls, and thus they operate under equal opportunity to perform. Tactical fouls may still represent a moral problem. If we find a high number of tactical fouls in a sport, there is a need for a critical evaluation. No practice can survive if key rules are commonly broken. If the tactical foul adds quality and skill challenge, a rule change and allowance of the foul may be a reasonable solution. On the other hand, if tactical fouls do not seem to add sporting qualities but on the contrary, for example, increase brutality and cynical conduct, the penalty system has to be revised. Tactical fouls build on a social logic in which penalties do not 'fit the crime'. Hence, as has been done in football with the introduction of a red card and expulsion from the game for bringing down a player in a scoring position, penalties should be imposed more strictly or increased. In this way, the very rationale for tactical fouls will disappear.

Figure 2 illustrates a proposed taxonomy of rule violations in sport and the degree of moral acceptability or non-acceptability together with what can be seen as appropriate reaction from the perspective of fairness and justice.

	Unintentional violation	Classic cheating	Professional foul	Play-acting
Restore	X	X	X	X
Penalty		X	X	X
Warning (degree of severity/harm)		(X)	(X)	XX

Figure 2   Varieties of cheating – a moral taxonomy

Doping, Justice and Human Excellence[29]

In public discourses in and around sport, there are blurred lines of what ought to count as athletic performance, each of them coloured by different views of what sport is good for, and what is human and inhuman, 'natural' and 'artificial'. Some of the most challenging discussions concern the use of performance-enhancing biomedical technologies, usually referred to as doping. What are acceptable and unacceptable biotechnologies in sport? And, what is the role of fairness and justice in this respect?

In spite of a reasonably high degree of public and political consensus on anti-doping, doping appears is a complex and challenging scientific and moral dilemma. Some scholars hold that the ban on doping is problematic and even unjustifiable.[30] And, as is evident from extensive doping cases in international elite sports such as athletics and professional cycling, some athletes and coaches seem to accept and indeed practise doping.[31]

A predominant argument in support of anti-doping is based on the fairness argument. If, as today, there is a ban on certain substances and means, those who use such substances and means break the rules to get an exclusive advantage. They cheat. For doping to be efficient, dopers 'prey' on the rule adherence of others. Doping is unfair.

In the justification of doping, however, the fairness argument is limited. Justifying a rule by reference to the wrongness of breaking it implies logical circularity and is invalid. What is at stake here is the very rationale for anti-doping. In fact, the fairness argument is sometimes used to reject anti-doping.[32] If a significant number of athletes break the rules without being caught, a minority of rule-adhering athletes have a disadvantage. Morality does not pay. The situation is unjust. The rules of the sport and its ethos dramatically diverge. The obligation on rule adherence becomes problematic. Thus, to restore justice an alternative could be to abandon anti-doping and leave the choice of performance-enhancing means and methods totally up to the athlete and athletes' supporting systems.

Stronger arguments in support of anti-doping can be found in the view of performance-enhancing means and methods as implying a significant risk of harm. This argument, however, has serious limitations as well. At elite levels, sport enhancement strategies often involve significant risks of harm. Long-term and hard training implies a constant balancing of the anabolic and catabolic processes of the body. Imbalances can result in overtraining and possibly injuries. Similarly, competition itself can lead to acute injury. In fact, in some sports risks are considered constitutive and valuable elements of the activity. In parachute jumping and downhill skiing there is an inherent possibility of serious harm and death. In professional boxing, avoiding pain and harm oneself and imposing pain and harm on opponents are important technical and tactical challenges. An argument on anti-doping due to health risks could be developed into a more general argument against elite sport as a whole.

Such a conclusion is unreasonable as no distinctions are made between kinds and relevance of health risks as related to the nature of sport. Different social institutions and practices are characterized by different goals and values. In medicine, the overriding goal is to prevent and treat illness and thereby to restore or maintain health. In other settings, health is not always the primary value. Sporting competitions aim at ranking competitors according to athletic performance. Some health risks seem to be integrated in and add value to sport. The challenge of the training process and of competing is to put in the necessary effort to succeed and at the same time to avoid injuries. One of the important challenges in both downhill skiing and boxing is the proper calculation and taking of risk. Health risks linked to doping seem to be of a different kind, though. The doping question seems to boil down to a question about what kind of inequality sport is supposed to cultivate.

Typically, performance-enhancing substances are biochemical agents that are intended to have performance-enhancing effects. Some substances such as anabolic androgen steroids (AAS) and erythropoietin (EPO) are agonists. They mimic the action of substances that occur naturally in the body. Others have antagonistic effects. They are not produced by the body and prevent biochemical agents produced in the body from interacting with their receptors (beta blockers). In general, it can be said that doping substances interact with biological targets and have desirable performance-enhancing characteristics independent of the efforts and training activities of an athlete.

Here, then, justice norms in athletic performance and relevant inequalities become applicable. Sport seems to cultivate performances that are primarily influenced by the efforts of the athlete him or herself and that are, as such, under the athletes' responsibility: avoiding injuries in training and competition, the calculation and taking of risk in typically risk sports, etc. Performances can to a large extent be identified with the performer. Performance-enhancement due to the use of doping substances implies administration of substances usually by, or on the advice of, external experts, and the substances interact with their biological targets without the athletes' interference. The associated health risks, therefore, are less relevant to sport. Such a view supports the position of anti-doping.

This, however, begs the question to a certain extent. We may think of performance-enhancing biotechnological means and methods without health risks. For instance, if the health risk using substances such as AAS and EPO is controlled, why could we not accept and use AAS and EPO and make them available to everyone?

The question brings us to the limits of the arguments of fairness and justice in sport. Rawls' understanding of the relationship between 'the right' (principles of fairness and justice) and 'the good' (individual, social and moral values) may serve as a background. Principles of fairness and justice secure the basic structure for realizing sport.[33] If followed, they enable sport to be realized in morally acceptable ways. They are, so to speak, necessary conditions for sport to arise. They are, however, not sufficient conditions. A fair competition is not necessarily a good competition when it comes to the realization of values among participants and spectators. Participants may not perform at their best, they may lack motivation, the contest may be one-sided, etc. According to the World Anti-Doping Agency (WADA), the position of anti-doping is based on an idea of 'the spirit of sport'; of the values sport is supposed to serve and realize.

A comprehensive answer to the question of anti-doping has to build on thicker normative theories of the meaning and value of sport than is provided by an analysis of fairness and justice. Philosophers of sport are concerned with the potential moral qualities in sport and have interpreted them in several ways.[34] For example, training to realize one's talent takes willpower, dedication, the ability of goal setting and hard work. Competing well takes courage, concentration, the ability to do one's best and never give in and honesty and dignity in both victory and defeat. Team sports have the potential of building qualities such as loyalty and solidarity and the ability to strive towards common goals.

The version of sporting fairness and justice presented here is built on a Kantian premise of mutual respect between free and moral agents independent of abilities and skills. Competition is considered an advanced form of cooperation in which individuals and teams do their utmost to outperform each other while at the same time treating each other as equals. Human qualities such as courage, honesty, loyalty and solidarity are often considered general virtues of value. These are moral virtues describing key characteristics of human excellence. Murray's view of the normative ideal of sport as the virtuous development of natural talent towards human excellence emphasizes the point.[35] Sport is not about any kind of performance; it is about performance developed by individuals' cultivation of talent primarily based on their own efforts. Sporting excellence becomes one kind of human excellence. In this way, sport performances become worthy of moral admiration and sport can be a valuable practice to the individual and society.

We can return to the doping issue. Fairness and justice are necessary but not sufficient premises for the development of human excellence in sport. Doping becomes a 'short cut'; it overruns 'natural talent' and deprives athletes of developing sporting excellence as human excellence.

Within this conceptual framework, traditional arguments on health and fairness can be reconsidered. The health risks involved in the use of performance-enhancing substances and methods do not add value to the practice of sport but imply unnecessary and non-relevant health risks. They put athletes in vulnerable positions without really adding value to sport. There is good reason to ban doping practices in sport. In this way we justify the ban on doping without references to the wrongness of breaking it, and the fairness argument becomes valid as well. Doping practices reduce the moral significance of sport and go against fairness and justice and against sport as a sphere for human excellence.

Concluding comments

After having given a brief background with references to scholarly work in the field, I have outlined a theory of sporting fairness and justice, and I have explored whether, and possibly how, such a theory can inform topical discussions in sport ethics.

Quite a few articles and book chapters discuss topics relevant to sport fairness and justice, but few works treat the topic from a more comprehensive perspective. I have pointed to an individual obligation of fairness prescribing competitors to keep to the ethos of the sport in which they voluntarily take part, and to structural norms of sporting justice in terms of equality of opportunity to perform, norms for relevant inequality (a normative interpretation of athletic performance), and norms for a reasonable relation between actual inequality and unequal treatment (performance and advantage, and rule violation and disadvantage [penalty]).

Moreover, I have tried to demonstrate the possibilities and limitations of this theory of sport fairness and justice when it comes to cheating and the use of performance-enhancing biotechnologies or doping. The theory proved useful in the categorization of cheating and relevant penalties to restore fairness and justice. The theory proved useful, too, in the analysis of performance-enhancing technologies, but demonstrated a limitation as well. A normative standpoint in the discussion over legal and illegal performance enhancement necessarily has to build on a view of the value of sport, or 'the spirit of sport', to use WADA's terminology. A theory of 'the right' has to be complemented by a theory of 'the good.'

Notes

1   Peter McIntosh, *Fair Play. Ethics in Sport and Education* (London: Heinemann, 1979).
2   Warren P. Fraleigh, *Right Actions in Sport: Ethics for Contestants* (Champaign, IL: Human Kinetics, 1984).
3   Robert L. Simon, *Fair Play: Sport, Values, and Society* (Boulder, CO: Westview Press, 1991); and idem, *Fair Play: The Ethics of Sport*, 2nd ed. (Boulder, CO: Westview Press, 2004).
4   Sigmund Loland, *Fair Play in Sport: A Moral Norm System* (London: Routledge, 2002).
5   William J. Morgan and Klaus V. Meier, eds., *Philosophical Inquiry in Sport* 2nd ed., (Champaign, IL: Human Kinetics, 1995).
6   Jan Boxill, *Sports Ethics: An Anthology* (Malden, MA: Blackwell, 2003).
7   William J. Morgan, *Ethics in Sport*, 2nd ed. (Champaign, IL: Human Kinetics, 2007). I refer to literature published in English. There is, of course, relevant literature on sport fairness and justice in other languages that deserves attention. German studies in particular have had an impact on the international literature. For an overview of articles, see Volker Gerhardt and Manfred Lämmer, eds., *Fairness und Fair Play: eine Ringvorlesung an der Deutschen Sporthochschule* Köln (Sankt Augustin: Akademia, 1993). For a collection of essays of scholars from both the English and German

tradition, see Claudia Pawlenka, *Sportethik: Regeln, Fairness, Doping* (Paderborn: Mentis, 2004).

8   John Rawls, *A Theory of Justice* (Cambridge, MA: Harvard University Press, 1971).

9   Loland, *Fair Play in Sport: A Moral Norm System.*

10   John Searle, *Speech Acts. An Essay in the Philosophy of Language* Cambridge, MA: Harvard University Press, 1969), 33–4.

11   Fred D'Agostino, 'The Ethos of Games', *Journal of the Philosophy of Sport* 8 (1981): 7–18.

12   The discussion is based primarily on chapter 3 of my book *Fair Play in Sport: A Moral Norm System*, and on my article 'Justice in Sport: An Ideal and Its Interpretations', *Sport, Ethics and Philosophy* 1 (2007): 78–95. The analysis deals with competitive sport in itself and not with sport as an instrument in the quest for more extensive social values such as social integration or public health. I believe this is a necessary analysis before instrumental concerns can be addressed thoroughly.

13   Aristotle, *The Ethics of Aristotle. The Nicomachean Ethics* (Harmondsworth and New York: Penguin, 1976).

14   Chaïm Perelman, *Justice, Law and Argument. Essays on Moral and Legal Reasoning* (Dordrecht: D. Reidel, 1980), 1–23.

15   Jon Elster, *Local Justice: How Institutions Allocate Scarce Goods and Necessary Burdens* (New York: Russell Sage, 1992).

16   Rawls, *A Theory of Justice*, 85–6.

17   Fraleigh, *Right Actions in Sport: Ethics for Contestants*, 71–9.

18   Kalevi Heinilä, 'The Totalization Process in International Sport', *Sportwissenschaft* 2 (1982): 235–54.

19   Adrian Walsh and Richard Giulianotti, *Ethics, Money and Sport: This Sporting Mammon* (London: Routledge, 2007), 82–106.

20   Dietrich Martin, Klaus Lehnertz and Klaus Carl, *Handbuch Trainingslehre* (Schorndorf: Hofmann (2001); Turod Bompa and Greg Haff, *Periodization. Theory and Methodology of Training*, 5th ed., (Champaign, IL: Human Kinetics, 2009); and Claude Bouchard and Eric Hoffman, eds., *Genetic and Molecular Aspects of Sport Performance* (Chichester and Hoboken, NJ: Wiley-Blackwell, 2011).

21   Tom Beauchamp, *Philosophical Ethics: An Introduction to Moral Philosophy* (New York: McGraw Hill, 2001), 372.

22   For further discussion of this point, see Loland, *Fair Play in Sport: A Moral Norm System*, 57–60; Claudio M. Tamburrini, *The 'Hand of God'? Essays in the Philosophy of Sport* (Gothenburg: Acta Universitatis Gothoburgensis, 2000), 10–33; and Torbjörn Tännsjö, 'Is it Fascistoid to Admire Sport Heroes?', in Torbjörn Tännsjö and Claudio M. Tamburrini, eds., *Values in Sport. Elitism, Nationalism, Gender Equality and the Scientific Manufacture of Winners* (London: E & FN Spon, 2000), 9–23.

23   Thomas Murray, 'Enhancement', in Bonnie Steinbock, ed., *The Oxford Handbook of Bioethics* (Oxford: Oxford University Press, 2007), 491–515.

24   After having won by a tenth of a second the 15-kilometre distance during the 1980 Lake Placid Olympic Winter Games, Swede Thomas Wassberg wanted to share his gold medal with the official number two, Finn Juha Mieto. Impressively, Wassberg considered their performances to be approximately identical. This demonstrates the more or less established understanding, at least in cross-country skiing at that period of time, of the significance of athletes' responsibility for performance.

25   Nicholas Rescher, *Luck. The Brilliant Randomness of Everyday Life* (New York: Farrar, Straus & Giroux, 1995), 31–4.

26   The discussion of the varieties of cheating is based on Loland *Fair Play in Sport: A Moral Norm System*; and idem, 'The Varieties of Cheating. Comments on Ethical Analyses in Sport', *Sport in Society* 8: 11–26.

27 The analytic distinction between unintentional and intentional rule violations is philosophically rough and empirically challenging. What can be said of an athlete who violates rules because of lack of sufficient knowledge, or lack of concentration, or because of carelessness, etc.? What can be said of an athlete who is socialized into a rule-violating ethos and breaks the rules more or less automatically and not really 'on purpose'? When can an athlete be said to be responsible for his or her actions? These questions lead into fundamental questions on human freedom and responsibility and cannot be discussed in detail here. In the practice of a sport, athletes, coaches and in particular referees seem to be able to draw these more or less subtle distinctions in reasonable ways based on some kind of psychological *fingerspitzgefühl* (instinct or intuition). In spite of its ambiguities, the distinction between intentional and unintentional rule violations will serve as my point of departure for further analysis here.

28 Ernest Cashmore, *Sports Culture. An A–Z Guide* (London: Routledge, 2000), 64–5.

29 The discussion is based on Sigmund Loland and Hans Hoppeler, 'Justifying Anti-Doping: The Fair Opportunity Principle and the Biology of Performance-Enhancement', *European Journal of Sport Science* 12 (2012): 374–53.

30 Terry Black and Amelia Pape, 'The Ban on Drugs in Sport: The Solution or the Problem?', *Journal of Sport and Social Issues* 21 (1997): 83–92; W. Miller Brown, 'Practices and Prudence', *Journal of the Philosophy of Sport* 17 (1990): 71–84; Julian Savulescu, Bennett Foddy and M. Clayton, 'Why We Should Allow Performance Enhancing Drugs in Sport', *British Journal of Sports Medicine* 38 (2004): 666–70; and Tamburrini, *The 'Hand of God'? Essays in the Philosophy of Sport.*

31 Ivan Waddington and Andy Smith, *An Introduction to Drugs in Sport: Addicted to Winning* (London: Routledge, 2009).

32 Tamburrini, *The 'Hand of God'? Essays in the Philosophy of Sport.*

33 Rawls, *A Theory of Justice*, 446–52.

34 Mike McNamee, ed., *Sports Ethics: A Reader* (London: Routledge, 2010); William J. Morgan, *Why Sports Morally Matter* (London: Routledge, 2006); Robert L. Simon, 'Good Competition and Drug-Enhanced Performance', *Journal of the Philosophy of Sport* 11 (1984): 6–13; and Paul Weiss, *Sport: A Philosophical Inquiry* (Carbondale: Southern Illinois Press, 1969).

35 Murray, 'Enhancement'.

The Ethics of Enhancing Performance

Sarah Teetzel

This chapter examines the historical development, social significance and ethical concerns associated with enhancing athletic performance. In discussing performance enhancement as an applied ethical issue, foundational arguments by key authors representing the fields of sport ethics, bioethics and medical ethics are reviewed and critiqued to provide an overview and analysis of the debates that have shaped and continue to challenge these areas of inquiry. This essay also discusses how the International Sports Federations (ISFs) determine which enhancements are allowable in competition and in training.

The World Anti-Doping Agency's (WADA) ban on substances and methods included on its *Prohibited List International Standard* is analysed in conjunction with the challenges that arise from doping detection protocols. These issues include concerns related to privacy, confidentiality, autonomy and paternalism, as well as the additional ethical issues that arise when testing vulnerable populations, such as child athletes. Stemming from this analysis, this chapter examines the ways the sports world has evaluated which forms of enhancement are acceptable and allowed, and the reasons given for why some enhancements are banned. The growing research literature addressing the ethical issues that arise from using genetic enhancements to maximize athletic performance, also referred to as gene doping, is reviewed and critiqued. In doing so, the idea of genetically modified athletes is raised to highlight the division between philosophers advocating individuals' autonomy to choose enhancements, and philosophers who encourage a more cautious approach that views the prospect of gene doping with suspicion.

The history of the therapy-versus-enhancement debate is discussed to highlight the potential futility in trying to maintain a distinction between therapies and enhancements for the purpose of justifying the current bans on performance-enhancing technologies in sport. While philosophers attempt to define enhancement and justify parameters for its acceptable use, sport scientists and engineers work with athletes and coaches to produce equipment and training methods that will help the athlete achieve excellence and push the boundaries of human capacities. This essay examines the fine line between extending the limits of human performance and preserving the values and traditions of sport.

Defining Enhancements

Philosophers of sport have given considerable attention to ethical issues involved in enhancement. Leon Culbertson, Mike McNamee and Emily Ryall note that 'in the last decade there is little doubt that the sub-field "ethics of sport" has seen the most growth and activity'.[1] Philosophers have consistently discussed the moral acceptability of performance enhancement, doping and drug bans. A starting point to these debates is the clarification of what the concept of enhancement involves. Enhancements are often defined in relation to health and therapy. A common view of enhancement considers enhancements to be medically unnecessary procedures that go above and beyond the treatment of illness and eradication of disease to make individuals 'better than well'.[2] In this case, enhancements are defined by how they differ from health and therapy; hence, an understanding of how both terms are applied is helpful. The World Health Organization's (WHO) often-cited definition of health, which states that 'health is a state of complete physical, mental and social well-being and not merely the absence of disease or infirmity', projects the idea that to achieve a state of health one must go beyond being free of disease or being unwell. By including elements of holism and happiness in its definition, the WHO sets a high standard for health.

In the pursuit of health, a distinction between therapies and enhancements is often invoked. Therapeutic interventions, which include 'treatment for a disorder or deficiency, which aims to bring an unhealthy person to health,'[3] are used to restore and maintain health. In its report, *Beyond Therapy: Biotechnology and the Pursuit of Happiness*, the President's Council on Bioethics defined enhancements as 'the use of biotechnical power to alter, by direct intervention, not disease processes but the "normal" workings of the human body and psyche, to augment or improve their native capacities and performances'.[4] Enhancements include drugs, procedures and methods of intervention that not only restore health to improve human functioning, but are intended to improve a person beyond 'the absence of disease or infirmity'. This can happen in more than one way: enhancements can involve attempting to raise a norm, so that a greater portion of the population is above the previous norm, or they can be used to raise humans to levels previously unattained.[5] It is not obvious that either form is acceptable.[6]

In sport, the former roughly equates to enhancements that enable more people to, for example, run 100 metres in under 14 seconds, while the latter amounts to enhancements that would enable the very best runners to cover 100 metres in eight seconds – well under the current world record. Many forms of enhancement cross beyond the professional obligations of medicine and are not medically necessary. Humans do not need to run 100 metres in under nine seconds, even if many people find the pursuit of this goal a meaningful and worthwhile challenge. Enhancements are used to improve the capacities of humans beyond what is required for good health and thus can cover a range of procedures from morally required, to morally permissible, to morally prohibited options. Examples of morally required enhancements include vaccines for children in high-risk areas, whereas morally permissible enhancements include elected cosmetic surgeries and providing short children with growth hormones. Enhancements that might be deemed morally prohibited in a society would be those that, for example, function to create social hierarchies among people or include an unacceptably high level of risk.[7] Much more ethical scrutiny has been directed at therapies that can treat illnesses and diseases than enhancements that seek to go beyond the restoration of health, as most research that requires ethical review and approval from research ethics boards is designed to treat, not to enhance.[8] Instead, when dealing with enhancement outside of the domain of medicine, these decisions are often governed by legal rules and debate can be lacking.

The utility of trying to maintain a therapy-enhancement distinction has been called into question by many philosophers. While moral boundaries are always hard to draw, the difficulty with the therapy-enhancement distinction is the inability to identify the point where a treatment is medically necessary and where it is merely a desirable option. For example, for an injured athlete who would prefer to heal faster and, if possible, strengthen or reinforce the injured joint in the process, elective surgery may not be necessary to ensure future health, but it could be an efficient and desirable option to return the athlete to competition sooner. Whether the surgery would constitute a therapy or an enhancement is not obvious. Moreover, as John Harris points out, many forms of enhancement are unproblematic and widely accepted. Music lessons and personal coaching serve as 'extra' education that can improve students' capacities, but we do not consider these activities to be enhancements, even though they may fit within a working definition of the word.[9] Beyond the moral acceptability of the procedure itself, ethicists are also concerned about the risk-to-benefit ratio, whether the enhancement promotes human dignity, and if providing only some members of a society with the enhancement is fair and equitable. As David Resnik has argued, 'some forms of enhancement are immoral, others are not; likewise, some types of therapy are immoral, others are not. The implication of this view is that we should not use the therapy-enhancement distinction as our moral compass in human genetics.'[10] Resnik's argument supports the view that moral boundaries are very difficult to draw, and can also be applied to show that not every enhancement possible in sport ought to be embraced.

The bioethics literature at the turn of the century was ripe with discussions of the moral acceptability and repercussions of human enhancements. These debates garnered considerable attention among the general public, with books such as Eric Paren's *Enhancing Human Traits* (2000), Carl Elliott's *Better than Well: American Medicine Meets the American Dream* (2003) and Sheila Rothman and David Rothman's *The Pursuit of Perfection* (2003) exposing a wide audience to ethical debates about enhancement. A common theme among these sources is the complexities involved in drawing a line between enhancements and therapies, and what types of enhancement we ought to embrace. Yet enhancements, generally, and enhancements in sport, specifically, are not new concepts; the history of sport is full of references to emerging technologies that functioned to enhance performance and enhance athletes' abilities to achieve athletic success.

Enhancing Performance and the Ways in Which Performance Can Be Enhanced

Sport historians chronicling the development of enhancements demonstrate the many ways that athletic performance can be facilitated. Beyond the obvious methods, such as strength and endurance training, access to excellent coaching and consuming an optimal balance of vitamins, minerals and nutrients, athletic performance can be affected by enhanced equipment, technology and sport medicine techniques. Enhancements are used to construct stronger, faster and more efficient bodies, which can be done using methods that range from spending countless hours training specific muscle groups using equipment recommended by highly trained coaches and sport scientists, to ingesting drugs, supplements and other ergogenic aids. In the quest to produce results in the form of stronger, faster and more effective athletes, the sport world has embraced innovations that promise to push athletes' limits continuously further.

Applied ethical problems examined by philosophers include the moral acceptability of new technologies, including carbon-fibre prosthetics, or 'blades', and racing wheelchairs.[11] The invention of new technologies can change how athletes train, what equipment they use and the conditions under which they compete, but the technology itself is value neutral. Since the technological revolution, technologies have been developed and used to increase athletic performance; these technologies function to enhance not only the athlete but also the athlete's capacity to train, equipment and the performing environment. For example, advances in sports equipment burgeoned in the late 1800s when mass production became a reality and factories could, for the first time, produce large quantities of inexpensive sporting goods for relatively low prices.[12] Technology in sport continued to proliferate throughout the 20th century. Professional sports became such competitive endeavours that the margin separating winners and losers was often reduced to millimetres, hundredths of seconds or mere tenths of points. As a result, many athletes embraced new technological enhancements to help gain an edge over their competitors.

Innovations such as smaller and lighter equipment for young athletes and equipment designed for left-handed players have made sports equipment more user-friendly, whereas the development of ergonomic, lightweight running shoes and moisture-wicking clothing has made training more comfortable for athletes. Electronic timing systems were first included at the 1912 Olympic Games in Stockholm, and since then the technology utilized in timing systems has advanced steadily to the present electronic equipment that can accurately measure competitors' times to the nearest thousandth of a second.[13] Technological advances in sport now function to rehabilitate injuries sustained through sport, help to prevent injury, improve equipment design and function, and exert control over previously unpredictable weather patterns. Examples of inventions include the use of electronic stimulation machines that expedite the healing of injured muscles at the cellular level, aerodynamic uniforms made from synthetic materials, high-altitude training chambers that mimic the effects of oxygen-deprived environments, and video replay systems that allow referees to make more accurate rulings and determine who crossed the finish line first in tight races. Whether or not each innovation is permitted and embraced, or prohibited and banned, is decided by the ISFs that govern each sport.

Enhancing human traits can take many forms, including: physical enhancements (such as increasing the strength or size of muscles or cosmetic surgeries), intellectual enhancements (such as improving mental alertness and decreasing the need for sleep), psychological enhancements (including making people less shy and more confident) and moral enhancements (for example, increasing one's ability to be empathetic or decreasing aggression).[14] The technology used to produce these enhancements can range from newly developed drugs to modifications of the human genome. In the next section, the complexities of determining the moral acceptability of banning and allowing enhancements in sport are examined through an analysis of doping and genetic enhancement in sport.

Doping and Genetic Enhancements

The 11th volume of the *Journal of the Philosophy of Sport*, published in 1984, remains a key source of information on the ethical issues arising from athletes' use of performance-enhancing drugs. Containing articles by Robert L. Simon, W.M. Brown and Warren P. Fraleigh on the moral acceptability of drug use and drug bans, this volume provides foundational readings in doping in sport.[15] Considerable attention is given to issues of paternalism and coercion involved in banning drugs and justifying why sports organizations can dictate to athletes what they cannot consume. In addressing the paternalistic nature of doping bans, Simon argued, 'at least two possible justifications of paternalistic interference are compatible with the harm principle. First, we can argue that athletes do not give informed consent to the use of performance-enhancing drugs. Second, we can argue that the use of drugs by some athletes does harm other competitors.'[16] Because sport involves a mutual quest for excellence by the competitors: 'even if the decision to use performance enhancers is a free and autonomous one, it changes the relationship between competitors and the nature of the sports contest in a morally inappropriate and indefensible way – one which transforms the sports contest so as to lessen (and if carried to extremes actually eliminate) the respect competitors show to each other as persons.'[17]

By distinguishing between empirical and moral concerns to address potential harms created by doping, Brown analyses the appropriateness of invoking paternalistic responses to justify doping bans. According to Brown, 'the soft paternalist could, of course, insist that where drug use or sports activities carry with them high risk, even risk of death or permanent injury, we are justified in intervening to prevent serious costs to the rest of us even when the athletes are willing to take the risks.'[18] Yet acting paternalistically toward competent adults functions to impose on them 'an alternative set of values.'[19] Brown's analysis suggests that 'we can indeed forbid the use of drugs in athletics in general, just as we do in the case of children. But ironically, in adopting such a paternalistic stance of insisting that we know better than the athletes themselves how to achieve some more general good which they myopically ignore, we must deny in them the very attributes we claim to value: self-reliance, personal achievement and autonomy.'[20] Moreover, Brown points out, 'athletes, as well as the rest of us, must weigh the risks and benefits of the choices they make; no one forces them to seek Olympic gold.'[21] Drawing on Simon and Brown's arguments, Warren P. Fraleigh summarizes, arguing that 'the use of performance-enhancing drugs by the individual is morally wrong because it changes the nature of the contest without agreement and exerts coercion on others to inflict self-harm'.[22]

Subsequent analysis of the ethical issues involved in enforcing a doping ban fine-tunes Simon, Brown and Fraleigh's arguments to expand the debates. Angela Schneider and Robert Butcher's article, 'A Philosophical Overview of the Arguments on Banning Doping in Sport,' addresses the arguments used to justify doping bans in sport.[23] The authors explain the strengths and challenges of the arguments based on naturalness, fairness, health, harm, coercion and setting bad examples for children. In taking an athlete-centred approach, Schneider and Butcher demonstrated that positive change will occur if 'athletes agree on the sorts of practices they do not wish to engage in and then request the assistance of international sports governing bodies in assuring compliance'.[24] Instead of a top-down approach where rules are imposed on athletes, more consideration needs to be given to consulting athletes on their preferences. This athlete-centred view is echoed in the philosophy of the International Network for Humanistic Doping Researchers (INDHR), which is an informal network of researchers studying the social, cultural and ethical aspects of doping who advocate fair doping policies that respect athletes' rights.[25]

Yet arguments calling for the elimination, or at least revision and relaxation, of the doping rules are equally concerned with respecting athletes' rights, particularly their rights to privacy and autonomy. For example, M. Andrew Holowchak has argued that 'all ergogenic aids that enhance skill should be promoted' because 'it seems impossible to give a principled justification of this unfairness, and there are often ways of remedying whatever it is we consider to be unfair'.[26] Philosophers have questioned whether a ban on drugs in sport can be justified and have argued that the doping ban ought to end. The arguments offered in support of this position focus on the ideas that the doping ban does more harm than good by failing to respect athletes' autonomy to decide what to put into their bodies. Claudio M. Tamburrini suggests that the harm that athletes might face if permitted to dope openly is no different to the harm people face in other occupations.[27] Conversely, John Gleaves examined whether arguments exist to prohibit the use of harm-free performance-enhancing drugs, ultimately arguing that even these drugs would have detrimental effects on the continuity of the test undertaken by the athletes.[28] Michael Burke raised the issue of whether Schneider and Butcher's anti-doping position is a defensible one or rather the preference of a community based on consensus, solidarity and social justification. He points out that 'in enforcing a ban on drugs, we may be intruding on a private space for the athlete in a way that would not be acceptable in other practice communities in liberal society', because 'actions that are private and are not cruel to others should remain under private control and should be protected from a public morality or legislation'.[29] Further, Michael Burke and

Terence Roberts have suggested that 'the pervasive dislike of athletes using drugs is not explained entirely by the "good" practice of sport and fairness, and that it also has something to do with the fear of transgressing socially constructed, gender boundaries'.[30]

While philosophers have examined the moral acceptability of the ban on performance-enhancing substances and methods in sport, it is the purview of WADA to enforce the banned substance list. The rationale provided by WADA in the *World Anti-Doping Code* is that substances and methods are prohibited in sport if they meet two of the following three criteria: they enhance performance, they cause harm and they violate the spirit of sport.[31] Yet much of the opposition to doping bans stems from ethical concerns arising due to the testing protocols used to ensure athletes comply with the banned substance list. The challenges that arise from applying the drug-testing protocols set out by the *World Anti-Doping Code* relate to concerns regarding athletes' privacy and the confidentiality of their test results and samples.[32] Requiring athletes to provide a urine sample in the presence of a doping control officer, simply to participate in sport, is not in line with acceptable practices outside of sport. Yet drug testing is not always an unacceptable infringement on a person's privacy and autonomy; it is used without controversy in cases where the need to protect the public interest is strong.[33] Thus drug testing is required in many nations for public transportation operators, health-care workers, jailed inmates and people on parole, among other groups, in order to protect the public trust. As a result, drug testing is usually conducted 'only in exceptional cases in which drug use constitutes a real risk to safety'.[34] Yet, as many philosophers point out, athletes' use of banned substances does not, on the surface at least, threaten public safety. Additional ethical issues arise when testing vulnerable populations, such as child athletes, who are too young to provide informed consent for their blood or urine to be taken and tested. The possibility of using genetic enhancements to improve athletic performance further exacerbates these concerns because methods of detecting genetic enhancements would require access to an athlete's genetic information.

The research literature examining the use of genetic enhancements to maximize athletic performance has exploded since philosophers began discussing 'gene doping' at the turn of the century. With advances in genetics and gene therapy research, a growing number of scholars and geneticists noted that therapeutic protocols designed to treat genetic diseases and disorders, such as muscular dystrophy, could be used to enhance athletic performance in healthy individuals. In an article published in the *Journal of the Philosophy of Sport* in 2001, Andy Miah identified genetic technology as the new ethical issue in sport and highlighted this emerging area of study.[35] Miah was correct and his article sparked a flurry of study in the area of gene doping in sport, which resulted in several manuscripts, articles and anthologies addressing the uncertainty for sport that the dilemma of genetic therapies used for performance-enhancement purposes creates. Parallel debates on engineering athletes to be predisposed to athletic success occurred concurrently.[36]

While some philosophers pointed out the problems that gene doping in sport creates, echoing WADA's views about upholding an elusive spirit of sport, a body of modest support for embracing genetic technology in sport followed. Miah's cautiously optimistic approach argued for accepting and embracing this technology rather than banning it outright and attempting to prevent athletes from utilizing it.[37] Miah's manuscript was followed one year later by Claudio M. Tamburrini and Torbjörn Tännsjö's edited collection, *Genetic Technology and Sport: Ethical Questions*, which contained arguments both for and against the use of genetic technologies in sport.[38] In the meantime, WADA included gene doping as a banned method in the *World Anti-Doping Code* and many philosophers weighed in on the social significance and ethical ramifications raised by using gene transfer technology, designed to restore health to individuals suffering from genetic diseases, to enhance athletic performance. Analysis of the prospects of gene doping in sport appeared in a wide variety of scholarly sources, encompassing journals dedicated to discussing not only ethical issues but gender studies, sociology, genetics and the life sciences. The debates on genetically modifying athletes highlight the division between philosophers advocating individuals' autonomy to choose enhancements and philosophers who encourage a more cautious approach that views the prospect of gene doping more suspiciously.[39]

Attempts to determine where to draw the line between legitimate and illegitimate enhancements led to renewed discussions of the therapy-enhancement distinction as it applied to performance enhancement in sport.[40] The human enhancement literature addresses the concerns of both 'bioconservatives' (who generally oppose genetic modification on the grounds of hubris and fears of 'playing God' and are thus anti-enhancement) and 'transhumanists' (who generally embrace human enhancement in order to determine the limits of human capabilities and can be considered pro-enhancement). Most ethicists contributing to these debates fall in the middle of the spectrum between the pro- and anti-enhancement positions.[41] However, Erik Parens suggests that the pro-enhancement and anti-enhancement camps have more in common than either side realizes. The overlap, according to Parens, occurs in recognition of the concept of authenticity.[42] Many ethical concerns about enhancement rest on the possibility of transcending human limits and what doing so would mean for living authentic lives. In applying ideas from the transhumanism literature to sport, Leon Culbertson's essays on theories of dehumanization and humanness provide a unique bridge to wider themes on human nature.[43]

As a result of human beings' desire for mastery and control, several philosophers concede that the technological enhancement of humans is an inevitable occurrence. Most arrive at this conclusion after considering several observations about human nature, including the ideas that humans are competitive beings who strive to exceed and surpass each others' accomplishments for recognition and other external awards. Being the first to invent or perfect an enhancing technique fuels many researchers' drive to investigate possible modes of enhancement. The capitalist market also leads to the inevitability of technological enhancements because as technology becomes available, there will be consumers willing to pay the required price to access the technology if they feel it will benefit them personally. With this demand in place, enhancements seem quite appealing to profit-driven producers and investors.[44]

There are several key arguments in favour of allowing technological enhancements of human traits and abilities. Most of these arguments are based on libertarian views of freedom, autonomy and the ability to live one's life as one pleases as long as doing so does not harm other people or violate their rights. These arguments stem from the belief that humans have a positive right to enhance and develop themselves, as long as it cannot be shown why they should not and they do not harm anyone in the process. In this light, humans have a duty to develop themselves in order to reach their maximum potential. Arguments of this sort are based on an individual's expectation that he or she has the right to alter his or her body as long as no one else is harmed in the process.[45] Respecting the individual's autonomy and right to make his or her own decisions factors strongly in the arguments advocating in favour of enhancing human beings.[46] If the technology is available, and an individual wants to use it and has the money to pay for it, prohibiting the individual from doing so is a violation of his or her autonomy. Furthermore, assuming the individual is a competent adult who understands the risks he or she is incurring via undergoing an enhancement procedure, prohibiting the individual from enhancing his or her performance is unjustifiably paternalistic. Other arguments in favour of allowing human enhancements focus on the thirst for knowledge and the curiosity and wonderment many feel regarding how strong, fast or efficient a human body can be made to be. Additionally, some philosophers argue genetic enhancements can be a way of compensating for a person's poor draw in the genetic lottery.

The above arguments meet opposition from individuals concerned about the direct consequences of improving human performance by genetic enhancements, the social and moral implications of such enhancements, as well as the intentions of the consumers looking to be enhanced. Opposition to the widespread use of technological enhancements is based on the uncertainty associated with the risks, benefits, consequences and intentions, particularly in light of the fact that we can never know the true intentions of the researchers developing the technology or the individuals who seek its use. Opponents thus fear the ends that genetic enhancements could be used for, such as supporting negative and restricting conceptions of the ideal and 'normal' woman and man, and reproducing damaging prejudices and discrimination. Others fear that researchers will never fully understand the complex and interconnected functions of genes or anticipate every potentially fatal side effect in every population. Questions of harm thus factor predominantly for philosophers who oppose using genetic enhancement to improve human performance. This view encapsulates the cautious stance that the risks outweigh the benefits and the potential harm to individuals and social groups would negate any benefits. Peter Singer has expressed fears about the social inequalities that are foreseeable by enhancing human beings. His concerns are based on the complexity of determining the potential negative societal effects enhancements might cause, such as squandering resources, aggravating inequalities and exacerbating the gap between rich and poor. Positional goods are also raised as an area of concern by Singer. For example, if everyone is enhanced to grow taller, the positional benefit of being tall is negated. Enhancements of this variety end up being futile and a drain on shared resources.[47]

A central issue that arises in the literature on the pros and cons of genetic enhancements is the perception that going down this route equates to 'playing God' or interfering with the divine rights of nature. People holding this view argue that humans are born as they are meant to be and unnecessary alterations, except to restore health and prevent or treat disease, crosses the line between acceptable and unacceptable applications of knowledge. Michael Sandel argues that one should invoke the metaphor of the giftedness of life and respect the fact that humans did not create themselves and thus should not attempt to alter future generations or speed up the rate at which humans are evolving. Sandel maintains that genetically altering germ-line cells fails to respect both the giftedness of life and the ability of an enhanced child to choose his or her own life path.[48] Bioengineered children could face the possibility of being pre-slotted into specific activities in which they were designed to excel.[49] Concern for maintaining children's right to open futures should make us hesitate to embrace any type of enhancement that will result in pressure for perfection in a specific area, such as steering a child toward a specific sport.

Additional reasons to oppose genetic enhancement include Francis Kamm's concern that humans are not innovative enough to choose beneficial enhancement, and would instead opt to promote stereotypical ideals that would cause more harm than good.[50] Other concerns include the fear that allowing those who desire the enhancement to get it would coerce others to follow suit in order to remain competitive and have a chance at success. The number of arguments that contest genetic enhancements to improve human abilities shows that there is a need for moral reflection on how technological enhancements should proceed. The need to proceed with caution and incorporate moral and social guidelines for the use of genetic enhancements is paramount. Yet allowing genetic enhancements in general does not mean that there is a place for them in sport.

Critiques of enhancement in sport suggest that medical means are used for non-medicinal purposes, and fear seeing sport divided into separate classes for enhanced and non-enhanced athletes. Concern has also been raised about the pursuit of designer athletes, and the possibility that people will use genetic enhancements to enhance their progeny through modification of their germ-line cells, which would be passed on to any children they produce. If humans can be made smarter or kinder, or able to jump higher, simply by taking a pill or undergoing minor surgery, questions about the nature of human beings and how we ought to treat enhanced humans emerge. Some philosophers, however, argue that resistance to performance enhancement technology in sport is unwarranted because performance enhancements do not necessarily fall beyond the limits of the spirit of sport.[51]

The arguments about harm, coercion and fairness in the philosophy of sport literature note that an athlete's autonomy and right to privacy are often violated by the requirement that athletes forgo using banned substances and methods, including gene doping. The fact that athletes consent to forgoing some of their rights when they adopt the *World-Anti Doping Code* is cited as justification for restricting their freedom and impinging on their autonomy. Yet sport is also an arena governed by its own code of conduct, and one that can apply rules and principles that do not hold in general societies. Enhancement technologies that alter a person's genetic code with the intention of making a person faster, stronger or more adept to participate in an activity are banned from sport. Athletes can undergo these procedures like any human being, but if they do they render themselves ineligible to compete in high-performance sport. As former WADA director Richard Pound frequently asserted during his time leading the agency, athletes can choose to opt out of sport if they do not agree with its rules, unlike their ability to opt out of society at large.[52]

Issues unique to sport are attributed to sport's positional advantages. According to Nick Bostrom and Julian Savulescu, 'competitive sport is characterized by certain features that are not present in many other enhancement contexts. The advantage that an athlete gets from doping is purely positional: he might win the race, but this benefit comes at the expense of all other athletes who rank lower as a result.'[53] Torbjörn Tännsjö responds, noting that in sport, enhancement is always viewed with suspicion and that there are no special medical ethics for sport.[54] Instead, Tännsjö describes the ethos of elite sport as a cultural phenomenon. Unlike cosmetic surgeries, for example, towards which most societies hold a neutral position and think that if a person can pay for the procedure he or she is free to obtain it, in sport the prevailing ethos is that providing oneself with an advantage over one's competitors is unfair, regardless of whether or not one pays for the enhancement oneself. As Tännsjö argues, the ethos of elite sport contains 'a very special notion of justice typical of it. This is a notion of justice insisting that we must all accept the ticket we have drawn in the genetic lottery. Genetic differences are *not* irrelevant to the outcome of the competition. Indeed, genetic differences are what *should* be decisive, once we have eliminated *other* differences.'[55] Tännsjö argues that this notion of justice is rejected in other areas of life, and sport should be no different; thus he suggests the ethos of sport needs to shift to allow 'fierce, fair and unpredictable competition – a sweet tension of uncertainty of outcome'[56] where athletes can use enhancements to push the limits of athletic accomplishment. Tännsjö's view does not represent the prevailing outlook on the ethics of enhancement, but he pushes philosophers to consider why, in fact, WADA's ban on gene doping in sport is or is not warranted. Recent debate on enhancements in sport has expanded to add discussions of reason and private rationalities, and rejection of the idea of splitting competition into competitions for the enhanced and the unenhanced.[57] The ethics of enhancement thus remains a topic within the sport ethics sub-discipline of particular interest to philosophers.

Where to Draw the Line

Sports governing bodies must make important decisions about what enhancements to accept and which ones to ban in sport.[58] Scientists and engineers continue to research innovative ways of enhancing performance, including new fibres in sportswear, advanced synthetic playing fields and supplements that enhance athleticism, meet WADA's strict criteria for use and will not cause an adverse analytical finding if an athlete is selected for doping control testing. Distinguishing acceptable technological interventions from unacceptable ones is difficult, and decision-makers need to understand the history, values and ideals attached to each sport in order to preserve the unique challenges of all sports. With the number of ways athletic performance can be enhanced, sports organizations have had to make decisions about which enhancements to permit in sport and which ones to prohibit and ban. Almost all the time, enhancements that make the overall goal or challenge of a sport too easy are banned so that sport will remain a test of athletic skill and ability, rather than a competition primarily between engineers, scientists and pharmacologists.

Enhanced equipment that an ISF deems to be in line with the goals of the sport must be available to all athletes before it is approved for use in competition. For example, prior to the blanket ban on 'fastskin' and similar swimming racing suits, some countries banned their athletes from wearing these suits because the technology was so limited and expensive that not all swimmers had access to the innovative style of racing wear that promised reduced drag and faster times. If only some athletes are provided with innovative equipment from their sponsors, or are wealthy enough to access newly released technologies, an unfair playing field emerges. Banning new and improved equipment until it is mass-produced and available to all competitive athletes who seek to purchase it can help level the playing field. For instance, the appearance of clapskates in speed skating prior to the 1998 Nagano Winter Olympics made it nearly impossible for top-ranked speed skaters to maintain their rankings and compete with the world's best using traditional speed skating skates. However, in this case, the accessibility of clapskates was not an issue as they had been available for several decades in Europe. Competitors only had to quickly adjust to the new competitive skates to maintain their position in the rankings.

The constitutive, regulative and auxiliary rules of sport, described first by gamesmiths and currently implemented by ISFs through their official rulebooks, specify which actions are allowable in competition and in training. By banning new and improved equipment until it is available to all competitors, ISFs can ensure that it is the athletes' skills and effort, and not the equipment itself, that leads to success. For example, the Fédération Internationale de Natation (FINA) banned the swimsuits described above after almost every world record was broken and implemented stricter rules on allowable competition swimsuits. ISFs must determine whether new technologies and equipment respect the artificial challenges that each sport contests and whether they are available to athletes worldwide, but more pragmatically the ISFs must determine the feasibility of enforcing a potential ban and the fairness of doing so.

With respect to the ethics of enhancement, maintaining a spirit of fair play often appears high up in a list of justifications for banning specific substances and methods in sport.[59] Brown points out that 'it seems artificial indeed to draw the line at drugs when so much of today's training techniques, equipment, food, medical care, even the origin of the sports themselves, are the product of our technological culture'.[60] At the crux of this debate in the sport context is the uncertainty over what acts, modifications and improvements can be considered acceptable enhancements that are embraced and permitted in sport, and which ones ought to be banned because they are not in line with the spirit of sport. Accepted enhancements must be in line with the ethos of the sport, which in turn must 'include a commonly accepted and clear interpretation of what are the non-relevant inequalities that ought to be eliminated or compensated for to ensure equal opportunity to perform'.[61] Drawing a line on permitted and banned genetic enhancements is much more complex than determining acceptable and unacceptable equipment and performance attire. The difference is that the latter addresses eligibility restrictions and the nature of the competition, while the former deals with potential permanent changes to human beings. The fine line between extending the limits of human performance and preserving the value of sport is not easily identifiable. Yet the ramifications of the distinction matter morally, socially and politically.

Notes

1   Leon Culbertson, Mike McNamee and Emily Ryall, *Resource Guide to the Philosophy of Sport and Ethics of Sport* (Oxford: Hospitality, Leisure, Sport and Tourism Network, 2008), 3.

2   Carl Elliott, *Better than Well: American Medicine Meets the American Dream* (New York: Norton, 2003).

3   President's Council on Bioethics, *Beyond Therapy: Biotechnology and the Pursuit of Happiness* (New York: Regan Books, 2003). This working group, which included 17 ethicists, legal experts and scientists, included the enhancement of athletic performance on its list of the four most pressing bioethical concerns.

4   President's Council on Bioethics, *Beyond Therapy: Biotechnology and the Pursuit of Happiness*.

5   Eric T. Juengst, 'What Does Enhancement Mean?', in *Enhancing Human Traits: Ethical and Social Implications*, ed., Erik Parens (Washington: Georgetown University Press, 2000), 29–47.

6   Frances M. Kamm, 'What Is and Is Not Wrong With Enhancement?', in *Human Enhancement*, eds., Julian Savulescu and Nick Bostrom (Oxford: Oxford University Press, 2009), 91–130.

7   A full discussion of the reasons why these enhancements are respectively morally required, permissible or prohibited is beyond the scope of this essay. See Angela J. Schneider and Theodore Friedmann, *Gene Doping in Sports: The Science and Ethics of Genetically Modified Athletes* (San Diego: Elsevier Academic Press, 2006).

8   Maxwell J. Mehlman, Jessica W. Berg, Eric T. Juengst and Eric Kodish, 'Ethical and Legal Issues in Enhancement Research on Human Subjects', *Cambridge Quarterly of Healthcare Ethics* 20 (2011): 30–45.

9   John Harris, *Wonderwoman and Superman: The Ethics of Human Biotechnology* (Oxford: Oxford University Press, 1992).

10 David B. Resnik, 'The Moral Significance of the Therapy Enhancement Distinction in Human Genetics', *Cambridge Quarterly of Healthcare Ethics* 9 (2000): 374. Resnik's remarks are made in the context of genetic interventions, but are nonetheless applicable to all forms of enhancement.

11 Carwyn Jones and David Howe, 'The Conceptual Boundaries of Sport for the Disabled: Classification and Athletic Performance', *Journal of the Philosophy of Sport* 32 (2005): 133–46.

12   John Rickards Betts, 'The Technological Revolution and the Rise of Sport, 1850–1900', *The Mississippi Historical Review* 40 (1953): 231–56.

13   Henning Eichberg, 'Stopwatch, Horizontal Bar, Gymnasium: The Technologizing of Sports in the 18th and Early 19th Centuries', *Journal of the Philosophy of Sport* 9 (1982): 43–59.

14   Frances M. Kamm, 'Is There a Problem With Enhancement?', *American Journal of Bioethics* 5 (2005): 5–14.

15   WADA's *Prohibited List International Standard* uses the language of 'prohibited substances' and 'metabolites or markers of prohibited substances' to discuss banned substances. This language is more precise than referring to banned substances as 'drugs', which can refer to any substance that creates a physiological effect in the body. Not all drugs are banned in sport. See World Anti-Doping Agency, *World Anti-Doping Code* (Montreal: WADA, 2009): 18–19.

16   Robert L. Simon, 'Good Competition and Drug-Enhanced Performance', *Journal of the Philosophy of Sport* 11 (1984): 8.

17   Robert L. Simon, 'Response to Brown and Fraleigh', *Journal of the Philosophy of Sport* 11 (1984): 32.

18   W.M. Brown, 'Paternalism, Drugs, and the Nature of Sport', *Journal of the Philosophy of Sport* 11 (1984): 20.

19   Ibid.

20   Ibid., 21.

21   Ibid., 35.

22   Warren P. Fraleigh, 'Performance-Enhancing Drugs in Sport: The Ethical Issue', *Journal of the Philosophy of Sport*, 11 (1984): 28.

23   Angela J. Schneider and Robert B. Butcher, 'A Philosophical Overview of the Arguments on Banning Doping in Sport', in *Values in Sport: Elitism, Nationalism, Gender Equality and the Scientific Manufacture of Winners*, eds., Torbjörn Tännsjö and Claudio M. Tamburrini (London: E & FN Spon, 2000), 185–99.

24   Angela J. Schneider and Robert B. Butcher, 'Why Olympic Athletes Should Avoid the Use and Seek the Elimination of Performance-Enhancing Substances and Practices From the Olympic Games', *Journal of the Philosophy of Sport* 21 (1994): 74.

25   INHDR is administered out of Aarhus University in Denmark. See <http://doping.au.dk/>

26   M. Andrew Holowchak, 'Ergogenic Aids and the Limits of Human Performance in Sport: Ethical Issues, Aesthetic Considerations', *Journal of the Philosophy of Sport* 29 (2002): 84.

27   Claudio M. Tamburrini, 'What's Wrong with Doping?', in *Values in Sport: Elitism, Nationalism, Gender Equality and the Scientific Manufacture of Winners*, eds., Torbjörn Tännsjö and Claudio M. Tamburrini (London: E & FN Spon, 2000), 200–16.

28   John Gleaves, 'No Harm, No Foul? Justifying Bans on Safe Performance-Enhancing Drugs', *Sport, Ethics and Philosophy* 4 (2010): 269–83.

29   Michael Burke, 'Drugs in Sport: Have They Practiced Too Hard? A Response to Schneider and Butcher', *Journal of the Philosophy of Sport* 24 (1997): 48.

30   Michael Burke and Terence Roberts, 'Drugs in Sport: An Issue of Morality or Sentimentality?', *Journal of the Philosophy of Sport* 24 (1997): 100.

31   WADA defines the 'spirit of sport' as 'what is intrinsically valuable about sport', the 'essence of Olympism', and 'the celebration of the human spirit, body and mind'. World Anti-Doping Agency, *World Anti-Doping Code* (Montreal: WADA, 2009): 14.

32   Paul B. Thompson, 'Privacy and the Urinalysis Testing of Athletes', *Journal of the Philosophy of Sport* 9 (1982): 60–5.

33   Privacy Commissioner of Canada, *Drug Testing and Privacy* (Ottawa: Privacy Commissioner of Canada, 1990), 22.

34 Ibid.

35 Andy Miah, 'Genetic Technologies and Sport: The New Ethical Issue', *Journal of the Philosophy of Sport* 28 (2001): 32–52. A year prior to the publication of this article, Munthe published a book chapter analysing the idea of using genetic technology to 'select champions'; however, his analysis focused on genetic selection, not genetic enhancement. See Christian Munthe, 'Selected Champions: Making Winners in the Age of Genetic Technology', in *Values in Sport: Elitism, Nationalism, Gender Equality and the Scientific Manufacture of Winners*, eds., Torbjörn Tännsjö and Claudio M. Tamburrini (London: Routledge, 2000), 217–31.

36 See, for example, Claudio M. Tamburrini, 'After Doping, What? The Morality of the Genetic Engineering of Athletes', in *Ethics in Sport*, 2nd ed, ed., William J. Morgan (Champaign, IL: Human Kinetics, 2007).

37 Andy Miah, *Genetically Modified Athletes: Biomedical Ethics, Gene Doping and Sport* (London: Routledge, 2004). This book was the first manuscript-length examination of genetic enhancement in sport.

38 Claudio M. Tamburrini and Torbjörn Tännsjö, *Genetic Technology and Sport: Ethical Questions* (London: Routledge, 2005).

39 These ideas are analysed in volume 36 of the *Journal of the Philosophy of Sport*. See, for example, Sigmund Loland, 'The Ethics of Performance-Enhancing Technology in Sport', *Journal of the Philosophy of Sport* 36 (2009): 152–61. See also Angela J. Schneider and Jim L. Rupert, 'Constructing Winners: The Science and Ethics of Genetically Manipulating Athletes', *Journal of the Philosophy of Sport* 36 (2009): 182–206.

40 See William J. Morgan, 'Athletic Perfection, Performance-Enhancing Drugs, and the Treatment-Enhancement Distinction', *Journal of the Philosophy of Sport* 36 (2009): 162–181. See also volume 1, issue 2 of *Sport, Ethics and Philosophy*, which contains papers presented at the conference 'Legitimate and Illegitimate Enhancement in Sport: Where to Draw the Line?' hosted by Tännsjö and Tamburrini in 2005.

41 Nick Bostrom and Julian Savulescu, 'Human Enhancement Ethics: The State of the Debate', in *Human Enhancement*, eds., Julian Savulescu and Nick Bostrom (Oxford: Oxford University Press, 2009).

42 Erik Parens, 'Toward a More Fruitful Debate About Enhancement', in *Human Enhancement*, eds., Julian Savulescu and Nick Bostrom (Oxford: Oxford University Press, 2009), 186.

43 See Leon Culbertson, 'Sartre on Human Nature: Humanness, Transhumanism and Performance-Enhancement', *Sport, Ethics and Philosophy* 5 (2011): 231–44. See also Leon Culbertson, '"Human-ness," "Dehumanisation" and Performance Enhancement', *Sport, Ethics and Philosophy* 1 (2007): 195–217.

44 Françoise Baylis and Jason Scott Robert, 'The Inevitability of Genetic Enhancement Technologies', *Bioethics* 18 (2004): 1–26.

45 Gerald Dworkin, *The Theory and Practice of Autonomy* (Cambridge: Cambridge University Press, 1988).

46 Tom L. Beauchamp and James F. Childress, *Principles of Biomedical Ethics*, 5th ed. (New York: Oxford University Press, 2001).

47 Peter Singer, 'Parental Choice and Human Improvement', in *Human Enhancement*, eds., Julian Savulescu and Nick Bostrom (Oxford: Oxford University Press, 2009), 277–90.

48 Michael J. Sandel, 'The Case Against Perfection: What's Wrong With Designer Children, Bionic Athletes, and Genetic Engineering', *Atlantic Monthly* 293 (2004): 51–62.

49 Ibid., 71–90.

50 Frances M. Kamm, 'Is There a Problem With Enhancement?', *American Journal of Bioethics* 5 (2005): 5–14.

51 Bostrom and Savulescu, 'Human Enhancement Ethics: The State of the Debate', 8.
52 Richard W. Pound, *Inside the Olympics* (Toronto: Wiley & Sons, 2004).
53 Bostrom and Savulescu, 'Human Enhancement Ethics: The State of the Debate', 13.
54 Tännsjö goes as far as suggesting that athletes could test out enhancements in sport to see how far the limits of human physiological function could be stretched by enhancements. See Torbjörn Tännsjö, 'Medical Enhancement and the Ethos of Elite Sport', in *Human Enhancement*, eds., Julian Savulescu and Nick Bostrom (Oxford: Oxford University Press, 2009), 315–26.
55 Ibid., 325.
56 Ibid.
57 See Silvia Camporesi and Paolo Maugeri, 'Genetic Enhancement in Sports: The Role of Reason and Private Rationalities in Public Arena', *Cambridge Quarterly of Healthcare Ethics* 20 (2011): 248–57. Michael R. King, 'A League of Their Own? Evaluating Justifications for the Division of Sport into "Enhanced" and "Unenhanced" Leagues', *Sport, Ethics and Philosophy* 6 (2012): 31–45.
58 Andy Miah and Simon B. Eassom, eds., *Sport Technology: History, Philosophy and Policy* (Amsterdam: Elsevier Science, 2002).
59 Claudia Pawlenka, 'The Idea of Fairness: A General Ethical Concept or One Particular to Sports Ethics?', *Journal of the Philosophy of Sport* 32 (2005): 49–64.
60 Brown, 'Paternalism, Drugs, and the Nature of Sport', 21.
61 Sigmund Loland and Mike McNamee, 'Fair Play and the Ethos of Sport: An Eclectic Philosophical Framework', *Journal of the Philosophy of Sport* 27 (2000): 68.

9 Disability and Sport

Carwyn Jones

The profile of disabled sport is high. With each successive and successful Paralympic Games, the stock of elite Paralympic athletes rises. From a philosophical and ethical point of view, disability in general and disabled sport in particular both raise unique questions and provide a unique context for the discussion of more general and familiar questions. In this essay, I aim to cover the following ground: definitions of disability, disabled sport and the classification process and the conceptual and normative status of categorized competition vis-à-vis mainstream sport. Sport for the disabled has featured in the philosophy and ethics of sport literature both as the focus of investigation and as exemplification of a more general investigation into sports ethics (for example, the implications of the principle of fairness applied to sport). Both the *Journal of the Philosophy of Sport* (vol. 32, issue 2) and *Sports, Ethics and Philosophy* (vol. 2, issue 2) have featured special editions on the topic. This essay covers some, but by no means all, of the ground featured in the essays published in those editions and elsewhere.

Disability

The concept of disability provokes significant and often heated debate among scholars, educators, medics and in society more broadly. Its meaning is contested and has genuine political, social and economic implications. Given the ubiquity of the term and how it is used to distinguish between people (an obvious example being competitors in the Paralympic and Olympic Games) one might think that the concept and its application are straightforward. 'Yet, when one attempts to specify just what it is that distinguishes those people who are disabled from the non-disabled, things quickly become very obscure.'[1] If the distinction between disabled and non-disabled is a viable one, then one would expect to find 'some characteristic by virtue of which one is accurately subsumed within that category'.[2] According to Steven Edwards, being disabled cannot mean the absence of *all* abilities just as being non-disabled cannot mean the presence of *all* abilities.[3] To some extent, we are all *relatively* abled or *relatively* disabled. As such, Edwards argues that disability is a relational concept. Comparison with others is built into the idea from the start, both in terms of physical/mental constitution and in terms of expected functioning. But it is also a value-laden concept. Disability, he argues, implies not only difference, but difference that is disvalued in some way. The term has negative connotations associated with a loss of independence and autonomy and a reduced capacity to live a good life. Significant implications follow from being classified as disabled, including access to social benefits, entry into sporting competitions and treatment by society. In fact, if disability is identified during pregnancy, in many countries termination is allowed to full term. Tanni Grey-Thompson, winner of countless Paralympic medals and successful broadcaster and journalist in the United Kingdom, tells her experience in her autobiography:

> […] there is an awful lot of prejudice and ignorance about disability. It's a taboo subject. People don't like it, so they shove it under the carpet. Like most disabled people, I have come up against the 'does-she-take-sugar?' syndrome on a few occasions. Because I am in a wheelchair some people assume I am mentally subnormal and treat me like dirt.[4]

Disability has been defined in different ways by different constituencies depending on their particular focus or agenda. The medical profession has featured prominently in shaping conceptions of disability because many disabilities are associated with illness, disease or injury. According to Ian Brittain, the medical profession has played a fundamental role in how we think and act in relation to disability:

> In modern-day Western societies, the power of the medical profession, gained through its ability to both define and name illnesses and body parts as well as the power to heal injuries and cure illnesses, has put it in a very strong position to create and perpetuate discourses with respect to many areas of life related to the body and mind including disability.[5]

In 1980, the World Health Organization (WHO) played a key role in the medical conceptions of disability. It developed and employed a taxonomy of disability – the International Classification of Impairments, Disabilities and Handicaps (ICIDH) aimed at 'analysing, describing and classifying the consequences of diseases'.[6] The ICIDH is a paradigmatic and systematic *medical* model of disability. Key concepts are disease, impairment, disability and handicap. Crudely speaking, a *disease* like cerebral palsy *causes* an *impairment* ('loss or abnormality of psychological, physiological or anatomical structure or function' – hypertonia caused by upper motor neuron lesions), which *might* cause a *disability* ('restriction or lack of ability to perform an activity in the manner or within the range considered normal for a human being', for example walking), which *might* constitute a *handicap* (if 'it limits or prevents the fulfilment of a role which is normal [depending on age, sex and cultural factors] for that individual', for example accessing public transport, buildings and so forth).[7] According to the ICIDH, impairment is a necessary condition of disability, but it is not sufficient. One might have impairments that do not result in disability or handicap (third nipple), or the impairment might be correctable, for example with the use of spectacles in the case of impaired vision. According to Edwards, the ICIDH believes the causes of disability to be twofold. 'They stem partly from factors within the body of the person (diseases, impairments), and partly from external factors (such as a social environment that is not wheelchair-friendly).'[8] Although disability is not defined solely in terms of impairment, the medical approach (medical model) foregrounds the impairment, for example blindness, which is seen as a property of the individual – disability is therefore a condition *of* or *in* the individual. The impairment manifests itself in contrast to 'normal' or 'species-typical' functioning criteria. The impairment that is caused by disease or illness is itself the *cause* of the disability. The focus for medicine therefore becomes: treatment, cure, correction, rehabilitation or adaptation of the impaired individual.

According to Carmelo Masala and Donatella Petretto, during the period when medical models were being developed, honed and implemented, there was growing concern that disabled people faced discrimination, were excluded from the workplace and marginalized in society (for example, disabled children were educated separately in special schools). Opponents of the medical model believed it contributed to discrimination. The promulgation of the idea that impairment was 'abnormal', coupled to the close association between disability and disease, coupled to the disvalue of disease and disability, led to the stigmatization and poor treatment of disabled people. In 1975, the Union of the Physically Impaired Against Segregation (UPIAS), which was an early disability rights organization in the UK, sought to challenge the dominance of the medical model in the disability discourse. A key aim for the organization (and for proponents of the social model) was to draw a sharp distinction between impairment and disability, thus rejecting the conventional wisdom of the time that it was the impairment that disabled an individual:

> What we are interested in are ways of changing our conditions of life, and thus overcoming the disabilities which are imposed on top of our physical impairments by the way this society is organized to exclude us.[9]

Impairment, the UPIAS believed, doesn't *cause* disability, society does. If disability is a social, rather than a biomedical issue, the problems disabled people face require social or political solutions.[10]

Since the formation of the UPIAS, significant progress has been made in terms of disability rights. Successes in combating discrimination manifest themselves in a number of ways including changes in laws regarding the physical environment (ramps and lifts), changes in policy and legislation such as the 1995 Disability Discrimination Act in the UK and the 1990 Americans with Disabilities Act in the United States, which prohibits discrimination (in specified circumstances) on the grounds of disability; and a change in the acceptable vocabulary used to refer to disabled people (the term 'handicapped' is no longer used in the UK; 'wheelchair user' is used instead of 'confined to a wheelchair').[11] The success of the Paralympic Games is also considered evidence of progress in cultural attitudes towards disability.

Despite the political gains associated with a shift in focus from the medical to a social model of disability, the latter has difficulties of its own. There are two important problems associated with downplaying or rejecting the role of impairment in definitions of disability. The first is a conceptual problem. Impairment is a *necessary* condition of *disability* and without it the definition of disability collapses (more of which later). The second is a political problem, which follows on from the conceptual. By rejecting impairment as essential, the UPIAS fails to 'acknowledge that the social exclusion referred to in the definition is at least partly a consequence of the presence of an impairment within the individual'.[12] Even if all the requisite changes are made such that individuals with impairments are purportedly no longer *disabled*, they will still have impairment that effects their movement, sight or some such that might be a problem for *them*. According to Edwards, if one bleaches the concept of disability or the role of individualized impairments completely, there will be no way to distinguish between discrimination based on disability from other forms of discrimination such as sex or race. He says that 'disability, in contrast to race and sex, is always accompanied by impairment ... impairment is a necessary condition of disability'.[13]

The WHO replaced the ICIDH in 2001 with the International Classification of Functioning, Disability and Health (ICF), partly in light of criticisms it received. It attempted to address the medical, environmental and social complexity of disability more explicitly while retaining impairment as a necessary but not sufficient condition of disability. Instead of impairment, disability and handicap, the ICF now includes reference to impairments, activity limitations and participation restrictions. The account of impairment remains similarly focused on 'body parts, functions and statistical abnormalities in structure or function',[14] but the disability dimension, activity limitations is defined as:

> [...] difficulties an individual may have in executing activities. An activity limitation may range from a slight to a severe deviation in terms of quality or quantity in executing the activity in a manner or to the extent that is expected of people without the health condition.[15]

The specific concerns of the proponents of a 'social model' (i.e. that it is the social conditions that are disabling) are putatively addressed by the 'participation restriction' idea, which replaces the handicap concept:

> Participation restrictions are problems an individual may experience in involvement in life situations. The presence of a participation restriction is determined by comparing an individual's participation to that which is expected of an individual without disability in that culture or society.[16]

This new model, according to the WHO, is a 'biopsychosocial' model. It purportedly rejects the biomedical model, but does not fully embrace the social model either. Rather it is an integration of the two perspectives. As we can see, the references to 'species-typical functioning' are toned down somewhat, but the concept remains a relational one; one is both impaired and disabled in relation to a norm, but this has been relativized to context (culture, age, etc.).

Disability and Vital Goals

Although the ICF account is an improvement on its previous incarnation, Edwards argues that both WHO definitions are similarly deficient.[17] Neither, he argues, takes the view of the disabled person into account. Whether the individual thinks he or she is disabled or not is immaterial in both the ICIDH and the ICF. Grey-Thompson reflects on her experience:

> What's it like being disabled? That's probably the one question I get asked more than any other. People think I must have overcome enormous obstacles to be a success as an athlete, but I don't see it like that at all ... I actually have a very fulfilling life. I don't think of myself as disabled but I know I am lucky.[18]

The voice of the individual is silenced in both the WHO definitions. Although Grey-Thompson has an impairment (spina bifida – little or no use of her legs) and an activity limitation (a severe deviation in terms of quality or quantity in executing the activity in a manner or to the extent that is expected of people without the health condition), and faced participant restrictions (problems an individual may experience in involvement in life situations), she does not feel disabled. Edwards believes that an alternative conception of disability can be established that avoids some of the problems identified with the WHO and UPIAS conceptions and allows us to make sense of Grey-Thompson's claim that she is not disabled.[19] It is a conception put forward by Lennart Nordenfelt: 'A disability, as well as a handicap, is a non-ability – given a specified set of circumstances – to realize one or more of one's vital goals (or any of its necessary conditions).'[20]

Individuals have many non-abilities. For example, at 5 foot 8, I have a non-ability to slam-dunk a basketball. This does not necessarily mean I am disabled. Firstly, for this to count as a disability, my non-ability must be a result of an inherent condition, namely an impairment. An impairment is identified in terms of a reduction in capacity for action. 'The capacity is what a person's inner resources permit him or her to do. By inner resources I mean the biomechanical, physiological and psychological conditions inherent in the person.'[21] This does seem to have a 'species-typical' element to it. In other words, not all reductions in capacities count as impairment, only those that are outside the normal range. The capacity to walk is a typical capacity for healthy human beings. A person who is born without legs lacks the capacity to walk because of their impairment (but as Grey-Thompson mentions above) for her the lack of the capacity to walk did not disable her because she has lived a fulfilling life, or, in Nordenfelt's terms, realized her vital goals).

Secondly, for it to count as a disability my inability to slam-dunk a basketball must stop me from realizing a vital goal. Being a basketball player is not one of my vital goals. I am not disabled, therefore, because my non-ability is not a result of impairment, nor do I have a desire to be a basketball player. From this account (as in the ICF) we can see that disability is a combination of internal and external factors. In summary, disability is the inability to achieve vital goals because of limitations and restrictions imposed by impairment.[22] A key strength (among many) of this theory, according to Edwards, is that it takes the individual's views into account. Nordenfelt's definition of disability does not depend upon statistical norms, but on the extent to which impairment interferes with an individual's vital goals.[23]

Disability, Sport and Physical Activity

In its early days, sport and physical activity for disabled people were closely linked to therapy and rehabilitation and took place under the gaze of doctors, physiotherapists and so forth. The focus was very much on the impairment, its cause and effects, and how physical activity could play a role in the maximal realization of impaired capacities. Sir Ludwig Guttmann, a neurologist at the Stoke Mandeville Hospital's rehabilitation facility, organized a competition in 1948 for 16 servicemen and women injured during the Second World War to improve their strength and self-respect. Veterans with spinal cord injuries competed in wheelchairs at sports like polo, basketball and archery.[24] These first competitions developed and expanded and over the years evolved into the Paralympic Games we see today. Early pioneers of sport for the disabled were interested in the treatment and rehabilitation of injury, but also the reintegration of the person more generally back into society. The Paralympic vision is, of course, a very positive one: 'To enable Paralympic athletes to achieve sporting excellence and inspire and excite the world'.[25] The current Paralympic discourse is very much about empowerment through sporting excellence.

Philosophers of sport have debated long and hard over the nature and essence of sports and the source of any value they might have for people. For some, the values of sport are play values, which include joy, spontaneity, voluntaries and autotelicity. It is by 'playing' sport that its values are realized – an approach whose tag line might be Pierre de Coubertin's 'the important thing is not winning, but taking part'. For others, sport is essentially about competition and striving to be better than one's opponents, and is about victory, medals and glory, an attitude captured by Vince Lombardi's famous dictum 'winning isn't everything, it's the only thing'. Attached to each conception is a set of sporting values, namely the intrinsic and extrinsic values or what Jane English calls the 'basic' and 'scarce' benefits.[26] The former (intrinsic/basic) are available to all who play sport whereas the latter are only available to those who excel. Both participation (basic benefits) and elite competition (scarce benefits) are political goals for disabled sport. Making sure that disabled people have the access and the opportunity to play sport for the recreational, health and enjoyment benefits it affords improves their quality of life, and the presence of high-profile, elite, disabled athletes challenges preconceptions and stereotypes of disabled people in general.

Another approach places sport in the context of a good life, either as a central plank (career) or as one of many social practices through which important goals are realized and key virtues are exercised. In Nordenfelt's language, sport can be a vital goal for many individuals. Without specific adapted sports for disabled people, opportunities for individuals with impairments to realize sporting or athletic vital goals would not exist, or at least would be severely restricted.

Adaptations and Classifications

Having certain impairments can severely restrict a person's capacity to engage and/or excel in sport and physical activity. Certain impairments would seem to make the rudimentary requirements of many forms of sport and physical activity beyond the reach of those with spinal injuries, amputations, and sight and hearing difficulties and so on. The modern Paralympic Games, however, are testimony to the fact that more and more disabled people, if given the opportunity, are able to participate, compete and excel in a range of sports. In order to create such opportunity, the Paralympic Games differ from the Olympic Games in a number of ways. From a structural perspective, they include sports contests not in the Olympic Games (for example, wheelchair racing), sports that are in the Olympics, but whose constitutive rules are adapted and changed (for example, tennis), sports whose rules are essentially the same (100 metres) and sports exclusively for one type of impairment (goalball for visually impaired people only). Each sport rewards excellence (winning) with gold medals, so the Paralympic Games are not simply about acquiring the basic benefits of sport. Of course, the crucial difference is that in the Paralympic Games most sports have competitive categories in which similarly impaired athletes compete together. Currently, the Paralympic Games include competitions for wheelchair athletes, amputees, athletes with cerebral palsy, athletes with loss of sight, athletes with intellectual disability and learning difficulties and 'Les Autres'.[27] Each group is represented by a federation (referred to collectively as International Organizations for Sport for the Disabled [IOSDs]), which 'were established with the explicit intention of creating opportunities for people with disabilities and using sport as a vehicle for their empowerment'.[28] A key task of the IOSDs is the structure and organization of sporting competitions, which includes establishing categories and classifying athletes under their jurisdiction. In other words, the range of sports to be played (for example, athletics, basketball and swimming), the number and structure of categories within each sport (for example, in athletics, athletes with cerebral palsy compete in categories T [track] and F [field] 31–38), and performing the classification process, which the ISODs define as follows:

> Classification provides a structure for competition. Athletes competing in Paralympic sports have an impairment that leads to a competitive disadvantage in sport. Consequently, a system has to be put in place to minimize the impact of impairments on sport performance and to ensure the success of an athlete is determined by skill, fitness, power, endurance, tactical ability and mental focus [...] Classification determines who is eligible to compete in a Paralympic sport and it groups the eligible athletes in sport classes according to their activity limitation in a certain sport.[29]

The aim is to establish the impairment and the extent of its incapacitating effects through a process of tests and assessments and then to allocate individuals to competitive classes/categories with others whose assessments have similar outcomes. This process differs from sport to sport and employs a range of classifiers with a medical background and experts in the sport. Implicit in the rationale and practice of classification seems to be the distinction between some inherent capacity (outside of our control) and the cultivation and execution of an ability (in which the capacity is implicated). An athlete with a greater capacity for explosive muscle movement in their legs will have a greater potential for certain sporting actions than an athlete with lesser capacity. The idea, then, is that they do not compete against each other because the former's ability to run faster than the latter (for example) will be a result of the former's greater capacity.

This rationale is predicated upon a certain picture of the nature and purpose of sports contests and the ethical principles that govern and define them. Very simply, victories in sport should be deserved; they should be just. Aristotle argued that justice involves receiving what is due and not receiving what is not due, or getting what one deserves – no more or less.[30] In sport, winners ought to deserve their victory; they should win, not because of superior capacity but by cultivating, mastering and executing the requirements of a certain sport. Gunnar Breivik argues that ideally, 'The athletes strive to control performance and make the result dependent on their own intended actions' and 'winning should be caused by the relevant sport-specific performance and not by accidental factors'.[31] In rowing, for example, athletes who have minimal or no leg and trunk function compete in different classes to those who can use legs and trunk because the latter's increased capacity (not merited) accounts for their increased ability/performance (merited). In principle, therefore, when rowers (or other competitors) of similar capacity compete, the victor is the one who has been able to develop greater sporting performance than others with the same or similar capacity.[32]

On the face of it, the principle and its application seem plausible. However, it is not clear how plausible it is to apply. It is not always clear which aspects of athletic performance one can justly claim responsibility for.[33] Carwyn Jones and David Howe argue that implicit in the classification idea (and perhaps many of the accounts of merit in sport) is an analytic or reductive account of 'sporting ability' or 'athletic performance' or whatever the label given to the variable (or collection of variables) through which competitors attempt to outdo each other.[34] The problem is that victories in sporting contests are brought about by a mixture of different factors, including talent, skill, tactics and character. Implied in the distinction above is the idea that 'sporting ability' is an acquired merit-based property of athletes that can be distinguished from other natural features or capacities over which the athlete has no control (height or impairment). Sporting ability, however, is an embodied property (mixture of properties) and is constitutive of both natural and acquired physical characteristics such as stature, strength, power and dexterity.

The point is highlighted when we compare with non-disabled sport. Of course, justice is central in non-disabled sport, but there is no attempt to control for, or minimize, the influence of inherent capacities (or lack thereof). It is clear that Michael Jordan and Usain Bolt were blessed by incredible physiques for which neither can claim responsibility, yet without them, neither would have been the best at their sport. Both were fortunate in the 'natural lottery'. One can legitimately pose the question, therefore, of why classify in disabled sport and not in other sports. Such a case could clearly be made.

For instance, Sigmund Loland argues: 'Competitors ought to be differentiated in classes only in cases in which inequalities in person-dependent matters that they cannot influence in any significant way and for which they cannot be held responsible have systematic and significant influence on athletic performance.'[35]

Both impairments and extraordinary height seem to fit the bill here. Perhaps the important difference lies in the conceptions of disability discussed above. It is the presence of a functional impairment (remember that impairment means the loss or abnormality of psychological, physiological or anatomical structure or function) that kick-starts the process, not just any difference – say in height or stature. These might be significant for athletic ability but they are not the result of impairment. 'Impairment is a loss or abnormality in body structure or physiological functioning (including mental functions). Abnormality here is used strictly to refer to a significant variation from established statistical norms (i.e. as a deviation from standard population mean).'[36]

Of course, one might further interrogate this definition by looking more closely at some of the key concepts like 'significant variation' and 'established statistical norms', but the 'loss or impairment' idea marks out the crucially relevant *cause* of the variation. The central role of the 'normal' or 'statistical norms' in the process reintroduces concerns about value discussed earlier. By focusing on impairments in this way and then dividing people into groups according to the severity of the impairment (or at least the severity of its impact), a de facto hierarchy is created. If desired, the evidence of value hierarchy can be read from the sporting achievements or ranking provided by times and distances. In other words, the most impaired will have slower times than the less impaired, who have slower times than the non-impaired. The question raised is whether comparison either between categories within Parlaympic sports or between Paralympic sport and Olympic sport makes any sense.

Scott Kretchmar argues that in sports contests, 'Opponents try to do the same thing as one another, only more so. They attempt to pass the same kind of test better, to a greater degree, higher on the scale, than another' and 'A minimal two persons must be doing the *same* kind of thing for valid comparisons of success to be made.'[37] Using Kretchmar's vocabulary, one view might be that in, say, the high jump, a competitor with impairment (IC) and a competitor without impairment (NIC) are attempting the same test (trying to clear the bar). Because of the impairment it is impossible for the IC to clear the bar at a level that the NIC finds easy. The test at that level is 'impregnable' for the IC and attempts to clear the bar would be 'wholly futile'.[38] Furthermore, there would not be any contest between the IC and the NIC; it would be too easy for the NIC to win. So, although the IC and the NIC could be said to be taking the same test they are not in an important sense part of the same 'testing family'. A testing family, according to Kretchmar, is formed by 'one tester recognizing another individual as a like tester'.[39] At least part of the process is finding one's level within sport and competing at that level. '[…] the beginner and advanced golfer do not see themselves as members of the same testing family.'[40] In sport generally, these testing families grow organically and naturally as individuals seek similarly skilled opponents to provide worthy tests. Within testing families, excellence is a property of very few – the elite. Only the most skilled and talented achieve excellence and the scarce benefits that go along with it. As we know, an IC cannot achieve excellence relative to the best standards of an NIC, which is why adapted competitions were created. If we take this approach, then, it implies that ICs are inferior to NICs (a fact often borne out in the statistics).

Another way to interpret our high jump contest between the IC and the NIC is that the test itself is not the same. Clearing the bar is a different test for the IC to what it is for the NIC (because of the IC's impairment). If this is the case, it makes no sense for the IC and the NIC to compete. Not because it is unfair, but because they are not trying to pass the '*same* test better, to a greater degree, higher on a scale, than another.'[41] The NIC cannot compete with the IC on this reading and his or her relative achievements are incommensurable because the achievement (height cleared expressed in centimetres) is as a result of measuring different things. In this picture, excellence is preserved for the IC under the current classification because the testing family is now not all high jumpers, but all F42 high jumpers (or whichever is the relevant category).

It's not clear whether either reading can be applied universally or whether either could provide general guidelines because each sport is different. A person who has an impairment that limits their ability to run will find the tests afforded by sports such as basketball challenging (but perhaps not by archery, target shooting, bowling or fishing) and in open competition (in basketball, but not archery) may not be very successful relative to others without the impairment. According to Karen De Pauw, athletes with impairments have competed within the same 'testing families' as other elite athletes in dressage (Liz Hartel's silver medal at the 1952 Olympic Games) and swimming (Jeff Float's swimming gold medal at the 1984 Olympic Games).[42] Given the nature of the test, they had the capacity to take the test (shoot and ride) and developed the ability to take the test successfully.

This question of whether an athlete is taking the same test or is in a different testing community can serve as a backdrop to the most prominent debate in Paralympic sports in recent years. Although the debate was triggered by sprinter Oscar Pistorius, the question is now more broadly relevant given the progress of Paralympic athletes in many sports. The focus has changed from disadvantage to advantage. Remember the Paralympic Games offer competitive opportunities for athletes whose impairments reduce their capacity for sport in such a way that competing with those similarly incapacitated provides the best opportunity for the realization of the values of sport (including winning). Remember also that certain capacities can only be realized as abilities with certain adaptations. In the case of Pistorius and others, his capacity to run can only be realized by the use of prosthetics. Technological advancement has produced prosthetics that seem to produce an ability to run that is thought to be beyond Oscar Pistorius' non-impaired ability (NIA) if such a thing could be calculated. This may not be a problem in Paralympic sports because ideally other similarly incapacitated individuals are also trying to maximize difference in ability from similar baseline capacities (determined by classifiers) *provided* they have similar or equal access to the equipment or technology. When competing against non-impaired athletes (taking the same test), however, the belief is that Oscar Pistorius is using means not available to his non-impaired competitors and these synthetic or artificial means give him an unfair advantage.[43]

There has been much debate about this question and scientists, biomechanists, doctors, ethicists and the practice community more broadly have all had an input. In many ways, the arguments about whether Oscar Pistorius ought to be allowed to use blades mirror arguments about the legitimacy of other purported performing-enhancing strategies and technologies in sport (e.g. performance-enhancing drugs) and are well rehearsed and evaluated in the literature.[44] Edwards concludes that 'whether the blades give him an unfair advantage [...] is beside the point. The central issue concerns whether or not what OP does counts as running.'[45] In other words, one can legitimately ask whether Oscar Pistorius is said to be taking the same test as non-disabled athletes.

This is not an easy question to resolve. A person who has an impairment that means he or she cannot use his or her legs might be said not to have the capacity to walk or run. They may never be able to achieve the *ability* to walk or run, but have the capacity for locomotion that can be realized with the use of a wheelchair. It is clear that although a wheelchair user is 'travelling' there is little doubt that a 400-metre wheelchair athlete is doing something different to a 400-metre runner (taking a different test – a propelling-a-wheelchair test). Oscar Pistorius' capacity to 'move' has been realized by the use of prosthetic blades. Outside the realms of sport it would seem churlish to deny that his moving should be called walking or running. But sports are institutionalized rule-governed activities 'separated from' ordinary life by rules and conventions that narrow the meaning of everyday concepts like 'car', 'bike', 'stick', 'helmet', 'ball' and so forth. It is an open question whether or not Oscar Pistorius' running and Michael Johnson's running are the same thing. Bernard Suits' definition of games and sports might help us see what is going on.[46] According to Suits, games (and therefore sports) have a prelusory goal – a goal specifiable independently of any game of which it may become a part; in the case of 400 metres – crossing the finish line. The test is created, however, not simply by the identification of the goal, but by the specification of the means permissible to achieve it – circumventing the track – and rules are then penned to specify precisely (or perhaps imprecisely) what counts as taking the test or playing the game. In some games the means are left fairly open (for example, football); in other games the means are fairly closed (for example, javelin throwing). Of course, the rules have to leave space for competitors to be more or less successful (see Kretchmar above), but the rules of each sport 'stipulate' accepted means. Silverstone is a 3.6-mile motor racing circuit in the UK. Competitors have to complete a designated number of laps around the circuit. Rules prohibit cutting corners and so forth. There are, however, various different types of race at Silverstone, including motorcycle races, Formula One, touring cars and so forth. Each type or class of motor sport stipulates very precisely the technical dimensions and limitations of the vehicles competitors are allowed to use to race. In other words, the test is specified very precisely and completing 40 laps of the circuit on a motorbike, in a Formula One car or in a touring car is not taking the same test using difference strategies and skills, but taking very different tests. It is the rules of the sport that create the different tests and sports have largely been given the autonomy to develop their own rules. As we have seen with the high-profile case of Oscar Pistorius, this autonomy has been questioned.

There are other examples of this potential clash. Anita Silvers and David Wasserman evaluate the case of Casey Martin, a talented golfer who had Klippel-Trénaunay-Weber syndrome, which caused serious impairment of his right leg.[47] The Professional Golfers' Association (PGA) did not permit Martin to use a golf cart, thus upholding their 'walking rule'. The rationale was that walking the course is an inherent part of playing golf, therefore using a golf cart was considered an unfair advantage. In his case, the courts, acting on Title III of the Americans with Disabilities Act, ruled that Martin ought to be allowed to use a golf cart. Interestingly, the Supreme Court commented directly on the rationale for the 'walking rule':

> After trial, the District Court entered a permanent injunction, requiring [the] petitioner to permit Martin to use a cart. Among its rulings, that court found that the walking rule's purpose was to inject fatigue into the skill of shot-making, but that the fatigue injected by walking a golf course cannot be deemed significant under normal circumstances; determined that even with the use of a cart, the fatigue Martin suffers from coping with his disability is greater than the fatigue his able-bodied competitors endure from walking the course; and concluded that it would not fundamentally alter the nature of [the] petitioner's game to accommodate Martin.[48]

The consequence of this ruling was that the PGA's autonomy to make its rules was undermined, particularly if these rules were judged to be discriminatory. Silvers and Wasserman conclude that the rules of the game or social practice 'depend to a large extent on conventions, habit and the practical imperatives of bygone eras' and as a consequence 'it will often be difficult to say whether they are essential, or why.'[49] What is clear is that such rules may be challenged by disabled athletes if they believe they are discriminatory.

Whether or not the Supreme Court was right depends on the resolution of a number of questions discussed above. As already mentioned, it seems that each sport is different. On the face of it, the skill of archery has little to do with whether one is standing or sitting (in a wheelchair), yet like the Martin example, competitors feel that an advantage is gained by using a wheelchair. At the London 2012 Paralympic Games, Oscar Pistorius himself was unhappy at being defeated in the T44 200-metre final. His complaint was that the prosthetic blades of the winner, Alan Oliveira, were too long, thus giving him an unfair advantage.[50] Although he later retracted his complaint, the practical, and therefore philosophical, problem of just competition was further highlighted. Sports ethics can provide various principles, test out various arguments and provide certain general guidelines, but often the judgement is a contextual and particular one where general principles are of limited value.

Equality of Opportunity

Of course, the purpose of the classification process in sports for the disabled was not merely borne out of a concern about just sports contests in the way discussed above. There is another goal behind the process, namely improving the lives of disabled people by promoting equality of opportunity to participate and compete in sport. In Nordenfelt's words, for many disabled athletes sport can become an important vital goal that ought not to be denied them because of impairment. The Paralympic Games are an institution that has undoubtedly created the opportunity for many disabled people to pursue vital goals and live good lives that may not otherwise have been available. To this end, the Paralympic Games are 'understood as "parallel Olympics", not special nor separate or inferior'.[51]

The London 2012 Paralympic Games were hailed as an important breakthrough for the issue of disability in general and for disabled athletes in particular in the UK. There was a concerted effort by the British media to provide a 'level playing field' and give comparable qualitative and quantitative coverage to both the Olympic and Paralympic Games. The desire not to discriminate between the Olympic and the Paralympic Games and the respective athletes became a national preoccupation. The media and the Paralympic Games cooperated to achieve similar status for the games and their athletes and to foreground admiration of athletic achievement rather than personal battles:

> The classical distinction between elite sports and the disabled athlete is blurring, as well as the distinction between the athlete as hero, excelling on the basis of what counts as 'normal,' and a (former) 'patient combating his limitations,' falling outside this normal variance. In this respect modern disability sports have made much progress in terms of admiration and respect.[52]

It is not clear whether the separate but equal model is either reasonable or realistic. As discussed previously, elite sports attract scarce benefits, but not in equal amounts. Scarce benefits (extrinsic goods) are largely a matter for the market. In a very successful Olympic year, 2012, Great Britain won a significant number of gold medals and many of its Olympians were honoured by the Queen. Only a few of those Olympians will become rich as a result of their efforts. It depends on whether their sport is popular and can sustain professionalism or attract significant endorsements. Their athletic abilities are not valued equally by the public, who prefer tennis to tae kwon do. Whether the skills and abilities associated with the former are intrinsically more valuable than the latter is probably a moot question. In the Paralympic Games the issue is exacerbated on a number of levels. First, there is the comparison with the Olympic Games. Pistorius' desire to compete in the Olympic Games might be seen as a tacit acceptance of the value hierarchy that exists between able-bodied and disabled sport. According to Ivo van Hilvoorde and Laurens Landeweerd:

> It would be as if Pistorius, being the best disabled runner, is promoted from an inferior division to the premier league of international sport. For most disabled athletes there is no reason (and no possibility) to aim for this kind of ranking and 'promotion'. Pistorius' 'promotion' may even contribute to a loss of credibility and appreciation of the performances of disability athletes.[53]

Then there is the difference between certain sports within the Paralympic Games; some sports are valued more highly than others because of their appeal to spectators. This is not exclusive to the Paralympic Games, but in disabled sport the appeal of different sports can track the severity of the disability. In other words, the T44 100-metre final might attract a large television audience whereas the Boccia contest might not be televised at all. This leads to a further issue of hierarchy between different disability categories. The limited athleticism of the most severely disabled and the marginalization of these events in terms of coverage can reinforce a hierarchy according to the type and nature of disabilities. Athletes with intellectual disabilities in particular can suffer in this respect and it's not clear whether the Paralympic Games help. Remember Grey-Thompson's desire to distance herself from the 'mentally subnormal'.

Two points can be made in conclusion to this part of the debate. First is that our admiration of sporting ability is relative. We admire sporting excellence in relation to its deviation from the normal. Bolt is admired because his speed is so much quicker than what 'we' could do. Our admiration of athletes is predicated on their ability to excel at certain physical tests. They are able to exploit their capacities in ways that we admire relative to our own abilities. Second, if we accept that (at least in some cases) the impairment itself partly creates the difficulty of the test, then our admiration of impaired competitors will inevitably (and perhaps logically) take the form of *'excellence considering the impairment'*. This is not to say that we fail to admire sporting excellence and focus on some other property such as courage in adversity, but that we are rightly recognizing that the impairment is partly constitutive of the test (in some, but not all Paralympic sports). It is inevitable, and in some cases right, that our admiration of disabled athletes' sporting achievements in some way takes their disability into account because we cannot separate the achievement from the disability. This does not mean that we resort to non-sporting-excellence vocabulary often associated with disabled athletes such as 'brave' and 'inspirational'. This is not to say that Paralympians, much like Olympians, can't be brave and inspirational, but this should be vis-à-vis athletic endeavour not vis-à-vis overcoming disability.[54]

I have provided an overview of some of the key issues pertaining to disabled sport. I have argued that Nordenfelt's definition of disability is superior to both the ICF and UIAP because it introduces the important (social or subjective) element of vital goals while retaining the key role of impairment. Disabled sport foregrounds impairment in its classification process and therefore tends to propagate a medical model. Movement restrictions are taken as the basis for classification and athletes of similar capacity compete against each other to discover which has cultivated the greater sporting ability. Controversy may arise in a number of ways: cheating the classification process, the type of technology permitted in developing athletic performance among others. I have also highlighted the relationship between Paralympic sport and mainstream sport. I have tentatively argued that disabled athletes (in certain paradigm cases) are taking different tests and playing different games. This view points to the conclusion (perhaps a gloomy one) that disabled athletes ought not to compete in non-Paralympic events (in certain paradigm cases; cases that need to be worked out on a sport-by-sport basis). This view, however, avoids the comparison problem where disabled sport achievements are evaluated relative to the norms of mainstream sport. If we accept that disabled sports, or more precisely each category within a disabled sport, is a unique test, then comparison with performance in different tests is irrelevant; to compare is to commit a category mistake.

Notes

1   Steven D. Edwards, *Disability: Definitions, Value and Identity* (Oxford: Radcliffe Publishing, 2005), 5.
2   Ibid, 6.
3   Ibid.
4   Tanni Grey-Thompson, *Seize the Day* (London: Hodder and Stoughton, 200), 100.
5   Ian Brittain, 'Perceptions of Disability and Their Impact upon Involvement in Sport for People with Disabilities at all Levels', *Journal of Sport and Social Issues* 28 (2004): 430.
6   Carmela Masala and Donatella R. Petretto, 'From Disablement to Enablement: Conceptual Models of Disability in the 20th century', *Disability and Rehabilitation* 30 (2008): 1235.
7   Ibid.
8   Edwards, *Disability: Definitions, Value and Identity*, 16.
9   'Union of the Physically Impaired Against Segregation', n.d., paragraph 15 <http://www.leeds.ac.uk/disability-studies/archiveuk/UPIAS/UPIAS.pdf> (accessed 12 February, 2013).
10 Ejgil Jespersen and Mike J. McNamee, 'Philosophy, Adapted Physical Activity and Dis/Ability', *Sport, Ethics and Philosophy* 2 (2008): 87–96.
11 In the United States, the reference now is to people with disabilities rather than to disabled people.
12 Edwards, *Disability: Definitions, Value and Identity*, 2.
13 Ibid, 39.
14 Ibid., 33.
15 World Health Organization, *The International Classification of Functioning, Disability and Health* (World Health Organization: Geneva, 2001), 191.
16 Ibid.
17 Edwards, *Disability: Definitions, Value and Identity*, 41.
18 Grey-Thompson, *Seize the Day*, 100.
19 Edwards, *Disability: Definitions, Value and Identity*, 43.
20 Lennart Nordenfelt cited in Edwards, *Disability: Definitions, Value and Identity*, 23.
21 Lennart Nordenfelt, 'Action, Theory, Disability and ICF', *Disability and Rehabilitation* 25 (2003): 1076.
22 Vital goals are not identical to the person's desires. Disability is not simply in the eye of the beholder. Vital goals have an objective dimension relating to general judgements about quality of life.
23 See earlier quote by Tanni Grey-Thompson.
24 Helen Bushby 'How Stoke Mandeville Put Paralympics on the Map', *BBC News*, 15 September, 2012 <http://www.bbc.co.uk/news/uk-14896776> (accessed 12 February, 2013).
25 International Paralympic Committee, *IPC Handbook 2003*, n.p., April 2003 <http://www.paralympic.org/sites/default/files/document/120203111830492_Sec_i_chapter_1.1_Paralympic_Vision_and_Mission_0.pdf > (accessed 12 February, 2013).

26 Jane English, 'Sex Equality in Sports', in *Philosophic Inquiry in Sport*, 2nd ed, eds., William J. Morgan and Klaus V. Meier (Champaign, IL: Human Kinetics, 1995), 285.

27 It is important to distinguish the Paralympic Games, which do provide competitive categories for athletes with learning difficulties and intellectual disabilities, from the Special Olympics, which cater exclusively for adults *and* children with intellectual disabilities. Where the former are for elite athletes with qualifying criteria and so forth, the latter are inclusive and welcome all participants regardless of sporting standard. The intellectual disability category was suspended indefinitely from the Paralympic Games (reinstated in 2008) after the 2000 Sydney Olympics following revelations that the Spanish basketball team was found to be in breach of the classification requirements.

28 P. David Howe and Carwyn Jones, 'Classification of Disabled Athletes: (Dis) Empowering the Paralympic Practice Community', *Sociology of Sport Journal* 23 (2006): 31–3. Currently, the International Paralympic Committee recognizes four International Organizations for Sport for the Disabled (IOSDs). The federations are the Cerebral Palsy International Sport and Recreation Association (CP-ISRA), the International Blind Sport Association (IBSA), the International Sports Federation for Persons with Intellectual Disability (INAS-FID) and the International Wheelchair and Amputee Sport Association (IWAS) – the amalgamation of the International Stoke Mandeville Wheelchair Sports Federation (ISMWSF) and the International Sport Organization for the Disabled (ISOD).

29 'Layman's Guide to Paralympic Classification', n.d., 1 <http://www.paralympic.org/sites/default/files/document/120716152047682_ClassificationGuide_2.pdf≥ (accessed 30 January, 2013).

30 Aristotle, *Nichomachean Ethics*, trans. J.A.K. Thomson (Penguin: Harmondsworth, 1953).

31 Gunnar Breivik, 'Against Chance: A Causal Theory of Winning in Sport', in *Values in Sport*, eds., Torbjörn Tännsjö and Claudio M. Tamburrini (London: Routledge, 2000), 15.

32 There are examples of athletes attempting to cheat the classification process in order to gain an advantage. Peter van der Vilet, the IPC's chief medical classifier, reported that at the London 2012 Paralympic Games many athletes were attempting to manipulate the classification process so they could compete in classes that would increase their chances of victory. See Gareth A. Davies, 'Paralympics 2012: Disabled Athletes Bending the Rules in Quest for Gold Medals', the *Telegraph*, 28 August, 2012 <http://www.telegraph.co.uk/sport/olympics/paralympic-sport/95025   02/Paralympics-2012-disabled-athletes-bending-rules-in-quest-for-goldmedals.html> (accessed 30 January, 2013). Athletes may also be re-classified, which has a significant impact on their chances of victory (Mallory Weggemann was reclassified into a category for less disabled athletes on the eve of her competition at the London 2012 Paralympic Games. See 'Paralympics: Mallory Weggemann Shocked by Classification Change,' *BBC Sport*, 30 August, 2012 <http://www.bbc.co.uk/sport/0/disability-sport/19429915≥ [accessed 30 January, 2013].)

33 For an extended discussion of this point see David Carr, 'Where's the Merit if the Best Man Wins?', *Journal of the Philosophy of Sport* 26 (1999): 1–9; and Paul Davis, 'Ability, Responsibility, and Admiration in Sport: A Reply to Carr', *Journal of the Philosophy of Sport* 28 (2001), 207–14.

34 Carwyn Jones and P. David Howe, 'The Conceptual Boundaries of Sport for the Disabled: Classification and Athletic Performance', *Journal of the Philosophy of Sport* 32 (2005): 127–40.

35 Sigmund Loland, *Fair Play in Sport: A Moral Norm System* (London and New York: Routledge, 2002), 60.

36   World Health Organization cited in Edwards, *Disability: Definitions, Value and Identity*, 33.

37   Scott Kretchmar, 'From Test to Contest: An Analysis of Two Kinds of Counterpoint in Sport', in *Philosophic Inquiry in Sport*, 2nd ed, eds., William J. Morgan and Klaus V. Meier (Champaign, IL: Human Kinetics, 1995), 39. Emphasis added.

38   Ibid, 37.

39   Ibid, 40.

40   Ibid.

41   Ibid, 39 emphasis added.

42   Karen De Pauw, 'The (In) Visibility of DisAbility: Cultural Contexts and "Sporting bodies"', *Quest* 49 (1997): 416–30.

43   See Steven Edwards, 'Should Oscar Pistorius be Excluded from the 2008 Olympic Games?', *Sport, Ethics and Philosophy* 2 (2008): 112–25 for an excellent and systematic analysis of the arguments for and against Oscar Pistorius competing in the Olympic Games.

44   See Edwards, 'Should Oscar Pistorius be excluded from the 2008 Olympic Games?'; and Carwyn Jones and Cassie Wilson, 'Defining Advantage and Athletic Performance: The Case of Oscar Pistorius', *European Journal of Sport Science* 9 (2008): 125–31. See also the essays by Sarah Teetzel and Alun Hardman in this volume for discussions of doping and technology.

45   Edwards, 'Should Oscar Pistorius be excluded from the 2008 Olympic Games?', 123. See also Jones and Wilson, 'Defining Advantage and Athletic Performance: The Case of Oscar Pistorius' for a similar discussion about conceptual and measurement issues in relation to athletic performance.

46   Bernard Suits, 'The Elements of Sport', in *Philosophic Inquiry in Sport*, 2nd ed, eds. William J. Morgan and Klaus V. Meier (Champaign, IL: Human Kinetics, 1995), 8–15.

47   Anita Silvers and David Wasserman, 'Convention and Competence: Disability Rights in Sports and Education', in *Ethics in Sport*, eds., William J. Morgan, Klaus V. Meier and Angela J. Schneider (Campaign, IL: Human Kinetics, 2001), 409–19.

48   PGA Tour, Inc. v. Martin, (00-24) 532 U.S. 661 (2001) 204 F.3d 994, affirmed. Available at <http://www.la w.cornell.edu/supct/pdf/00-24P.ZS≥ (accessed 4 February, 2013).

49   Silvers and Wasserman, 'Convention and Competence: Disability Rights in Sports and Education', 411.

50   Saj Chowdhury, 'Paralympics 2012: Oscar Pistorius Beaten by Alan Oliveira in 200m', *BBC Sport*, 2 September, 2012 <http://www.bbc.co.uk/sport/0/disability-sport/19460 868> (accessed 4 February, 2013).

51   Ivo van Hilvoorde and Laurens Landeweerd, 'Disability or Extraordinary Talent: Francesco Lentini (Three Legs) Versus Oscar Pistorius (No Legs)', *Sport, Ethics and Philosophy* 2 (2008): 103.

52   Ibid, 105.

53   Ibid, 108.

54   The following article appeared in the British media around the time of the Paralympics and illustrates the point. Damon Rose, 'Paralympics 2012: Is It OK to Call the Athletes Brave?', *BBC News*, 4 September, 2012 <http://ww w.bbc.co.uk/news/magazine-19466064> (accessed 30 January, 2013).

10 Sport, Risk and Danger

Leslie A. Howe

When is a sport a 'risk sport'? Conversely, we might also ask, when is a 'risk sport' a *sport*? I shall approach the second of these questions near the end of this chapter, but first we must attempt to gain some clarity concerning the place of risk and danger in sport in general.

Many, perhaps most, mainstream sports incorporate some degree of personal danger, whether that is because they involve the use of equipment that can cause injury or because movement is required that may subject the body to stress that is beyond its current capacity to withstand. Thus, a ball or racquet may deliver a contusion or a lunge after an errant pass may cause a tear to a muscle or tendon, even in relatively sedate sports. Normally, such injury is unfortunate but not life-threatening, though it may in some relatively infrequent cases be life-altering, such as, for example, a cruciate ligament injury or a severe concussion.[1]

The possibility of such injury in sport raises questions concerning proper care or negligence for those who provide facilities and opportunities for sport activity, but these issues of responsibility for risk management will not be addressed here. Our concern in the next few pages is primarily with those sports in which risk or danger plays a central and defining role in the activity itself, though we must also consider the possibility that risk and sport are in some way inseparable, such that attempting to remove all possibility of hazard to participants is counterproductive.

What Sports Are We Talking About?

The taxonomy of risk sport is complicated by a proliferation of, and lack of hard consensus in the use of, terms to designate different varieties of sport that take a positive approach to risk, in the sense that they do not attempt to eliminate it altogether but embrace the presence of danger or of encounters that are inherently or highly likely to be dangerous to the participant. For example, does the term 'risk sport' cover the same activities as 'extreme sport'? That, in part, depends on in what sense any given 'extreme' sport is *extreme*. Formula One racing is extremely fast and carries a strong element of risk, but would seem to fall into the category of conventional sport, as would American football, which happens to carry a significant risk of future debilitation to its participants, especially at its highest levels. Likewise, cage-fighting is 'extreme' but does not appear to offer greater overall risk to its participants than conventional boxing.

Many of the sports generally classified as 'extreme', where this epithet is more than mere advertising hyperbole, originated as *independent* sports, outside conventional sport organizational structures. Alterity, or 'otherness', is an important characteristic of many so-called 'extreme' and many 'adventure' sports; what defines them is, supposedly, their non-conventional, non-mainstream ethos: they are not, in origin or in spirit, part of a sport establishment that governs how its participants engage in the sport. In reality, this claim may be somewhat overstated. Many 'extreme sports' have been domesticated to a greater or lesser degree and the alterity has been largely limited to a matter of independence from external governance; as far as gender and class boundaries are concerned, extreme sports are at least as conventional as they are alternative.

These sports are also often described as 'lifestyle sports', indicating that those participating in them have tended to adopt their chosen sport as an integral element in an (alternative) way of life, identifying themselves with both, rather than viewing their sport as a recreation separated from their other pursuits. This is not a very useful designation, as most sports require lifestyle commitments if the participants are determined to excel in them, and most sports do, in fact, generate a particular style of life around themselves. The designation, however, tends to carry the connotation of 'alternative', i.e. not mainstream.[2]

'Adventure sports' are also often identified as risk sports, and vice versa, and it is true that many risky sports are so because they take place in wilder spaces and centrally concern interaction with more or less natural environments, such as mountains, white-water rivers, big surf, etc. In this case, it would be reasonable to regard 'adventure sports' as those that incorporate direct participation in natural environments, whose environments or activities may, though need not, involve some element of real danger, often at an elevated level. The 'adventure' aspect of such sports derives from the relative remoteness or exoticism of the location, combined with the extremity (intensity) of the experience the location offers. Not all nature-based sport qualifies: Nordic skiing on groomed trails in a local park, for example, would presumably not, regardless of the physical intensity of the skier's endeavour.

The exact importance of risk in adventure sport is less than clear-cut. Remoteness always elevates the impact of risk, but a fully organized and guided canoe or raft trip *may* qualify as adventure, but not as especially risky. 'Intensity of experience' is not as helpful a designator as it might seem either, as any seriously competitive sport can offer potentially unbearable levels of intensity. The question really concerns the source of the intensity: competitive pressure and expectations on performance can explain mainstream sport intensity; in risk sports this is provided in large measure by the (potential) danger. Adventure and extreme sports *may* be risk sports but the intensity may also be provided by the extraordinary quality of the surroundings (their exoticism), and certainly not all risk sports need be adventure sports. Nevertheless, in the pages to follow, a large part of the discussion will focus on risk sports that are also adventure or extreme sports. Many are also non-traditional but, so far as risk is concerned, this is not necessary. For example, the running of the bulls in Pamplona is arguably a risk sport but it is also highly traditional, though not so in the usual sport sense. Moreover, what will concern us is not this taxonomy as such, but the relative importance placed on risk or danger in those sports commonly designated as risk sports.

Risk in Sport

The risk present in sport may be incidental, something that may occur and against which we expect some degree of vigilance, but that does not and perhaps should not be a primary focus of attention for those involved. Negligent play on the part of participants may increase such risks but these are, in principle, avoidable, for example, through officiating, or improvement of equipment and of the fitness of participants. Sport participants may experience injuries, even fatalities, that would not have occurred had they not played, but this does not necessarily mean that they are at greater risk of any injury than if they did not play. A person is unlikely to be hit in the eye with a shuttlecock unless they venture on to a badminton court, but that does not make badminton a risk sport.

In the current philosophical literature that treats risk as a positive aspect in sport experience, we see two main positions: first, that the risk experience is valuable for individuals as a catalyst for personal development, either as an occasion for self-affirmation or as a backdrop to the cultivation of certain kinds of virtue; and second, that while danger is an ineliminable and constructive component of certain kinds of sport experience, such that the sport itself or the special character of the experience it affords could not occur without it, the risk is emphatically not the point of the activity itself. The former might be characterized as taking the risk in certain sports to be a defining feature of the value of those sports and the latter as assigning risk an ancillary if highly significant role.

Following this distinction through, risk in sport may be something that one seeks out. Those who wish to test their courage or resolve in the face of danger, or who believe that their self-knowledge will be enhanced by the confrontation with their own mortality, or that one can only win at life if one lays one's very existence on the line, may be drawn to a sport that has a central defining element of personal risk. Alternatively, danger of serious injury or death may be merely the price of inattention to a task that is itself the focus of one's efforts. In such a case, one pursues the sport for the intrinsic benefits it has to offer as the particular sport it is, but to do so requires that one put oneself into situations that demand active response to the possibility of final disaster.

Risk sport can fall into either the first or the second category depending upon the participant's attitude to his or her activity. Many of those who advocate activities that may fall under the rubric of risk sport argue that focusing on the risk element is a distraction and that those who actually do these sports are primarily directed to the activity itself and, in any case, expend considerable effort in minimizing possible risk. Climbers, in particular, emphasize the care taken to ensure safety in order to then concentrate on the climbing itself. In such cases, we must draw the conclusion that the activity is one that presents risks but that, while acknowledging and responding to it, participants do so in order to seek some other value than the courting of risk itself.

There is not always a clear distinction between characterizations of sport that stress risk as a central feature and those that treat it as facilitating for some other goal, but there is a tendency in the former to valorize the individual as such and the importance of the individual's relation to the risk for him or her *self*, whereas the latter approach tends to put more stress on, or is at least more open to, the value of the participation in a particular kind of *activity*. This distinction between two kinds of value derived from dangerous sport as an outcome of two kinds of relation of self to activity is developed by Pam Sailors from an initial distinction drawn by Jonathan Simon between narrowly self-in-goal fixated 'summiteers' and more broadly context-aware 'mountaineers'.[3] As Sailors elaborates the distinction, summiteers are characterized by their goal orientation, their ambition for self-knowledge or self-affirmation in attainment of their goal, and a predilection to put self and pursuit of goal before concern for others, whereas mountaineers are process-oriented, achieve self-transcendence or negation, and through this, self-knowledge, and have a stronger sense of responsibility to others.[4] As Sailors argues, these characteristics are interconnected; thus, insofar as one is process- rather than goal-oriented, one would be likely to see success more in terms of the way in which one reached an activity goal, including how others involved in the pursuit were affected, and how the procedure of doing so, and not just the having done, affected the agent. This distinction, between the goal-centric and the process-centric, is one that we shall see reiterated throughout the rest of this essay, not only because it captures a fundamental division in views about the purpose and value of sport as such, but because it is also reflected in the relative significance given to danger in risky sports. That is, what risk or danger in sport is *for* is a question that will be answered differently depending upon whether the approach is directed to the development of self or to the development of the broader activity in which the self plays a role.

Naturalism

In the 19th century, 'wilderness' pursuits were increasingly advocated as an antidote to the allegedly weakening and even feminizing influence of modern civilization and urban industrialized life. Man was (i.e. males were) becoming soft, modernity was increasingly separating him from his basic nature. Wilderness began to be seen not as the terrifying other to be guarded against, or brought under saving domestication, but the wellspring of a primitivist regeneration.[5] A modern version of this ideal is expressed in the view that our daily lives are too safe, too controlled, too predictable. When it comes to sport, we cannot step on to the ice, pitch or court without all the requisite safety gear and supervisory personnel in place. To participate in a truly dangerous sport, then, is sometimes interpreted as something like an act of natural rebellion against such constraint and an expression of a basic human need to seek freedom and excitement by risking our very being – an existential defiance of the ever-vigilant nanny state.

Gunnar Breivik puts forward a version of this claim that centres on the tension between rational(ized) safety-oriented society and the individual's need for escalating levels of excitement and self-expression. Breivik suggests that the risk attitude is traceable to our evolutionary background[6] and that some humans are simply genetically predisposed to high sensation-seeking behaviour,[7] though he also remarks that the seeking out of excitement need not be explained by some biological need, 'but rather by the inherent pleasure and satisfaction that such pursuits provide'.[8] Breivik's is not the only expression of this view and it is not clear just how much weight he is willing to place on it, especially given his much stronger emphasis on the pleasure generated by such activities, but it is worth making a few comments about these sorts of explanations and justifications of human behaviour.

Naturalistic claims are in general subject to at least two points of criticism: 1) is it *really* natural? and 2) what follows if it is? With respect to 1), claims about what is natural are notoriously open to dispute: even if the basic 'facts' are indeed factual, what they then mean (what they describe *and* what they further entail) is open to considerable interpretation. As for 2), that something is 'natural', supposing that we can agree that it is, tells us little if anything about how we ought to act with respect to it. This should be particularly evident in risk-seeking behaviour as such behaviour not infrequently affects those who have no desire to be so affected.

Claims of naturalism also need to be filtered through a careful gender critique, as what is claimed to be 'natural' frequently corresponds to a social construction of either original humanity (the inevitable hunter-gatherer model) or of essential masculinity. This certainly comes across in the claims of 'feminization' due to excessive civilization. Insofar as dangerous sport is advocated as a means of recovering a supposedly suppressed masculinity, especially a perceived need to demonstrate masculinity, or a humanity conceived in conventional masculine terms, we need to question both its accuracy and its value.

Agency: Benefitting Self

One of the two central areas of discussion in the philosophical literature concerning risk sport is agency, that is, the right and necessity for individuals to determine their own way of life and the particular choices therein. As this characterization implies, there are two streams in this discussion: those who argue that risky or dangerous sport provides an important means of self-development, particularly in respect of the development of agency itself, and those who argue that it is an individual's right to so express him or herself, whatever may be the consequences for that individual. Both these positions challenge what they perceive as paternalistic constrictions on self-determination.

J.S. Russell has argued that the confrontation with significant danger in sport is valuable for the project of self-affirmation. Specifically:

> Dangerous sport in its best exemplars, particularly those in which substantial bodily danger is an immediate and ever-present risk, represents an opportunity for confronting and pressing beyond certain apparent limits of personal, and indeed human, physical and psychological capacities in ways not afforded by other normally available human activity. Thus, I say that the dominant, distinctive value of dangerous sport consists of an activity of self-affirmation because dangerous sport invites us to confront and push back the boundaries of the self by creating contexts in which some of the ordinary

bounds of our lives can be challenged. Hence, we discover and affirm who we are and what we can be by confronting and attempting to extend these boundaries. In this sense, dangerous sport is perfectionist. It tests us by requiring us to make the most of our whole selves, of our bodies and our minds working together as a unity, when (or because) everything, or almost everything, is at stake.[9]

By 'dangerous sport' Russell means 'sport that involves activity that itself creates a significant risk of loss of, or severe impairment to, some basic capacity for human functioning'.[10] This definition he further explicates in terms of Martha Nussbaum's catalogue of central human functional capacities, such as living a life of normal length, good health, the capacity for free movement and the use of the senses for characteristically human purposes (reasoning, imagining, etc.), though Russell discounts the importance of social capacities for affiliation, which Nussbaum includes in this list.[11] The view that Russell advances builds upon the tradition of romantic militarism, but insofar as it places the endeavour in sport rather than military exploits it avoids the tremendous cost to others of individual achievement. Thus, in Russell's view, dangerous sport 'can incorporate a challenge to capacities for judgement and choice that involves all of ourselves – our body, will, emotions and ingenuity – under conditions of physical duress and danger *at the limits of our being*'.[12]

The value of dangerous sport, then, is in this cultivation of the human capacity for self-affirmation, but is this sufficient to justify the potential cost? Self-affirmation is presumably intrinsically valuable for the self that affirms, but that does not rule out its needing to be weighed against other such values in a life. Russell refers to perfectionism; thus, insofar as we hold that an individual ought to cultivate their inherent and acquired capacities to the utmost it seems reasonable to expect that he or she ought to push him or herself to the limits of their being. Yet, this is a potentially narrow and, if things go badly, shortened road to maximal flourishing of self. Moreover, self-affirmation in and of itself seems a thin sort of goal to have for oneself. The more convincing answer to this question is perhaps in the connection that Russell draws in another paper between the self-affirmative potential of dangerous sport and the development of our moral capacity.[13]

Responding to contemporary efforts to make children's play as safe as possible, he declares that the 'presence of physical risk in children's sport and recreation has important value and its complete elimination – so that children face zero-risk of physical danger in their lives, including in sport and recreation – would indeed be a bad thing. Physical risk or danger does contribute some important value, albeit indirectly, to a child's good.'[14] To make his argument, Russell distinguishes what he calls the 'common sense view', that some physical risk is important for developing rational agency, from the 'uncommon sense view', which he favours, that physical risks are to be tolerated and choices respected even if the risks are greater than what is necessary to develop the goods of rational agency.[15]

The point Russell argues here is that children must be encouraged to develop the ability to stand up for themselves in difficult situations, which is an integral part of being a responsible moral agent, and to develop a moral imagination. We can understand the latter in terms of the capacity to anticipate the possible outcomes of one's actions, how they will affect oneself and others, and, in particular, the cost of failing to think things through adequately. To protect children from this kind of moral education, with the result that they are only confronted with the circumstance that their choices may have unpleasant consequences once they are nominally responsible adults, is a pedagogical cost that society can ill afford.

Russell's argument is again directed primarily, however, to the good of self-affirmation, which in his view is not a matter of developing 'the skills and virtues necessary to pursue human flourishing' but about 'achieving flourishing by pressing individual boundaries and thus defining new self-understandings and conceptions of the self'.[16] In other words, it's not about getting the tools one could use to flourish, but about actually flourishing, and this one does precisely by stretching oneself *beyond* what one is now – in effect, making oneself anew by risking what one is now. Thus, what the participant in dangerous sport does is not just discover herself but recreate herself as more than she was in exceeding her previously conceived limits. This, then, is affirmation of self not simply as inventory ('this is who I am/have been') but aspiration ('this is what I aim at'). As Russell points out, for children, this aspirational affirmation of self is critical to the development of autonomy and well-being.

One clear objection to this position is that adults, especially parents and those · acting in their stead, such as educators and coaches, have a strong obligation to ensure that children are not exposed to risks that are beyond their capacity with which to cope and it would appear that Russell's view is at odds with our responsibility to ensure an open future for children, as he himself points out.[17] As he suggests, however, the route from child to adult is not fixed and to protect the child for the sake of a future adult, whose future is in flux and the advent of which is not precisely determinate, is counterproductive.[18] A quite different objection arises from the likelihood that not all the practical expressions of autonomous responsible agency and well-being are compatible. While the process Russell describes is valuable in itself as an abstract description of self-creation, and especially valuable for children, its abstraction passes over the difficulties. The concrete realization of this process may yield favourable results but also ones that end the process of flourishing as well as mutually incompatible results for multiple individuals. Simply, Tim's self-affirmation may radically prevent Sarah's, in which case the inherent value of self-affirmation runs aground on the circumstance that the human world is social at least as much as it is individual.

The Right to Risk

While Russell's argument could be characterized as presenting the case for dangerous sport in terms of the value of *self*, Breivik argues, among other things, its value *for* selves. In particular, he puts the case for the *right* of individuals to pursue the activities, including dangerous ones, that give them pleasure. In Breivik's case, the explicit justification of risk-seeking is simply 'the inherent pleasure and satisfaction that such pursuits provide'.[19] High-risk sports, then, must be justified by their high pay-off relative to their increased possibility of serious injury or death if the participant fails to execute correctly. Breivik also criticizes the modern tendency to annul all risk, including that to children,[20] but is not an advocate of random risk, or danger, just for the sake of it:

> One should avoid or eliminate risks when there are no rewards. Risks should be minimized when other people are involved. One should, however, be willing to take risks when the rewards are obvious and the total expected outcome is positive. One should not only accept, but even seek risks when the odds are good enough, mastery is possible and the total expected outcome is positive.[21]

Those risks that should be pursued are 'those that can be predicted, controlled, mastered and dealt with by me through the use of my skills'.[22] Given that the point of these skills is an enhanced ability to participate in and appreciate certain pleasurable experiences of embodied agency, their development is *instrumentally* valuable; their exercise allows one to have experiences that count as expressive of human flourishing. Hence Breivik's insistence that the experience must be worth the risk.[23]

This raises a number of questions concerning both the content of the experience and the reasonableness of it. For Breivik, the pleasure gained by participants is one of several reasons in favour of its pursuit and for the non-interference of others with that pursuit.[24] Indeed, his view is that people have a right to live as they choose and to follow their own values.[25] Even weighing conflicting interests, such as the concern of families for their risk-taking members, he remarks that the 'deeper question here is whether concerned and worried families can cripple a person's right to flourish and live a life that is rich for him/her, a life where BASEjumping is a central part'[26] – though he later concludes that jumpers' right to jump has to be balanced against competing interests such as those of their families.[27] The paramount consideration, though, is the right of individuals to take the risks they choose to take in the pursuit of a life and pleasures that are of defining importance to them, though it would seem that there is the expectation that these are risks that those individuals are well equipped to manage.

Paternalism is thus ruled out by Breivik as not beneficial and as contravening a deontological right held by dangerous-sport participants. The assumption of mastery in the constitutive skills of the activity does seem to open a small window of objection, but presumably the right is not contingent upon this mastery as one could only acquire it through exercise of the relevant activity. Nevertheless, it might be reasonable to ask whether it would be appropriate to intervene where an individual was about to attempt an activity that was well beyond their ability to successfully complete, where death was a certain outcome and failure to complete the activity inevitable. A justification of intervention in such cases might be offered on the grounds that the incompetent individual presents an unwarranted risk to other participants and to rescue personnel, but this is then not a case of paternalism, but of adjudication between competing rights and interests.

Marcus Agnafors explores the collision between the right an individual is generally supposed to have to do as he wishes and the rights of others in the context of free solo climbing.[28] While agreeing that generally we do have such a right, it becomes much more problematic once our activities impinge upon the rights of others, which must certainly include not having free soloists hurtling down upon one's head, and which may also require others to rescue us (or clean up afterwards) when things go wrong. The problem with the individualist rights stance is that 'there is no such thing as a private sphere where we are allowed to do whatever we want, since everything we do affects others. We have no absolute moral right to do things that may harm others. Free soloing seems only to be permissible if you climb on a deserted island, where society doesn't have to share the costs of your actions.'[29]

Breivik touches on the question of risk imposed on rescuers but it is more directly taken up by Heidi Howkins Lockwood in an essay responding to recent attempts to require those who need rescuing from remote areas to pay for the service. The issue, as Lockwood portrays it, is that we tend to regard certain kinds of risk, or risky activities, as justifiable or even heroic (e.g. that incurred by astronauts) and others as gratuitous and therefore unjustifiable; this is the asymmetry thesis.[30] Of course, sport is by definition gratuitous and thus the asymmetry thesis would entail that all risk in sport is unnecessary and avoidable, and therefore unjustifiable. More to the present point, though, the asymmetry thesis accounts for our asymmetrical appraisal of the actions of, for example, snowboarders or climbers who get stranded in remote and difficult locations and those who are called upon to rescue them. The 'Rule of Rescue', as Lockwood explains,[31] impels responsible human beings to risk their own lives to save others who are in danger, including those who, it may seem, could have avoided putting themselves into the position of needing rescue – since they didn't need to do what they were doing before rescue became necessary. Thus, certain varieties of dangerous sports are sometimes regarded as unjustifiable not only for the risks incurred by their participants but those they impose on others who are morally or legally compelled to rescue or recover those participants.

Lockwood's argument against pay-for-rescue measures is simply that it is inequitous in that it supposes that activities that involve gratuitous risk are unworthy of care and because it makes the mistake, in fact, of supposing that participants in at least certain risk sports (i.e. climbing) are in it for the risk (and therefore irresponsible). Though what they do does carry a significant degree of risk, Lockwood maintains that the risk is not the point of the activity.[32]

This question of the relation to risk remains fundamental to understanding what risk sport is and possibly to the question of whether any given risk sport constitutes *sport*. Is it the risk itself that matters, or is risk the background condition of a particularly heightened version of an experience that could otherwise be had, if in a more pallid form, without risk? Breivik concedes that for some, it appears,

[…] the risk is part of the experience one seeks. To be able to control one's body and mind and perform complicated and difficult things under stress, knowing that things can go wrong, is part of what they seek. In the case of BASEjumping the experience is impossible to have without the risk and for most BASEjumpers the risk is an intrinsic and valuable part of the experience itself.[33]

But to express the situation this way is, in fact, to deny that risk or danger is the crux of the matter; rather, it is performance in dangerous conditions that is at issue – the thrill of testing oneself at the utter limits of one's expertise, knowing that one succeeds or fails on one's own or with a select group of people, and that getting it wrong means the possibility or even certainty of death. The dangerousness of the activity may indeed be responsible for the intensity of awareness that this must be done correctly, but there must also be the making sure that one does it correctly. Simply deciding to walk off a high fixed point isn't BASEjumping and if one only wants danger, taking a chainsaw to a nail-encrusted telephone pole would do, but neither would be satisfactory examples of the superior exercise of skill in an environment that requires it in an absolute sense, nor would either be likely to generate the heightened pleasure of the successful exercise of skill at the edge. So, if it is not the putting oneself into a situation of danger as such that is the draw of such sports, but the intensity of experience that is the result of *both* skill *and* awareness of danger, then we need to consider the other major approach to risk sport.

Being in Risk

Risk sports can be interpreted as expressions of their participants' fundamental human search for meaning and transcendence over the inevitability of physical being. Such an interpretation relies on an ontological-phenomenological analysis that owes its origins to philosophers such as Martin Heidegger and Jean-Paul Sartre. Ivo Jirásek, for example, taking a Heideggerian perspective, argues that the predilection for dangerous sport is symptomatic of a 'crisis of experiencing', 'existential frustration' and 'the absence of the reflective meaning of one's own life'.[34] He argues that such sports answer our need in post modernity to 'obtain extraordinary experiences, to overcome the boundary of normality and to step out from the zone of sureness and security'[35] while bringing to the fore the ambiguity and fragility of the boundary between life and death by seeking out situations that challenge the subject's response. Like Breivik, Jirásek calls attention to the dulling effect of modern society, though here the emphasis is less on obsessive safety culture than on the mediation of experience. Where all our experiences are, in effect, second-hand, there will be some who must seek out an authenticity of lived experience, especially experience that stretches the very possibility of experience. Thus, the appeal of dangerous sport is the way in which it makes one feel so much more 'alive' playing in the jaws of death, and in its alteration of perception, including the passage of time.[36] From this it might also be added that in dangerous sport the subject's experience of agency itself is enhanced; that is, our ordinary mundane lives seem largely outside our own control, but choosing to face down the possibility of our own annihilation through the kind of play opened to us in dangerous sport gives us an *immediate* experience of agency and returns to the participant the prospect of ownership over not just his or her experience but existence itself.

At the level of phenomenological analysis, one might say that the individual wholeheartedly engaged in dangerous sport lives a more authentic existence, since she is not racked by fear of the death that comes to us all, but anticipates it, owns it, by welcoming its real possibility into her self-expression through play. It is as if one were to say: I know that I shall die some day but I refuse to be diminished by this; I do not live in fear that what I do may kill me but I choose to do what is the best expression of me even though it may be my final act – but then my act will be a true expression of my being. I am mortal and as a mortal being I express my mortality thus and thereby transcend it; I own my death; death, and the fear of death, do not own me.

This aspect of the existential-phenomenological approach comes out in the work of a number of authors, including Breivik and Jesús Ilundáin-Agurruza. Breivik draws on the work of Hans-Georg Gadamer to make the point that in risk sports, especially those that involve interaction with the natural environment, athletes not only *play*, but are *played with* by nature.[37] Kevin Krein also explains the attraction of adventure sports in terms of the opportunity to play with features of the natural environment, while strongly discounting the importance of risk as decisive in this respect. Krein argues that while there is risk in such sports in the sense that there are hazards that are out of one's control, there are many others that are considerably mitigated with skill and knowledge. Thus he remarks that 'the goal of adventure athletes is not to leave survival up to chance, or to gamble with one's life, but ... they seek situations in which they have control and responsibility for their lives and in which survival depends on their judgement and skills.'[38] However, it is his characterization of the natural environment as a partner in the sport experience that is of special interest at this juncture:

> In adventure sports, the other 'participant' in the game might be a 10 meter wave, 800 meter, 60-degree couloir, or an 8,000 meter peak, rather than a human competitor. It is my claim that the opportunity to play with such awesome partners is one of the principal sources of the attraction of adventure sports.
>
> For one who takes sports seriously, the opportunity to take part in sports activities under conditions that make it possible to engage with natural features more powerful than any conceivable human being is at least worth considering.[39]

The notion that one doesn't only play *on* a mountain or river, but *with* it, and *it* with you captures the notion that play is not an individualistic endeavour but a contextual one, involving place and an other, in relation to which play unfolds, not necessarily as a single player dictates, but according to the ingenuity and imagination of the player to respond.

The motif of *play* performed in proximity to natural danger is especially captured in Ilundáin-Agurruza's two-part essay on running with the bulls in

Pamplona. The *encierro*, as Ilundáin-Agurruza points out, is not strictly a sport, though it shares many sporting elements.[40] Yet, perhaps for that very reason it has an exemplary value in that, in common with so many 'risk sports', it is the activity itself and the manner of one's performance that count rather than the competitive totals that normatize most conventional sport. It is important that the activity (in this case, the *encierro*) 'is done freely, disinterestedly and for the *fun* of it … the *encierro* is primarily play, very risky, but play'.[41] Nevertheless, this play and the *jouissance* it generates in the player depend on the presence of danger: 'Actual peril is an integral part of the *encierro*: it is appealing precisely because the "ultimate sacrifice" or serious injury are *real* possibilities,'[42] and again: 'The *encierro*, as a vehicle for jubilation, is what it is to a great extent because of the danger inherent in it: it is *appealing* largely because one has the chance to confront one's *own* mortality in a very real and concrete fashion that may lead to a richer experience of life – or end it.'[43]

Such an outcome, however, depends on the individual's approach to the activity. Ilundáin-Agurruza is emphatic that although one can participate in the running of the bulls as a show of courage or presumed masculinity, to do so is to fail to participate in it as the event it is. The awareness of risk is not just a test of courage, but of one's ability and readiness to respond appropriately to the flow and alterations of circumstance in a situation that presupposes, among other things, that one has an adequate understanding of one's situation vis-à-vis the danger posed by the activity. But the danger is *not* the focus of the activity.[44]

Breivik, Krein and Ilundáin-Agurruza all stress that risk in and of itself is not the point; risk is necessary and it must be real, but the point is the *playing* in front of the horns of the bull that could end your life if you fail to execute the necessary skills correctly. In the case of the *encierro*, restrictions demanded by tradition and for the sake of aesthetically pleasing play constrict the possibility of real success further than simple survival (as climbers often value style at least as much as completion). The activity of such risk sport is not just about confronting mortality, but confronting it by playing, and playing *well* – and this is what allows these activities to be *sports* and not just inefficient attempts at daredevilry or suicide. As Breivik, Krein and others have pointed out, certain groups of risk sport participants, climbers in particular, tend to expend a great deal of time and effort on controlling the effect of risk on their activity. A climb may be particularly significant because of the difficulty of the route, and failing to cope with the difficulty may result in severe injury or death, but the point is to do the climb safely and go home – not to take idiotic risks just to prove that you can.[45]

But is it Sport?

Clearly, the conclusion must be that risk cannot be entirely removed from risk sports and still have them be the sports that they are. Even if two activities were to involve exactly the same movements, if danger is wholly removed from one and not the other, we cannot consider them identical, not least because there will be a divergence in the skills developed. Thus, indoor sport climbing, even with a high degree of ingenuity, resources and attention to detail in replicating outdoor routes, cannot be the same sport as free soloing; the use of ropes and other safety equipment must change the skill emphasis, movement and the decision-making of participants given the differing effects of risk.

Are risk sports *sport*? We have seen a number of considerations that bolster their claim to be accounted as such, but this will not be determined on the issue of risk but on the movement and structure of the individual sports themselves. As Russell observes, having oneself flung from a catapult may be dangerous or extreme, but it cannot reasonably be regarded as a sport; neither can bungee jumping, as it requires no skill or self-directed physical activity other than allowing oneself to fall.[46] Supposing that some basic requirements are met, individual sports may yet remain a matter of dispute; this is not something that risk sport brings anew to sport – people have argued for years about whether activities as diverse as boxing and figure skating are properly designated as sports.

One issue that may give more difficulty is that of repeatability. Because of the remote and natural environments in which many of these sports take place, in which climate and other physical conditions may vary, no two performances may be wholly comparable or repeatable. This is compounded by the multiple factors that may go into determining a level of risk, and an individual's response to it in any given instance. In most sports, especially but not exclusively games, the activity of that sport is, in principle, infinitely repeatable; performance is a moment in the life of the sport that vanishes only to be replayed on another day, by another player, in another place. Sport defines an abstract space in which a set of artificially constricted movements is given form and then disappears, to give way to another. While many dangerous or extreme sports fit into this conventional mould, and thus can be assessed as sports in the same way as more mainstream ones, those that take place in natural environments are not like this. Their performances have a higher possibility of uniqueness and thus two individuals following the same activity plan may have radically different experiences even with identical skill and preparation levels. Thus, their performances are not comparable, and this is something normally supposed to be possible in sport. But this is because sport is often defined in terms of a contest between opponents[47] and this in turn presupposes a conception of sport as a process of reaching certain measurable, quantitative goals, rather than as a process-orientated, relational experience for the individual participants. This, then, is the crux of the matter: when is a sport a sport? But to ask this is also to question what sport is for. If sport is an expression of the player's being through movement, a statement of existence, then risk sport is sport *par excellence*.

Notes

1   In particularly rare cases, exercise may trigger an undiagnosed condition causing death, but it seems unreasonable to blame these incidents on sport as such.

2   See Wheaton, Belinda, ed., *Understanding Lifestyle Sports: Consumption, Identity, and Difference* (London: Routledge, 2004); and Robert E. Rinehart and Synthia Sydnor, eds., *To the Extreme: Alternative Sports, Inside and Out* (New York: SUNY Press, 2003).

See also Leslie A. Howe, 'Remote Sport: Risk and Self-Knowledge in Wilder Spaces', *Journal of the Philosophy of Sport* 35 (2008): 4.

3   Jonathan Simon, 'Risking Rescue: High Altitude Rescue as Moral Risk and Moral Opportunity', in *Risk and Morality*, eds., Richard V. Ericson and Aaron Doyle (Toronto: University of Toronto Press, 2003), 375–406; and Pam R. Sailors, 'More Than Meets the "I": Values of Dangerous Sport', in *Climbing-Philosophy for Everyone: Because It's There*, ed., Stephen E. Schmid (Oxford: Wiley-Blackwell, 2010), 82.

4   Sailors, 'More Than Meets the "I": Values of Dangerous Sport', 83.

5   See William Cronon, 'The Trouble with Wilderness; or Getting Back to the Wrong Nature', in *Uncommon Ground: Toward Reinventing Nature*, ed., William Cronon (New York: W.W. Norton and Company, 1995), 69–90. See also J.S. Russell, 'Children and Dangerous Sport and Recreation', *Journal of the Philosophy of Sport* 34 (2007): 11 regarding historical views on the perceived ill effects of modernity.

6   Gunnar Breivik, 'The Quest for Excitement and the Safe Society', in *Philosophy, Risk, and Adventure Sports*, ed., Mike McNamee (London: Routledge, 2007), 17.

7   Gunnar Breivik, 'Trends in Adventure Sports in a Post-Modern Society', *Sport in Society* 13 (2010): 267.

8   Breivik, 'The Quest for Excitement and the Safe Society', 21.

9   J.S. Russell, 'The Value of Dangerous Sport', *Journal of the Philosophy of Sport* 32 (2005): 2.

10   Ibid., 3.

11   Ibid., 4.

12   Ibid., 14.

13   Paul Charlton also presents an argument to the effect that, as well as having intrinsic value, climbing has significant instrumental values in that it cultivates human excellence in 'Risk and Reward: Is Climbing Worth It?', in *Climbing-Philosophy for Everyone: Because It's There*, ed., Stephen E. Schmid (Oxford: Wiley-Blackwell, 2010), 24–36. Brian Treanor in the same volume argues that it cultivates the virtues: 'High Aspirations: Climbing and Self-Cultivation', 67–80.

14   Russell, 'Children and Dangerous Sport and Recreation', 176–7.

15   Ibid., 177.

16   Ibid., 182.

17   Ibid., 183.

18   Ibid., 184–8.

19   Breivik, 'The Quest for Excitement and the Safe Society', 21.

20   Ibid., 20.

21   Ibid., 12.

22   Ibid., 19.

23   Gunnar Breivik, 'Can BASEjumping Be Morally Defended?', in *Philosophy, Risk, and Adventure Sports*, ed., Mike McNamee (London: Routledge, 2007), 174.

24   The least compelling of these is Breivik's contention that the commercial success (sales of videos, etc.) of BASEjumping indicates that, for society, the benefit of the sport outweighs the cost ('Can BASEjumping Be Morally Defended?', 176).

25   Breivik, 'Can BASEjumping Be Morally Defended?', 173.

26   Ibid., 175.

27   Ibid., 184.

28   Free soloing is defined by Agnafors (fine-tuning common usage) as climbing that is done without any safety equipment (ropes, etc.) on vertical or near-vertical surfaces at a height of six metres or more and from which a fall would be likely to cause severe injury or death. Marcus Agnafors, 'The Ethics of Free Soloing', in *Climbing-Philosophy for Everyone: Because It's There*, ed., Stephen E. Schmid (Oxford: Wiley-Blackwell, 2010), 160.

29 Agnafors, 'The Ethics of Free Soloing', 164.
30 Heidi Howkins Lockwood, 'Jokers on the Mountain: In Defence of Gratuitous Risk', in *Climbing-Philosophy for Everyone: Because It's There*, ed., Stephen E. Schmid (Oxford: Wiley-Blackwell, 2010), 49.
31 Ibid., 50–4.
32 Ibid., 61–3.
33 Breivik, 'Can BASEjumping Be Morally Defended?', 174.
34 Ivo Jirásek, 'Extreme Sports and the Ontology of Experience', in *Philosophy, Risk, and Adventure Sports*, ed., Mike McNamee (London: Routledge, 2007), 139.
35 Ibid., 147.
36 Ibid. Note that these comments apply to the *active participant*; the way that most people encounter dangerous sport is vicariously, mediated through television and video representations that attempt to persuade their audience of their contemporaneity with the events and their authors.
37 Gunnar Breivik, 'Dangerous Play with the Elements: Toward a Phenomenology of Risk Sports', *Sport, Ethics, and Philosophy* 5 (2011): 321.
38 Kevin Krein, 'Nature and Risk in Adventure Sports', in *Philosophy, Risk and Adventure Sports*, ed., Mike McNamee (London: Routledge, 2007), 87.
39 Ibid., 91.
40 Jesús Ilundáin-Agurruza, 'Between the Horns: A Dilemma in the Interpretation of the Running of the Bulls – Part 1: The Confrontation', *Sport, Ethics, and Philosophy* 1 (2007): 339–40.
41 Jesús Ilundáin-Agurruza, 'Between the Horns: A Dilemma in the Interpretation of the Running of the Bulls – Part 2: The Evasion', *Sport, Ethics, and* Philosophy 2 (2008): 28.
42 Ibid., 25.
43 Ibid., 22.
44 Ilundáin-Agurruza, 'Between the Horns: A Dilemma in the Interpretation of the Running of the Bulls – Part 1: The Confrontation', 337.
45 There is further discussion of this point in Howe, 'Remote Sport: Risk and Self-Knowledge in Wilder Spaces'.
46 Russell, 'The Value of Dangerous Sport', 5.
47 See Warren P. Fraleigh, 'An Examination of Relationships of Inherent, Intrinsic, Instrumental, and Contributive Values of the Good Sports Contest', *Journal of the Philosophy of Sport* 10 (1984): 52–60 for a classic statement of this view.

Sport and the Environment – Ecosophical and Metanoetical Intersections

Ron Welters

Since the Centennial Olympic Congress in Paris in 1994, the International Olympic Committee (IOC) has considered 'ecological concern' as one of its essential missions. And yes, we had quite green Winter Olympics in Vancouver in 2010 and a fairly green *Grand Départ* of the Tour de France in Rotterdam, also in 2010. We even have the promise that the FIFA World Cup 2022 in Qatar will take place in an eco-friendly soccer utopia. Certainly, these are interesting developments, but we need to dig deeper, philosophically. One important question is: How to be a good sports(wo)man – from Usain Bolt and Serena Williams to John and Jane Doe – that takes his or her environment seriously into account?

To develop a tentative ecological philosophy (or 'ecosophy') of sport that may lead to a radical (or 'metanoetical') change in the way people live their lives, in this essay I will constantly intertwine the deep and the shallow, the practical and the ideal. To live a worthy sporty life with as little environmental pressure as possible, this is the heart of the matter.

Turning the Tide

In *Sportfilosofie*, their comprehensive overview of the continental and analytic philosophy of sport published in 2000, Jan Tamboer and Johan Steenbergen argue that in the ethics of sport there traditionally was, and still is, a strong focus on the proper behaviour of the individual sports(wo)man.[1] They argue that due to recent developments the often complex interrelation between sport and the environment should be at the forefront of any attempt to formulate a comprehensive contemporary ethics of sport. Referring to an article written in 1987 by Klaus Cachay,[2] the two Dutch philosophers of sport distinguish four actual practices where the detrimental effects of sports on our natural habitat are manifested: the vast use of natural reserves for sport (from sports fields to stadium car parks), direct (car racing) and indirect (travelling to matches and sports tourism) pollution, the increasing pressure on and even destruction of ecologically vulnerable communities (e.g. the devastating effects of skiing on local communities, flora and fauna) and, finally, sound pollution.

Tamboer and Steenbergen detect a growing awareness of the harmful effects of sport on the environment among sports associations. Environmental advisors are hired and sportspeople are being environmentally educated to make sports practices sustainable at least to some extent. On the one hand, there is a movement to limit the explosive growth of 'nature sports' and thus the negative effects on our natural habitat. This would be salubrious for the environment as such. On the other hand, at the same time, governmental measures for enhancing the health of the citizens by practising outdoor sports are flourishing.

In a chapter on sport ethics and environmental ethics, the German, philosophically inclined sports pedagogue Eckhard Meinberg also observed in 1991 that until then the natural environment of sport was self-evident and unproblematic, and therefore anathema in mainstream ethics. Building on a rich German culture of philosophical anthropology, Meinberg sets forth his position. He argues: 'We always encounter non-human nature, including the natural environment, never directly, non-natural, but always in a prefabricated cultural context ... either if we want to dominate or we want to feel her and the like ... To the watchful observant of the world of sports it will be dawning that sport, not only elite sport in many of its manifestations, has become a first-rate moral provocation, and it increasingly becomes clear that lately the relation between sport and the environment is ethically dubious.'[3]

Alpine skiing is a ruthless land-consuming activity that causes deforestation. Motor car racing, as already mentioned by Cachay, is polluting, Meinberg proceeds. Furthermore, notwithstanding the fact that they took up environmental issues as early as in the 1970s, 'clean sports' like kayaking and sailing cause irresponsible and irreversible negative environmental effects. Also, the ever more popular cross-country skiing is seen as a real environmental threat, because of the fact that this activity threatens the natural habitat of animals and plants. And even horse riding and jogging are becoming environmentally suspect, Meinberg concludes.[4]

The expanding importance of elite as well as mass sport has a double-edged effect: sport becomes hostile to the environment and there is an environment that becomes hostile to sport. Meinberg suggests a blueprint for an ethics of sport that is environmentally conscious. Such a coexistential ethics, which respects nature and sport equally, is clarified by four 'particulars'. First, the idea of coexistence should not only be descriptive but should also be a *normative touchstone* for sporting behaviour. In this respect, for example, producing artificial snow for alpine skiing – fruitful for humans but potentially harmful to flora and fauna – becomes a matter of moral questioning.

Second, Meinberg argues that a comprehensive coexistential ethics of sport should have a *macro character*. Not just sports(wo)men but also institutions, systems, the natural environment and non-human life that is involved one way or another with the effects of sport should be taken into account in any coexistential effort. Third, Meinberg insists on the *pluralist character* of a coexistential ethics of sport. Not just sport-intrinsic norms (fair play, the principle of equality of competitors, etc.) but also external value systems should be taken into account. The ethics of sport inevitably has to consider and cooperate with other forms of applied ethics (for the sake of this argument, notably with ecological ethics, which is, due to the current state of planet earth, also an ethics of survival, Meinberg argues). So the question is: What is an appropriate and well-matched relation between humans and nature? Meinberg pleads for a democratic 'plural ecology' instead of radical and coercive ecological straightforwardness: 'Plurality is a protection against dogmatism, tyranny and absolutism, for which reason the plurality-commandment itself is morally motivated.'[5]

Meinberg's non-speciecist attempt to design an up-to-date coexistential ethics of sport may look circular. He seems to be aware of this. Therefore, he makes an anthropological turn: for him, humans are *homo compensators,* beings opposed to nature, but at the same time embodied in and dependent on the natural world, so in this respect humans are rather participants in nature. Thus, Meinberg ends with his fourth particular: a plea for good-natured, obliging and moderate human sporty selfishness, or *'benevolent anthropocentrism,'* that uses nature as a playground for sport practices only reluctantly. '*Homo sportivus* should – and because it is more honest this is the real benevolent anthropocentrism – therefore protect natural spaces, truly cultivate them, to protect himself. Yet a coexistential ethics of sport cannot decide if such an insight also will be followed by appropriate acts. He who knows how hard it is for people to convert thinking into moral acting will most certainly not glow with optimism.'[6]

Nature under Siege

In their comprehensive and recently re-edited book *Sport, Culture and Society: An Introduction,* Grant Jarvie and James Thornton raise the issue of the specific power of sport as a transformative tool. The authors distinguish radical or 'dark green' and reformist or 'light green' approaches to environmental ethics in sport.[7] The first mindset is rooted in anti-capitalism, tends to be proactive and relies on the beneficial effects of deep ecology (there is intrinsic value in nature and sport is not above nature), social ecology and eco-socialism. The second school of thought tends to be reactive and is based on conservatism, preservationism, stewardship, free-market liberalism and social (but free-market!) reformism, which, in essence, means 'tradeable pollution rights plus voluntary agreements plus regulation'.[8] Jarvie and Thornton end the book with a carefully worded conclusion that says: 'Sport may not be able to halt major environmental catastrophes but its undoubted popularity in many parts of the world means that it provides a popular target for organizations such as Greenpeace, the anti-golf movement and the IOC to deliver on environmental messages. Perhaps the real question for environmentalists is: can we have sport at all without nature?'[9]

The answer, naturally, depends on how we interpret and frame 'nature'. Do we see nature as fixed, something pristine out there, untouched by humans? Or do we see nature as dynamic and intertwined with human activity? For Baruch Spinoza (1632–1677), *natura naturata,* or 'nature natured', refers to nature as a passive product of an infinite causal chain, whereas *natura naturans*[10] denotes the self-causing activity of nature, or 'nature in the active sense', as Samuel Taylor Coleridge (1772–1834) phrases the issue of how to deal with the often used but rarely well-defined theoretical term 'nature', which generally seems to refer to something like 'non-human' or something – more or less – 'beyond human control' or 'sublime'.

Meinberg's theses of 'coexistence' and 'benevolent anthropocentrism' implicitly imply the *naturans* modus. In his view, there is no opposition between (unnatural) sport and (natural) nature. Even more, the concept of 'nature' is anthropomorphic by its very own nature, since this theoretical term always operates in a 'prefabricated cultural context'. This *natura naturans* stance also fits perfectly well with the two authors I will introduce, analyse and synthesize hereafter: Norwegian Sigmund Loland and German Peter Sloterdijk.

Ecosophy of Sport

The most analytic attempt to develop a comprehensive ecological philosophy, or 'ecosophy of sport', so far has been made by Loland. Over the last two decades, this leading Norwegian philosopher of sport has constructed a theoretical framework that can stand analytical as well as continental philosophical hair-splitting. Here is a rendition of his view.

In his 'Outline of an Ecosophy of Sport', an article published in 1996 in the *Journal of the Philosophy of Sport*, Loland argues that in the ecological movement 'to a certain extent, competition has been seen as the very counter-principle to ecologically sound practice in which cooperation and symbiosis are considered key values'.[11] Based on the work of the Norwegian philosopher Arne Naess, one of the founding fathers of the ecological movement in the 1970s and the man who coined the term 'deep ecology', Loland develops a set of hypotheses and norms that give philosophical evidence for the idea that sport can be ecologically justified. Key values in this effort to mitigate, to radically change the way humans deal with sport (and consequently with their natural habitat) are 'Self-realization' (indeed with capital s), on the one hand, and the idea of 'biospheric egalitarianism' or 'the democracy of all life forms', on the other.

Loland is aware of possible controversial consequences of his position. 'For example, we might, under certain circumstances, reach the conclusion that human beings ought to recommend their own withdrawal as the dominant life form on earth to promote other life forms to live and blossom; this withdrawal may contribute more to the Self-realization for all. Such norms, critics could argue, cannot serve as a common basis for society at large.'[12]

However, rather than staying at home, which would be by far the best for the environment, we try, for example, to develop cleaner ways of travelling. We tend to see nature as something co-evolutionary with our uncontrollable desire to conquer planet earth – so we prefer *naturans* rather than *naturata*. This persistent habit of solving problems by applying 'techné'. the technological fix, in one way or another, is very hard to break. Accordingly, Loland argues that 'Naess's slogan of "simplicity in means, richness in ends" is true in sport as in other areas of life. At the same time, technology can add to the ecosophical joy of sport and thus serve the Self-realization process. In sport, we can establish meaningful relations to technology, and technology can expand our experience of the unity and diversity of life. If increase in joy is able to outweigh on a long term-basis the ecological costs of production and application, sport technology can be ecologically justified.'[13]

Applying the ecological/ecosophical calculus to the admissibility of the introduction of new specific sport practices means a full 'yes' to the introduction of the carving ski and telemark technology, which according to Loland increased the joy of skiing significantly. And the ecosophical fairness principle means a full 'no' to the introduction of integrated bicycle brakes in time trials and triathlons, to switch over to a sport practice that Loland doesn't mention in his article, which makes the top-level riders just a few seconds faster over 40 kilometres in a non-drafting time trial.

Loland's most controversial norm in his sophisticated effort to develop a comprehensive ecosophical framework with a proper set of hypotheses and norms is the call to practise 'sport in closeness to nature!' This means that sports that have been practised indoors for decades – handball, basketball, etc. – have to change dramatically. But also sports that are still performed 'in the wild' are at odds with true ecosophy, because – as Meinberg has already concluded – 'Alpine and telemark skiers demand energy-consuming ski lifts and machine-prepared snow'.[14] These technological developments evoke the paradox of naturalness by unnatural means.

Intermezzi in the Woods, the Crystal Palace and on the Road

On a larger scale, which includes sports as a health-enhancing technique for the masses, rather than the more or less organized and more or less serious competition, the intuitive appeal of striving for sport in closeness to nature becomes more complicated even under Loland's ecosophical outline. How close to nature can we get in sport? Abstract (deep) visions of nature that cyclists hold dear are often dissonant with their (shallow) actual behaviour.

An anecdote. In my home town, I observe on a regular basis the weekend masses driving (often four-wheel drive) from suburbia to the woods, riding an hour or so on their mountain bikes, experiencing nature and driving back home. In the lovely medium-sized university town where I live, the grey-haired weekend-walking squad, usually dressed up in green (natural!) wax coats, is definitely not amused by the reckless armada of mountain bikers, dressed in bright-coloured spandex (unnatural!). The members of this aggrieved army put small tree trunks right across those tricky parts of the official mountain bike track where you really do not want to have such obstacles – a nasty habit that made me have a serious crash and a broken front wheel once. And since I was the last one on the track just before sunset (and since I do not own a mobile phone nor a driving licence – unlike my natural opponents I often observe), the cunning ambush arranged by the complacent walking squad made me drag myself home for many kilometres.

We could have it all – walking, running, mountain biking and even nordic walking – since the wooded area around my home town is vast enough. But in reality, there is a clash of different 'cultures of nature' (which is not a paradox in the *naturata* idea!).

A second observation comes from my university sports centre. This is mistakenly called the Gymnasion, since there are no free men sporting naked and having shrewd philosophical conversation in the open, but students and teachers from both sexes working out, spinning, or running on treadmills under energy-consuming climate-controlled circumstances in crystal palaces, as the post-Heideggerian German philosopher Peter Sloterdijk calls the immensely popular modern gyms. Yet, a simple walk at lunchtime or an outdoor bike ride would probably promote health better for most of us. How far away from nature and ecosophical joy can we get in sports?

Except for the massive turn to the crystal cocoon, in my part of the world there is also a massive turn to large-scale versions of classic bike rides specifically designed for tourists, for instance, the cyclo-tourist version of the Milan–San Remo race or the Tour of Flanders, usually held one day before the professionals ride the same stretch at double speed. These mass events with often as many as 10,000 'competitors' are indirectly polluting, because of the commute to and from their residences and because of the numbers of events, but also directly damaging planet earth, because of the waste the ever-hungry pack produces by throwing away power gel and power bar wrappers. That is what the professionals do the next day, so that is what the mimicking pack does the day before.

Also, in finding the balance between technology and ecosophical joy amateur cyclists are sometimes even less ecosophical than the real ones they imitate and through all possible means. The most striking example of this hyper-compensation through high-end technology is the following. Where professional cycling has imposed itself material limits by introducing the *Union Cycliste Internationale* norm of the minimum bike weight of 6.8 kilograms in 2000, the free market for fun, mass-event and amateur riders hasn't. So if you can afford it, you can bike even lighter than a professional.

The Sport Record as External Axiom

Back to the tricky thin and slack rope over the winding and slippery slope that leads to Friedrich Nietzsche's athletic *Übermensch*.[15] In 2001, Sigmund Loland published his article 'Record Sports: An Ecological Reconstruction' in the *Journal of the Philosophy of Sport*. There he distinguishes three categories of sports. First, 'record sports', sports where exact measurements in mathematical-physical entities within a standardized spatio-temporal framework are possible, for example swimming, athletics and weightlifting. Second, 'quasi-record sports', such as marathon and road cycling; sometimes people talk of records here, but this is inaccurate since conditions (weather) and trails (flat or mountainous) differ from race to race. Loland's third category consists of 'games' such as football, baseball, etc. These are non-record, but nevertheless highly competitive sports, and in this sense they also raise severe ecosophical concerns, from aggression on the pitch – which is at odds with the ecosophical plea for peaceful coexistence and the flourishing of all creatures, great and small – to the environmental impact of football, I argue.

Because they are exemplary, Loland concentrates on record sports – notably Olympic athletics – and puts forward his challenging 'record sport dilemma', which replaces the pre-modern logic of *Enough is enough!* by the modern logic of *Enough is never enough!* This ruthless quest for records – 'the external axiom of sport', according to Pierre de Coubertin, the founding father of the International Olympic Committee (IOC) – is the very equivalent of the problem of unlimited growth in limited systems. Every new record has to be broken, over and over again, by tenths, hundredths or maybe even thousandths of a second. This is perfectly expressed in the official motto of the Olympics: *citius, altius, fortius*, ever faster, higher, stronger.[16] But there is a flip side to the record as the external axiom of sport. Thus, Loland argues that 'The continuous quest for new records is built on the impossible quest for unlimited growth in limited systems.'[17]

In 2006, Loland publishes an article entitled 'Olympic Sport and the Ideal of Sustainable Development,' once again in the *Journal of the Philosophy of Sport*. In it, he reflects on the ambition of the IOC 'to engage in protection of the environment'.[18] Here Loland recaptures his record dilemma and connects it to ecosophical issues in sport. Loland argues that 'On the 100 metre sprint, a race on 10 seconds requires runners that run below 10 seconds in the current and next generation of sprinters. From the record perspective, performances above 10 seconds are used once and for all. Hence, every new record represents the use of a non-renewable performance resource in the sport to which it belongs. Every record means a missed opportunity for performance for other current and future athletes. Record sports are non-sustainable in that they require unlimited growth in limited systems ... If Olympic sporting life is to continue indefinitely, record sports have to be either abandoned or reformed.'[19]

Loland, therefore, advises the IOC to skip the idea of measuring performance in absolute units. His alternative is an ordinal ranking for competitors according to the order in which they cross the finishing line or – if sprint competitions are made up by a series of competitions – by giving points such as five for a win, three for a second place and so on. But this is not enough to achieve 'ecosophical justice'. Thus, Loland continues: 'Requirements on standardization of record events can be transformed into requirements on equal conditions in a variety of ways. For instance, competition schemes could be varied by introducing a variety of distances (sprinters could run from between 30 and 300 metres, but never the exact same distance twice) and surfaces (sand, running tracks, turns, slightly uphill, slightly downhill, etc.) ... In such a reformed sprint-running scheme, a larger variety of sprint talents can blossom.'[20]

Loland furthermore argues: 'Nature's curved lines and unpredictable diversity are being replaced by the straight, geometrical coordinate system of the arena ... The ideal of record sports portrays a one-dimensional social logic and a mono-culture version of sport. All athletes strive for the same objective goal of record setting, and they prepare for and specialize in exactly the same kind of performance over and over again. Hence record sports have the characteristics of a non-sustainable system.'[21]

One could question, however, what the consequences are of this ecosophical revision of sprinting for real ecology out there in the remains of what we still consider nature. How do diversified running tracks, varying from sprinting some 300 metres on permafrost in the very northern tip of Sweden to 30 metres on high-altitude soft soil in Kigen, Kenya, contribute to a more ecosophical conception of sport? There certainly is an analogy between blossoming varied sprint challenges and talents and the blossoming of biological species. One could even ponder on the special merits of the idea of an ecosophized sprint circus for a better intercultural understanding of people all over the world.

History, however, shows that, in all probability, we will ever be longing for athletes that challenge and push the limits in terms of hundredths or even thousandths of a second. I find it hard to imagine the Olympics, with its tradition of a strong focus on athletics, changing in the ecosophical direction Loland suggests. I could imagine, however, a world record-breaking 100-metre sprint race that can be ecologically justified. Imagine Usain Bolt converting himself into a vegetarian hermit, an ascetic who keeps on sprinting, never leaves Jamaica but is still able to set a 9.49 world record on an outdated Kingston athletic track. What's wrong with this unlimited growth in a definitely more sustainable system? A group of athletes travelling all over the world to visit the ecosophical and multicultural sprint series that requires a series of diversified sprinting skills, Loland suggests, will probably do more harm to the environment.

Therefore my advice to the IOC is the opposite of Loland's call to concentrate first and foremost on our deep ecological thoughts on our (sporty) being in the world: redefine your institutions, minimize the ecological footprint of the games within the current system, and then switch over to sensitizing concrete sport practices and individual sports(wo)men towards more self-realization through symbiosis with 'nature'.

Three Central Ecosophical Questions and Answers

Loland ends his decisive 1996 essay 'Outline of an Ecosophy of Sport' *by* proposing three pivotal questions. As a practical philosopher and as a philosophical practitioner, I will try to answer them from the perspective of (outdoor) endurance sports, such as running and cycling. These endurance sports do not fare well in celebrating the multitude of motor and physical skills Loland pleads for, but they are nevertheless popular with the masses and are within their reach, since perseverance and stamina are these sports' prerequisites rather than sheer talent.

1. What are the implications of the norm on ecosophical joy in my sport practice?
For many 21st-century people, sport is not a *homo ludens*-like recreational activity, but a truth- or knowledge-seeking lifestyle.[22] Many of us, even if we are non-professional athletes, may work out six times a week.[23] Imagine yourself as someone who is not just into cycling, but also into running, because you simply like it and it is very effective in terms of time input and output and in terms of ecosophical joy.

Since you might be doing fairly but not extremely well in both and because you do not like to ride in a 'peloton' – a closed pack, which provides aerodynamic advantages (less drag) – you have specialized yourself in the duathlon,[24] or run-bike-run, with non-drafting rules on the bike, which means that you are biking on your own, without the aerodynamic profit of a pack. Usually there are some 150 competitors during a duathlon, so there is not too much pressure on the environment, even during the off-road mountain bike version in the muddy winter season. To lower your environmental impact even more, you travel to races by train or by sharing a car. But you have to admit, you do have more bikes – maybe up to six – than you really need, and you do own more than just one pair of running shoes. So your overt materialism lessens your ecosophical joy, when you are honest with yourself.

Because you'll probably run and bike on different tracks under different conditions at different speeds and lengths, you are doing quite well on Loland's scale of challenging your bio-motor abilities. (This might balance your ecosophical scale slightly, which due to your excessive use of high-end carbon bicycles tips toward the negative.) But you are probably very limited in your bio-motor abilities, and in this sense not celebrating life in full. But then again, what is the problem for the environment as such?

What about your ecosophical mindset as a duathlete, which seems to be of the greatest importance in Loland's view? Your deepest ecological thoughts might pop up during a lunchbreak run of an hour or so or an evening bike ride. This is about enjoying nature, about being as such, maybe even about Martin Heidegger's concept of *Gelassenheit* (releasement or letting-go).[25] But even when competing with opponents in a race there still may be some idea of ecosophical closeness to 'nature' or 'life' somewhere deep inside. In Loland's terminology: 'The immediate joy of the "interconnection between all there is" in competitive moments might be a microcosmos reflecting a macrocosmos in terms of an athlete's fundamental total view of the world.'[26]

This probably is what the Dutch cyclist Peter Winnen, twice winner of the Alpe d'Huez, a famous ascent in the infamous Tour de France, means when he writes in a column that though during his winning ascents in 1981 and 1983 he simply wasn't able to think anymore, let alone watch the beautiful surrounding massif, the Alpe d'Huez nevertheless entered his body in an unconscious, subliminal way – or 'muscle memory,' the words David Kilpatrick used in his paper on 'Poetics and the Beautiful Game'.[27]

2. How should I, in my sport context, relate to norms for developing skills in width and depth, for playing to win and for applying only ecosophically sound sport technology?
'Depth' and 'width' are the norms you probably hold dear as an endurance athlete in your efforts to improve yourself. 'Playing to win' can be threefold in this case: trying to end as high as possible in the total ranking, trying to end as high as possible in your age group and, finally, trying to be faster than you were before on this specific duathlon or half-marathon, in terms of minutes or even seconds. This triplicate notion of record-setting – from overall ranking to age-group ranking to personal best – is 'wider' and consequently more ecosophical than the uncompromising hunting down of opponents during a 100-metre dash.

Your relation to technology as an endurance athlete is probably ambivalent. What is the optimum between gear and training? Imagine you possess a rather expensive time trial bike, not as expensive as some of your opponents, but more expensive than some rivals who are better than you. How to deal with this dilemma? Riding a high-end aerodynamic carbon bicycle increases the joy you experience during training and racing and might outweigh on a long-term basis the ecological costs of production.[28]

But how to philosophically weigh the devilish dilemma of just enough and too much technology, since *homo sapiens* does not simply use ever more sophisticated tools, but to some extent has become him or herself technological? Sloterdijk argues that an assessment of the pervasive techno-sciences of the present has to build on a broad historical and cultural understanding of the ways in which science and technology have played a crucial role in the coming into existence of human beings as entities that are, to a significant extent, self-made and open to change, which also means an openness to ecosophical change in the way we deal with sport at large.

In *Du mußt dein Leben ändern* (*You Must Change Your Life*),[29] Sloterdijk argues that the call for *metanoia*, a turning point in life, radical reform, personal mitigation, is something that has always occurred, but it differs in how it manifests itself in each era. Nowadays the athletic ideal, which already flourished in Ancient Greece, is very influential once again. What we seem to have forgotten, however, Sloterdijk emphasizes, is that becoming an athlete takes a lot of *askesis*, the Greek word for 'training' or 'practice'. The good life doesn't simply come without effort. For Sloterdijk, those who explicitly and repeatedly train, rehearse and practise are the ones that really embody true existence. Or, as Loland writes in his ecosophical essay, 'periods of monotonous hard work are sometimes necessary to reach deeper insight and values'.[30]

For Sloterdijk, who managed to climb Mount Ventoux in France in about two and a half hours, road cycling is one of the modern variants of ancient heroism. He believes that 'Anyone can fight on flat stretches, but those who remain capable of fighting a duel on the worst of mountains already deserve to be called Hector or Achilles … Cycling represents for me a return to the primal man of the savannahs, who during a hunt spends the entire day running, and is constantly high in the process.'[31]

The noble art of cycling, with its sheer physicality, enables us to overcome the dichotomy of human beings and tools in a magnanimous and up-to-date way, one that allows us to attenuate our energy and resource-consuming lifestyle without forcing us to go back to a simple life of staying at home.[32] This is what Steen Nepper Larsen expresses proficiently in his essay, 'Becoming a Cyclist'.[33] Larsen, a 6 foot 7 inch-tall Danish cycling giant condemned by his height to ride a custom steel bike, ascends an *hors catégorie* philosophical mountain in proper cadence: 'My consciousness is embedded in things and cognition is incarnated in a restless body. My *being-in-the-world* is transformed to a *body-on-a-cycle-in-motion*, being able to do more than it knows. My identity is in a process of becoming an "inter-being" between the bike, the experience and an ocean of interpretations. To cycle is an extended, mind-stimulating rendezvous with and in nature.'[34]

Larsen cautions that the environmental benefits of a cycling life cannot be justified in the long run by sheer utilitarianism. Rather, he justifies cycling philosophically, pointing out that in contrast to a modern sports utility vehicle, primitive bike technology 'fosters an ecstatic-present-attentive being. One might say that I become bigger than my own flesh.'[35] Larsen refers to Sloterdijk, who thinks mountains are not to be messed with; either you climb them or you leave them alone. 'Emanating from the mountains of the world, a vertical imperative hits the horizontal human. Pull yourself together, leave the lowlands and conquer the summit!'[36]

Nonetheless, just *askesis*, in the sense of 'training', is not enough. In order to attain ecosophical joy one needs to take care of the bicycle. The dichotomy between 'hip' or 'romantic' and 'square' or 'classicist' bikers that Robert M. Pirsig makes in his famous 1970s novel *Zen and the Art of Motorcycle Maintenance: An Inquiry into Values*[37] clarifies my point. As a hip romantic (John Sutherland, the supporting role) you could be overwhelmed, and nearly speechless, by the sheer beauty of, say, the Alps. You could even be flowing, not even aware that you were pushing the pedals quite hard. And yes, sometimes you do take the unknown and unpaved road. At the very same time, however, you can be as square and 'classic' as hell (Phaedrus, the leading character and Pirsig's alter ego), since you are meticulous when it comes to bike care, and you are the kind of cyclist that wants to know in advance where the road is going and how long and steep the ascents are.

During a long-distance run-bike-run you could be totally possessed by square and unhip thoughts: your bike must be in optimal form, force yourself to eat five power bars, four bananas and three power gels during the 150-kilometre ride, watch out for potholes, stay in heart rate zone 3 as long as possible, etc. And during the second, extremely hilly 30-kilometre run your motto will probably be: don't think of the killing kilometres to come, just accept the pain, take a drink every 2.5 kilometres, keep going, etc.

Applying the only-ecosophically-sound-sport-technology principle in this case simply means defining the right mean between training not harder but more efficiently and/or deciding if spending 1000 extra euros on a full carbon tri-spoke wheel outweighs the hypothetical gain of two minutes on 150 kilometres. At a glance, such a high-impact endurance race, which will probably take more than eight hours of sporting activity, is about *andreia*, the cardinal virtue of courage. But on second thoughts *sōphrosunē*, temperance, and *phronēsis*, practical wisdom, are the preferential virtues by far. Only knowing how to be confident but not foolhardy and an acquired routine of taking in food and fluid at the right moment will help one to survive in the long run.

3. What can I do to promote sport training and competition in closeness to nature?
Jung Hyun Hwang and Scott Kretchmar argue that 'the golden mean is neither an arithmetic midpoint nor a lukewarm state of being noncommittal, tentative, or otherwise uncertain … It incorporates elements of each extreme but, with its location at the mean, avoids the evils that are found in the unbridled end points. Moreover, this mean is a state that takes into account the unique person and his or her specific environment.'[38]

This also goes for the way we should deal with (lots of) training and (some) competition in the domain of nature. Ken Glah, a 28 consecutive Ironman World Championships finisher in Kona, Hawaii, advises athletes to stay engaged by finding ways to enjoy training. Glah, who prefers training in his Pennsylvanian backyard, simply doesn't understand people who compete at the classic triathlon distance, 3.8-kilometre swimming, 180-kilometre cycling and finishing by running a marathon, and declare that they love racing but hate training. 'I have no idea why they're in the sport. Even if you were to race 10 or 15 times a year, you're spending 95 per cent of your time training. If you don't enjoy the training, why would you do something you don't enjoy 95 per cent of the time, just to enjoy it 5 per cent of the time?'[39]

And that's what we could or even should do in our effort to reach the Elysian fields of harmless ecosophical sport as well: skip the naturalistic romantic idealism of letting flourish as many talents as possible, and look for practical philosophical arrangements that can bring about willingness for *metanoia* towards a more sustainable lifestyle in, and for, concrete individuals. Or to give the simplest of all possible answers to Loland's question of how to promote sport in closeness to nature: tell people of the joy of outdoor sporting, especially of the long and lonely rides and runs, I argue, referring to the Dutch psychiatrist and philosopher Jan-Hendrik van den Berg's provocative and poetic plea for solipsism in telegram style. He maintains that 'The masses do not make up their minds. The crowd is driving a car. Leave this path, contemporary. It is still possible. Chose the path that is too narrow for a spinal mass. You should go alone, or by two or three. Only in a small group, or in solitude, can one find life. Only to a small group, to the individual, does existence reveal its possession, its destiny. In the way of the crowd one cannot discern a direction. The crowd moves among itself. He who is in search of life goes alone. He leaves the broad road, which leads to doom and destruction, and chooses the narrow, unpaved path, that demands full attention at every single step.'[40] The problem in real life is that the proclivity for leaving the beaten track may cause a lot of harm to fragile habitats, but the metaphysical point that Van den Berg scores is clear: do not yield to 'spinalism' or herd instinct, be thyself.

Sport philosopher Leslie Howe also gives good philosophical reasons for sporting close to nature. She argues that 'All sport has the potential to develop self-understanding and personal growth by offering various kinds of tests, but sport carried out in the remote and wilder places of the earth elevates this benefit because it commonly demands a higher than usual awareness of and response to risk, as well as presenting participants with a practical revelation of their relative significance (or lack thereof) in the natural environment. It can teach us not only about ourselves as human individuals, but also as humans placed in a wider world than the purely human. My claim is not therefore that remote sport is better than conventional sport as such, but that it does have some special benefits to offer.'[41]

Finally, even the paved road has special ecosopshical benefits to offer. Magnanimous cyclist Larsen, frozen to the marrow after a climb on Palma de Mallorca during which the weather changed dramatically, contends that 'We have to listen to our vivid memory and create our own narratives. The work of the biking man's legs and muscles are his embodied thought.'[42] Only experiencing nature directly can make sport ecosophically significant.

Metanoetic Olympism

Commissioned by Olympic Fire, a task force of the Netherlands Olympic Committee-Netherlands Sport Federation, in 2011 I worked with 24 students of the Top Sport Programme of the HAN University of Applied Sciences (Nijmegen, The Netherlands) on 'the ecological legacy' of the Amsterdam bid for the 2028 Olympics.[43] The rationale was that 100 years after the 1928 Amsterdam Olympics, the Amsterdam 2028 Olympics should become as 'green' as possible.

A quick search taught us that many aspects of the modern Olympic Games we consider 'classic' were actually introduced during the 1928 Amsterdam Olympics. The Olympic flame was lit for the first time (although for security reasons the honour went to an employee of the national gas company and not to an athlete). The Olympic parade with the Greek delegation at the start and the host country at the end also occurred for the first time in Amsterdam. Since then, athletics has been contested on a 400-metre track. A marathon has measured exactly 42.195 metres ever since, and the games have lasted for 16 days instead of several months since 1928.[44]

The 1928 Amsterdam Olympics were also the first with an official commercial sponsor (Coca-Cola), and also hosted the first sports icon (swimmer Johnny Weismuller), who soon after became a movie star (*Tarzan*). For the first time there were women's athletics. German Lina Radke won the inaugural title in the 800 metres in a world record time of 2 minutes and 16.8 seconds, which would last until 1944. Also, from the viewpoint of Loland's plea for applying only ecosophically sound sport technology, the 1928 Amsterdam Olympics were interesting since Englishman Jack London, who won the silver medal in the 100-metre dash, was the only athlete using starting blocks, whereas the rest still dug little holes in the gravel with their hands. This caused a thorough discussion of fairness and the use of technology. The most important conclusion of this little historical retrospective is that the modern Olympics are flexible and open to change. Even more, they could be the blueprint for a broader ecosophical Olympism, which opens up for 'the deep identification with all life forms characteristic of an extended, ecological Self.'[45]

In the scenario this group developed for a potential Amsterdam 2028 Olympics, the students linked such themes as climate change, water management and energy production in various ways with solutions for stadiums, infrastructure and accommodation for athletes. There was also consensus on the idea that in the wake of the celebration of elite sport, the Amsterdam 2028 Olympic Games should pay special attention to recreational sport, social justice and public health. To mention four refreshing recommendations:

1. *Stadiums with different post-Olympic Games use:* from a temple for elite athletes during the Olympic Games to a home for the elderly, a school or a community centre afterwards.
2. *Praise the all-round runner:* introducing an ordinal ranking in a sprinting competition over several distances to let a larger variety of talents blossom, and abandoning the impossible quest for unlimited growth in limited systems.

3. *Earth, water, wind and fire: Olympics of the four pre-Socratic elements*: a plea for using as many renewable resources as possible for (public and athlete) transport during the event, which in the Dutch case means a special focus on the aqueous and the aerial, since we have plenty of waterways and a good deal of fair wind.
4. *Diving clean*: an outdoor Olympic diving contest in Rotterdam Harbour, where the water quality has improved exceptionally over the last few years.

In addition to their attempts to socialize and ecologize the Olympic Games, the students also acknowledged Sloterdijk's idea of *Vertikalspannung*, our longing for verticality that overcomes the drudgery and monotony of everyday life: 'A vertical imperative hits the horizontal human. Pull yourself together, leave the lowlands and conquer the summit.'[46] To determine the right mean between horizontal and vertical dimensions, we reassessed Sloterdijk's plea for revaluing *askesis*. As Sloterdijk argues, the athletic ideal has become influential again, one century after the introduction of the modern Olympics. 'He who is in search of humans will find acrobats.'[47]

To achieve a true ecosophical and metanoetical Olympics in 2028 we made three suggestions to Olympic Fire:

1. At the Sydney Olympic Games in 2000, the triathlon was introduced: 1500-metre swimming, followed by 40-kilometre road cycling (drafting permitted, to make it more spectacular for the audience) and finally a 10-kilometre road run. This manifestation of *askesis*-light should be replaced by the classic triathlon, as the ultimate expression of *askesis*.
2. To show that the overarching ideology of faster, higher, stronger also has an aesthetic dimension. The group proposed re-introducing the 'Pentathlon of the Muses', the competition in music, sculpture, painting, literature and architecture that, as a result of de Coubertin's efforts, went along with the 'physical' side of the Olympics from 1912 until 1948.
3. Introduce parkour, or free-running, a sport where practitioners aim to move from one place to another, negotiating the obstacles in between, often in an urban setting. 'By dissolving the boundaries of the game's field of play, parkour has immersed itself into the environment like no other sport can. There are no longer stadiums, tracks, or determined pathways that force nature to concede to human power and privilege. Parkour integrates the environment, whether urban or rural, into the sport, and, in essence, allows nature to decide the rules of play. This fresh connection between athlete and environment creates many new perspectives of the world and the athlete's place in it.'[48]

Sloterdijk argues that while it is true that humans produce themselves, this does not happen through work and the actual results of work, neither by the recently so much-praised 'working at yourself' nor by 'interaction' or 'communication,' they do so by 'a life in exercises'.[49] Although Meinberg, who in his mentioned appeal to a non-committal 'benevolent anthropocentrism' to change our hyper-consuming lifestyle does not glow with optimism, Sloterdijk is positive-minded. To him, the long-awaited collective form of *metanoia* is a 'renaissance', which in his exuberant philosophical grammar is not bound to 14th-century Europe but denotes a massive ideological shift that can occur at any time and at any place. And the signs for a sporty renaissance that produces more health for humans and the environment – less meat, less pollution, more cycling – are promising: 'All over the world you can see a new form of reflection, there is a new generation who thinks over life in the new perspective I suggest. This ethical avant-garde can be recognized by the high standards they demand and fulfil.'[50]

I started this essay with an overview of recent attempts to develop an environmentally friendly philosophy of sport. Then I brought Loland's ideas on the ecosophy of sport to the forefront, the most sophisticated and motley attempt by far, but with shortcomings when it comes to real-life applicability. Renouncing Loland's focus on elite sport and on developing sporting skills in width and depth, I thereupon concentrated on repetitive and numb mass sports like running and cycling, and confronted these with Sloterdijk's provocative ideas on *askesis* as the fit means for a radical change of our unsettled lives. I ended with some rudimentary ideas on how to make the Olympics more sustainable.

We must change our lives. 'It cannot be denied: the only fact of universal ethical importance is the ubiquitously growing insight that we cannot continue like this.'[51] Ecosophical sport is a perfect tool for arousing the *metanoia* we need.

Notes

1 Jan Tamboer and Johan Steenbergen, *Sportfilosofie* (Leende: Damon, 2000), 183.
2 Klaus Cachay, 'Sport und Umwelt: Zur Entwicklung und Reflexion eines Konfliktes', *Sportunterricht* 3 (1987): 102.
3 Eckhard Meinberg, *Die Moral im Sport: Bausteine einer neuen Sportethik* (Aachen: Meyer & Meyer, 1991), 132.
4 Ibid., 133.
5 Ibid., 139–40.
6 Ibid., 151.
7 Grant Jarvie and James Thornton, *Sport, Culture and Society: An Introduction* (London and New York: Routledge, 2012).
8 Ibid., 272.
9 Ibid., 280.
10 '[By] *Natura naturans* we must understand what is in itself and is conceived through itself, *or* such attributes of substance as express an eternal and infinite essence, that is … God, insofar as he is considered as a free cause. But by *Natura naturata* I understand whatever follows from the necessity of God's nature, *or* from God's attributes, that is, all the modes of God's attributes insofar as they are considered as things which are in God, and can neither be nor be conceived without God.' Baruch Spinoza, *Ethics* (London: Penguin, 1996), 26.
11 Sigmund Loland, 'Outline of an Ecosophy of Sport', *Journal of the Philosophy of Sport* 23 (1996): 70.
12 Ibid., 76.
13 Ibid., 84
14 Ibid., 85.
15 Which for Nietzsche was an ideal construct rather than a real aspiration.

16 Loland points at an internal contradiction in Olympic ideology. 'Coubertin's perhaps best known aphorism is really a quote from a bishop of Central Pennsylvania, Ethelbert Talbot, who, in a pulpit sermon during the 1908 London Games, claimed that "… the important thing in these Olympiads is less to win than to take part in them." In other words, Olympism praises the ethos of excess while at the same time prescribing participation in sport with the disinterested attitude of the English gentleman amateur.' Sigmund Loland, 'Coubertin's Ideology of Olympism from the Perspective of the History of Ideas', *Olympika: The international Journal of Olympic Studies* 4 (1995): 64.

17 Sigmund Loland, 'Record Sports: An Ecological Critique and a Reconstruction', *Journal of the Philosophy of Sport* 28 (2001): 130 (emphasis in original).

18 Sigmund Loland, 'Olympic Sport and the Ideal of Sustainable Development', *Journal of the Philosophy of Sport* 33 (2006): 144.

19 Ibid., 147.

20 Ibid., 150.

21 Sigmund Loland, 'Record Sports: An Ecological Critique and a Reconstruction', 133.

22 Heather L. Reid, 'Sport, Philosophy and the Quest for Knowledge', *Journal of the Philosophy of Sport* 36 (2009): 40.

23 I refer to the group of quite serious endurance athletes of a certain age with often an academic background, to which I indeed belong myself.

24 You, of course, know that the classic triathlon is the *condition sine qua non* for a successful life as an endurance athlete, but since swimming demands an investment in technique and fixed training hours, you keep postponing this switchover to the real thing.

25 For an account of how *Gelassenheit* got lost in translation in the context of a discourse on ski-jumping, see Lev Kreft, 'Lost in Translation: Heidegger and Ski Jumping in Slovenia', *Physical Culture and Sport Studies and Research* 49 (2010): 13–20.

26 Sigmund Loland, 'Outline of an Ecosophy of Sport', 85.

27 David Kilpatrick, 'Poetics and the Beautiful Game' (paper presented at the annual meeting of the International Association of Philosophy of Sport, Rome, Italy, 15–19 September, 2010).

28 I will use the bicycle as a running gag from now, since it is the perfect grindstone for philosophical thinking on the (ecosophically) proper use of technology in sport. I will rely on the 'thick theory' Sigmund Loland suggests in his 'Technology in Sport: Three Ideal-Typical Views and Their Implications', *European Journal of Sport Science* 2 (2001): 1–11. For Loland, the thick interpretation 'does not just require equality of opportunity; its basic premise is that sport should be an arena for moral values and for human self-development and flourishing' (1).

29 Peter Sloterdijk, *Du mußt dein Leben ändern: Über Anthropotechnik* (Frankfurt: Suhrkamp, 2009).

30 Sigmund Loland, 'Outline of an Ecosophy of Sport', 80.

31 Lothar Gorris and Dirk Kurbjuweit, 'Philosopher Peter Sloterdijk on the Tour de France: "The Riders are Just Regular Employees"', *Der Spiegel Online International*, 10 July, 2008 <http://www.spiegel.de/international/eur ope/philosopher-peter-sloter dijk-on-the-tour-de-france-the-riders-are-just-regular-employees-a-565111.html> (accessed 19 February, 2013).

32 The next paragraphs on Steen Nepper Larsen and Sloterdijk are based on my review of *Cycling Philosophy for Everyone: A Philosophical Tour de Force*, eds., Jesús Ilundáin-Agurruza and Michael W. Austin (Chichester, Malden, MA: Wiley-Blackwell, 2010), *Sport, Ethics & Philosophy* 5 (2011): 182–4.

33 Steen Nepper Larsen, 'Becoming a Cyclist – Phenomenological Reflections on Cycling', in *Cycling Philosophy for Everyone: A Philosophical Tour de Force*, eds. Jesús

Ilundáin-Agurruza and Michael W. Austin (Chichester, Malden, MA: Wiley-Blackwell, 2010) 27–39.

34   Ibid., 29.
35   Ibid., 30.
36   Ibid.
37   Robert M. Pirsig, *Zen and the Art of Motorcycle Maintenance: An Inquiry into Values* (New York: William Morrow, 1974).
38   Jung Hyun Hwang and Scott Kretchmar, 'Aristotle's Golden mean: Its Implications for the Doping Debate', *Journal of the Philosophy of Sport* 37 (2010): 103.
39   Kim McDonald, 'Long Course For Life', *Triathlon Europe* 346 (2013): 66–7.
40   Jan-Hendrik van den Berg, *De reflex, metabletische, tegelijk maatschappijkritische studie* (Nijkerk: Callenbach, 1973), 170.
41   Lesley A. Howe, 'Remote Sport: Risk and Self-Knowledge in Wilder Spaces', *Journal of the Philosophy of Sport* 35 (2008): 1.
42   Steen Nepper Larsen, 'Becoming a Cyclist – Phenomenological Reflections on Cycling', in *Cycling Philosophy for Everyone: A Philosophical Tour de Force*, eds., Jesús Ilundáin-Agurruza and Michael W. Austin (Chichester, Malden, MA: Wiley-Blackwell, 2010), 38.
43   The new Dutch government, installed in late summer of 2012, has withdrawn the bid until further notice to push back budget deficits.
44   Paul Arnoldussen, *Amsterdam 1928: de Spelen in Nederland* (Amsterdam: Thomas Rap, 2008).
45   Sigmund Loland, 'Outline of an Ecosophy of Sport', 85.
46   Larsen, 'Becoming a Cyclist – Phenomenological Reflections on Cycling', 30.
47   Sloterdijk, *Du mußt dein Leben ändern: Über Anthropotechnik*, 29.
48   James C. Greening, 'A Fresh Perspective: Parkour and the Infinite Potentiality of the Environment' (paper presented at the annual meeting of the International Association for the Philosophy of Sport, Rochester, New York, 8–11 September, 2011).
49   Ibid.
50   Peter Giesen, 'Peter Sloterdijk, Duitse filosoof: Naar de sportschool om de planeet te redden', *De Volkskrant*, April 30, 2011, 7.
51   Sloterdijk, *Du mußt dein Leben ändern: Über Anthropotechnik*, back cover.

12 The Aesthetics of Sport

Stephen Mumford

Sport sees the realization of many aesthetic values.[1] In sports such as gymnastics, ice dance, ski jumping and synchronized swimming, aesthetics are to the fore. Beauty can be found in other sports too, though sometimes it requires an expert eye to see it. The greater one's tactical understanding of football, for instance, the more aesthetic appreciation is available; and the greater one's expertise in baseball, the more one is likely to find its beauty. With some sports, there is more of a struggle to identify the aesthetic elements: in weightlifting and pistol shooting, for instance. But even here it is at least possible for someone to view these sports aesthetically and this no doubt happens. It has to be accepted, however, that not everyone likes sport, let alone likes it from an aesthetic point of view. Whether one sees sport in an aesthetic way can be to a large extent a matter of choice. One can choose to watch it in all sorts of ways, from the partisan fanatic to the educated purist. Those watching the same event may be seeing it in a whole host of ways.

The popularity of sport as a spectator activity must surely be in some degree due to its aesthetic appeal. Perhaps some are watching it because they support one particular athlete or team and want them to win. Others might watch because they have bet on the outcome, and more might be coaches, family members of competitors, journalists or scouts. But many will watch because of the spectacle of sport. It sets up moments of brightly coloured drama replete with some of the glamour of the theatre and circus. Spectators have to be attracted to make their investment of time and money and those sports that are able to produce aesthetic elements regularly will be those that do best.

There are a number of questions we should consider in relation to the aesthetics of sport if we are to advance beyond these starting observations. What are the aesthetic values that sport elicits? Does sport produce aesthetics essentially or merely incidentally? Do different kinds of sport produce different aesthetic values? How do sporting values relate to other values in sport, namely ethical and emotional ones? And how do sport's aesthetics relate it to other aesthetic arenas, art in particular?

In this essay, I will not, however, address the more general and broad questions of aesthetics.[2] I will not consider the objectivity or otherwise of aesthetic judgements, for instance, nor say what I take an aesthetic judgement to be. These questions are too big to resolve here, but also most of the claims to be made about aesthetic judgements in sport can be made regardless of adherence to any particular theory of aesthetics. The following observations should be neutral on that front. All we need really accept is that sport very often is appreciated aesthetically and in a variety of ways.[3] It can also be accepted that standards of taste differ to a greater or lesser extent. Some find no aesthetic pleasure in sports at all while for others it may be their primary aesthetic consumption.

The Possibility of Sporting Aesthetics

There is a view that what makes something a work of art depends at least in part upon 'something the eye cannot descry'.[4] One cannot tell just by looking at or listening to the intrinsic properties of the work whether it is art or not. A pile of bricks at an art gallery may be art while an indistinguishable pile just outside is not.[5] The status of a work as art must depend also, therefore, on some 'nonexhibited characteristic'.[6] We need not go into the exact details of this additional non-visible feature. The general idea suggests, however, that there is something about the context of the art gallery that invites the pile of bricks to be viewed in a certain way: a way that we are not expected to view bricks in the builders' yard. And while the purpose of art is no doubt not solely to provide aesthetic experiences, it is a context in which one may feel it appropriate to do so. As one steps through the door, one crosses a boundary into an aesthetic context.

It is arguable that the same happens in sport. There are a number of boundaries that mark out the sporting context from non-sporting ones and thereby separate sport off from 'normal' life. Christopher Cordner points out various borders between sport and the outside world.[7] Entering a sports stadium is a bit like entering an art gallery. One is there for a different kind of seeing, one that invites an aesthetic perception. One thus enters an 'aesthetic situation' in both the art and sport cases.[8] They are contexts in which the taking of aesthetic pleasure is accepted and encouraged. Hence, one is indeed free to admire the athletes' bodies, an activity that in other contexts might be deemed wholly inappropriate. One is free to enjoy any drama that unfolds in the stadium. There could be other situations with just as many twists and turns – a military campaign, for instance – but that would be wrong to enjoy dramatically. And one can enjoy colours, sounds, even smells that in different contexts would be considered entirely mundane. Other experience of sport are no doubt extraordinary. Sport encourages physical excellences and displays it to spectators. That very exhibition can be taken as an invitation to an aesthetic perception, however, in a way that that same excellence exercised in a training situation does not. The athletes, too, cross a boundary when they enter an arena of public performance.

There are, however, a number of challenges to this view. Paul Ziff, for instance, argues that we should not understand aesthetics to be an aspect of sport because much sport occurs without it.[9] Aesthetics cannot, then, be essential to sport. Certainly there are events or games of sport with little or no aesthetic value. Some sports have ugly players who 'win dirty'. Not every game of football, nor goal within a game, can be beautiful. But we can allow that while still taking the subject of sporting aesthetics seriously. Many sporting events manifestly do have aesthetic value and we can consider what it is about them that makes them so pleasing, as well as what kind of aesthetic value is gained in watching sport.

There may be another concern behind Ziff's position, however. This has been articulated by Ray Elliott, who says: 'The goddess of sport is not Beauty but

Victory, a jealous goddess who demands an absolute homage. Every act performed by the player or athlete must be for the sake of victory, without so much as a side-glance in the direction of beauty.'[10]

The point is that aesthetics is not just inessential to sport, but that it could be a hindrance to it. Beauty should have no place in sport, certainly from the point of view of the athletes. Their aim should always be to win. Creating beauty is never a goal. If it were, it would come at the expense of the sport. One would have effectively stopped playing and started doing something else: making art, for instance.

We can add to this a point from David Aspin on the nature of aesthetic experience.[11] One thought is that an aesthetic perception is a disinterested one. When one views the pile of bricks in the gallery aesthetically, for instance, it is not because one is planning a kitchen extension. And if one understands the essence of sport, with its goddess of Victory, then one should never be viewing it disinterestedly. Sport should be seen as being for the sake of winning. It is about the competition and the striving for mastery of the opponent, not for some detached aesthetic experience.

Now there are some sports fans that purport to see sport in precisely this disinterested kind of way, namely, the purists who watch not because they are fans of one of the teams but because they seek aesthetic experience in sport. But this means, according to Elliott, that they misunderstand sport:

> [...] the ordinary spectator ... does not fully enjoy a football match unless he has an interest in the victory of one side or the other. We have no right to tell him that he ought to adopt a detached aesthetic attitude unless we can assure him that by doing so he will gain more than he loses. In fact, he will gain very little and lose a great deal.[12]

The purist does not gain the full and authentic experience of sport, it is alleged. They miss out on what is essential to it.

Elliot's view can be challenged, however. At the heart of this challenge is what Terry Roberts calls the 'Best equivocation'.[13] The idea that has been presented is that the aesthetic is always incidental in sport, whereas in art it is typically the principal aim. This claim was urged by David Best.[14] In sport, one attempts to score goals, hit runs, reach the finishing tape first, jump the highest and so on. If a spectator happens to find beauty in someone doing these things, then so be it. But the athletes were not aiming to provide aesthetic experiences to others; they were just aiming to win.

Roberts points out, however, that something entirely analogous can be said in the case of the arts and that Best is able to separate sport and art only on the basis of an equivocation. When he talks of the principal aim of sport, he talks about specific sports with their individual lusory (game-playing) goals. When he talks about art aiming at the aesthetic, he is talking of art in general rather than specific art forms. If he did speak of specific arts, we would see that sport and art are in similar positions. Hence, the aim in painting is not to create beauty but to paint a picture, in sculpture it is to make a three-dimensional object, in fiction it is to tell a story, and in music it is to produce harmonious and structured sounds. In no such case in the arts is one aiming directly to produce beauty. Indeed, how could one possibly do so without producing some particular work within a specific form? To that extent, beauty looks to be just as much a by-product of art as it is of sport. If the study of aesthetics has no place in sport, then it has no place in art either. That would make no sense, so with many provisos accepted – that not all sport is beautiful, that not everyone finds sport aesthetically pleasing, that some sports have greater aesthetic values than others, that aesthetics may be incidental, and so on – we can progress on the basis that the consideration of aesthetics in sport is a worthwhile pursuit.

The Aesthetic Hypothesis

Having pointed out the Best equivocation, and seen that in neither sport nor art do its specific instances necessarily aim towards the aesthetic, we can consider next the aim of sport at the general level. We can consider what the purpose of sport is, and compare it with the aims of art in general. A reason to do this is that it brings sport and aesthetics closer than it seemed when we considered its specific instances. Some support will be found for what could be called the aesthetic hypothesis: that *aesthetic considerations are essential to the being of sport and continue to shape its development.*

The aesthetic hypothesis is in clear contrast to Elliott's view, cited above. Elliott's argument suggests that victory is the whole point of sport. But does sport really serve that general purpose? Why would it do so? Was sport created to serve a pre-existing need for victories, and is that the reason we continue to keep it? What would look odd about that claim would be the fact that sport is not a terribly efficient way of producing victory. At least as many competitors gain defeat from sport as victory and for some sports there are far more losers than victors.[15] A game of football might produce one of each, but in a sprint race, for instance, there are usually seven losers for every winner. And in a marathon race there can be thousands of losers.

This point is pushed home by Joseph Kupfer:

> Scoring is not the *raison d'être* of competitive sport. It was not that in virtue of which the sport came to exist or is engaged in. 'The play's the thing' and it includes scoring and winning. Since neither scoring nor winning is the reason or basis for competitive sport, it cannot be its purpose.[16]

It is not as if there was a pre-existing need for goals, for golf balls to be in holes, for darts to pierce boards, and so on. So what was the need that sport satisfied?

At this stage, one does not wish to offer mere *a priori* speculations that might lack any basis in history or sociology. Work on those topics exists. And no doubt the origins of sport are complex and multifactorial. Readers of Bernard Suits might point to the intrinsic pleasure in play and see sport as its codification.[17] According to the aesthetic hypothesis, however, one of the drivers of the development of sport is its ability to provide aesthetic pleasure.

Aesthetic experiences are inherently desired for their intrinsic value. There is one question of why we do sport – to get fit, rich and famous, for instance – but there is another question of why we consume sport as spectators. And arguably, the development of sport has been shaped just as much by the needs of those watching as it has been by the needs of those playing. After all, a desire for competition and fitness could have been satisfied in much simpler ways, and in private too. Sports that have become spectator sports, however, have to compete with others over popularity and one way in which to gain this is to be aesthetically pleasing.

A corroboration of the aesthetic hypothesis, then, would be if rule changes had been selected with aesthetic considerations in mind and whether their success or abandonment was based to an extent on their aesthetic reception. Does a rule change allow a game to flow more freely? Does it excite the spectator? Does it increase the possibility of dramatic tension and release? Does it encourage more aesthetically pleasing bodily forms or does it discourage them?

It cannot be emphasized enough that not all sports are for the benefit of spectators. When someone goes jogging, for instance, or rock climbing, or for a game of squash with a friend, the concern is primarily for the participant's own sphere of interest, whether it be with one's own fitness, personal challenges or social life. But many of the sports that currently flourish do so because of what they offer to those watching and also because of how they adapt to those spectators' needs. Again, not all those needs will be aesthetic, but many are and the development of sports supports this view.

In football, the rule for a defender passing back to the goalkeeper changed so that the ball could no longer be picked up but had to be kicked away. This had the intended consequence of speeding the game up by disallowing a negative but safe tactic that had no aesthetic appeal to the spectator. In cricket, rules were introduced over field placings to stop the field being heavily loaded on one side, down which the bowler could monotonously aim. And Australian rules football, at its very birth, was designed as a spectacle. The game was created somewhat artificially by selecting all the best rules from similar sports that would make the most exciting game to see.

As well as these formal rules, selected on aesthetic grounds, however, the less formal conventions around sport are aimed clearly towards aesthetic enhancements. The shirts of the teams, for instance, which originally had no purpose but to allow the two sides to be distinguished, are now a matter of studied design. An appealing shirt sells to the fans, of course, but there is a much bigger sale to be made. The fans are also buying tickets to the game and TV subscriptions to watch at home. That a sport is a visually pleasing spectacle disposes towards its survival and growth.

As well as considering the very direct and immediate aesthetic values instantiated in sport, in the next section, we should acknowledge that there are many other seemingly peripheral aesthetic enhancements to sport. In football, the lush green grass upon which two teams in beautifully designed contrasting kits play against a spectacular backdrop of colourful and noisy fans, hosted in an architecturally pleasing stadium, all make it an extraordinary experience to the senses. And while some of these factors seem peripheral, they are all part of what looks to be a markedly aesthetic experience of sport.

Who is to say, then, that aesthetic value is not one of the primary aims of sport? There is evidence that the game is shaped to a significant degree by aesthetic considerations. And there is also some plausibility in the idea that aesthetic pleasure is a very basic human need, desired for its own sake, and for which sporting spectacle is one avenue for its satisfaction.

The case for the aesthetic hypothesis would be assisted further if we could show that certain sports, by their very nature, will have tendencies to produce the kind of aesthetic experiences that we have identified. Is there something about sports, embodied in their rules of play, that elicits our aesthetic enjoyment? In the next section, we will look at some distinct types of sport and argue for the types of aesthetic they tend to produce.

Aesthetics in Different Categories of Sport

Different sports facilitate the instantiation of different aesthetic values. How exactly we divide up sports into different kinds is to a large extent an arbitrary matter. Some are clearly more closely related than others, for example, rugby and American football have more in common with each other than with swimming. But the division we make would always be relative to some interest and indeed there is no reason why the basis for division couldn't include aesthetic considerations.

It may help, however, if we start from a division made by Kupfer between different types of sport.[18] We can then progress to another relevant distinction made by Scott Kretchmar and then to consider some of the overarching aesthetic categories for sport.

Kupfer distinguishes three general kinds of sport and we can think of each as producing its own distinctive type of aesthetic. These are sports that are:

1. Quantitative/linear: concerning going the fastest or furthest, highest or heaviest. This will include races of all kinds (running, swimming, cycling), throwing events (discus, shot putt, javelin), jumping events (long, high, pole vault) and weightlifting events.
2. Qualitative/formal: emphasis on style and performance and can be highly aesthetic, including aesthetic considerations in the scoring. A high level of technical ability is usually required in order to manifest those aesthetic qualities (examples include ice dance, synchronized swimming, gymnastics, diving).
3. Competitive: requires the overcoming of an opponent, not just playing to the best of your ability but doing so in the face of opposition, and equally stopping that opposition from playing (football, field hockey, tennis).

It is arguable that the different demands of each sport shape a different kind of accompanying aesthetic. In many sports – those of the first two varieties listed – there is nothing that one can do legally to stop an opponent playing and doing their best. In long jump, for instance, each athlete takes their turn to jump and must be allowed to do so unhindered. And in a 100-metre sprint race, competitors are not allowed to leave their lane and block an opponent, nor squirt a slippery oil on the track ahead of an opponent. In competitive sports, as defined above, it is in contrast an essential part of the game that one hinders the opponent, obviously within certain defined parameters. This feature adds a possible aesthetic dimension to be found in the striving, the tussle. The direct opposition creates the need for tactics of overcoming that concern how one can work around the problems posed by competitors who are adapting to one's moves and trying to counter them at each stage. Thus in football, patterns of play emerge that often require apprehension at a high level of abstraction and which, it can realistically be maintained, have an aesthetic dimension. Sometimes it requires the educated eye to appreciate these tactics, to be able to see the formations, changes of pace and patterns of passing.

Tactics are, of course, possible in other kinds of sport, not just competitive ones. In distance races, for instance, pacing is a tactical issue and each runner will have his or her own plan for the race. And even in short cycling races there are tactics around slipstreaming and timing one's attack so that it comes in the final few metres. In the case of quantitative/linear sports a different kind of aesthetic is often to the fore, however.

Such sports encourage for success the pushing of the human body to its peak of performance. To win the sprint, one must run the fastest. To win the high jump, one must jump higher than all the others and so on. The successful athletes will tend to be those that instantiate the highest aesthetic values because speed, form, extension, suppleness, power, strength and so on, as well as being those that contribute towards athletic success, are those we also admire aesthetically. Why exactly this should be is a matter we can leave to the specialist aestheticians, or perhaps the empirical psychologists. But we do naturally seem to prefer seeing a fast and fluid runner to a slow, irregular and jerky one. Similarly, the form of a body as it arcs over the sandpit in long jump is admired much more than if we saw a cumbersome form make a slow and crater-forming landing in the sand. And being able to throw the javelin far requires both a beautifully toned and muscular body, which itself is considered pleasing, but also a fluid and powerful throwing technique, the motion of which has an additional appeal.

Standards of taste can vary among us, of course, because humanity is itself varied, including our aesthetic sensibilities.[19] But it is perhaps no coincidence that many of the bodily shapes and movements required for competitive success are also replicated in artistic dance, where aesthetic values are even more obviously the aim. Sport creates an environment, therefore, in which the instantiation of aesthetic value is rewarded, not necessarily directly, but because the qualities that tend to athletic success are also ones with a high aesthetic value.

Qualitative/formal sports from Kupfer's classification have been left until last, partly because it is easiest here to make the case for the aesthetic in sport. In cases such as gymnastics, the issue of winners and losers is often secondary for the casual spectator watching on TV. Sport is watched here for relaxing entertainment where the viewer can be lost in contemplation of the amazing physical feats that occur: the incredible twisting and turning, balance, grip, control and comportment.

There will, of course, be some involved in these sports who are highly concerned with the competition and the winning. Among the participants, teams and coaches, a qualitative sport can be just as competitive as any other and fiercely so. But the popularity of such sports among spectators seems bound to have a big aesthetic appeal. And these are the sports that can so easily be represented artistically, in photography and painting (which is not to overlook the slightly different topic of sport represented in art, in which any sport could be the subject).

Kupfer's is only one classification of sports, however, and another division is also worthy of comment in that it has aesthetic relevance. Kretchmar distinguishes E games from T games.[20] E games are based on running through a series of required events. In golf, a series of 18 holes have to be played before the round is complete and in baseball there are nine innings. T games are instead time limited. One plays until time is up, irrespective of how many episodes of skilful interchange have occurred. Football is an obvious example. The game ends after 90 minutes of play, irrespective of how many goals have been scored, passes completed, or cautions issued (there are exceptions such as in cup finals where a winner has to be decided, sometimes by resorting to penalty kicks).

Kretchmar argues that T games are flawed because they permit stalling. A team that is winning can slow the game down to limit the number of skilful interchanges and thereby increase their chance of hanging on for a win. What Kretchmar's analysis does not explain, however, is why T games are often so popular among spectators. Football is by many measures the most popular spectator sport in the world. One could accept Kretchmar's claim that T games are 'flawed' in the sense that they make it easier for the weaker team to win – through limiting the number of skilful interchanges – but this would only be a flaw if one thought the purpose of sport was always to reward the stronger competitor with victory. Instead, an 'underdog' victory can have a high dramatic appeal and for spectators come to represent the struggle against the odds that they face in their own lives. Those lives, as every mortal knows, are also time limited. T sports mirror life, in that respect, and are far from flawed if one accepts aesthetic criteria rather than mere efficiency in determining the strongest competitor. If there is any truth in this interpretation, then we may have further confirmation of the aesthetic hypothesis.

Aesthetic Categories in Sport

We advance now to the aesthetics themselves, setting aside the issue of how different sports tend towards one or another of these aesthetic categories. Given the preceding discussion, we can see a useful division taking shape, which are the first three categories below. To these, a fourth is added that has not yet been discussed.

1. Bodily Motion, Form and Grace
Although the lusory goals of sport are required for the purpose of victory, the attainment of those goals tends to the production of beautiful and gracious bodily forms and movements.[21]

A sporting context permits an admiring gaze upon the human body, a pleasurable admiration in seeing the athlete's exercise of their causal powers.[22] To look admiringly at another's body in other contexts might be considered intrusive or even sexually threatening. Speaking generally, in sport this is not the case and a plausible explanation of this would be that the admiring gaze is an aesthetic one as opposed, for instance, to a sexual one. This is not to deny that beautiful bodies in sport can be exploited in a sexual way, as Charlene Weaving has demonstrated in various places.[23]

An example of an aesthetic category that has attracted detailed scrutiny in the case of sport is grace. One might think of a swimmer's body cutting through the water,[24] a fluid tennis stroke, a smooth running motion and a gymnast perfectly balanced on the beam. But what does such grace actually consist of? Best suggested that grace was a matter of perceived functionality.[25] The graceful athlete was efficient in the manner in which they achieved their lusory goals. There was no wasteful energy expelled on redundant moves, for instance, such as 'extraneous waggles, rolls or jerks'. In reply, however, Cordner pointed out that it is at least possible to be perfectly functional and efficient without having grace, Martina Navratilova's tennis style being cited as an example.[26] Cordner's positive account also looks suspect, however. He spoke of grace consisting in a 'unity of being in the performance'.[27] Apart from it being somewhat vague what this might consist of, it also seems possible to construct counterexamples. A practised professional might easily be able to play a perfectly graceful shot while thinking of that evening's dinner, if they are playing an amateur, for instance. Because such analyses of grace are likely to permit these counterexamples, Paul Davis argues that grace just consists of pleasing superficial appearances.[28] Those movements are graceful that appeal to us and we label graceful. It is not, for instance, as if we could mistakenly find something graceful that in reality was not, just as we mistook fool's gold (iron pyrite) for real gold. Gold has an underlying essence: something that makes it gold beyond its superficial observable qualities. But we cannot say the same for grace. If it seems graceful to us, it is graceful. Such a feature could be considered response-dependent. What makes it graceful is at least in part down to our response to it.

This doesn't answer all the questions about grace. There are various aesthetic categories about which we could say exactly the same. They are all about features that we find immediately pleasing. But what distinguishes them? Isn't there something about grace that is different from sporting drama, for instance? There is still room, it seems, for detailed descriptive work on the various aesthetic categories of sport, even if no such description constitutes an analysis of the relevant concept.

2. Higher-level, Abstract Forms

There is an old theory of aesthetics known as formalism, in which art was seen as an attempt to produce certain abstract forms within the work, forms that had an inherent aesthetic appeal.[29] This is worth mentioning in relation to the second kind of sporting aesthetic category, which concerns patterns of play and forms of tactics, which can be discerned at only a relatively high level of abstraction. Thus, some football fans may see the individual players running and kicking, and follow the movement of the ball, but be missing out on the overall pattern of play because they are unable to understand the game on a higher intellectual level.

An ability to abstract is something that most humans have, however, even if it requires some nurturing. A pattern in play is something that will have to be discerned over an extended space and time. The pattern will develop, involving many players and their movements, sometimes behaving as if they are a single organic entity. Brazil's fourth goal in the 1970 World Cup final provides a good example. The beauty of the goal was to be found in the whole. It was a move that included the full length of the pitch and nine of the team's players were involved. There were immediate and superficial aesthetic properties to be found in the players' bodies, their attractive yellow shirts against the background grass and so on, but arguably the unfolding of the move was a higher aesthetic that could be appreciated only through an intellectual understanding of the game. As with many cases of aesthetic appreciation, it is something that needs to be cultivated and educated. One can learn to see aesthetically through practice and learning. The more one understands the particular sport in question, the more one will be empowered to appreciate it aesthetically.

3. Drama

An even higher level of aesthetic abstraction allows us to appreciate the drama of sport. There are last-second wins when the clock is almost up, unexpected triumphs over tragedy, victory snatched from the jaws of defeat – with its correlated opposite – and so on. Sports fans regularly talk of the drama they find in sport, with the cliché being that sport is 'unscripted theatre'. There are many of the twists and turns to be found in novels, for instance, but here, of course, the drama is real rather than contrived.

This very point has been used by Best to argue that sport is not real drama. Best argues that in theatre it is the character rather than the actor that we see on display.[30] Julius Caesar dies in the play, not the actor who fills the role. The objects of drama are imagined. In sport, however, it is real people who suffer victory and defeat, the occasional sprained muscle or broken leg.

There are two ways in which this claim can be challenged, however. One would have to admit the disanalogy, accepting that the objects of fiction or theatre are imagined and of sport are not, but argue that this difference is not an adequate basis for saying that one activity is real drama and the other isn't. Why concede that it is not real drama just because someone suffered a real defeat instead of only a fictional one such as on the stage? Perhaps one could say that the drama of sport is even more real.

The other response, however, would be to deny the disanalogy.[31] Perhaps when one enters the field of play one is indeed playing a role or character, as if on the stage. Perhaps one has a role in the team that one is expected to live up to. One has to take an adversarial stance towards the opposition, for instance, irrespective of any personal feelings one has towards them. In professional football, for instance, where transfers between teams are quite frequent, players will often come up against personal friends but be sporting adversaries playing just as hard against whoever it is. And just as something of one's own personality may be evident in how one plays that ascribed role within a team, so too, of course, can actors bring something of themselves to the role they play. One actor will play Richard III differently from another, even if given the same directions, and this is why it is a matter of interest to us which actors are in which roles. The case remains open, therefore, that there is aesthetic appreciation of real drama in sport.

4. Innovation and Genius

The aesthetic category that has not yet been discussed is that of innovation, sometimes ascending to the height of genius.

There is a particular aesthetic fascination with innovation.[32] How exactly we define genius is unclear; arguably one thought is that genius should be indefinable. We may think of sporting genius in terms of an exceptional innovator, able to make a major breakthrough in sporting problem solving, or able to make a number of smaller breakthroughs. A couple of examples might be Dick Fosbury, whose 'flop' was a completely novel and effective way of tackling the problem of clearing a high bar, and Johan Cruyff, who first showed the 'Cruyff turn' on the highest stage in football, the 1974 World Cup Finals. The turn was a way of tricking an opponent into thinking a pass was to be played but then turning behind his defensive lunge and dribbling away.

The reason it is worth mentioning innovation as a distinct aesthetic category in sport is because of the following possibility. It seems plausible to think that the Cruyff turn or the Fosbury flop could be replicated in almost every respect. Indeed, the flop was universally adopted in elite-level high jump. Now many of the jumps that have been performed will have been indistinguishable from Fosbury's first and one might be tempted to say that they must therefore be of identical aesthetic value. If one is beautiful, all are, one could say, and beautiful to the same degree. But this is contentious and there may again be 'something the eye cannot descry' that is involved. The context of being the first such performance – the moment of innovation – seems to add aesthetic value to the original instance. Similarly, one can argue that the original Mona Lisa has a higher aesthetic value than all the copies (even if indistinguishable) simply because it is the original.

Sport involves in many instances the overcoming of obstacles. There are distances to be run, hurdles to be surmounted (literally) and opponents in the way of the goal. Sheer athletic fitness suffices for a lot of the obstacles but many sports involve problem solving. And it is here that the innovator can gain an advantage with an unexpected solution: a new move or tactic. And if the innovation gains a clear advantage that revolutionizes the way the game is played, then we start to talk in terms of sporting genius.

Aesthetics and Other Values

Aesthetics are not the only values to be found within the domain of sport. We can also point to the many ethical values at play. There is cheating and various other vices as well as sporting virtues. Another area of value is the emotions.

Sport is very frequently emotionally engaging, sometimes strikingly so, leading to great joy or deep sorrow. There is a clear emotional value to sport. It is worth considering how these other domains of value relate to the aesthetic domain. Do they enhance or interfere with its aesthetic value?

In the case of ethics, there is a strong case for the argument that moral vice can detract from aesthetic value in sport and moral virtue can enhance it. The argument for this comes from the examples of known cheating being revealed that thereby ruin the aesthetic of the event. Ben Johnson was believed to have won Olympic gold in 1988, for instance, and for a few days the race was widely admired. When the doping test eventually revealed Johnson to have used performance-enhancing drugs, the aesthetic of his race was destroyed. In other circumstances, the motion of his smooth and powerful run would have been attributed some of the highest aesthetic value but his cheating seemed to immediately invalidate it. Cheating is not the only case of this nature, however. A footballing triumph for a club thought to be run by a deeply immoral owner is unlikely to be appreciated aesthetically by any neutral spectator. The other side of this would be the virtuous, heroic win, which seems all the more beautiful. When this was discussed elsewhere,[33] the example given was the comeback from cancer of Lance Armstrong to win the Tour de France cycle race, which was thus perceived to be aesthetically enhanced as a result. The fact that since then the opposite has become apparent only serves to confirm the thesis. Armstrong has now admitted to routine drug use to win his titles and the aesthetic value of his races, once enhanced, now seems virtually negated to zero.

The idea that ethical considerations can detract from or enhance aesthetic value is known in mainstream aesthetics, though with remaining controversy.[34] One might think of the Leni Riefenstahl films *Triumph of the Will* (1934) and *Olympia* (1936), which superficially have a high artistic value but when understood as Nazi propaganda are seen in a less favourable light.[35]

The other sphere of value mentioned was emotional, where sport clearly has a significant capacity for the production of both positive and negative emotional responses. An interesting question concerns whether the aesthetic perception of sport hinders or enhances the possibility of an emotional engagement. Similarly, would an emotional engagement with sport hinder or enhance its aesthetic appreciation?

Recent work suggests that on the whole there is a trade-off to be made.[36] The partisan supporter will have a deep emotional engagement in sport but at the cost of experiencing it aesthetically. The beauty of sport is secondary to the victory, and any beauty enjoyed is only in one's own side's victory. On the other hand, the purist who watches sport aesthetically, without an interest in who wins and who loses, is thereby unable to gain the deep emotional experiences of the partisan. This is why Elliott, in the passage quoted above, thinks that purists will lose a lot if they adopt a detached aesthetic attitude to sport. Elliott's point can be challenged, however. The partisan, too, suffers a loss: a loss of potential aesthetic experience.

The trade-off between aesthetic experience and emotional involvement is not, however, absolute. The most sublime moment of supreme beauty may come from the dramatic win. When that happens, one must be a partisan – it is a precondition – but one also has a deep aesthetic appreciation of the sport in that moment. The aesthetic experiences of partisans may be fewer, but they could be the ones who have the deepest aesthetic experiences.

Sport and Art

Thus far the question of whether sport is art has been deliberately avoided. There was a time when this was a matter of healthy debate,[37] though it is increasingly being seen as a rather uninteresting or irrelevant question. Certainly, that sport contains aesthetic values is in no sense dependent upon it having any status as art. Many things are valuable aesthetically without being art, such as an evening sunset, birdsong or a newborn baby. And we will happily talk about the aesthetic properties of these things regardless of them lacking the status of art. It is not, therefore, as if sport requires the status of art for its aesthetics to be validated. They are valid independently and sport's separation from art perhaps makes it a more important topic for aesthetics. It is a *sui generis* aesthetic domain in its own right, rather than *qua* art.

There are, nevertheless, arguments to the effect that sport is not and never could be art. We have encountered already some of the points. Best, for instance, urged that the drama of sport was not real and that the principal aim of sport was winning rather than the aesthetic. He has other arguments besides, claiming that art allows for the possibility of expression of a conception of one's life situation.[38] How can sport do this? What does it express? What is it about? Furthermore, in art the end can never be fully separated from the means of achieving it. What is achieved in Sergei Prokofiev's *Lieutenant Kijé* could not have been achieved in any other way than that piece of music. In sport, however, there is a clear means-end separation. The end is to score a goal, for instance, and they all count the same whether they are beautiful or ugly goals.

It is possible to contend these points. Maybe at a suitably high enough level of abstraction, sport is about something and indeed expresses something about our life situation: as embodied, physically empowered agents, for instance. But, again, it is not necessary to resolve this debate. Art and sport are clearly different forms of social practice, occupying different spaces in human social history.[39] They are certainly distinct but that distinctness may come down to relatively trivial and contingent facts about our social practices rather than any profound philosophical cleavage.

It should be clear from the above that there are many worthy areas of investigation in the aesthetics of sport. Irrespective of discussions in the philosophy of art, sport seems to present a distinct area of aesthetics, one that raises numerous questions about the nature of human culture. That we find sport aesthetically pleasing is interesting enough in its own right. But that we go to such lengths to provide this pleasure is perhaps a finding of even greater significance and profundity.

Notes

1   Hans Gumbrecht, *In Praise of Athletic Beauty* (Cambridge, MA: Belknap Press, 2006).

2   Alan Goldman, 'The Aesthetic', in *The Routledge Companion to Aesthetics*, 2nd ed., eds., Berys Gaut and Dominic McIver Lopes (London: Routledge, 2005), 255–66; and Stephen Davies, *Definitions of Art* (Ithaca: Cornell University Press, 1991).

3   Wesley Cooper, 'Do Sports Have an Aesthetic Aspect?', *Journal of the Philosophy of Sport* 5 (1978): 51–5.

4   Arthur Danto, 'The Artworld', *Journal of Philosophy* 61 (1964): 580.

5   Jeffrey Wieand, 'Perceptually Indistinguishable Objects', in *Institutions of Art: Reconsiderations of George Dickie's Philosophy*, ed., Robert Yanal (University Park: Pennsylvania State University Press, 1994), 39–49.

6   George Dickie, *Art and The Aesthetic* (Ithaca: Cornell University Press, 1974), 37.

7   Christopher Cordner, 'Differences Between Art and Sport', in *Philosophic Inquiry in Sport*, eds., William J. Morgan and Klaus V. Meier (Champaign, IL: Human Kinetics, 1988), 425–36.

8   Marjorie Fisher, 'Sport as an Aesthetic Situation', in *Sport and the Body: A Philosophical Symposium*, ed., Ellen Gerber (Philadelphia: Lea and Febiger, 1974), 318.

9   Paul Ziff, 'A Fine Forehand', *Journal of the Philosophy of Sport* 1 (1974): 92–109.

10 Ray Elliott, 'Aesthetics and Sport', in *Readings in the Aesthetics of Sport*, eds., H. Whiting and D. Masterson (London: Lepus, 1974), 111.

11 David Aspin, 'Sport and the Concept of "The Aesthetic"', in *Readings in the Aesthetics of Sport*, eds., H. Whiting and D. Masterson (London: Lepus, 1974), 117–37.

12 Elliott, 'Aesthetic and Sport', 110.

13 Terry Roberts, 'Sport, Art, and Particularity: the Best Equivocation', *Journal of the Philosophy of Sport* 13 (1986): 49–63.

14 David Best, 'The Aesthetic in Sport', *British Journal of Aesthetics* 14 (1974): 197–213.

15 Anthony Skillen, 'Sport is for Losers', in *Ethics and Sport*, eds., Mike McNamee and Jim Parry (London: Routledge, 1988), 169–81.

16 Joseph Kupfer, 'Sport – the Body Electric', in *Philosophic Inquiry in Sport*, eds. William J. Morgan and Klaus V. Meier (Champaign, IL: Human Kinetics, 1988), 460.

17 Bernard Suits, *The Grasshopper: Games, Life, and Utopia* (Peterborough, ON: Broadview Press, 2005).

18 Kupfer, 'Sport – the Body Electric'.

19 David Hume, 'On the Standard of Taste', in *Essays, Moral, Political and Literary*, ed. Eugene Miller (Indianapolis, IL: Liberty Fund, 1987), 226–49.

20 Scott Kretchmar, 'Game Flaws', *Journal of the Philosophy of Sport* 32 (2005): 36–44.

21 V. Hohler, 'The Beauty of Motion', in *Readings in the Aesthetics of Sport*, eds., H. Whiting and D. Masterson (London: Lepus, 1974), 49–56' and David Best, *Philosophy and Human Movement* (London: George Allen and Unwin, 1978).

22 Stephen Mumford, *Watching Sport: Aesthetics, Ethics and Emotion* (London: Routledge, 2011), ch. 14.

23 Charlene Weaving, 'Unraveling the Ideological Concept of the Female Athlete: A Connection Between Sex and Sport', in *Philosophical Perspectives on Gender and Sport*, eds., Paul Davis and Charlene Weaving (London: Routledge, 2010), 83–94; 'Buns of Gold, Silver, and Bronze: A Critical Analysis of the State of Olympic Women's Beach Volleyball', in *Olympics and Philosophy*, eds., Michael Austin and Heather Reid (Lexington, KY: University Press of Kentucky, 2012), 370–92; and Pam Sailors, Sarah Teetzel and Charlene Weaving, 'No Net Gain: A Critique of Media Representation of Women's Olympic Beach Volleyball', *Feminist Media Studies* 12 (2012): 1–5.

24 Armando Vilas Boas and Teresa Oliveira Lacerda, *Water/Água* (Porto: Porto University Faculty of Sport, 2006).

25 Best, 'The Aesthetic in Sport', 204.
26 Christopher Cordner, 'Grace and Functionality', *British Journal of Aesthetics* 24 (1984): 305.
27 Ibid., 308.
28 Paul Davis, 'Issues of Immediacy and Deferral in Cordner's Theory of Grace', *Journal of the Philosophy of Sport* 28 (2001): 89–95.
29 Immanuel Kant, *Critique of Judgement* [1790], trans. James Meredith (Oxford: Oxford University Press, 2007).
30 Best, 'The Aesthetic in Sport'.
31 Mumford, *Watching Sport: Aesthetics, Ethics and Emotion* ch. 6.
32 Teresa Oliveira Lacerda and Stephen Mumford, 'The Genius in Art and in Sport: A Contribution to the Investigation of Aesthetics of Sport', *Journal of the Philosophy of Sport* 37 (2010): 182–93.
33 Mumford, *Watching Sport*, 75.
34 See Berys Gaut, 'The Ethical Criticism of Art', in *Aesthetics and Ethics: Essays at the Intersection*, ed., Jerrold Levinson (Cambridge: Cambridge University Press, 1998), 182–203; and *Art, Emotion and Ethics* (Oxford: Oxford University Press, 2007).
35 Mary Devereaux, 'Beauty and Evil: the case of Leni Riefenstahl's *Triumph of the Will*', in *Aesthetics and Ethics: Essays at the Intersection*, ed., Jerrold Levinson (Cambridge: Cambridge University Press, 1998), 227–56.
36 Stephen Mumford, 'Emotions and Aesthetics: an Inevitable Trade-off?', *Journal of the Philosophy of Sport* 39 (2012): 267–79.
37 David Best, 'Sport is Not Art', in *Philosophic Inquiry in Sport*, eds., William J. Morgan and Klaus V. Meier (Champaign, IL: Human Kinetics, 1988), 527–39; and Geoffrey Gaskin and Don Masterson, 'The Work of Art in Sport', in *Readings in the Aesthetics of Sport*, eds., H. Whiting and D. Masterson (London: Lepus, 1974), 139–60.
38 Best, 'The Aesthetic in Sport'.
39 Monroe Beardsley, 'Is Art Essentially Institutional?', in *Culture and Art*, ed., Lars Aagaard-Mogensen (Atlantic Highlands, NJ: Humanities Press, 1976), 194–209; Robert Yanal, 'The Institutional Theory of Art', in *The Encyclopedia of Aesthetics*, ed., Michael Kelly (Oxford: Oxford University Press, 1988), 508–12; and Larry Shiner, *Invention of Art: A Cultural History* (Chicago: Chicago University Press, 2001).

13 Sporting Knowledge

Gunnar Breivik

The problem of knowledge has been discussed in philosophy since Early Greek philosophy. Central problems were raised by Plato and Aristotle that have been at the core of *epistemology* as one of the central philosophical disciplines. The goal of the Greek philosophers was to secure timeless truths – *episteme* – as opposed to mere opinions among people – *doxa*. Scepticism was a serious challenge in Greek philosophy as well as modern philosophy. René Descartes' basic aim was to secure true knowledge that could withstand scepticism. The rationalists (Descartes, Gottfried Leibniz, Baruch Spinoza) and empiricists (John Locke, George Berkeley, David Hume) discussed whether perception or thinking could best provide true knowledge. Also, in present-day discussions in epistemology one of the most important tasks is to defend knowledge against the threat of scepticism.[1]

The discussion of knowledge in epistemology takes knowledge in a narrow sense, mostly centred around problems relating to theoretical or propositional knowledge. However, Aristotle discussed *praxis* and *techné* as knowledge forms. The practical knowledge of politics and the technical knowledge displayed in art and handicraft are different from theoretical knowledge. In modern philosophy, the practical knowledge forms have received more attention. The discussion of 'knowing how' versus 'knowing that' in analytic philosophy, as well as the discussion of various forms of practical knowledge in phenomenology, have widened the perspective of knowledge and introduced a broader conceptualization.

Sport is a practical activity and it is no surprise that the discussion of theoretical epistemological problems in sport has received little attention. Sporting knowledge is, however, strongly related to practical knowledge, to the discussion of know-how, learning and skill. Therefore, this essay will deal mostly with the various forms of practical knowledge displayed in sports. However, with the strong development of sport sciences since the 1970s, the discussion of theoretical knowledge has become more important to sport philosophers, mostly as a 'philosophy of sport sciences'. In this essay, I will therefore start with a short discussion of the development of sport sciences and then go into the more specific problems relating to practical sporting knowledge.

Conceptual Clarification

Epistemology can be defined as 'the study of the nature of knowledge and justification; specifically the study of a) the defining features, b) the substantive conditions, and c) the limits of knowledge and justification'.[2] This general definition allows for different kinds of knowledge. Propositional knowledge states that something is so and so. This type of knowledge may be empirical (a posteriori) or logical and mathematical (a priori) knowledge. Philosophers also mostly accept knowledge that is non-propositional, like knowledge *by acquaintance* or *by direct awareness*. Some philosophers, like Robert Audi, distinguish between knowledge *de dicto*, about propositions and facts, and knowledge *de re*, about objects and their properties.[3] In addition, an important form of knowledge is self-knowledge or knowledge *de se*. A special kind of knowledge, which is important in sport, is knowledge of *how to do* something.[4]

This means that as a sportsperson I have direct knowledge of myself, who I am, my abilities and so on (knowledge *de se*). Furthermore, I know how to do things in my sport, I have certain sporting skills (know-how). I also have direct knowledge of my sports equipment (knowledge *de re*). I also have direct knowledge of fellow athletes (knowledge by acquaintance). I also know things about my sport, how it developed, its rules and so on (propositional knowledge). I also have a lot of experience, both episodic memories of past events and experiences, that predisposes me to behave in certain ways in different situations. As we will see later, a sportsperson also has a lot of background knowledge that lets him or her find meaning and behave in relevant ways in different situations. If one looks at sports today, especially at a higher level of sports, one finds a lot of knowledge developed by scientific research and, not to forget, thousands of hours of experience, accumulated by athletes, their coaches, leaders, service people, team doctors and so on.

Sporting knowledge is thus diverse and of many kinds. Some of the knowledge is explicit, but much is implicit or tacit. In what follows, I will not be able to cover the whole domain of sporting knowledge, so I have selected some of the most relevant topics and issues. Since sport is a practical bodily activity, it is reasonable that the main focus be practical knowledge.

1. Theoretical Knowledge

The Development of Sport Scientific Knowledge

According to John Massengale and Richard Swanson,[5] the various sport scientific sub-disciplines had their origins towards the end of the 19th century, their first organizational events took place after the Second World War, and the development of the specific sub-disciplines with their international organizations finally happened in the late 1960s and early 1970s. During the 1960s, many sport scientific sub-disciplines were developed and gained some independence and identity in relation to their mother disciplines (sport psychology, sport sociology, exercise and sport physiology and so on). At the Pre-Olympic Scientific Congress before the Munich Olympics of 1972, the German philosopher Hans Lenk gave a presentation on the philosophy of sport as a field of study[6] and described the quite different philosophical interpretations of sport by philosophers, authors and commentators. Shortly after the Munich conference, *The Philosophic Society for the Study of Sport* was founded in the United States in 1973 and the first scholarly sport philosophy journal, the *Journal of Philosophy of Sport*, appeared a year later.

From the 1970s onward, sports sciences developed differently in different countries. In some countries they were organized as a specialty or a sub-discipline of a mother discipline. In other countries specific sport scientific schools were set up, educating people to various professions, like sport manager, sport psychologist, sports coach, outdoor life instructor, physical education teacher, researcher, fitness instructor and so on.

As sport sciences were developed in teaching as well as research, at colleges and universities in various countries in the 1980s, the need for clear paradigms and organizational efficiency became pressing. In this regard, Karl Newell made an important distinction between two fundamental types of knowledge, called 'declarative' and 'procedural'.[7] Declarative knowledge encompasses theoretical knowledge related to activity-cognate sub-disciplines, but also to practitioner knowledge, which 'is associated with the role of a specific professional activity (such as teaching, coaching, etc.) and might be viewed generally as practical competence'.[8] Procedural knowledge is related to what one can execute as a practical act or behaviour. We will come back to this type of knowledge later.

The search for relevant paradigms also included efforts to counteract the increasing split between different sub-disciplines and the separation of theory and practice. Roland Renson discussed various models in the United States, France, Germany, Great Britain and the Low Countries, and suggested an integrated model for the 'Study of Man in Movement'.[9] Renson's idea was to include sport, play, work and exercise into the new integrated science of *kinanthropology* and he distinguished between several cross-disciplinary areas like developmental, differential, social-cultural, clinical and agogical approaches and connected this with a practice-based or professional application. Since these efforts in the early 1990s, it seems that the sport-related programmes at university level have developed in different directions. In some countries, many practice- and skill-based knowledge areas have been outsourced to practical experts. Activity-related research has since then lost its academic foundation.

In general science as well as in sport sciences, the standard account of knowledge has been the model developed in relation to the most advanced natural sciences, like physics. In the standard account, knowledge is defined as 'justified true belief'. It holds, according to Jonathan Dancy, that 'a knows that p if and only if 1) p, 2) a believes that p, 3) a's belief that p is justified'.[10] During the 19th century, the goal of the natural sciences was to establish true objective knowledge by verification of eternal causal laws. In the 20th century, Karl Popper, Thomas Kuhn, Imre Lakatos and others contributed to more contextual views of science and accepted the differences between natural sciences, social sciences and humanities. Parallel developments in philosophy, epistemology and theory of science led to views amenable to relativism, constructivism and even deconstructive theories.[11] We see the results of this development in two recent books that show that philosophy of science has now entered the philosophic discussion of sport. In *Philosophy and the Sciences of Exercise, Health and Sport*, edited by Mike McNamee, scholars from various disciplines and fields of study discuss various problems in the philosophy of science in relation to sport.[12]

The most encompassing discussion of philosophy of science in relation to sport sciences has been presented by Graham McFee in his book *Ethics, Knowledge and Truth in Sports Research*.[13] It deserves a short discussion. McFee's book has a special focus on social sciences and humanities. He rejects 'an ahistorical and universal "one right answer" conception of truth which drives many scientistic misconceptions concerning research into human situations, including setting inappropriate goals for social science'.[14] McFee discards both scientism and postmodernism and instead, inspired by Ludwig Wittgenstein, he develops *contextualism* as his position. From a contextualist perspective, the search for truth is meaningful, but only relative to a certain social and historical context. For instance, scoring a goal in football is only meaningful relative to a context where football is developed in a certain way to make the scoring of goals meaningful and true.

For McFee, explanation in social sciences and humanities takes the form of intentional explanations: 'The intentional explanation of an event depends on how the event is appropriately characterized (and such like) by its agent.'[15] Therefore the 'world' of social sciences is not determined by exceptionless laws and strict causality, where one can predict future events on the basis of these laws. Whereas in natural sciences one can set up a finite set of causal factors to explain what happened, such a thing is impossible in social sciences. McFee's position leads to a form of naturalism, which means that persons must be studied in natural contexts. More important than a distinction between quantitative and qualitative methods is a distinction between those who take people seriously as research subjects and those who do not.

2. Practical Knowledge
Sport Philosophy and Knowledge: the Beginnings

The connection between sport and knowledge has a background in Greek ideas. In the incipient sport philosophy of the 1970s the subject was raised again by several authors.

In his article 'A Fine Forehand', Paul Ziff raised some questions that Margaret Steel and Spencer Wertz later developed and tried to answer.[16] Ziff asked us to imagine a coach that tells a tennis player that he is not bending his knees enough when hitting a forehand. In many cases, athletes seem not to be aware of, or not know precisely, their bodily position and where their limbs are. How is it with this 'knowledge without observation'? How do players manage to remember the positions of their body?

Steel went directly into the problem of what is happening when we learn a new sport.[17] She distinguished between 'inductive learning' and 'learning by exemplars'. She discarded the inductive model because it is unable to analyse the totality of a technique. Instead she used Kuhn's idea of paradigms and maintained that we learn a sport in a similar way to how we learn a paradigm in science. In order to learn a science, one must identify the specific science and its disciplinary matrix, and one must be presented with an exemplar of the practice of such science. Similarly, to learn a sport one needs to learn what the sport is about, its paradigmatic totality and what it means to take part in the sport. There is, therefore, a distinction between the specific movements, skills and techniques that one must learn and the totality of a performance as an instance of that sport. During the process, the learner must be guided by 'gestalts' presented by the instructor or other sportspersons as role models. Accordingly, 'sports and games are acquired by demonstration, and not by teaching in the sense of being told'.[18] In contrast to science, knowledge in sport is not knowledge of facts but rather of gestalts and processes.

Wertz followed up on the questions posed by Ziff and Steel.[19] Wertz distinguished between two theories about knowledge in sport. The 'result theory' is used when players only look at whether they succeed in what they aim to do. The other theory is called the 'feel theory'. Here the focus is on the feeling one has when executing a movement. Some athletes try to memorize this feeling in order to succeed over time. Wertz refers to Timothy Gallwey and examples from good tennis players who focus on feeling rather than result. But this feeling is not an inner feeling. It is not like, say, the feeling of confidence. It is the feeling of a bodily movement. There is, thus, a difference between an emotional feeling and a bodily feeling. The bodily feeling, in turn, can be a perceptual feeling or a feeling as a sensation. In contrast to the more specific sensation, say in one's hand, the perceptual feeling is a totality, a gestalt. Wertz here followed Steel and the idea of a paradigmatic learning by exemplars. He called this 'the skill model'.

Ziff, Steel and Wertz in various ways brought the practitioner into view and looked at how we come to know a sport and become proficient in it. Scott Kretchmar then brought a new twist to the discussion.[20] He argued that, instead of being absorbed in concrete involvement, 'athletes commonly achieve a uniquely human distance from their sport environment by reason of abstract thinking engaged in by these performers during play'.[21] According to Kretchmar, human behaviour is characterized by intentional activity where we can distance ourselves from the immediate surroundings and focus on certain objects, goals or things to do, and thereby open up a space of possibilities for thinking and action. This opening up of possibilities is developed on the background of absorption. Thus 'there is nothing inherently incompatible between spontaneous, "thought-less" play and distancing'.[22] Kretchmar builds on Martin Buber, Maurice Merleau-Ponty and Michael Polanyi, and discusses especially how athletes receive 'multiple invitations to act' and how distancing makes possible the most relevant and most functional choices, among these invitations. Kretchmar seems to argue for a form of 'thinking' in sports practices that is of its own kind. 'Distancing, it was shown, does not necessarily produce knowledge. Nor does it inherently beg for the use of language. The "medium of exchange" in sport is "feel," and meaningful distinctions in this realm typically outrun any verbal ability to refer to them.'[23] Accordingly, Kretchmar maintains that athletes have their own 'brand of thinking'. It is obvious that this thinking does not result in knowledge of the common kind. It rather seems to be a sort of thinking in doing or thinking in playing.

'Knowing that' and 'Knowing How': Gilbert Ryle as Sport Philosopher

The sport philosophy authors of the 1970s who wrote about knowledge in sport already had access to the works of Ryle and Polanyi. In his book *The Concept of Mind*, Ryle made the important distinction between *knowing how* and *knowing that*.[24] His point of departure is ordinary life. Whereas science and philosophy typically discuss the nature, source and credentials of theories, in ordinary life 'we are much more concerned with people's competencies than with their cognitive repertoires'.[25] When we describe people as knowing how to do something, we normally imply that they perform well, that they perform correctly or efficiently. According to what Ryle called the *intellectualist legend*, knowing how could be assimilated to knowing that 'by arguing that intelligent performance involves the observance of rules, or the application of criteria'.[26] This means that an agent first has to go through an inner mental operation producing maxims or rules for what to do and then apply these rules in the execution of the performance. Ryle criticizes this view by maintaining that many performances, for instance jokes, show intelligence but no rules. More importantly, the idea of inner operations in accordance with rules would lead to an endless regress since in order to perform the inner operation correctly one would need new rules in order to perform the inner operation right. Therefore, Ryle concludes: 'Efficient practice precedes the theory of it; methodologies presuppose the application of methods.'[27]

Performing something intelligently, therefore, does not mean first considering rules or prescriptions and then executing it according to the rules. Ryle gives the example of learning to play chess where a novice would gradually, with the help of an instructor, learn the rules and become skilled. He might then play without being aware of the rules or thinking about them at all. 'At this stage he might even have lost his former ability to cite the rules. If asked to instruct another beginner, he might have forgotten how to state the rules and he would show the beginner how to play only by himself making the correct moves and cancelling the beginner's false moves.'[28] This means that a person's ability to play chess is verified by his playing chess and not by hidden operations in his or her head or whether he is able to describe the rules. Ryle does not deny that one can have inner thoughts, inner operations of the mind, but he maintains that the inner operation has its own success criteria.

Ryle also makes a distinction between *habit* and *intelligent practice*. 'It is of the essence of merely habitual practices that one performance is a replica of its predecessors. It is of the essence of intelligent practices that one performance is modified by its predecessors. The agent is learning.'[29] This is typical for elite sport since athletes are all the time trying to *optimize* their performance in contrast to daily life where *satisficing*, showing acceptable performance, is good enough to get by.

Another important distinction is between theory and practice. 'A man knowing little or nothing of medical science could not be a good surgeon, but excellence at surgery is not the same thing as knowledge of medical science; nor is it the product of it.'[30] The surgeon must have learned by theory and by practice. One may be good at practising but bad at theorizing and vice versa.

Both knowing how and knowing that come from learning, but not in the same way. 'Learning *how* or improving in ability is not like learning *that* or acquiring information. Truths can be imparted, procedures can only be inculcated, and while inculcation is a gradual process, imparting is relatively sudden. It makes sense to ask at what moment someone became apprised of a truth, but not to ask at what moment someone acquired a skill.'[31] To have a skill or be skilled is thus to have acquired a stable disposition to perform an act at a certain level. To be skilled admits of grades, but normally higher levels are implied.

Michael Polanyi: Personal Knowledge

After Ryle had made the distinction between knowing how and knowing that, Polanyi introduced the distinction between *personal* or *tacit knowledge* as opposed to *objective* or *scientific knowledge*. Polanyi criticized the traditional objective view of knowledge and maintained that even in the natural sciences there is a 'personal participation of the knower in all acts of understanding'.[32] According to Polanyi, this does not make science subjective, but it means that the subject relates to the objective world with passion, interest and the indeterminacy and probabilities that such a relation entails. It is, however, on the personal knowledge that is displayed in the practice of skills that Polanyi makes a lasting contribution.

Polanyi introduces the idea of unconscious rules that has been much discussed recently. He maintains that 'the aim of skilful performance is achieved by the observance of rules which are not known as such to the person who is following them'.[33] For instance, the swimmer adheres to the rules and laws of nature that must be followed if one wants to keep oneself afloat and move forward through the water. Even better known is the example of cycling, used by Peter Hopsicker and others. According to Polanyi, cyclists observe rules unknown to themselves. 'When he starts falling to the right he turns the handlebars to the right, so that the course of the bicycle is deflected along a curve towards the right.'[34] But this kind of rule is different from a rule that can be obtained by a biomechanical analysis, like 'for a given angle of imbalance the curvature of each winding is inversely proportional to the square of the speed at which the cyclist is proceeding'.[35] The cyclist does not know this last analysis or at least does not follow the result of the analysis. A biomechanical analysis can be useful but it does not determine how to execute the act of bicycling. Such analysis can at best be integrated with the practice.

Especially relevant for the discussion of performance in sports is Polanyi's distinction between two types of awareness: 'When we use a hammer to drive in a nail, we attend to both nail and hammer, *but in a different way*. We watch the effect of our strokes on the nail and try to wield the hammer so as to hit the nail most effectively.' By executing the stroke 'I have a *subsidiary awareness* of the feeling in the palm of my hand which is merged into my *focal awareness* of my driving in the nail'.[36] The feeling in the palm of the hand is subsidiary and thus instrumental in bringing about what the person focuses on and aims at. There is thus a *from-to* movement of one's awareness, away from the subsidiary to the focal. Polanyi then extends this distinction to the relation between the body and the surrounding world. The hammer or the blind person's stick is an extension of the body and it may be experienced as parts of the body. Polanyi says that 'We pour ourselves out into them and assimilate them as parts of our own existence. We accept them existentially by dwelling in them.'[37] But Polanyi later adds that through this process we render these instruments unconscious. We become unconscious of how we use a racquet in tennis. But we become conscious of the target. Thus, we have three factors operating: the knower, the focal targets and the subsidiary particulars. Polanyi calls it *dwelling* when the knower has a tacit awareness of the subsidiaries and a focus on the target or purpose of the movement. If there is a focus on subsidiaries the performance breaks down, which happens, for example, when a pianist starts watching his fingers.

But dwelling is not enough. 'Moving to higher levels of skilful performance requires one to move beyond dwelling within the triad of subsidiary awareness, focal targets and personal integration. A conscious effort is needed to acquire knowledge and skilfully apply it.'[38] In order to reach higher performance levels, one needs goal-directed striving by a combination of intuition, imagination and ideas. 'Through intentional striving by performers, the imagination actively casts forth potential ideas and solutions to confronted challenges. This latter mechanism is catalyzed through one's intuition which spontaneously integrates subsidiaries to create explicit solutions.'[39] Thus, Polanyi has a room for tacit immediate absorption as well as creative imagination and conscious striving.

A Combination of Knowing How and Knowing That? Sigmund Loland and the Example of Alpine Skiing

The *knowing that* perspective uses theoretical knowledge to explain sport performance, whereas personal *knowing how* may help explain to the athlete why some performances succeed or fail. Can both types of knowledge be combined? Loland has presented an example of a possible combination with a demonstration from Alpine skiing.[40]

Alpine skiers have personal 'inner' experiences but their performance can also be analysed from 'the outside', by coaches with video cameras. Loland asks us to 'Imagine watching a skilled skier carving round, harmonious turns down a steep mountainside'.[41] The skier demonstrates good skiing technique. According to Loland, there are two alternative approaches to understanding movements of this kind: an analytic approach and a holistic approach. The analytic approach is the one of natural science with its claim to objective knowledge. The other is the holistic approach, which makes reference to the subjective experience of the skier. In contrast to the meristic view of analytic science, where a whole is just the sum of its parts, the whole in the holistic approach is a gestalt, which is more than the sum of its parts. In contrast to the theoretical mechanical laws of natural science, phenomenologists like Merleau-Ponty and Hubert Dreyfus are better equipped to give a description of the 'know-how' of the skilled skier. But the holistic view also has its limitations, according to Loland, since holists are not able to present theories that are open to empirical testing and other requirements of traditional scientific methodology. Holistic findings, therefore, need to be discussed and defended on the basis of rational arguments. One could think that the two approaches complement each other or are able to be integrated into a broader framework. Instead, Loland presents them as alternative positions with distinct methodologies inside what he calls an open possibilist framework.

1. Phenomenological Knowledge

Martin Heidegger and Knowledge

In addition to Ryle and other analytical approaches to knowing how, many philosophers in the phenomenological tradition have discussed the problem of knowledge in relation to practical activities like sports. A recent book, *Phenomenological Approaches to Sport*, edited by Irena Martínková and Jim Parry, shows the many new approaches to sport philosophy coming from phenomenology.[42] The works of Heidegger and Merleau-Ponty have many implications for sporting knowledge.

Husserl is the founder of phenomenology.[43] Husserl wanted to develop an exact science where the goal was to give a precise description of the essential structures (*das Wesen*) of the phenomena that showed themselves to the subject. The phenomenological description was obtained by moving away from the empirical reality and the individual variations of phenomena, and concentrating only on the essences (*eidetic reduction*) presenting themselves to the intentional subject. Instead of causal explanations, phenomenologists wanted to give precise descriptions of phenomena, of their relations and meaning.

Building on Husserl, Heidegger wanted to describe the basic structures of human existence, since the human being is the entry point to an understanding of the world as such. Knowledge, whatever it is about, is always human knowledge and not God's knowledge or animal knowledge.

Heidegger defined the human mode of being (*Dasein*) as *being-in-the-world*, thereby indicating the strong bond between humans and the environing world.[44] Heidegger's goal in his early philosophy was to reach an understanding of the basic ontological structures of the human being-in-the-world. One of these basic structures is *understanding* (*verstehen*), since humans always have an understanding of their situation in the world. The understanding is directed towards the future, since the goal is to take care of oneself in relation to what comes. By looking into the future, being aware of the past and relating to the present, the human being carries his or her life project towards death. Heidegger shows how the understanding is linked to human existence and thus defined by deep interests. We can call this knowledge a basic *existential knowledge* since it means that we understand our own existence in the world as 'being towards death'. According to Heidegger, one can hide from this insight and live like all the others do in their everyday existence, or one can live authentically, facing death and realizing one's deepest possibilities.

According to Heidegger, there are two other forms of knowledge, one theoretical and the other practical. Whereas theoretical knowledge, and especially scientific knowledge, has a high prestige in modern society, this type of knowledge is, according to Heidegger, not the primary one. Our primary mode of understanding the world is not to describe things as objects but to use them as equipment. Most of the time entities in the world are discovered in their functionality, which is taken in a very wide sense by Heidegger. 'In our dealings we come across equipment for writing, sewing, working, transportation, measurement.'[45] That which makes things suitable for such uses is what he called 'equipmentality' (*zeughaftigkeit*). The carpenter thus has a practical grip on the world. A hammer is a piece of equipment; it is used in an equipmental context of hammer, nails, planks, walls, house, etc. To describe the hammer as an object with a certain form, weight, colour and so on is a secondary way of relating to it. According to Heidegger, we have, then, at least three forms of knowledge: existential knowledge, practical knowledge and theoretical knowledge.

Heidegger's idea of being-in-the-world means that humans have an immediate understanding of the environment that is developed early in childhood and onwards. Play in children gives the brain models that answer questions like 'what can I do?' or 'what is possible?' This bodily relation to the environing world is explored in extreme forms in some sports. Building on Heidegger, Breivik studied how climbers explore vertical cliffs, skydivers play with wind resistance in empty space, and kayakers dance with, and on, the waves of white water.[46] Dangerous play with the elements presupposes a knowledge of 'what I can do' and of 'how I can do it' in relation to specific natural elements. Based on long experience, some people simply understand water and how it behaves, how air resistance builds up in free fall, and how hard rock allows for finger holds and grips.

2. Maurice Merleau-Ponty and Bodily Knowledge

Heidegger described very well the practical human being, but in his theory the human body was not clearly visible and remained in the background. The hand that held the hammer, the arm and body that directed and gave momentum to the hand, disappeared. And it was not clear how the existential knowledge of being-in-the-world included the body. This was corrected by Merleau-Ponty, who showed convincingly how the human body is not only a *body-object* but a *body-subject*.[47] It is through the active body as a *medium* that we relate to the world and immediately know how to behave and handle tools.

Merleau-Ponty underlined the intentionality of the body. Central for Merleau-Ponty is that 'my body appears to me as an attitude directed towards a certain existing or possible task'.[48] This intentionality of the body is a form of knowledge that, according to Breivik, is exemplified in many ways on the sporting field.[49] For instance, the movements and positions of football players on the field are defined and solicited by the movements of the ball and the other players. It is the situation that defines the body, its movements and positions. And more than that, good football players are able to read the situation before the ball is played. Therefore, the best players tend to be at the right place at the right time. And even more than that, they are ready for the action that the situation demands.

Merleau-Ponty speaks about what he calls the body as a motor power, a 'motor project' or a 'motor intentionality'. This motor intentionality operates in various contexts as an optimizing agent. We have an ability to find the right relations to sizes and distances in our environment. 'For each object, as for each picture in a gallery, there is an optimum distance from which it requires to be seen, a direction viewed from which it vouchsafes most of itself.'[50] This involves a dynamic attitude. Merleau-Ponty calls it 'a tension which fluctuates round a norm'.[51] He thinks that in general we come to grips with things by placing ourselves in them. We break forth into them and in a sense transcend into them.

It is by establishing this bond that we can come to feel what the optimal grip is and explore the various perspectives of whatever we are dealing with.

Merleau-Ponty gives several examples of this motor understanding of the world. For instance, when driving a car one can see that one can get through an opening without having to compare the width of the opening with the outline of the car. Through our bodies we thus have a knowledge about the world that is implicit and that makes it possible to move around efficiently. Merleau-Ponty also distinguishes between *body image* and *body scheme*. Body image is the passive view 'from the outside' of how I look and behave. Body scheme is the operative body experienced 'from the inside' that makes me aware of 'what I can do'. Brian O'Shaughnessy further elaborates on this and notes that through our body scheme we know 1) what is possible for me now, 2) what I can do at my best, and 3) what is possible for experts.[52] This is very relevant in relation to sports. It seems that as people reach higher performance levels they get more precise understandings of what they can do now, at their best, and what the very best athletes can do.

Building on the work of Samuel Todes, Breivik also underlines the importance of the basic bodily orientations in space.[53] Humans always know whether they are balanced or not, where they are directed. The vertical space with gravity forces limits our movement upwards, whereas the free 360-degree horizontal space opens up for movement in many directions. Todes calls the intention of the active body its *poise* in dealing with things and distinguishes it sharply from the *pose* of the inactive body.[54] As soon as I am poised, I know what I am doing and I know about the surrounding objects. Poise is therefore both the internal coordination of the body and the skilful handling of things and persons around us.

This fundamental bodily knowledge of how we are oriented in space and how we interact with the surroundings is mostly a form of tacit knowledge. It is, as Heidegger claimed, only in situations of 'breakdown', where things do not function as expected, that we become aware of our normal well-balanced relations to the surrounding world.

3. Hubert Dreyfus: Critique of Cognitivism and the Importance of Background Knowledge

Dreyfus builds his philosophy on Heidegger and Merleau-Ponty but develops phenomenology in his own direction. Dreyfus' book *What Computers Can't Do: The Limits of Artificial Intelligence* was first published in 1972.[55] Here Dreyfus attacked the computer models of how the human mind works, arguing that the human mind is not a computer. The mind does not relate to the brain as software to hardware. Humans have capacities that computers lack, like elegant walking, telling jokes, building violins, expressing feelings or making innovations. The expert knowledge used by the best violin makers, like Antonio Stradivari and Andrea Guarneri, was tacit and intuitive. For instance, the computer programs that are used by artificial intelligence experts are not able to catch the complexity and fine discriminations that are needed to select the right material to build a violin. Dreyfus' critique of cognitivism and computer models was followed up by Vegard Moe.[56] He makes a strong critique of cognitivism and the information-processing models that have dominated research in motor control and learning. Moe's key term is *intentional movement*. His premise is that movements in sport are intentional actions. Cognitivism instead assumes '1) that athletes are processors of information, and 2) that intentional movement is set up in advance by one or several motor programmes'.[57] Moe maintains that, instead of relating to cognitive representations or executing motor programmes, athletes deal with the surroundings directly in an absorbed and non-representational manner. Sport is thus an extension of our daily dwelling in the world. Movements in sport are intentionally directed at bringing about certain states and the way success is reached is a sign of how skilled the behaviour is.

In accordance with the phenomenological tradition, Dreyfus underlined the importance of experiential knowledge and how expertise is built on long and varied practice. Together with his brother, Dreyfus studied how airline pilots reached the highest performance level. With input also from activities like chess and sport, the Dreyfus brothers developed a five-stage skill model that showed how performers went from novice to expert level. At the beginners level, practitioners learn by instruction and by following rules. With more experience, they become able to make finer discriminations and act according to variations in context and situation. At the expert level, practitioners perform with direct intuitive reactions to the relevant features of the situations without using rules, concepts or mental representations of any kind. Experts are characterized by 'absorbed skilful coping'. As we will see later, this model has been heavily debated by sport philosophers.

Dreyfus underlines the importance of 'background knowledge' both in daily situations and in sport. The gestalt theorists thought that a figure is impossible without a background. Similarly intentions are made possible by various forms of knowledge, which has accumulated through a person's life and which is dependent upon the experiences and kind of life the person has had. It is this complex and vast area of knowledge that is impossible to model in a computer program and that makes computers unable to perform even seemingly simple daily-life activities. The situational and environmental background is lacking.

Dreyfus here got support from his philosophical adversary, but personal friend, John Searle, who from his analytic point of view underlined the importance of background knowledge in intentional actions. Moe has shown how Searle and Dreyfus shared some common viewpoints and how they differed in others. According to Searle, an intentional state is related to other intentional states in a 'Network' and is dependent upon a certain 'Background'. According to Moe's interpretation of Searle, 'the Background is a set of "nonrepresentational" or "preintentional" "mental capacities" that provides the preconditions for intentional states'.[58] The idea is that 'what one simply takes for granted fits into the Background, and the things we learn through consciously acquired rules and facts fit into the Network'.[59] Whereas Dreyfus placed the background knowledge 'out there' in the environment, Searle in his later views understood the Network and the Background as 'neurophysiological brain capacities'. Searle's neurophysiological and causal approach to background capacities is therefore quite different from Dreyfus' fundamental ontology and hermeneutic everydayness.

4. Phenomenal Knowledge

According to Dreyfus, people performing at expert level are totally absorbed in what they are doing. The performance is non-conscious and non-representational. As Breivik has maintained, Dreyfus' view almost makes elite athletes look like zombies.[60] As a consequence of this, the knowledge they have must be implicit or tacit. But is this the whole story?

In a famous article, Thomas Nagel maintained that only a bat can have an experience of 'what it is like to be a bat'.[61] This experience has a qualitative feel, called *qualia*. Alan Chalmers then introduced the distinction between two forms of consciousness. Whereas *phenomenal consciousness* is characterized by the experience of *qualia*, the feeling of *what it is like to be* in a certain way, *psychological consciousness* is the mental machinery that makes us perceive, decide and act. As Chalmers says, 'On the phenomenal concept, mind is characterized by what it feels; on the psychological concept, mind is characterized by what it does'.[62] This opens up for two types of knowledge. The question is whether phenomenal consciousness is unique and whether it generates knowledge that is different from knowledge obtained from psychological consciousness. I may drive my car to work and be completely absent-minded, thinking about other things than driving and not being aware of traffic lights and what I have been doing. Obviously, the psychological consciousness, the mental machinery, is working. But what is lost when I do not attend to what I am doing? The question is related to the famous article by Frank Jackson, 'What Mary Didn't Know'.[63] Mary is colour-blind but has learned everything that there is to know about colours. Is there anything she has lost, from a knowledge point of view? Breivik argues that something is lost. Using examples from elite sport, Breivik maintains that elite athletes are consciously monitoring and correcting what they are doing based on conscious experience of what is happening.[64] Elite downhill skier Aksel Lund Svindal consciously experiences deviations from the optimal course in his downhill run and corrects his position. Michael Johnson consciously attends to his running and immediately corrects the next steps based on what just happened.

Following Breivik, Jens Birch argues that specific sport experiences include specific qualitative states, specific phenomenal experiences. 'These features make the experience of outdoor rock climbing unidentical to the indoor plastic climbing, even though the attention mechanisms and the mere movements might be identical. Phenomenal consciousness is not an epiphenomenon … it is causally potent.'[65] This means that a pure physical or physiological explanation can never give the whole picture. As Birch argues, 'we can probably find mechanistic analysis for all joints in a pole vault. We could perhaps also find all neuronal events in the brain, and all forces working on the body, ground and pole. But is this identical to how it feels to do a six-metre jump? The suggestion is "no" and the reason is that the reference between the angles, the neuronal events and my feeling of what it's like does not refer both ways.'[66]

Furthermore, Breivik argues that not only the conscious awareness during a competition but also the conscious planning before the competition is often overlooked in phenomenological analyses of sport. Athletes spend a lot of time making plans, preparing, evaluating alternatives, going through things in their minds before competitions, elaborating on strategies, etc. All this includes knowledge of different kinds.

5. Neuroscience and Mirror Neurons

The neurosciences have developed fast and have generated new knowledge about how the brain works. What is called the *easy problem* is related to the brain location of consciousness states. The *hard problem* is related to how the subjective conscious experience of something (*qualia*) is related to the neurophysiology of the 'soggy grey matter' that is called the brain. The gap between the neurophysiological description of the working brain and the correlated subjective experience of a specific person defines what is called 'the explanatory gap'. Philosophers and neuroscientists are still far away from an explanation of this gap. Some philosophers, like Colin McGinn, think that our brains may not be wired in such a way that we can bridge this gap.[67]

Neurophysiological research has, however, opened interesting new vistas for sport philosophers. Imitation and copying are important ways of learning skills. Neurophysiological studies have shown that imitation is founded in our brains at a much deeper level than we thought. Giacomo Rizzolatti and co-workers have found that the brains of monkeys and humans respond directly to motor actions performed by other agents.[68] When I see a person lifting her hand to her mouth to eat, I respond not only with a visual response, but a motor response that is a copy of the original one. My brain fires at the same location as the brain of the other person. The response is somehow not carried through but the motor neurons in the brain fire as if I was lifting my own hand to my mouth. This means that we have an immediate motor understanding of what other agents do. And, furthermore, it seems that it is the intentional character of the action that is important. I know immediately what the action is about and respond with the relevant intentional pattern (lift the hand to eat). So knowledge is related to intentions of other people in an immediate sensorimotor copying pattern. As Birch and others conclude, this new insight has consequences for our understanding of basic skills in sports like copying, imitation and taking the perspective of others.[69]

Concluding comments

Sporting knowledge is of many kinds. I have tried to give an overview of quite different forms of knowledge and I have used different approaches that are not easily combined to a coherent whole. What is unique to sport is the form of knowledge we call know-how. Aristotle was aware of *techné*, the technical and practical knowledge needed in painting, sculpturing and manual work. But Greek philosophers and philosophy in modern times were mostly occupied with discussions of theoretical knowledge. In recent philosophy, the seminal distinction made by Ryle between knowing how and knowing that led to a discussion of various forms of practical knowledge. The discussion of the relation between know how and know that is alive and is unresolved. Intellectualists maintain that know how is a form of or is dependent on know that. Most philosophers lean in the anti-intellectualist direction and think that these are two distinct and different forms of knowledge.

In addition to this discussion, the distinction between personal knowledge and objective knowledge made by Polanyi became important. Polanyi also underlined the tacit dimension. Most of the personal knowledge is tacit or implicit. Dreyfus had views similar to Polanyi but he came from another tradition, building his work on Heidegger, Merleau-Ponty and phenomenology. Dreyfus also underlined the immediate, direct, non-representational form of dealing with the environment. Absorbed skilful coping became a standing expression for expertise in daily life and in sport. Also, from Dreyfus' viewpoint, knowledge in sport is non-conscious. In contrast to these views, Breivik, Birch and others have maintained that it is not only the psychological machinery working on automatic pilot that plays a role in sport but also the conscious experience of *qualia*. Phenomenal consciousness thus adds something to our experiences in sport and thereby makes a specific contribution to sporting knowledge. With the introduction of the neurosciences and the new knowledge of mirror neurons, new dimensions of immediate knowledge of other persons, their intentions and actions are opened up. Maybe the understanding, especially of team sports, will be deeply changed by such new discoveries.

We saw at the beginning of this chapter that scientific knowledge has become important in sport. Since the 1970s, sports sciences have had an increasing impact on how sports, both at mass and elite level, are practised. The development of sport scientific paradigms, the organization and focus of sports sciences, will be important in the coming years, since new practitioner roles and new professions of a sports-related nature are spreading rapidly. The same is true of the global dissemination of new forms of physical activity, which have cultural ramifications. At the heart of sporting knowledge, however, lies the unique experience each of us has when, after mastering a new skill, we exclaim: 'Yes! I know how to do this!'

Notes

1 See the thorough treatment by Robert Nozick in *Philosophical Explanations* (Cambridge, MA: Harvard University Press, 1981).

2 Robert Audi, ed., *The Cambridge Dictionary of Philosophy* (Cambridge: Cambridge University Press, 1995), 233.

3 Ibid., 233.

4 Ibid., 234.

5 The sub-disciplines mentioned are sport pedagogy, sport sociology, sport history, sport philosophy, motor behaviour, sport psychology, biomechanics and exercise physiology. See John D. Massengale and Richard A. Swanson, eds., *The History of Exercise and Sport Science* (Champaign, IL: Human Kinetics, 1997).

6 Hans Lenk, '*Sport in Philosophischer Sicht*', in *Sport Im Blicpunkt der Wissenschaften*, eds., Ommo Grupe, Dietrich Kurz and Johannes Marcus Teipel (Berlin, Heidelberg, New York: Springer-Verlag, 1972).

7 Karl M. Newell, 'Physical Activity, Knowledge Types and Degree Programs', *Quest* 42 (1990): 243–68.

8 Ibid., 249.

9   Roland Renson, 'From Physical Education to Kinanthropology: A Quest for Academic and Professional Identity', *International Journal of Physical Education* 27 (1990): 10–23.

10 Jonathan Dancy, *Introduction to Contemporary Epistemology* (Oxford, UK and Cambridge, MA: Blackwell, 1985), 23.

11 For a discussion of truth and knowledge from a constructivist perspective, see Pirkko Markula and Richard Pringle, *Foucault, Sport and Exercise. Power, Knowledge and Transforming the Self* (London and New York: Routledge, 2006), 51–71.

12 Mike McNamee, ed., *Philosophy and the Sciences of Exercise, Health and Sport. Critical Perspectives on Research Methods* (Abingdon and New York: Routledge, 2005).

13 Graham McFee, *Ethics, Knowledge and Truth in Sports Research. An Epistemology of Sport* (London: Routledge, 2010).

14 Ibid., 20.

15 Ibid., 21.

16 Paul Ziff, 'A Fine Forehand', *Journal of the Philosophy of Sport* 1 (1974): 92–109.

17 Margaret Steel, 'What We Know When We Know a Game', *Journal of the Philosophy of Sport* 4 (1977): 96–103.

18 Ibid., 101.

19 Spencer K. Wertz, 'The Knowing in Playing', *Journal of the Philosophy of Sport* 5 (1978): 39–49.

20 Scott Kretchmar, '"Distancing": An Essay on Abstract Thinking in Sport Performances', *Journal of the Philosophy of Sport* 9 (1982): 6–18.

21 Ibid., 6.

22 Ibid., 9.

23 Ibid., 17.

24 Gilbert Ryle, *The Concept of Mind* (Harmondsworth: Penguin Books, 1963).

25 Ibid., 28.

26 Ibid., 29.

27 Ibid., 31.

28 Ibid., 41.

29 Ibid.

30 Ibid., 48.

31 Ibid., 58.

32 Michael Polanyi, *Personal knowledge. Towards a Post-Critical Philosophy* (Chicago: The University of Chicago Press, 1962), vii.

33 Ibid., 49.

34 Ibid.

35 Ibid., 50.

36 Ibid., 55.

37 Ibid., 59.

38 Ibid., 83.

39 Ibid., 84.

40 Sigmund Loland, 'The Mechanics and Meaning of Alpine Skiing: Methodological and Epistemological Notes on the Study of Sport Technique', *Journal of the Philosophy of Sport* 19 (1992): 55–79.

41 Ibid., 55.

42 Irena Martínková and Jim Parry, eds., *Phenomenological Approaches to Sport* (London and New York: Routledge, 2012).

43 For a presentation of the development of phenomenology from its beginnings to the present day, see Dermot Moran, *Introduction to Phenomenology* (London and New York: Routledge), 2000.

44 Martin Heidegger, *Being and Time*, trans. J. Macquarrie and E. Robinson (New York: Harper and Row, 1962).

45 Ibid., 97.
46 Gunnar Breivik, 'Dangerous Play With the Elements: Towards a Phenomenology of Risk Sports', *Sport, Ethics and Philosophy* 5 (2011): 314–30.
47 Maurice Merleau-Ponty, *Phenomenology of Perception*, trans. Colin Smith (London and New York: Routledge, 2002).
48 Ibid., 114.
49 Gunnar Breivik, 'Bodily Movement – The Fundamental Dimensions', *Sport, Ethics and Philosophy* 2 (2008): 337–52.
50 Merleau-Ponty, *Phenomenology of Perception*, 352.
51 Ibid.
52 Brian O'Shaughnessy, 'Proprioception', in *The Body and the Self*, eds., J.L. Bermúdez, A. Marcel and N. Eilan (Cambridge, MA and London: MIT Press, 1995).
53 Breivik, 'Bodily Movement – The Fundamental Dimensions'.
54 Samuel Todes, *Body and World*, with an introduction by H.L. Dreyfus and P. Hoffman (Cambridge, MA and London: MIT Press, 2001).
55 Hubert Dreyfus, *What Computers Can't Do* (New York: Harper & Row, 1972).
56 Vegard F. Moe, 'Understanding Intentional Movement in Sport' (PhD diss., Norwegian School of Sport Sciences, 2007).
57 Ibid., 40.
58 Ibid., 51.
59 Ibid.
60 Gunnar Breivik, 'Zombie-Like or Superconscious? A Phenomenological and Conceptual Analysis of Consciousness in Elite Sport', *Journal of the Philosophy of Sport* 40 (2013): 85–106.
61 Thomas Nagel, *The View from Nowhere* (New York and Oxford: Oxford University Press, 1986).
62 David J. Chalmers, *The Conscious Mind. In Search of a Fundamental Theory* (Oxford: Oxford University Press, 1996), 11.
63 Frank Jackson, 'What Mary Didn't Know', *The Journal of Philosophy* 83 (1986): 291–95.
64 Breivik, 'Zombie-Like or Superconscious? A Phenomenological and Conceptual Analysis of Consciousness in Elite Sport', 85–106.
65 Jens E. Birch, 'In the Synaptic Cleft: Caught in the Gap between Neurotransmitter Release and Conscious Experience in Sport' (PhD diss., Norwegian School of Sport Sciences, 2011), 79.
66 Jens E. Birch, 'A Phenomenal Case for Sport', *Sport, Ethics and Philosophy* 3 (2009): 40.
67 Colin McGinn, *The Problem of Consciousness* (London: Basil Blackwell, 1991).
68 See Giacomo Rizzolatti and Corrado Sinigaglia, *Mirrors in the Brain: How our Minds Share Actions and Emotions* (New York: Oxford University Press, 2008).
69 Birch, 'In the Synaptic Cleft: Caught in the Gap between Neurotransmitter Release and Conscious Experience in Sport', 82.

14 Sport and Ideology

Lamartine P. DaCosta

The current notions of ideology include one proposed by Edward Shils, which became significant as it consisted of a revision of key sociological issues. For this distinguished sociologist, 'ideology represents a comprehensive pattern of cognitive and moral beliefs about man, society and the universe', which, when compared with other beliefs, are relatively highly coherent with one or multiple consensual values.[1] Shils also claims that adherents of a particular ideology are expected to be in complete agreement with each other. Also, those who adopt this consensual belief speak for a transcendent entity – a stratum, a society, a species – or an ideal value that is supposedly broader than the group to which these believers belong.

As far as sports go, an empirical research conducted by Sigmund Loland and Yngvar Ommundsen in Norway revealed that its findings were remarkably compatible with Shils' understanding of ideology.[2] This investigation aimed to identify Norwegian children's sport's 'values' and 'ideologies' as they are perceived by the general population. In addition, quantitative data collected for the study conclusively demonstrated that the majority of respondents emphasized the development of positive attitudes through sport along with the acquisition and implementation of a wide spectrum of athletic skills. For Loland and Ommundsen, the apparent ambivalence meant a distinction between a pattern of beliefs – that is, ideology – and sport's intrinsic values cultivated by respondents of the investigation.

The empirical evidence detected by Loland and Ommundsen may also raise pertinent questions about the intersections between social and philosophical interpretations of ideology. In short, those intersections seem primarily to be an interplay of values in which sport would have a causal and functional role.

Regarding Shils' thought-provoking approach to ideology, the thesis of intersections might include various areas of knowledge, as for him every ideology – whether progressive or traditionalistic, revolutionary or reactionary – arises in the midst of an ongoing culture. In other words, ideology cannot entirely divest itself of important elements of a particular culture in addition to philosophical or, in this case, sporting traditions, not to mention other specific epistemic influences. In this context, Shils emphasized historical evidence revealing that ideological groups forced themselves into the political arena, because, as he argued, 'since the 17th century, every ideology has had its views on politics'.[3]

Having Shils' understanding of ideology as the scope of this essay, the central focus shall then be the intersections of ideology as juxtaposed to sport, society, philosophy and politics. As such, distinct and multidisciplinary approaches are characteristically found in specific ways of thinking in North American, European and also Latin American countries. So, the aim of this essay is to explore the leading theories of ideology and sport articulated in these geographical areas, albeit emphasizing the North American perspectives due to their relatively long tradition as well as their attempts at conceptual clarification and critical assessment.

The Role of European and North American Philosophy

Formally, the choice of North American thought as the basis for a broad review of ideology in sport may be supported by the 'Resource Guide to the Philosophy of Sport and Ethics of Sport',[4] whose extensive annotated bibliography shows that 'ideology' was incorporated as one of its 11 organizational sections under the title 'Social and Political Philosophy'. However, 'ideology' as a specific theme in that disciplinary resource had just a few citations mostly referencing North American academic productions.

The relatively low importance of 'ideology' as a topic of research in the philosophy of sport is, then, assumed to be a consequence of its roots, which originally lay in sociology, history and political science. As a result, philosophical concerns of ideology are informed by multidisciplinary configurations, as assumed in the previous definition proposed by Shils. Therefore, insights and overviews related to sport and ideology generally combine different disciplinary perspectives and reveal the complexity of their characteristics and conceptions. As already mentioned, this conceptual effort is reflected in the sustained work of several North American sport theorists, in addition to seminal European authors who have extensively explored the ideological meanings of sport.

Generally speaking, the most recent and dynamic discussions of the relationship between sport and ideology come from North American sport theorists such as John Hoberman, Allen Guttmann and William J. Morgan. From their theoretical advances, sport has been understood as a category that permeates multiple areas of knowledge including society and ideology, in addition to philosophy when this discipline puts forward questions related to, for example, the social access to and participation in sport, its political meanings, freedom and justice in sporting contests and various epistemological issues. European and Latin American contributions often also consider sport as an expression of ideological motivations and purposes, as may be initially ascertained by the example of Fascist and Communist sport.

A Brief Analysis of Fascist and Communist Sport Ideologies

The collective work edited by the British historian J.A. Mangan putting the focus on the 'fascist body as a political icon', indeed revealed a manipulation of sporting practices towards Fascist ideological commitments during the 1930s and 1940s in nine countries from different continents.[5] In Brazil, for instance, the Nazi party (one million members in 1931) gave explicit priority to sport as a tool for popular mobilization.[6] Although the details of this conclusive remark varied in each of the countries studied, the historic survey conducted by Mangan came to the general conclusion that the Nazi ideology was portrayed by male sporting practices and through the aesthetic portrayal of the body, which was infused with political purposes. In this regard, Mangan concentrated his analysis on the cult of the body and its communicative power whereas a pertinent philosophical question – for the sake of this essay's appropriation – should primarily focus on the meaning of the political construction of Nazi sport as an ideological commitment.

The close connection between ideology and sport, having as background Fascist activism, arguably became a common approach in many countries with the rise of Nazism in the 1930s, on account of post-Second World War interpretations. In this case, it is important to mention the now classical terminology proposed by Richard Mandell,[7] which coincides with the term coined by Guttmann[8] for the 1936 Olympic Games held in Berlin: the 'Nazi Olympics'. Guttmann, specifically for that sport event, emphasized the statement of Pierre de Coubertin himself for whom 'the Games had been organized with "Hitlerian" strength and discipline'.[9] In fact, Guttmann described the Nazi Olympics as a mix of international politics, racism, nationalism and Fascist ideology,[10] a context in which sport clearly played more than a supportive political role.

Unsurprisingly, after the analyses of Mandell and Guttmann, the expression 'Nazi sport' became broadly used and recognized. Again, lessons coming from the culmination of the Fascist pre-war era are likely to show compatibility with Loland and Ommundsen's fact-finding study. That is, ideology (consensual belief) may be associated with sport (intrinsic values) despite their different meanings.

Similar remarks to that of Guttmann's related to the connection between sport and ideology at the Berlin Olympics are found in a book edited by Arnd Krüger and William Murray,[11] researchers who challenged the view that sport was a trivial matter, laying the groundwork for the examination of Fascism in many countries that took part in the Berlin Games. Simply put, the Nazi Olympics did not prove to be an isolated phenomenon; rather, they suggested, the event emerged from a context of political changes – mostly concentrated in Europe – creating the conditions to infuse ideology into sport in novel ways. In particular, Krüger and Murray's work coincides with the general conditions found by Mangan some years earlier, despite the fact that their emphasis was more philosophical than Mangan's.

The contextual interpretation should, then, be seen as a valid way to distinguish patterns of belief from internal values in some sporting manifestations. James Riordan adopted this view observing the changes of directions during times of political and institutional shifting in the former Soviet Union (USSR).[12] He studied the evolution of sport in that country from its early development in the 1920s, with physical education oriented towards the increase of labour productivity and defence goals. Contrariwise, the post-war booming phase in the USSR searched openly to enhance the political power of that nation and the Communist ideology internationally. Moreover, Riordan had a study with Pierre Arnaud in which they emphasized the impact of either Fascism or Communism on sport in some selected European countries during the interwar period.[13]

These academic contributions showed how sport became an instrument to give support to both ideologies in different styles and core meanings, especially in terms of political propaganda.

Historical and Theoretical Constructions of Ideology

The examples shown above may be regarded as historical and evidence-based theoretical constructions connecting sport with ideology claims. These are starting points in order to fully bring the philosophy of sport into this essay. For the sake of the argument, therefore, let us explore more deeply the meaning of ideology at large and its historical relationship with other areas of knowledge. Central to this aim lies the understanding of ideology first proposed by Antoine Destutt de Tracy in 18th-century France when he developed a 'science of ideas' proposal.[14] As demonstrated by Emmet Kennedy, this conception was equally pedagogical and political, and it was intended to mould social behaviour towards the so much needed harmonious social order.[15]

The initial conception of 'ideology' was a typical product of the French enlightenment, which gave science a radical capacity to explain and understand social life. Unexpectedly, during Destutt de Tracy's lifetime, renowned intellectuals in France were called *idéologues* – or even *doctrinaires* – in the French language, expressions often used with a pejorative connotation. According to José Ferrater Mora, this fact signals the multiplicity of meanings carried by the term 'ideology', especially when it emerged from different political views and social groups.[16] Ferrater Mora also identified, among the diversity of these 'ideas', an attempt to consider ideology as a philosophical category as seen in the texts elaborated by Hippolyte Taine, one of the most distinguished French intellectuals of the early 19th century.[17]

Still, taking into account Ferrater Mora's interpretations, the focus on 'idea' as a basis for ideology had a progressive maturation from its origins with several different connotations. Furthermore, there was another generation of French thinkers after Destutt de Tracy that became famous in the mid 19th century for the manner in which they connected their ideas with social claims, including Pierre Leroux, Claude Henri de Saint-Simon and Auguste Comte. Such *idéologues* had distinct philosophical positions but afterwards, in one way or another, they supposedly influenced Karl Marx, for whom the category of 'idea' became central in its transition to 'ideology'.[18]

In the late 19th century, a full reversal of meaning occurred to ideology, giving way to one of its main interpretations: the historical materialism of Marxist thought. This new theory adopted ideology as a composition of ideas that exerts a masked domination using descriptive or prescriptive proposals by social groups, which were called 'ruling classes' by Marx and his followers. Classical examples of these ideas, according to Marxist supporters, are religious beliefs and moral claims. Marxist doctrine also implies understanding social reality as a 'false consciousness' as well as ideology as opposition to true knowledge. Moreover, ideology here equally implies a special sort of criticism that calls into question the beliefs and values of a particular society.[19]

Classic Marxism nevertheless rejected philosophy as a discipline, including its approaches to ideology, due to its presumed bourgeois origin. To put it differently, philosophy was understood by Marxists as an ideological product, a position never fully clarified or dismissed by Marxists themselves. Ironically, 'Marxist ideology' became a philosophical category broadly accepted today even by neo-Marxist theorists.[20] Most post-Marx ideologies have furthermore come to be preponderantly political, a tendency also pointed out by Shils in the late 1960s.

At any rate, the term 'ideology' and its variants – mostly in sociology, political science and philosophy – consolidated their importance after Marx's reappraisal and as a result of the growth of Marxism beyond the 19th century. This drive apparently created an intellectual ambience in Germany for the appearance of Karl Mannheim, who developed a more consistent understanding of ideology during the mid 20th century. This new approach included an epistemological discussion insufficiently explored before either by Destutt de Tracy and his followers or Marx and his companions. According to Ferrater Mora,[21] Mannheim actually elaborated a sociology of knowledge whose content might be opened to social and historical particularities, that is to 'ideologies'.[22] For this reason, when the concept of ideology is examined, it is important to take into account its multiple variations.

Although with some uncertainty – an admitted risk of relativism in the analysis, for instance – Mannheim brought into light a theoretical framework that overcame the one-sided political identification of ideology, especially the false consciousness of capitalist social relations proposed by the Marxist vision of the world. In this sense, Mannheim argued that it was a mistake to see the viewpoint of one social class as wrong and another as right; sociologically, it was more valuable to consider all belief systems as representing the interest of particular groups.[23]

Mannheim's claims have also been brought to discussion today by philosophers such as Jürgen Habermas and Paul Ricouer or cultural studies authors such as Norberto Bobbio and Gilles Lipovetsky, as argued in a recent report by Gláucia Villas Bôas.[24] The long-time pertinent interpretations by Mannheim are probably due to the methodological path chosen by him, consisting in the elaboration of counterpoints to the Marxist main propositions, completed by arguments taken from history, culture and epistemology mostly from European thinkers of the early 20th century.[25]

To fully appreciate ideology, specifically in the context of philosophy and sport, some of Mannheim's ideas, as well as those of his followers, were therefore selected as follows. First, Mannheim's book *Ideology and Utopia* from 1929 must be taken into consideration for its long-time influence over 20th-century intellectuals.[26] In this famous text, Mannheim concluded that knowledge is a result of social life from several influences exerted over individuals as knowers. Therefore, this concept originated the 'sociology of knowledge' (*Wissensoziologie*), a valid thesis even today by means of the new disciplines of 'knowledge management' and 'social epistemology'.[27]

The proposal of a 'Sociology of Knowledge' implies the acceptance of conflicts within and between different social groups as emphazised by Mannheim, which generates two tendencies: one supporting conservative positions and another one favouring change. The former creates or reinforces ideologies whereas the latter brings out utopias, that is, changes in the social structure. In other words, Mannheim kept the focus of ideology on self-interest – socially constructed as proposed by Marxism – but he moved away from Marxist determinism, making changes according to the elaboration of knowledge, again created by different social groups. Also, Mannheim called upon these changes as a context defined by values and free choices from a collective willingness.[28] In another approach to the exchange between ideology and free choices, Mannheim emphasized the meaning of the context when it is socially favourable to a common language of understanding, whether this language is based on ideology or free will.[29]

In summary, the tradition of Western thought related to ideology submitted to synthetic approaches might be peculiarly concerned with epistemological evaluations in the area of philosophy as well as with a socially constructed relationship akin to sporting practices. Actually, reviews from Destutt de Tracy to Marx and Mannheim's classic contributions might also disclose different kinds of ideology such as political, social, cultural and ethical.

French, German and Latin American Approaches to Ideology and Sport

Again putting the focus on sport, French intellectuals, for instance, have often been concerned with its political meaning, even regarding it as a carrier of ideological propositions, either related to a search for consensus or to a manifestation of 'false consciousness'. In this regard, Frédéric Baillette pointed out the dualistic nature of sport in terms of ideology, being integrated into the capitalist system with its values of radical competition as well as representing a means of autonomy among participants.[30] This author also emphasized the historical association of sport with totalitarian regimes in contrast to its capacity to depoliticize those who participate in sporting activities.

In his book *L'idéologie du sport en France depuis 1880: race, guerre et religion* the French historian Michel Caillat agreed with the polysemic nature of sport; nevertheless he added that 'the ideology of sport is similar to religion with its expansionist trend and militant predication'.[31] In this sense, Caillat identified three modes of discourse that give support to sport ideologies: the foundational, exemplified by Pierre de Coubertin's works for the restoration of the Olympic Games; the didactic, mostly referred to learning and morality; and the apologetic, often offered as a defence of sport in terms of social development.

In his book, Caillat also put forward that the strength of sport ideologies was not concentrated on its discursive structures but instead on sport's seemingly non-ideological resemblance. The demonstration of this peculiarity was attributed to Friedrich Engels' explanation of ideology per se, which after being consolidated by his adherents became independent from external influences. In summary, for Caillat sport clearly seems distinct from the outlooks, creeds and other ideologies existing in the same society; therefore, the task of the critic is mostly to unmask those self-reflexive constructions.

However, the seminal thinker of the French tradition on sport ideologies is Jean-Marie Brohm for whom modern sport is a sound expression of the self-destructive nature of capitalism as it reproduces bourgeois social relations such as selection and hierarchy, subservience, obedience, competition, individualism, success, etc.[32] Certainly, this Marxist position is difficult to reconcile with theory-based dualisms like those exposed by Baillette and Caillat. Besides this constraint, the historical synthesis of Marxist doctrine and its solid application to sport may explain the unquestionable influence of Brohm over studies exploring ideology and sport not only in France but also abroad.

In other words, the past and present interpretations of the connection between sport and ideology assumed by Brohm are likely to coincide with the Marxist claim of universalism. This convergence became more acceptable with the positions taken by the Frankfurt School thinker Theodor Adorno during the 1930s in Germany. In a nutshell, the often recognized 'neo-Marxist' Adorno argued that sport, like many other cultural manifestations, was a frivolous activity that increases the inequalities of the capitalist system. Therefore, Adorno and Brohm might be considered together, sharing the same philosophical tradition with universal appeal.

Despite this apparent supranational coincidence, Adorno did not adopt the category of 'false consciousness', preferring the attribute of 'instrumental reason' to criticize the social deviations of sport in favour of the materialism and consumerism of bourgeois society.[33] What was actually going on in this presumed convergence is that Brohm never disregarded the original roots of Marxism, leaving aside the polysemic nature of ideology. Symptomatically, in 2006 Brohm published the book *Théorie critique d'un opium du peuple* putting together his central theses from past decades into one approach in which sport is simply seen as an 'opium of the people', using the famous expression originally coined by Marx in the 19th century.[34]

In a general overview of the topic ideology and sport, Brohm's positions may be taken as a classical, continuing and reiterative account lasting over four decades, revealing a stable interest in the topic and a demand for synthesis. According to Paulo C. Nunes Junior and Janir C. Batista, this possibility is particularly valid in contemporary sport organizations, mostly concerned with commercial interests and financial transactions typical of capitalist and hegemonic social relationships.[35] In these circumstances, those Brazilian authors, followers of Brohm's ideas, defined his approach as a 'model' for their critiques and analysis.[36] A similar understanding to that of Nunes Junior and Batista may be found among other Latin American sport theorists, as well as in current academic production from European countries not always referred to as Marxist. In Brazil, for example, Brohm's one-dimensional and radical model was used by Leandro M. Beneli, Eduardo F. Rodrigues and Paulo C. Montagner to survey the management conditions of basketball at the national level.[37]

In France, a study of Brohm's academic legacy done by the sociologist Henri Vaugrand[38] suggested that his Marxist-based approach to sport became hybrid due to the work of Brohm's followers. Something similar happened with Pierre Bourdieu. Vaugrand argued that 'Two approaches have had an important impact on the development of French sport sociology. The first, based upon the work of Pierre Bourdieu, can be termed *sporting field theory*. The second, developed by

Jean-Marie Brohm, is often labelled Neo-Marxist theory, but is more accurately denoted as a *critical theory of sport*.'[39]

Vaugrand's overview also created the nexus between paradigms in order to accommodate diverse interpretations of sport in terms of politics and ideology. As a whole, the polysemic characteristic of the relationships between ideology and sport can be confirmed by the methodological arrangements adopted by different analysts and critics, as previously described.

In Germany, in turn, Bero Rigauer, a seminal thinker equivalent to Brohm in France, kept the tradition of neo-Marxism proposed by the Frankfurt School, stressing the structural connection between sport and work as organized in capitalistic environments. This assumption was actually discussed by Rigauer in his book *Work and Sport*, originally published in 1969 in Germany prior to Brohm's impact in France.[40] In 1983, Ian Taylor suggested that Rigauer's conceptions influenced Guttmann, one of the key researchers of ideology and sport in North American thought.[41]

Italian and Spanish Approaches to Ideology and Sport

Some European sport historians not directly dedicated to the subject of this essay also revealed the multiple meanings and manifestations of ideology and sport without emphasizing much theoretical frameworks such as those advanced by Brohm and Rigauer. For example, in Italy, Simon Martin reviewed the history of sport of that country focusing on politics and the ideological influences behind it. He did so by studying how the right and the left as well as their political parties and their politicians' interests intersected with sport.[42] This kind of approach is more thematic and descriptive than analytical. However, it reveals relevant expressions of the connection between sport and ideology. This peculiarity may also be appreciated in the work of Gigliola Gori, who recovered selective sport activities from 1920 to 1930 in Italy as related to female adherents to the Fascist party.[43] In this investigation, also grounded in historical methodology, descriptive narratives were naturally favoured for the sake of demonstrating the effective connections between sport and ideology.

Another example in line with the multiple facets of sport and ideology is the Spanish historian Eduardo González Calleja, who analysed the history of the famous football club Real Madrid to identify the club's social and political impacts in Spain and Europe.[44] This analysis acknowledges that Real Madrid's triumphs at the continental level up to the 1960s created a promotional platform for Francisco Franco's dictatorship. Still, according to Calleja, this meant the use of sport as an ideological instrument, despite its apparent neutrality. In addition, all of this, in turn, exposed the key role of institutional relationships in favour of political power as a typical attribute of sport.

Ideology and Sport in North America

Turning to contributors from North America, John Hoberman's 1977 article 'Sport and Political Ideology' in effect set the tone for interpreting the categories of sport and ideology as mutually influenced and often combined with other social or political structures.[45] As later confirmed, his central thesis considered sport and ideology as expressions of political doctrines.[46] Specifically, he declared that 'Historical evidences suggest that sport is not a neutral entity with respect to the ideological spectrum. Crucial to the thesis is what I shall call the appropriation of sport by ideologically oriented observers of all kinds: political figures, novelists, sociologists and others. Sport, according to this view, is indeed innocuous if viewed as a mere physical act.'[47]

Supported by historical evidence, Hoberman did not dismiss the sheer cultural and physical nature of sport but he emphasized that societies at large view sport as a subject open to political interpretation, despite the fact that sport in itself is apparently innocuous.[48] In some cases, societies are supportive of sport activities as a means of neutralizing ideological interests, resulting in a completely new political culture.

A peculiar conservative tradition often labels sport according to experiences from its many institutions, the International Olympic Committee (IOC) being an outstanding example since Pierre de Coubertin created it in 1894. The Baron himself became a model of conservatism in spite of his public position of political neutrality. These observations made by Hoberman[49] also brought to light one key disclosure: 'It must be admitted at the outset that to claim in an overall sense that the politically nuanced literature of sport is predominantly a right-wing phenomenon, and that the enormous Marxist literature which has been accumulating for a century contains relatively less and reveals in addition a basic lack of affinity for the subject itself is of necessity a somewhat impressionistic judgment rather than one subject to quantitative verification.'[50] Indeed, Hoberman finally claims that sport has not been integrated into the Marxist ideology even considering the high value attributed to sporting practices by socialist nations.[51]

This conception strengthens the interpretation of sport as having a prevalent and non-deterministic instrumental role when it comes to its association with ideology, as confirmed by Hoberman in his 1984 book *Sport and Political Ideology*. Hoberman showed an early preference for philosophy as a basis for a better understanding of that instrumentality: 'For ideological dispositions to sport, we realize, are grounded in political psychology, which in turn finds its own sources in questions of philosophy. In this sense, sport can function as a powerful instrument in the search for the origins of ideology itself.'[52]

Another prominent North American theorist of the relationship between sport and ideology is Allen Guttmann. To approach his contributions to the topic, the basic text is *From Ritual to Record: The Nature of Modern Sports*, published in 1978.[53] But in relation to this essay's reappraisals, the book *Games and Empires: Modern Sports and Cultural Imperialism* published by Guttmann in 1994 will also be used to explore his take on the issue.[54] To begin with, it is important to mention that in Guttmann's appreciation of modern sport, there are many indications of the natural association of sport with ideology; following this lead he adopted a philosophical vision later in the 1990s when his arguments focused on sport as a means of support to provide freedom 'to' (no restrictive conditions to act) as opposed to freedom 'from' or previous restrictions to individual actions. More explicitly he claims that 'Despite imperfections and false emphases, modern sports hold forth the possibility of a realm of relative if not absolute freedom'.[55]

Later the proposal of sport as a means of intrinsic and optional freedom was put into a simple formulation. Guttmann argues that 'When we are surfeited with rules and regulations, when we are tired – like Robert Frost's applepicker – of the harvest we ourselves desired, we can always put away our stopwatch, abandon the cinder track, kick off our spiked shoes, and run as Roger Bannister did, barefoot, on firm dry sand, by the sea'.[56] In other words, the voluntary and autonomous practice of sport is very similar to the acceptance of the rational-scientific order in society, since in both cases individuals search to get better results in an organized group rather than as individuals acting alone.

The search to consolidate the associative conception between sport and ideology achieved its maturity in 1994, when Guttmann understood modern sport as transcending national boundaries and nationalistic ideological limitations. For this macro interpretation, sport already meant an ideological instrument and a common and consensual property of the word at large. In addition, the practical example of this prominent characteristic was the Olympic Games, which originally incorporated an imperialist ideology, and then became a practice with universal appeal.[57] This idea presents sport as both an independent instrument to support social, cultural and ideological constructions and an ideology in itself providing free choices to participants.

The point here, though, is that Guttmann's liberal-democratic argument constitutes the starting point of a sport ideology that brings within itself an apparent contradiction, having an explicit and close connection with free and democratic choices, in addition to an underlying utilitarianism or commodification. This tendency often means a predatory commercialism of sport with side effects such as corruption, doping, victory at any cost, overtraining and other non-communal and unhealthy practices.

Certainly here also lies the criticism of the previously cited Marxist interpreters selected for this essay, including Rigauer, who explicitly defined sport as a commodity early in 1969. Much of Rigauer's argument, that sport mirrors alienated labour and focuses on the sport training process, is an argument that still persists nowadays.

Would the ambivalent mainstream positions on ideology and sports be related to the intrinsic nature of sports and their contradictory elements? On account of Guttmann's approach with his conclusive remark on the mix of influences over the Nazi Olympics, a positive answer to this question would be consistent. After all, throughout this essay, sport has revealed a coherent role as supportive to a diversity of politically oriented ideologies and to different social and cultural constructed values as well. Philosophically speaking, however, the question of how sport can be considered a socially liberating or constraining human activity requires an analysis that is less ideology-bound and more related to the idea of the social contract. This understanding was elaborated by Dennis A. Hemphill, who revisited Guttmann's works and concluded that sport reconciles freedom with its structural restrictions.[58]

In this context, Morgan may represent the consolidation of both Hoberman's and Guttmann's insights, especially because of his commitment to philosophical argumentation. This conceptual effort found in Morgan's works also helped to clarify the intersections of ideology and sport with sociology, history, political science and so forth.

Morgan's approach to sport and ideology can be primarily seen in two distinguished books that have framed his academic production since the 1970s: *Leftist Theories of Sport: A Critique and Reconstruction*[59] and *Why Sports Morally Matter*.[60] But in opposition to Brohm's four decades of unchanged tradition, Morgan elaborated in a similar time span a progressive construction firstly providing critiques to radical ideologies – mostly rooted in Marxism – and then outlining reconstructed theories of sport.

Consider, for example, the early critique of Theodor Adorno's claim that sport is an agent of social domination in capitalist society. Morgan argues that 'Adorno has been reproached for glossing over the emancipatory potential of the popular sports and leisure pursuits of mass culture, and for producing hyper-critical doctrines of the body and of modern sport based on Fascist political paradigms'.[61] That is, Morgan thought that those criticisms were misguided. Previously, Morgan had evaluated two major versions of the 'new critical theory of sport', the Marxist and the hegemonic sport theory, suggesting that 'radical theory's conceptions of sport as social practice is in error, and that this error receives its impetus and plausibility from the social circumstances that presently prevail in capitalist society'.[62] His conclusion stressed that the 'radical theory of sport is not a radical but a reactionary theory and that a genuine critical theory must be based on its formal autonomy'.[63]

Almost two decades later, Morgan was still breaking down the so-called leftist theories but at the same time was adding his own proposal by stressing the importance of the logical integrity of sports. These perspectives all together can be interpreted through his reference to the contemporary German philosopher Habermas as a bearer of the Frankfurt School legacies: 'Although critical social theorists of sports have had plenty to say about … shortcomings of contemporary sports, little of what they say touches on their specifically moral character. Habermas's critical theory of society is a notable exception, claiming, as it does, that if one wants to understand contemporary social practices such as sports, one cannot turn their back on the moral ideals and values that drive them.'[64] In his approach, however, Morgan has progressed from particular critiques to a broader focus emphasizing the moral significance of sports, searching for explanations in the realms of social and political philosophy. Overall, Morgan became heavily critical of sport in capitalist society but he also recognized sport as a means for the moral development of individuals and societies. In this sense, he followed a similar path already embarked on by Hoberman and Guttmann, both supportive of a socially liberating sport.

In conclusion, putting together the contributions of Hoberman, Guttmann and Morgan, there is an emerging vision of the Janus-like opposing roles of sport with two faces: one is looking in ideology-bound directions, the other into the constructive social values that challenge the dominant ideology. The call to reinforce the intrinsic value of sport or to create a new politically based culture of sport is another common convergence found among the three leading thinkers of ideology and sport in North America.

In this particular sense lie the ultimate commitments from Morgan as seen in his recent interventions in academic events. For instance, at the XVII Congress of Panathlon International held in Stresa, Italy in 2010, whose topic was 'The Primacy of Ethics. Also in Sports?', he stated: 'I will claim that nothing short of breaking the dominance of money over sport is likely to change appreciably the present day culture of sport. This will not require that we forbid the market from operating in sport at all, but that we significantly curtail its influence, in short, that we learn to appreciate the value of sport not the (market) price it is able to fetch.'[65] At the 2011 Annual Conference of the International Association for the Philosophy of Sport held in Rochester, New York, Morgan made a conclusive remark. He said: 'The basic idea here is that sports, and kindred perfectionist practices, are valuable because they affirm our freedom to shape and contour social practices suited to our specific self-determination, and to find sources of meaning and intrinsic value that make life worth living in the first place.'[66]

Current Perspectives

The review of conceptions and justifications presented in this essay implies the presence of the topic ideology and sport in the philosophy of sport literature, initially with a politically based recognition and then progressing to a debate on the morals of sport, either by its deviations or virtues. This peculiar development became a recurrent and residual theme within the field of 'Social and Political Philosophy' during the 2000s, as we observed earlier.

Despite the relatively loose delimitations of the subject of study, new approaches to the relation between sport and ideology could be considered as the basis for advances at least in terms of the methodology of research. This is the case of Teun A. van Dijk, who has summarized today's understanding of ideology per se.[67] In short, those visions are primarily closely connected with a system of beliefs and values, covering an increasing area of knowledge and disciplines, ranging between diversified views and extreme positions. As such, this positioning scenario supports the theories of sport and ideology developed mostly in the past four decades by pre-eminent North American sources. Indeed, in terms of sport, the value-led and belief approaches in recent years have got a renewed interest, particularly in the areas of gender, disability claims, doping, commercialization, media, nationalism, race, cultural identity, globalization, governance, public policy, poverty, environmental issues and so forth.

Still addressing the system of value and beliefs as the main delimitation of ideology, it can be argued in terms of past and present concerns that sport has been proposed to enforce the values of a wider society, though it was not seen as a source of value within itself as demonstrated by Loland.[68] This retrospective account of value-led sport is still giving grounds to the common association of ideology with sport as found in particular areas as here exemplified by children's sport and the Olympic Games.

A better clarification of that association comes up through a recent research report from Peter Hatemi, Lindon Eaves and Rose McDermott.[69] In this study, the particular meanings of ideology per se, emphasizing global environments, established the possible range of understanding, from macro to micro reviews. This double-level approach is apparently the upcoming mainstream of ideology and sport studies and investigations.

This prevalent tendency has early academic commitments here already defined by investigations on particular countries' sport movements backed by political ideologies. For instance, the Nazi Olympics already described by Mandell[70] and the connection between the military political power and soccer in Argentina as reported by Joe Arbena[71] are both micro representations of macro-level ideological dominance already described by Hoberman during the 1970s.

Ultimately, whether or not it is possible to give substantive theoretical content to the concept of ideology in a variety of social contexts, it is thought-provoking to paraphrase Terry Eagleton[72] and argue that ideology and sport remains a challenging blend of social aspirations, ideas and myths.[73]

Notes

1 Edward Shils, 'Ideology', in *International Encyclopedia of the Social Sciences*, ed., David L. Sills (New York: Macmillan and Free Press, 1968), Vol. 7, 66–77.
2 Sigmond Loland and Yngvar Ommundsen, 'Values and Ideologies of Norwegian Children's Sport as Perceived by the General Population', *European Physical Education Review* 2 (1996), 133–42.
3 Shils, 'Ideology'.
4 Leon Culbertson, Mike McNamee and Emily Ryall, *Resource Guide to the Philosophy of Sport and Ethics of Sport*, Hospitality, Leisure, Sport and Tourism Network: Oxford: 2008.
5 James A. Mangan, ed., *Shaping the Superman: Fascist Body as Political Icon-Aryan Fascism* (Portland: Frank Cass, 1999).
6 Lamartine P. DaCosta and Plinio Labriola, 'Bodies from Brazil: Fascist Aesthetics in a South American Setting', in *Shaping the Superman: Fascist Body as Political Icon-Aryan Fascism*, ed., James A. Mangan (Portland: Frank Cass, 1999), 1–23.
7 Richard D. Mandell, *The Nazi Olympics* (Urbana, IL: University of Illinois Press, 1987).
8 Allen Guttmann, 'The Nazi Olympics', in *The Olympic Games in Transition*, eds., Jeffrey O. Segrave and Donald Chu (Champaign, IL: Human Kinetics, 1988), 216.
9 Ibid.
10 Ibid., 203–215.
11 See William J. Murray, 'Introduction', 13–16; and Arnd Krüger, 'Germany: The Propaganda Machine', 17–21 and 'Epilogue', 229–41 in *The Nazi Olympics: Sport, Politics, and Appeasement in the 1930s*, eds., Arnd Krüger and William J. Murray (Urbana, IL: University of Illinois Press, 2003).
12 James Riordan, *Sport in Soviet Society: Development of Sport and Physical Education in Russia and the USSR* (Cambridge: Cambridge University Press, 1977), 10.
13 James Riordan and Pierre Arnaud, eds., *Sport and International Politics: Impact of Fascism and Communism* (Oxford: Taylor and Francis, 1998).
14 The original proposal of Destutt de Tracy distinguished three elements, namely ideology (generic term of the subject), general grammar (meaning) and logic (reason), as components of his new 'science of ideas'. For further details see Emmet Kennedy,

'"Ideology" from Destutt De Tracy to Marx', *Journal of the History of Ideas* 40 (1979): 353–68.

15 See Kennedy, '"Ideology" from Destutt De Tracy to Marx'.

16 José Ferrater Mora, *Diccionario de Filosofía* (Madrid: Alianza Editorial, 1982), 1610–15.

17 The *Diccionario de Filosofía* by Spanish philosopher José Ferrater Mora (1912–91) is often considered a precursor of 'Companions', which introduces extended explanations of different philosophical topics instead of simple definitional entries. He was quoted in this essay for a summary of international contributions to the topic of 'ideology' beyond European sources.

18 Ferrater Mora, *Diccionario de Filosofía*, 1610–15.

19 Ibid., 1613.

20 Ted Honderich, *The Oxford Companion to Philosophy* (New York: Oxford University Press, 1995), 526–8.

21 Ferrater Mora, *Diccionario de Filosofía*, 1613.

22 In addition, Ferrater Mora also stressed the influence of the German philosopher Max Scheler (1874–1928) over Mannheim in relation to the social and historical dimensions of ideology.

23 Karl Mannheim, *Ideologia e Utopia* (Rio de Janeiro: Zahar Editores, 1972), 11.

24 Gláucia Villas Bôas, 'Os portadores da síntese: sobre a recepção de Karl Mannheim', *Cadernos CERU* 13 (2012): 128.

25 See Pedro H. Batista, 'Uma recuperação do conceito Ideologia: Karl Mannheim e a validade da noção de ideologia para a análise de produtos culturais audiovisuais ficcionais', *RELEM – Revista Eletrônica Mutações* 1 (2012): 3. Karl Mannheim's books have been translated into Spanish, Portuguese and French, becoming classic literature in many Latin American and European countries. This fact signals the important presence of Mannheim's sociology in other countries besides Germany, especially by means of subsidiary theories of ideology.

26 See note 23.

27 See Lamartine P. DaCosta, Ana Miragaya and Valeria Bitencourt, 'Epistemological Experiments in the Perspective of Sport in the Global Era', *Revista Portuguesa de Ciências do Desporto* 12 (2012): 74–7; and Lamartine P. DaCosta, Ana Miragya and Valeria Bitencourt, 'Epistemological Experiments in the Perspective of Sport in the Global Era' (paper presented at the annual meeting of the International Association for the Philosophy of Sport, Porto, Portugal, 12–15 September, 2012).

28 Mannheim, *Ideologia e Utopia*, 33.

29 Ibid., 31.

30 Frédéric Baillette, 'Les arrière-pensées réactionaires du sport', *Quasimodo* 1 (1996), 19–25.

31 Michel Caillat, *L'idéologie du sport en France depuis 1880: Race, Guerre et Religion* (Paris: Editions de la Passion, 1989). See Michel Caillat, 'Idéologie du sport' <http://1libertaire. free.fr/MCaillat14.html≥ (accessed 14 April, 2013). The original sentence in French is *'L'idéologie sportive est de type religieux et de tendance expansionniste; elle part à la conquête des firmes dans une sorte de prédication militante.'*

32 Jean-Marie Brohm, *Sociologie politique du sport* (Paris: Jean-Pierre Delarge, 1976).

33 Peter Millward, 'Ideology, Sport and Society', in *Blackwell Encyclopedia of Sociology*, ed., George Ritzer (Oxford: Blackwell, 2006), <www.sociologyencyclopedia.com> (accessed 2 May, 2013).

34 Jean-Marie Brohm, *La tyrannie sportive: théorie critique d'un opium du people* (Paris: Beauchesne, 2006).

35 Paulo C. Nunes Junior and Janir C. Batista, 'Ensaio sobre a organização capitalista do esporte: resgate das contribuições de Jean Marie Brohm para o entendimento do sistema esportivo atual', *EFDeportes.com, Revista Digital* 167 (2012) <http://www.

efdeportes.com/efd167/a-organizacao-capitalista-do-esporte-jean-marie-brohm. htm> (accessed 13 April, 2013).

36   Nunes Junior and Batista introduce their text as follows: 'This essay aims to discuss the question of the capitalist organization of sports on the model proposed by Jean Marie Brohm in the 1970s. From the reading of his work and dialogue with the authors who had supported his theories, we will make reflections about the current dynamics of the sport in our society, offering new interpretations of the theme.'

37   Leandro M. Beneli, Eduardo F. Rodrigues and Paulo C. Montagner, 'O modelo de Brohm e a organização do basquetebol masculino brasileiro', *Conexões* 4 (2006): 48–63. The book by Brohm that inspired and framed the survey proposed by Beneli and his co-authors was *Sociologie politique du sport*.

38   Henri Vaugrand, 'Pierre Bourdieu and Jean-Marie Brohm. Their Schemes of Intelligibility and Issues towards a Theory of Knowledge in the Sociology of Sport', *International Review for the Sociology of Sport* 36 (2001): 183–201.

39   Ibid., 183.

40   Bero Rigauer, *Sport and Work* (New York: Columbia University Press, 1981).

41   The translation into English and the Introduction of Rigauer's *Sport and Work* had the signature of Allen Guttmann, suggesting a close connection between these two authors. Furthermore, Ian Taylor's observations on this connection are found in his review '*Sport and Work* by Bero Rigauer; Allen Guttmann', *The Canadian Journal of Sociology* 8 (1983), 486–88.

42   Simon Martin, *Sport Italia. The Italian Love Affair with Sport* (London: I. B. Tauris, 2011).

43   Gigliola Gori, *Italian Fascism and the Female Body: Sport, Submissive Women and Strong Mothers* (London: Routledge, 2004).

44   Eduardo González Calleja, 'Deporte y poder: El Caso del Real Madrid C. de F.', *Memoria y Civilización* 7 (2004), 79–127.

45   John M. Hoberman, 'Sport and Political Ideology', *Journal of Sport and Social Issues* 1 (1977), 82.

46   John M. Hoberman, *Sport and Political Ideology* (Austin: University of Texas Press, 1984), 2.

47   Hoberman, 'Sport and Political Ideology', 82

48   Ibid., 83.

49   Ibid., 84–92.

50   Ibid., 84.

51   Ibid., 85.

52   Ibid., 110.

53   Allen Guttmann, *From Ritual to Record: The Nature of Modern Sports* (New York: Columbia University Press, 1978).

54   Allen Guttmann, *Games and Empires: Modern Sports and Cultural Imperialism* (New York: Columbia University Press, 1994).

55   Guttmann, *From Ritual to Record: The Nature of Modern Sports*, 157.

56   Guttmann, *Games and Empires: Modern Sports and Cultural Imperialism*, 117.

57   Ibid., 171–88.

58   Dennis A. Hemphill, 'Sport, Political Ideology and Freedom', *Journal of Sport and Social Issues* 16 (1992), 15–33.

59   William J. Morgan, *Leftist Theories of Sport: A Critique and Reconstruction* (Urbana: University of Illinois Press, 1994).

60   William J. Morgan, *Why Sports Morally Matter* (London: Routledge, 2006).

61   William J. Morgan, 'Adorno on Sport. The Case of the Fractured Dialectic', *Theory and Society* 17 (1988), 813.

62   William J. Morgan, '"Radical" Social Theory of Sport: A Critique and a Conceptual Emendation', *Sociology of Sport Journal* 2 (1985): 56–71.

63   Ibid., 71.
64   William J. Morgan, 'Social Criticism as Moral Criticism: a Habermasian Take on Sports', *Journal of Sport and Social Issues* 26 (2002), 281.
65   William J. Morgan, 'What Morally Ails Contemporary Elite Sports?' (paper presented at the XVII congress of Panathlon International, Stresa, Italy, 14–15 May, 2010).
66   William J. Morgan, 'What Makes Athletic Excellence Good' (paper presented at the annual meeting of the International Association for the Philosophy of Sport, Rochester, New York, 8–11 September, 2011).
67   Teun A. van Dijk, 'Ideology and Discourse Analysis', *Journal of Political Ideologies* 11 (2006), 115–40.
68   Sigmund Loland, 'Normative Theories of Sport: a Critical Review', *Journal of the Philosophy of Sport* 31 (2004), 111–121.
69   Peter K. Hatemi, Lindon Eaves and Rose McDermott, 'It's the End of Ideology as We Know It', *Journal of Theoretical Politics* 24 (2012), 345–69.
70   Mandell, *The Nazi Olympics*.
71   Joseph L. Arbena, 'Generals and Goles: Assessing the Connection between the Military and Soccer in Argentina', *International Journal of History of Sport* 7 (1990), 120–30.
72   Terry Eagleton, *Ideologia: uma introdução* (Sao Paulo: UNESP-Boitempo Editora, 1997), 141.
73   The blend of social aspirations, ideas and myths assumed by Eagleton to define ideology per se was actually inspired in the work of Pierre Bourdieu (1930–2002).

15 Competitive Sport, Moral Development and Peace

J.S. Russell

Competitive sport is often defended and praised for its potential to foster moral growth and development of individuals and relations between communities. As a result, the massive expense and effort that goes into international competitions like the Olympic Games and the World Military Games is often justified on moral grounds as contributing to cooperation and respect, and ultimately peace, among nations and among athletes and fans. These claims form what is arguably the key foundation of the Olympic ideal.[1] Within various sport and recreational communities that recognize a moral role for sport, they are widely accepted as settled and beyond controversy. More recently, these ideas have supported the efforts of international organizations like the United Nations to use sport as a development tool to assist rebuilding broken communities and to promote peace.[2]

Philosophers of sport have acknowledged a greater degree of uncertainty about the connection between sport and moral values, but they too have come to a near consensus regarding the morally enlightening potential of sport. Robert L. Simon speaks for many in arguing that competitive sport is best understood as a 'mutually acceptable quest for excellence through challenge'[3] that incorporates a number of significant internal moral values. Specifically, competitive sport must be colour- and culture-blind and respect and recognize a principle of equal opportunity across individuals and nations, since the quest for excellence demands seeking out worthy opponents regardless of race or nationality. More generally, the 'dialogic' character of any mutual quest for excellence requires respect and tolerance toward others, including respectful exchanges that fairly and honestly recognize the contributions of others. In sport, this means a commitment to fairness in observing the rules of play and honest acknowledgement of the strengths and weaknesses of one's opponents' and one's own abilities.[4] More abstractly, we can say that the pursuit of excellence in any area of common human endeavour imposes duties among all contributors to foster a context in which excellence can flourish and that this presupposes a commitment to moral equality.[5]

I am convinced that these now familiar arguments correctly identify some of the key moral foundations of sport and their implications, but I have become increasingly sceptical about the potential of sport to promote these and other moral virtues. Notice that it is one thing to acknowledge the presence of certain moral ideals as being internal to sport, but it is quite another to argue that sport is a promising basis for spreading those ideals. Not to distinguish these claims carefully and defend them separately is to confuse what are mainly conceptual arguments with causal empirical ones. The conceptual evidence for the moral foundations of sport is compelling, but just as compelling is the empirical evidence all around us that sport does not make for either better individuals or better relations between communities. Indeed, there is plenty of evidence that sport has the opposite effect. So we seem to have a tension or maybe even a paradox here that demands to be understood and, if possible, resolved.

Of course, philosophers of sport do not make the elementary mistake of supposing the identification of moral ideas that are embedded in sport suffices to show that competitive sport has morally salutary effects on those who play or watch it. Their arguments are typically that if we could only educate people to understand or take seriously the values that are embedded within sport, then sport *properly understood* has the potential to be used as a tool for promoting important moral values. They argue, and again there is near consensus about this, that what stands in the way are misunderstandings about sport that are encouraged by the corrupting effects of modern society, for example, the effects of creeping moral relativism in a postmodern age and capitalist culture and its promotion of professional win-at-all-costs sport.[6] In short, then, the problems realizing and promoting the moral values that are internal to sport are all external to sport. These corrupting forces include failures of moral insight and various ideological influences that are not attributable to sport per se.

Again, I am sure philosophers of sport are correct in supposing there are external forces that interfere with the recognition and appreciation of moral ideals that can be found within competitive sport. But I suspect that even these qualifications and apologies on behalf of sport represent a too brisk and optimistic defence of the potential of sport to morally enlighten. Despite the progress that has been made answering some bad arguments for the corrupting features of competition in sport,[7] there is a need to consider more carefully whether the moral ideals that are internal to sport are significantly at odds with morally problematic elements that are equally internal or fundamental to sport. For sport, like many (perhaps all) human institutions, may be morally flawed. Just as democracy or adversarial systems of law or the nuclear family each has troubling moral limitations, so may sport. And so, just as we recognize the moral limitations of democracy (for example, the perils of an uninformed and inexpert populace choosing a government, the potential for democracies to tyrannize minorities, the difficulty of devising a truly representative system of government, and so on), and we adopt practices and institutions in attempts to address those limitations, we may need to take a similarly cautious and reformist approach to sport. Just as democracy remains morally messy and a work in progress, so may competitive sport. But like democracy, any measures for addressing moral shortcomings within competitive sport may also turn out to be partial and less than fully satisfying.

The problem with competitive sport is that it gets in the way of its own potential to morally enlighten and to serve as a school for moral virtue. I argue that this is reflected in two partly connected features of competitive sport. First, there is a certain amorality built into competitive sport. From the perspective of sport as a quest for athletic excellence, moral virtues are useful only to the extent that they facilitate such excellence. Virtue is not necessarily superior to vice *as a means* to sporting excellence, and thus vice is to be preferred over virtue where it is more effective as such a means. Unfortunately, there is plenty of evidence of the special utility of vice in promoting athletic excellence. A second problematic feature of competitive sport is the idea of sporting competition itself, which values a certain conception of success that I shall argue is morally flawed.

Cooperation and Moral Failures in Competitive Sport

It will be helpful to lay the ground for this discussion by reviewing claims about cooperation as a moral virtue in sport and then examining some of the empirical evidence of moral failure in sport. The empirical evidence is well known, but it is worth reviewing because it presses the issues under consideration. Cooperation, by contrast, seems to be an obvious moral virtue that competitive sport promotes, because cooperation is a condition of any competitive sporting activity. This is another obvious place to start, then. The problem, however, is that cooperation, while it is a condition of any common human activity, does not by itself reflect any evidence of moral virtue. Glaucon shows us this in *The Republic* by arguing that the unjust person will readily cooperate with others, but only when it is to his personal advantage. Even more to the point, Immanuel Kant anticipates modern economists and political scientists in arguing that given the right set of personal incentives even the most challenging of human social institutions can be set up to serve moral ends. Thus, he argues that with the right incentives the problem of creating a modern government and civil society 'can be solved even by a nation of devils'.[8]

Glaucon and Kant are correct that pursuit of personal interests may require cooperation, and can even be enlisted to establish reasonably stable cooperative practices and institutions that serve moral ends. But this also means that cooperation is not on its own evidence of morally virtuous behaviour. We have to be careful, therefore, about claims that the cooperation required in competitive sport either reflects or promotes personal moral virtue. Given the abiding human love of competition, games and physically challenging activity that are combined and reflected in competitive sport, both the angels and devils among us have profound personal incentives to cooperate to engage in it. But such cooperation may not make the devils better disposed toward the angels or better persons generally. This does not mean that sport cannot be used as a tool to promote or encourage the learning of cooperation or that cooperation is not an important social good.[9] It means, however, that if people play competitive sport together, this is not yet good evidence that they either have, or are learning to have, respect for each other or are developing any other moral virtues. They may come to do so through sport, but it remains to be seen how potent a vehicle sport is for these purposes, or if it is one at all.

Unfortunately, the empirical evidence regarding the connection between sport and moral growth and development is bleak to say the least and should invite a thoroughly self-critical inquiry about sport's potential to morally enlighten. At the level of individual athletes, psychological studies done over the past 50 years have uniformly shown lower levels of moral development among elite athletes as compared to their peers.[10] These studies should give serious pause to anyone who thinks sport has special potential to make better people, for these studies beg the question about what makes sport specially problematic. More troublingly, if elite athletes are corrupted by external societal forces and their own lack of attention to conceptual moral argument, then why aren't their peers corrupted to a similar degree? It is at least puzzling why competitive sportsmen and women appear more susceptible to such corrupting influences, and the comparison with their peers suggests we should look at other factors besides ones that are external to sport.

We should also consider the behaviour of fans. I am not aware of any systematic scientific studies of the morality of sports fans, but the public evidence we have looks at least as discouraging. Sport is used around the world by its fans as a stand-in or proxy for conflicts, jealousies and animosities that exist between them, both as supporters of teams and as representatives of communities. At one level, this is reflected in the boos and catcalls that typically meet the introduction of the visiting teams at home games, but fan abuse of opponents is almost always more systematic than this. In almost all sports, partisan fans have various ritual chants and activities that involve derision of other teams. This is raised to a sort of competitive art of its own in United States collegiate sports. As a Canadian attending Cornell University in New York, I recall my first college sporting event, which was a match for the Ivy League (American) football championship. The Cornell fans' insults towards the opposing team (University of Pennsylvania) and its band were so well organized and fierce that I wondered how either could perform, which of course was exactly the point. The University of Pennsylvania supporters responded with the following parody of the Cornell school song, which seemed to me entirely apt in the circumstances:

> Far above Cayuga's waters,
> There's an awful smell.
> Some say it's Cayuga's waters.
> We say it's Cornell.

All good fun? Well, maybe, but it certainly does not seem plausible that people are being morally educated or enlightened by attending these games. Are these types of behaviour the product of creeping moral relativism and capitalist values? Well, maybe, but this hardly appears to be the whole story, particularly since these types of behaviour can be found in non-capitalist and morally conservative societies. And, of course, these are far from being the most extreme examples of fans' poor sportsmanship and misbehaviour.

Fans of football from around the world often regard their clubs as vehicles for expressing historical prejudices and animosities. One of the most famous is the conflict between the Protestant Glasgow Rangers and the Catholic Glasgow Celtic. At games between these two fierce rivals, you can hear chants that are considerably more offensive and vulgar than anything you can hear at a United States college game. One chant parodies the children's nursery song 'If you're happy and you know it, clap your hands …' The Protestant fans' version goes: 'If you hate the fuckin' Fenians clap your hands (clap, clap). If you hate the fuckin' Fenians, clap your hands …' Many of the Protestant fans' chants refer to the Pope being the object of sexual acts that are mortal sins in orthodox Catholicism. The Catholic fans repay these compliments in their own way, of course, presenting predictable challenges for preserving public order. Again, it is difficult to see any moral enlightenment going on at these events. And while the Rangers-Celtic fan rivalry seems particularly bitter, it is neither the only such example nor the worst. Variants of this sort of behaviour are common throughout the football-playing world, which is to say they exist everywhere. The worst case I know is discussed by Franklin Foer in his book *How Soccer Explains the World*.[11] In it, Foer chronicles how Serbian football fan clubs in the former Yugoslavia because of their violent tendencies were readily organized into groups that became a leading force in the murder and ethnic cleansing of Croatians and Bosnians. We might well ask why these sorts of problems are basically unknown at other displays and celebrations of human excellence, such as academic conferences and film, music or literary festivals. Again, we need to inquire about what makes competitive sport special in this sense. (I will say more on this later.)

What of larger communities like nations? It hardly needs recounting how the Olympics have been used as propaganda by major powers. Perhaps the worst example is the Berlin Olympics of 1936, but when superpowers put on these events, the organizers are doing it in part to display and attempt to expand their dominance. Thus, the Cold War era was predictably a bad one for the Olympics, and there is no end in sight to the use of the Olympics as politics by other means. It is more than plausible that there are external forces that contribute to some of these behaviours, but we should ask what makes sport so especially attractive to those who would use it for political purposes.

In the face of all this sad evidence, we need to consider seriously whether competitive sport contains within itself certain elements that are morally problematic and that account significantly for some of the moral failures that are associated with it. I make two main claims about this. The first is that, for several reasons, competitive sport naturally engages morally suspect or malign motivations in order to promote excellence. If I am right about this, competitive sport may often require a choice between athletic excellence and moral excellence. It is not self-evident, or even clear, what sort of excellence we should prefer. Frankly, I confess I would probably prefer some athletic progress even at the cost of some moral progress among athletes, and I am sceptical that there is a good argument that we should always prefer moral excellence in this context. I suspect I have company. The second claim is that competitive sport contains within itself a corrupt ideal of value, and this is a source of moral problems both within sport and for the influence of sport on society.

The Problem with Competitive Sport

For more years than I can readily count, my family has holidayed each New Year at a Canadian mountain lodge that has an outdoor ice hockey rink. There we spend many hours playing a watered-down version of ice hockey called 'shinny'. No one keeps score, anyone can play regardless of age or ability, and the rules are adjusted accordingly (no lifting the puck or slapshots, for example). Similar pickup games involving versions of other sports can be found on fields and playgrounds around the world. Not surprisingly, these types of game playing tend to be friendly affairs, marked by good sportsmanship, good humour and respect for others. However, they have obvious drawbacks from the perspective of sport and games. The main one is that they are not conducive to the development and display of sporting excellence. There is no expectation that players will play at their highest level of exertion and ability, and play will not reflect a sophisticated understanding and execution of game strategy and teamwork. All this, of course, changes when competition is formally added and the goal is to strive wholeheartedly to win. Sportsmanship and friendliness and respect for opponents are no longer givens in this context. They have to be taught and reinforced. This should not be so puzzling. Once sport becomes competitive, it is not evident that the familiar moral virtues of friendliness, sportsmanship and respect for others will be conducive to the highest level of sporting excellence and achievement. In fact, there is good reason to believe that striving for excellence or playing one's best can for some individuals, and perhaps for most or all individuals at least some of the time, require motives that are morally disturbing or even destructive of personal character. In a thoughtful discussion of the costs of competition, the Canadian philosopher Thomas Hurka (taking his cue also from his experience of shinny) puts the matter this way:

> It would be nice if we could always do the best thing from the best motive, playing the most skilful hockey without wanting anyone to lose. But we aren't like that. Often we need extra motives for excellence, and what comes with these motives isn't always attractive.[12]

Hurka is thinking of dislike of opponents as providing an edge, particularly in contact sports, but there is no doubt that many competitors in all sport find this a source of useful motivation. Coaches also look for it in their players. Perhaps the most extreme (and frank) example was baseball coach/manager Leo Durocher, who was famous for the line 'nice guys finish last'. Here is what Durocher looks for in a teammate: 'Give me some scratching, diving, hungry ball players who come to kill you … That's the kind of guy I want playing for me.'[13]

Even participants in non-contact sports adopt similar attitudes. Tiger Woods once admitted in an interview that for him the desire to compete, in anything from cards to golf, was fundamentally about wanting 'to kick your butt'.[14] His mother (whom Woods credits with giving him his competitive attitude) went further in the same interview: 'That's sport. You have to. No matter how close friend [sic] you are, you must kill that person.' Of course, one does not have to look far to find similar ideas expressed in any competitive sport. Even Olympians are not shy about expressing such ideas. In the 2010 Winter Olympics in Vancouver, Canada, a leading member of the United States national ice hockey team, Ryan Kesler, explained that the reason some of his best performances had come against the Canadian team was because 'I hate them'.[15] (Ironically, Kesler was also at that time, and remains to this day, a well-loved member of the NHL Vancouver Canucks ice hockey team.)

These are all morally offensive metaphors and remarks. They are ubiquitous in competitive sport and are used freely by players and coaches as motivating devices. Of course, perhaps some athletes never need such motivation to achieve their best. They may be the few philosopher kings and queens among sportsmen and women. But the simple and regrettable fact is that these sorts of motivations have a place in human psychology precisely because they wonderfully focus the mind and are highly effective as motivational tools. It is likely that these motivations can and do often help many of us excel in conflicts with others, perhaps especially in physical conflicts, and this may help to explain some of the discouraging evidence about the lesser moral development of elite-level athletes. Indeed, we might think such vices can be competitive virtues in an Aristotelian sense: kept under control so that there is not too much or too little emotion, there is a sort of mean to be sought with malign motives that is relative to the circumstance and supports the display of athletic excellence.

Malign motives are not strictly or logically internal to sport in the sense that they are not conceptually entailed by sport. It is logically possible to engage in sport without these motives. Angels can play hockey. Nevertheless, the pursuit of sporting excellence will seek and utilize whatever means are the most effective to this end. This amorality within competitive sport will therefore exploit whatever resources humans bring that can contribute to athletic excellence and are permitted by the competition. There is another important connection between competitive sport and these motives. This can be traced to the fact that competitive sport is a type of *ritualized partisan physical conflict* (to amend Mary Midgley's gloss on games as a 'ritualized conflict'[16]). That is to say, competitive sport is an artificial, rule-governed conflict involving competing physical excellences. These sorts of motives are typically found, and undoubtedly have their biological origins, in the context of human conflicts, and in physical conflicts in particular, so it is to be expected that competitive sport as a ritualized physical conflict will tend strongly to engage them. The connection is not one of logical necessity, but the internal nature of competitive sport as a type of partisan conflict will quite naturally elicit these motives from evolutionary aspects of human psychology – and the more so if they can be used effectively to encourage excellence. Later, I shall give another argument that further explains why these emotions are such a common feature of competitive sport. For now, I want to emphasize how this sort of competition differs from other human activities that involve pursuit of excellence through competition and how these differences also help to explain the greater prevalence of these motives in competitive sport.[17]

Excellence and the Varieties of Competition

It is interesting that many other areas where human excellence is pursued are not similarly beset by intense desires to visit various types of physical domination or revenge over others. I am thinking in particular of pursuit of excellence in science and the arts. Thus, we do not typically find academics or artists announcing that they had as a motive during their careers 'to kick the butts of' or 'to kill' their peers. Rather they, at least in the usual case, engage in these sorts of activities because they value the result for its own sake, at least in significant measure. Thus, to be 'the best philosopher' is a statement about contributing to knowledge, not about demonstrating superiority over others (although it might do that indirectly). Of course, competition may be required sometimes to develop skills, or to allocate scarce resources or opportunities, or to compare or demonstrate ability or the importance of one's contributions. And people may be motivated by the competitive pursuit of public recognition or honour. But even allowing for these qualifications, it is still the case that the pursuit of scientific or artistic excellence does not measure success in terms of competition with others per se, but rather in terms of the realization or production of knowledge or artistic value. While cancer researchers may be in competition with each other in some sense, we measure their success by their contributions to the treatment of cancer. By contrast, we measure Tiger Woods' success in the number and quality of his victories over others. This is a difference that bears careful consideration.

Simply put, competitive sport conceptually requires striving to win over others, intellectual inquiry and art require striving for knowledge and aesthetic value. Even if we add or recognize competition as an element in science and art (as we often do and sometimes must), it is readily understood, or at least can easily be explained, that art and science are not themselves *about* demonstrating personal superiority in excellence over others. Competitive sport is not like this. The pursuit is about attempting to measure and determine personal superiority. We might exhort people to focus on the process, not on winning or losing, but competitive sport is ineluctably also about engaging in a sort of competitive ritualized physical conflict with others (the conflict being that each competitor desires to win and, at most, only one can) and striving one's best to resolve that conflict in one's favour. The motive to win is always there in any sporting competition. You can *say* it should not be the goal of competition, as many sport philosophers do, but it is a goal that cannot be ignored. It is always there. Intellectual competition, by contrast, is not fundamentally about resolving a conflict in one's favour, but resolving it to advance knowledge – whoever 'wins'. It is thus not ultimately partisan about the outcome of the competition. These are fundamentally different measures of competitive success and it is plausible to believe that their differences will tend to influence the attitudes of those who engage in them.

One way to think of this is that competitors in intellectual inquiry are more like teammates than opponents. You are trying to find ways to succeed together, rather than simply to overcome each other. Although there will often be internal competition for roles on a team, including highly challenging competition, teammates are expected ultimately to cover up or put animosities and dislikes aside, put the team first, and participate in a cooperative fashion to promote the success of their common enterprise (i.e. the success of the team). By contrast, their relation to their opponents is strictly partisan in the sense that their goal is to achieve victory over their competitors. For reasons I have given, certain morally questionable motives are both predictable and useful in partisan contexts where the goal is to demonstrate relative superiority over another, but they are, of course, toxic to and readily undermine more immediately cooperative activities and so they are understandably discouraged in this context. This explains why it is very poor form for teammates to take the same competitive attitudes toward each other as they do toward opponents. Such individuals often find themselves ostracized or 'off the team' very quickly. It barely needs to be mentioned that it is highly inappropriate to adopt such attitudes to opponents in intellectual debate.

In certain important respects, competitive sport is closer to the competition we find in adversarial systems of law than to adversarial practice in intellectual inquiry. It will be instructive to draw this comparison to illustrate and support the points just made.[18] In a thoughtful account of why the adversarial method in law should not be compared to adversarial processes in philosophical inquiry, Nicholas Dixon has noted that the main problem is that success from the perspective of the legal adversaries is measured by whether their side wins and the decision goes in their favour, not by whether the truth is discovered and justice is done.[19] As Dixon puts it, 'the legal adversary method is a competitive pursuit of victory', and adversarial philosophical inquiry is properly regarded as 'a *cooperative* search for the truth or the most reasonable position'.[20] Lawyers within adversarial systems of law are thus partisans for their clients, and are to do what they can within the rules of the court to succeed on their behalf. Since they have no general overriding commitment to the truth or justice or excellence, it is no surprise that they sometimes use tactics that would be utterly inappropriate in the context of intellectual inquiry but often have analogues in competitive sport, such as gamesmanship, intimidation or bullying of witnesses, withholding key information and knowingly introducing misleading theories or evidence, to the extent these are permitted by the rules.

Dixon's argument can be supported in a different way. Notice that intellectual inquiry fails if it degenerates into a game of one-upmanship, but this is, of course, a tool of adversarial legal method and it is just what competitive sport institutionalizes. An anecdote will illustrate this point.[21] The Cornell philosopher Max Black was once facing a particularly persistent and apparently annoying questioner at a public talk. He eventually became exasperated and tried to end the exchange by saying, 'Well, now you are just trying to score points.' The metaphor of 'scoring points' Black chose is revealing. Intellectual debate and inquiry is not a sport or a game. Success there is not properly measured by scoring points but by contributing in as wholeheartedly constructive and impartial a way as possible to the goal of advancing knowledge and understanding. In competitive sport, there is nothing wrong with one-upmanship and scoring points, but it is a failure of intellectual inquiry if it falls to this level. Thus, we draw a distinction between sophism and philosophy.[22] Sophism reduces intellectual inquiry to a partisan contest or a game. Philosophy does not. Sophists are strict partisans for their side in an argument whatever the evidence, philosophy and philosophical debate require being open to changing positions on the basis of evidence.

This distinction demonstrates that measuring success in some types of competition is fundamentally different from in others. There is *partisan success*, which requires victory over others, and *non-partisan success*, which does not. The latter measures success by achievement of a common objective, such as the production of knowledge or artistic value. At times, it can enlist competition to serve this purpose. As such, victory over others is in no way the real measure of the success of non-partisan competition, whereas it is at least partly the measure of success in partisan competition. The distinction helps to explain the greater presence of certain tactics in one type of competition and their more common absence in another. Intimidation and bullying and veiled or openly malign attitudes toward opponents can be quite useful as means in partisan contexts such as competitive sport (including for encouraging sporting excellence and pursuing victory), but they will generally be poisonous to the openness and cooperation needed for non-partisan competition to succeed.

Philosophers of sport have often drawn the comparison with competition in other areas to argue that there is nothing especially problematic about competition in sport. But they compare apples and oranges, in particular partisan and non-partisan varieties of competition. Simon explicitly draws the comparison between competition in intellectual inquiry and sport. Despite identifying some notable moral parallels (mentioned at the outset of this article), his discussion overlooks the important differences.[23] Jan Boxill points out that we often accept competition as a cooperative challenge to better ourselves or make contributions to society, and she rightly argues that there need be nothing that is morally flawed about this. She argues that competitive sport can adopt this model, too.[24] But this overlooks the important differences between the partisan nature of competition in competitive sport and more benign forms of competition. A similar point is arguably true about Simon's position that sport is 'a mutually acceptable quest for excellence through challenge'. I accept this claim and Simon's arguments for the moral values that can be drawn from it, but it softens and leaves ambiguous the nature of the challenge that is involved, for there are many non-competitive examples of mutual quests for excellence through challenge. Researchers may agree to work together on the challenge of finding a cure for cancer. The 'challenge' in this sense refers to a test of human abilities and resources in overcoming a difficult obstacle. This seems to be what Simon has in mind. He proposes that 'the value in sport lies not in winning but in overcoming the challenge presented by a worthy opponent'.[25] But 'challenge' in competitive sport goes beyond this to express a call to engage in a fundamentally partisan conflict or confrontation. Such partisan conflict or confrontation is intrinsic to the competition and striving to win. Arguably, competitive sport is more accurately (if less elegantly) described as a 'mutually acceptable quest for excellence through ritualized partisan physical conflict'. But stated in this way, it is easier to recognize the distinctive competitive character of competitive sport and its moral flaws, which in turn help to explain some of the morally troubling evidence that is associated with it.

Simon also argues that given the accessibility and cross-cultural nature of sport, the internal moral values of sport are not culture-specific, and so sport can be used as a vehicle for educating and promoting important moral values across cultures.[26] But the counterpoint is that competitive sport may also be a vehicle for spreading moral vices across cultures, if there are vices that are internal or deeply connected to sport. If so, it is possible those vices may qualify, or even overwhelm, the potential to use sport as a tool of moral education. Boxill is arguably even more optimistic than Simon about the potential of sport to promote healthy human relations. She claims that the virtues that are associated with competition generally – perseverance, honesty, cooperation and courage – make competition 'a perfect vehicle for friendship'.[27] Simon is almost as optimistic. He says that sport as a mutual quest for excellence represents 'a paradigm case' of treating others as moral equals.[28] But the empirical and philosophical evidence of the moral messiness of competitive sport casts doubt on whether it truly is a perfect vehicle for promoting friendship or an exemplary model for reflecting moral equality.

I am confident that the idea of non-partisan intellectual dialogue and debate affords a better model for promoting both friendship and moral equality, even if it is often imperfectly realized in practice. Admittedly, as with any mutual quest for excellence, respect for intellectual opponents is consistent with disliking them, perhaps intensely, and with heartfelt competition. But when it dissolves into mere one-upmanship or valuing getting ahead of others as the primary goal, it is easy to identify potential threats to the enterprise and the openness and cooperation that it relies upon (even if in some circumstances such motives can produce useful results). Indeed, it is relatively easy to show that such an approach to intellectual debate fails to reflect moral equality and respect for others, since it uses one's adversaries as unwitting means to further an individual's partisan or personal goals rather than to contribute to what is assumed to be a common non-partisan goal. It is sophists (or maybe fanatics for a cause) disguising themselves as philosophers. Scandals involving falsification of research data or withholding data from adversaries in order to embarrass others or manipulate them into errors reflect extreme versions of this sort of moral failure. A less egregious failure is also reflected in the Max Black example discussed earlier. But unlike intellectual inquiry and debate, getting ahead of others and one-upmanship are unexceptionable within the terms of competitive sport. And because personal partisan conflict is intrinsic to the activity, it quite naturally enlists certain malign motives and certain types of non-cooperative behaviour (e.g. intimidation and gamesmanship) because these presume partisan conflict. Arguably, then, these can be found more prevalently, or at least more openly, in competitive sport because they appear to pose less of a threat of undermining the enterprise or calling it into question, since the goal of the activity is defined by the pursuit of partisan victory. Given their role in partisan physical conflicts, they may often be useful to many participants in promoting athletic excellence, as discussed above. I doubt this is nearly as plausible in non-partisan competition.[29] However, Simon could still argue that since the adversaries accept a partisan approach to competition at the outset, this is consistent with recognizing moral equality and respect for others within competitive sport. I accept this, but it must be acknowledged to be in some tension with these other features of competitive sport. If we are at all Aristotelian about moral virtue, then habituating ourselves to these dispositions will not be a good thing for moral development. Finally, and unfortunately, there are other, deeper reasons to be concerned that the mutual quest for excellence in competitive sport is a flawed model for reflecting moral equality and respect for others.

The other main argument I have for the morally problematic nature of competitive sport is developed from the connection between competitive sport and Kant's account of human jealousy.[30] Kant's treatment of jealousy reflects his dark assessment of how personal ambition – the desire to be superior to and to dominate others and to be recognized for this – is both a basic element of human nature and its most fundamentally corrupting feature.[31] According to Kant, jealousy reflects the fundamental human desire not to be inferior to others. We have two jealous responses to someone we perceive to be better than us. One is 'to snipe at' or 'cut down' another to make ourselves at least feel superior. Kant calls this type of jealousy 'grudging'. The other type of jealousy aims to make ourselves better just so we can be demonstrably as good as or superior to others. Kant calls this 'emulating jealousy' or 'jealousy of emulation'. Of the two types of jealousy, jealousy of emulation is less common because it requires personal efforts to make oneself better. However, Kant argues that jealousy in both its forms reflects a corrupt idea of value, since it regards *relative excellence* as an end rather than pursuit of excellence for its own sake. According to Kant, comparing oneself to an ideal of perfection, or something that is valuable for its own sake, is the only proper way of arriving at an opinion of one's worth. By contrast, pursuit of relative excellence is a corrupt idea of value and will frequently lead to a result that is opposed to our own perfection, including our moral perfection.

It should be pretty clear how these Kantian vices, and in particular jealousy of emulation, are reflected in competitive sport, for competitive sport institutionalizes the motivation and striving to be superior to and dominate others through competitive conflict. Thus, competitive sport institutionalizes relative excellence as an end rather than pursuit of excellence simply for its own sake. The basic moral failure here, to put it in Kantian terms, is that by regarding personal worth in comparative or relative terms, I will regard myself as worth more (or less) than others based on my value relative to others. The danger, then, is that I will fail to see the absolute worth of individuals (including myself). In extreme cases of pursuit of relative excellence, I will not be able to recognize the absolute worth or moral equality of individuals at all. Thus, I will find it easy to come to think of using others as mere means, for example, to hate those I am competing with, or to want to kill them, or to kick their butts, and so on, because I am consumed by the desire to feel and be superior to them. I will also regard the superiority of others as a challenge to my own worth. By contrast, if I forsake the pursuit of relative value as a goal and pursue perfection for its own sake, my success and worth is not measured specifically by interpersonal comparisons of worth. Since achieving favourable comparisons with others is not the object of my activity, I have no reason to measure my worth in this way, and I will be less prone to overlook the moral value of others.

It is not difficult to see the relevance of this to sport. Indeed, we can see grudging and jealousy of emulation at work in any genuinely competitive sport activity from a small town league rivalry to Olympic and professional sport. It is present in the statement 'Yankees suck!' that follows the Bronx Bombers into every foreign ballpark and in Tiger Woods' assertion that his goal has always been to be dominating. Unlike the pursuit of excellence in science and art, it is a conceptual truth that competitive sport institutionalizes the aim to seek relative superiority over others, and generally the greater and more public the relative superiority the better. Even if one is trying to run farther or faster, jump higher or be stronger, competitive sport institutionalizes this as fundamentally a relative comparison between individuals. Winning, despite whatever else it may be, is a statement of superiority or dominance over others. This, of course, explains competitive sport's profound attraction as a political tool. But if Kant is right, it also explains its attraction to all of us at a deep and frankly disturbing psychological level. This provides another, deeper explanation for the sorts of malign motivations discussed earlier. It also explains the profound sense of failure that athletes sometimes experience in losing, one that goes beyond simple disappointment to a feeling that they have somehow lost something, or are less worthy, as persons, even though they may have given their greatest performance in defeat. Kant is surely right that if one measures personal success in such relative terms, these sorts of responses are bound to ensue. The problem is that competitive sport is conceived around just this sort of relative valuation. We can encourage people to ignore it, as sport philosophers commonly do (thus implicitly giving this Kantian argument its due), but it is always there nevertheless.

Reforming Competitive Sport

These problems with competitive sport help to explain the ubiquity of the vices that are associated with it and their apparent resistance to reform. They persist at a deeper level than explanations grounded in inattention to philosophical arguments and corrupting social forces. They should be given prominent weight in discussions of the morally troubling aspects of sport. A disturbing aspect of them is that they may also have effects beyond sport. That is, given the immense influence of sport in contemporary society, it may become a vehicle for promoting certain vices outside sport.[32] The corrupting influences may move in two directions. Society may encourage or reinforce poor moral attitudes in competitors and their fans but the example of competitive sport may similarly encourage or reinforce troubling attitudes within society, in particular the pursuit of superiority or dominance over others as an end.

It is fair to say that international sporting events and sport educators have done little to either recognize or respond to these internal problems. Until now, the great genius of international sporting institutions like the Olympics has been to create a context where different peoples can come together in peaceful competition and learn from each other through vehicles like the Olympic Village, the opening and closing ceremonies and promotion of Olympic-related cultural events. But while these are important and justly celebrated achievements and symbols, they are themselves external to the activity of competitive sport itself and so do not directly address the problems within sport. If we are serious about using sport to promote moral progress and peace, then we should publicly recognize the moral tensions within it and its limitations and take seriously the need to adopt measures to amend sporting practice, so that it is more conducive to moral progress.

What these changes might be remain to be worked out. At a minimum, frank recognition of the moral limitations and pitfalls of competitive sport should be part of educating sports officials, coaches and participants generally. But more creative responses need to be considered. In a Kantian vein, we might amend competitive events where it is possible to emphasize the progress of human sporting excellence in addition to relative individual excellence. For example, we might begin to keep records of aggregate accomplishments in individual sports, so that, for example, records for total times in the final medal heats or rounds are kept and awards are given, not only for top individual finishes, but also for aggregate local, world or Olympic records, depending on the venue. Arguably, this would measure and acknowledge local, transnational and transcultural human athletic achievement and progress at a deeper level than through the awarding of individual medals. It would mean that all participants would be recognized as striving to contribute to the collective advancement of human sporting excellence and de-emphasize the pursuit of relative excellence through ritualized personal conflict. Other similar measures could be taken, for example, new national or personal records that are broken at events could be publicly recognized at medal ceremonies. Such proposals will not work, of course, for many team sports. But other types of proposals should be considered. For example, we might end national team competitions, and draft the players into truly transnational teams where they have, say, a year to prepare for the games, under the direction of transnational teams of coaches. This is a radical idea, but it is certainly possible to implement in a world of modern transportation and communication, and it could at one stroke remove some of the national politics from Olympic and other international sporting events. It is encouraging that the recently inaugurated Youth Olympic Games have moved significantly in this direction.[33] John Gleaves and Matthew Llewellyn have recently argued that transnational competition is also required by a commitment to athletic excellence, and they have responded to various arguments that national teams should be preserved.[34] A virtue of their proposal is that it would tend to draw the focus toward the realization of sporting excellence for its own sake and away from conceiving of international sport as contests for assessing national superiority and dominance over others.

We might also encourage or invent competitive sports that are more likely to contribute to moral growth. For example, some sports, like golf, curling and ultimate, are what we might call 'honour sports', since they are largely or entirely self-officiated. They have obvious advantages from a moral perspective, since (among other things) participants do not accept what they recognize as undeserved advantages, which can be a flaw of officiated sports. I have argued elsewhere that encouraging some measures of self-officiating (say, for disputed calls) would help to put competitive sport on a better moral ground.[35] Sports where conflicts are not immediately one-on-one may also have some advantages in downplaying some types of motives. Judged sports like figure skating, diving or gymnastics, and sports where the conflict is more directly with nature or oneself, like golf or high jumping or some types of downhill skiing, should perhaps be emphasized more.

Clearly, more thought and investigation need to be given to some of these proposals. And it is an open empirical question to what extent these sorts of changes can assist moral development. Nevertheless, a frank awareness of, and investigation into, the moral limitations and costs of competitive sport is long overdue and should be part of any informed discussion about its moral value. If I am right about this, proposals like these should be on the table. They cannot eliminate all the moral tensions within competitive sport, but they may help to clarify further some of the moral ideals within sport and do a better job of promoting them. Finally, the obligation to pursue these avenues falls most strongly on institutions that wish to use sport to promote moral development and peaceful relations between individuals and communities. Amateur athletics and the Olympic Movement arguably bear the heaviest burden to take a clear-eyed look at the current moral limitations of competitive sport and to devise ways and means of responding to them. They should not be blinded by their love of sport from seeing its moral flaws and doing what can be done to address them.[36]

Notes

1   Cesar R. Torres, 'Morally Incompatible? An Analysis of the Relationship between Competitive Sport and International Relations at the Olympic Games', *SAIS Review* 31 (2011): 3–16.

2   United Nations Office on Sport for Development and Peace (UNOSD) <http://www.un.org/wcm/content/site/sport/>. See also Simon Darnell, *Sport for Moral Development and Peace* (London and New York: Bloomsbury, 2012).

3   Robert L. Simon, *Fair Play: The Ethics of Sport*, 2nd ed. (Boulder, CO: Westview Press, 2004), 27.

4   Robert L. Simon, 'Sports, Relativism, and Moral Education', in *Sports Ethics: An Anthology*, ed., Jan Boxill (Malden, MA: Blackwell, 2004), 20–5.

5   J.S. Russell, 'Broad Internalism and the Moral Foundations of Sport', in *Ethics in Sport*, 2nd ed., ed., William J. Morgan (Champaign, IL: Human Kinetics, 2007), 51–65.

6   Simon, *Fair Play: The Ethics of Sport*; William J. Morgan, *Why Sports Morally Matter* (New York: Routledge, 2006); and Jan Boxill, 'The Ethics of Competition', in *Sports Ethics: An Anthology*, ed., Jan Boxill (Malden, MA: Blackwell, 2004), ch. 5.

7   Simon, *Fair Play: The Ethics of Sport*, ch. 2.

8   Immanuel Kant, 'On Perpetual Peace', in *Kant's Political Writings*, ed., Hans Reiss (Cambridge: Cambridge University Press, 1970), 112.

9   Thus, sport is often used to teach cooperation to children and to help repair communities broken by civil strife or war. See note 2. There is nothing in the argument that I am presenting that rejects these uses of sport. Nevertheless, we shall see that it is important to have a clear-eyed awareness of the limitations of sport to promote cooperation and moral virtue generally.

10   Sharon K. Stoll and Jennifer Beller, 'Moral Reasoning in Athlete Populations – A 20 Year Review', Center for Ethics, University of Idaho <http://www.educ.uidaho.edu/center_for_ethics/research_fact_sheet.htm> (accessed 12 July, 2011). J.S. Russell, 'The Moral Ambiguity of Coaching Youth Sport', in *The Ethics of Sports Coaching*, eds., Alun R. Hardman and Carwyn Jones (London: Routledge, 2011), 87–103.

11   Franklin Foer, *How Soccer Explains the World: An Unlikely Theory of Globalization* (New York: Harper Collins, 2004). Foer also chronicles the Rangers-Celtic rivalry.

12   Thomas Hurka, *Principles: Short Essays on Ethics* (Toronto: Harcourt Brace and Company, 1994), 271.

13   Leo Durocher (with Linn, E.), *Nice Guys Finish Last* (New York: Simon and Schuster, 1975), 5–6.

14   Daniel Schorn, 'Tiger Woods Up Close and Personal: Golf Superstar Talks to Ed Bradley About Planning a Family', *60 Minutes*, 2 December, 2009 <http://www.cbsnews.com/stories/2006/03/23/60minutes/main1433767.shtml?tag=contentMain;contentBody> (accessed 15 April, 2013).

15   Ben Kuzma, 'Kesler Fired Up With Hate: Canucks Center Takes Bitter Shot at Team Canada', *The Province* (Vancouver, BC), 21 February, 2010, A 84.

16   Mary Midgley, 'The Game Game', in *The Ethics of Sport: A Reader*, ed., Mike McNamee (London: Routledge, 2010), 37.

17   It is worth noting that psychologists have wondered about the effects of competition on human aggression. Thus, there is, for example, a relevant lively debate among experimental psychologists as to whether it is the violent content of gaming or competition that explains evidence of players' aggression toward others. See Paul Adachi and Tina Willoughby, 'The Effect of Video Game Competition and Violence on Aggressive Behaviour: Which Characteristic Has the Greatest Influence?', *Psychology of Violence* 1 (2011): 259–74. The arguments presented in this essay can help to explain why psychologists should be looking at connections between competitive sport and aggression and other antisocial tendencies. However, the argument presented here does not claim that all types of competition are morally problematic. In this sense, the argument of this essay can be regarded as providing a deeper explanation of why competitive sport, and some other types of competition, are morally problematic than was given in Alfie Cohen's now classic critique of competition, but it does not present a general argument against competition as Cohen did in *The Case Against Competition* (Boston: Houghton Mifflin, 1992). The studies mentioned in Stoll and Beller's review cited above frequently identify a greater tendency to 'egoistic reasoning' in athletes. The analysis presented here may help to clarify some of the sources for that reasoning and suggest other avenues for investigation.

18   Other comparisons are apt too, for example, partisan politics or competition in the marketplace. I will focus on a comparison with adversarial systems of justice, since the goal of the partisans is so clearly to win without being guided by justice, all things considered. In partisan politics, the goal is to win, but also to pursue political justice. This adds a further level of complexity.

19   Nicholas Dixon, 'The Adversary Method in Law and Philosophy', *The Philosophical Forum* 30 (1999): 13–29.

20   Ibid., 17, original emphasis.

21   This event was related to me by Robert L. Simon at the International Association for the Philosophy of Sport's Annual Meeting in Rochester, NY in September 2011.

22   See Dixon, 'The Adversary Method in Law and Philosophy', for a discussion.

23   Simon, 'Sports, Relativism, and Moral Education', 20–2.

24   Boxill, 'The Moral Significance of Sport', in *Sports Ethics: An Anthology*, ed. Jan Boxill (Malden, MA: Blackwell, 2004), 6. See also idem, 'The Ethics of Competition'.

25 Simon, *Fair Play: The Ethics of Sport*, 26–7. Simon's position is that sport is 'most defensible ethically when it is understood as a mutual quest for excellence' (38). This is consistent with there being moral tensions and flaws within sport that get in the way of that understanding.

26 Simon, 'Sports, Relativism, and Moral Education', 26.

27 Boxill, 'The Ethics of Competition', 113.

28 Simon, *Fair Play: The Ethics of Sport*, 35.

29 Admittedly, this is an empirical claim. Just to be clear, I am not suggesting that such motives cannot have pay-offs in excellence in other contexts. I am sure they can. It is rather that they can be more dangerous in a variety of ways if used in non-partisan competition. A further part of the evidence for this is that people are usually quite careful about hiding such motives if they have them.

30 Immanuel Kant, *Lectures on Ethics*, trans. Louis Infield (New York: Harper Row Torchbooks, 1963), 215–17. See also discussions of these issues in J.S. Russell, 'The Moral Ambiguity of Coaching Youth Sport', and idem, 'Coaching and Undeserved Athletic Success', in *The Ethics of Coaching Sports: Moral, Social, and Legal Issues*, ed., Robert L. Simon (Boulder, CO: Westview Press, 2013), 103–20.

31 Allen W. Wood, *Kant's Ethical Thought*, (Cambridge University Press, 1999), 264–5, 289–90.

32 Russell, 'The Moral Ambiguity of Coaching Youth Sport'.

33 International Olympic Committee, 'Youth Olympic Games Fact Sheet' <http://www.olympic.org/Documents/Reference_documents_Factsheets/The_Youth_Olympic_Games.pdf> (20 February, 2013).

34 John Gleaves and Matthew Llewellyn, 'Ethics, Nationalism, and the Imagined Community: The Case Against Inter-national Sport', *Journal of the Philosophy of Sport*, forthcoming.

35 Russell, 'Coaching and Undeserved Athletic Success'.

36 For helpful comments on this paper, I am indebted to Robert L. Simon and Cesar R. Torres and to an audience at the Seminário 'Desporte, Desenvolvimento e Paz' that was sponsored by the Centro Conjunto de Operações de Paz do Brasil e a Academia Brasileira de Filosofia held during the World Military Games in Rio de Janeiro in July 2011, and to an audience at the International Association for the Philosophy of Sport's Annual Meeting in Rochester, NY in September 2011.

16 Sport, Spirituality and Religion

Simon Robinson

The opening of the London 2012 Olympic Games underlined the links between sport, religion, spirituality and culture. At one level, the opening ceremony attempted to link back to the original Olympics through the lighting of the Olympic flame. The flame was lit some months before at a ceremony and site linked to the original Olympics. The flame is symbolic of the high values at the heart of the Olympics, but also links back to the sacred nature of fire, which burned outside Greek temples, and which, in myth, Prometheus stole from the gods. This sense of a link to the transcendent is reinforced by the fire being lit for the modern Olympics from the sun with the aid of only a lens. From such a religious connection a whole series of symbols and rituals have been added, including an anthem (composed in 1896), an oath (added in 1920), a flag with the symbol of five rings (designed in 1912), the release of doves (1896) and a relay for the flame torch carriers (1936).

With these symbols and rituals the actual religious context of the Olympics has become superseded by a broader sense of spirituality. This looks to develop a sense of common good and shared responsibility and stewardship for the global community, focusing in a non-theistic transcendence of individual and national identity. Hence, the rings symbolize the interdependent nature of the five continents. The oath involves commitments to the core values and focuses on the honour and integrity of the athletes and officials, based in the 'spirit' of the games and the Olympic community. The anthem focuses on the importance of tradition and upholding ancient values. It is of little surprise that all this should have emerged from what Pierre de Coubertin referred to as the *religio athletae*.[1] This non-theistic religion (which does not exclude theistic religions) is, of course, very broad in its scope and engages many different narratives, some of which might conflict with other values. Perhaps most notably, the ritual of the Olympic relay for the flame torch in 1936 was the creation of Joseph Goebbels, focused in a nationalistic narrative.[2] Problematic narratives of a different sort have emerged more recently with the sponsorship of multinational corporations, which, it is argued, contradict the core spiritual identity of the Games.[3]

The dynamics and growth of the Olympics reveal much about the relationship between sport, spirituality and religion, not least the initial association of sport with religion, the development of a wider sense of spirituality, and questions about how both relate to ethical and wider cultural values and how they relate to the experience of athletes and the wider sporting community. This essay will begin to unpack these.

Definitions and Developments

The term 'religion' comes from the Latin *religionem*, respect or care for what is sacred. There is also *religiare*, attested by St. Augustine, meaning to bind fast, to place obligation on. At the heart of the term, then, is commitment to something, be it a way of life, an idea or belief. Religion is mostly now associated with formal groups or institutions, whose task is to maintain the community of commitment through rituals that focus on the history and narratives of the community, their core meaning and implications for personal development and practice. In effect, formal religions try to hold together community discipline, shared meaning and personal commitment. This offers something of a range between the formal religious expression of commitment and the personal expression of commitment, and involves maintaining structures but also individual agency. Inevitably, this means that all the major religions have dynamic, sometimes turbulent, histories, involving institutional ossification and defensiveness (often involving association with political power) and moments of great change, which try to focus on a return to core practices and personal agency, commitment and care. Examples of figures who created such change include Luther and St Francis. Not surprisingly, this dynamic leads to plurality within formal religions, from different denominations to different schools of jurisprudence.

The level of personal commitment and focus is often where the term 'spirituality' is focused. The term 'spirit' is derived from the Latin *spiritus* (Hebrew *ruach*, Greek *pneuma*), meaning breath, wind and even essence or life principle. Hence, any idea of spirituality is holistic, not simply based on rational agency, and involves understanding and practising the essence of humanity and thus developing holistic meaning in relationships. The term 'soul' is often seen as synonymous with spirit, and has been seen by many as not just the essence of the person but also a non-material entity that is distinct from, and can possibly even survive, the physical body. This has introduced a dualism into spirituality, leading to distinctions between mind, body and spirit, contrasting with perspectives of the spirit as essentially holistic – involving rational, affective and somatic elements together, in relationships.

Formal religions in the West dominated the cultural discourse about human essence and significant life meaning, until the rise of modernity and then post or late modernity. The first of these, arising from the Enlightenment, stressed the rationality of the individual and questioned the metaphysical foundations of religion.[4] While this did not inevitably lead to a challenge to formal religion,[5] it did encourage the questioning of power structures, and the questioning of myth, in the sense of the core narratives that underpin significant meaning. So-called postmodernity saw a more aggressive questioning of dominant narratives. Postmodern scholars argued for new ways of understanding language and social constructs.[6] Jean Baudrillard,[7] for instance, sees the division between art and life as breaking down, with no objective sense of reality and each person having to create their own reality and underlying life meaning. This works against privileged and normative views of spirituality. Instead of meta-narratives there were local narratives, determined by groups or individuals. This was reinforced by the 'new age' in the second half of the 20th century. More a collection of different movements, this asserted the importance of holistic meaning making, as distinct from orthodox doctrinal meaning, and defended the freedom to develop generic spirituality, based on individual choice, against the imposition of institutional spirituality.[8]

Sociology suggests that such diversity was further reinforced by, and also contributed to, a breakdown of patterns of behaviour and moral institutions such as marriage and the family, caused partly by the increase in wealth and mobility, and partly by changes in attitude towards the sanctity of marriage and the notion of securing a partnership for life. Alongside this was a greater development and awareness of cultural and religious diversity within society, caused by increased migration and global awareness.[9]

Philosophy and psychology further reinforced the emergence of individualized holistic spirituality that was not necessarily connected to religion, through phenomenology,[10] existentialism,[11] transpersonal psychology[12] and social constructionism.[13] Phenomenology and existentialism, in particular, were concerned to move away from looking at phenomena from the outside, and to focus on the stuff of experience. Existentialists argued that experience and being precede rational analysis. This also emphasizes feeling at the heart of such experience, and the way in which experience could not be easily described in self-contained concepts. Existentialism was never a single or simple school. Part of it shares with postmodern thinking a rejection of narratives that attempt to impose meaning on experience. Life is absurd, it is argued, and of itself does not make sense. Nonetheless, humans need to make sense of their alienating and ambiguous experience and engage their social environment. Central to this was authenticity, being true to the self and the social and physical environment.[14] For Jean-Paul Sartre, this meant breaking through mechanisms that encouraged people to avoid the engagement of the individual with the self and the ambiguous environment. Every individual thus bears responsibility for such engagement, for the social and physical environment, and for making significant meaning and practice of these. This involves personal responsibility for how we see the world and respond to it. Other philosophers such as Charles Taylor, Iris Murdoch and Robert Solomon[15] encouraged philosophy, and ethics in particular, to engage with wider views of metaphysics and underlying world views as a means of fuelling the imagination and expanding consciousness of the social and physical environment. This encouraged the ownership of wider meaning, without it being institutionally imposed, but argued for a spirituality that tied into the major narratives and also experientially into relationships with the wider social and physical environments. The importance of a community that enables this, as distinct from a directive institution, was seen to be acceptable.

All of this suggests that there are many different views of spirituality. Nonetheless, despite its contested nature, it is possible to broadly describe a generic spirituality, which may or may not involve formal religion. This focuses in consciousness of the social and physical environment, interaction with that environment, and the making of significant life meaning. Spirituality would thus involve:

- Developing *awareness* and *appreciation* of the other over time (including the self, the other person, the group/community/wider society, the environment and, where applicable, deity).
- Developing the capacity to respond to the call of the other. This involves putting spirituality into practice, *embodying* spirituality, and thus the continued relationship with the other.
- Developing *ultimate life meaning* based in significant relationships with one or more member of the social and physical environment, and in creative response to the network of those environments.[16]

Awareness and appreciation involves knowledge of the holistic other; the other as both same and different, and hence ambiguous; the interdependent other; the other as always emerging, always learning and therefore never totally knowable; the other as involving imminence, awareness of the self and transcendence, a movement beyond the self.

Response to the other is essentially about the articulation of spirituality in practice. It involves roles that express something of the relationship to others, and the contribution towards these relationships. The working out of these roles involves the expression of the uniqueness of the person and their particular part in any relationship. The response to the other can be seen in terms of *vocation* (calling), or response to the *calling*, or needs, of the other and in terms of placing *trust* in the other. The idea of vocation has tended to be either restricted to particular purposes, or professions or in practice to the Christian spirituality, with God calling the Christian. However, in terms of a broader human spirituality, all the different others 'call' the person in some way. The environment calls the person or group to be aware of the complexities and interconnectedness and to respond with responsible stewardship. The group calls the person or other groups to be aware and to respond to need with a particular contribution. The other person calls for response as her needs are disclosed. Al McFadyen[17] argues that such a call is the basis of personhood. Any calling, of course, has to be critically tested, and, as shall be seen below, it also involves negotiation about how responsibility is to be shared.

The response of the person to the other, then, becomes an embodiment of spirituality, life meaning in action. In this sense, the response is another aspect of transcendence, with action going beyond the self. The embodiment may be individual or collaborative. Importantly, the embodiment of this spirituality is in itself a working out of the life meaning, not simply the applying of a set meaning to the situation. Indeed, it is not possible to fully understand any life meaning other than in and through the practical testing and working out of it.

Developing life meaning is often identified purely with the development of doctrines – belief systems that set out something about the nature of life and its different aspects. Such world views naturally emerge from awareness of, and reflection on, the other. However, life meaning in the light of the holistic and community perspective cannot be simply confined to conceptual beliefs. It is rather located in and understood in two major ways:

- *Holistic meaning*: this involves whole person awareness.
- *Value-based meaning*: meaning here is discovered in the value the person recognizes in herself and others. It is therefore based in the perceived identity of the person. Such value is based on both a sense of unconditional acceptance from the other and a sense of the worth, expressed in contribution, to the other and the wider community, a sense of purpose.

Meaning is then based in the relationships that give value to life and includes the development of faith and hope. Fowler defines faith in two ways:

1) The foundational dynamic of trust and loyalty underlying selfhood and relationships. In this sense, faith is a human universal, a generic quality of human beings.
2) A holistic way of knowing, in which persons shape their relationships with the self, others and the world in the light of and apprehension of and by transcendence.[18]

Fowler argues that faith develops through discernible stages. Each of these stages is about the development of the self and the relationship of the person to the different others, leading to a point of spiritual maturity in which individual agency and community relationships are held together.

All of this provides a view of reality that is not just 'given' but also created, and this begins to generate *hope*. Hope in this sense becomes the capacity to envision the future positively.[19] Both faith and hope have been characterized as theological virtues,[20] but can also be seen as general spiritual virtues.

All this views spirituality as relational, reflective, holistic and dynamic. It involves meaning based in faith, hope and purpose, with transcendence not as a loss of the self but rather the discovery of identity in relationships and creative action. It also involves energy[21] generated by meaning and relationships. The tension between structure and agency remains, not least because as meaning is found in relationships some form of community is required to enable such a dynamic and sustain meaning development. Hence, the emergence of a more generic spirituality does not exclude religious or any other communities. Most formal religions would argue that they aim for an interrelated community of spirituality and that where the survival of an institution of religion takes precedence, this involves teleopathy,[22] an imbalance of purposes.

Spirituality in Practice

Increasingly, spirituality has been focused in areas of practice, such as work and organizational leadership, health care and education. Research from the Leeds Church Institute, for example, examined spirituality in work organizations, focusing in particular on how members of these organizations relate their work to life meaning, and how the organization of work might enable this.[23] Among other things, this suggests that those with a religious background often do not relate this to their experience of work. Those with a non-religious background tend to develop a spirituality of work, in the sense of consciously finding significant life meaning there. Much of the work in leadership and spirituality looks to how the community of work can foster such meaning.[24]

Spirituality in practice has been focused most securely in education and health care. In one sense this is hardly surprising, as the development of both areas has been historically linked to institutional religion.[25] However, the focus of spirituality in both areas has become wider than simply the religious. Spirituality is not something that is brought *to* the practice of learning or caring but something that is bound up in it, with spiritual meaning emerging from reflection upon the experience and the practice.[26] In health care, spirituality has been focused in general medicine, psychiatry and especially palliative care, and in organizational and professional spirituality. This has involved the development of tools of spiritual assessment and focus on spiritual techniques, which enable developing awareness, responsiveness and life meaning, as part of therapy.[27]

Attacks on the Concept of Spirituality

Writers such as Lee Crust[28] (sport) and John Paley[29] (health care) argue against the use of the term 'spirituality'. First, they argue, the concept is not clear. There are many different uses of it, with different criteria for determining what is correct or reasonable. Second, the term derives from religion and is still associated with that. Crust argues that many writers begin with a generic definition and revert to a religious definition, not least when reporting experiences that refer to help from a transcendent source. Third, Crust argues that the very term 'spirit' is vague and not open to empirical verification. Fourth, it is not clear whether the reported empirical work actually points to something termed spirituality as distinct from psychology. Many writers on spirituality refer to psychological and spiritual needs as if it were obvious what the difference was. Crust suggests that the term 'psychological' is quite sufficient – in terms of need for significant relationships, need for meaning, and so on. Fifth, Crust suggests that qualitative empirical work can easily lead to an uncritical approach to the data. In the end, all the data can point to is sets of beliefs that are held by the practitioners. It does not support either a religious view of spirituality or a domain that is distinct from psychology or social psychology.

Use of the term has been defended in several counterarguments. John Swinton and Stephen Pattison[30] argue that the idea of spirituality does not have to be specific. On the contrary, there are many different words that are vague or general that precisely find their meaning in reflection on practice. Simon Robinson[31] argues that a working definition is reasonably clear, and that it is based in enabling agency and meaning in relationships. It is not clear that the term, as such, derives from religion; indeed, it came to be used in religion comparatively late. For example, the new-age movement claims that that wider sense of spirituality, focused in consciousness of the environment, predated the major institutional religions.[32] The fact that some writers confuse or conflate religious and wider senses of spirituality does not falsify the concept. Moreover, it is not clear that any concept, as such, is open to 'empirical verification'. Crust rightly draws attention to problematic uses of the term. The distinction of physical, psychological and spiritual needs, for instance, presumes that spirituality is an area (possibly with an attendant academic discipline) that is different from the other two areas. This also suggests a dualistic view of spirituality, which it is not possible to verify empirically. However, the description of spirituality above, focused in the development of holistic meaning, suggests rather that spirituality is centred in holistic experience, and, as such, connects to all aspects of the person in relationships. Hence, it is not a separate area or discipline and is open to the investigation of several different academic disciplines, including psychology, sociology, philosophy and theology. Qualitative research enables us to see precisely how people make holistic meaning in their lives, what prevents or enables it, and what effect the practice of such meaning making can have on individual or corporate (in a general sense) lives.[33]

Sport as Religion

Sport does not have any of the drivers, professional or legal, that motivate the integration of spirituality into education or health care. Nonetheless, in several contexts there are real overlaps. The concern for personal development is traditionally linked to sport, with the idea that the practice of sport can enable transformation, liberation, health and well-being and character development.[34]

As I noted in the introduction, de Coubertin argued that sport itself could function as a form of civic religion, enabling the transmission of core values through a community, and establishing significant meaning and purpose that were focused in the common good beyond the particular sport.[35] A good example of this is Barcelona FC. Its motto is 'more than a club' and it focuses on meaning and identity as part of Catalonia and Spain and as part of a global network.[36] Their cooperative structure enables the supporters to be part of this meaning making, and the meaning making moves out to engage global responsibility. Michael Novak's analysis of baseball looks further at the structure of meaning making and related rituals affirming sport as a civic religion.[37] At the heart of that is joy, suggesting the importance of gratification based in physical action and in communities based around that. This is the joy of the creative act, which in Christian theological terms involves the balance of *agape* with *eros*, inclusive care of the social and physical environment and care based in the attraction of the other. Michael Grimshaw[38] notes, however, that successful clubs can easily be seen in terms of the worship of perfection. He suggests that, in fact, sport might better be seen in terms of fallible heroes, enabling the fan to focus more on reality, and to accept the less than perfect. This ties in closely with the idea of spirituality seen as awareness of the self and others, and thus an awareness and acceptance of the limitations as well as the potential of the athlete. In all these ways sport can represent and embody meaning, and act as the ground of significant meaning. Such meaning can extend from personal fulfilment to the more complex community meaning including the idea of serving society, expressed once more in the Barcelona FC vision. Hence, sport as a social organization communicates significant meaning. It is not surprising that Grimshaw[39] points to different kinds of epiphanies (revelations) that can be communicated in experience of different aspects of sport.

Certain forms of negative spirituality, in particular those based in non-questioning authority of the leader or ecstatic experience, can lead to ethical and social problems. The Berlin 1936 Olympic Games were based in ritual, ancient myths and modern martyrs.[40] The belief system was precisely one that denied the presence or value of the other, working directly against de Coubertin's vision. Combined with the oratory of Adolf Hitler it produced an ecstatic response from the crowd – a feeling of purpose and hope, and of transcending their situation. All this would suggest two things. First, sport cannot be of itself a fundamental ground of faith. It is rather a means to expressing more fundamental relational values. Second, attention has therefore to be paid to the ends of sport, and what makes spirituality in sport acceptable. This reinforces the need for critical testing of meaning, and the expression of meaning in the other, as part of the development of any spirituality. Any organization that claims to generate significant meaning should be tested for the arbitrary exclusion of others, the encouragement of dependency and discouragement of mutual reflection or critical autonomy, and the denial of responsibility for their own thinking or for their response to the other. The stress on critical thinking as a key part of the development of spirituality is comparatively new to contemporary debate.[41] However, it recaptures a genuine sense of holism, against a largely affective view of the 'new-age' movement. It also underscores a dynamic relationship between spirituality and ethics.[42] Against traditional views of religion, which derive ethics from scripture or core doctrinal principles, this sees any spirituality as itself subject to ethical challenge. Drawing from the existentialists, this also stresses the close relationship of responsibility to spirituality, both for making meaning and for creatively responding to the call of the social and physical environment. The relationship between ethics and spirituality is also reinforced through the virtues, ethical and spiritual, not least with the stress on the relationship between virtues and meaning generated by community narrative.[43]

There is an ongoing debate about whether sport may be seen as religion in an existential sense of providing ways to an experience of the numinous, not least through the experiences of extreme sports such as rock climbing or skiboarding.[44] This comes down to how one might define the numinous, or sublime, any awareness of that which is greater than the self, and whether this can be associated with the divine as defined by formal religious doctrines. It also raises questions as to whether such experiences are genuinely relational (i.e. involve awareness and appreciation of the other, or are focused simply in, possibly gratuitous, attention to the experience itself). Narrowly focused, such experiences are more likely to lead to negative behaviour, including addiction to the experience itself and exclusion of awareness of the wider social and physical environment, one's identity in relation to that, and the related 'call'.

Sport and religion

The relationship of sport to different religions is more problematic, partly because religions come to sport with specific values and identities and related potential conflicts. Buddhism, for instance, comes to sport with a concern not to cause harm by physical action, placing it in conflict with many sports. At the same time, there is great concern for mindfulness and holistic health, which makes Buddhist meditation very useful in focusing the sportsperson (see below the discussion on spiritual techniques). Despite critiques from St Augustine about negative relationships to sport,[45] Christianity has a long tradition (not least of St Thomas and St Ignatius) of associating spiritual development (in a religious sense) with physical development.[46] In Victorian Great Britain, this developed into the idea of muscular Christianity, a movement that saw sport and physical activity expressing something of the glory of God.[47] This extended to the use of sport as a means of evangelism, but also became associated with the wider growth of the British Empire. Such associations have themselves caused problems with other religions, including Islam. Islamic theology, like the other Abrahamic religions, has a positive view of sport. Islamic scholars stressed the importance of balancing the mind and the body. Some sports, including running, horseback riding, wrestling, swimming and archery, were practised from the beginning of the faith.[48] However, some Islamic scholars (largely Salafī) view sport as based in Western culture and the globalization of such culture as an attack on the Muslim faith, leading to a social and moral vacuum. Other scholars (largely Wasaṭī), while suspicious of Western cultural influence, argue rather for an integration of Muslims into sporting practice. Historically, some scholars have argued that Islam should emulate muscular Christianity in order to effect the growth of Islam.

All this aptly demonstrates two things: that relationships between religion and sport are often mediated by other factors, such as cultural and political identity, and that these are always different perspectives about religion itself. Hence, increasingly in Islam, this issue has become a matter for taking out *fatwa*, rulings, by the local imam about a solution to how the Muslims may relate to sport.

Of course, sport and any religion may well in different ways lead to value conflicts. Simple issues such as beliefs about the holiness of the Sabbath may lead to sportspersons withdrawing from events. The classic case was Eric Liddell withdrawing from an Olympic 100-metre heat in 1924. More recently, the increase in multiculturalism in the West has led to problems about the accommodation of religious practice to sport. There are several examples of Muslim women being asked to remove the *hijab* during football, basketball or swimming competitions.[49] On closer examination, the problems reveal several different factors, from health and safety to the politics of *laïcité*. In the London 2012 Olympic Games, one female swimmer was refused permission to swim in an overall bodysuit because it might have given her an advantage. Broadly, these cases involve issues where the core values of sport, such as fairness and health, trump religious rights, issues where it is reasonable to accommodate religious duties and rights (such as the provision of 24-hour restaurant facilities during Ramadan), and issues where there are more contentious value conflicts (such as between the right to wear religious symbols and a secular job or political policy against this). Even the last of these is not a simple matter, given that some religious scholars argue that Islam requires its followers to be fully citizens of their chosen country and thus adhere to its laws. Against this, basketball player Mohamud Abdul-Rauf was repeatedly suspended by the NBA for failing to stand for the national anthem.[50] His interpretation of Islam as 'the only way' led to this conflict. Increasingly, however, the stress in Islam and sport is on developing *ijtihad*, interpreting the scriptures in context.

Increasingly, spirituality, religious or wider, is seen as normative. This does not refer to normativity as ethically prescriptive but rather as based in a critical awareness of the different value narratives in the social environment. Such plurality militates against any totalizing or cultic view of spirituality, enabling mutual challenge through engaging different narratives. This relates to the growth of critical interculturalism,[51] i.e. the possibility of both accommodating rights and also challenging practices that go against either human rights or the greater good. The different perspectives within religions and between them and other cultures themselves provide another approach to critical challenge.[52]

Religious/Spiritual Techniques

Traditional religious spirituality was always concerned about techniques and discipline, the aim being to deepen relationships with God. Such techniques as the Ignatian Spiritual Exercises involve prayers and meditation that enable the development of a consciousness of God, having a direct effect on the perception, attitude and capacities of the person. With development of a more generic spirituality, spiritual techniques tend to focus less on relationships and more on capacities and virtues. In health care and medicine, this is well exemplified by the school of positive psychology.[53] Positive psychology looks to certain techniques to develop virtues that will directly strengthen the patient, enabling him or her to take responsibility for therapy. The classic example is the 12-step approach to addiction. This focuses on the 12 steps leading to recovery. Critical to success are the first steps in which the patient learns humility and dependence on others through the acceptance that he or she needs others to help recovery. It also provides a strong sense of community support, with patients themselves becoming an active part of that community of mutual care.

The use of spiritual techniques in sport also seeks to enable focused and holistic states that improve performance. Susan Saint Sing,[54] for instance, stresses that such techniques enable the balance of mind, body and emotions and how important this is in enabling the person to develop the best performance. There may be several different approaches to this from the overtly religious, based in prayer, as lived out by triple jumper Jonathan Edwards,[55] to the development of positive psychology, expressed through techniques such as meditation.

Meditation

Meditation has a long history in Western and Eastern religious spirituality. It is often associated with relaxation, and therefore a useful technique for addressing anxiety. In the mental health context, it is now increasingly being used to develop 'mindfulness'. Mindfulness is the capacity for the human mind to transcend its preoccupations with negative experiences – with fears, anxiety, anger and obsessions – and bring a holistic attention to the experience of each moment.[56]

It focuses precisely on the observing self, providing epistemic distance from negative perceptions of the self and the social and physical environment. This aims not to change the content of thoughts but rather to enable the person to alter attitudes to or relationships with those thoughts. Hence, it enables effective and flexible thinking and understanding and control of emotions.

Meditation, then, is associated with two main processes. Firstly, it leads to an experience of, and acceptance of, 'impermanence', the way in which perceived reality is constantly changing. This process involves the transcendence of thoughts and feelings, enabling both metacognitive awareness and interoception. Metacognitive awareness[57] is the awareness of thought and how we think. Hence, we can begin to distinguish between a thought that we are responsible for and intersubjective reality. Interoception involves physical awareness as part of holistic awareness, and with that an openness to new perspectives. Secondly, meditation enables the capacity to monitor the self from the perspective of a detached observer. Involved in most meditation practice is the heightened but detached awareness of sensory and thought experience. For the sportsperson, this both contributes to focus, being 'in the zone' so that performance can be optimized, handling stress and anxiety, and also enables focus on the wider sport environment, empowering a balanced response when emotions are heightened in a game.

William Glasser[58] suggests that meditation can also be seen in terms of a 'positive addiction', one that is intrinsically rewarding. Research has shown a wide constellation of physical and psychological effects including:

- Reduced oxygen consumption and carbon dioxide and lactate production.
- Reduced adrenocorticotropic hormone (ACTH) excretion. This produces the opposite effects of stress.
- Reduced heart rate and blood pressure.
- Reduced activity in the sympathetic branch of the nervous system.
- Changes in electroencephalographic brain wave activity and function. These are consistent with slowing down of brain and body activities.[59]

Meditation also assists in enabling the experience of 'flow' in sport. Mihály Csíkszentmihályi[60] refers to this as a state of complete immersion in an activity. Flow is 'being completely involved in an activity for its own sake. The ego falls away. Time flies. Every action, movement and thought follows inevitably from the previous one, like playing jazz. Your whole being is involved, and you're using your skills to the utmost.'[61] This involves several factors, though flow does not have to involve all of them. Central to this is strong concentration and focused attention around a sporting action that is attainable but that challenges the participant to stretch her skills. Action and awareness are merged, such that the sporting experience itself becomes a form of meditation. This leads to a feeling of serenity and a loss of self-consciousness. Consciousness of time is also affected, with feeling so focused that one loses track of time passing, hence a sense of timelessness, and feedback on what is happening is immediate. With all that, there is a lack of awareness of physical needs, such that the person can cope with concomitant pain and suffering. Indeed, the Buddhist origins of meditation aim for a transcendence of the self, which involves a transcendence of suffering and all negativity connected to self-obsession. Inevitably this leads to feelings of control over both the situation and the outcome. This control is associated with the development of key virtues. The virtues of the individual sportsperson are often seen as the strengths of character that enable better performance. Saint Sing[62] relates this to the Greek concept of *arete*, a state both of grace and excellence. Holistic techniques can enable the so-called 'runner's high', which leads to the activity of running itself experienced as akin to the mystical or transcendent. The activity then becomes intrinsically meaningful and rewarding. It becomes autotelic, done for its own sake. Tensions remain, however, between virtues centred in the moment and the individual athlete (potentially excluding the wider social environment), and virtues focused in wider relationships.[63] Positive psychology looks to deeper developments, such as resolution and forgiveness,[64] and this includes how to handle failures positively. G. Alan Marlatt and Jean Kristeller[65] suggest that this transcendence also enables the person 'to become more comfortable with compassion, acceptance and forgiveness',[66] hence the practice of other virtues more associated with sport as a wider community of meaning and practice. In the case of sport, this includes the moral framework of justice, fairness and respect.[67] In a related area, the use of spiritual techniques in counselling sportspersons has also been noted.[68]

Spirituality has often been seen in terms of energy and power.[69] This might be in terms of a transcendent model, with external power being given or infused to the sportsperson. Or it may be seen as energy that comes from holism and from positive relationships in the community of meaning.

Prayer

Prayer and associated rituals have had similar effects on meditation. This is summed up in research on the effects of the rosary and yoga mantras. Both forms of prayer involve on average six breaths per minute, leading to 'striking, powerful and synchronous increases in cardiovascular rhythms'.[70] There are several forms of prayer associated with well-being, including ritual, petitionary, colloquial and intercessory:

Ritual prayer can simply involve repetition of well-known words. However, ritual prayer tends to be part of public worship and this also builds up awareness, in this case of the community. It is associated with the development of related virtues, not least empathy.

Petitionary prayer involves prayer about specific needs. This is often associated with times of crisis and coping techniques.

Colloquial prayer involves informal conversation with God. It can include conversation about anything, and is associated with increased intimacy with the divine presence. Such prayer can also involve an articulation of feelings and tensions, exemplified in the Hebrew psalms.

Intercessory prayer involves a conscious focus on issues, practice and other people, in the context of relating to the divine other, and often in the context of the ritual community. As such, this promotes both the awareness of different stakeholders in the local and global community and their need. It is therefore action oriented and relates strongly to practical wisdom and the development of hope.

In the light of this, Jay Coakley[71] suggests six reasons athletes utilize religious prayer: as a coping mechanism when faced with stress, support of ethical living, a religious offering of the athlete's sport skills, placing sport into perspective, enabling a strong bond of attachment between teammates and as enabling social control. A number of investigations have shown the use of prayer by athletes before, during and after competition to be a common and valuable practice for enhancing performance and overall well-being.[72] These help the athlete to be focused in the face of stress, and remain above negative dynamics on the field. Other studies suggest that prayer can reinforce a strong sense of worth in the sporting activity.[73] While research is increasing into prayer and its effects, much remains speculative about the nature of the effects and their causation.

Prayer has also been associated with religious evangelical witness. This is exemplified in the very public praying of quarterback Tim Tebow.[74] Tebow's praying involved a witness to his personal faith, a focus for evangelism, associating success with religious faith and the assertion of a constitutional right to pray. Perhaps the most appropriate challenge for or against such a use of prayer is that of Jesus himself, who argues that it is wrong to pray publicly, i.e. to draw attention to the fact that one is praying.[75] Again this suggests the possible teleopathic use of spiritual techniques, i.e. focused on personal or institutional achievement rather than focus on relationships.

The relationship between spirituality and sport is complex and multifaceted. This essay has suggested that views on spirituality are continuing to develop, focusing on awareness of the social and physical environment and developing holistic meaning in response to them, such that the physical and affective mediation of meaning is balanced with critical challenge, and community of practice is balanced with agency. This suggests a dynamic relationship between spirituality and ethics, focused in responsibility, the development of virtues and the working through of continued mutual challenge. In the light of that, spirituality is becoming increasingly focused on how the individual engages with the plural narratives that make up the social and physical environment rather than one static narrative. This would characterize postmodern spirituality not in terms of asserting individual narratives but in terms of critical and creative dialogue with the plural narratives of the social and physical environment. The work of philosophers such as Paul Ricoeur[76] suggests that what brings such engagement together is responsive, creative and shared action. It also suggests that the poles of spirituality as agency and religion as a formal institution come together in active community.

Sport is an equally complex phenomenon, which looks to see how meaning is mediated through the engagement of the whole person in physical activity. In all of that, the very activity of sport has been seen as an individual spiritual or mystical experience, as relating directly to formal religious practice, as a practice focused in a community of meaning (implicit religion) and as a community that mediates holistic and relational meaning to the wider society.

A great deal of the literature on and research in sport and spirituality has been focused on the justification of spirituality, as a discernible concept, as a state, virtues, or practice, that can contribute to performance, well-being or happiness in sport, sport management and sport counselling. The danger of justification is that it narrows boundaries and hides complexity. Equally problematic are conceptions of happiness. The developments in spirituality and its relationship to sport might suggest research should now explore complexity and well-being in sport. Even within sport, there are plural narratives around individual, professional, corporate, community, social, environmental and theistic vocations, calls to those who identify themselves, and thus find meaning and worth in and through sport. Are connections being made between each of those levels? How do practitioners make sense of them? What prevents the critical dialogue or creative response? And what can enable more meaningful and effective responses to those calls? These are among the many questions that need to be addressed in working through the relationship between spirituality and sport.

Notes

1 Jim Parry, 'The *Religio Athletae*, Olympism and Peace', in *Sport and Spirituality: An Introduction*, eds. Jim Parry, Simon Robinson, Nick Watson and Mark Nesti (London: Routledge, 2007), 201–14.

2 David Large, *Nazi Games* (New York: W.W. Norton, 2007).

3 Andrew North, 'Legacy of Bhopal Disaster Poisons Olympics', *BBC News Asia*, 30 May, 2012 <http://www.bbc.co.uk/news/world-asia-18254334> (accessed 28 February, 2013).

4 Robin Lovin, 'Moral Theories', in *The Blackwell Companion to Religious Ethics*, ed., William Schweiker (Oxford: Blackwell, 2005), 19–26.

5 Roy Porter, *Enlightenment* (London: Penguin, 2000).

6 Jean Baudrillard, *Simulations* (New York: Semiotext, 1983); Jean-Fancois Lyotard, *The Postmodern Condition* (Manchester: Manchester University Press, 1979); and John Reader, *Beyond All Reason* (Cardiff: Aureus, 1997).

7 Jean Baudrillard, *Simulations* (New York: Semiotext, 1983).

8 Michael Perry, *Gods Within* (London: SPCK, 1992).

9 Ian Markham, *Plurality and Christian Ethics* (Cambridge: Cambridge University Press, 1999); Steven Connor, *The Postmodernist Culture* (Oxford: Blackwell 1989); and Grace Davie, *Religion in Britain since 1945: Believing without Belonging* (Oxford: Blackwell, 1994).

10 Irena Martínková and Jim Parry, 'An Introduction to The Phenomenological Study of Sport', *Sport, Ethics and Philosophy* 5 (2011): 185–201.

11 Steven Crowell, *The Cambridge Companion to Existentialism* (Cambridge: Cambridge University Press, 2012).

12 Brian Cortright, *Psychotherapy and Spirit: Theory and Practice in Transpersonal Psychotherapy* (Albany: SUNY, 1997).

13 Andy Lock and Tom Strong, *Social Constructionism Sources and Stirrings in Theory and Practice* (Cambridge: Cambridge University Press, 2010).

14 Jean-Paul Sartre, *Existentialism and Humanism* (London: Methuen, 2007).

15 Charles Taylor, *Sources of the Self* (Cambridge: Cambridge University Press, 1989); Iris Murdoch, *Metaphysics as a Guide to Morals* (London: Vintage, 1993); and Robert Solomon, *Spirituality for the Skeptic: The Thoughtful Love of Life Spirituality for the Skeptic* (Oxford: Oxford University Press, 2002).

16 Simon Robinson, 'Spirituality a Working Definition', in *Sport and Spirituality: An Introduction*, eds. Jim Parry, Simon Robinson, Nick Watson and Mark Nesti (London: Routledge, 2007), 22–38.

17 Al McFadyen, *Call to Personhood* (Cambridge: Cambridge University Press, 1990).

18 James Fowler, 'Faith/Belief', in *Dictionary of Pastoral Care and Counseling*, ed., Ray Hunter (Nashville: Abingdon, 2000), 394–97. Fowler's two other definitions are overtly religious.

19 Simon Robinson, *Spirituality, Ethics and Care* (London: Jessica Kingsley, 2008).

20 I Corinthians 13. Jane Gillham, ed., *The Science of Optimism and Hope* (Radnor: Templeton Foundation Press, 2000).

21 David Aldridge, *Spirituality, Healing and Medicine* (London: Jessica Kingsley, 2000).

22 Kenneth Goodpaster, *Conscience and Corporate Culture* (Oxford: Blackwell, 2007).

23 David Randolph-Horn and Katherine Paslawska, *Spirituality at Work* (Leeds: Leeds Church Institute, 2002).

24 Simon Robinson and Jonathan Smith, Co-charismatic Leadership: A Critical Examination of Spirituality, Values and Leadership (Oxford: Peter Lang, 2014).

25 James Beck, 'Spiritual and Moral Development and Religious Education', in ed. Adrian Thatcher *Spirituality and the Curriculum* (London: Cassell, 1999), 153–80.

26 Rowan Williams, 'Spirit in the Curriculum', in *Values in Higher Education*, eds. Simon Robinson and Clement Katulushi (Leeds: Leeds University Press, 2005), 24–35.

27 William Miller, ed., *Integrating Spirituality into Treatment* (Washington: American Psychological Association, 1999); L. George, D. Larson, H. Koenig, and M. McCullough, 'Spirituality and Health: What we Know, What we need to Know', *Journal of Social and Clinical Psychology* 19 (2000); 102–16; and William Miller and Charles Thoresen, 'Spirituality and Health', in ed., William Miller, *Integrating Spirituality into Treatment* (Washington: American Psychological Association 2003), 3–18.

28 Lee Crust, 'Challenging the "Myth" of a Spiritual Dimension in Sport', *Athletic Insight, The Online Journal of Sports Psychology* 8 (2006): 17–31.

29 John Paley, 'Spirituality and Nursing: A Reductionist Approach', *Nursing Philosophy* 9 (2008): 3–18.

30 John Swinton and Stephen Pattison, 'Moving Beyond Clarity: Towards A Thin, Vague, and Useful Understanding of Spirituality in Nursing Care', *Nursing Philosophy* 11 (2010): 226–37.

31 Simon Robinson, *Spirituality, Ethics and Care* (London: Jessica Kingsley, 2008).

32 Michael Perry, *Gods Within*. (London: SPCK, 1992).

33 Martínková and Parry, 'An Introduction To The Phenomenological Study of Sport', 185–201.

34 A. Cooper, *Playing in the Zone* (Boston: Shambhala, 1998), 121.

35 M. Ashley, 'Secular Spirituality and Implicit Religion: the Realisation of Human Potential', *Implicit Religion* 1 (2000): 31–50; and Michael Grimshaw, 'I Can't Believe My Eyes: The Religious Aesthetics of Sport as Postmodern Salvific Moments', *Implicit Religion* 2 (2000): 87–100.

36 Simon Robinson, 'The Spiritual Journey', in *Sport and Spirituality: An Introduction*, eds. Jim Parry, Simon Robinson, Nick Watson and Mark Nesti (London: Routledge, 2007), 38–58. See also Nick Hornby, *Fever Pitch* (London: Penguin 2000).

37 Michael Novak, *The Joy of Sport* (Lanham, MD: Madison Books, 1994).

38 Michael Grimshaw, 'I Can't Believe My Eyes: The Religious Aesthetics of Sport as Postmodern Salvific Moments', 90.

39 Ibid., 95.

40 Michael Burleigh, *The Third Reich* (London: McMillan, 2000) and David Large, *Nazi Games* (New York: W.W. Norton, 2007).

41 Robinson and Smith, Co-charismatic Leadership: A Critical Examination of Spirituality, Values and Leadership. (Oxford: Peter Lang, 2013).

42 Simon Robinson, *Spirituality, Ethics and Care* (London: Jessica Kingsley, 2008).

43 Alasdair MacIntyre, *After Virtue* (London: Duckworth, 1981).

44 Nick Watson, 'Nature and transcendence: the mystical and sublime in extreme sports', in *Sport and Spirituality: An Introduction*, eds. Jim Parry, Simon Robinson, Nick Watson and Mark Nesti (London: Routledge, 2007), 95–116.

45 Mark Hamilton, 'An Augustinian Critique of Our Relationship to Sport,' in *Sport and Spirituality: An Introduction*, eds. Jim Parry, Simon Robinson, Nick Watson and Mark Nesti (London: Routledge, 2007), 25–35.

46 Patrick Kelly, 'Flow Sport and Spiritual Life', in *Sport and Spirituality: An Introduction*, eds. Jim Parry, Simon Robinson, Nick Watson and Mark Nesti (London: Routledge, 2007), 107–48.

47 Nick Watson, 'Muscular Chrstianity in the Modern Age, "Winning for Christ" or "Playing for Glory"', in *Sport and Spirituality: An Introduction*, eds. Jim Parry, Simon Robinson, Nick Watson and Mark Nesti (London: Routledge, 2007), 80–94.

48 Uriya Shavit and Ofir Winter, 'Sports in Contemporary Islamic Law', *Islamic Law and Society* 18 (2011): 250–80; and Ahmad Shalaby, *History of Muslim Education* (Beirut: Dār al-Kashshāf, 1954), 173–4.

49 Mafoud Amara and Ian Henry, 'Deconstructing the Debate around "Sport" and Muslim Minorities in the West', in *Islam and the West*, eds., Max Farrar, Simon Robinson, Yasmin Vali and Paul Wetherly (Basingstoke: Palgrave, 2012), 138–53.

50 Ibid.

51 Max Farrar, Simon Robinson, Yasmin Vali and Paul Wetherly, eds., *Islam and the West* (Basingstoke: Palgrave, 2012).

52 Robinson, *Spirituality, Ethics and Care*.

53 William Miller, ed., *Integrating Spirituality into Treatment* (Washington: American Psychological Association, 2003).

54 Susan Saint Sing, *Spirituality of Sport: Balancing Body and Soul* (Cincinnati, OH: St. Anthony Messenger, 2004).

55 M. Folley, *A time to Jump: The authorized Biography of Jonathan Edwards* (London: Harper Collins, 2001).

56 G. Alan Marlatt and Jean Kristeller, 'Mindfulness and Meditation', in ed. William Miller, *Integrating Spirituality into Treatment* (Washington: American Psychological Association, 2003), 68.

57 Ibid., 67–84.

58 William Glasser, *Positive Addictions* (New York: Harper and Row, 1976).

59 H. Benson, *Timeless Healing* (New York: Scribner, 1997).

60 Mihály Csíkszentmihályi, *Flow: The Psychology of Optimal Experience* (New York: Harper and Row, 1990).

61 Mihály Csíkszentmihályi, interview by John Gierland in 'Go with the Flow', *Wired* 4 (1996): 1–2.

62 Saint Sing, *Spirituality of Sport: Balancing Body and Soul*, 12

63 Nick Watson and Mark Nesti, 'The Role of Spirituality in Sport Psychology Consulting: An Analysis and Integrative Review of Literature', *Journal of Applied Sport* 17 (2005): 228–39

64   E.L. Worthington Jr., ed., *Dimensions of Forgiveness* (Philadelphia: William Templeton Foundation, 1998), 341–54.
65   Marlatt and Kristeller, 'Mindfulness and Meditation', 67–84.
66   Ibid., 68.
67   Simon Robinson, 'Spirituality, Sport and Virtues', in *Sport and Spirituality: An Introduction*, eds. Jim Parry, Simon Robinson, Nick Watson and Mark Nesti (London: Routledge, 2007), 173–86.
68   Watson and Nesti, 'The Role of Spirituality in Sport Psychology Consulting: An Analysis and Integrative Review of Literature', *Journal of Applied Sport Psychology* 17 (2005), 228–39.
69   David Aldridge, *Spirituality, Healing and Medicine* (London: Jessica Kingsley, 2000), 41; and N.C. Goddard, 'Spirituality as Integrative Energy', *Journal of Advanced Nursing* 27 (1995): 15–23.
70   L. BernardI, P. Sleight, G. Bandinelli, S. Cencetti, J. Fattorini and L. Lagi, 'Effect of Rosary Prayer and Yoga Mantras on Autonomic Cardiovascular Rhythms: Comparative Study', *British Medical Journal* 323 (2001): 1446–9.
71   Jay Coakley, *Sport in Society*, 8th ed. (Boston: Irwin McGraw-Hill, 2003).
72   Nick Watson and Daniel Czech, 'The Use of Prayer in Sport: Implications for Sport Psychology Consulting', *Athletic Insight: The Online of Sport Psychology* 7 (2005): 26–36.
73   Ibid.
74   Greg Bishop, 'In Tebow Debate, a Clash of Faith and Football', *New York Times*, 7 November, 2011 <http://www.nytimes.com/2011/11/08/sports/football/in-tebow-debate-a-clash-of-faith-and-football.html?pagewanted=all&_r=0> (accessed 21 April, 2013).
75   St. Matthew's Gospel Chapter 6, verse 6.
76   Paul Ricoeur, *Oneself as Another* (Chicago: Chicago University Press, 1994).

17 Violence in Sport[1]

Danny Rosenberg

Violence has been associated with sport since ancient times. One need only recall the ancient Greek sport of pankration, a combination of boxing and wrestling that included kicking, throwing and punching between two competitors. In a later period, Roman gladiatorial contests displayed gruesome and lethal forms of sports violence to entertain the masses. During the Middle Ages, melees were no-holds-barred events that could involve hundreds engaged in fighting and combat, and jousting tournaments then were also violent affairs. Remnants of these activities exist today in sports like boxing, mixed martial arts (MMA), rugby, American and Australian Rules football, soccer and ice hockey, which require severe physical force that often causes pain, injury and suffering among participants.

The presence of violence in sport today is explained in part by the manifestation of masculinity, the role of the media and the power of multinational organizations and governments that foster a climate of violence.[2] In post modern society, influential sport organizations structure and promote sport to elicit maximum public displays of violence by mostly male subgroups, and certain males like 'enforcers' in professional ice hockey, who sometimes assert their power recklessly by engaging in and encouraging systematic sport violence. In this atmosphere, bullying in playground and schoolyard games, abusive conduct by coaches and teachers, hurling invective at sport officials, dangerous behaviour exhibited by sports fans, technological forms of violence against the body, mistreatment against women and minority athletes and actions by athletes both on and off the field of play are ubiquitous expressions of violence in contemporary sport.[3]

That sports violence has a long history and broadened meanings indicates that it has a consistent and prevalent status within our sport experiences and practices. Some argue that sport in previous generations and eras was far more brutal and was motivated for different reasons to today. Still, few can deny that unacceptable and harmful forms of physical assault are part of today's sport landscape.[4]

Whereas the bulk of the literature on violence and sports exists in the sub-disciplinary fields of sport psychology and sociology,[5] less published research appears on the topic in the extant sport philosophy literature. There are, however, some notable exceptions and it is on these sources that this essay will focus. To proceed, this essay will: 1) characterize the meaning of violence in sport, 2) address philosophical and ethical issues related to sports violence and 3) present a concluding remark.

A Characterization of Sport Violence

As will be seen, trying to define violence in the context of sport is difficult. For example, Jim Parry states that violence 'is centrally to do with intentional hurt or injury to others, as well as attempts to harm, recklessness as to harm and negligence'.[6] He distinguishes violence from assertion and aggression that may involve harm, but for the most part the latter are morally acceptable ways of playing sport. These distinctions are less clear in sport psychology and sociology, which often conflate the meanings of violence, assertion and aggression within sport.[7] Parry maintains that violence is morally wrong in most social circumstances even though a distinction can be discerned between legitimate and illegitimate violence, especially in certain political and social situations.[8] For example, violence may be justified in times of war and in personal self-defence, and unlike most sports, boxing and MMA sanction and are inherently characterized by legitimate violence. Thus the rules of boxing and MMA stipulate and permit violence. Illegitimate violence is wrong, usually condemned, and typically outside the written and unwritten rules of sport. Finally, Parry makes an important distinction between acts of violence and violent acts. The latter describe actions that are performed with lots of vigour, energy and fierceness, while the former are distinguished by intentional behaviour that causes and results in harm, injury and suffering.

What is lacking in Parry's initial definition is direct reference to the physical dimension of violence in sport. In a discussion paper distributed by the Canadian Centre for the Ethics of Sport (CCES), the following definition is offered: 'Violence in sport is a physical assault or other physically harmful actions by a player that takes place in a sports context and that is intended to cause physical pain or injury to another player (or fan, coach, game official, etc.), where such harmful actions bear no direct relationship to the rules and associated competitive goals of the sport.'[9]

The discussion paper itself identifies a number of shortcomings with this definition. For example, intention is very difficult to assess, inflicting physical harm is permitted according to the rules of many combat and contact sports, violence in sport is not just a participant problem, the principle of informed consent raises a host of questions, and there are instances of accepted or expected violence outside the rules of some sports.

To elaborate on these points, the ability to clearly discern between intentional and unintentional action can be difficult in normal, everyday situations. In a sport context, especially in fast-paced, interactive sports, this distinction can be less clear-cut from an athlete's perspective, as well as from a non-player's vantage point. Sport is also associated with spectator violence unlike many public, audience-based performances. Football hooliganism is an example of fan violence peculiar to the realm of sport. A number of perplexing questions can be raised on the matter of informed consent. For example, if athletes were to agree to play in a violent way, can such an agreement be made explicit and legally binding? At what age can athletes give consent to such an agreement? Are athletes aware of and do they agree to assume all the risks involved in sport? Finally, rugby is a sport where violent episodes occur outside the rules, like kicking or punching an opponent after the whistle stops play, yet these are accepted and expected actions to some degree in the contest.

The point of the preceding discussion is to say that rather than offer a precise definition of violence in sport it may be more advantageous to describe various meanings of this concept. Robert L. Simon, for example, acknowledges several interpretations of violence linked to the use of force as in psychological and institutional forms of violence, and the wrongful use of force.[10] However, these conceptions of violence do not account for the fact that not every use of force is violent, and that the wrongfulness of an act embedded within a definition leads to a circular argument. Instead of a formal definition, Simon describes a pragmatic sense of violence and asserts that 'violence involves the use of physical force with the intent to harm persons or property',[11] and more specifically, 'sports, to the extent that they involve violence at all, generally involve the use or threat of use of physical force to harm opponents'.[12] This description and the definitions above of violence do not specifically include the use of physical force that results in harm to oneself as can happen in diving, figure skating and gymnastics when high-risk manoeuvres are performed or in long-distance endurance races or cycling competitions.

A further approach to characterize sport violence is Michael Smith's socio-legal typology.[13] He classifies four types of violence: 1) brutal body contact that conforms to the official rules of sport and the law of the land; 2) borderline violence that violates the official rules of sport and the law of the land but is widely accepted; 3) quasi-criminal violence that violates the official rules of sport, the law of the land and to a great extent informal player norms, and is more or less not accepted; and 4) criminal violence that violates the official rules of sport, the law of the land, informal player norms, and is not accepted. Smith claims 1) and 2) are relatively legitimate (e.g. body-checking and fighting in ice hockey), whereas 3) and 4) are relatively illegitimate (e.g. shoulder checks to the head and clubbing an opponent's head from behind with one's stick in ice hockey). The difficult cases in this classification scheme occur in the two middle areas; however, Smith provides a useful way to situate sport violence in social contexts where varying degrees of violence are permissible or unacceptable in relation to sport rules, player norms and criminal law.

Given the above characterization, the following section will only focus on in-contest violence by athletes, even though there is substantial literature on out-of-contest violence committed by athletes and others in the sport community.[14] This delimitation shifts the emphasis to athletes, who are the central agents involved in the execution of physical violence on the field of play. As core producers, the motivations and interests of athletes are more intimately and directly connected to the internal goods and practices of sport. Thus, participants who resort to or exhibit violent behaviours during a contest impact most directly on the nature and character of sport itself.

Philosophical and Ethical Issues Associated with Sport Violence

Sport is a human endeavour infused with moral rules and replete with moral dilemmas. Violence happens to be one of the more pressing ethical issues in sport. Most philosophical and ethical studies of violence in sport focus on boxing and more recently MMA because in part these sports require constitutive actions defined by the intentional use of physical force that harms others. Unlike these combat sports, contact sports such as American football, rugby and ice hockey contain behaviours that require physical force like tackling and body checking but need not involve the intent to harm others. On the other hand, violent episodes do occur even in contact sports.

Robert Butcher and Angela Schneider point out that in the course of everyday life, forcefully pushing and shoving people is prohibited, whereas in rugby they are constitutive movements for playing the game. Moreover, a wrongful 'act of violence in rugby might be a punch or a kick but not a crushing tackle. (And, of course, this is true even if the tackle causes more physical harm than the punch.)'.[15] Stanley Eitzen observes that the ethos of many contact sports goes beyond legal, expected and morally permissible hits, blocks, tackles and checks. Instead, athletes are taught to physically punish their opponents to fulfil game strategies.[16] From a different perspective, Peter McIntosh discusses self-inflicted injuries resulting from risky manoeuvres in some sports that may be described as violent.[17] When specific sport actions are deemed too dangerous, like head tackling in American football, they are banned. However, elite gymnasts, figure skaters and divers seem to always be pushing the envelope to exhibit more elaborate skills and dangerous sequences of movements where physical force can lead to self-inflicted harm. While acknowledging that all sports carry risk of physical harm, some sports may fail to adequately protect the well-being of participants from others and themselves. This can be most egregious in organized youth sport. Finally, television and other media outlets sometimes promote the public celebration of violence in sport. Such promotion has seen the meteoric rise in popularity of MMA over the past decade or so. Although the motives, consequences and influences of all these instances of sport violence may be ambiguous, this author has argued that moral insensitivity explains in part why athletes (and others in the sport community) mostly tolerate, rationalize, legitimize, 'are indifferent to and fail to actively and seriously reduce the level of violence in sport'.[18]

Contact sports pose other difficult issues as to what counts as a legitimate tackle or body-check and when do these actions become acts of violence? A hard body-check in ice hockey, for example, makes use of physical force to achieve strategic ends and does not have to include intent to cause injury. Part of the reason for this is that ice hockey players are taught to properly execute and absorb body-checks, similar to tackling taught to American football and rugby players, to minimize serious injury. It is also understood in ice hockey that athletes assume a certain level of risk and are susceptible to harm and injury when engaged in the sport. However, Simon raises an important issue when he states, 'The key ethical question in fair competition may be whether the use of force takes advantage of an opponent's physical vulnerability.'[19] Here is another element toward understanding violence in sport that has particular relevance to contact sports.

Based on the above observation, Simon presents a novel concept called the vulnerability principle (VP) as follows: 'According to the VP, for the use of force against an opponent in an athletic contest to be ethically defensible, the opponent must be in a position and condition such that a strategic response is possible and it is unlikely that injury will ensue.'[20] Acts that violate the VP include 'undercutting' from behind a basketball player who is in the air. While this example appears to be a clear violation of the VP, Simon recognizes that some acts, like a blind-side tackle against a receiver in American football, are 'ethically dubious'.[21] In ice hockey, it would seem that body-checking complies with the VP, but shoulder checks to the head may be 'ethically dubious' as well. And, similar to American football, ice hockey may be condemned for having too much violence or producing too many harmful risks to players, but it need not be by its nature a violent sport. The question of taking advantage of an opponent's vulnerability in relation to sport violence may be useful to discern violent acts from acts of violence in contact sports, but the VP requires further study and its application is likely helpful only on a sport-by-sport basis.

For example, in recent years the National Hockey League (NHL), North America's premier ice hockey league, has been plagued with on-ice violence specifically related to hits to the head. The issue of violence in ice hockey generally, and more specifically in terms of hits to the head, is a controversial topic. The NHL brand of the sport is known for its aggressive and violent character within a wide range of behaviour. The mix of skills like shooting, passing, stick handling, forechecking, net minding, and the speed and precision of skating, combined with body-checking, often makes for thrilling action. Moreover, organized male ice hockey, particularly in Canada, from youth leagues to the pros, often teaches and encourages violent play like stick work and fighting. Some violent actions in ice hockey are accepted and institutionalized, like fighting, while others are not, and this often makes it difficult to determine whether behaviour like hits to the head is ethical or unethical.

In a recent article,[22] the VP was applied to determine the ethical status of hits to the head in the NHL. But first one must understand what it means to be vulnerable in sport. In general, taking advantage of the physical weaknesses of opponents, either related to a lack of proficient skill, poor reflexes or an athlete's return to competition after an injury, is not considered unethical. Receivers in American football often make catches in positions of vulnerability, and no one expects defensive backs to hold back from taking advantage of this vulnerability by not executing a blind-side tackle. If such blind-side tackles produce too many serious injuries, then rules could be implemented to protect receivers, perhaps similar to those that protect quarterbacks. In tennis, a player is not chastised for hitting consistently to an opponent's backhand to aggravate a previous wrist injury. If the opponent is just returning to competition from a wrist injury, testing the vulnerability of that injury is a legitimate strategic option.

The introduction of protective rules to curb VP violations indicates that the VP is partially grounded in the concept of paternalism, in addition to the intent to harm. Certain sport actions that have the potential to violate the VP should either be prohibited or restricted through the enforcement of rules. So spearing or head-tackling has been outlawed in American football as being too dangerous and this form of tackling is no longer taught. In Canada, there is controversy related to the appropriate age for the introduction of body-checking in ice hockey. As a paternalistic notion, the VP is linked to consequentialist concerns like the incidence, rate and severity of injury, the opportunity to respond strategically and the unlikelihood injury will ensue. As we know, paternalism has its limits when it comes to individual liberty among adults who can and do assume greater risks. Adults who enjoy and feel exhilaration in playing team contact sports would likely want few paternalistic restrictions and are willing to be more vulnerable than most. Moreover, they would likely acknowledge that opponents would take advantage of such vulnerability and this is something they are prepared to accept. The paternalistic character of the VP is needed in some sport contexts, but in other settings it would face strong opposition.

Returning to hits to the head in the NHL, these acts of violence are extremely difficult to curtail because they are an extension of body checking that is often legitimate and may or may not take advantage of player vulnerability. Those who are against a ban refer to 'slippery slope', 'blame the victim' and rule-utilitarian arguments. In brief, these positions argue that removing hits to the head in the NHL would necessarily lead to other forms of desirable contact being banned, that most hits to the head are the fault of the victim who receives a headshot for not being alert enough, and finally, no ban is warranted because there are existing NHL rules that regulate hits to the head and empirical evidence about the risks and harms of headshots is inconclusive. The 'slippery slope' argument is fallacious because banning a specific act of violence would not necessarily diminish the fierce and aggressive playing style of NHL ice hockey. The 'blame the victim' viewpoint is faulty because it absolves all responsibility of the player who hits the head of an opponent and denies that victims can be in vulnerable positions where the head is targeted, which is patently not the case. Finally, rule-utilitarians rely on the fact that if there are no rules that ban hits to the head, then such acts of violence are legitimate because no rules are violated. Moreover, since the risks and harmful consequences of headshots are 'judged' inconclusive, rule-utilitarians exploit such findings to claim that head injuries are not severe and frequent enough to warrant a ban. At the moment, NHL officials are reluctant to enforce a complete ban on hits to the head, though new rules are now in place to reduce them.

By contrast, advocates of no headshots in the NHL believe there is sufficient medical evidence related to concussions and head trauma to implement and enforce a ban on hits to the head. They also point out that given the NHL's violent style of play there is not enough respect between players and awareness of player vulnerability to hold back meting out punishing blows to the head. In other words, a ban would alter the consciousness of players so they would refrain from intentionally and unintentionally targeting the head. A headshot ban in the NHL would create a clearer yardstick or demarcation between legal and illegal, acceptable and unacceptable action in the game. It would give on-ice referees an opportunity to enforce the rules with less ambiguity and greater consistency. NHL ice hockey is one of the most difficult sports to officiate and a ban on hits to the head would go a long way to improving the sport in a significant way. Finally, supporters of a headshot ban in the NHL claim that league officials are disingenuous when they say they are concerned for the safety and welfare of players, yet promote a 'blood and guts' style of ice hockey that includes hits to the head. A ban on headshots would demonstrate a supreme test of league accountability for the safety of players, engender respect among players, curtail and hopefully eliminate dangerous play, and assist in the enforcement of the rules in a consistent and fair manner. In addition to hits to the head, elite-level male ice hockey has another peculiar and common violent feature not found in virtually all other sports, namely, bare-knuckled fighting.

Unlike other sports and for at least a century, fighting at the highest competitive levels of male ice hockey has been institutionalized and is a popular, acceptable part of the game. Young male ice hockey players are socialized into a culture of violence supported by the community so that by the time they enter the elite ranks fighting is an expected and accepted component of the competition. The NHL has no moral qualms about fighting; fans enjoy fights that break out during the course of a game, and the rules that govern fighting are fairly lax when compared to any other sport. For example, NHL players who fight without spilling blood receive a five-minute penalty in the penalty box and can then return to play in the game.[23] In most sports, fighting results in the immediate ejection of players from the game. Of course, fighting is not a prescribed necessary sport-specific skill in ice hockey like skating, stick handling, passing and shooting and does not directly relate to scoring goals. Fighting is prohibited in most youth leagues and in women's ice hockey, and if the NHL had the will to do so, it could ban fighting and much of the aggressive nature of the game would remain intact. One must also recognize that an ice hockey fight is a highly circumscribed, choreographed and short-lived affair and more often than not no serious injuries result from such conflict. Linesmen usually break up fights after a few minutes, penalties are handed out and play resumes after a short break. There are several explanations for the institutionalization of fighting in high-level male ice hockey.

Leagues do not take fighting very seriously. The relatively weak punishments for fighting are in place merely to ensure that such public entertainment does not get excessive or is portrayed negatively. In other words, fighting is good for business at the professional ranks and fans are not bothered by momentary pauses for fights in the game. Another explanation for fighting in ice hockey refers to the notion that players are engaged in a kind of self-policing when they feel officials have missed fouls and penalties. This is so even when players know that by fighting they will be sent to the penalty box. Fighting demonstrates traditional expressions of masculinity that include such values as aggression, domination, courage, respect, honour and risk-taking. Some researchers maintain that fighting in contact sports, especially in ice hockey, has a cathartic effect and serves as a release valve when frustration and anger builds up in athletes. Without an occasional fight in ice hockey, athletes might resort to more serious and harmful forms of violence like using their sticks as a weapon.[24]

Finally, players who do not shy away from fighting become an asset to their team by displaying toughness and can confront opponents by either threatening to or actually fighting them. The so-called 'goon' or 'enforcer' in elite ice hockey is known primarily for their fighting prowess. They have adequate hockey and skating skills to play at an elite level but their role is mainly to protect star players, intimidate opponents, instigate fights and seek retribution when unwritten codes of the game are violated. Ice hockey fighters can set the tone and influence how fierce any given contest is and they are typically celebrated by the ice hockey community, which reinforces the idea that fighting is a 'natural' aspect of the game. Coaches are also known to pressure and send out enforcers to pick fights against opponents or 'take out' certain players to achieve strategic goals. Such 'orders' are well understood by 'enforcers', who are placed in a difficult situation because if they don't 'follow orders' they can be easily replaced by those who will.[25] That certain ice hockey players are designated and identified as fighters and can build a reputation around this element of the sport is ethically questionable. Yet from a philosophical perspective one may raise another issue.

While fighting in elite male ice hockey does not contribute directly to scoring goals, it can influence a win or a loss in the game by shifting any number of conditions. Instigating a fight may lead to a penalty against a key star opponent, offer a respite if one team dominates and is pressuring another team, and settle a score against an opponent who executed an egregious foul that the officials did not call. However, even if these 'reasons' and explanations in favour of fighting are unconvincing and fighting itself is unnecessary, one may still ask, is fighting in elite male ice hockey desirable, or perhaps tolerable and relatively harmless from an injury standpoint? The consensus today is that fighting, especially in the NHL, is desired by most of the ice hockey community. Whether this desire is misguided and fighting cannot be fully justified, for now it is an accepted, institutionalized part of elite male ice hockey and its ethical status, will likely be debated for many years to come.

In a recent article relevant to some of the preceding discussion, Nicholas Dixon critiques violent retaliation in sport as a specific instance of sport violence.[26] His analysis arises mainly from the example of pitchers in baseball who throw 'beamers' or 'bean balls' at the heads of batters to retaliate for unpunished wrongdoing that either the batter or his teammate committed against a member of the pitcher's team. Dixon convincingly demonstrates that the only justification for private retaliatory violence occurs when one faces imminent death or bodily harm by acting in self-defence or in defence of another person. Once an unpunished wrongdoing has occurred one must rely on the legal system to seek redress and one must refrain from any kind of vigilantism. Given this sense of defensible violent retaliation, Dixon argues that no amount of 'athletic vigilantism' is justified in sport, including pitchers throwing 'bean balls', whether the retaliation is executed as a deterrent to avoid some future unpunished wrongdoing or is carried out to promote team unity and other sport values like pitching excellence.

Unfortunately, Dixon does not make reference to the VP whereby elite batters are trained and experienced to avoid getting hit by wild pitches and 'beamers'. While the VP does not guarantee highly skilled batters always avoid getting hit, they cannot be said to be 'sitting ducks'. Moreover, the case of pitchers throwing 'bean balls' is a discrete and open instance of retaliatory violence that can be much more easily recognized and criticized than the multiple ways players retaliate in contact team sports. Athletes in football, ice hockey, soccer and rugby have numerous opportunities to settle scores and retaliate violently in very nuanced and subtle ways. A clandestine punch, kick or slash may go unnoticed by referees; a tackle or body-check may contain a little extra fierceness yet it appears to be an acceptable move. Perhaps Dixon's critique of retaliatory violence requires further inquiry into these instances where the intent to cause physical harm may or may not be less discernible.

Even if retaliatory violence is part of the ethos of sports, as it is in baseball and ice hockey where league authorities minimally punish such behaviour, Dixon holds that retaliation should be rejected by forming new leagues where such violence is unacceptable. While this suggestion seems drastic, it is consistent with Dixon's critique. However, as an alternative, perhaps the players' association should educate players about the immorality of violent retaliation and seek a pledge that they refrain from such violence. By way of conclusion, Dixon makes an appeal that sport not be perceived and conceived as immune from external moral scrutiny. 'Sporting exceptionalism' is no defence to support retaliatory violence and preclude criticism against this form of sport violence.

Turning away from team sports like baseball and ice hockey, when one examines the more difficult cases of boxing and MMA, additional moral issues and principles arise in trying to answer whether these sports are ethically justifiable and whether they should be banned or modified. The following will discuss the two main arguments to ban boxing and MMA, namely, boxers and MMA athletes require protection from themselves due to the severe harm they inflict upon each other, and both sports create unacceptable indirect broader social harms.

The idea of banning boxing and MMA to protect boxers and MMA athletes from harming themselves is known as paternalism, which 'refers to interference with the liberty of agents for what is believed to be their own good'.[27] For example, a mandatory helmet law for motorcyclists is a classic case of paternalism. Yet some object to such laws because it restricts the freedom of motorcyclists to decide what is in their best interests. That is, interference in self-regarding acts is unjustified. Paternalism seems to be a patronizing principle because it meddles in personal decision-making; it can impose biased views on others, or interfere for the wrong reasons, in the wrong places and at the wrong times. And too much interference would stifle independent thinking and limit our autonomy to think, feel and judge for ourselves. Finally, we generally like to think that people should have control of their lives to pursue their own interests and decide what is best for themselves, yet paternalism hampers these basic rights.

Those who support boxing and MMA claim that if boxing and MMA were banned, it might not create more personal and social good. And even if a ban promoted more good, it would deny boxers, MMA athletes and spectators the choice to participate and watch boxing and MMA privately and publicly. Lastly, a ban would deny the rights of boxers, MMA athletes and spectators to control and live their lives as they see fit.

The call to ban boxing and MMA on paternalistic grounds is usually endorsed by those who claim that boxers and MMA athletes inflict severe harm against each other and participants do not know or appreciate the severity of these injuries. This is the stance of many national and international medical associations who have been calling for a boxing ban for a number of decades, and now include such a ban of MMA.[28] Aside from the controversial empirical claims such a position raises that are so far inconclusive, Daniel Sokol demonstrates an internal inconsistency in the call by medical associations to ban boxing and MMA. The overriding principle in contemporary medical ethics is patient autonomy such that if a patient is deemed rational and competent he or she may refuse medication and medical treatment to prolong life. Yet the same level of autonomy to refuse medical interference is being denied to boxers and MMA athletes by those who call for a ban of these sports on paternalistic grounds. To date, the medical ethics community who favour a ban of boxing and MMA has not responded to this criticism.

Another powerful argument against paternalism is known as the harm principle, which states that the only justification for limiting liberty is to prevent harm to others. Yet there are exceptions to the harm principle in the case of children, the mentally incompetent and those not informed of harmful risks in certain activities. For these groups, acting on their behalf in a paternalistic manner is justified. The question, then, is should boxers and MMA athletes also be considered exceptions to the harm principle?

A number of reasons can be given to answer this question in the affirmative. First, perhaps choosing to box or engaging in MMA in the first place is an irrational choice and demonstrates incompetence. However, if this were so, one could declare a priori that all sorts of choices, like earning a college degree, are irrational and demonstrate incompetence. Clearly independent reasons, rather than the mere fact one elects to box or participate in MMA, are needed to determine irrationality or incompetence. Second, boxers and MMA athletes are exceptions to the harm principle because by engaging in these activities they will lose their future status as rational, autonomous agents given the excessive harms they will face including brain damage. This is a strong motive for acting in a paternalistic way in the case of young children, but as they develop and mature less paternalistic interference is typically warranted. Nicholas Dixon, however, believes this sort of pre-emptive paternalism provides sufficient justification to eliminate punches to the head in boxing.[29] The difficulty with this paternalistic reason for young and mature adults is that the long-term, severe physical harms in boxing and MMA are not guaranteed such that all boxers and MMA athletes end up losing their future autonomous decision-making status.[30] A third reason to make boxers and MMA athletes exceptions to the harm principle is that they cannot give full consent to participate in boxing and MMA either due to ignorance, impoverished socio-economic backgrounds, their minority status, or some other hindrance 'beyond' their control. In this sense, their decision to box or engage in MMA is perhaps socially coerced or a kind of forced choice where few alternatives exist for a brighter future. Such a reason may be questionable because there are educated, informed people who know the harmful risks in these sports yet they still elect to box or practise MMA. Moreover, perhaps boxing and MMA organizations have an obligation to educate potential boxers and MMA athletes on the risks of these sports so participants are not ignorant. Lastly, rather than deny choices to those from impoverished backgrounds or minority groups, boxing and MMA are, for some, reasonable life choices and provide the poor or disenfranchised room to control their lives as they see fit. Given this exposition and critique of paternalism and the harm principle, these views have some force but they do not justify in a foolproof way a complete ban of boxing and MMA.

The second major approach that advocates a ban on boxing and MMA is the harm they promote within society. So rather than direct physical harm inflicted by boxers and MMA competitors against one another, perhaps these sports should be banned for the indirect harm they cause because they promote moral insensitivity, diminish a civilized way of life and desensitize us to violence in sport and in society generally. According to Robert L. Simon, there are two versions of this argument. The first claims that individual spectators or consumers of boxing and MMA become insensitive to violence and become violent themselves.[31] However, this empirical point has not been shown to be the case.[32]

The second version of harm to society states that boxing and MMA debase community standards of decency and civility. Since we are all a product of and are defined by a community with shared values, sport violence cannot be tolerated on a communal basis because it would lead to the erosion of civil society, which would negatively influence people as individuals. A presumption of this view is that the good of a community exists prior to and is undifferentiated from the good of the individual. Criticism of this view focuses on the idea that if we are wholly defined by our community, individual choice and autonomy are impossible. As such, individuals would be incapable of resisting a community that promotes racism, sexism, slavery and other abuses and discriminatory practices since we completely identify with community standards. Clearly this is not the case and community norms are not necessarily the final and only arbiters of deciding practices deemed moral and just. Contrary to the harm-to-society position, Nicholas Dixon claims that legal moralism – the view that some practices are repugnant and immoral and ought to be prohibited even if they result in no direct social harm – can justify, together with pre-emptive paternalism, reforms in boxing like the elimination of punches to the head.[33] This argument is limited to altering not banning sports like boxing and MMA. Therefore, in the case of boxing and MMA, indirect societal harm and the corruption of community standards are insufficient arguments to warrant a complete ban on these sports, although for most they provide sufficient grounds to reform boxing and MMA.

In addition to these points of view, another approach toward sport violence is gaining currency and relies on an understanding of the phenomenology of pain, injury and suffering.[34] This view in part states that boxers, MMA athletes and those who participate in contact and other high-risk individual sports inflict and/or experience harm and endure pain in ways non-participants cannot fully understand or appreciate. As sports with constitutive and regulative rules that are accepted on a voluntary basis, they are not free-for-all, no-holds-barred events resembling mayhem.[35] Even in sports that are defined as violent like boxing and MMA, or contain acts of violence as in American football and ice hockey, or commit violence to the body because they are extremely physically demanding sports like cycling or ultra-marathons, there are those in society who mutually agree to mete out and receive crushing blows to the body or 'punish' the body because they find it exciting and exhilarating to experience collisions and/or pain and suffering and this gives significant meaning to their lives.[36] Moreover, in addition to formal rules, within each of these sports communities and sub-cultures there exist codes of behaviour and shared values that regulate and condemn egregious and reckless behaviour. In Olympic wrestling, for example, athletes have the capacity and opportunity to inflict severe harm on their opponents, like dislocating their limbs, however, they are taught to withhold exerting such physical force and confine their moves to legitimate ones. When one speaks to boxers, for example, virtually all view their opponents with mutual respect as embodied subjects and not as objects to be vanquished and eradicated.[37] Those who participate in violent and violent-like sports are rarely asked to express what draws them to these sports and to describe their experiences in the ring or on the playing field. Although questions and judgements from non-participants can and should be raised and critically assessed, an insider's perspective of violent and contact sports may reveal experiential dimensions that offer an alternative understanding and conception of violence in sport that may make these sports ethically justifiable.

Concluding Comments

In the sport philosophy and ethics literature, therefore, there are no ironclad moral arguments to ban sports like boxing and MMA as well as contact or high-risk sports because they are themselves violent activities or acts of violence are contained within them. Most scholars, and those who govern sport, endorse various programmes of reform to lessen the amount and severity of the intentional use of physical force to inflict harm on others or on athletes themselves. An earlier example was cited about the ban on head tackling in American football. In the same sport, a protection-of-the-passer rule exists in part to reduce the amount of physical harm that could be inflicted on the quarterback. Very recently, North American professional ice hockey implemented rules to minimize shoulder checks to the head partly because victims of such checks were in positions of vulnerability. A growing concern in both these sports, as well as boxing, is the frequency and long-term consequences of concussions and brain trauma and injury. As result, some scholars have called for boxing to eliminate punches to the head. Others endorse protective helmets in boxing and greater emphasis on the scoring system, which might discourage boxers from focusing on the knockout to secure a victory. Although it began with few rules less than two decades ago, MMA has undergone extensive reforms by employing light equipment, shorter rounds, several options to end matches, close scrutiny by referees and intensive medical supervision to minimize severe harm and injury to athletes.[38] Thus reasonable reforms that reduce the severity and frequency of acts of violence in contemporary sport are being implemented and these will likely continue in the future.

There is clear recognition that violence exists in sport at the participant level to some degree and at other levels not examined here. Whether or not violence is ethically defensible in sport is still contentious and under debate, perhaps because sport violence is constrained by many rules and regulations. Contemporary sport is also heavily monitored by sports organizations, government agencies, the justice system, the media and many community sports groups who influence and mediate the degree and type of sport violence society is willing to tolerate. These processes of negotiation may be ineffective or too slow for some who feel the amount of gratuitous violence in sport has reached an intolerable state. Others believe all sports carry a certain amount of physical risk and harm, and a safe and justifiable balance can be reached to ensure sport participation is significant and meaningful. Philosophical and ethical concepts and principles are certainly part of this discourse and may assist those in the sport community to comprehend the nature of violence in sport and reach reasoned, thoughtful decisions about its presence in society.

Notes

1   Parts of this entry are adapted from Danny Rosenberg, 'The Banality of Violence in Sport and the McSorley Affair', *Avante* 9 (2003): 30–42.
2   Toby Miller, 'Sport and Violence', *Journal of Sport & Social Issues* 21 (1997): 235–239.
3   Aleš Sekot, 'Violence in Sports', *European Journal for Sport and Society* 6 (2009): 37–49.
4   Eric Dunning, *Sport Matters: Sociological Studies of Sport, Violence and Civilization* (London and New York: Routledge, 1999).
5   See, for example, John H. Kerr, 'Issues in Aggression and Violence in Sport: The ISSP Position Stand Revisited', *The Sport Psychologist* 16 (2002): 68–78; Kevin Young, 'Sport and Violence', in *Handbook of Sport Studies*, eds., Jay Coakley and Eric Dunning (London: Sage, 2000), 382–407; and Kevin Young, *Sport, Violence and Society* (London: Routledge, 2012).
6   Jim Parry, 'Violence and Aggression in Contemporary Sport', in *Ethics and Sport*, eds., Mike J. McNamee and Jim Parry (London and New York: E & FN Spon, 1998), 209.
7   Mitch Abrams, *Anger Management in Sport: Understanding and Controlling Violence in Athletes* (Champaign, IL: Human Kinetics, 2010); and John H. Kerr, *Rethinking Aggression and Violence in Sport* (London: Routledge, 2005).
8   See Hannah Arendt, *On Violence* (New York: Harcourt, Brace & World, 1969), who examines these meanings of violence.
9   Canadian Centre for Ethics in Sport, *Building a New Brand of Sport©—What about Violence?* (Ottawa: Canadian Centre for Ethics in Sport, 1999), 1.
10   Robert L. Simon, *Fair Play: Sports, Values, and Society* (Boulder, CO: Westview Press, 1991), 52–53.
11   Ibid., 53.
12   Ibid., 54.
13   Michael D. Smith, *Violence and Sport* (Toronto: Butterworths, 1983), 8–23.
14   See, for example, Gordon A. Bloom and Michael D. Smith, 'Hockey Violence: A Test of Cultural Spillover Theory', *Sociology of Sport Journal* 13 (1996): 65–77; and Laura Robinson, *Crossing the Line: Violence and Sexual Assault in Canada's National Sport* (Toronto: McClelland & Stewart, 1998).
15   Robert Butcher and Angela Schneider, 'Fair Play as Respect for the Game', *Journal of the Philosophy of Sport* 25 (1998): 4.
16   D. Stanley Eitzen, *Fair and Foul: Beyond the Myths and Paradoxes of Sport* (Lanham, Md: Rowman & Littlefield, 1999), 45–6.
17   Peter McIntosh, *Fair Play: Ethics in Sport and Education* (London: Heineman, 1979), 186.

18 Rosenberg, 'The Banality of Violence in Sport and the McSorley Affair', 34.
19 Robert L. Simon, *Fair Play: The Ethics of Sport*, 2nd ed. (Boulder, CO: Westview Press, 2004), 104.
20 Ibid.
21 Ibid., 105.
22 The following discussion on hits to the head is adapted from Danny Rosenberg and Julie Stevens, 'Head's Up: Violence and the Vulnerability Principle Revisited', *Sport in Society* 16 (2013): 283–94.
23 Sarah K. Fields, Christy L. Collins and R. Dawn Comstock, 'Conflict on the Courts: A Review of Sports-Related Violence Literature', *Trauma, Violence, & Abuse* 8 (2007): 363.
24 Ibid.
25 Nick T. Pappas, Patrick C. McKenry and Beth Skilken Catlett, 'Athlete Aggression on the Rink and Off the Ice', *Men and Masculinities* 6 (2004): 300–4.
26 Nicholas Dixon, 'A Critique of Violent Retaliation in Sport', *Journal of the Philosophy of Sport* 37 (2010): 1–10.
27 Simon, *Fair Play: The Ethics of Sport*, 94.
28 George D. Lundberg, 'Boxing Should be Banned in Civilized Countries – Round 4', *Medscape General Medicine* 7 (2005): 52; and Daniel Sokol, 'Boxing, Mixed Martial Arts and Other Risky Sports: Is the BMA Confused?' *British Medical Journal* 343 (2011): 6937.
29 Nicholas Dixon, 'Boxing, Paternalism, and Legal Moralism', *Social Theory and Practice* 27 (2001): 342–44.
30 Patrick McCrory, 'Boxing and the Risk of Chronic Brain Injury', *British Medical Journal* 335 (2007): 781; and Eric C. Rainey, 'Determining the Prevalence and Assessing the Severity of Injuries in Mixed Martial Arts Athletes', *North American Journal of Sports Physical Therapy* 4 (2009): 190–8.
31 Simon, *Fair Play: The Ethics of Sport*, 93–4.
32 Paul Davis, 'Ethical Issues in Boxing', *Journal of the Philosophy of Sport* 20 (1993): 49–50.
33 Dixon, 'Boxing, Paternalism, and Legal Moralism', 342.
34 Sigmund Loland, Berat Skirstad and Ian Waddington, *Pain and Injury in Sport: Social and Ethical Analysis* (London and New York: Routledge, 2006).
35 Davis, 'Ethical Issues in Boxing', 50–1.
36 See Dale Spencer, *Ultimate Fighting and Embodiment: Violence, Gender, and Mixed Martial Arts* (New York: Routledge, 2012).
37 See Michael Burke, 'Is Boxing Violent? Let's Ask Some Boxers', in *All Part of the Game: Violence and Australian Sport*, ed., Dennis Hemphill (Sydney: Walla Walla, 1998), 111–32.
38 David T. Mayeda and David E. Ching, *Fighting for Acceptance: Mixed Martial Artists and Violence in American Society* (Lincoln, NE: iUniverse, 2008).

Part IV
Future Developments

18 Sport and Technological Development

Alun Hardman

In the 1970s, two non-golfing scientists developed an oddly dimpled golf ball that was taken to market in the guise of Polara's 'Ultimate Straight'.[1] The ball, which minimized flight deviation due to slice and hook, caught on quickly with hackers, but was banned by the United States Golf Association (USGA) in 1981.[2] A settlement of $1.4 million stopped its sale.[3] A new company acquired the technology in 2005, and through marketing their ball strategically as a 'training device' for amateur players, thus circumventing the USGA rule, a renewed surge in its use is underway.[4]

Another well-recognized example of the indeterminate role technology plays in sport is the debate as to whether athletes with disabilities using prosthetic limb technology ought to be allowed to compete against able-bodied athletes in events such as the Olympic Games. In the London 2012 Olympics, Oscar Pistorius, the South African Paralympic athlete, did just that with the aid of Ossur flex-foot Cheetah prosthetics.[5] He was permitted to enter the 400-metre event after he won a legal case on appeal via the Court of Arbitration for Sport (CAS) where the evidence involved demonstrated that the biomechanical functionality of his competition prostheses provided no significant advantage over able-bodied competitors.[6]

These stories, like many others, capture the essential ingredients and the fundamental issue regarding the relationship between technology and sport. It is a story of deciding the correct balance, or 'sweet tension',[7] between, on the one hand, a view of the sport seen as an impromptu challenge faced spontaneously to examine our reservoir of skills and experiences in overcoming gratuitous difficulties and, on the other, a carefully crafted experiment that draws on all possible means to achieve the required physical task with maximal efficiency.

The examples also demonstrate that philosophy has a role to play in understanding and resolving debates about the relationship between 'technology' and 'sport'. We encounter the effects of technology in the world of sport so frequently and in such varied ways that even the least curious and most accommodating sportsperson cannot venture too far without wanting to know what the technology does, and whether such effects are a good thing.

Technology influences how sportspersons prepare through the way we manage and supplement our diet, ensure effective rest, optimize our psychological state, embed technical skills and plan strategy. It is present when we compete and seek to monitor and optimize our performance as well as anticipate and counteract the efforts of our opponents. We also use technology after competition to optimize psycho-physical recovery, to scrutinize areas for skill and tactical modification, and otherwise inform how to plan for and improve future performances. The plan-perform-evaluate cycle is sustained with zeal by an ever-increasing array of specialist tools, machines, equipment, products, coaches and support staff that have 'technologized' the goal of improved performance. Technology further shapes sport and its practitioners when it is used as a vehicle for officiating, both increasingly as a decision aid for human umpires, judges and referees, and also for determining participant eligibility through out-of-competition testing (for drugs, excessive and sudden weight loss, injury recovery, etc.).[8]

The upshot is that sporting practices exist within a constant spectre of innovation and change, where sport necessitates a technological approach and technology industries are eager to respond. In this state of affairs, philosophy has an important role in clarifying exactly what changes to sport are likely as a result of this or that technology, as well as asking for robust justifications as to the merits of those changes.

This essay examines the philosophical literature on technology and sport, and in particular concentrates on what Sigmund Loland considers to be the three most important questions that philosophy must ask in relation to technology and sport.[9] The first is: what is sports technology? The second asks: what does sporting technology do? The essay concludes by examining the third and most important question: is sport technology good?

The Concept of Technology

Before we focus on the relationship between technology and sport, some brief but absolutely essential conceptual work is needed. It is needed, not because it's what philosophers always do, but because in the case of sport, what we understand technology to mean in a more fundamental sense will impact upon our understanding of its relationship with sport.

The etymological roots of 'technology' are Greek, where *technē* was understood as 'craft' or 'art' – those skills needed for the efficient performance of a functional task or production of an object or artefact.[10] These qualities are embodied in the work of tradespeople and artists, carpenters, cooks, mechanics and information technology (IT) specialists, etc. Those who possess good technique or a technical outlook are considered as having practical knowledge, or 'know-how' – a set of skills that are held in regard for their efficiency and effectiveness in relation to performing an identified task. Technical knowledge is often contrasted to theory generated by policymakers, academics or researchers whose purpose is to establish the knowledge and information ('knowing that') that underpins the development of a technology. The historical relationship is one where theoreticians with theoretical knowledge provide a route map that technologists try to implement with technology. Resolving the problems and challenges of life involves theorizing as to what can be done – technology tells us how to do it.

A more modern and narrower view tends to further refine theoretical knowledge as primarily scientific knowledge and understands practical know-how as predominantly the technological application of science. The dominant view, then, is that technology is the handmaiden of scientific discovery and thus earlier ideas about the relationship between theory and practice become limited to one where resolving problems of modern life is a technological issue where science tells us what is possible and technology shows how it can be done.[11]

This populist view of both the nature and role of knowledge and those of science and technology may be a crude caricature of modern perceptions, but its influence is largely unchecked and can have significant implications as to the way human beings live their lives, and also understand and appreciate sport. There are two real issues here. The first is a tendency to compartmentalize knowledge in such a way that technological issues become exclusively conceived as a matter of know-how. The second is the extent to which a fragmented view of knowledge also evolves to be a hierarchical one, where the dominant knowledge forms and their associated spheres of theoretical and practical activity account for all questions of human living. The core issue is whether the answer to all human challenges can really be explained through scientific contemplation coupled to a technological remedy.

To examine the first of those issues further (the belief that technology involves only practical knowledge), let us consider the task of house building. One can see technology at work in how the building materials are made and in the skills of the construction workers who put the building together. However, building a good house is not merely the completion of a set of technical tasks because the goodness of the house is not exclusively to be derived in the technical qualities of its construction. A good house, more comprehensively understood, takes into account who will live there, where the house is built, what resource implications arise from the materials used, the impact of the building on the existing environment and so on. In short, house building is not exclusively a problem of technical performance, but a problem that resides within a complex interrelation of far-reaching concerns that are social, cultural, economic and humanistic. While technology can contribute to improving human lives in terms of providing warm, safe, comfortable and affordable homes, the knowledge required to determine what constitutes the improvement of human lives is not merely a task for technicians with narrow expertise. Employing better architects, bricklayers, plumbers and electricians is important in order to build better houses, but those who understand the construction industry fully will see the goodness of a house as encompassing a broad set of considerations. The important point that comes from this is that the knowledge required for understanding what constitutes the best kinds of human living cannot be understood simply as technological knowledge. The example also suggests that a far more comprehensive and relational account of knowledge is required to understand what technology is.

The second issue relates to that of a hierarchical understanding of the relationship between different notions of rational activity – one that elevates theoretical knowledge above that of practical know-how. The sources of this view are old and multiple, but the upshot is the belief that those engaged in theoretical activity rather than practical work have more important and meaningful things to do.[12] There is a connection here to dualistic notions of the body which include such notions as an elevated regard for the thinking mind having control over the performing body.[13] In modern times, this normative view of rationality is shaped in such a way that natural science and its systematic methods are seen as the epitome of good thinking. What is more, the popular view of technology is one that has become synonymous with science – or, at the very least, a view that science is what brings about technological innovation. The result is, according to Jacques Ellul,[14] that in technology we begin to recognize the emergent single dominant way of answering all questions concerning human action, partly based on a view that understands science as the single dominant way of answering all questions concerning human knowledge.[15] In what subsequently leads to a 'domination of objects',[16] the modern alliance between science and technology forces all human life to conform to a single, partial principle of rational maximum efficiency.[17]

Mary Tiles and Hans Oberdiek[18] make this customary understanding more specific when they talk of technology as 'material devices designed and manufactured to make existing human activities easier or to make possible activities which people have dreamt of engaging in but to which they are not biologically adapted.'[19] Generally, technology refers to tools and equipment ranging from the simple knife and fork to mobile phones, the automobile and spaceships. Technology is thus typically understood as *human-made means* to reach *human interests and goals*. This view, as Loland indicates, also predominates in sport. He says: 'sport technologies, then, are human-made means to reach human interests and goals in, or related to, sport.'[20] Crucial to our evaluation of sport technology, therefore, is a good understanding as to what these interests and goals are.

Sport Technology: A Review of the Literature

Modern sport, where ideals of performance enhancement, competitive success and maximal efficiency prevail, provides fertile ground for technology and technological thinking. Steve J. Haake[21] notes that the degree of improvement in Olympic events measured by time and distance during the last 100 years ranges from 24 per cent (100 metres) to 221 per cent (one-hour cycle ride). Such changes, he argues, represent a compulsion to overcome constraints experienced by the physical body by various environmental forces. Breaking records is not just an indicator of social progress but is derived from a deeper desire to break free from the resisting forces of gravity, air and water. This explains why fibreglass replaces bamboo for pole vaulting, the Fosbury flop is preferred to the straddle in high jumping, cyclists wear Lycra skin suits, and competitive swimmers shave their body hair.

This commonplace picture of the relationship between sport and technology often mistakenly presumes a one-way relationship between the sportsperson as subject and the technology as object – as if it is always persons who shape technology while the reverse is never true. A number of authors writing in the philosophy of sport have questioned the extent to which this view is the case.

John Hoberman, in his seminal article 'Sport and the Technological Image of Man',[22] first suggests technology is an issue of significant interest for the philosophical study of sport. This work, a precursor to *Mortal Engines*,[23] his much acclaimed book on drug use in sport, argues that the ethics of performance-enhancing drugs in sport is a consequence of the more fundamental metaphysical question regarding the nature of being-in-the-world. Sport, in his view as with a number of other practices (such as medicine, communications and engineering), should provoke reflection upon the relationship of the human self in the face of increasing technology. He suggests that:

> The problem is that whereas science and technology can be progressively transformed, the human body cannot be. The temptation to treat the human body as if it were a machine comes into conflict with our most basic ideas of what human beings should be, and the result of this conflict is the idea of human limits.[24]

Hoberman's work thus establishes a relationship between sport and technology that drills down to a moral issue rooted in foundational existential premises. Hoberman's concern is 'that the comprehensive technologizing of high-performance sport contains, and at the same time conceals, an agenda for human development for which high-performance athletes serve as ideal models'.[25] For Hoberman, modern sport has a distorted anthropological agenda that includes and transcends certain body types for sporting purposes – high-performance sport has become the perceptible cultural arena for propelling not only imaginative desires about future athletic types, but also ideals about impending human types as well.

For the last 20 to 30 years the issue of technology in sport has principally been played out in sporting reality, and in the philosophy of sport literature as a moral debate about the rights and (primarily) wrongs of the use of performance-enhancing drugs in sport. This focus on the issue of drug use in sport, while understandably imminent and critical, tends to sidetrack the debate on the basic metaphysical roots of the issue identified by Hoberman. It does so in three ways. First, the debate on the use of drugs in sport is often confused with the socially broader 'war on drugs'. This explains why the World Anti-Doping Agency's (WADA) list of prohibited substances and methods includes non-performance-enhancing cannabinoids and cocaine.[26]

Second, the focus on drugs tends to be presented as exclusively an ethical rather than a metaphysical one. It is principally conceived as one of relational morality between competitors, practice communities and social institutions.[27] Inevitably, then, the dominant discourse about drug use in sport concerns justice and fairness, autonomy and paternalism, and individual rights and collective duties, which culminate in a series of anti-doping rules aimed at ensuring healthy and fair competition. The downside to this ethics-dominated philosophical discourse is that the broader debate about an ominous technological *Weltanschauung* – the very source of such moral concerns in the first place – largely disappears.

This narrowing of the debate, from that of technology and sport to one of the morality of drug taking, is perhaps clearly shown in the ways that arguments about the unnatural and dehumanizing effects of drug use are marginalized. Angela J. Schneider and Robert B. Butcher's view is typical in suggesting that pursuing this line is problematic because we are unable to give a satisfactory account of what it is to be human. They express the perceived philosophical impasse in the following way:

> The dehumanization argument is interesting but incomplete. It is incomplete because we do not yet have an agreed-upon conception of what it is to be human. Without this it is difficult to see why some practices should count as dehumanizing.[28]

Ironically, of course, it transpires that the moral arguments about drug use in sport are equally incomplete and contested because the views underpinning fairness, autonomy and paternalism in sport are themselves not yet agreed upon. What this tells us, suggests Leon Culbertson,[29] is that trying to uncover the essence of concepts such as fair competition and human-ness is likely to be ill-fated because such terms are occasion-sensitive and context-dependent. They are better understood as ostensive concepts whose meaning and cogency appear by pointing out relevant examples and the range of ways in which the term is used. Our understanding of these terms, together with the normative force they convey, is not to be found by correspondence to a yet-to-be-determined ultimate ideal, but arises through appreciating the function of context and contrasts in how they are used, who is using them and for what purpose. So, while it remains true that technology in sport presents fundamental challenges to realizing a shared view of what it means to be human or what is natural, we should not shelve the debate because we are yet to determine the basis upon which such challenges are to be evaluated. Instead, the task is to engage enthusiastically in the issues, understanding that there is nothing more to guide such discussions than the meanings that evolve and gain acceptance as new technological possibilities in sport become realities. What is needed more than ever before in dealing with new technologies such as biogenetics and transhumanistic technology, therefore, is conceptual reflexivity because they require that we understand differently, and evaluate better, the relationship between such technologies and who we (currently) are as human-selves.[30] Such an approach allows the development of a balanced tension between 'the need for a significant ostensive element to our understanding of such terms as "dehumanize" and cures us of the tendency to look for an essentialist metaphysical account.'[31] In doing so, there is the possibility that those on different sides of the debate on biogenetics can both find a common starting point to address the various challenges that technological advances in this area bring to sport, and at the same time be more candid about the reasons that drive their understanding.

The third problem that arises from the debate on drug use in sport is that it redirects attention away from the wider debate about the different ways in which other technologies challenge our existing sense of what is meant by being a sportsperson. Here it is important to note that while biogenetic technology will pose significant ethical problems for sport in the future, what is scientifically imagined and technologically possible are years apart.[32] The ethics of biogenetics are also largely irrelevant to all but the most advanced and wealthy high-performance sport systems and instead concerns involving the use of existing sport technologies in ways that respect the autonomy and integrity of disempowered athletes are more pressing. It is also evident that unless we are able to resolve the moral concerns that existing technologies present to sport right now, there is little hope that the challenges presented by technologies of the future will be managed any better.

Sigmund Loland and Sport Technology

One author who has attempted more than others to provide a comprehensive framework for looking at the relationship between technology and sport is Sigmund Loland. In an eclectic body of work, Loland's attempt to provide sport technology with both classificatory and normative frameworks stands apart.[33] This work tries to draw out some common principles useful for understanding technology in sport and focus on three fundamental and related questions. What types of sporting technology are there? What functions do sporting technologies have? And how do we decide if a sporting technology is good? These questions and Loland's work are examined below.

Loland's work on a typology of technologies identifies *body techniques, sports equipment, training technology* and *expert-administered technologies* as four central forms of sports technology. A range of examples for each is as follows:

Body techniques
What we do that is new and different with the movements of our bodies in order to improve competitive performance:

- Fosbury flop
- Jan Boklov V-style ski jump
- Rugby spin pass
- Backstroke dolphin leg kick
- Tkachev release skill on horizontal bar
- Cycling time trial riding position

Sports equipment
What we use that is new and different in order to improve competitive performance:

- Shock-absorbing running shoes
- Carbon-fibre bikes
- Hydration regime
- Bike handlebar design

Training technology
What we use and what we do that is new and different in preparation for competitive performance:

- GPS timing devices
- Circadian rhythm-embedded training
- Opposition SWOT analyses
- Course reconnaissance
- Nutritional supplementation
- Power output measurement
- Heart rate monitoring

Expert-administered technologies
What we use and do outside of sport in order to improve competitive performance:

- Biogenetic blueprinting
- Physiological testing
- Medical screening
- Psychological profiling
- Biomechanical movement mapping
- Pedagogic analysis

Some of these technologies might overlap – an expert-administered technology might also result in a new approach to training. The physiological testing of a cyclist, for example, reveals responses to different workloads and at the same time might report findings associated with optimal biomechanical pedal stroke efficiency.

Loland outlines three functional roles for technology – as a *constitutive technology* necessary for the game itself (i.e. a ball for soccer), to *prevent harm or injury* (i.e. a helmet for American football) or to *enhance performance* (i.e. a strength and conditioning programme). A range of examples for each is as follows:

Constitutive technology
- Playing surfaces/arenas
- Measuring devices – times, distances, height, etc.
- Equipment
  - Projectiles (balls, javelins)
  - Striking tools (bats, racquets, boxing gloves)
  - Propelling tools (poles, paddles)
  - Balance/steadying tools (ski poles)
  - Conveyances …
    - Motorized vehicles (racing cars, motorbikes, powerboats)
    - Self-propelled vehicles (bikes, canoes)

Harm or injury prevention
- Body protection (helmets, gloves, abdominal guards, shin guards)
- Release technology
- Securing technology …
  - Climbing carabina
  - Harness

- ○ Wrist/ankle tethers
- Impact protection …
  - ○ Worn by athletes (training shoes, shoulder pads)
  - ○ Their moving vehicles (seat belts)
  - ○ External environment (matting, sandpits)

Performance enhancement
- Nutritional programmes
- Pharmacological products
- Biogenetic therapy
- Blood doping

Evidently, again certain technology may cross over from one functional category to the next. For example, while a quick-release binding mechanism for Alpine skiing is necessary for attaching skis to boots, it reduces risk of injury as it allows skis to detach in a fall, and, based on the binding's relative responsiveness, allows for quicker and sharper turning on the snow. Of these functional categories, Loland argues that the constitutional role is the least controversial (though there may be technologically dependent constitutive features of a sport that are inherently morally problematic such as boxing gloves).

The third and final question – should a sports technology be used? – is the most difficult yet the most important question to answer. In his normative work, Loland attempts to draw lines between *unacceptable, acceptable* and *valuable* technologies in sport based on the development of ideal-typical theories.[34] His initial work draws these lines according to three emerging prototypical views in common use – an axiological foundation that has informed later ideas and revisions about the role of technology in sport.[35]

The first perspective, he suggests, is a *relativist* approach where the rationale for implementing a sporting technology is an instrumental one based upon the personal desires and wishes of an individual or group of individuals without regard for constraints that might be informed by the inherent goods of sport. He describes this understanding of technology in sport as a 'non-theory' because from an ethical perspective the ethics of performance take on a descriptive quality.

He calls his second account a 'thin theory' or *narrow* understanding of performance enhancement. It builds on the single ideal that sport is all about testing the limits of a performing body, primarily in Olympic sports (where the magnitude of movement of a physical quantity of mass in time is typically measured). Here, according to Loland, technical innovation is considered justified when it enhances the reliability and validity of a standardized sporting test, such that an equal opportunity to complete is maintained. The theory is thin/narrow because the focus is on in-competition technology and the normative evaluation is limited to a particular account of sport – one based on the goal of ensuring equality of opportunity to compete while at the same time attempting to transcend current sporting achievements. As this account requires that the use of a given technology is deemed acceptable only on the basis that all competitors agree to use it, Loland acknowledges that where there is an obsession with improving performance it is likely that 'a no-regulation approach to both traditional performance-enhancing drugs and to genetic technologies'[36] emerges as the dominant ethos.

Loland's third, and preferred, 'thick theory' or *wide* account argues that 'that sport should be an arena for moral values and for human self-development and flourishing'.[37] He develops this normative account of sport, and thus the context within which we are to understand technology, in the following way:

> Inspired by Rawls' (1971) Aristotelian principle, competitive sport is interpreted based on a perfectionist ethics in which individuals are seen to flourish only and insofar as they realize their innate and trained abilities and skills to increased levels of complexity. If practised in the right way, sport becomes part of a cultivation project where the development of performance is part of a general development of athletes as free and responsible moral agents. Sporting excellence is a particular expression of human excellence.[38]

Loland asks that we evaluate technology in sport on the basis of its contribution to human excellence, while at the same time leaving the exact content of such excellence open for debate and pluralistic possibility. From a philosophical point of view, this indicates that a debate about the goodness of technology in sport involves consideration of both the *means* and the *ends* of sport. What follows is a brief overview as to how such a philosophical approach might be undertaken. It principally takes a virtue ethics approach and develops further Loland's appeal to Aristotle. More specifically, it attempts to recapture how practical rationality is to be understood and the implications as to how we evaluate technology in sport.

It is difficult to get a handle on the role Aristotle sees for ethics without considering his full account of the nature and forms of knowledge. He classifies knowledge into three different types: *theoria*, the kind of knowledge gained through observing or contemplating and then comprehending through consciousness, *praxis* or the kind of knowledge that comes form deliberating about the means appropriate to one's actions in a particular situation and *poiesis*, the knowledge that comes through the production or making of an object or artefact.[39]

Of particular relevance to technology in sport is the idea of *praxis* and in particular how it differs from *poiesis*. Though *praxis* is largely absent from contemporary discourse, it is a term that captures a distinct form of rational understanding involved in how we attempt to organize and justify conduct in a public space with others in which persons (such as sportsmen and women) pursue types of activity in particular ways both as means to certain ends and for their own sake. In doing so, sportspersons are able to realize excellence considered by his or her community as constitutive of a worthwhile way of life. As *praxis* involves development of other people and at the same time is productive of the self, it binds those involved emotionally and socially to what they do in ways that contribute significantly to the revelation and formation of character and personality. The defining quality of *praxis*, according to Aristotle, is that it is constituted by diverse and contingent human interactions and requires for its comprehension and regulation a more personal and experiential form of knowledge. He called this specific practical knowledge *phronesis*, or practical wisdom, and differentiated it explicitly from *technē*, technical or productive knowledge, another tradition of rational activity affiliated with *poiesis* (the art or craft of making an object).[40]

What is important here is that with the loss of any great sense of *praxis*, and with it the normative significance of practical wisdom, the core of the critical debate on the nature and value of sport technology is no longer grounded on rival conceptions of rational action. Performance enhancement is understood as requiring technical productivity (*technē*) where the need for practical wisdom (*phronesis*) is mainly relevant insofar as it makes possible, rather than requires, a responsible justification for a technical approach to sport.

Debates on technology are likely to provoke different emotional responses as the examples with which I opened the essay show. The Polara golf ball, for example, is loathed by golf traditionalists who decry such innovations because they remove the essential challenge of being able to control the flight of the ball due to one's own efforts. Innovations like this, they argue, 'de-skill' the game and are ultimately self-defeating, for they remove the very ingredients that entice millions to play in the first place.[41] Sports innovators, on the other hand, favour such changes because they consider that game playing is all about probing the most efficient means to overcome the 'gratuitous difficulties'.[42] If game players devise a technology to make the task easier, then should it not be celebrated as an example of the kind of rationality the game encourages.[43] After all, other advances in golf club design, training regimes, laser range finders and the quality of greenkeeping suggest that the use of sophisticated dimple patterns in golf balls ought to be understood and accepted as merely one of many similar technological innovations that aim at improving performance. Moreover, it can be argued that a technological approach to sport is a transhistorical, rather than a new phenomenon – the story of the Greek wrestler Milo of Croton lifting a bull calf every day to improve his strength is an ancient example of a technological approach to improving sporting performance that remains true today.[44]

From a *praxis* perspective, the decision by the USGA to ban the ball seems to be both reasonable and proportionate. The decision suggests that while the technology is *acceptable* in the broad sense that it is inherently morally insignificant, in the context of professional golf it is *unacceptable* according to how professional golfers themselves are able to articulate the best interpretation of the game. This statement requires further clarification and is crucial, for it suggests that judgements as to the efficacy of some technologies are a matter of degree – that there are cases that prove to be more or less taxing for a sporting community's practitioners to resolve. How a sporting community responds to 'hard cases' that have to do with technological change will therefore also be indicative of the moral character of the practice community itself. 'Hard cases' ought to engage all who are members of the sporting community in ongoing discourse that debates and argues the various possibilities that technology has to offer. A reflective community will treat seriously the alternative sporting visions that technological innovation might bring. Such a community will also challenge such alternative ideas with the strongest possible arguments it has at its disposal, in the same way that those who believe that technological innovation presents an improvement will also challenge the existing sporting order. The hope is that through a multilayered, continuous, inclusive and receptive discourse that emerges, a community can demark what is of moral significance and what is not.

What also begins to emerge is that the difference between a technological 'hard case' and less taxing technological innovations is to be understood according to the intensity, durability and persistence of the discourse. The history of sport is replete with technologically driven challenges that have sparked briefly to life, but soon fade, either because they failed to resonate at all with the existing norms of the practice community or because they were wholeheartedly embraced. Of far greater interest, from both a philosophical and a technological point of view, are those changes that are difficult to resolve and refuse to go away, or if they do, they re-emerge at some later historical juncture in a new guise. It is here that we need to better understand sport as *praxis*, and the necessary role *phronesis* plays in practical judgements.

Our golf ball example shows through the nature and import of the arguments used by debating parties, how the rationality of *phronesis*, acts to constrict the rationality of technology. The crucial issue rests on the degree to which the design technology limits the skill demands of the game. While it may be the case that every golfer would prefer the game to be easier to play from a self-interested point of view, it is also the case that such a personal preference resides with a broader, and ultimately constraining, communal rationality that accepts that a key ingredient of golf is the ludic challenge that the game entails. In the absence of a well-crafted challenge, the entire project of golf is likely to be less attractive. At some hard-to-determine point, these two principles must 'bottom out' – technology that demands increasingly less skilled performance and a practice community that demands an interesting challenge of skill at some point will be incompatible.

For the USPGA, the design of the Polara golf ball, supported by the empirical evidence available, represents the current measure as to where the tipping point exists between what is possible technologically and what is 'good' for golfing *praxis* in which that technology must reside and defer. That there are alternative golfing communities – particularly weekend duffers – who collectively might welcome the use of technological innovation to make the game easier for them presents no problem. One need not go as far as to say that playing with a techonolgically advanced golf ball invalidates the entire enterprise – all we can say is that playing the game in such a way is incompatible with the USPGA's current understanding of its convention.

The use of technologically advanced golf balls then may be entirely permissible for amateurs and non-competitive golfers. Its current aerodynamic properties, however, make its use impermissible in competitive professional golf because the degree to which the competitive outcome of the game is determined by which golfer consistently produces the most proficient golf stroke seems to be significantly eroded. By de-skilling the game in this way, the Polara ball also has an adverse affect on other areas of technique, namely in diminishing the biomechanical understanding and mechanical demands needed by the golfer to control the flight of his or her shots through imparting 'draw' or 'fade'. It can be argued using Loland's conceptual framework for sports technology, and with the rationality of *praxis* in mind, that the Polara golf ball actually constitutes a technological regression rather than a progression.

Not all technological examples are straightforward for sports organizations, however. For example, the USGA prohibited Casey Martin, a golfer with a disability, the use of a cart on the grounds that doing so contravened the constitutive rules of golf.[45] This argument was rejected by the courts, who acknowledged, however, that if the USGA were concerned that Martin might gain a significant advantage over his competitors, his competitors should also be allowed the use of a cart. Beyond issues of fairness of competition, however, the courts judged his use of a cart constituted no significant de-skilling of the game.

A similar set of arguments broadly supported Oscar Pistorius' right to compete in the Olympic 400 metres – the CAS decided his blade technology provided him with no significant advantage over his competitors. The CAS found that his current prosthetics matched the norms of current elite athletes in terms of power generation, stride length and ground reaction forces.[46] Encouraged by this ruling, it is likely that sports technology companies will respond in two ways. The first will be to aim for technological improvements within a non-normalized framework through a pure design ideal that aims for better blades. The second will involve technology that responds to increased standardization through identifying relevant differences between individual athletes and minimizing their effect. The first approach aims to improve performance technology in ways that challenge the limits (and therefore the regulatory framework) of the performance potential of non-bladed athletes. The second aims to improve the specific performance potential of each athlete within the given limits of current regulations. Both approaches, however, are likely to encourage a technological arms race in prosthetic technology for both have performance enhancement as their ultimate goal. Thus, the imposition of regulatory frameworks often has the unintended consequence of becoming just one more variable to manage effectively in the technological design process. In all cases, the underlying rationality remains the same – a monological view that what counts as rational development in sport is technologies that deliver performance improvement. The crux of the problem is that all such attempts to regulate the influence of technological advancement do so merely on technological grounds – they provide 'artificial' performance limits that then reshape but do not fundamentally change how 'improving' competition is understood.

The rational response to artificial limits on performance-enhancing technology in sport continues to be a technologically driven one. This will remain the case as long as the dominant view of sport is a performative one. It is only when, as has been argued towards the end of this chapter, sport is perceived as *praxis* – aimed at improving a much broader set of human qualities – that technological advances, aimed at improving a narrow set of performative capacities, might be better balanced.

Notes

1   For extended explanation of the biomechanical ball's properties see Chang-Hsien Tai, Leong Jik-Chang and Chien-Yao, 'Effects of Golf Ball Dimple Configuration on Aerodynamics, Trajectory, and Acoustics', *Journal of Flow Visualization and Image Processing* 14 (2007): 183.

2   J. Nadine Gelberg, 'The Rise and Fall of the Polara Asymmetric Golf Ball: No Hook, No Slice, No Dice', *Technology in Society* 18 (1996): 93–110.

3   Mike May, 'The Athletic Arms Race', in *Building the Elite Athlete*, ed., Scientific American (Guilford, CT: Lyons Press. 2007), 157–166.

4   Bill Pennington, 'A Golf Ball that Won't Slice Comes With a Catch: Its Illegal', *New York Times*, 9 May, 2011 <http://www.nytimes.com/2011/05/10/sports/golf/10ball.html> (Accessed 10 March, 2013).

5   Sarah A. Curran and Richard Hirons, 'Preparing Our Paralympians: Research and Development at Össur, UK', *Prosthetics and Orthotics International* 36 (2012): 366–369. For an extended discussion on the relative merits of different prostheses on the market, see Lee Nolan, 'Carbon Fibre Prostheses and Running in Amputees: A Review', *Foot and Ankle Surgery* 14 (2008): 125–129.

6   The International Amateur Athletics Federation banned Pistorius from competition on grounds of fairness. It argued that the biomechanical and physiological evidence indicated his prostheses were in contravention of Rule 144.2, which forbids the use of any technical device (such as prosthetic limbs) that provides the user an advantage over another athlete. The nature and size of athletic advantage and the basis for determining its validity are crucial for determining an account of fairness. Similar difficulties apply to 'relevant athletic performance'. See Carwyn Jones and Cassie Wilson, 'Defining Advantage and Athletic Performance: The Case of Oscar Pistorius', *European Journal of Sport Science* 9 (2009): 125–131.

7   This phrase related to the logic and appeal of game playing originates from Warren Fraleigh in *Right Actions in Sport Ethics for Contestants* (Champaign, IL: Human Kinetics, 1982). It has subsequently been extensively quoted (see Scott Kretchmar, 'From Test to Contest: An Analysis of Two Kinds of Counterpoint in Sport', *Journal of the Philosophy of Sport* 2 [1975]: 23–30; Sigmund Loland and Mike McNamee, 'Fair Play and the Ethos of Sports: An Eclectic Philosophical Framework', *Journal of the Philosophy of Sport* 27 [2000]: 63–80; and Scott Kretchmar and Tim L. Elcombe, 'In Defense of Competition and Winning: Revising Athletic Tests and Contents', in *Ethics in Sport*, 2nd ed, ed., William J. Morgan [Champaign, IL: Human Kinetics, 2007], 181–194) and receives extended discussion in Douglas W. McLaughlin and Cesar R. Torres, 'Sweet Tension and Its Phenomenological Description: Sport, Intersubjectivity and Horizon', *Sport, Ethics and Philosophy* 5 (2011): 270–284.

8   For out-of-competition drug testing, see David R. Mottram, 'A Historical Perspective of Doping and Anti-doping in Sport', *Routledge Online Studies on the Olympic and Paralympic Games* 1 (2012): 21–34, and for their ineffectiveness, Paul Dimeo and John Taylor, 'Monitoring Drug Use in Sport: The Contrast between Official Statistics and Other Evidence', *Drugs: Education, Prevention and Policy* 20 (2013): 40–47. The biological effects of rapid body mass loss are presented in Ciro José Brito, Aendria Fernanda Castro Martins Roas, Igor Surian Souza Brito, João Carlos Bouzas Marins, Claudio Córdova and Emerson Franchini, 'Methods of Body-Mass Reduction by Combat Sport Athletes', *International Journal of Sport Nutrition and Exercise Metabolism* 22 (2012): 89–97. A 2000 NCAA ruling has done much to prevent the adverse effects of cutting weight. See Alan C. Utter, 'The New National Collegiate Athletic Association Wrestling Weight Certification Program and Sport-seasonal Changes in Body Composition of College Wrestlers', *The Journal of Strength & Conditioning Research* 15

(2001): 296–301. For the benefits of ice baths after intense exercise, see Giuseppe Banfi, Giovanni Lombardi, Alessandra Colombini and Gianluca Melegati, 'Whole-body Cryotherapy in Athletes', *Sports medicine* 40 (2010): 509–517.

9   Sigmund Loland, 'Technology in Sport: Three Ideal-typical Views and Their Implications', *European Journal of Sport Science* 2 (2001): 1–11.

10   Joseph Dunne, *Back to the Rough Ground* (Notre Dame, IN: University of Notre Dame Press, 1993), 9.

11   Jürgen Habermas, *Theory and Practice* (Boston: Beacon Press, 1973).

12   Jürgen Habermas, *The Structural Transformation of the Public Sphere: An Inquiry into a Category of Bourgeois Society* (Cambridge: Polity, 1962), 255.

13   For a clear development of the mind-body problem in the context of physical culture see Jan Rintala, 'The Mind-Body Revisited', *Quest* 43 (1991): 260–279; W. Miller Brown, 'Comments on Simon and Fraleigh', *Journal of the Philosophy of Sport* 11 (1984): 33–35; and Scott Kretchmar, *Practical Philosophy of Sport and Physical Activity* 2nd ed (Champaign, IL: Human Kinetics Publishers, 2005), 45–62.

14   Jacques Ellul, *The Technological Society* (New York: Vintage Books, 1964).

15   Jürgen Habermas, *Toward a Rational Society* (Boston: Beacon Press, 1970).

16   Henning Eichberg, 'Stopwatch, Horizontal Bar, Gymnasium: The Technologizing of Sports in the 18th and Early 19th Centuries', *Journal of the Philosophy of Sport* 9 (1982): 55.

17   Jacques Ellul, 'Technology and Democracy', in *Democracy in a Technological Society*, ed., Langdon Winner (Dordretch: Kluwer Academic Publishers, 1992), 35–50.

18   Mary Tiles and Hans Oberdiek, *Living in a Technological Culture: Human Tools and Human Values* (New York: Routledge, 1995).

19   Ibid., 5.

20   Loland, 'Technology in sport: Three ideal-typical views and their implications', 2–3.

21   Steve J. Haake, 'The Impact of Technology on Sporting Performance in Olympic Sports', *Journal of Sports Sciences* 27 (2009): 1421–1431.

22   John Hoberman, 'Sport and the Technological Image of Man', in *Philosophic Inquiry in Sport*, eds., William J. Morgan and Klaus V. Meier (Champaign, IL: Human Kinetics, 1988), 319–327.

23   John M Hoberman, *Mortal Engines: The Science of Performance and the Dehumanization of Sport* (New York: Free Press, 1992).

24   Hoberman, 'Sport and the Technological Image of Man', 319.

25   Ibid., 320.

26   World Anti-Doping Agency, *Prohibited List* <http://www.wada-ama.org/en/World-Anti-Doping-Program/Sports-and-Anti-Doping-Organizations/International-Standards/Prohibited-List/> (accessed 11 February, 2013).

27   This idea is presented in a number of ways. Mike Lavin, for example, presses the idea of a democratic consensus as the basis for normative judgement (see his article, 'Sports and Drugs: Are the Current Bans Justified?', *Journal of the Philosophy of Sport* 14 [1987]: 34–43). Nicholas Dixon discuses the morality of a communitarian-based account (see his article, 'Rorty, Performance-enhancing Drugs, and Change in Sport', *Journal of the Philosophy of Sport* 28 [2001]: 78–88). Others identify the issue with regard to individual justice (see John Sabini and John Monterosso, 'Judgments of the Fairness of Using Performance Enhancing Drugs', *Ethics & Behavior* 15 [2005]: 81–94).

28   Angela J. Schneider and Robert B. Butcher, 'A Philosophical Overview of the Arguments on Banning Doping in Sport', in *Values in Sport: Elitism, Nationalism, Gender Equality and the Scientific Manufacture of Winners*, eds., Torbjörn Tännsjö and Claudio M. Tamburrini (New York: E & FN Spon, 2000), 196.

29   Leon Culbertson, '"Human-ness", "Dehumanisation" and Performance Enhancement', *Sports, Ethics and Philosophy* 1 (2007): 195–217.

30 Ibid.

31 Ibid, 208.

32 See Giuseppe Lippi, Umile Giuseppe Longo and Nicola Maffulli, 'Genetics and Sports', *British Medical Bulletin* 93 (2010): 27–47. Also, for an ethical response to these possibilities see Andy Miah, 'Genetics Sport: Bioethical Concerns', *Recent Patents on DNA & Gene Sequences* 6 (2012): 197–202; and Ryan Purcell, 'Performance Enhancement: To Embrace Doping in Sport is Absurd', *Nature* 488 (2012): 157. For a comprehensive discussion on biogenetics the following resources provide a good grounding: Mike McNamee, 'Performance Enhancing Technologies in Sports: Ethical, Conceptual and Scientific Issues', *Journal of the Philosophy of Sport* 38 (2011): 128–31; Andy Miah, *Genetically Modified Athletes. Biomedical Ethics, Gene Doping and Sport* (London: Routledge, 2004); and idem, 'From Anti-doping to a "Performance Policy" Sport Technology, Being Human, and Doing Ethics', *European Journal of Sport Science* 5 (2005): 51–7.

33 The body of work of Sigmund Loland is fairly extensive. Several of his publications are cited in this essay.

34 Loland, 'Technology in Sport: Three Ideal-typical Views and Their Implications'.

35 Sigmund Loland and Arthur Caplan, 'Ethics of Technologically Constructed Hypoxic Environments in Sport', *Scandinavian Journal of Medicine & Science in Sports* 18 (2008): 70–5; and Sigmund Loland, 'The Ethics of Performance-enhancing Technology in Sport', *Journal of the Philosophy of Sport* 36 (2009): 152–61

36 Loland, 'The Ethics of Performance-enhancing Technology in Sport', 157.

37 Loland, 'Technology in Sport: Three Ideal-typical Views and Their Implications', 6.

38 Loland, 'The Ethics of Performance-enhancing Technology in Sport', 158.

39 The differences between theoretical and practical knowledge in Aristotle's thought are sketched out in Book VI: I of his *Nicomachean Ethics*. See Aristotle, *Nicomachean Ethics*, trans. Terence Irwin (Indianapolis, IN: Hackett Publishing Co.), 1988.

40 Dunne, *Back to the Rough Ground*, 10.

41 For a comprehensive discussion on this aspect, see Heather Sheridan, 'Tennis Technologies: De-skilling and Re-skilling Players and the Implications for the Game', *Sport in Society* 9 (2006): 32–50.

42 See William J. Morgan, 'Toward a Critical Theory of Sport', *Journal of Sport & Social Issues* 7 (1983): 30.

43 William J. Morgan, *Leftist Theories of Sport: A Critique and Reconstruction* (Urbana; IL: University of Illinois Press, 1994).

44 David W. Masterson, 'The Ancient Greek Origins of Sports Medicine', *British Journal of Sports Medicine* 10 (1976): 196–202.

45 Andrew I. Warden, 'Driving the Green: The Impact of PGA Tour, Inc. v. Martin on Disabled Athletes and the Future of Competitive Sports', *NCL Review* 80 (2001): 643.

46 Gert-Peter Brüggemann, Adamantios Arampatzis, Frank Emrich and Wolfgang Potthast, 'Biomechanics of double transtibial amputee sprinting using dedicated sprinting prostheses', *Sports Technology* 1 (2008): 220–7; Wolfgang Potthast and Gert-Peter Brüeggemann, 'Comparison of Sprinting Mechanics of the Double Transtibial Amputee Oscar Pistorius with Able Bodied Athletes' (paper presented at the annual meeting of the International Society of Biomechanics in Sports, Marquette, Michigan, 19–23 July, 2010); and Peter G. Weyand, Matthew W. Bundle, Craig P. McGowan, Alena Grabowski, Mary Beth Brown, Rodger Kram and Hugh Herr, 'The Fastest Runner on Artificial Legs: Different Limbs, Similar Function?', *Journal of Applied Physiology* 107 (2009): 903–11.

19 Conceivable Horizons of Equality in Sport

Pam R. Sailors

The realm of sports would seem to be ideally situated to embody equality. After all, participants in athletic contests compete together under apparently identical conditions. The same rules govern all, while precise timing devices and consistent distance markers measure the performances of all athletes. Yet closer examination shows otherwise. Inequalities may be generated by differences of race and sex, social class, conditions of disability, nationality and religious belief, among other variables. Confining the focus here to only the first three categories – race, sex and class – reveals an extensive list of examples of sporting inequalities.

Persons who belong to traditionally disadvantaged racial groups are rarely found in positions of power in sports. Owners, managers, head coaches and members of legislative sporting federations are almost always a racially homogeneous group. In the vast majority of cases, white men control who, when and how sport participation occurs.[1] Native tribes are often represented only in an offensive or demeaning manner by team mascots exhibiting stereotypical dress and behaviour.[2] Organizers of mega-events, like the Olympic Games, exhibit no qualms about staging such events on native lands, with little consideration of the fact that those lands might be sacred sites, trivializing any indigenous opposition.[3]

Inequalities based on sex are also easily identified in sport. Women are regularly denied the opportunity to compete under equal conditions to men. Women's sports are expected to make do with inferior facilities and smaller budgets than men's sports. The rules for many women's sports constrain them to a diminutive version of participation, requiring that they cover less distance, or use a smaller ball, or play fewer sets or minutes, sometimes on a shorter field. Even when they do compete under the same conditions as men, women are often awarded less prize money than their male counterparts. Sex segregation is taken to be an immutable fact, with virtually no serious consideration given to the idea of mixed competition between women and men. And the treatment of transgender and intersex athletes, who do not fit exactly into either of the two usual categories of male or female, has been discriminatory at best and often hostile.[4]

Equality would seem to require that differences between competitors that affect the outcome of contests be a matter only of athletic ability. This assumption, however, runs into two challenges when examined in the light of actual circumstances. Firstly, the opportunities to participate in sport, and which sports are available, are more limited for potential athletes in lower socio-economic classes. Some sports simply are not available to people who do not enjoy a certain level of wealth. Golf, equestrian events and tennis are examples of sports that have traditionally been the exclusive province of athletes whose circumstances allowed them to invest in expensive equipment and club memberships. Secondly, the degree of one's athletic ability will often depend upon the external advantages one's social position makes available. Athletes without access to the most sophisticated coaching techniques, technological advancements in equipment and top-notch facilities are unlikely to attain the level of athletic excellence of their competitors who have such access. And that access is, to a large degree, a function of the wealth one (or one's location) possesses.

As is often the case, we may see something more clearly by contrasting it with its opposite, so these examples of conditions of inequality offer a beginning point to imagination of an alternative state, and a suggestion for a method to move us closer to that state. I will examine some oft-cited philosophical accounts of equality, then move to more sport-specific accounts to construct a framework for equality. This will allow for consideration of how the landscape of sport would be changed and conceivable horizons of equality in sport expanded if the framework were employed.

The concept of equality has been explored by many, and the exploration often begins by citing Aristotle, who took up the matter most fully in *Politics*. Aristotle notes a general agreement among people on the idea that equals ought to be treated equally. The issue, however, is by what criteria equals are determined and what is meant by equal treatment. Surely all are not equal, so there will necessarily be unequal treatment. It is too simplistic, however, to distribute positions or goods based on a mere superiority in any area. The superiority must be relevant to the position. Thus, Aristotle says we should not award someone who is particularly tall, dark or handsome with greater political rights than a less attractive peer, as one's appearance is not relevant to the deserving of rights in the political arena. He illustrates the meaning with the example of musical talent, asserting that:

> When a number of flute-players are equal in their art, there is no reason why those of them who are better born should have better flutes given to them; for they will not play any better on the flute, and the superior instrument should be reserved for him who is the superior artist ... For if there were a superior flute-player who was far inferior in birth and beauty, although either of these may be a greater good than the art of flute-playing, and may excel flute-playing in a greater ratio than he excels the others in his art, still he ought to have the best flutes given to him, unless the advantages of wealth and birth contribute to excellence in flute-playing, which they do not. Moreover, upon this principle any good may be compared with any other.[5]

Transferring his example from the world of music to the world of sport indicates that Aristotle would disapprove of race, sex or class being the criteria upon which athletic inequalities rest. Just as the most talented flute player should receive the best instrument, the most talented athletes should receive the best equipment and training, and have access to the best facilities, since their race, sex and socio-economic class are not directly relevant to athletic ability.

Echoing Aristotle, John Stuart Mill claims that people agree that one's treatment ought to be tied to relevant factors, most importantly to the factor of desert. In his treatment of justice, Mill says that 'it is universally considered just that each person should obtain that (whether good or evil) which he *deserves*; and unjust that he should obtain a good, or be made to undergo an evil, which he does not deserve'.[6] Where Aristotle took a single example to be sufficient to explain his view, Mill provides far more detail regarding the ingredients of justice; of particular importance for him is impartiality. Impartiality is the most important ingredient in justice because it is the prerequisite for the satisfaction of any of the other ingredients. Impartiality requires that we not 'show favour or preference to one person over another, in matters to which favour and preference do not properly apply'.[7] This is important because it is tied to equality, which Mill says 'often enters as a component part both into the conception of justice and into the practice of it, and, in the eyes of many persons, constitutes its essence'.[8] Connecting impartiality and equality to each other and, further, to the overall moral duty to increase the sum of happiness in the world, Mill argues that:

> If it is a duty to do to each according to his deserts, returning good for good as well as repressing evil by evil, it necessarily follows that we should treat all equally well … who have deserved equally well of *us*, and that society should treat all equally well who have deserved equally well of *it*, that is, who have deserved equally well absolutely. This is the highest abstract standard of social and distributive justice; towards which all institutions, and the efforts of all virtuous citizens, should be made in the utmost possible degree to converge. But this great moral duty rests upon a still deeper foundation … It is involved in the very meaning of Utility, or the Greatest Happiness Principle. That principle is a mere form of words without rational signification, unless one person's happiness … is counted for exactly as much as another's. Those conditions being supplied, Bentham's dictum, 'everybody to count for one, nobody for more than one', might be written under the principle of utility as an explanatory commentary.[9]

The connection to the Greatest Happiness Principle indicates the sole consideration that can trump equality – utility. Because the highest moral duty we have is to increase the total amount of happiness, it alone pardons impartiality and/or inequality. At the same time, increasing the total amount of happiness requires impartiality, which requires, in turn, that no individual's happiness count more than any other's.

Following Mill requires that all athletes be treated impartially, unless one of two conditions is met. First, unequal treatment might be justified by relevant differences, presumably in athletic ability, among the athletes that make partial treatment appropriate. Or, second, overall social utility (an increase in the sum of happiness) would justify unequal treatment. This second condition seems problematic, on the face of it. How could unequal treatment actually be of social utility? To answer this question, it will be useful to turn to the work of John Rawls.

Rawls asks us to imagine that we know nothing about our own particular circumstances. Whether we are rich or poor, old or young, black or white, able-bodied or disabled, gay or straight, genius or dullard, all is hidden behind what he calls a 'veil of ignorance'. In this, the 'original position', we choose the principles that will govern us, without the specific knowledge that would allow anyone to establish principles that would be prejudiced to his or her own advantage. Through this procedure for choice, Rawls believes he has eliminated unfairness from his theory of justice. Thus, it is justice as fairness, since the choice takes place under fair conditions.[10]

Behind the veil of ignorance, no one would choose principles that would sacrifice the happiness of any individual for the sake of increasing the total amount of happiness since the one choosing is aware of the possibility that she might also be the one whose happiness would be sacrificed. This is where Rawls appears to disagree with Mill's suggestion that social utility might trump equality. Still, in the end, the two may not be so far apart in application, because the principles Rawls says would be chosen in the original position themselves allow for inequality. Rawls's assertion of the two principles is as follows:

> […] the first requires equality in the assignment of basic rights and duties, while the second holds that social and economic inequalities … are just only if they result in compensating benefits for everyone, and in particular for the least advantaged members of society. These principles rule out justifying institutions on the grounds that the hardships of some are offset by a greater good in the aggregate. It may be expedient but it is not just that some should have less in order that others may prosper. But there is no injustice in the greater benefits earned by a few provided that the situation of persons not so fortunate is thereby improved.[11]

So, both Mill and Rawls allow that inequalities might justifiably exist, but the conditions of justification differ. For Mill, it is social utility (the greatest happiness), while for Rawls it is the benefit of the least advantaged. Of course, one might argue that a society in which inequalities harm the least advantaged would not be a society in which the greatest happiness is realized. Or, to put it positively, social utility requires that inequalities work to the benefit of the least advantaged members of society.[12]

In any event, what we get from Rawls is a way to evaluate the conditions we find in sport, including the inequalities that currently exist. We ask, first, whether the governing principles would be chosen in a sort of sporting original position. Then we ask whether the inequalities that have been allowed work to the benefit of the least advantaged. Unless a reasonable argument can be advanced to conclude that the inequalities are justified in this way, we have no grounds for their continued existence. In fact, we have a moral obligation to eliminate the inequalities.

Moving now to more sport-specific accounts of equality, the preceding theories are not supplanted, but serve a foundational role. For example, Warren P. Fraleigh's characterization of sports participants as 'rational contractors' evokes Rawls' rational agents, in the original position, choosing the principles by which they will be bound. Fraleigh even borrows Rawls's terminology to refer to the sports participants as being behind a veil of ignorance in the original position. As he puts it, the participants:

> assume a hypothetical stance in their deliberations, and this stance presumes that all sports participants are free, equal, rational, and wish to pursue general human self-interests. This hypothetical stance is called the original position; to reach agreement from that position the sports participants/ rational contractors must also assume the veil of ignorance. Behind this veil of ignorance, each sports participant/rational contractor operates as if he/ she does not know his/her own particular desires, abilities, status, and circumstances. In principle, before agreement on the guides and ends of action, no sports participant knows whether he/she is old or young, amateur or professional, male or female, athlete or coach, or athletic trainer or contest official, or exhibits any other individual characteristics.[13]

Just as in Rawls, since none of the participants knows his or her particular circumstances, none will propose or agree to rules that could disadvantage even the least advantaged, since he or she might be that individual. The result is that the system will be just since no one can take a chance on suffering from injustices of one's own creation.[14]

Having established the conditions for choosing guidelines, Fraleigh posits as the most important guide one that is focused on equality. His 'Guide of Equal Opportunity for Optimal Performance' prescribes that 'Athletes, coaches and athletic trainers shall seek and sustain, by their acts, like equal opportunity for themselves and for opponents to achieve oppositional superiority within sports contests'.[15] This is the most important guideline because it is required to guarantee that athletes perform at the highest levels of which they are capable. Without this guarantee, we would not be able accurately to compare performances and, thus, assess which athlete is the best, defeating the entire purpose of the sporting contest. Of course, the guide requires that contestants follow the rules of the particular contest in which they are engaged, but it requires much more, as Fraleigh describes:

> This guide means that all participants shall actively seek and sustain the same kind of liberty to perform well in the sports contest. Such equal liberty includes, prior to a contest, access to effective coaching, adequate facilities and equipment, effective sports medicine services, and sufficient practice time. Equal access to such essentials prior to the sports contest is necessary for maximum preparation by all so that they can perform to their capacity.[16]

Fraleigh's emphasis on pre-event conditions and advantages is evidence of a deep commitment to equal opportunity. In his view, sport requires that participants perform at the highest individual levels possible, which entails equal preparation; thus, all must be equally situated in terms of access to all of the means to the end of athletic excellence. Of course, equal opportunity will not guarantee equal performance, and we wouldn't want it to anyway since the point is to make a comparative assessment of athletic ability. The concern here, instead, is to ensure as much as possible the conditions that enable superior athletic performance.[17] Most obviously, this view conflicts sharply with any state of affairs in which some sports opportunities and athletic accomplishments are closed solely as a result of race, sex or class.

Robert L. Simon takes a similar path in his treatment of inequalities in sport, carefully establishing the distinction between equal treatment and equal opportunity. Athletes should be guaranteed the latter, but not the former, as the treatment will depend upon the advantage the athlete is able (and chooses) to make of the opportunity.[18] To put this another way, athletes should be treated as equals, but this does not entail identical treatment. Simon also shares Fraleigh's appropriation of Rawls' decision-making procedure, suggesting that the 'use of this limited "veil of ignorance," suggested by John Rawls's theory of justice, forces the athletes to be impartial and unbiased rather than to vote according to personal self-interest'.[19] Given this, it is unsurprising that Simon objects to the exclusion of athletes based on sex. 'Males and females,' he says 'have an equal claim to participation because members of both sexes may seek the challenges presented by competitive sports.'[20] Still, Simon shares a concern for social utility that harkens back to Mill, supporting sex-segregated contests on the grounds that this provides the best chance of equal opportunity. That is, he argues that sex segregation, or sex pluralism, is necessary in most circumstances to ensure that women have opportunities to participate, since few of them are physiologically capable of competing against men. This is not an absolute prohibition, however, as Simon goes on to suggest that 1) men and women could compete together at the recreational level, and 2) individual women who are physiologically capable of competing with men should be allowed to do so. 'A reasonable understanding of equal opportunity minimally would provide persons on an individual basis the chance to compete if qualified to do so, and not prohibit them from doing so on grounds (such as sex) not related to their athletic qualifications.'[21]

Again, we are brought back to the notion that athletic ability is the only relevant criterion for inequality in sport and it must even be assessed in terms of effects on the least advantaged in augmenting opportunities to compete. Inequality may exist so long as it would be agreed to in the original position. Distinguishing between race and sex, Simon says, 'unlike the doctrine of "separate but equal" in the context of racial segregation, separate athletic programmes do not stigmatize one group or the other, are not imposed against the will of either sex, and actually enhance the freedom and opportunity of the previously disadvantaged group.'[22] All of the preceding concerns are incorporated here as the conditions are freely chosen, based on relevant factors, work to the advantage of all, and would seem to increase social utility.

I have focused primarily on circumstances of inequality for individuals, but it is likewise important to take a wider view of systematic inequalities. Sigmund Loland's work in this area is particularly helpful, beginning with his very Aristotelian principle that 'relevantly equal cases ought to be treated equally, cases that are relevantly unequal can be treated unequally, and unequal treatment ought to stand in reasonable accordance to the actual inequality between cases'.[23] The relevant difference, as we have already seen, is athletic ability. Any other inequalities should be eliminated, such that all athletes have an equal opportunity to perform to the best of their capabilities.[24] This includes, of course, inequalities in the preconditions for competition, a requirement that Loland echoes, both on the individual level and the wider level. As others have noted, there are serious inequalities in access to equipment, coaches, support staff and facilities, but Loland draws our attention to the fact that these inequalities occur among teams and even countries, not merely among individual athletes. 'Athletic performances are developed within large "systems" of material, technological and scientific resources, including facilities and equipment, trainers, medical and administrative apparatus, exercise scientists, technologists and so on. Given all this, the public admiration of the winning athlete or team appears to be based on false premises. We do not just measure, compare and rank competitors according to skills; rather, we are measuring the strength of whole systems.'[25] When access to financial resources, rather than athletic ability, becomes the relevant factor in determining athletic success, wealthy teams will always triumph over poor teams. Beginning from the premise that athletic ability should be the only relevant inequality in sport, this state of affairs violates the principle that relevantly equal cases be treated equally. Thus, Loland concludes, access to resources on the system level must be compensated for or eliminated.[26] Loland's attention to groups and systems rather than merely individuals leads to a consideration of why some groups have been excluded historically and how we may move toward their inclusion.

What prompts humans to extend the boundary of moral concern to include groups previously excluded? Peter Singer suggests it is the realization that what we have in common is greater than the differences that distinguish us. In particular, possession of the capacity to suffer is the trait that Singer asserts as decisive for inclusion in the moral community. All members of the moral community are owed equal consideration of their like interests.[27] However, history reveals that this is not always persuasive, even when we are assured that members of some group can suffer. This explains why the history of humanity has been a story of the gradual expansion of consideration.[28] Singer illustrates this process by pointing to Thomas Jefferson's realization that the interests of his African-American slaves should be taken into account, which led him to oppose the institution of slavery, and Sojourner Truth's argument that the interests of women should be taken into account, which led eventually to women's full participation in the political process.[29]

It is important to note two aspects of Singer's view. Firstly, Singer's claim does not commit him to supporting equal treatment. In line with the positions already examined, this is a prescription for equal consideration, or opportunity, not for equal outcome. Actual treatment, outcome and even rights may turn out to be different under equal consideration of interests.[30] Secondly, Singer is not making a factual claim that all humans are equal, a claim that would too quickly be disproved by empirical examination; instead, he is making a moral claim about how humans ought to be treated. As he puts it:

> […] the claim to equality does not depend on intelligence, moral capacity, physical strength, or similar matters of fact. Equality is a moral idea, not an assertion of fact. There is no logically compelling reason for assuming that a factual difference in ability between two people justifies any difference in the amount of consideration we give to their needs and interests. *The principle of the equality of human beings is not a description of an alleged actual equality among humans: it is a prescription of how we should treat humans.*[31]

Adding Singer's notion of the gradual expansion of our moral boundaries and his principle of equality to the theories already examined provides the final piece of the framework for evaluating particular instances of inequality in sport and speculating about how sport might be changed in eliminating those instances.

We ought to inquire of any instance of inequality in sport by asking how it answers five questions, which together incorporate the tools pulled from Aristotle, Mill, Rawls, Fraleigh, Simon, Loland and Singer. First, does it treat athletic equals equally? Second, does it avoid partiality, or, if not, does it increase social utility? Third, is it, or would it be, chosen under fair conditions, ones which preclude bias toward any individual's self-interest? Fourth, does it work to the advantage of the least advantaged of those affected? And, finally, does it give equal consideration to like interests of all members of the moral community, and/or expand the boundaries of inclusion? Affirmative answers to all five questions are required to justify an instance of inequality. Now we can return to the cases mentioned at the outset for evaluation of their current status and imagination of an improved future.

In the area of race, the current state of affairs regarding leadership positions in sport fails to provide an affirmative answer to any of the five questions, so these positions should be opened up to include persons who belong to traditionally disadvantaged racial groups. Turning our attention to supporting characters, certainly someone behind a veil of ignorance would not choose to have one's race depicted in a disparaging way by a team mascot, so, such mascots must be eliminated. Finally, current practices in Olympic staging fail to include in a meaningful way input from indigenous groups, thus failing to give equal consideration to like interests, so the practices must be revised to include voices from all stakeholders.

The framework suggested here also points to new directions regarding inequalities based on sex. Most obviously, reforms are needed to enable an affirmative answer to the first question, which asks about treating athletic equals equally. Women who are physiologically capable of competing with men should be allowed to do so. But all women should not be forced to compete against men, since that would decrease social utility. To avoid a negative answer to all five questions, the preconditions that enable athletes to perform at the top of their capability must be guaranteed to women as well as men. Finally, the interests of transgender and intersex athletes must be given equal consideration as our moral community expands and we recognize that such is what would be chosen from behind a veil of ignorance.

Since socio-economic class is not relevant to athletic ability, equality requires that it does not determine the sports in which one can participate or the level of athletic ability one can attain. So, conditions that limit access to certain sports, or equitable equipment, facilities, technologies and coaching, must be changed, such that the conditions work to the advantage of even the most disadvantaged in terms of wealth and access.

To conclude, I have suggested that we can extract, so to speak, five questions from existing work in philosophy and philosophy of sport to use to evaluate any instance of perceived inequality in sport. Such questions also allow us to begin to conceive new horizons of equality in which race, sex and class, among other variables, do not determine in any way one's opportunity to participate in sport to the height of one's capability. Of course, the horizon will not hold perfect equality, as equality of performance or outcome would defeat the very purpose of sport. Treating athletes equally does not mean treating them identically. We may find in some cases that social utility would be increased by allowing partiality, as in instances of policies designed to increase the hiring of minority group members to positions of power, since such policies would arguably expand the boundaries of inclusion. We may find that procedures that work to the advantage of the least advantaged require inequality of possible benefits, as when standardization of equipment or access to coaches requires athletes in wealthier countries or systems not to take advantage of all the assistance that might be available to them. Most importantly, we will find that the adoption of the evaluative criteria suggested here justifies the elimination of illegitimate inequalities and expands opportunities for participants to enjoy the best of sport.

Notes

1   In the NFL's hiring cycle that concluded in 2013, for example, not a single person of colour was chosen to fill any of the eight head coaching or seven general manager positions that were available. See Jarrett Bell, 'Playing Field Still Not Level', *USA Today*, 22 January, 2013, 4C. The leadership situation is no better for women. For example, only 17 per cent of Olympic team coaches in Canada are women. See Megan Stewart, 'Canadian Women Shut Out from Sport Leadership Roles', *Vancouver Courier*, 27 November, 2012 <http://www.canada.com/sports/Canadian+women+shut+from +sport+leadership+roles/7618061/story.html> (accessed 28 November, 2012). And only 22 per cent of sports organizations' board members in the UK are women. See Hannah Kuchler, 'Sports Groups Lack Women in Boardrooms,' *The Financial Times*, 4 March, 2013, <http://www.ft.com/intl/cms/s/2/2cea863e-8290-11e2-8404-00144feab dc0.html#axzz2PtzTFGXj> (accessed 5 March, 2013).

2   For instance, a group of Native Americans is currently suing the Washington Redskins football team, claiming that the team name should be prohibited by a law that disallows names that are 'disparaging, scandalous, contemptuous or disreputable'. See 'Redskins Face Name Challenge', *USA Today*, 7 March, 2013, 3C.

3   For an excellent account of how indigenous protests of Olympic events are dismissed, see Christine M. O'Bonsawin, '"No Olympics on Stolen Land": Contesting Olympic Narratives and Asserting Indigenous Rights Within the Discourse of the 2010 Vancouver Games', *Sport in Society* 13 (2010): 143–56.

4   See 'Sport in Transition: Making Sport in Canada More Responsible For Gender Inclusivity', a report from the *Canadian Centre for Ethics in Sport*, October 2012. See also John Coggon, Natasha Hammond and Soren Holm, 'Transsexuals in Sport – Fairness and Freedom, Regulation and Law', *Sport, Ethics and Philosophy* 2 (2013): 4–17.

5   Aristotle, 'Politics', in *Introduction to Aristotle*, ed., Richard McKeon, trans. Benjamin Jowett (New York: Random House, 1947), 1282b 15–1283a 5.

6   John Stuart Mill, 'Utilitarianism', in *Utilitarianism and Other Writings*, ed., Mary Warnock (New York: Penguin, 1962), 299.

7   Ibid., 300.

8   Ibid., 301.

9   Ibid., 318–319.

10 John Rawls, *A Theory of Justice* (Cambridge, MA: Harvard University Press, 1971), 12.

11 Ibid., 15.

12 This move requires an emphasis on the rule utilitarian aspects of Mill's theory. While it might satisfy Mill, I recognize that Rawls would likely object to being linked to utilitarianism in this way.

13 Warren P. Fraleigh, *Right Actions in Sport: Ethics for Contestants* (Champaign, IL: Human Kinetics, 1984), 108.

14 Ibid., 109.

15 Emphasis in original.

16 Ibid., 114.

17 Ibid., 115.

18 Robert L. Simon, *Fair Play: The Ethics of Sport*, 3rd ed. (Boulder, CO: Westview Press, 2010), 33.

19 Ibid., 86. In this passage, Simon's use of Rawls is in regard to athletes choosing whether to use performance-enhancing drugs, but the decision-making procedure itself can be extended to cover other issues, and nothing in Simon indicates that he would disapprove of such an extension.

20 Ibid., 113.

21 Ibid., 118–19.

22 Ibid., 124.

23 Sigmund Loland, *Fair Play in Sport: A moral norm system* (New York: Routledge, 2002), 43.

24 Ibid., 46.

25 Ibid., 60–1.

26 Ibid., 61–2.

27 Peter Singer, *Animal Liberation: A New Ethics For Our Treatment of Animals* (New York: Avon Books, 1975), 5.

28 Mill has a similar description of the expansion of the boundaries of moral concern, although he attributes the expansion to social utility rather than enhanced sympathetic identification. Thus, Mill ('Utilitarianism') writes, 'The entire history of social improvement has been a series of transitions, by which one custom or institution after another, from being a supposed primary necessity of social existence, has passed into the rank of a universally stigmatized injustice and tyranny. So it has been with the distinctions of slave and freemen, nobles and serfs, patricians and plebeians; and so it will be, and in part already is, with the aristocracies of colour, race and sex' (320).

29   Singer, *Animal Liberation: A New Ethics For Our Treatment of Animals*, 6.
30   Ibid., 3.
31   Ibid., 5.

20 'Spoiled Sports': Markets and the Corruption of Sport

William J. Morgan

To corrupt a person or a thing is to defile it, to treat it in a way that belies its true worth or value. The same goes for the corruption of a social practice like sport. For to corrupt sport is also to defile it by treating it in a way that undermines the central goods it traffics in. When this happens the purpose and point of athletic enterprise is deformed, and the standards of excellence, values and social meanings that inform such enterprise are spoiled.

To talk of the corruption of sport does not entail or imply that it possesses some sort of essence that must be vigilantly protected. Rather, it suggests that sport is a cultural artefact, something made and remade rather than discovered, and that this process of making and remaking is a thoroughgoing social and historical matter in which various cultural features, meanings and values are affixed to sport and regarded as vital to its flourishing. Put another way, sport is a kind of normative laboratory in which we (players, spectators, critics, etc.) work out what its purpose should be, what sorts of skills, virtues and excellence it should embrace and aspire to, and, more generally, how its worth should be determined and assessed. That means that as our social conceptions of the point of sport change, so do the sources of its possible corruption. There have been, then, in the history of sport different things that have been considered as corrupting of sport. Two relatively recent examples include an amateur conception of sport that defined athletic excellence in such a narrow way that only the well-off were considered suited to pursuing athletic glory, which meant all the ills of sport were blamed on the ill mores of working-class interlopers and an international conception of sport that championed the cause of peace through sport, which attributed the failings of sport to nationalistic excess. Today, however, I want to claim that the major threat to the integrity of sport is the market, specifically, its all too familiar tendency to dominate sport and everything else it comes into contact with. For what results when the market dominates cultural practices like sport is that it installs its own distinctively egoistic logic and mode of valuation in place of the distinctively social logic and mode of valuation generally considered to be central to the flourishing of sport. That is why, in my estimation, the commodification of sport can't but corrupt its central purpose and value, and with it the social meanings that account for sport's special standing in our contemporary culture.

The Point and Value of Athletic Enterprise

Since I have claimed that talk of the corruption of sport requires we be clear about just what is defiled in sport when it is so corrupted, it is necessary to say something first about what is the point and value of athletic enterprise. The obvious place to begin in this regard, I think, is to note that sport is first and foremost a perfectionist practice, in which the achievement of athletic excellence is, therefore, primary.[1] But determining what constitutes genuine athletic excellence, and what bundle of skills, virtues and the like it comprises, not to mention how hard we should strive to be excellent in this athletic sense, are not matters, as noted, for armchair metaphysical speculation. Rather, they are very much bound up with, as also noted, our social and historical circumstances, and, in particular, our reigning conventional background understandings of the purpose of athletic enterprise. In this conventional sense, then, athletic excellence in its current iteration differs from its predecessors in several respects. First, by our present lights athletic excellence only counts as such if it is achieved in a fair and equitable manner, that is, if it results from a competition open to all-comers with the requisite talent. Second, an important part of the mix of skills that constitute genuine athletic achievement today includes a well-honed strategic approach to the game, which includes the select strategic violation of the rules. Third, striving for athletic excellence is in the present context considered to be a full-time, full-throated enterprise that requires intense training and specialization. The days of sport being a pastime that needn't be pursued too strenuously to accomplish something of athletic note are long gone.

It is also an important feature of our contemporary conventional understanding of sport that getting paid to play it is not only an acceptable way to take it up, but a necessary one. That's because if the pursuit of athletic excellence is to be a full-blown undertaking requiring nothing less than our wholehearted commitment, in other words, a serious vocation rather than a less-than-serious avocation, then one must be able to make it one's career. In a market economy like ours, that means getting paid to play sports. Obviously, then, when I claim markets are corrupting of sport I don't mean simply getting paid to play it is corrupting, that because sport is now considered a bona fide career on a par with other professional occupations open to talent it is, therefore, no longer truly sport.

The Anomalous Sport Market

So just what is it about markets and their trademark norms that prove corrupting of sport? We can begin to see the answer by first observing that even though professional-styled elite sports are a kind of market, they are a very odd one on several accounts. The first and perhaps most obvious is that some sports are accorded special legal status that exempt them from anti-trust regulation on the grounds that they are special social undertakings and as such cannot be considered strictly business ventures. The second, less obvious feature of the anomalous sport market is that allowing sports franchises to operate as cartels (monopolies), which follows, of course, from granting them legal protection against anti-trust laws, is not intended to drive their competitors out of business as is the typical aim of market actors, and as is the direct aim of forming monopolies in the first place.[2] That is because sports cannot exist, let alone thrive, in a competitive vacuum, in the absence of competitors. This would further explain why sport franchises sometimes share their revenue with one another, institute salary caps, and conduct a draft to allocate players to teams based on their order of finishing (not, as one might expect from business-oriented enterprises, from best to worst, but worst to best) to ensure not only that their competitors survive to compete another day, but to ensure competitive balance among the existing teams to make for more competitive, athletic contests.

None of these particular measures to accommodate sport, it goes without saying, typify the daily, business-as-usual, activities of markets. So while commodifying sport by putting its goods on the open market to be bought and sold, which privileges the exchange value of those goods (what they command on the open market) over their athletic-specific, internal features, is easy enough to do, it must make allowances for these goods in ways that are uncommon to most market dealings. I have claimed this is telling because it suggests that the goods particular to sport and to the social logic of its practice are not amenable to wholesale commodification. That means that if the market were to penetrate too deeply into the internal affairs of sport, or were to extend its reach too widely over all things athletic such that it is no longer clear where the business of sport ends and the game begins, it would prove corruptive of these athletic goods and that distinctive social logic. To understand why sport is vulnerable to such market intrusions requires we consider the kind of practical rationality and mode of valuing characteristic of the market.

Markets, Preferences and Cost-Benefit Analyses

The chief virtue claimed for the market is its supposed efficiency in meeting the needs, wants and desires of people. This efficiency presupposes a certain conception of practical reasoning and valuing that evidently all agents, at least rational ones, depend on in making important decisions about their lives. Specifically, it holds that all rational agents rightly so called seek to maximize their welfare, which is just another way of saying to satisfy as many of their subjective desires and preferences as is feasible. Based on this market conception, then, the basic unit of welfare is the agent's preference whatever it might be, and whatever object or practice it might target. That means that so far as the market is concerned the expression 'I want' doubles as both a preference and a reason. Indeed, preferring something based on this market model is not just one reason among other possible reasons, but the best and strongest sort of reason to procure some good whether it be in the form of an actual object or the tangible reward for engaging in some activity or other.

If preferences are to do the work they are supposed to do in our market dealings, then no qualitative distinctions between and among them are to be allowed. In other words, all preferences are to be accorded equal standing and worth, which rules out any attempt to treat some as better, or higher, or more worthy of satisfaction than others. That is because markets are not in the business of evaluating our desires but satisfying them. And it is precisely because the market eschews any effort to evaluate critically people's subjective desires that it proves to be so efficient in sating them. This speaks to the epistemic primacy markets according to individual actors; after all, who knows better what individuals want than the individuals themselves? Any attempt to second-guess, or to challenge them in this regard, is, therefore, only likely to frustrate what they desire, to be, in a word, inefficient. As Elizabeth Anderson avers, 'To respect a customer is to respect her privacy by not probing more deeply into her reasons [preferences] for wanting a commodity than is required to satisfy her want',[3]

So critical reflection is no friend of the market. The thought, therefore, that putting some goods up for sale might appreciably alter it, might even undermine it, is one thought too many so far as market actors are concerned. More pointedly, it is one thought that has no place allotted to it in the logical space in which such actors determine just what it is that they want. Such actors depend instead on a cost/benefit analysis, on calculating what gains and losses they might incur in satisfying their various wants. For it is only such calculation, such weighing of pros and cons, that is required to maximize one's personal welfare.

It should be clear by now that what drives the market and accounts for its vaunted efficiency is nothing other than naked self-interest. David Gauthier was on to something important, then, when he characterized the market as a zone of 'mutual unconcern'.[4] That doesn't mean that market actors ignore each other's presence, or take no account of their often competing interests and desires. For the ability to size up one's fellow actors, to gauge accurately their motives and aims, is an important, if not indispensable, market skill. But it does mean that whatever interest we take in others in this 'zone' is predicated on our own self-interest, on making sure that our interactions with others serve that self-interest rather than frustrate it. So maintaining one's egocentric focus and edge in our dealings with others in the market is a virtue rather than a vice, since, to reiterate, the central purpose of the market is to make sure people get what it is they want.

That the market is an egoistic device that is meant to further rather than disappoint our self-interest is, from a personal welfare standpoint, neither mysterious nor controversial. But how, it may be asked, can such an egoistic mechanism further the social welfare, that is, the collective interests and preferences of larger society? From what has been said so far, it seems that the market could not be more ill suited to promoting the aggregate good of any social grouping let alone an entire society. To this conundrum, defenders of the market offer an easy, ready and, to their mind at least, knockdown reply, which is that if everyone pursues his or her own self-interest the welfare of all will take care of itself. The basic idea here is that trying to maximize one's own personal welfare is the best, meaning the most expeditious, way to maximize the social welfare of all. This is what Adam Smith meant by his famous metaphor of the 'invisible hand', and by his no less famous point that we depend on the butcher not for his generosity but for his self-interest. That is, it is in the self-interest of the butcher to sell us the goods he has to offer that we desire, and in our self-interest as consumers to buy those goods, presuming, of course, we have the cash to pay for them.[5] So when we follow our self-interests rather than relying on less dependable, disinterested, and supposedly scarce resources like fellow-feeling or altruism, all of us are made better off and none of us are made worse off. According to Smith and other market enthusiasts, then, maximizing one's personal welfare turns out to be the best way to maximize the social welfare. Any suggestion of tension between what is in my personal interest and what is in the larger social interest is, therefore, if Smith and his epigones are right, at best an illusion, at worst crass propagandizing.

Because the market is so effective at the egoistic work it does, and because that egoistic work is able evidently, by virtue of its very egocentric focus, to maximize our social welfare as well, killing, as it were, two birds with one stone, it is unsurprising that it has been given wide berth in societies like ours. So much so that our market economy is in danger of becoming, if it has already not become, a market society, in which the market's trademark norms and self-styled cost-benefit analysis have become the tools of choice not just for solving our economic problems but our most pressing social problems as well.[6] No matter the problem, then, coming up with the right monetary incentives is more often than not viewed as the preferred solution. So if academic underachievement is the concern, then paying kids to read is the answer, or if pollution is the problem, then buying and selling pollution permits (cap and trade) is the ticket, or if immigration is the pressing issue, then setting a significant financial sum to ensure only a select few are able to emigrate is the way to go.[7] And since the only thing that counts in assessing such financial inducements is their efficiency, their success in actually changing people's behaviour in the requisite way, questions like does paying Johnny and Mary to read undermine whatever intrinsic love they presently have, or in the future might have, for reading never get asked let alone given the slightest consideration. It is because such normative questions have no purchase in the market, as I will argue in the next section, that we should be wary of giving it too much latitude in governing the affairs of social practices like sport.

Markets and the Corruption of Sport

I have argued thus far that paying players to play sports at elite levels, whether it be in the form of scholarships or salaries or commercial endorsements, is not in itself corrupting of sport. I have also argued, however, that if the market figures too centrally or widely in the conduct of sport then it is corrupting of sport. That we have good reason to worry that the market does exercise such undue influence on sport should also be apparent from what I have said so far, since monetary incentives are especially powerful ones, and the cost-benefit analyses they come packaged in are now seen as the main, if not only, way to assess practically everything we contemporaries do and value. If my argument is cogent in this respect, then sport is especially vulnerable to market intrusions precisely because it matters, really matters, to so many of us. So I turn next to the question of whether or not the market has, in fact, overstepped its boundaries in the case of sport, and in doing so has violated sport's distinctive perfectionist aims and goods.

I have already suggested that there are two main ways in which the market proves corrupting of sport, namely, when it ranges too widely over, or plumbs too deeply into, its affairs. That these two sources are not the same is evident from my own earlier claim that if we can limit the scope of the market's influence over sport, by restricting it to the pay athletes receive that enables them to make a career out of sports, we can safeguard its central goods. It is also evident that we are dealing here with two different corrupting forces by what follows from this claim. And that is if financially remunerating athletes to play sports were to become their dominant motive, which would mean that the pursuit of the almighty dollar would be the main goal of their athletic enterprise, then that single change in the market's reach into its internal affairs would be corrupting of sport even if we were successful in blocking all other market overtures.

We, however, quickly reach a point of diminishing return in terms of this contrast. For as a general rule of thumb, empirically not conceptually speaking, when the scope of the market's involvement in sport is excessive, that means it has successfully penetrated to the very heart of athletic endeavour and compromised its perfectionist goals. And that, I contend, is the sad state most elite sports find themselves in today, in which their wholesale saturation by the market has left few, if any, of their main goods unscathed.

Since I have claimed that the far-flung hold the market presently has on sport leaves little to the imagination, I would be hard-pressed to say just what part of sport has not been significantly affected by that influence. Consider, for starters, the various athletic paraphernalia associated with record-breaking athletic accomplishments that have become, of late, hot commodities. The best examples come from Major League baseball, and, in particular, record-setting home run baseballs such as Mark McGwire's 62nd home run ball and Barry Bonds 73rd, which fans fought over mostly for their monetary value as commodities rather than their athletic value as keepsakes. Once these balls cleared the outfield fence they were treated largely as the private property of those fortunate enough to snag them. It is true that only one of these examples, Bonds' ball, was not returned to him but sold by its new proprietors at auction for the hefty sum of $450,000. However, that the fan that caught McGwire's ball did return it to him does not disconfirm my point here. For that fan's action sparked a robust public commentary, a portion of which lauded him for returning the ball as an act of rare generosity, but a comparable portion of which roundly criticized him for acting stupidly, for not realizing the ball was his to sell to the highest bidder, which according to one *Time* financial columnist revealed a 'mindset that leads many of us into grave errors in daily money matters'.[8] In this case, both those who viewed the return of the ball as a praiseworthy act on the one hand, or as a financially ill-considered act on the other, exemplify what amounts to the sporting public's only plausible reaction once a record-setting baseball is viewed as a marketable commodity. For once the ball is seen in this exclusively economic light, as Michael Sandel sharply but rightly puts it, returning 'it to the player who hit it is no longer a simple gesture of decency ... but either a heroic act of generosity or a foolish act of profligacy'.[9]

Naming rights for sports stadiums reveal yet another way the market has left its unmistakable stamp on the sporting world. So, just as sports memorabilia, such as players' autographs, are now bought and sold on the open market, so, too, are the names affixed to the arenas in which athletic exploits take place. Corporations of all stripes are only too happy to pony up large sums of money for this purpose for the obvious advertising opportunities it provides.

Speaking of advertising, corporations are no longer content simply to have their wares displayed on outfield baseball fences or stadium walls. For what better way to get their commercial messaging across than by inserting that content into the narrative play-by-play accounts emanating from the broadcast booth, and in the analyses of games featured in the countless television programmes devoted to such commentary. When, for example, Bank One purchased the naming rights for the Arizona Diamondbacks' stadium (Bank One Ballpark), as part of the deal, they required the team's broadcasters to call each home run struck by a member of the home team a 'Bank One Blast'. The New York Life Insurance Company took this a step further, cutting a deal with 10 Major League teams to air a commercial plug every time a player slides safely into a base. For those players who manage to slide safely into the most coveted base of all, home plate, an image of the company's corporate logo is flashed on the TV screen accompanied by the announcer's contractually obligated declaration, 'Safe at home. Safe and secure. New York Life'. By smuggling their commercial messaging into the narrative of the game itself and the commentaries of the actions as they unfold, rather than in breaks from that action, advertisers can be sure that audiences won't be able to escape what they want them to hear. As to the supposed salutary contribution of these inside-the-game advertising pitches, I can do no better than quote the following confident words of one of New York Life's advertising directors, it 'is a great reminder to fans who are cheering for their favourite players to reach bases safely, that they too can be safe and secure with the largest mutual life insurance company in the United States'.[10]

Yet another example of the market's grip on sport is the much heralded 'moneyball' approach to the game itself made famous by Michael Lewis's book, which was later turned into a Hollywood film of the same name. The book features the general manager of the Oakland Athletics, Billy Beane, who was able to field a competitive team that won as many games as the mighty New York Yankees despite having a payroll one-third of that of the Yankees. Beane accomplished this feat by hiring a PhD in econometrics, who was able by means of sophisticated statistical techniques to determine what baseball skills and strategies contributed most to a winning team. By employing these statistical devices, the As discovered, for instance, that a high on-base percentage is more important to winning than a high batting average or slugging percentage, and that base stealing decreases rather than increases a team's chance to score. So they signed players who could draw walks rather than high percentage hitters and sluggers, and whose speed on the base paths was no longer a high priority, at salaries considerably lower than the players they replaced. Beane's innovative statistical take on the game and clever pricing of heretofore 'undervalued' players worked for a time. But it didn't take the richer clubs long to copy it, and to regain their athletic supremacy because they had the financial wherewithal Beane and company lacked to pay the increasingly higher salaries now commanded by these players, not to mention the escalating salaries of the statisticians whose counsel they eagerly sought. As a consequence, money came to figure more rather than less in baseball, and not just in terms of players' salaries and owners' fortunes, but most importantly in the new, conservative way the game itself came to be played.

As the moneyball example shows, once the market was able to get, as it were, its foot in the door it didn't take long for it to seize control of the game itself, dictating not only who played it but also the manner in which it was to be played, seen and organized. This is why I have been arguing that most of the ills that plague sport today can be traced back in one form or another to the undue influence of the market on its production and consumption. On the top of any list of such market-induced ills, I would have to put the win-at-all-costs mentality that pervades sport today, in which the effort to gain a competitive edge over one's opponents by hook or by crook not only imperils its perfectionist ideals but spoils as well the social relations that take place within its precincts. High on that list would also be the top-down hierarchical way sport is presently organized and conducted, in which owners at the top, who typically know little about the intricacies of the games they preside over, insist the coaches in their employ win now rather than later, which is why most coaches at this level try to control as much of what happens on the field of play as possible (calling plays, etc.), and, as a consequence, typically resort to a more conservative, less daring style of play. We would further have to include the structuring and scheduling of games around the commercial advertising that pays a lion's share of the bills racked up by elite sports. And any such list would be woefully incomplete if it didn't have on it the search for new, larger markets to consume its product, a driving force of markets everywhere, which is why athletic franchises (for example, professional ice hockey) are sold to parts of the country (for example, Phoenix and Los Angeles) whose inhabitants have no tradition in, and therefore lack even a basic understanding of, the games peddled to them. Little wonder, then, why such fans often have scant appreciation of the sports themselves, of the excellence that defines them, and need to be distracted, depending on the sport, by overt displays of violence or exploding scoreboards, or Laker girls, etc.[11]

In singling out the market as the main culprit behind the present corruption of sport, I am not saying it is the sole cause of its decline in value and meaning – corruption on the scale we see in sport today is seldom attributable to a single source. Nor am I saying the market only has a corrupting effect on sport, that nothing good of a genuinely athletic kind can come from its preference-friendly rational calculus. After all, I noted earlier how paying athletes to play sports has made it possible for them to make a career of their playing. There is further evidence that strategic advances in the game have been partially abetted rather than hindered by market incentives and pricing schemes (the previous moneyball example is a prominent one). No doubt, other positive, innovative changes in the game could also be credited to the market. But I am arguing that whatever positive things can be said on behalf of the market in this regard, we must not lose sight of the considerable damage done to sport by that same market. For by commodfying sport the market has largely succeeded in getting many of us today to regard and treat it as just another business, to include the players themselves, who increasingly see themselves as entertainers paid to put on a good show, and those vast throngs who flock to watch them, who increasingly see themselves as consumers of that show expecting, therefore, to be titillated and amused rather than uplifted. That this selling of sport as a mass spectacle militates against the perfectionist challenges and excellence that are essential to its flourishing should, therefore, come as a surprise to no one.

It might be asked, however, how I can be so sure that the market is indeed the main culprit that stands in the way of a richer, more nuanced way of understanding and appreciating sport, and therefore richer, more nuanced ways of engaging in and watching it that 'capitalize' on its perfectionist value rather than its exchange value. After all, the monetary incentives and pricing mechanisms at work in market transactions give players and spectators alike another reason (incentive) to play and watch sport. Rightly understood, then, these financial incentives complement rather than contravene the perfectionist aims of sport, add to rather than subtract from the excellence sought there. This would suggest I have been barking up the wrong tree here all along in trying to impugn the appropriateness of monetary incentives in pursuits like sport in which the achievement of excellence is the main point.

This objection has some force for precisely the reason I earlier conceded that if the market for sport is suitably constrained, so that it doesn't intrude too deeply or too much into its perfectionist logic and attendant goods, it can have a salutary effect on sport in at least two ways: 1) by giving players two reasons (a monetary and an excellence-friendly one) rather than one for engaging in sport, and 2) by making it possible to pursue sport as a secure, full-time enterprise rather than a tenuous, occasional pastime. The problem, however, as I have been arguing, is that the market is notoriously difficult to contain because the egoistic preferences and desires that fuel it lack any determinate 'satisfaction conditions'. This is the point Aristotle was getting at when he claimed that the pursuit of money is an activity without a *telos*, an end goal.[12] For the absence of such an end goal means that such pursuit not only lacks an answer to the question 'how much money is enough' to count as meeting that goal, but crowds out other reasons people might have for engaging in sport or other kindred social practices above and beyond their financial compensation. This is why the pursuit of money, when unchecked, has a tendency to trump all other aims and purposes, why left to its own devices it installs itself, to use market jargon, as the proverbial 'bottom line' by virtue of which the worth of any enterprise that contemporary human agents care enough to pursue is gauged.

We can see why unfettered monetary incentives invariably overpower the kind of perfectionist goods particular to sport by recalling our earlier discussion that people's subjective preferences in the market double as reasons, indeed the strongest sort of reasons, for engaging in an activity or procuring an object. That is because, as also previously noted, the vaunted efficiency of markets has precisely to do with the fact that they cater exclusively to making sure those preferences are satisfied rather than adequately reflectively vetted. So the market in sport, as is true of the market in any social practice or object, takes human subjects just as it finds them, which is to say with whatever mix of needs and wants that presently comprise, to borrow a term of art from Bernard Williams,[13] their subjective motivational sets (hereafter referred to as their S).[14] On this market conception, one can have a reason to act in a certain way in sport if and only if it is relative to some preference or other of a person's S. If such a connection to the subjective desires of a person's S is absent, that person cannot be rightly claimed to have a reason to act in sport no matter what relevant others (fellow members of that sport practice community) may think such a person has good reason to do. This market conception of reasons for engaging in sport, therefore, not only requires preferences be treated as reasons, once again the most powerful reasons, for acting in particular ways in the athletic arena, but limits consideration of just what reasons or preferences to act on exclusively to weighing their relative costs and benefits.

From a market perspective, then, so long as the monetary incentives are consonant with the self-interests of the relevant athletic parties they can do what they are supposed and designed to do, which is either to nudge people to take up sport in the first place or to sustain or perhaps ramp up their previous involvement in it. But, and this is the crucial point, what they cannot do, and what they were not designed let alone conceived to do, is to get these athletic parties to take on board the perfectionist aims of sport itself, to act on the excellences that inform them. This is not because, to reiterate, these monetary incentives are necessarily hostile to perfectionist and other kinds of motives people may have for engaging in sport, but rather because such extra-monetary motives and aspirations don't figure at all in the rational calculus that goes into divining these monetary incentives. And they don't figure at all because every inch of the logical space in which markets operate is given over to indulging our private preferences, not to vetting or transforming them.

The market's single-minded focus on the private preferences of would-be athletic actors is corrupting of sport, therefore, because, at its root, sport is not in the private-preference-satisfying business but the public (social)-excellence-aspiring one. For sport is an irreducibly social practice, which is to say its central goods and excellences are common, shared ones. So in the athletic realm subjective preferences do not count as reasons as such unless they are consonant with the perfectionist purpose and goods of sport itself. But achieving such consonance entails an intersubjective move, that is, taking one's marching orders from the (conventional) aims and values of sport itself as opposed to the subjective desires of an agent's pre-existing S.[15] It is only in this fashion that private preferences can become fully fledged reasons, such that what I regard as a reason for engaging in or watching sport is also regarded by my athletic peers as a reason for playing or watching sport.[16] It is by transforming whatever our private designs on sport might be by internalizing the social aims and norms of sport itself, which would make those latter aims and norms now integral features of each athletic party's S, that a logical space is created in which to entertain better and worse ways of participating in and observing sport, a space without which a reflective evaluation of the qualitative distinctions between and among higher and lower ways of playing and watching sports is not possible.

If I'm right, that means that in social practices like sport, as opposed to the market and other similarly preference-based activities, everything depends upon achieving, to use a Hegelian turn of phrase, a common human-mindedness. For it is this kind of common-mindedness, in which we think and deliberate about sport not as individuals but as individuals and members of an athletic practice community, that allows us to shed our subjective skins and rationally take up how we ought to engage and observe sport in ways appropriate to the particular goods it puts on offer. This is, of course, the reason why I have been arguing that an unalloyed market take on sport, one dominated by the creation of shrewd financial incentives and the implementation of equally shrewd pricing schemes, is an imminent threat to sport, since these trademark market instruments sap rather than supplement the shared perfectionist ideals of sport.

The Domination of the Market

In closing, I want to borrow and tweak an example that bears on my argument from Alasdair MacIntyre's magisterial book, *After Virtue*, to illustrate why market forces should not be allowed to have their way, as is their tendency, with a social practice like sport. I have in mind here his oft-cited example of a young person whom an adult mentor is trying to get to take up chess by offering her candy as an external reward.[17] I want to change the example to the sport of tennis, and the external reward to money to suit my present purpose – which, I think, doesn't change the point he is trying to make here one iota. What is so telling about this example as modified, I hope to show, is that even the mere offer of money to a person to play a sport, which I previously have suggested is unproblematic for those already initiated in a sport and not excessively given to financial rewards, is for those uninitiated in a sport itself enough to spoil their involvement in and appreciation of it. If money can exert such a powerful pull on would-be players and observers of sport, it doesn't take much imagination to see how it could exert a similar corrupting pull on actual players and observers of sport by undercutting their initial commitment to athletic excellence.

The problem the mentor faces in MacIntyre's hypothetical case is that the child at present has no interest in playing tennis, indeed, knows next to nothing about the game. What the mentor does know, however, is that she can be plied by a financial reward to play the game, which she can readily cash in to satisfy her craving for candy and the like. So the mentor makes her an offer that she can hardly refuse, which is to give her a small stipend if she plays tennis with him once a week, and which he offers to double if she manages to beat him on any given occasion. The child now has a 'reason' not only to play tennis but to play it to win because her desire for the sweet things that can be had by means of her monetary reward is already a feature of her S. So we can reasonably expect both that she will show up at the appointed time to play and try mightily to win. But what we can't nor should expect, MacIntyre claims, is that from this same subjective standpoint she won't cheat if she can get away with it. Nor can we or should we expect, something MacIntyre doesn't consider and I won't pursue further to stay true to his account, that she won't quit tennis the moment she is presented with a better alternative to get what she wants. After all, it's not the game she's invested in – nor could it be since the subjective perspective she brings to it has nothing specifically to do with the game – but the monetary pay-off.

Now the fact that the child considers cheating an unobjectionable way to get what she wants is precisely the problem with the financial incentive featured in this example. For it is that incentive itself that distorts the way she sees the game, that prompts her to think there is nothing normatively unseemly if she has to cheat to achieve her goal. Indeed, she has no reason to think she is not seeing the game aright, since cheating is as acceptable a way to win at tennis as any other way she might choose to best her mentor that can plausibly be traced back to some feature or other of her S. But, of course, when considered from the perfectionist standpoint of the game, that she considers cheating an appropriate way to win is a sure sign she is not seeing the game aright. For it suggests that while she has a firm rational handle on what she wants to achieve by means of playing tennis, she has no rational handle, firm or otherwise, on the game itself, on the normative demands tennis makes on her and her athletic peers if she and they are to fulfil the standards of excellence that are central to the challenges it poses.

Of course, the reason MacIntyre introduced an external reward to induce the child to take up chess – in his example, tennis in mine – is that he was holding out for the possibility that she might eventually find the game compelling in its own right, that is, that she might find another reason intrinsic to the game itself to pursue tennis. The rub, however, is that the monetary incentive itself is more likely to pre-empt rather than elicit such a normative transition, since once the financial reward is either withdrawn or loses its grip on our hypothetical tennis player she is more apt than not to cease playing tennis altogether rather than to ramp up her game to a new perfectionist level.[18] That is not to say that a sport like tennis is not capable on its own of effecting such a transition, of capturing the fancy of novices unfamiliar with its perfectionist ways, but it is to say that a financial reward of this sort often discourages such a transition given its motivational pull in the opposite direction.

MacIntyre's example of how money beguiles the athletically uninitiated is illustrative of how the market exercises its corrupting influence, as it were, upstream, before players and spectators have had a chance to sample its intrinsic goods for themselves. But, by showing just how powerful those market forces are it also, I want to claim, reinforces my argument in this essay of how the market corrupts sport downstream, after players and spectators have absorbed the perfectionist lessons it has to offer. The difference, of course, is that the market corrupts the athletically initiated by crowding out, rather than pre-empting, the perfectionist motives needed to acquire and to appreciate the internal goods of sport. So while paying these players to play is not, to reiterate, corrupting in itself, allowing the market to dominate how sport is conducted and governed is. And that, alas, is the fate I have argued has befallen contemporary sport today, in which the market controls almost everything that goes on in elite sport circles.

The domination of sport by the market is an important part of the story I have tried to tell in my essay, and of the argument that underpins it. For when athletic stadiums more resemble billboards than storied places of significant athletic accomplishment, when sporting memorabilia are valued primarily as commodities rather than keepsakes, when broadcasts of games and the commentary that accompany them are little more than running advertisements, when econometricians who are adept at manipulating numbers and devising ingenious pricing schemes are heralded as the new sports experts, and when the game itself is tailored to the demands of the money changers it is beholden to, precious little of the game itself, of its perfectionist ideals, remains to savour. That loss is no trifling matter. For when so much of what attracts us to sport in the first place is eviscerated by the 'almighty' dollar, what Hubert Dreyfus and Sean Kelly aptly call the public 'gathering force' of sport, its capacity to unite us with our fellow human beings 'in the celebration of something great', in which the striving for athletic perfection 'burst[s] forth and shine[s]' for all to see and appreciate in ways not typically experienced in our everyday lives[19] is also eviscerated. I can think of no worse fate for sport to suffer, and a fortiori, no better reason why we ought to devote our wholehearted efforts to protecting sport and its kind from domination by the market.

Notes

1   By a perfectionist practice I mean simply that the aim of the endeavour is to achieve some form of excellence. I have in mind here, besides sport, practices such as art and music.

2   Sport cartels most assuredly do, however, protect existing sport franchises from competition from new, upstart sport franchises that seek to set up business in their locale.

3   Elizabeth Anderson, *Value in Ethics and Economics* (Cambridge, MA: Harvard University Press, 1993), 159.

4   David Gauthier, *Morals By Agreement* (New York: Oxford University Press, 1986), 87.

5   That markets feed off both our willingness *and* ability to pay for the goods they put on offer raises an issue of fairness in addition to the corruption issue I am focusing on in the present essay, which given its obvious importance deserves a separate essay in its own right.

6   We can add here our personal problems as well. For the University of Chicago economist Gary Becker has provocatively endorsed an economic approach to such intimate personal decisions as whether to get married or not, and, unsurprisingly, whether to divorce one's spouse or not, based on a calculation of one's personal utility, of the benefits of doing so versus the costs. See Sandel's illuminating discussion of Becker in this regard (Michael Sandel, *What Money Can't Buy: The Moral Limits of Markets* [New York: Farrar, Strauss and Giroux, 2012], 50).

7   For a thorough analysis of the astonishingly wide range of problems that economists are entrusted to solve by recourse to market incentives, see Sandel, *What Money Can't Buy: The Moral Limits of Markets*.

8   This example, and many of the other examples I cite in the ensuing discussion, to include the quotation in the text, come from Sandel, *What Money Can't Buy: The Moral Limits of Markets*, 167.

9   Ibid.

10 Ibid., 171.

11 I speak in this latter regard from personal experience having just attended my first Los Angeles Lakers basketball game since moving to the area. And what a spectacle it was, in which the actual game was overshadowed by, among other things, the

stream of advertisements projected on the video screens of the huge scoreboard hanging over centre court, which because they were shown during the frequent television breaks taken to air commercials for the viewing audience at home were a constant, ongoing distraction, and the Laker 'girls', who changed outfits during the game so many times, each time festooned with different corporate logos, I lost count. Amid all the hoopla, one could be forgiven for forgetting a game was actually being played.

12 I owe this point to Adrian Walsh and Richard Giulianotti's excellent analysis of the effect commodification has on sport; see their book *Ethics, Money, and Sport* (New York: Routledge, 2009), 41.

13 Bernard Williams, *Moral Luck* (New York: Cambridge University Press, 1981).

14 I should point out, however, that Williams' account of what he calls his internalist conception of practical reason, which is keyed to an agent's S, differs in several important respects from the market conception of practical reason I offer in the text. These important differences make it clear that Williams's conception of practical reason was not intended by him to be an account of market reasoning. See Williams, *Moral Luck*.

15 This intersubjective move that I insist is crucial to transforming a preference for engaging in sport to a reason for doing so does not entail, I want to make clear, that all subjective, idiosyncratic features of a person's S must be expunged, but only those that are at odds with the perfectionist aims and ends of athletic enterprise.

16 I hasten to add that doesn't mean my athletic peers must find my reasons to be persuasive ones, for that would suggest a kind of myopic group thinking in which there is no room for dissent, but only that what I offer as a reason can be recognized by others as such because it speaks to the social perfectionist goods of sport rather than my private preferences. This opens the door, as I suggest in the text, for rational deliberation about how persuasive my reasons actually are. As Anderson astutely notes in this regard, 'collective willing does not require … unanimity at the individual level, but simply a willingness to accept the collective decision as authoritative of the group' (Elizabeth Anderson, 'The Epistemology of Democracy', *Episteme. A Journal of Social Epistemology* 3 [2006]: 16).

17 Alasdair MacIntyre, *After Virtue* (Notre Dame, IN: Notre Dame University Press, 1984), 188.

18 The brunt of the empirical evidence regarding use of financial rewards to cajole people to behave in certain ways backs up my claim that when these rewards are removed people overwhelmingly stop doing the activity rather than acquire new practice-specific motives to continue doing it. See Daniel Pink, *Drive: The Surprising Truth About What Motivates Us* (New York: Riverhead Books, 2009).

19 Hubert Dreyfus and Sean Kelly, *All Things Shining* (New York: Free Press, 2011), 193.

21 Sport Philosophy Around the World

Peter M. Hopsicker and Ivo Jirásek

Philosophic inquiry into sport and physical activity can be found throughout much of the modern world. Having roots primarily in philosophy of education and physical education, broad examinations into the nature and value of human physical activity developed into the recognized discipline of sport philosophy in the second half of the 20th century. Arguably, philosophic treatments of sport and physical activity have occurred sporadically around the world for centuries, or *in a wide sense*, by scholars not defined as sport philosophers, but rather as educators, physical educators or general philosophers. However, when one considers only the work of scholars who call themselves sport philosophers and whose efforts and achievements reflect that title, sport philosophy as a discipline *in a narrower sense* is considerably younger, with its formative years being the late 1960s through the 1970s in most regions.[1]

In this essay, we briefly examine the development and regional characteristics of sport philosophy throughout the world proceeding geographically from the Far East to the West. We present the discipline's origins in the wider sense, its development during the formative years, and its current status and qualities in the narrower sense, paying significant attention to the effects of regional and cultural nuances. Key scholars, publications and scholarly associations provide notable benchmarks in the discipline's regional and global advancement.

Significant detail for the development of each region was not possible. However, footnotes include references to other publications, websites and academic associations that provide extensive detail for further investigation.[2] By no means do we suggest that our presentation is inclusive of all authors, publications and academic associations in sport philosophy. Nor do we suggest that the discipline is static, and it is hoped that the following pages depict a dynamic and growing international field of inquiry whose continued progress depends on several factors summarized at the conclusion of this essay.

Japan[3]

Japan has a rich history of integrating physical activity and philosophy. Traditional Japanese philosophies and religions such as Shintoism and Zen Buddhism (with its 'cult of warrior' samurai ethics) influenced traditional Japanese sports such as archery and sumo wrestling, and martial arts such as ju-jitsu, judo, karate and aikido. The inception of sport philosophy in Japan, however, lies with physical educators interested in philosophy, not philosophers interested in physical activity. From these pedagogical roots came a progressive nationwide recognition of sport philosophy as a subject of serious academic inquiry including the establishment of the Japan Society of Health and Physical Education in 1950, the creation of a section of that society focused on the philosophic study of physical education five years later, the founding of the Japan Society for the Philosophy of Sport and Physical Education in 1978[4] and its *Journal of the Philosophy of Sport and Physical Education* in 1979,[5] and the inaugural publishing of a second journal in 2003, the *International Journal of Sport and Health Science.*[6]

Japan's heightened interest in Western conceptions of sport and physical education in the mid 19th century, a time when the country opened its borders to foreigners for the first time, significantly changed the nation's view of physical activity. 'Sport', understood as games, competition and contest, and physical education or 'gymnastics', understood as training, exercise and physical improvement, quickly found homes in high schools and universities. After the Meiji Restoration (1868–1912), physical education became an essential part of the school curriculum as a means to develop strong bodies and, ultimately, a strong nation. While the pedagogical benefits of physical education grew, philosophers and other intellectuals continued to view sport as having little scholarly value. In fact, 'The Structure of My Feelings When Playing Sport', published by Japanese philosopher Masakazu Nakai in 1933, was the only essay treating sport philosophically before the Second World War.

Sport found its way into physical education programmes as a means to build health and character in the latter half of the 20th century. The 1964 Tokyo Olympics, the country's growing economy and a strengthened link between sports and education further stoked Japan's interest in philosophic treatments of sport – specifically the social meanings and ethical problems of competitive sport. The translation of several books written by Western sport philosophers in the late 1960s continued the discipline's growth.

Theories of the body, often using phenomenological methods, represent the main sport philosophy scholarship in Japan. Fumio Takizawa, for example, has published several articles comparing Japanese and Western perspectives of the body, asked questions of the relationship between body and society, and emphasized the educational value of the body culture in contrast to the modern sports culture. In recent years, some Japanese sport philosophers, such as Masami Sekine, Takayuki Hata, Yoshitaka Kondo and Naofumi Masumoto, have redirected their focus to consider such topics as gender verification, the ethics of Olympism and the problem of doping.

Future scholarship may be guided by a resurgent interest in Japanese traditional philosophies, specifically the re-emergence of common consciousness or a non-individualist culture found in traditional Japanese sports and martial arts, rather than the self-consciousness characteristic of Western culture. Several articles written by Sekine, Koyo Fukasawa, Kenji Ishigaki, Koji Takahashi and Ai Tanaka explore solidarity and communication with others and the ethics of interpersonal relations rather than personal ethics in the context of sport.

Australasia[7]

Terry Roberts described sport philosophy in Australia in the early 1990s as a 'generally bleak scene' apart from the 'glimmer of hope' provided by his place of employment, Victoria University of Technology, which he described as comparable to North American institutions. Roughly two decades later, Michael Burke and Dennis Hemphill of the same institution (now known simply as Victoria University or VU) suggest a similar perspective: the discipline 'clings to life' throughout Australasia with VU remaining the flagship programme.

The challenges facing the discipline in Australasia emerge from an evolving appreciation of sport and a subsequent shift in institutions' undergraduate curriculums. Elite, high-performance sport in this region has transformed into big business and an instrument of national identity. In response to this transformation, university programmes have shifted away from social science- and humanity-based programmes in favour of a scientific and management focus – a shift that has been compounded by the demands of external accreditation bodies, funding cuts and the necessity to streamline programmes to include more biological science areas and clinical practice. Ironically, the rise of elite sport carries with it a growing public concern over ethical sport issues such as doping, match fixing, gender discrimination, violence and athletes' rights to name a few. Yet apart from VU, few philosophy of sport-related classes are offered in Australian universities, and while the University of Otago in New Zealand has a stronger focus on the sociocultural studies of sport than other programmes, it appears to offer no specific philosophy of sport units.

In contrast to the meagre undergraduate offerings, research outputs in Australasia have been significant. Most notable have been Terry Roberts (aesthetics, artistic and semiotic issues, and Rortian perspectives of sport), Dennis Hemphill (doping control and human rights, cybersport, embodiment and ethics, diversity and inclusive curriculum) and Michael Burke (Foucault, feminism and doping) at VU. Others, such as Chris Cordner and Chuck Summers from the University of Melbourne, Robert Paddick of Flinders University and Fred D'Agostino at the University of Queensland, have also contributed to the discipline through essays in international refereed journals.

Sport in Australasia remains fertile ground for philosophical analysis. While these scholars will most likely continue to contribute to the literature, unless educational programmes devote serious attention to the discipline, and reinstitute the importance of humanities-based courses in sport, exercise and physical education programmes, sport philosophy will continue, as Burke and Hemphill have noted, to 'cling to life' in this region.

Taiwan and Mainland China[8]

Philosophy and physical activity also have deep ties in Chinese-speaking regions of the world. Traditional Chinese philosophy emerges from both Confucius' harmony between *jin* and *jang* and Lao-Tse's (Taoism) harmony between the individual and the Tao path. Humanism, tolerance and strong connections to nature are central to Chinese thinking and factor heavily in traditional Chinese martial arts such as kung fu and tai chi.

Similar to Japan, philosophic treatments of physical education instigated the development of sport philosophy in Taiwan, but Western inspirations have significantly shaped the discipline in the last three decades. In the wider sense, the German-trained Jiang, Liang-Gwei's 1965 book, *On New Perspectives of Principles of Physical Education*, served as the initial influential contribution. Fifteen years later, sport philosophy in the narrow sense gained traction when Japanese-educated scholar I-Hsiung Hsu at the National Taiwan Normal University arranged for the translation of Western sport philosophy essays allowing Taiwanese students to experience Western sport philosophy and research methods for the first time. One of the two pioneers of sport philosophy in Taiwan, I-Hsiung Hsu would later found the Body Culture Society of Taiwan in 2004 and initiate two journals: the *Body Culture Journal* and the *Journal of Sports Studies*, first published in 2005 and 2007, respectively.[9] About the same time, the other pioneer of Taiwanese sport philosophy, I-Min Liu, returned from earning his doctorate at Purdue University to teach sport philosophy at the National Taiwan Normal University, both at the undergraduate and graduate levels.

Taiwanese sport philosophers progressively shifted their efforts from translation to production between 1980 and 1998, publishing investigations into the essence and nature of play, games and sports, philosophy of body, sport and Eastern philosophy and sport ethics. Liu I-Min's 1991 collection of essays, *Sport Philosophic Research: Play, Sport and Life*, is representative of this growing body of scholarship. Concurrently, the translation of Western works inspired many young scholars to not only read more Western sport philosophy, but also to attend both national and international conferences and publish papers in a variety of journals.

Tein-Mei, Hu, professor at the National Taipei Teacher University, for example, is the first female sport philosopher in Taiwan and is interested in the works of Bernard Suits and issues of gender and class. At the National Taiwan Normal School, professor Simon Shih, a national-level basketball coach, uses his experience as an avid mountain climber to inform his research on sport and spirituality, particularly the Eastern philosophy of Zen. Leo Hsu of Da-Yeh University is the founder of the International Olympic and Multicultural Studies programme in Taiwan and focuses on Olympic studies, sports rules and ethics.

Sport philosophy in Mainland China lagged behind the progression of Taiwan and seemed to have developed slowly through national sport conferences. Several important steps for the discipline occurred following the first national conference on the 'dialectic studies' of sport held at Shenyang Sport College in 1981, including the development of a Chinese sport philosophy discipline in 1982, the formation of the Chinese Sport Society in 1984, and the official recognition of sport philosophy research by the Chinese Sports Science Society in 1985.

There continues to be very few Chinese publications in sport philosophy taken in the narrow sense, and no unified textbook for universities and colleges exists. Still, scholars defined as sport philosophers in the wider sense address topics such as the implication of ancient Chinese philosophy for modern sport, the impact of Western sport philosophic research on China, ontological examinations of play, games and sport, and sport aesthetics. Examinations may narrow in the future and publications such as Dao-Jie Lee and Jin-Wu Pan's works on sport ethics may become more prominent for addressing new ethical issues created by the commercialization of the Chinese football league.

The Slavonic Countries: Czech Republic, Poland and Slovenia[10]

Little remains of 19th-century efforts to unify the language, literature and cultures of Slavonic countries into a pan-Slavic ideal. After two world wars and the fall of socialism, the region resembles a patchwork of 14 independent nations. Consequently, diverse regional, social and cultural differences and political ideologies shaped sport philosophy in this part of the world.

Three Slavic scholars spawned initial ideas of sport philosophy in the wider sense. Czech John Amos Comenius and Russian Petr Francevich Lesgraft integrated physical education into the pedagogical process in the 17th and 19th centuries, respectively. During that same era, Miroslav Tyrš, considered the first philosopher of sport in Czechoslovakia,[11] created a system of gymnastics known as *Sokol*, or Falcon, as a means of physical development as well as a pathway to political and national freedom.

The former Soviet Union's ideological and political dominance provided the greatest impact on the development of Czech sport philosophy in the second half of the 20th century. Rather than philosophy of sport, only a 'theory of physical culture' from a Marxist point of view existed. Because of this, social and political topics, such as social justice and equality of opportunity, remain rarely discussed in Czech philosophy of sport. Other philosophic modes of inquiry developed instead, including phenomenology, made popular by Czech philosopher Jan Patočka between the 1960s and 1980s. Patočka's phenomenological and holistic understanding of human movement, as not only the movement of bodies but also of personalities, has provided significant inspiration for modern Czech sport philosophers, yet his anti-dualistic and existential interpretation of movement is rarely found in the English-speaking world.

Other approaches to the study of human movement and sport are also utilized. Anna Hogenova, Miloš Bednář and Irena Martínková at Charles University in Prague focus on such topics as games and play, Olympism, existential phenomenology, 'kinanthroposophy' (wisdom through human movement) and the linking of thought and movement through Martin Heidegger's conception of *Dasein*. At Palacký University in Olomouc, Ivo Jirásek promotes the term 'philosophical kinanthropology' (the investigation of what it means to be human through the phenomenon of human movement) as superior to sport philosophy. He further examines the importance of culture, body and movement in the movement culture as well as topics such as leisure, nature and experiential education. In 2011, Jirásek, Martínková and Jim Parry founded the philosophy of sport section of the Czech Kinanthropological Society.[12] While this society does not have its own journal, *Acta Universitatis Palackianae Olomucensis. Gymnica*[13] and

Czech Kinanthropology[14] provide space for sport philosophy articles in both English and Czech, respectively.

In Poland, the philosophy of sport appears to be strongly driven by Jerzy Kosiewicz, professor at Josef Pilsudski University of Physical Education in Warsaw.[15] Founder of the International Society for the Social Sciences of Sport (ISSSS),[16] editor-in-chief of the journal *Physical Culture and Sport. Studies and Research*,[17] and author of *Sport and Philosophy: From Methodology to Ethics*, Kosiewicz focuses on philosophical and methodological topics of physical culture such as the anthropological themes of body and corporality in Christian thinking, the ontological and epistemological nature of leisure, and philosophies of recreation and aggression in sports. Kosiewicz's colleagues, Jakub Mosz and Alicja Przyluska-Fisher, further add to the literature with aesthetic studies and short sport films as lines of inquiry for the former, and bioethics, medical ethics and the ethics of sport as lines of inquiry for the latter.

Polish sport philosophers are also quite active at other universities. Marek Kazimierczak and Tomasz Sahaj, both from the Eugeniusz Piasecki University School of Physical Education in Poznan, address the philosophical foundations of tourism and recreation, and the background, conditions and forms of public perception of disorderly behaviour in sport, respectively. At the University School of Physical Education in Wroclaw, Tomasz Michaluk uses Charles Peirce to understand the properties, meaning, semiotics and symbolism of contemporary sport. Krzysztof Pezdez and Katarzyna Salomon-Krakowska of the same university examine issues of axiology, and the ethical and phenomenological dimensions of sport for persons with disabilities. Finally, Maria Zowislo at the University School of Physical Education in Krakow uses a combination of philosophic paradigms, mythology and religion in her sport inquiries. These authors regularly attend and present their research at the annual conference for the Polish Society of Social Sciences of Sport.[18]

Of the remaining Slavonic countries, Lev Kreft, who focuses on aesthetics of sport, and Milan Hosta, who focuses on sport ethics, Olympism and inclusive Kinesiology, both at the University of Ljubljana, Slovenia, are notable scholars as well as Vladyslav Stolyarov from Russia who contributes in the field of methodology and aesthetics of sport. Although other scholars from this geographic region include philosophy of sport sections in larger works, few stand-alone publications exist and those that do are mostly unknown to the rest of the world. Still, the founding of the Slovene Philosophy of Sport Association in 2003 holds promise for future development in this region.[19]

The Nordic Region: Norway, Finland, Sweden and Denmark[20]

Sport philosophy in the Nordic countries gained significant traction after the 1972 Pre-Olympic Scientific Congress in Munich, Germany. At this conference, the first to bring science and sport together in connection to the Olympic Games, the German philosopher Hans Lenk argued for sport as a suitable philosophic topic. His presentation symbolized a very real turning point for the philosophy of sport as a serious academic discipline in the Nordic region and throughout the world.

Norway maintains the strongest position in sport philosophy among the Nordic countries. Here, sport philosophy finds its cultural roots in the 9th- to 12th-century Viking concept of *idrett* ('strong deeds' such as running, swimming, sailing and horse riding, or in a modern sense narrowly defined as *sport* to include such things as play, games, dance and outdoor activities), and in an identity intimately linked to skiing and *friluftsliv* ('life in the open air' – a specific approach toward nature, movement and outdoor activities). The introduction of English sport to the region in the late 19th century would further diversify its sport culture to incorporate the prominence of football, Olympic sport and recreational sport.

While German philosophers such as Georg Wilhelm Friedrich Hegel, Ludwig Wittgenstein, Edmund Husserl and Heidegger influenced the early development of sport philosophy in a broad sense, local philosophers such as Arne Næss in Norway have advanced the discipline in more specific ways. As a professor at the University of Oslo, Næss linked his expertise as a mountain climber to his environmental philosophy called 'deep ecology'. He was also friend, colleague and mentor to two of the most prominent sport philosophers in Norway, Gunnar Breivik and Sigmund Loland, both of whom would eventually become professors at the Norwegian School of Sport Sciences (NSSS)[21] and acquired teaching responsibilities in the philosophy of sport. Breivik's works include links between *friluftsliv* and risk sports, *friluftsliv* and the human relation to and responsibility for nature, elite sport, mass sport, doping and phenomenology. Loland's primary scholarly areas include fair play, doping, an ecological view of sport, Olympism and sport and technology.

The only other Nordic country with a strong sport sciences school is Finland (University of Jyväskylä). However, this school focuses little on sport philosophy, favouring instead biomechanics, pedagogy and sociology. In fact, the most well-known sport philosopher in Finland is the theologian Mikael Lindfelt, who studies sport and ethics at the theological academy in Åbo.

Sweden does not have one strong sport sciences institution, and most Swedish sport philosophers emerge from specializations in master and doctoral programmes found in general university philosophy programmes. Claudio M. Tamburrini (originally from Argentina) and Torbjörn Tännsjö, who started in the general philosophy programme in Gothenburg but now teach at the University of Stockholm, exemplify this situation and work closely together on sport philosophy projects. Other scholars include Christian Munthe in Gothenburg and Kutte Jönsson in the sports sciences programme in Malmö – the college that has taken the leading role in the country's sport philosophy discipline. Sweden's traditional emphasis on utilitarianism in ethics and social philosophy influences its sport philosophy. Sport ethics, including biomedical considerations, spectator sports, gender, doping and genetic technologies are of primary consideration.

Denmark, while influenced by the gymnastics movements of Germany (Friedrich Ludwig 'Turnvater' Jahn) and Sweden (Per Henrik Ling's gymnastics) as well as the philosophical works of Søren Kierkegaad, has not developed any courses or programmes in sport philosophy at university level. As such, there are few sport philosophers in Denmark taken in the narrow sense apart from perhaps Verner Möller, who maintains the central Danish perspective on the anti-doping and performance enhancement debate, and Ejgil Jespersen, who specializes in Maurice Merleau-Ponty and various forms of situated and non-scholastic learning.

Germany[22]

In the wider sense of the term 'sport philosophy', such philosophers as Theodor W. Adorno, Karl Jaspers, Ernst Bloch, Max Scheler and Helmuth Plessner made isolated philosophic treatments of sport in the early 20th century. Yet as the significance of sport in Germany grew, so did the philosophy of sport discipline. Hans Lenk, the founder of German sport philosophy, focused German scholarship to the narrow sense of the term in the 1960s and 1970s. Other scholars, such as Gunter Gebauer, Jürgen Court, Herbert Haag and Volker Caysa, would also produce standard works and significantly promote the discipline through the 1990s.

While the philosophy of sport in Germany initially had much in common with the Anglo-American community through connections with the Philosophic Society for the Study of Sport (PSSS) founded in the 1970s, this transnational attitude faded somewhat in the following years. Hence, German sport philosophy acquired its own profile, one not couched in physical education or the particularities of the German sporting culture, but rather in the regional philosophic traditions of such philosophers as Hegel, Wittgenstein, Plessner, Friedrich Nietzsche and Immanuel Kant.

Sport ethics holds the dominant position in Germany, but with methodological differences from other regions of the world. German sport ethics takes a 'bottom-up' approach by using the implicit norms of sport practice as a point of departure as opposed to the 'top-down' approach of simply applying ethical theories to sport. Theories on discourse ethics and philosophy of language also influence philosophic inquiries. Particular concerns include whether following rules constitutes a moral action, whether the morality in the world of games and that of real life are comparable, and how to define the concepts of play, games and sport. Sport anthropology and sport aesthetics constitute additional areas of inquiry, and include the works of Ommo Grupe, Elk Fanke and Peter Röthig.

Recent developments in German sport philosophy include inquiries into naturalness, doping and the technologization of the body, all of which attempt to address current societal problems. For example, Arno Müller of Leipzig University examines risk sport from an existential and phenomenological perspective, and Claudia Pawlenka of Heinrich Heine University stands on the Anglo-American traditions of sport ethics. Yet no more than a dozen German scholars currently pursue the philosophy of sport in the narrow sense, and, more often than not, hold chairs in sport pedagogy or sport sociology.

Most academic discourse in this area is rooted in the German Association of Sport Science, which includes the division of Philosophy of Sport founded in 1976.[23] Three journals, *Sport Science*,[24] *Sport and Society*[25] and *Leipzig Sport-Scientific Writings*, provide German publication outlets for this association, although no

German-speaking journal specifically for the philosophy of sport exists. Recent efforts have created dialogues between sport philosophers, the area of cultural studies and the general philosophy milieu, opening the potential for new analyses and publication outlets.

Italy[26]

Philosophy of sport in Italy did not gain significant attention until the early 1990s with Fabrizio Ravaglioli's evaluation of sport as part of popular culture. While the discipline remains small in Italy, and the philosophy of physical education continues to be more visible than the philosophy of sport, the efforts of Emanuelle Isidori at the University of Rome 'Foro Italico' hold promise. He recently hosted the 2010 International Association for the Philosophy of Sport (IAPS) annual conference, co-authored the first Italian sport philosophy book in 2011 (with Heather Reid) and has published a text on the philosophy of sport education. These publications, as well as his continued enthusiasm for sport philosophy, will hopefully produce future dividends for the discipline.

The Netherlands and Belgium[27]

In the wider sense, Johan Huizinga's 1938 volume *Homo Ludens*, with its relatively normative conception of play, greatly influenced the development of the sports sciences in the Low Countries and eventually throughout the world. However, Huizinga's work created strong demarcations between pedagogical and philosophical sport and physical education research and the more empirical sciences of sport psychology and sociology – a polarization that would perhaps contribute to the delay in the inception of sport philosophy in the narrow sense until the 1990s.

Twentieth-century Low Country general philosophy mediates between the traditional tenets of continental and Anglo-Saxon philosophy. This international perspective influenced the development of philosophy of physical education. Sport, however, was resisted as unpedagogical, focusing too much on competition, the body as an object and winning. Still, philosophers of the first half of the 20th century sowed the seeds for the eventual acceptance of the discipline. Dutch psychologist and philosopher F.J.J. Buytendijk brought philosophical anthropology to the forefront of modern thinking, and later the phenomenological and existential works of Merleau-Ponty and Jean-Paul Sartre held influence.

Carl Gordijn came from these same traditions and focused on their implications for physical education, transforming it from a medically and physiologically oriented practice to one influenced by anthropology and pedagogy, promoting movement education over physical education. By the 1960s, however, analytic and positivistic methodologies had reduced the importance of phenomenological approaches due to strong neo-positive, analytic and Marxist tendencies.

It could be argued that Dutch students had been exposed to the philosophy of sport in the wide sense by the end of the 1980s, primarily under the guise of philosophy of physical education. In the narrow sense, Jan Tamboer, one of

Gordijn's students and the first Dutchman to contribute to the *Journal for the Philosophy of Sport* (1992), taught the first philosophy of sport class at VU University Amsterdam in 1990. Ivo van Hilvoorde took Tamboer's place in 1996, and VU University Amsterdam remains the only Low Country university that offers sport philosophy as an autonomous academic discipline.

Sport ethics dominates Dutch sport philosophy, and Anglo-Saxon sport philosophy writings became launching pads for several Dutch authors, such as Johan Steenbergen, Agnes Elling and Van Hilvoorde, to publish papers on fair play, gender, doping, genetics and human enhancement. Others pursue different lines of inquiry such as Ron Welters of Radboud University Nijmegen, who is interested in sport and the environment and how endurance sport can lead to a more ecologically sustainable lifestyle. In addition, the Netherlands and Belgium's failed attempt to secure the 2018 World Cup, current efforts to bid for the 2028 Olympics and nationalistic debates over talent identification through sport education (rather than physical education) as the Netherlands ambitiously strives to become one of the top 10 sports countries worldwide have publicly promoted the importance of independent, critical reflection on sport.

While football and cycling are near and dear to Belgians' hearts, compared to the Netherlands, sport seldom attracts the interest of Belgian ethicists and philosophers, although the interest is increasing. Scholars at the Catholic University of Leuven and Ghent University hold courses on sports and ethics. Recently, Marc Maes of the former university founded the International Centre for Ethics in Sport[28] in response to an increasing number of sport organizations seeking workshops, practical guidelines and reflections on ethics in sport. The University of Leuven also founded a new research group on ethics and sport at the Research Centre for the History of Sport and Kinesiology. In the end, sport philosophy in Belgium remains marginalized by universities due to its infancy and the strong division between the departments of health and sports and philosophy and ethics. However, Belgian sport scandals in the first decade of the 21st century have instigated requests to philosophers of sport to critically contribute to these public debates.

France

In the narrow sense, sport philosophy in France is considerably younger than in other regions and holds little academic ground. In the broad sense, sport philosophy began in the 20th century with Jacques Ulmann's history of physical education research and the pedagogical philosophies of Bertrand During. Other scholars, such as Bernard Jeu, André Rauch and Georges Vigarello, have contributed to the discipline on topics such as self-expression through movement and aesthetics. France would wait until 2005 for the Faculty of Sport of Nancy to create a seat dedicated to sport philosophy. However, French philosophy departments remain relatively closed to philosophic treatments of sport and body. While seemingly marginalized, Bernard Andrieu of the University of Nancy is preparing a philosophy of sport handbook written in French and is one of the leaders in the development of the French Association for the Philosophy of Sport.[29]

The Iberian Peninsula: Spain and Portugal

At the beginning of the 20th century, Spanish philosopher José Ortega y Gasset published some works concerning the relevance of sport in society, but the impetus for Spanish sport philosophy would not take root until Spain's economic and social recovery from its civil war (1960s–1970s). During that time, José Maria Cagigal mused about the social meaning of sport and its increasing significance to Spanish society. Gregorio Robles' 1982 publication comparing legal rules and game rules also holds significance for the discipline's development. In a more narrow sense, current scholars such as Francisco Javier López Frías and José Luis Pérez Triviño have examined issues such as morality, doping, commercialization and technology in sport and have published in both Spanish- and English-speaking outlets over the last five years. Cesar R. Torres (originally from Argentina) and Jesús Ilundáin also contribute to the literature in Spanish, remain active in English-speaking publications and represent valuable and needed connections between Spanish and English sport philosophy. Sport philosophy in Spain continues to suffer from a lack of attention, a lack of university departments willing to support the discipline and a resultant lack of young scholars. However, the recent publication of the first sport philosophy journal in Spanish, *Fair Play. Journal Sport Philosophy, Ethics and Law*,[30] holds promise for the future of the discipline in this region.

In the wide sense, the origins of philosophy of sport in Portugal began with Manuel Sérgio's and Jorge Bento's positions on the naming of the physical education discipline – the former scholar arguing for 'science of human kinetics' while the latter argued for the term 'sport sciences'. In the narrow sense, Teresa Lacerda's work in the aesthetics of sport at the University of Porto, Faculty of Sports, has generated steady interest in the discipline over the past 10 years to include masters and doctoral students, a consistent body of publications, and the hosting of the IAPS annual conference in 2012.

The United Kingdom[31]

Sport philosophy developed in the UK when the reorganization of higher education in the late 1960s to early 1970s caused the merging of physical education teacher training colleges and universities. This motivated universities to 'beef up' the original three-year teacher programmes to four-year human movement programmes by incorporating educational theory (as well as history, psychology and sociology) into their curriculums, thus sowing the early seeds of sport studies programmes. Hence, like many other regions of the world, sport philosophy in the UK grew from physical education programmes rather than philosophy departments.

Scholarship in the discipline began in a similar fashion, addressing pedagogical concerns of physical education rather than philosophic treatments of sport. Robert Carlisle's 'The Concept of Physical Education' and the response by Mollie Adams in the same issue of the *Journal of Philosophy of Education* (1969), and David Aspin's 'Ethical Aspects of Sport and Games and Physical Education' in the same journal six years later, represent early works. During the same time period, British educational philosopher R.S. Peters marginalized physical education, arguing that education is only valuable if it develops the rational mind, an idea that continued to garner discussion by philosophers Andrew Reid and David Carr in the late 1990s and by sport philosopher Mike McNamee in a 2005 book chapter.

Philosophy of sport in the narrow sense remained insignificant in the UK until the mid 1980s. During this time, philosophers such as Jim Parry and David Carr (working in the philosophy of education) and David Best and Graham McFee (working in the philosophy of human movement) not only contributed to the growing scholarship but also became mentors to budding sport philosophers. Arguably, it would not be until Mike McNamee (Swansea University, Wales) attended the PSSS conferences in the early 1990s that sport philosophy in the UK experienced significant growth. Educated in movement studies, physical education and philosophy of education, he has written, edited and co-edited several works and anthologies, including the first sport philosophy text in the UK, *Ethics & Sport* (1998) with Jim Parry. He helped spawn new courses at undergraduate and postgraduate levels, founded the British Philosophy of Sport Association (BPSA) in 2001[32] (an organization that formally accepted the European Association for the Philosophy of Sport's [EAPS] affiliation in 2008[33]) and launched *Sport, Ethics and Philosophy*[34] in 2007, a journal concerned with the analysis and interrogation of key ideas and issues in games, play and sport and related movement activities.

Apart from some well-known names, sport philosophers remain scarce in the UK. Scholars such as Andrew Edgar at Cardiff University, and Alun Hardman and Carwyn Jones at Cardiff Metropolitan University, continue to pursue the discipline in the narrow sense focusing on moral development in sport, ethics in sport and coaching, aesthetics, technology and doping. Emily Ryall at the University of Gloucestershire is instrumental in the organization of the Philosophy at Play Conference and the editing of the related book *The Philosophy of Play*, published in 2013.[35] In addition, Stephen Mumford at the University of Nottingham conducts aesthetic and metaphysical investigations of sport, and Andy Miah at the University of West Scotland continues to publish (among other things) on the ethics of emerging technology and sport and the Olympics. However, these philosophers (as well as others) continue to carry the profession, with few developing scholars ready to join their departments or eventually take their place. One could say that sport philosophy is more prevalent than ever in the UK, but its lack of a disciplinary home divides its focus between philosophy, sport studies and physical education departments, somewhat inhibiting the discipline from progressing through the combined efforts of a common community of academic interest.

Latin America[36]

Latin American countries share a common political and historical heritage as well as cultural and linguistic similarities rooted in the past colonization efforts of Spain, Portugal and France. Modern sport philosophy in this region, however, stands in relationship to parts of the English-speaking world and the Iberian Peninsula. Similar to its development in North America, sport philosophy in Latin America, in the wider sense, developed from the philosophic concerns of late-19th- and early-20th-century educational reformers such as Argentinians José B. Zubiaur and Enrique Romero Brest, Brazilians Fernando de Azevedo, Renato Kehl, Jorge de Souza and B. Vieira de Mello, Mexican Moisés Sáenz and Chilean Luis Bisquertt Susarte, each articulating their own visions of physical education and often including pedagogical, hygienic and moral goals. Philosophy of sport in the narrow sense, however, struggled during the first half of the 19th century with few publications or dedicated scholars outside of the philosophy of education.

While Latin American physical educators continued to think philosophically of their discipline in the 1950s to the 1970s, journalists began considering the philosophical quandaries created by sport – specifically football. Although untrained as philosophers, thousands likely read their investigations into the nature, status, value and beauty of sport. Several books, including Dante Panzeri's *Football: Dynamic of the Unthought* (1967), critically examined football from perspectives of race, economics, ethics and cultural expression and prefigured some of the ethical concerns sport philosophers would have with football in the following years.

In the decades that followed, philosophy of sport in North America enjoyed considerable progress. The same cannot be said for Latin America, which struggled slowly and unmethodically to promote the discipline. It was not until the 1980s and 1990s that Latin American academics began to view sport as worthy of academic attention, yet this largely rested with social scientists interested in sport as part of the gestalt cultural phenomena. Some philosophers, such as Mexican Juan Parent, Uruguayan Homero Altesor and Argentine Graciela Scheines, concentrated briefly on the ethics, meaning and phenomenology of sport as well as analyses of play and games, yet these were short-lived efforts. While physical educators continued to pursue the philosophical foundations of their subject matter and writers, journalists and intellectuals continued to show increasing interest in football, these authors were largely not philosophers and their books did not garner much philosophical interest.

The new millennium, however, brought with it signs of gradual expansion in Latin American sport philosophy. Argentine Claudio M. Tamburrini published the first comprehensive approach to the discipline in Latin America in 2001: *The 'Hand of God'? Essays in the Philosophy of Sports*. Other prominent scholars, such as Cesar R. Torres and Daniel G. Campos, furthered the profession through edited works, journal publications and pieces in Latin American newspapers. In 2006, they co-edited a volume dedicated to philosophical examinations of football. In 2008, Torres edited a second work focusing on youth sport and physical activity. Three years later, he published a book discussing some central elements of sporting practice. Other Latin American scholars have recently pursued such philosophic inquiries as justice in sport, feminism in sport, body philosophy, Olympism and perspectives on Asian martial arts.

In spite of these recent efforts, philosophy of sport in Latin America remains undeveloped due to the lack of a disciplinary organization, specialized scholarly associations, undergraduate or graduate programmes, introductory or advanced textbooks for required undergraduate philosophy classes, academic credibility and a continued belief that philosophic inquiry does not lead to any practical applications in physical education. While daunting, overcoming these challenges may be significantly facilitated by the 2016 Rio de Janeiro Olympics – a venue that may present various opportunities to foster sport philosophy throughout the region.

North America[37]

According to Scott Kretchmar, philosophy of sport in North America experienced three periods of academic growth. From the late-19th century through the mid 20th century, sport philosophy in the wider sense linked to the progressive education movement and, most influentially, Jesse Feiring Williams' *The Principles of Physical Education* (1927) and his pedagogical philosophy of 'education through the physical'. While significant in promoting physical education, Williams and other interested scholars were more pedagogists than philosophers. In the 1950s and through the mid 1960s, sport philosophy continued in the wider sense but shifted methodology to one describing and comparing how different systems of philosophic thought applied to the field of physical activity. Yet the validity, utility and quality of scholarship were questioned, its methods deemed by some to be overwhelming and tedious, and the frame of reference remained physical education – not philosophy. Therefore, this 'systems' approach garnered only fleeting attention.

Over the next decade, sport philosophy in the narrow sense began to take shape in North America. Early ground-breaking analyses in the 1960s from Eleanor Metheny, Howard Slusher and Paul Weiss broke away from pedagogical concerns and used the tools of philosophy rather than science to examine sport. Weiss' book *Sport: A Philosophic Inquiry* (1969) was not only the first modern text to philosophically treat sport written by a philosopher, but it would also become significantly influential to the development of the discipline both in North America and abroad.

The discipline became institutionalized in 1972. Weiss and Warren P. Fraleigh instigated the formation of the Philosophic Society for the Study of Sport (PSSS), with its first full disciplinary conference held the following year and the creation of a scholarly journal, *Journal of the Philosophy of Sport*, a year later.[38] With the mission of 'fostering interchange and scholarship among those interested in the scholarly study of sport', the PSSS conceived itself as international in membership and programme – a value that motivated the renaming of the PSSS to the International Association for the Philosophy of Sport (IAPS) in 1999.[39]

Favouring a brand of scholarship closer to philosophy, little attention was paid to the practical application of sport philosophy research to physical education and sport. Efforts were further made to ensure that the quality of these works would be acceptable to that of the parent discipline. This esoteric turn made it somewhat difficult for lay people to understand sport philosophy writings. The perceived lesser importance of philosophy to science and a lack of respect and comprehension of the need for it offered additional early struggles for the discipline in North America. Resistance from traditional philosophers to examining what they considered the 'trivial' matters of play, games and sport, department heads unwilling to support the research activities of sport philosophers and the lack of production of new scholars through graduate programmes compounded the early challenges.

In recent years, however, sport philosophers in the narrow sense at institutions such as Pennsylvania State University, Purdue University, Ohio State University, the University of Idaho, the University of Tennessee and Western University have produced not only a great deal of scholarship but also a number of young scholars at both the masters and doctorate levels. Several books, anthologies and textbooks have aided in the process. Bernard Suits' work, *The Grasshopper. Games, Life, and Utopia* (1978), for example, remains a seminal text on games and play. Fraleigh's *Right Actions in Sport: Ethics for Contestants* (1984) and Robert L. Simon's work *Fair Play: The Ethics of Sport* (1991) explore ethical theory and its connection to concrete moral dilemmas in competitive sport. William J. Morgan has written two important works, *Why Sports Morally Matter* (2006) and *Leftist Theories of Sport* (1994), both of which ethically consider the impact of sport on society. Morgan has also edited or co-edited several anthologies including *Philosophic Inquiry in Sport* (with Klaus V. Meier, 1995) and *Ethics in Sport* (2007). Kretchmar produced the first textbook designed specifically for sport philosophy classes titled *Practical Philosophy of Sport and Physical Activity* (2005). Heather Reid followed suit with her *Introduction to the Philosophy of Sport* (2012) text. She has also published a work that advocates a philosophic approach to the sports experience titled *The Philosophical Athlete* (2002) and others that examine sport through the use of ancient Greek philosophies. Each of these works, as well as others, has progressively contributed to the development of the discipline in North America and, in some cases, throughout the world.

While analytic philosophy dominated the first 20 years of the *Journal of the Philosophy of Sport*, regular reviews of selected philosophy of sport journal articles by the *International Journal of Physical Education*[40] reveal a diversifying trend in scholarship to include inquiries into the value and meaning of sport and play, ancient Greek philosophy and Olympism, ethical issues in sport, phenomenology, doping and technology, officiating, sport and spirituality, and aesthetics. Given this disciplinary body of work, it could be argued that North America has produced the greatest number of sport philosophers and sport philosophy publications in the narrow sense. However, the ideas of these scholars are somewhat contained within the English-speaking world. If IAPS truly values the international development of the discipline, efforts toward the regular and consistent translation of works from English to other languages and vice versa need to be strongly considered.

The future development of the sport philosophy discipline will rely on several factors. First, the translation and exchange of research across borders and cultures is imperative. During its formative phase, translations of sport philosophy writings, such as Abe Shinobu's *Sport Philosophy*, Weiss' *Sport: A*

Philosophic Inquiry (1969), Kretchmar's textbook *Practical Philosophy of Sport* (1994) and McNamee and Parry's *Ethics and Sport* (1998), greatly influenced the development of the discipline in Japan, Taiwan and China and, to some degree, Germany and the UK. The same global impact could be expected with modern translation efforts, and journals and academic associations have recognized this need. *Sport, Ethics and Philosophy* includes abstracts for its articles in four different languages, and IAPS has proceeded with the translation of important works from English to Chinese, German, Japanese and Spanish and vice versa.[41]

Second, sport philosophers almost exclusively communicate through sport science journals and conferences. This continued isolation is not beneficial for future development, and sport philosophers would be wise to consider communicating with such domains as general philosophy and medical and engineering ethics. Sport bureaucracies and other policymakers could also benefit from the insight of applied sport ethicists – an effort that could promote segments of the sport philosophy discipline from an esoteric perspective to a more practical application. This could also move sport philosophy out of the academy and into the public sphere, subsequently increasing visibility and acceptance of the profession. Further, the perceived value of philosophic inquiry in sport can benefit from joining, augmenting and enhancing empirical studies of sport and physical activity. Sport philosophers need to not only help empiricists find value in our work as beneficial to their research needs and products, but also need to utilize and appreciate empirical sport scientists' research in their investigations.

Finally, the production of new scholars will be imperative to the continuation of the discipline. Programmes at both the masters and doctoral level must be sustained in their current geographic region and must be developed and created where they are budding or non-existent. As sport philosophers leave the academy, all efforts should be made to maintain their chairs. Such durability will most likely be tethered to the discipline's ability to garner value in the sport sciences, with links to empirical studies, and with connections to the public sphere.

The cultural significance of sport continues to grow throughout the world – a world that is shrinking through the development of technology. The need to critically examine sport policies, practices and outcomes from a global perspective will become equally if not more important in the discipline. The discipline of sport philosophy, through its growing international perspective and scholarly activity, remains in the best position to provide such analyses.

Notes

1   'Wide sense' and 'narrow sense' are found in Claudia Pawlenka, 'Philosophy of Sport in Germany: An Overview of its History and Academic Research', *Journal of the Philosophy of Sport* 37 (2010): 271.

2   For example, see the Resource Guide in this volume for an overview. In this essay, all university and association names as well as publication titles have been translated from their native language. Consult their respective websites, listed in this essay, for their original titles.

3   Takayuki Hata and Masami Sekine, 'Philosophy of Sport and Physical Education in Japan: Its History, Characteristics and Prospects', *Journal of the Philosophy of Sport* 37 (2010): 215–24.
4   See
5   See <www.jstage.jst.go.jp/browse/jpspe/>
6   See <www.jstage.jst.go.jp/browse/ijshs>
7   Michael Burke and Dennis Hemphill, 'Philosophy of Sport in Australia and New Zealand', in *A Companion to Philosophy in Australia and New Zealand*, eds., Graham Oppy, Nick Trakakis, Lynda Burns, Steve Gardner and Fiona Leigh (Clayton, Victoria: Monash University Publishing, 2010), 440–3 and Terence J. Roberts, 'Reflections on the Philosophy of Sport in Australia', *Journal of the Philosophy of Sport* 20/21 (1993–1994): 113–21.
8   Leo Hsu, 'An Overview of Sport Philosophy in Chinese-Speaking Regions (Taiwan & Mainland China)', *Journal of the Philosophy of Sport* 37 (2010): 237–52.
9   See <www.bodyculture.org.tw>. This organization also includes the Taiwan Sport Philosophy Society.
10   Ivo Jirásek and Peter Hopsicker, 'Philosophical Kinanthropology (Philosophy of Physical Culture) in Slavonic Countries: The Culture, the Writers, and the Current Directions', *Journal of the Philosophy of Sport* 37 (2010): 253–70; Douglas Hochstetler and Tim L. Elcombe, 'A Summary of Selected Research in North America & Western Europe (2003–2004)', *International Journal of Physical Education* 41 (2004): 144–59; Peter Hopsicker and Ivo Jirásek, 'Selected Philosophy of Sport/Movement Culture Texts in English and Slavonic (2005–2006)', *International Journal of Physical Education* 43 (2006): 140–55; Peter Hopsicker and Ivo Jirásek, 'Selected Philosophy of Sport/Movement Culture Texts in English and Slavonic (2007–2008),' *International Journal of Physical Education* 45 (2008): 162–76; Peter Hopsicker and Eman Hurych, 'Selected Philosophy of Sport/Movement Culture Texts in English and Slavonic (2009–2010)', *International Journal of Physical Education* 4 (2010): 2–16; and Eman Hurych and Jim Parry, 'A Review of Selected Philosophy of Sports Texts in English and Slavonic (2011–2012)', *International Journal of Physical Education* 49 (2012): 2–16.
11   At this time, Czechoslovakia was not yet divided into the Czech Republic and Slovakia. This occurred on 1 January, 1993.
12   See <www.ftvs.cuni.cz/knspolecnost/>
13   See <www.gymnica.upol.cz/index.php/gymnica>
14   See
15   Jerzy Kosiewicz, 'Philosophy of Sport in Poland: Observations', *Physical Culture and Sport. Studies and Research* 54 (2012): 86–102.
16   See <http://www.issss.net/>
17   See <www.degruyter.com/view/j/pcssr>
18   See
19   See <www.fsp.uni-lj.si/eng/>
20   Gunnar Breivik, 'Philosophy of Sport in Nordic Countries', *Journal of the Philosophy of Sport* 37 (2010): 194–214.
21   See <www.nih.no/en/>
22   Pawlenka, 'Philosophy of Sport in Germany: An Overview of its History and Academic Research', 271–91.
23   See <www.sportwissenschaft.de/index.php?id=20#134>
24   See <www.springer.com/medicine/journal/12662>
25   See <www.sportundgesellschaft.de/index.php/sportundgesellschaft>
26   Emanuele Isidori and Heather Reid, *Filosofia dello sport* (Milano: Bruno Mondadori, 2011); and Emanuele Isidori, *Filosofia dell'educazione sportiva. Dala teoria alla prassi* (Nuova Cutura: Roma, 2012).

27   Ivo van Hilvoorde, Jan Vorstenbosch and Ignaas Devisch, 'Philosophy of Sport in Belgium and the Netherlands: History and Characteristics', *Journal of the Philosophy of Sport* 37 (2010): 225–36.

28   See <www.ethicsandsport.com>

29   See <www.staps.uhp-nancy.fr/SFPS/index_SFPS.htm>

30   See <www.upf.edu/revistafairplay>

31   Mike McNamee, 'Sport, Ethics and Philosophy; Context, History, Prospects', *Sport, Ethic and Philosophy* 1 (2007): 1–6; Mike McNamee. Interview by author, 16 January, 2013; and Jim Parry. Interview by author, 18 February, 2013.

32   See <www.philosophyofsport.org.uk>

33   See <philosophyofsport.eu>

34   See <www.tandfonline.com/toc/rsep20/current>

35   See <www.routledge.com/books/details/9780415538350/>

36   Cesar R. Torres and Daniel Campos, 'Philosophy of Sport in Latin America', *Journal of the Philosophy of Sport* 37 (2010): 292–309.

37   Scott Kretchmar, 'Philosophy of Sport', in *The History of Exercise and Sport Science*, eds., John D. Massengale and Richard A. Swanson (Champaign, IL: Human Kinetics, 1997), 181–201; Douglas Hochstetler and Tim L. Elcombe, 'Sport philosophy: A Summary of Selected Research (2001–2002)', *International Journal of Physical Education* 39 (2002): 4–20; Hochstetler and Elcombe, 'A Summary of Selected Research in North America & Western Europe (2003–2004)', 144–59; Hopsicker and Jirásek, 'Selected Philosophy of Sport/Movement Culture Texts in English and Slavonic (2005–2006)', 140–55; Hopsicker and Jirásek, 'Selected Philosophy of Sport/Movement Culture Texts in English and Slavonic (2007–2008)', 162-176; Hopsicker and Hurych, 'Selected Philosophy of Sport/Movement Culture Texts in English and Slavonic (2009–2010)', 2–16; and Hurych and Parry, 'A Review of Selected Philosophy of Sports Texts in English and Slavonic (2011–2012)', 2–16.

38   See <www.tandfonline.com/toc/rjps20/current>

39   See <www.iaps.net>

40   See <www.m-m-sports.com/shop/en/international-journal-of-physical-education.html>

41   The first phase of this project is expected to be completed by 31 December, 2019.

Part V

Glossary of Key Terms and Concepts

Glossary of Key Terms and Concepts

Cheating

Warren P. Fraleigh

Cheating is a word used to describe many actions.[1] It ranges from cheating in marriage, to cheating on one's taxes, to cheating in sport. I will focus on the concept of cheating in individual contests, doubles contests, one-among-many contests and team contests in sports. I will not discuss equipment, sport facilities or eligibility to compete.

Cheating is dealt with in three ways. From the comments of a television golf announcer, formalism, 'If you want to play this game, you have to know the rules', to conventional actions in sport, such as a base-runner in baseball going out of the baseline to impede a possible double play,[2] to reference to the internal structure of sport.[3]

Most commentators discuss cheating in relation to the rules. Many state that cheating is a violation of the rules because the rules say what *must* be done in a contest, for example, passing, dribbling or shooting in basketball, what methods to use in pursuing the *goal of the sport*, for instance, throwing the ball through your own basket and what *must not* be done, for instance, in basketball, holding, tripping or hacking an opponent. The *intentional* violation of the rules is at the heart of what is called cheating. Thus, here is a stipulative definition of cheating: *'Cheating is an intentional act that violates an appropriate interpretation of the rules shared by the participants, done to obtain advantage for oneself and/or one's teammates, while trying to avoid detection so as to escape penalty.'*[4]

The justification of the intentional violation of the rules being cheating comes from the formalist position of 'definitional deception', that is, when someone 'has contracted to participate in one sort of activity and then engages in another sort of activity'.[5] A strict formalist position maintains that a sport 'is no more (in terms of its careful definition) than its rules',[6] thus all intentional rule violations fail to honour one's contractual obligation.[7]

Reacting to the formalist position on cheating, conventionalists maintain that the social context of sport must be included in our understanding of sport. Claudio M. Tamburrini says that 'The sport practitioners' ethos – the particular understanding of the game entertained by the players – is the most relevant indication of how the game should be played.'[8] Randolph Feezell argues that each sport has its prescriptive atmosphere.[9] He states: 'The problem of course is that the prescriptive atmosphere is only partly constituted by the central, explicit rules of the game in question.'[10] He cites instances of things that are 'part of the game', things that have been acknowledged, for example, by practitioners of baseball, such as batters digging up the chalk line at the back of the batter's box, illegally placing their rear foot outside the box or pitchers learning to throw inside to intimidate. Historically, being 'part of the game' is 'why they do not constitute cheating'.[11] Critics of this position say that conventionalism 'confuses social description with normative justification' and results in existing conventions becoming immune to criticism.[12]

Now, if we examine part of the previous definition of cheating, *'an appropriate interpretation of the rules shared by participants'*, we note how rules are to be interpreted and agreed upon by participants. Neither the rules (formalism) by themselves nor the historically accepted conventions (conventionalism) decide the interpretation of the rules. Such a decision comes from broad internalism.[13] Broad internalism is a 'theory of the nature and function of sport … [that] is not part of the constitutive rules but may be thought as the best explanation of why the rules' create artificial obstacles, such as passing, dribbling, shooting to the goal and throwing the ball through the basket, that can be done easily outside a basketball contest,[14] for instance, by standing on a ladder and throwing the ball through the basket. The presupposition of the rules is that they are the artificial barriers that facilitate the expression of excellence. J.S. Russell states that 'Rules should be interpreted in such a manner that the excellences embodied in achieving the lusory goal of the game are not undermined but are maintained and fostered'.[15] Thus, for internalists, cheating is when an intentional act undermines excellence in what *must be done* or increases what *must not be done* to achieve *the goal of the sport* in order to get an advantage for oneself or for one's team while avoiding penalty.

An illustration of internalism is Cesar R. Torres' analysis of skills.[16] He talks of constitutive skills, those skills that *must be done* (i.e. dribbling, passing and shooting in basketball) to accomplish the goal of the game that 'define and shape the character of games … [and] in terms of such skills, players are to show their superiority',[17] that is, to fulfil the internal excellence of games. Also, there are restorative skills, which put games back on track (such as throw-ins or foul shots in basketball) and act as penalties when an intentional or unintentional rule violation occurs and interrupts the game of constitutive skills. Torres demonstrates the internal superiority of *what must be done*, constitutive skills, over restorative skills for acts that *must not be done*. Warren P. Fraleigh applies Torres' differentiation to intentional strategic fouls and finds very few categories of such fouls that are acceptable.[18] Robert L. Simon, in reaction, critiques Fraleigh's analysis.[19]

Now, we have a revision of internalism offered by William J. Morgan.[20] He states that broad internalism results in an abstract internal concept of excellence that changes over history, for instance, from amateurism to present professionalism. For Morgan, internalism's broad idea of excellence, however, makes it difficult to specify normative judgements in different sports, at different times, in different places. He suggests that 'deep conventions' need to be a part of internalism. Here 'deep conventions' are different from the 'part of the game' conventionalism cited earlier. At this point, a more thorough illustration of 'deep conventions' in different sports is needed.

So, we have three bases for judgements on cheating: formalism, conventionalism and broad internalism. They reveal not only the complexity of cheating as a moral phenomenon but also the increasing complexity of its analysis in the sport philosophy literature over the years.

Competition

Jan Boxill

One of the most controversial features of our society is competition. It is condemned by Marxists, championed by capitalists, deemed a necessary evil in education, and is necessary to and dramatized in sport. Alfie Kohn argues that competition is bad both psychologically and morally. As he sees it, competition is a vice, the very antithesis of cooperation – a virtue.[21] For him, competition is intrinsically immoral; it is selfish and egoistic; it involves treating others as means or as obstacles thwarting one's victory. Further, the consequences of competition are harmful; in aiming for success, competitors view their opponents as enemies, and focus on winning by whatever means possible. Sports may not hold a monopoly on the 'win at all costs syndrome' nor on the harmful effects of competition, but because competition is dramatized and exaggerated in sport, and because the competitive spirit is first fostered in sport, where it is publicly reinforced and approved, the characteristics of competition are best seen in sport.

The word *competition* comes from the Latin *petere*, meaning 'to strive' or 'to seek', combined with the prefix, *com*, meaning 'with'. Thus competition is not 'to strive *against*'; rather, it is 'to strive *with*'. When you strive with someone, you seek to bring out the best in each other through presenting a worthy challenge. You strive for and achieve excellence together. Thus, competition in sport is *'a mutually acceptable quest for excellence through challenge'*.[22] It becomes clear that far from being mutually exclusive, competition and cooperation are complementary. Competition requires cooperation. By competing with each other we cooperate with each other and so enter a partnership. Each requires the other to bring about the best in each.[23]

Competition inevitably produces winners and losers. But winning isn't everything. There is the effort and excellence achieved by trying to win. As David Shields argues, 'Within true competition, winning and losing are required because these outcomes enable the process. Winning is significant because it allows striving to win.'[24] The opposite of competition is 'decompetition', which according to Shields is 'competition that has devolved into something that is really the antagonist of the original'.[25] In decompetition, winning becomes everything. True competition maintains a balance of seriousness and play, the process and the outcome, the intrinsic and extrinsic. So, according to Shields, 'the true competitor is motivated to pursue values intrinsic to the game, while the decompetitor is motivated by the pursuit of values extrinsic to the game'.[26]

We see both competition and decompetition in sport. When viewed as a challenge to achieve excellence, when it involves others, as a 'mutual quest for excellence',[27] competition leads to friendship rather than enmity; to mutual respect and esteem rather than to mutual disrespect. When competition has harmful effects, these are due largely to a deviation from the ideal of competition, or to circumstances outside the competition itself.

At its clearest, competition in sport is an attempt to secure victory within the appropriate constitutive rules defining the contest and the rules of decency, fair play and sportsmanship. Officials are present not just to police the game by enforcing the rules, but to facilitate the competitive process. Competitors treat each other as partners in the process not as enemy opponents to be destroyed. Competition does involve participation where victory by one is another's defeat. But 'winning and losing are required because these outcomes enable the process'.[28] There is a winner and a loser of the game, but both win in the effort and excellence of trying to win the game. This is different from competition in economics, which may be described as an attempt according to agreed-upon rules to get or keep any valuable thing either to the exclusion of others or in a greater measure than others.

While competition exists in many aspects of society, it is seen most clearly in sports. Sport by definition is agonistic, derived from the Greek *agonia*, which embodied the notions of struggle, toil, hardship and risk in striving for victory. Unfortunately, our contemporary practice of sports often fails to adhere to the Greek ideal. In emphasizing the victory, an external outcome becomes the symbol of success and the importance and the significance of the process is de-emphasized. It is this that leads to claims that competition is bad. And in examining the different kinds of sports, from individual pursuits in nature (skiing) to full contact sports (American football), one can see the progression leading from the emphasis of the process to the outcome, from the emphasis of internal basic benefits to the external scarce benefits, where comparisons are emphasized. The rewards of the outcome become excessive; the competition is blurred by financial gain, where the process itself is perverted in the pursuit of these ends.

Unfortunately, those who object to competition in sports focus only on decompetition, or the deviations that are dramatized in sport. Competitive sports neither have a monopoly on these deviations, nor are these deviations essential to them. Competition when viewed as a mutual challenge to achieve excellence, no matter the field, leads to progress, to respect for others, to friendships, and to excellence. This is the essence of competition.

Conventionalism

Peter F. Hager

Conventionalism is the view that sports, as unique, socially constructed activities, cannot be completely understood or explained without an account of the unwritten norms, customs and rules that guide the conduct of athletes, coaches, officials, administrators and spectators within sporting contexts. Conventionalists contend that this set of informal conventions carries normative as well as descriptive power, and that its normative strength complements that of the formal, constitutive rules of sports.

Historically, it was conventionalism's descriptive value that allowed it to pose a strong challenge to the well-established formalist position in the early 1980s.[29] It was Fred D'Agostino who first clearly framed the formalist/conventionalist debate.[30] Descriptively, D'Agostino argues that 'any particular game has an *ethos* as well as a set of formal rules', and defines the *ethos* as 'those conventions determining how the formal rules of that game are applied in concrete circumstances'.[31] In his view, the *ethos* provides a set of guidelines that helps officials and players recognize which formal rules can be suspended or ignored in a sport, and the conditions under which it is permissible to suspend or ignore them. For example, D'Agostino points out how the *ethos* of professional basketball facilitates an understanding between officials and players regarding what kinds of formally illegal contact are conventionally acceptable, and when more or less contact is permissible.[32] The descriptive strength of this 'non-formalist' position allows it to clearly distinguish between 'permissible' behaviour, which is either formally legal or conventionally acceptable, 'impermissible' behaviour, which is punishable by penalty because it is formally and conventionally unacceptable, and 'unacceptable' behaviour, which constitutes a failure to play the game. D'Agostino contends that formalism presents a weaker account of sport because it lacks the ability to make distinctions between these three types of action.[33]

Although D'Agostino's position appears strong, it suffers from weaknesses that reduce its normative value substantially. Descriptively, this view fails to account for the fact that conventions are rarely assessed as having the same normative value by everyone in a sporting community. The conventional use of specific illegal tactics, for example, is frequently questioned by a minority of community members who would prefer that such rule-breaking be eliminated.[34] The communities' majorities, who represent the conventional status quo as it were, tend to shield such conventional practices from criticism by granting them privileged status as 'part of the game'. Implicit within this attempt to immunize the *ethos* against criticism, Robert L. Simon notes, is an attempt to deny the validity of challenges presented by reformist minorities by simply ignoring their existence.[35] Thus, ironically, conventionalism has a descriptive Achilles heel: its failure to recognize dissenting viewpoints that might help to normatively bolster sporting practices and communities.

Normatively, Simon contends that because conventionalists like D'Agostino have produced neither strong moral arguments for favouring conventions over formal rules in instances in which these conflict nor criteria or methods that could be used to ethically assess conventions, they have failed to demonstrate the primacy of conventions in sporting contexts. Additionally, Simon recognizes that conventionalists have not supplied sporting communities with the kinds of tools they need to determine whether established conventional practices should be jettisoned or changed.[36]

Given the weaknesses noted above, the general consensus has concluded with Simon that D'Agostino's version of conventionalism lacks normative power as an account of sport. However, there are some who believe the position has yet to be presented in its strongest form. More recent articles by William J. Morgan[37] and Bogdan Ciomaga[38] present conventionalist positions designed to more precisely categorize the types of conventions that operate within sporting contexts and more accurately portray how they normatively function to guide the conduct of community members in sporting practices.

Ciomaga contends that philosophers like Simon and Nicholas Dixon[39] are responsible for constructing the normative conventionalist position at which the primary criticisms of the conventionalism in sport are aimed, from the work of D'Agostino and Richard Rorty, respectively. More specifically, he claims that D'Agostino's 'non-formalist' view – the one that many sport philosophers believe is most representative of the conventionalist viewpoint in sport – is actually intended as 'a form of local conventionalism about language', which does not entail the kind of normative conventionalism it is alleged to represent.[40] Because no specific philosopher appears to hold the most widely accepted and criticized rendition of normative conventionalism, Ciomaga concludes that this account is 'to a large extent a construct of its critics', and, as such, is 'illegitimate' and constitutes a 'straw man'.[41]

Ciomaga has developed a conventionalist position grounded in axiomatic geometry to address the aforementioned criticisms.[42] Morgan, on the other hand, accepts the criticisms levelled at D'Agostino's conventions, claiming that the latter ascribes unwarranted normative value to them based solely on their social acceptance, without providing any normative justification for them.[43] However, he argues that the same critique does not apply to 'deep conventions' – conventions that help us determine the normative value of sporting practices by understanding 'what sport demands of us in our efforts to be excellent, to meet its challenges, and why such demands warrant our pursuing them in certain ways rather than others'.[44] Although assessments of Morgan's and Ciomaga's positions are just developing, the introduction of these more robust theories has already enriched the debate regarding conventionalism and its value for sport philosophy and sporting communities.

Cybersport

Dennis Hemphill

Conventional sports are increasingly being digitalized, that is, converted into computer-generated replicas, sometimes for use as training simulators, but more often for arcade and home entertainment. By virtue of their status as simulations, these computerized versions of sport are often considered to be virtual (i.e. unreal), disembodied or merely 'games'. However, the term 'cybersport' has been coined in the sport philosophy literature to mean electronically extended human actions in computer-mediated or -generated sporting worlds.[45]

Contrary to the claim about them being virtual or merely games, sport-themed computer games that involve human immersion and skilful, physical interactivity can be considered sport, at least in the classic formulation of sport as the demonstration of physical prowess in a game.[46] That is, there exists a human interface with a digitally mediated or created sporting world, where bodily movements in one spatial and temporal plane are translated into movements in a computer-generated one. The keyboard, mouse, foot pedal or cycling ergometertype game controller dexterity required to make a difference in determining the outcome of the computer game can be thought of as sufficiently physical to qualify the computer activity as sport.

As for the view that they are disembodied, digital sports can be described differently as a form of electronically extended embodiment. Just like any prosthetic device or telepresence surgical procedure, the technology literally extends the reach of the agent so as to be effective from a distance. In phenomenological terms, as the technology is in(corp)orated, the body recedes into the background as the agent immerses him/herself in the sporting action. However much the body is forgotten when the athlete is immersed in cybersport, or conventional sport for that matter, the body is always there lurking behind the scenes as the foundation of sport experience.

The type of learning that occurs in cybersport can be likened to 'skilful coping' in conventional sport.[47] That is, the preoccupation with rudimentary information and conscious control of discrete body parts and movements (e.g. keyboard, mouse or game controller) is similar to what Hubert L. Dreyfus[48] refers to as 'novice'-level skill acquisition. When moving from the novice stage to the more advanced, 'expert' stage, there is a gradual shift of focus away from conscious decision-making to a more intuitive sense of engagement. In other words, once the fundamental computer-mediated or translated skills and rules about their application are learned, the cyberathlete becomes less reliant on rules, more attentive to situational factors, develops a broader and more refined repertoire of responses, and applies them almost automatically and effortlessly in the particular cybersport.

Cybersport can also be theorized as a MacIntyrean practice community, with its standards of excellence, virtues and the way of life it can sponsor.[49] Online gaming/sporting communities have proliferated in recent times, offering a range of activities eligible to participants ranging in prowess from novice to professional. Knowing no borders, these communities are open to all and are largely self-regulated, with participants often self-selecting cybersport communities based upon achieved skill level and cohesive, effective team dynamics.

The ability to represent one's sporting self in electronic form may enhance opportunities to participate on the basis of ability and interest, sidestepping other embodiment issues (e.g. age, gender or disability) that might otherwise encourage some and discourage others from playing conventional sports. At the same time, cybersport communities develop a range of unwritten rules to penalize forms of play or performance enhancers considered to be cheating or unsporting.

Cybersport can be thought of as alternative, but nonetheless real sport. In one sense, cybersport challenges conventional philosophical understandings of games and sport, and what it means to be an athlete. In another sense, it extends conventional renderings of sport and games in a way that captures the new skills, lived experiences and communities ushered in by the rise of computer technologies.

As computer technology becomes more sophisticated, it will likely expand further the range of activities that can be called sport and cater to an even wider range of abilities and interests.[50] Moreover, advances in technology will permit fuller (visual, auditory and tactile) immersion and interactivity, thereby creating fantastically possible lived and social experiences.

At the same time, cybersport will continue to raise questions, not just about the nature of sport and what constitutes sporting skill, but also the understanding of sporting community and ethics. These questions, some of which are being addressed, focus on moral autonomy and self-regulation, the nature of virtues and online cheating, not to mention the relationship between the cybersport practice communities and commercial organizations. No longer simply considered an underground or alternative activity, cybersport has entered mainstream culture in a way that presents opportunities to refresh our sense-making about sport.

Deception

Adam G. Pfleegor

Deception is an often implemented general concept in many personal and professional endeavours. Although research in fields such as philosophy, language and business has considered deception, there is little consensus on what the concept actually entails.[51] However, applying definitional efforts by philosopher Harry Frankfurt and psychologist Paul Ekman, deception can be considered a deliberate attempt to make another individual believe something false.[52] Considering this, it becomes apparent that games and sport contain many deceptive acts, and furthermore, many skills and strategies of games and sports are built on a foundation of trickery and deception.

In her 1973 work on deception, Kathleen Pearson championed that athletic deceit is too complex to define without further categorization and examination. Pearson presented two distinct categories of deception in sport, strategic deception and definitional deception.[53] For Pearson, strategic deception occurs 'when an athlete deceives his opponent into thinking he will move right when he actually intends to move left – that he will bunt the baseball when he intends to hit a line drive – that he will drive the tennis ball when he actually intends to lob it'.[54] This type of deception is closely aligned to various athletic skills implemented by athletes.[55] Somewhat contrarily, she contends that definitional deception 'occurs when one has contracted to participate in one sort of activity, and then deliberately engages in another sort of activity'.[56] She elaborates these types of acts by exploring the ethical nature of the intentional or 'good' foul in basketball.[57] Until recently, Pearson's dual categorization was the standard for defining deception in the sport philosophy literature.

Using Pearson's pioneer analysis, Adam G. Pfleegor and Danny Rosenberg expanded the discussion on sport deception by creating a more complex taxonomy.[58] Pfleegor and Rosenberg begin by identifying deceptive acts that occur within the contesting periods of competition from those that are preconceived and implemented before or after such contesting periods or during an extended break in the action, such as half-time or a timeout. By focusing on in-contest deceptive acts, they further categorize deception into five distinct categories: constitutive deception, restorative deception, gamesmanship, verbal sport deception and non-athletic physical deception.[59] Constitutive deceptive acts occur within the flowing phase of a contest and involve practices directly associated with constitutive skills as defined by Cesar R. Torres. These skills are central to a game and are meant to be tested.[60] This category closely aligns to Pearson's understanding of strategic deception. Similarly, restorative deception is inseparable from Torres' understanding of restorative skills, those that are used to put a game back on track.[61] These kinds of deceptive skills are implemented when the game or sport is returning to the flowing, contesting phase. Both constitutive and restorative deceptions are skill-based forms of deceit. However, the same does not hold true for the remaining three categories.

Gamesmanship, verbal sport deception and non-athletic physical deception all utilize trickery in different contexts, without involving sport-specific skills, in order to gain a competitive advantage over an opponent. Gamesmanship occurs when the rules of a contest are artfully manipulated, yet not specifically broken.[62] In these instances, opponents are deceived through the use of various tactics (e.g. intimidation), and fall victim to a competitive disadvantage to the deceiving athlete. Verbal sport deception occurs when an athlete employs language to manipulate an opponent into believing something false. This is a common occurrence in many sports, especially American football with the use of quarterback cadence calls.[63] Although, more often than not, no constitutive rule is broken in these instances, there is still deception going on but it does not involve the use of a sport-specific skill. The final category is non-athletic physical deception, which entails an athlete deceiving an indirect contest participant such as a referee, coach or fan. In these instances, a player attempts to fool an indirect participant in order to gain an advantage over an opposing direct participant.[64]

Deception in sport is a complex phenomenon that is only now beginning to receive clarification in sport philosophy literature. Although many classifications and types exist, deception in sport can be considered 'conscious, intentional efforts by athletes to alter the movement expectations of opponents, and sometimes other contest participants, through sport-specific or non-sport-specific skills to acquire a competitive advantage'.[65] These actions can take place both within and outside the contesting periods of competition, and can potentially alter the outcome of the contest at hand in a significant manner. Determining the ethical permissibility of various deceptive practices in sport is a significantly cumbersome task. Although potentially illuminating, this process should not be undertaken until a firm comprehension of the main tenets and features of sport deception are realized. Ultimately, Pfleegor and Rosenberg found that deceptive categories that maintain a significant connection to sport-specific skills and support the proper treatment of opponents (i.e. constitutive deception, restorative deception and verbal sport deception) should be viewed as acceptable practices in contests. Conversely, those forms that lack connections to sport-specific skills and treat opponents as obstacles to surmount (i.e. gamesmanship and non-athletic physical deception) may be unethical due to their dubious nature.

Doping

Angela J. Schneider

Prior to the inception of the World Anti-Doping Agency (WADA) in 1999 and the World Anti-Doping Code (2003), banned substances (e.g. drugs) and practices (i.e. blood doping and gene doping) in organized sport were identified by the International Olympic Committee (IOC). The use of these banned substances and practices is referred to as *doping*. In the philosophy of sport literature, there are categories of arguments to justify the ban on doping: cheating, unfair advantage, harm, perversion of the nature of sport and that doping is unnatural and dehumanizing.

Cheating and unfairness: The moral disapprobation of doping is seen as coming from the fact that doping is cheating and/or unfair. The major problem with this position is that an activity only becomes cheating once there is a rule prohibiting it. Alternative interpretations imply a notion of *unfair advantage* of one competitor over another. However, for this view to justify banning doping, the notion of unfair advantage must be independent of the rules of sport (unlike cheating). If *unfair advantage* turns out to be just rule-breaking, then it cannot do the work that the concept of 'cheating as rule-breaking' could not do. This raises a variety of philosophically interesting questions like 'why should doping be banned?'

Harm: The second most commonly cited argument used to justify the ban on doping is that it is harmful. Doping is viewed as being: 1) harmful to users, 2) harmful to other athletes, 3) harmful to society, and 4) harmful to the sports community. The argument that a ban is justified because doping is harmful to the user assumes that a particular substance or practice is harmful, and that potential users need to be protected from the substance or practice. It can be argued that the desire to protect competent adults from the consequences of their own actions is paternalistic. Paternalism has both acceptable and unacceptable forms. Some would argue that it is inconsistent, and even hypocritical, for the governing bodies of sports to attempt to justify a ban by appealing to the athlete's well-being.

The argument that doping harms other athletes is sometimes called the *coercion* argument. The same liberal tradition that prohibits paternalistic interventions permits interventions designed to prevent harm to others. What must be determined is how great the harm is to other athletes, and how severe the limitation is on personal action.

There is also the argument that doping harms others in society, especially children who see athletes as role models. The argument here is that if children see athletes using drugs to attain sporting success, then other drugs may be seen as a viable means to other ends. The limitation of this argument is that there are many things that are considered appropriate for adults but not for children. Alcohol and cigarettes are obvious examples, but, in North America at least, these substances or activities are not banned for adults simply because they would be bad for children. Why should more be expected from athletes than from other public figures? So it is not even the case that athletes are asked to meet the standards every one else meets, but rather, at least in regard to substance use, they must meet more rigorous standards.

One other group that is potentially harmed by doping is the sports-watching public. These people will be harmed, the argument goes, if they are being cheated – if they expect to see dope-free athletes battling it out in fair competition and are denied this form of entertainment. One could, for example, remove the expectation that athletes be dope-free. Of course, this does not address the question of why people value doping-free competition.

Because any bans that are imposed need to be enforced, there are potential harms caused by the bans themselves. Enforcement of bans requires year-round, random, unannounced, out-of-competition testing. This is an intrusion into the private lives of athletes.

Perversion of sport: Arguments related to the perversion of sport do not operate from moral principles, but from metaphysical ones. What the arguments seek to show is that there is some feature of sport that, if properly understood, would be demonstrably incompatible with doping. Thus, doping should be banned because it is somehow antithetical to the true nature of sport. Part of the problem when dealing with this position is that sport is socially constructed, and there is no obvious reason why it could not be constructed to include doping.

Unnaturalness and dehumanization: It is also argued that doping should be banned because it is either unnatural or dehumanizing. The unnaturalness argument does not get very far for two reasons. The first is that it is not clear what would count as *unnatural*. The second is that it is inconsistent. Some things designated unnatural are permitted (e.g. spiked shoes) while certain natural substances (e.g. testosterone) are banned. The dehumanization argument is interesting but incomplete. There is no agreed-upon conception of what it is to be human. Without this it is difficult to argue why some practices should count as dehumanizing. We also have a problem with consistency. Some practices, such as psycho-doping (the mental manipulation of athletes using the techniques of operant conditioning), are not banned, whereas the reinjection of one's own blood is banned.

While neither of the arguments discussed above are conclusive, a two-tiered approach has been proposed that could justifiably prohibit doping in sport. This approach tries to show: 1) why athletes should not want to dope, and 2) why the community should support doping-free sport.

Sports are practices that provide the opportunity for individuals to acquire and demonstrate skills. The joy of sport comes from acquiring the goods that are internal to sport, the goods that come with the mastery and demonstration of skill. If this joy is the primary reason for participation in sport, then doping is irrelevant to the internal goods of sport. The sporting community is in a position to defend a view of human excellence that can put limits on the pursuit of performance excellence in sport. This community can promote a view of sporting excellence that places it within the context of a complete and excellent human life. Thus, this community is in a position to put limits on its support, limits that come from the desire to promote human excellence across a complete lifetime.

Gene doping has brought new ethical dilemmas to sport. One challenge lies in drawing the line between therapy and enhancement. Because of the relation of sport to society, the language used in the World Anti-Doping Code attempts to deal with the development of genetic technology. In regard to genetic enhancement, even if sport organizations decided that enhancements should not be permitted, if it became standard medical and social practice to enhance memory and mental acuity, or to enhance muscle growth and strength in the elderly, it would be extremely difficult for sport to stand apart in opposition. There are many areas where enhancement is not only accepted but encouraged, valued and highly rewarded (e.g. cosmetic surgery) and even in sport. If it is socially acceptable in some settings, why not in sport?

A number of themes and issues related to genetic therapy and genetic information have yet to be fully discussed in the sport context. The first of these is the ethics of *genetic design*, which involves 'designing' babies for specific (athletic) traits. The second of these issues is *germ-line*, or heritable, therapy.

Embodiment

Irena Martínková

Embodiment (or corporeality) emerged as a central topic in philosophical thinking mainly due to the 'continental' philosophical tradition (i.e. phenomenology), beginning with the work of Edmund Husserl and Martin Heidegger. Until then, in philosophy, the body was usually either overlooked or examined through the lens of scientific description, and conceived as an object. This understanding is represented mainly by ontological dualism, as described especially by René Descartes,[66] who posits mind and body[67] as two separate substances. This generates the problem of the relation between the two substances, in which the body is conceived as mindless and the mind as disembodied. In ontological dualism, the body is conceived as a *res extensa*, a material object, a complicated machine (a sum of small parts or particles) and/or as a carcass or cadaver that functions on mechanical principles. The mind, then, functions, as Gilbert Ryle put it, as 'the Ghost in the Machine'.[68]

Phenomenology, with its critique of the 'objective' approach and its questioning of the nature of first-person human experience,[69] opened a new way of examining human embodiment. To illustrate this new approach, two German words are sometimes used: *Körper* and *Leib*.[70] The word *Körper* depicts the body as an object, while the word *Leib*, often translated as 'the lived body', stands for embodiment as experienced from within human existence. However, *Körper* and *Leib* are not contradictory concepts; rather, *Körper* is correlative to *Leib* as the perceivable body (i.e. the body conceived in terms of how we perceive it).

The lived body is a much more complex and fleeting phenomenon than the objective body, enabling many different conceptions, such as those of Maurice Merleau-Ponty,[71] Jean-Paul Sartre,[72] Michel Henry[73] and others.[74] In brief, the lived body is 'my' own body – 'my' in quotation marks means that my body is not always in my hands, because sometimes I am in the hands of the body. The lived body can be described as the centre of human existence, for it is only through the body that human existence is situated and open to the world. The body enables an individual perspective of the world, orientation in it, perception of things in it, movement within it, and doing things within it (practical endeavours, use of instruments, etc.). According to Mearleau-Ponty, our existence happens between 'a double horizon' (background) of the body and the world as well as 'a double horizon' of the past and the future,[75] which creates a specific human space and time, inhabited and filled with personal projects. In his later work, Merleau-Ponty introduces the notion of 'the Flesh' (*la chair*), which expresses the complex intertwining of the experiencing body and things in the world (the sensate and the sensible).[76]

Putting the lived body at the centre of one's philosophical work, and thinking about existence as embodied, often also gave rise to a rethinking of phenomenology and of philosophical method and knowledge. The body brings opacity into human existence since it involves processes that we cannot directly grasp. Whereas the Cartesian disembodied mind can bring absolute clarity, the embodied subject's experience is always conditioned by (in the hands of) the body, and therefore opaque and ambiguous.[77]

In the philosophy of sport, the topic of embodiment has not received much attention so far, and what there is draws mainly from the work of Heidegger and Merleau-Ponty. While there are a few works that deal directly with the human body,[78] the most recent topics focus rather on related topics, such as human movement,[79] embodied learning,[80] the skilled coping of athletes,[81] embodiment with respect to anorexia[82] and play[83] among others.

In 'analytical' philosophy, we find discussions of 'embodied mind' and 'embodied cognition' taking place mainly within the philosophy of mind and artificial intelligence, and drawing on non-phenomenological philosophers, such as, for example, Immanuel Kant. However, some recent analytical philosophers have also been inspired by research in psychology, psychopathology, neuropsychology, linguistics, cognitive science and artificial intelligence sometimes also by phenomenology and Buddhism.[84]

Although the analytical tradition has a strong presence in the philosophy of sport, the topic of embodiment has not yet been considered to any great extent by analytical philosophers of sport, and sometimes they do not avoid the dualistic language.[85] A more promising direction would seem to include embodiment within a holistic approach to human beings and all their endeavours, including sports.[86]

For the overall enrichment of the topic of embodiment, Dan Zahavi[87] suggests looking into both camps, and recommends a dialogue between both phenomenological and analytical traditions, so that there is no unnecessary overlapping of effort (an example of this dialogue is Shaun Gallagher[88]). Each tradition can profit from the strengths of the other. Phenomenology can benefit from related analytical discussions, from the conceptual clarity and from the problem-oriented approach of analytical philosophy. And analytical philosophy should not ignore the extensive phenomenological discussions of embodiment and related issues such as spatiality, temporality, intersubjectivity, awareness and self-awareness, which are the grounds for all of our experiences.

Enhancement

W.M. Brown

Enhancements in sports are generally considered to be improvements in the normal capacities or functions of athletes. But even with this seemingly straightforward characterization, controversy begins. The term has deep roots in medicine and various forms of biomedical treatments of human diseases and injuries. Many treatments result in improved capacities and can be considered as enhancements. Many forms of preventive medicine, such as vaccination, function to enhance our immune systems. The notion also has its origins deep in human history. The development of literacy, of agriculture, of printing, of industrial capitalism, of computers and other forms of technology, all have functioned to enhance human capacities. In sports, the development of various forms of enhancement has been as pervasive as it has been problematic. Methods of training, diets, equipment, playing venues and the application of the growing knowledge of human biology have all vastly enhanced the ability of athletes to develop their skills and perform with increasing proficiency and competitive zeal.

Discussion of enhancement in sports has largely focused on the use of drugs and biomedical techniques for improving performance in competitive sports, most noticeably in professional sports such as baseball, American football, cycling and in Olympic sports.[89] There has been little discussion of enhancements in sports such as ice climbing, international sailing, ultra marathons or beach volleyball. Perhaps this is a reflection of where the money is.

But the discussion in sports is only part of a larger debate about the prospects of biomedical enhancement of human life in a more pervasive and general way. For those favouring such enhancement (for example, improved immune systems, greater memory capacity, longer lives, more powerful cognitive powers, and increased capacities for empathy, cooperativeness and moral sensibility) we can look forward to a 'posthuman' world where our descendants are scarcely to be considered humans like us. For its detractors, we face a profound loss of our sense of ourselves, of human nature in its best aspects, and a decline in the levels of moral character, even an abandonment of our sense of ourselves as living authentic and rich lives.[90] Clearly this debate has profound implications for the future of sports since the changes that enhancements could bring (*are* bringing) to the lives of everyone will mean that those choosing to play sports will have capabilities far surpassing those of even the best athletes of today.

In no area is the debate more vociferous than in regard to genetic enhancement. Modification of the human genome is already a part of medicine as pharmacogenetics seeks to find medical solutions to diseases by examining individual genetic profiles and developing remedies specific to individual needs. And although there is currently a moratorium on experimentation at altering individual genetic profiles by inserting new genes into cellular DNA to correct for genetic mutations, it will no doubt soon continue with results that will make not only treatments feasible, but enhancements as well. It is a small step to modifying germ-line cells, gametes, in ways that change the genetic profiles of embryos. How will we decide who can play our sports when the candidates were born with enhanced capacities? Indeed, the issue has already risen with athletes born with physiological capacities above the (statistical) norms used by sports associations to test for illicit drug use. It is hardly fair to deny participation to an athlete who is born with a haematocrit level above those induced by the use of exogenous erythropoietin (EPO).[91]

These 'all-purpose' enhancements are also clearly not designed for 'positional' advantages, the competitive edge in sports of someone who uses an enhancement technique not available to others. It is this tactic that is considered by some to be unfair or a form of cheating, though usually only when it violates some rule. How these rules are determined and justified remains controversial. Hypobaric rooms and high-altitude training seem permissible; EPO is not.

Efforts to justify prohibitions of enhancement in sports have faced daunting problems. The claim that they are 'unnatural' would seem to disqualify all medicine and other interventions in human lives. The claim that they cause great harm lacks convincing evidence. The worry that they will conflict with the essence of sport fails to find support from a plausible account of that essence. The insistence that their use is sometimes unfair or a form of cheating, though true, misses the point: why should their use be banned in the first place? The concern that their use undermines the development of character and the sporting virtues of determination, fair play and self-knowledge may be warranted in a culture where their prohibition is inconsistent, poorly justified and erratically enforced. But this, too, begs the question.

A number of conceptual issues bedevil enhancement discussions:

1. How to distinguish biomedical enhancements from medical treatments.
2. How to show that biomedical enhancements (drugs, genetic modifications, etc.) are ethically different from other kinds of enhancements (training techniques, food, equipment, etc.)
3. How ethically to justify the use of enhancements.
4. How to incorporate enhancements into broader social policies to ensure just distribution and safe use.
5. How to develop regulatory mechanisms in a free society to oversee changes in genetic medicine and enhancement technologies both in sports and in the larger population.

As biomedical science develops, and these issues are resolved, the impact on sports will come not from 'doping' scandals but from changes in the general population, which begins to adapt to enhanced 'all-purpose' capabilities affecting health, cognition, sociability and longevity.

Fair Play

Claudia Pawlenka
The concept of 'fair play' is closely related to the concepts of 'sportsmanship' and 'fairness'; for the most part, it initially found use in the language of sports. Fairness, the core of sport ethics and the epitome of morality in sports, is viewed

as its 'innermost daughter'.[92] Terminologically speaking, sports and games provide the predominant frame of reference for the concepts of fair play and sportsmanship whereas the concept of fairness is more neutral and thus rather suitable for application to other realms of life such as economics and politics.[93] Language usage is culturally determined, with the concepts of fair play and sportsmanship[94] dominating the English-speaking world and fairness forming the focus of the discourse on sport ethics in the German-speaking world. Randolph Feezell claims that:

> Some have made extraordinary assertions about the importance of this notion [sportsmanship], as if it is *the* most important virtue in American cultural life. The interpretations of the essence of sportsmanship have included numerous other virtues: self-control, fair play, truthfulness, courage, endurance and so forth.[95]

Historically speaking, the sport ethos of fair play is an English invention of the 19th century. A notion of sports oriented towards character formation and moral education that was subscribed to in English public schools, fair play quickly spread throughout the entire world. Aesthetically pleasing games and the ideal of the English gentleman constitute one of the two roots of the notion of fair play in sports; the other is related to competition and economics, with correct or rather fair behaviour forming the foundation for business relations.[96]

The notion of fair play has changed since it originated in Victorian England.[97] In modern-day commercialized sports, reference is made to 'fair fouls' or so-called 'tacit agreements', which tolerate violations of the rules to a certain extent.[98] Moreover, the concept of fair play has found its way into everyday life, appearing in connection with advertising campaigns addressed to the driving public, for example, where slogans like 'Play fair!' are used. The concept of fairness has established itself in philosophical ethics as well, in particular through John Rawls' theory of 'justice as fairness'.

Although fair play is often described as a fair *disposition* (Latin: *habitus*/Greek: *hexis*), associated with such virtues as equity, reasonableness and propriety, its *subject* is difficult to determine. This is due, in part, to the question concerning the *particularity* of fair play (i.e. the question as to whether the concept holds validity outside the realm of sports or whether it is applicable to other realms of society as well).[99] There is also controversy concerning *the point* at which morality starts to play a role in fair behaviour. Does merely following the rules already constitute moral action or does being 'genuinely fair' start with the spirit of rules?[100] There is also disagreement regarding the question as to who the *addressee* of fair behaviour is. Does the concept of fair play in sports go beyond rules and opposing players to include teammates, spectators, the sport itself or the sportsperson's own body?[101]

In sport ethics as well as ethics at large, the concept of fairness and fair play is closely connected with the concept of *rules* for practices and institutions.[102] And yet, whereas fair play in sports is oriented towards *individual* participants (i.e. towards fair behaviour in practice), the philosophical concept of fairness focuses primarily on the *institutional* framework of such practices (i.e. whether the rules of the practice are themselves fair).[103]

Contrary to common belief, the two notions of fairness, the sports-related one and the ethical one, do not present irreconcilable *contradictions*. On the level of individual ethics, one in fact encounters distinctions that are made between *formal* and *informal* norms of fairness in regard to both concepts. Thus, in both cases, mere compliance (i.e. behaviour that fulfils the letter of the norm), or formal fair play, is distinguished from behaviour guided by the spirit of the rules, or informal fair play, which goes beyond mere compliance.[104] According to John Rawls:

> Usually acting unfairly is not so much the breaking of any particular rule, even if the infraction is difficult to detect (cheating), but taking advantage of loopholes or ambiguities in rules, availing oneself of unexpected or special circumstances which make it impossible to enforce them, insisting that rules be enforced to one's advantage when they should be suspended, and more generally, acting contrary to the intention of a practice. It is for this reason that one speaks of the sense of fair play: acting fairly requires more than simply being able to follow rules; what is fair must often be felt, or perceived, one wants to say.[105]

Moreover, besides the so-called 'internal differentiation' of fairness, the Rawlsian notion of the so-called *participatory fairness* in regard to social duties can be transferred to the practice of sports as well. This is so because 'it is usually considered unfair if someone accepts the benefits of a practice but refuses to do his part in maintaining it'.[106] According to this notion, a footballer who profits from the fact that the other participants comply with the rules and nevertheless commits a foul *acts unfairly in the same way* as a tax evader who enjoys all the advantages of the tax system but refuses to make his or her own contribution to it.

However, fair play in sports does not exhaust itself in the so-called 'free-rider problem'. In other words, when we encounter violations of fair play in sports, we do not automatically think of 'free-riders' or instances of parasitic behaviour as purely 'process-oriented' (*trying activities*). For unfair actions in sports are not only process-oriented (focused on *trying*), but are also goal-oriented (*achieving activities*)[107] (i.e. they are unfair in regard to the outcome of the competition). Unfair actions that occur in the course of a competition always constitute the attempt to intentionally influence the outcome of the contest to the disadvantage of the opponent and the advantage of oneself. In relationships like those found in competitive sports, *taking advantage of* the opponent is usually intended. Thus, *unfair* actions in competitive sports are not primarily free-rider actions but rather actions that are intended to be deceitful and/or aggressive.[108] By implication, *fair* actions in sports are those that do not illegally impair the opponent's chances of winning and his or her inviolability beyond what is allowed by the rules. Thus a concluding definition of fair play in sports could read as follows:

> In the context of sports competitions, fairness manifests itself in the endeavours of sportspersons to follow the rules consistently and deliberately

(even under difficult conditions) or at least to only violate them rarely and, in the interests of equal opportunity in competition, neither to take improper advantage of the opponent nor to create an improper disadvantage for him or her and to view the opponent not as an enemy but to respect him or her as a person and partner.[109]

Formalism

José Luis Pérez Triviño

The formalist account of sport establishes that the rules, or its formal structure, comprise its very definition. The written rules are those that shape and determine the purpose and the sense of sports. That is, what counts as a valid movement, a correct action in the frame of the sport practice, scoring a goal or committing a foul, is determined and specified by the rules of the sport in question.

Bernard Suits was probably the first author to offer a conception of sport in which the rules play a crucial role.[110] But perhaps a more precise explanation of this conception can be found in the work of William J. Morgan. For him, in formalism 'the various derivative notions of a game are to be defined exclusively in terms of its formal rules. What it means to engage in a game, to count as a legitimate instance of a game, to qualify as a bona fide action of a game, and to win a game is to act in accordance with the appropriate rules of that game.'[111]

While rules are crucial to formalism, different theses about sport can be distinguished within it: 1) an ontological thesis about the nature of the sport, according to which there is no understanding of sport without appealing to its rules; 2) a thesis about the application and interpretation of the rules of sport, which says that judges and referees are limited to applying only the written rules. And if the need to interpret the rules arise, they have to choose the rules' normative sense in strict accordance with the literal meaning of the rules, leaving aside other kinds of interpretation; and 3) an ethical conception about sport in which the idea of respect for the rules of the game prevails. Under this view, the participants have to follow the rules exactly as written when engaged in sport. The justification of this perspective is based on the idea that sports are institutional activities, which are guided by rules, where the correct action is to follow the rules.

In spite of the different formalist approaches in the philosophy of sport, the first one has had particular importance. However, following the paragraph above, it would be simplistic to say that there only exists a unique version of formalism. It would be more accurate to state that its main ideas have been modified as a result of the criticisms the theory has received. In this way we could distinguish between a radical conception and a moderate one. The first is the one that exclusively defines a sport in terms of its formal rules, and the second is the one pointing out that rules must be supplemented with an account of other elements (social context or moral principles) but retains the primacy of the rules.

The main objections that have been directed at formalism are the following. On the one hand, rules cannot provide an account of all the possible cases that could arise in the practice of sport, and consequently there will always be a margin for indeterminacy and, therefore, judges and referees will have some discretion when they face indeterminate or hard cases.[112] And if new rules or types of rules are added to existing ones (whether they are constitutive, regulative or auxiliary), the problem would remain. Indeterminacy is unavoidable.

On the other hand, it has been pointed out that the formalist characterization of sport lacks intuitiveness, because if to participate in sport means only to act in agreement with the rules, every time that a player violated a rule she would be participating in a different game or it would be a defective instance of the game. And this seems odd. Thus, Fred D'Agostino suggests that there is a difference between playing a game and playing fairly.[113] For instance, the player who commits a foul does not stop playing football, although she is playing it defectively.

Finally, the formalist conception of sport overlooks or does not adequately consider that sport practices are not only nourished by the formal rules that establish the basic normative framework, but also by the social conventions of a group and by principles that govern the interpretation of the rules. Those have been the main objections of the theories known as conventionalism and interpretivism, respectively. According to conventionalism, the description of sport should not focus on the rules but rather on the ethos of games: the unofficial system of conventions that determines how the official rules are to be applied in concrete circumstances.[114] The interpretivist account points out that sport should be interpreted taking into consideration elements such as ethical principles,[115] the constitutive abilities or excellences,[116] and internal goods.[117]

But beyond these criticisms, formalism's basic position remains strong: the appeal to rules is unavoidable in identifying the phenomenon of sport, and any rival theory can allude to other components (conventions or principles), but they will not be able to avoid reference to the fundamental role that is played by the rules.

Games

Chad Carlson

Philosophers have found games to be a relatively intriguing and philosophically rich phenomenon, and it has inspired provocative scholarly discussions. Two scholars, in particular, have provided theoretically opposing positions regarding the metaphysics of games. Ludwig Wittgenstein, on the one hand, argued that the category of activities we call games resembles a family. Many family members share similar and overlapping traits, but there are no traits that everyone in the family has. In the same way, many games share certain characteristics, but there is no trait that is present in all games. Some games involve the manipulation of objects, others occur in water, and others require no physical activity, for instance. Wittgenstein argues, then, that in answering questions about the metaphysics of games, we should focus less on defining their essential characteristics and more on determining their similarities and relationships. 'Don't think but look!' he urges when trying to determine what a game is.[118]

Bernard Suits, on the other hand, ardently espoused metaphysical endeavour to find the essence of games. 'Those who are incurably opposed to the construction of definitions,' he proposes, half-jokingly, 'are persons I think of as terminal

Wittgensteinians.'[119] While Suits' definition of games has received some criticism, it also provides the basis for virtually all discussion among sport philosophers regarding their nature. He argues that 'playing a game is the voluntary attempt to overcome unnecessary obstacles'.[120] More thoroughly, he defines games as having four necessary and sufficient conditions. All games, he asserts, are goal-directed activities. Suits calls the most basic description of a game's goal the 'prelusory goal'. This is a 'specific achievable state of affairs', and includes such examples as putting the football in the net, getting to the other end of the swimming pool first or collecting all of the poker chips. However, a game player can achieve these states of affairs in any number of ways. One could put the ball into the net on a football field however one wants – by throwing it in, carrying it in or using a giant slingshot to propel it in – but the game of football specifies, with a few allowances, that one must not use hands or arms when doing so. Thus, Suits' second necessary element of a game refers to the means that are permitted in trying to achieve the prelusory goal. When using permitted means within the game of football to put the ball into the net, one is trying to achieve the other type of game goal, the lusory goal – trying to win the game.

In order to win the game, Suits argues, one must use permitted means to achieve the prelusory goal. And a game player will know the permissible and impermissible means based on a set of proscribed actions stipulated in the rules – Suits' third necessary condition of a game. Rules that define which actions are permissible and impermissible in attempting to attain the prelusory goal are called 'constitutive rules'. These rules explain how to play the game (do not touch the ball with one's hands, and do not let the ball go outside the boundary lines, for instance). These rules make accomplishing the prelusory goal more difficult than it would be in their absence. Suits also recognizes a different set of rules – rules of skill – that describe how to play the game well (use the inside of the foot to pass the ball, keep one's knee over the ball when shooting at the goal, and so on).

Suits' last necessary condition for a game, the lusory attitude, may be the most complex and the most important. He argues that the game-player must adopt a particular attitude, among others, in which he or she willingly accepts the restrictions on permissible means available to achieve the prelusory goal. The lusory attitude separates games from the many other activities that have goals, means and rules. Games are different because game players recognize and accept the gratuitous, and therefore unusual, logic of games.[121] In non-game activities, we strive for the most efficient means and productive goals. In games, however, we go against this standard mindset and knowingly embrace less efficient means and unnecessary goals for the sake of the activity such embracing makes possible. In baseball, the pitcher has to throw to the batter from an elevated mound. In golf, each player must use relatively small metal clubs to hit a ball in the hole. We embrace these unnecessary difficulties in baseball and golf because they help provide challenges that are interesting, uncertain and stimulating.

Accepting the gratuitous logic of game conventions is what makes them so valuable in our lives. Games help us fulfil our human nature as problem solvers. When we encounter problems, we try to solve them. In the absence of problems, we create new ones. Games, therefore, expand our domain of problems to solve.

As such, Suits boldly argues that games are *the ideal human activity*.[122] He believes that game playing constitutes the good life. On this account, games are the most durable non-essential activities – even more so than play activities that are not games. And durability is the key. Well-crafted games have obstacles to overcome or challenges to face that are neither too hard nor too easy, leaving them as just right, interesting and attractive projects to the participant and/or spectator. Other scholars have taken slightly more moderate but no less game-loving positions by asserting different value claims. One way or the other, games, it has been contended, may be among the best ways of displaying human intelligence, distinguishing human abilities from lesser animals, and revealing truths about human cultures.

Gamesmanship

Mark Hamilton

Gamesmanship is a legal but morally questionable method of gaining an advantage by competitors in games or sporting contests. The term originates from Stephen Potter's 1947 satirical book *The Theory and Practice of Gamesmanship*, where he calls it 'The Art of Winning Games Without Actually Cheating'.[123] Gamesmanship is not essentially considered to be cheating because the one who practises it does not actually violate the formal rules of the game. Though gamesmanship may not explicitly be cheating, it uses every lawful though not necessarily ethical means to win a contest. It compromises the integrity and moral commitment to the game by using dubious strategies to better one's position to gain an unwarranted benefit or to secure victory while technically remaining within the constitutive rules of the game. Gamesmanship, considered to be the opposite of sportsmanship, ruthlessly pursues precarious actions by walking right up to the line demarcating cheating but not quite crossing that line. Leslie Howe characterizes it 'as an attempt to win one game by playing another ... [it] is a deliberate strategy of competition ... designed for winning regardless of athletic excellence'.[124] While gamesmanship may not technically violate the written rules of the contest, it uses manoeuvres that threaten the spirit of the rules and as such is generally considered unsporting.

Forms of gamesmanship include, but are not limited to, attempts to gain competitive advantage by 1) an artful manipulation of the rules, 2) withholding information, 3) outright deception, or 4) intimidation.[125] Manipulation of the rules occurs when one looks for obscure loopholes or technicalities in the rules and uses this information for personal advantage. Withholding information may include delaying handing over line-up cards or hiding injury reports from opponents. Outright deception includes stunts like trick plays, stealing signs, faking injuries or verbal bantering. Intentionally breaking the flow of a contest by, for example, sending a ball out of play or feigning ignorance of the game is also an unacceptable form of deception. Throughout his book, Potter describes getting 'inside one's opponent's head' by such ploys as disturbing the opponent's focus by fidgeting, getting the opponent to 'over think' their moves, or disrupting an opponent's attention.[126] He provides the example of an intentional false accusation of cheating against an opponent to unsettle his or her focus.[127] These actions cause opponents to become conscious of something other than the game.

Intimidation includes verbal confrontation or threatening physical violence, both of which might have detrimental psychological consequences. There is also a broad range of serious examples involving interfering with the opponent's emotional preparation by interrupting his or her concentration in an intense moment by calling timeouts to 'ice' a shooter or kicker, by taunting, throwing inside in baseball, firing slapshots at a goalie's head or loading the ice with thugs.[128]

At the higher levels of sport there are psychological strategies of gamesmanship that are arguably part of the accepted regulative approach to the game. This is their justification: 'The opponent who directs a strategy of gamesmanship against a competitor constructs an opportunity for the opponent to fail, but the decisive move, the failure, belongs to the target. If the gamer's behaviour is within the rules, it cannot be unfair, and the competitive failure of the target is not the result of any unfair advantage.'[129] This is so because the target did not successfully meet the psychological element of the contest, which is undoubtedly part of the challenge.

Consider whether an American football receiver running a pattern over the middle who is hit hard by a linebacker will mentally recover from the linebacker's intimidating hit to repeat the pattern. Does the field goal kicker attempting the game-winning kick on the last play of the game withstand the pressure of the defensive team calling a timeout? Can the visiting college free throw shooter withstand the pressure of the screaming home-town crowd? These are all mental challenges that can be considered part of the tests found in these contests and to remove these forms of gamesmanship might alter in undesirable ways the contemporary challenges of these sports.

Forms of gamesmanship that are truly demeaning are always immoral but there may be 'forms of gamesmanship that are compatible with an ideal of sport as a "mutual challenge to achieve excellence"'.[130] The criterion that needs to be applied, then, in attempting to distinguish between appropriate and inappropriate forms of gamesmanship is to determine whether the practice improves both participants or not and whether it contributes to the merit of the challenge.[131] As Howe argues, 'Certain kinds of gamesmanship are indeed wrong because they are athletically self-defeating, as well as morally suspect, whereas others are valuable, possibly even required'[132] if they do not degrade the contestants and if they contribute to the success of the challenge.

Internalism

Francisco Javier López Frías

Internalism is a normative account of sport that was born in part as a response to Marxist analyses of sport. Such leftist theories presented sport as simply mirroring capitalist relations, that is to say, the *external* conditions found in the larger society. In contrast, internalism claims that philosophically relevant features of sport are *internal* to them, enjoying considerable autonomy from other social realms. Thus, internalist philosophers defend the belief that sport can only be correctly analysed by attending to the intrinsic logic that makes it different. In so doing, some have claimed that the philosophy of sport should not even take concepts from other areas of philosophy and apply them to sport but that it should attempt to offer its own particular concepts and theories. For instance, Graham McFee claimed that one cannot 'find concepts or ideas "ready to hand" in *general* philosophy to apply straightforwardly to the philosophy of sport'.[133]

According to Robert L. Simon, internalism is divided into broad internalism and narrow internalism.[134] The latter is mainly composed of formalism while the former is composed of interpretivism. Bernard Suits' classic book *The Grasshopper: Games, Life and Utopia* could be considered to be the first work that proposed a formalist approach. It was conceived as an answer to Ludwig Wittgenstein's claim that there is no definition of the word 'game'. To do so, Suits adopted the methodology of analytic philosophy that emphasized the role played by rules. Following Suits' proposal, formalism claims that to correctly define games and sports it is enough to solely appeal to the rules that constitute them.

Fred D'Agostino's famous essay 'The Ethos of Games'[135] firmly rejected formalism and proposed an anti-formalist approach, which has become known as 'conventionalism'. According to D'Agostino's position, philosophers of sport should not focus on the rules but rather on the ethos of games, understood as an unofficial system of conventions that determines how the official rules are to be applied in concrete circumstances. Thus, contrary to the formalist's emphasis on rules, conventionalism highlights the social nature of sports.

Simon takes conventionalism to be exclusively a type of externalism. However, conventionalism can also be understood within the tenets of internalism since the social conventions that determine the application of the rules of games might also be solely related to the intrinsic nature of sports. In fact, William J. Morgan holds a position that could be defined as an internalist type of conventionalism. In a recent paper, he asserts that there are two different varieties of conventions: coordinating conventions and deep conventions.[136] For Morgan, deep conventions constitute sports' normative inner nature. These conventions have been historically constructed and accepted by practice communities through careful deliberation. On the other hand, coordinating conventions are arbitrary agreements that serve to solve concrete practical problems (they could be grounded in elements external to sports, for instance, economic interests). According to Morgan's interpretation, D'Agostino's ethos is exclusively formed by coordinating conventions. Therefore, he overlooked the relevance of those deep conventions that socially construct sports' logical space from within.

Following conventionalism's emphasis on the social nature of sports, the philosophy of sport reached a turning point in the 1980s when both *After Virtue* written by Alasdair MacIntyre and *Right Actions in Sports: Ethics for Contestants* by Warren P. Fraleigh were published. The influence of such works in the philosophy of sport was twofold. First, the MacIntyrean concept of 'social practice', also used by Fraleigh, deeply influenced the way in which the term 'sport' was conceived. Second, MacIntyre's hermeneutical methodology became a widespread philosophical way of analysing sporting practices. According to hermeneutics, philosophy should not oversimplify the complexity of reality. To do so, it has to meet the following criteria. On the one hand, since there are no timeless concepts, philosophy has to pay attention to the concepts' historical development. On the other hand, philosophy has to avoid overlooking the complexity of sports by picking out some of its features and elevating them to a paradigmatic status.

Since then, the philosophy of sport's main aim has been to infer the best *interpretation* of sports' current key elements in order to articulate a comprehensive *understanding* of such a complex realm. Formalism and conventionalism are too narrow since they reduce sporting practices to either their formal rules or the conventions stipulating how to apply such rules.[137] So, the philosophy of sport moved from the narrow analysis of rules and social conventions to a much wider analysis that encompasses elements such as the constitutive abilities of sports, their internal goods, their models of excellence and their gratuitous logic. As a consequence, it is neither formalism nor conventionalism but interpretivism that is the dominant approach within the philosophy of sport.

It could be claimed that such a widening process is still ongoing.[138] As a consequence, the philosophy of sport is facing a new challenge: the blurring of the limits drawn between internalism and externalism. Since sports are understood as social practices, they are already in permanent relationship with other social practices. Should not they all share some minimum common elements? According to this intrinsic relationship between social practices, some authors like Andy Miah,[139] Scott Kretchmar[140] and J.S. Russell[141] have claimed that internalism should embrace external principles in order to properly deal with the reality of 21st-century sports. Thus, it might well be that the evolution of internalism is pointing to a future beyond the internalism/externalism distinction.

Kinesiology

Gregg Twietmeyer

Kinesiology means the 'study of motion'. In early 21st-century academic circles, however, it has generally been meant and understood as the 'study of physical activity'. Since the 1990s, at least in North America, kinesiology has increasingly become the preferred umbrella term for all of the sub-disciplines that grew out of physical education in the 1960s (e.g. athletic training, exercise science, sport management, sport philosophy, etc.).[142] Today, for example, the most highly regarded PhD-granting programmes in these areas are usually housed in departments or schools of kinesiology.[143]

Several questions arise from this reality. First, a historical question: why and how did this shift occur? Why did the discipline settle on the name kinesiology? Second, an important philosophical question: what does kinesiology *mean*? It may seem an obvious indication of the frivolousness of philosophy to raise this question again. Wasn't it ably answered in the first two sentences of this entry? Nevertheless, such criticism is superficial. As the historical questions have already indicated, the name 'kinesiology' was *chosen* for the field, but on what philosophic grounds? Even if one posits 'the study of physical activity' as the meaning of the term 'kinesiology', that still begs the question what does 'physical activity' mean? Is sport elemental or incidental to the field? What of dance or manual labour for that matter? Furthermore, how should the day-to-day practice of the discipline be understood? Should kinesiology be a broad and diverse field, or a narrow and scientific discipline? Do the sub-disciplines currently under the umbrella of kinesiology really belong together? What principles should guide kinesiology? What principles or interests do all kinesiologists have in common?

Consider the matter this way. Just as the ancient theologians wrestled with the question 'what has Athens to do with Jerusalem?', that is, what if anything has pagan learning to do with Christian faith? Those who study the philosophy of kinesiology must attempt to examine and answer a similar set of questions, related to the relationship between the various sub-disciplines in the field. In other words, the question could be put, for instance, something like this: 'What has biomechanics to do with sport sociology?'[144]

These questions, both the historical and the philosophical, have and have had various answers. Although there is little controversy over which sources are the most worthwhile in trying to understand the history and development of kinesiology, interpretations of that evidence do differ to some degree. Nevertheless, the most unsettled questions remain the philosophical ones. Put bluntly, the philosophic core of kinesiology *is still there for the taking.*

It seems wise, then, in the space that remains, to briefly offer an answer to the questions proposed and then to point readers to the *further readings* listed in the foonotes for this entry, so that they can begin to engage with other voices and evidence. This is vital because an overview, by definition, cannot be comprehensive and the reader is urged to use the resources listed as a jumping-off point rather than a terminus for their investigation.

Here is, in brief, what I have proposed as a proper philosophy of kinesiology. Kinesiology should be understood as a broad discipline that examines physical activity from a variety of perspectives including both scientific and humanistic methodologies. For example, both exercise physiology and sport history belong in kinesiology because kinesiology necessarily depends on all aspects of the human person. The human person is neither a 'meat-based machine' nor a 'mind trapped in a body' but rather an organic whole.[145] It is human beings not mere human bodies that participate in physical activity. In other words, it is human beings not minds that philosophize, or write, or analyse data and it is human beings not bodies that play football, or baseball, or go jogging. The entire person is present whether we are deep in contemplation or, as they say in baseball, 'deep in the count'.

Physical activity should be understood as 'the placeholder term for culturally significant and recreative movement forms. Games, play, sport, exercise, dance (among others) are central to who we are and what we do.'[146] Kinesiologists must remember that it is specific activities (e.g. jogging, swimming, square-dancing, field hockey, etc.) not abstract generalizations that make up the core of the field. 'Human *kinesis* is a function of all aspects of the human person whether those aspects are physiological *or just plain logical*. Kinesiology is neither a pure science nor solely a member of the humanities, but rather a field that necessarily encompasses both.'[147]

While science sheds light on the how and even to some degree the why of physical activity – at least insofar as the answers have some roots in our biological nature – science cannot by definition evaluate the 'experiences of meaning'[148] found in physical activity.[149] To do so is to move into the realm of culture, history, ethics and metaphysics. That is, the realm of the humanities. Similarly, humanists must evaluate, discuss and debate the meaning of physical activity upon a foundation that includes factual claims about the empirical world. The firmest foundation yet devised by human beings for making and testing factual claims about the empirical world is that of the scientific method. In short, both description and evaluation matter. It follows that scientists and humanists in kinesiology need each other.

What, then, is the future of kinesiology? It is dangerous to speculate. It is possible that the field will begin to coalesce behind some form of the 'broad' vision proposed here. Unfortunately, the field presently seems content to drift along in the philosophic wind. If this continues, then I see kinesiologists being guided by an unspoken but nevertheless comprehensive philosophy: an essentially pragmatic, technocratic and utilitarian view of the discipline, where scientific research and health – in the narrow medical sense – are the chief concerns. Should this come to pass, those in the discipline concerned with specificity in principle, and sport in particular, will come under increasing pressure, as concern for 'human experience and human culture' fades in the face of an overriding commitment to 'the abstract, the generalizable and the measurable'.[150] If, in contrast, a broad (inter/multidisciplinary) vision of kinesiology is to succeed, it will require deliberate, consistent and sustained action by the leaders of the field.[151] Some signs of hope exist, but much work remains to be done.

Play

Stephen E. Schmid

Thelonious Monk is quoted as saying 'I don't have a definition of jazz ... You're just supposed to know it when you hear it.' The same might be said about a definition of play. We all know it when we 'see' it, but defining it is notoriously difficult. One reason is that 'play' has metaphorical, colloquial and technical uses and disentangling these (and even deciding what counts as metaphorical, colloquial and technical) is part of the debate surrounding the nature of play.

The general strategy is to define play in contrast to what it is not. The list is lengthy and changes from one thinker to another: play is not work, is not serious, is not real or ordinary life, is not ordered, is neither instrumental nor extrinsic, is not purely physical, is not about what one does, is not reducible or rationally analysable, is not determined, is not coerced, is not a duty, is not unbounded, is not productive, is not certain, or is not miserable.[152] Most thinkers define play in relation to one or more of these (or other) contrasting qualities. One might argue, as Mihály Csíkszentmihályi[153] has, that one can play only if one thinks of one's action in contrast to non-play. From this perspective, play is fundamentally a subjective and relational attitude depending on what one conceives as non-play.

Some analyses of play assert that it is neither necessary nor sufficient for participating in games or sports.[154] One might play independent of games and sports (as do children in a sandpit), or one might participate in a game or sport without playing it in the technical sense (as might be the case for professional athletes). Nonetheless, play is often incorrectly conflated with games and sports. Of course, this very distinction presupposes a conception of play activities that distinguishes the technical conception from games and sports.

Many modern philosophical, sociological and psychological accounts of play note Johan Huizinga's influence. His expansive list of play activities promotes play as cultural, social and psychological identity. In his summary definition, Huizinga states that play is 'a free activity standing quite consciously outside "ordinary" life as being "not serious", but at the same time absorbing the player intensely and utterly'.[155] Despite this definition's relative simplicity, it leads Huizinga, as Bernard Suits observes, 'to find play under nearly every rock in the social landscape'.[156] From animal and child's play to sacred ritual activities, Huizinga conceives of these and other activities as being play whenever participants are 'transported' to another world.[157] Roger Caillois[158] rejects both Huizinga's tendency to relate play with the sacred and his tendency to consider play only in competitive contexts. Most notably, Caillois focuses on the player's attitude in distinguishing different types of play. In the context of games, Caillois emphasizes that '*ludus* proper' occurs when one's striving to overcome a challenge has no other purpose than pleasure or enjoyment for its own sake. This conception of play activity being an end in itself is the dominant conception of play in the philosophy of sport and was influentially advanced in Suits' article 'Words on Play'.

'Autotelicity' is the term used to describe play activities that are ends in themselves. Play is an autotelic activity pursued for intrinsic factors, and these intrinsic factors set these activities apart from extrinsic or instrumental activities. Most who ascribe to autotelicity think it is necessary for play activities, while fewer think it alone is both necessary and sufficient.[159] Stephen E. Schmid[160] identified three conceptions of autotelicity in the literature, which are frequently blended into a single account of play. The Metaphysical Account treats play as an activity that is an end in itself. The Intrinsically Valued Account conceives of play as an intrinsically valuable activity. And the Intrinsic Reasons Account asserts that play is an activity pursued for intrinsic reasons. Schmid argues that the first two, in addition to other conceptual problems, presuppose the motivating reasons of the agent, thus making the Intrinsic Reasons Account foundational. Later, Schmid[161] argues that the Intrinsic Reasons Account should eliminate autotelicity because the concept is incompatible with the dynamic nature of play. Instead, he defers to empirical research about motivation and suggests grounding the 'intrinsic' of Intrinsic Reasons in the innate psychological needs of the agent.

In light of the many distinct ways play exhibits itself, Randolph Feezell[162] advocates a pluralist conception of play. Under this pluralist account, each of five approaches to play needs to be respected when considering a conception of play: play as behaviour or action, play as motive or attitude, play as formal structure, play as meaningful experience and play as an ontologically distinct phenomenon. While recognizing play phenomena as diverse, this account returns to a broad characterization of play akin to Huizinga's.

Outside the philosophical circle, other play theorists have examined the nature and role of play in human development, well-being and survival. One of the most prolific and influential, Brian Sutton-Smith,[163] contrasts play not with work but with depression. Sutton-Smith's analysis of play reveals overlapping themes appearing in ancient and modern 'rhetorics'. While these rhetorics are sources of the ambiguity of play, he finds a coherent theme throughout. Play is a kind of adaptive variability analogous to adaptive variability in evolutionary biology. In effect, play is an imitation or model of evolutionary processes of natural selection.

Rules

John Gleaves

Scholars in the philosophy of sport have long examined game rules both as a subject in itself and as a means to understanding normative behaviour in sport. Rules play an essential role in understanding sport because they define testing and contesting elements of each particular sport. For example, it is because of rules that marathon runners must *run* the 26.2 miles rather than use a bicycle or a car to cover the same distance. In this most basic sense, rules create the challenges that rest at the very heart of athletic contests. But rules also do much more than that. They define the problem but they also perform other functions as well. Rules establish how a sport starts and stops and also explain what to do in the event that a rule is broken. Many sporting institutions have also introduced rules to ensure players maintain decorum or certain moral behaviours. Such rules can range from stipulations over kit to rules that prohibit spitting at an official.

To add conceptual clarity to the range of rules, scholars often point to categories or descriptions of game rules that capture their primary role. The two most commonly used categories are constitutive rules and regulative rules. Both were developed by John Searle to help explain language, but have been successfully applied to game rules.[164] According to Searle, constitutive rules are rules that 'create or define new forms of behaviour, and … have the form: X counts as Y in context C'.[165] An example of a constitutive rule is that a ball passing through a goal counts as one point in the context of football. In general, constitutive rules also include rules that define the boundaries, stipulate permitted actions or indicate what counts as success. In that sense, constitutive rules often define a game's challenges.

A second common category is regulative rules. Regulative rules, although often interpreted differently, are generally rules that support constitutive rules by explaining behaviours that aid in successful occurrences of the game and may only be tacit rules, such as rules of skill,[166] or auxiliary rules that govern the play of the game but are not central to establishing the game, such as those specifying players' eligibility and admission. Other examples of regulative rules include rules that define a punishment for violating a game's rule, such as how many yards a team is punished in American football for having too many players on the field. Often rules governing controversial practices ranging from illicit doping to fighting and verbal abuse are considered regulative rules as such practices have little or no influence on a game's challenges.

However, much debate exists in the literature over game rules as scholars attempt to explain how rules fit within games. Gordon Reddiford argues that constitutive and regulative rules do not create or define new forms of behaviours in games, but rather 'create the possibility of *new descriptions* of behaviour'.[167] Others, including Klaus V. Meier, have pointed out that such efforts to categorize game rules may be flawed since 'it is by no means clear that an absolute dichotomization [between constitutive and regulative rules] may be supported' and that '[regulative] rules are perhaps best viewed as extensions, or as a subset of constitutive rules rather than as indicators of the termination, however temporary, of the "constitutional internalities" of playing the game'.[168] William J. Morgan, in perhaps the most common explanation of game rules, explains that constitutive rules are those 'upon which the very existence of the game is logically dependent', and they are 'to be distinguished from another kind (regulative rules) which regulates antecedently or independently existing forms of behaviour, and to which specific penalties are attached'.[169]

However, some scholars have called into question the entire Searlean-inspired approach to game rules. Fred D'Agostino asserts that the rigid dichotomy between constitutive and regulative rules has indefensible 'Platonistic implications'[170] by formalizing an 'essence' of a game. On the other hand, Chad Carlson and John Gleaves argue that the categorical approach leads to interpreting each game rule as if it only fits into one category when often a single rule can function in a constitutive, regulative or auxiliary role depending on the rule being invoked.[171] Such ambiguity in practice indicates that perhaps categories are useful as descriptions but not indicative of any real or permanent truth about game rules. In that sense, a constitutive rule does not really define a new kind of behaviour but rather acts as a descriptive signpost indicating how a rule functions in a particular instance.

Despite the ongoing debate about game rules, such research has helped clarify games while also informing ethical investigations of sports. Philosophical accounts of sport, including formalism, conventionalism and broad internalism, often rely heavily on basic explanations of game rules. Scholars including Robert L. Simon and Sigmund Loland have used various accounts of game rules to develop normative frameworks for ethical behaviour in sport.[172] Other scholars have applied principles from rules to assist with studying ethical issues ranging from diving in football[173] to doping[174] to officiating.[175] Thus, while debate may continue over the correct description of game rules, their essential role in creating and governing games means that scholars will consistently rely on such investigations as the foundation for deeper inquiry into sport.

Skills

Daniel G. Campos

In general, a skill is an ability to do something well. Skills are thought to be central to sports, especially when these are conceived as activities designed to solve artificial problems or overcome unnecessary obstacles[176] and thus to involve the testing of skills. According to one definition along this vein, skills are 'acquired, intentional and purposeful capacities to negotiate solutions to problematic situations'.[177] In this view, the rules that constitute and regulate a sport 'generate a need for skilful behaviour by erecting artificial barriers that are unlikely to be hurdled in the absence of those capabilities'.[178] Sport thus demands the development of purposeful, cultivated abilities or skills. Moreover, since sports have constitutive and regulative rules, skills can be classified as constitutive – when they are the central abilities required to solve the problem posed by the rules – or restorative – when they are the peripheral abilities required to restore the contest after a rule infraction or some other kind of interruption.[179] This initial characterization is helpful to raise some issues surrounding the notion of skill in sport.

An important issue is whether skills are the only, or even the main, abilities tested in sport. This can be approached, for instance, by asking what is the relationship between, and value of, skills and chance in sport? Against the view that chance – understood as an effect that exceeds an intended action – is central to sport, it has been argued that what determines the outcome of a sporting game is the intentional play of the participants and that not every unintended outcome is the result of chance.[180] Alternatively, it has been argued that what is colloquially referred to as chance or luck by sport practitioners is often the result of a spontaneous interaction of causes, some of which are under skilful control of the players and others that are beyond such control, but that what constitutes good sports playing is the spontaneous, creative use of cultivated skill.[181] Others have argued that when the most skilful performance does not prevail there is not necessarily a failure in a sporting contest. Rather, other qualities such as nerve and courage can sometimes overcome skill, and poor execution of a few specific skills can result in the failure of the more skilful performance overall.[182] The case of poor execution still makes skill the central feature of a sporting context. The case of nerve and courage, however, suggests that sport may test qualities other than skill. It should be observed, nonetheless, that this rests on an understanding of skill as purely physical. However, qualities such as nerve and courage can be understood as the 'minded' or mental aspect of body-minded sporting skill.

This leads to the question of the nature of skill in sport. In light of the structure of sports, the skills used to accomplish their goals are typically labelled as physical. Nonetheless, are they only physical and thus reducible to physicalist scientific-philosophic accounts? Against the view that skills may be reduced to biology, mechanics, chemistry and physiology – for instance, against the view that explanations for skill are exhausted by investigating the neuronal structures and events related to memory[183] – it has been argued that the conscious experience of sportspersons is difficult to identify with the physical events described by mechanics or neurophysiology.[184] This suggests that skills are not reducible to mechanics and neurophysiology either. It may be added that the reductive approach to skill conceives of the player as only body. However, if the sportsperson is conceived as body-mind – as the continuity of psycho-physical processes where the psychical is not reducible to the physical or vice versa – sporting skills must be conceived as body-minded or bodily and mental at once. Under this view, of pragmatist origin, skills are body-minded habits or cultivated psycho-physical capacities that can be activated or enacted in the specific context of sporting tests or contests for specific purposes.[185] Thus mechanical and intellectual processes are continuous with and inseparable from each other in skilful activity. Additionally, it has been argued that sporting skill involves 'knowing how', and this knowledge is not reducible to the propositional knowledge that the reductive, scientific-philosophic approach yields.[186] Presumably, many types of embodied knowledge are involved in sporting skill.[187] Examples may be knowing how to control the ball with the chest in football or knowing how to position one's body and use one's glove to field a difficult ground ball in baseball. The body-mind knows how to do it in ways that are not reducible to propositional knowledge.

The relationship between skill and knowledge is thus a crucial philosophical question. This is not surprising since the very word 'skill' is synonymous with expertise and in fact originates from the late Old English *scele* (knowledge) and from Old Norse *skil* (discernment, knowledge).[188] Sporting skills have been described as tacit or procedural knowledge concerned with performative competences for accomplishing practical goals.[189] A recent investigation reconciles several accounts of the relationship between background, subsidiary or tacit knowledge and conscious attention and deliberation in goal-directed, skilful performance.[190] It argues that the relationship is mediated by intuition, imagination and ideas.[191] Surely, the relation between knowledge, imagination and skilful performance in sport deserves further investigation, and research is ongoing in this and other issues related to skill in sport. While this research will deepen the understanding of skilful behaviour in sport, it is clear that such behaviour constitutes and manifests complex forms of knowledge. It is also clear that skill proficiency, and sportspersons' attempt to accomplish it, lie at the centre of people's attraction to sport.

Sport

Jeff Fry

The worldwide enjoyment of activities heralded as sport by participants and viewers belies underlying difficulties of delineation. What is sport? Etymological considerations are of limited utility in attempting to delimit the contours of sport with precision. The word 'sport' derives from the Anglo-Norman *disport* and Old French *desport*. Uses of the noun *disport* included references to 'diversion from serious duties: relaxation, recreation, entertainment, amusement'. By the 18th and 19th centuries the word 'sport' was applied to 'hunting, shooting and fishing'. By the 19th century the idea of sport involving competitive physical activities was also current.[192]

The origins of sport are obscure, but early sport-like activities were associated with religion.[193] This was manifestly the case in the ancient Olympic Games. Sport has evolved. Allen Guttmann claims that modern sport has recognizable characteristics: 'secularism, equality, rationalization, specialization, bureau-cratization, quantification and the quest for records'.[194] Administrators of modern sport sought to distinguish between professional and amateur sport, which were categories tied to class distinctions in Britain.[195] The professional/amateur distinction has now eroded. Conspicuous manifestations of sport today are the quadrennial Olympic Games and football's FIFA World Cup. But there is continuous worldwide consumption of sports today by different means, of which the internet is becoming ever more prominent.

The philosophical literature displays debates waged around the ontology of sport and the sources of value in sport. What Bernard Suits labelled 'the tricky triad' (sport, play and games) has been the subject of lively discussion.[196] Suits understood game playing as crucially involving the acceptance of constitutive rules that demarcated the legitimate means to achieve a goal. As he pithily put it, 'Playing a game is the voluntary attempt to overcome unnecessary obstacles'.[197] While at one time Suits held that all sports are subsumed under games,[198] he later retracted this position in favour of the view that some sports are games (refereed), while other sports are performances (judged).[199] In turn, Klaus V. Meier argued that Suits' performances meet the requirements of games.[200] Regardless of whether all sports are games, philosophers widely accept the view that sports involve tests of physical skills.[201] Games and sports can be classified in a number of ways. An illustrative taxonomy includes the following: 'invasion' games (basketball), 'net' games (badminton), 'wall' games (racquetball), 'fielding/run-scoring' games (baseball) and 'target' games (golf).[202]

Philosophers also disagree over the sources of value in sport. Internalists argue that sport generates values. The formalist version of internalism sees the key to games as rules, which are constitutive of the sport. Not abiding by the rules is tantamount to not playing the game. Broad internalism (a term coined by Robert L. Simon), or interpretivism, maintains the importance of rules, but views sport as also embodying internal norms and principles that go beyond rules and assist in adjudicating conflicts lying outside strict application of the rules. In contrast to internalism, externalism holds that sport is not an independent source of value, but rather absorbs values from its context. An example of externalism is conventionalism, which holds that practices in violation of rules may become part of the game and thus be exhibited in valid instantiations of a sport.[203] In light of differing views on the roles of rules, internalists and externalists disagree, for example, on the nature of cheating.

Sport continues to face a number of practical challenges. Conspicuous examples include the use of performance-enhancing substances, violence and the domination of sport by market forces.[204] Is big-time sport, on balance, a good thing? Some philosophers suggest that the problem lies not in sport itself, but in the corruption of sport.[205] Thus Simon argues that the ideal form of sport, a 'mutual quest for excellence', is morally defensible.[206] On the other hand, Alfie Kohn claims that competitive sport is structurally, and thus inherently, flawed because of its promotion of competition, a zero-sum game with damaging psychological consequences, a natural vector towards cheating, and inefficiencies.[207]

Defenders of sport argue that elite sport raises the profiles of ethnic minorities and thereby challenges dominant cultural values.[208] In a similar way, it is arguably the case that the participation of women in sport at a high level has contributed to challenges to widespread preconceptions about women. Beyond this, and as evidenced by the Paralympic Games, sport today allows for the display of the potential of individuals with disabilities. Thus, sport may be taken to possess liberationist aspects insofar as it allows for the recognition and unleashing of human potential.

The future of sport is no doubt tied to emerging technologies. These will continue to have an impact on training techniques, equipment and, most intimately, athletes themselves. Emerging technologies may further broaden opportunities for participation. On the other hand, some fear that technologies hold the potential for transforming sport into a transhuman activity.

To date, enthusiasm for sport seems to have no saturation point. Some even argue that parallel structures point to some kind of identification of sport with religion.[209] Joan Chandler denies this equation, arguing that sport lacks the central characteristics of religion, such as providing answers to fundamental questions about our origins.[210] But 'religion' is itself a contested notion. Even if sport is not, strictly speaking, religion, the masses are 'religiously' devoted to it.

Sportsmanship

Diana Abad

Sportsmanship, we may say following James Keating,[211] is conduct befitting a person involved in the practice of sport. Thus it requires certain modes of conduct from those involved in sports, from sportspersons. These modes of conduct are directed at other people involved in sport, and hence the notion of sportsmanship is only applicable when at least two sportspersons are involved in its practice, although these two or more sportspersons need not necessarily be involved in a sports contest. Clearly, sportsmanship is a moral notion.

But what exactly sportsmanship is seems to be difficult to explain. In the last few decades, there have been a number of quite disparate attempts to define sportsmanship. For example, the literature refers to sportsmanship as fair play,[212] as generosity,[213] as altruism,[214] as honour,[215] as respect for the game,[216] as play spirit[217] and more. Each of these attempts captures something important about sportsmanship, but the problem is that they never seem to get all there is to it, because they concentrate on one or other feature of sportsmanship and try to reduce the rest of it to that feature. This is misguided. Rather, sportsmanship is not one virtue but a conglomerate of four virtues that tie in with the different elements of sport, that are not reducible to one another and between which a balance needs to be held.

The four virtues, or the four elements, of sportsmanship are derived from the elements of sport. Sport is, first, a rule-governed activity that is, secondly, about honing a skill or achieving excellence, as well as, thirdly, knowing how to play the game and, finally, in competitive sports, about winning.

The elements of sportsmanship tie in with the respective elements of sport and are best considered negatively, that is, by examples of unsporting behaviour. The first sort of unsporting behaviour is gaining an unacceptable advantage by breaking the rules of the game in question, or unfairness, like preventing the ball from hitting the floor by using your foot in volleyball. This ties in with the first element of sport. The second sort is gaining an unacceptable advantage by going against the spirit of the game while adhering to the letter of the rules, or inequity, like going on playing when there is an opposing player down with an injury in football. This sort, like the next, ties in with the third element of sport. The third sort is bad form, like not shaking hands after a match.

The fourth sort of unsporting behaviour can only be found in contests, and it consists of not displaying an adequate will to win, like giving up without an effort. Note that advanced players playing against beginners ought to tone down their efforts so that, while not getting a test of their own excellence, they test that of the other contestants. Note also that, on the one hand, not all contestants may be in a position to actually win, but then they are competing for the best position possible; and, on the other hand, not all sportspersons in a given contest may be in the business of actually competing at all, like runners in a marathon who only want to finish. As long as a serious test of the excellence of the other contestants is given, these actions are not problematic.

Accordingly, the four elements of sportsmanship are fairness, equity, good form and the will to win. However, even though these four elements are all equal elements of sportsmanship, they may conflict. For example, what is fair may be inequitable, as in the football example where one player is down injured and the opposing team do not put the ball out of play. This kind of conflict is contingent; it is not necessarily the case that what is fair is also inequitable. Indeed, most often, fairness and equity are on the same side, as it were.

But there is a second sort of conflict, namely, between good form, fairness and equity on the one hand, and the will to win on the other. Unlike the first sort of conflict, this one is not contingent but systematic in that these elements direct the sportsperson towards conflicting actions. The will to win requires the sportsperson to fight the opponent, while the former three require that no dishonourable means be used in achieving this goal.

So, it is important in being sporting to harmonize these differing tendencies of the four elements. This harmonizing, however, should not be seen as fairness, equity and good form posing a boundary on the will to win, natural though this might seem. This is so because it is just as unsporting to be so honourable as not to fight at all, as it is to fight dishonourably. Hence, a balance needs to be upheld between the four elements of sportsmanship, and this balance is the fifth element.

So, the elements of sportsmanship are fairness, equity, good form, the will to win and the balance held between the first four elements.

Notes

Cheating

1   Randolph M. Feezell, 'On the Wrongness of Cheating and Why Cheaters Can't Play the Game', *Journal of the Philosophy of Sport* 15 (1988): 57–68.
2   Ibid., 60.
3   J.S. Russell, 'Are Rules All an Umpire Has to Work With?', *Journal of Philosophy of Sport* 26 (1999): 27–49; Robert L. Simon, 'Internalism and Internal Values in Sport', *Journal of the Philosophy of Sport* 27 (2000): 1–16; and Cesar R. Torres, 'What Counts as Part of a Game? A Look at Skills', *Journal of the Philosophy of Sport* 27 (2000): 81–92.
4   Warren P. Fraleigh, 'Intentional Rules Violations – One More Time', *Journal of the Philosophy of Sport* 30 (2003): 163.

5   Kathleen M. Pearson, 'Deception, Sportmanship and Ethics', in *Philosophic Inquiry in Sport*, 2nd ed, eds., William J. Morgan and Klaus V. Meier (Champaign, IL: Human Kinetics, 1995), 184.

6   Ibid., 183.

7   Warren P. Fraleigh, *Right Actions in Sport: Ethics for Contestants* (Champaign, IL: Human Kinetics, 1984), 71–81.

8   Claudio M. Tamburrini, *The 'Hand of God'? Essays in the Philosophy of Sports* (Göteborg: Acta Universitatis Gothoburgensis, 2000), 21.

9   Feezell, 'On the Wrongness of Cheating and Why Cheaters Can't Play the Game', 60.

10   Ibid.

11   Ibid.

12   William J. Morgan, 'The Logical Incompatibility Thesis and Rules: A Reconsideration of Formalism as an Account of Games', in *Philosophic Inquiry in Sport*, 2nd ed, eds., William J. Morgan and Klaus V. Meier (Champaign, IL: Human Kinetics, 1995), 57.

13   See Russell, 'Are Rules All an Umpire Has to Work With?', and Simon, 'Internalism and Internal Values in Sport'.

14   Simon, 'Internalism and Internal Values in Sport', 10.

15   Russell, 'Are Rules All an Umpire Has to Work With?', 35.

16   Torres, 'What Counts as Part of a Game? A Look at Skills', 81–92

17   Ibid., 86.

18   Fraleigh, 'Intentional Rules Violations – One More Time', 171–6.

19   Robert L. Simon, 'The Ethics of Strategic Fouling: A Reply to Fraleigh', *Journal of the Philosophy of Sport* 32 (2005): 87–95.

20   William J. Morgan, 'Broad Internalism, Deep Conventions, Moral Entrepreneurs, and Sport', *Journal of the Philosophy of Sport* 39 (2012); 65–100.

Further reading

Oliver Leaman, 'Cheating and Fair Play in Sport', in *Sport and the Humanities: A Collection of Original Essays*, ed., William J. Morgan (Knoxville, TN: Bureau of Educational Research and Service, University of Tennessee, 1981), 25–30.

Sigmund Loland, 'The Varieties of Cheating – Comments on Ethical Analyses in Sport', *Sport and Society* 8 (2005): 11–26.

S.K. Wertz, 'The Varieties of Cheating', *Journal of the Philosophy of Sport* 8 (1981): 19–40.

Competition

21   Alfie Kohn, *No Contest: The Case Against Competition*, rev. ed. (Boston: Houghton Mifflin, 1992).

22   Robert L. Simon, *Fair Play. The Ethics of Sport*, 3rd ed. (Boulder, CO: Westview Press, 2010), 27.

23   David Shields, 'Rethinking Competition', *TrueCompetition.Org*, 14 April, 2010 <http://truecompetition.org/resour ces/rethinking-competition/> (accessed 1 May, 2013).

24   Ibid.

25   Ibid.

26   Ibid.

27   Simon, *Fair Play. The Ethics of Sport*, 27.

28   Shields, 'Rethinking Competition'.

Further reading

Jan Boxill, 'The Ethics of Competition', in *Sports Ethics. An Anthology*, ed., Jan Boxill (Malden, MA, Blackwell, 2003), 107–15.

Scott Kretchmar, 'In Defense of Winning', in *Sports Ethics. An Anthology*, ed., Jan Boxill (Malden, MA, Blackwell, 2003), 130–5.

David L. Shields and Brenda L. Bredemier, *True Competition. A Guide to Pursuing Excellence in Sport and Society* (Champaign, IL: Human Kinetics, 2009).

Conventionalism

29   For examples of formalist views, see Bernard Suits, 'The Elements of Sport', in *The Philosophy of Sport: A Collection of Original Essays*, ed., Robert G. Osterhoudt (Springfield, IL: Charles C. Thomas, 1973), 48–64; Kathleen M. Pearson, 'Deception, Sportsmanship and Ethics', *Quest* 19 (1973): 115–18; Edwin J. Delattre, 'Some Reflections on Success and Failure in Competitive Athletics', *Journal of the Philosophy of Sport* 2 (1975): 133–9; and Warren P. Farleigh, 'Why the Good Foul Is Not Good', *Journal of Physical Education, Recreation and Dance* 53 (1982): 41–2.

30   For examples of other anti-formalist views, see Oliver Leaman, 'Cheating and Fair Play in Sport', in *Philosophic Inquiry in Sport*, eds., William J. Morgan and Klaus V. Meier (Champaign, IL: Human Kinetics, 1988), 277–82; and Craig K. Lehman, 'Can Cheaters Play the Game?', *Journal of the Philosophy of Sport* 8 (1981): 41–6.

31   Fred D'Agostino, 'The Ethos of Games', *Journal of the Philosophy of Sport* 8 (1981): 7.

32   Ibid., 14.

33   Ibid., 15.

34   For a basketball example, see Robert L. Simon, *Fair Play: The Ethics of Sport* 3rd ed., (Boulder, CO: Westview Press, 2010), 49.

35   Ibid.

36   Ibid., 49–50.

37   William J. Morgan, 'Broad Internalism, Deep Conventions, Moral Entrepreneurs, and Sport', *Journal of the Philosophy of Sport* 39 (2012): 65–100.

38   Bogdan Ciomaga, 'Conventionalism Revisited', *Sport, Ethics and Philosophy* 6 (2012): 410–22.

39   See Nicholas Dixon, 'Canadian Figure Skaters, French Judges, and Realism in Sport', *Journal of the Philosophy of Sport* 30 (2003): 103–16.

40   Ciomaga, 'Conventionalism Revisited', 412.

41   Ibid., 411–13.

42   Ibid., 413–20.

43   Morgan, 'Broad Internalism, Deep Conventions, Moral Entrepreneurs, and Sport', 79.

44   Ibid., 72.

Further reading

David Lewis, *Convention: A Philosophical Study* (Oxford: Blackwell, 2002).

William J. Morgan, 'Interpretivism, Conventionalism, and the Ethical Coach', in *The Ethics of Coaching Sport: Moral, Social and Legal Issues*, ed., Robert L. Simon (Boulder, CO: Westview Press, 2013), 61–77.

Robert L. Simon, 'The Ethical Coach: An Interpretivist Account of the Ethics of Coaching', in *The Ethics of Coaching Sport*, ed., Robert L. Simon (Boulder, CO: Westview Press, 2013), 41–59.

Cybersport

45   Dennis Hemphill, 'Cybersport', *Journal of the Philosophy of Sport* 32 (2005): 195–207.

46   See Klaus V. Meier, 'Triad Trickery: Playing With Sport and Games', in *Philosophic Inquiry in Sport*, 2nd ed, eds., William J. Morgan and Klaus V. Meier (Champaign, IL: Human Kinetics, 1995), 16–35; and Bernard Suits, 'The Elements of Sport', in *Philosophic Inquiry in Sport*, 2nd ed, eds. William J. Morgan and Klaus V. Meier (Champaign, IL: Human Kinetics, 1995), 8–15.

47 Gunnar Breivik, 'Skillful Coping in Everyday Life and in Sport: A Critical Examination of the Views of Heidegger and Dreyfus', *Journal of the Philosophy of Sport* 34 (2007): 116–134.

48 Ibid.

49 Alasdair MacIntyre, *After Virtue*, 2nd ed. (Notre Dame, IN: University of Notre Dame Press, 1984).

50 Dennis Hemphill, 'Revisioning Sport Spectatorism', *Journal of the Philosophy of Sport* 22 (1995): 48–60.

Further reading

Tim Crick, 'The Game Body: Toward a Phenomenology of Contemporary Video Gaming', *Games and Culture* 6 (2011): 259–269.

K.K. Kimppa and A. K. Bissett, 'The Ethical Significance of Cheating in Online Computer Games', *International Review of Information Ethics* 4 (2005): 31–38.

Miguel Sicart, *The Ethics of Computer Games* (Cambridge, MA: The MIT Press, 2009).

T.L. Taylor, *Raising the Stakes: E-sports and the Professionalization of Computer Games* (Cambridge, MA: The MIT Press, 2012).

Deception

51 Leslie Boldt-Irons, Corrado Federici and Ernesto Virgulti, eds., *Disguise, Deception, Trompe-l'oeil: Interdisciplinary Perspectives* (New York: Peter Lang, 2009); and Paul Ekman, *Telling Lies: Clues to Deceit in the Marketplace, Politics, and Marriage* (New York: Norton, 1991).

52 Harry G. Frankfurt, *On Bullshit* (Princeton: Princeton University Press, 2005); and Ekman, *Telling Lies: Cues to Deceit in the Marketplace, Politics, and Marriage.*

53 Kathleen Pearson, 'Deception, Sportsmanship and Ethics', *Quest* 19 (1973): 115.

54 Ibid., 115.

55 Ibid., 116.

56 Ibid.

57 Ibid.

58 Adam G. Pfleegor and Danny Rosenberg, 'Deception in Sport: A New Taxonomy of Intra-Lusory Guiles', *Journal of the Philosophy of Sport*, forthcoming.

59 Ibid.

60 Cesar R. Torres, 'What Counts as Part of a Game? A Look at Skills', *Journal of the Philosophy of Sport* 27 (2000): 85.

61 Ibid., 87.

62 Leslie A. Howe, 'Gamesmanship', *Journal of the Philosophy of Sport* 31 (2004): 213.

63 Pfleegor and Rosenberg, 'A New Taxonomy of Intra-Lusory Guiles'.

64 Ibid.

65 Ibid.

Further reading

Warren P. Fraleigh, *Right Actions in Sport: Ethics for Contestants* (Champaign, IL: Human Kinetics, 1984).

Kathleen Pearson, 'Deception, Sportsmanship and Ethics', *Quest* 19 (1973): 115–118.

Adam G. Pfleegor and Danny Rosenberg, 'Deception in Sport: A New Taxonomy of Intra-Lusory Guiles', *Journal of the Philosophy of Sport*, forthcoming.

J.S. Russell, 'Are Rules all an Umpire has to Work With?', *Journal of the Philosophy of Sport* 26 (1999): 27–49.

Cesar R. Torres, 'What Counts as Part of a Game? A Look at Skills', *Journal of the Philosophy of Sport* 27 (2000): 81–92.

Doping

Further reading

W.M. Brown, 'Paternalism, Drugs, and the Nature of Sports', *Journal of the Philosophy of Sport* 11 (1984): 14–22.

Robert L. Simon, 'Good Competition and Drug-Enhanced Performance', *Journal of the Philosophy of Sport* 11 (1984): 6–13.

Angela J. Schneider and Robert B. Butcher, 'Why Olympic Athletes Should Avoid the Use and Seek the Elimination of Performance-Enhancing Substances and Practices in the Olympic Games', *Journal of the Philosophy of Sport* 21 (1994): 64–81.

Embodiment

66 René Descartes, *Meditations on First Philosophy* (Cambridge: Cambridge University Press, 1996).

67 The leading historical analysis of the concepts of body and mind is described in John P. Wright and Paul Potter, eds., *Psyche and Soma* (Oxford: Clarendon Press, 2000).

68 Gilbert Ryle, *The Concept of Mind* (Harmondsworth: Penguin, 1963), 17. See also G.N.A. Vessey, *The Embodied Mind* (London: George Allen and Unwin, 1965).

69 In other words, 'subjectivity', which depicts experience as 'universal personal', should not be confused with subjective experiencing, which means 'my particular perspective'. See more in Irena Martínková and Jim Parry, 'An Introduction to the Phenomenological Study of Sport', *Sport, Ethics and Philosophy*, 5, no. 5 (2011): 185–201.

70 Edmund Husserl, *Ideen zu einer reinen Phänomenologie und phänomenologischen Philosophie. Zweites Buch: Phänomenologische Untersuchungen zur Konstitution* (The Hague: Martinus Nijhoff, 1952). These two concepts are also used beyond phenomenology; see, for example, Henning Eichberg, 'Body, Soma – and Nothing Else? Diversity of Body Semantics', *Sport, Ethics and Philosophy* 3 (2009): 382–407.

71 Maurice Merleau-Ponty, *Phénoménologie de la perception* (Paris: Gallimard, 1945); and idem, *Le Visible et l'Invisible* (Paris: Gallimard, 1964).

72 Jean-Paul Sartre, *L'être et le néant: Essai d'ontologie phénoménologique* (Paris: Gallimard, 1943).

73 Michel Henry, *Incarnation, une philosophie de la chair* (Paris: Seuil, 2000).

74 See, for example, Jan Patocka, *Body, Community, Language, World* (Chicago and La Salle, IL: Carus Publishing Company, 1998); and Bernhard Waldenfels, *Das leibliche Selbst: Vorelsungen zur Phänomenologie des Leibes* (Frankfurt am Main: Suhrkamp, 2000).

75 Merleau-Ponty, *Phénoménologie de la perception*, 117, 277.

76 Merleau-Ponty, *Le Visible et l'Invisible*.

77 Drew Leder, *The Absent Body* (Chicago: The University of Chicago Press, 1990), 36 ff. See also: Klaus V. Meier, 'Embodiment, Sport, and Meaning', in *Philosophic Inquiry in Sport*, eds., William J. Morgan and Klaus V. Meier (Champaign, IL: Human Kinetics, 1988), 96–7.

78 Meier, 'Embodiment, Sport, and Meaning', 93–101; and Calvin O. Schrag, 'The Lived Body as a Phenomenological Datum', in *Philosophic Inquiry in Sport*, eds., William J. Morgan and Klaus V. Meier (Champaign, IL: Human Kinetics, 1988), 109–118.

79 Gunnar Breivik, 'Bodily Movement – The Fundamental Dimensions', *Sport, Ethics and Philosophy* 2 (2008): 337–52; and Irena Martínková, 'Anthropos as Kinanthropos: Heidegger and Patocka on Human Movement', *Sport, Ethics and Philosophy* 5 (2011): 217–30.

80 Øyvind F. Standal and Vegard F. Moe, 'Merleau-Ponty Meets Kretchmar: Sweet Tension of Embodied Learning', *Sport, Ethics and Philosophy*, 5, no. 3 (2011): 256–69.

81 Bryan Hogeveen, 'Skilled Coping and Sport: Promises of Phenomenology', *Sport, Ethics and Philosophy* 5 (2011): 245–55.

82 Anna Hogen, 'Cartesian Bodies and Movement Phenomenology', *Sport, Ethics and Philosophy* 1 (2009): 66–74.

83 Ana Zimmermann and John Morgan. 'The Possibilities and Consequences of Understanding Play as Dialogue', *Sport, Ethics and Philosophy*, 5, no. 1 (2011): 46–62.

84 Francisco Varela, Evan Thompson and Eleanor Rosch, *The Embodied Mind: Cognitive Science and Human Experience* (Cambridge: MIT Press, 1991); George Lakoff and Mark Johnson, *Philosophy in the Flesh: The Embodied Mind and its Challenge to Western Thought* (New York: Basic Book, 1999); Lawrence A. Shapiro, *The Mind Incarnate* (Cambridge, MA: MIT Press, 2004) and *Embodied Cognition* (New York: Routledge, 2011); and Andy Clark, *Supersizing the Mind: Reflections on Embodiment, Action, and Cognitive Extension* (Oxford: Oxford University Press, 2008).

85 Paul Weiss, *Sport: A Philosophic Inquiry* (Carbondale, IL: Southern Illinois University Press, 1969).

86 Scott Kretchmar, *Practical Philosophy of Sport* (Champaign, IL.: Human Kinetics, 1994).

87 Dan Zahavi, 'First-person Thoughts and Embodied Self-awareness: Some Reflections on the Relation between Recent Analytical Philosophy and Phenomenology', *Phenomenology and the Cognitive Sciences* 1 (2002): 7–26.

88 Shaun Gallagher, *How the Body Shapes the Mind* (Oxford, New York: Clarendon Press, 2011).

Further reading

Paco Calvo and Antoni Gomila, eds., *Handbook of Cognitive Science: An Embodied Approach* (London: Elsevier Science, 2008).

Maurice Merleau-Ponty, *Phenomenology of Perception* (London and New York: Routledge, 2004).

Donn Welton, ed., *The Body: Classic and Contemporary Readings* (Malden, MA, Oxford, UK: Blackwell, 1999).

Enhancement

89 The literature, especially journalism, is vast. An excellent review of historical, legal and ethical issues for biomedical enhancement is Maxwell J. Mehlman, *The Price of Perfection: Individualism and Society in the Era of Biomedical Enhancement* (Baltimore: The Johns Hopkins University Press, 2009).

90 A useful collection of essays on human enhancement is Julian Savulescu and Nick Bostrom, eds., *Human Enhancement* (Oxford: Oxford University Press, 2009).

91 Eeva Juvonen, Eero Ikkala, Frej Fyrhquist and Tapani Ruutu, 'Autosomal Dominant Erythrocytosis Caused by Increased Sensitivity to Erythropoietin', *Blood* 78 (1991): 3066–9. The International Ski Federation makes dispensations for high levels of haemoglobin in skiers certified by its experts. See <http://www.fis-ski.com/uk/medical/fisanti-doping/medicalantidoping/dispensation-naturally-h.html> (accessed 4 December, 2012).

Further reading

W.M. Brown, 'The Case for Perfection', *Journal of the Philosophy of Sport* 36 (2009): 127–139.

W.M. Brown, 'As American as Gatorade and Apple Pie: Performance Drugs and Sports', in *Ethics for Today and Tomorrow*, ed., Joram Graf Haber (Sudbury, MA: Jones and Bartlett Publishers, 1997), 324–41.

Allen Buchanan, *Beyond Humanity? The Ethics of Biomedical Enhancement* (Oxford: Oxford University Press, 2011).

Michael Sandel, *The Case Against Perfection: Ethics in the Age of Genetic Engineering* (Cambridge: Harvard University Press, 2007).

Fair Play

92 Hans Lenk, *Erfolg oder Fairness? Leistungssport zwischen Ethik und Technik* (Münster, Hamburg, London: Lit, 2002), 94.

93 Hartmut Gabler, 'Fairness/Fair play', in *Lexikon der Ethik im Sport*, ed., Ommo Grupe and Dietmar Mieth (Schorndorf: Hofmann, 1998), 150.

94 Concerning the topic of fair play, see, for example, Peter McIntosh, *Fair Play. Ethics in Sport and Education* (London: Heinemann, 1979); Robert L. Simon, *Fair Play: The Ethics of Sport*, 2nd ed. (Boulder, CO: Westview Press, 2004); and Sigmund Loland and Mike McNamee, 'Fair Play and the Ethos of Sports: An Eclectical Philosophical Framework', *Journal of the Philosophy of Sport* 27 (2000): 63–80. Concerning the nature of 'sportsmanship' as a 'moral category', see James W. Keating, 'Sportsmanship as a Moral Category', in *Philosophic Inquiry in Sport*, 2nd ed., eds., William J. Morgan and Klaus V. Meier (Champaign, IL: Human Kinetics, 1995), 144–151; and the critical view of Randolph M. Feezell, 'Sportsmanship', in *Philosophic Inquiry in Sport*, 2nd ed., eds., William J. Morgan and Klaus V. Meier (Champaign, IL: Human Kinetics, 1995), 153.

95 Feezell, 'Sportsmanship', 153.

96 Gabler, 'Fairness/Fair play', 150.

97 See Gunter A. Pilz and Wolfgang Wewer, *Erfolg oder Fair play? Sport als Spiegel der Gesellschaft* (München: Copress, 1987); and Allen Guttmann, 'Ursprünge, soziale Basis und Zukunft des Fair play', *Sportwissenschaft* 17 (1987): 9–19.

98 Oliver Leaman, 'Cheating and Fair Play in Sport', *Philosophic Inquiry in Sport*, 2nd ed., eds., William J. Morgan and Klaus V. Meier (Champaign, IL: Human Kinetics, 1995), 193–7; and Fred D'Agostino, 'The Ethos of Games', in *Philosophic Inquiry in Sport*, 2nd ed., eds., William J. Morgan and Klaus V. Meier (Champaign, IL: Human Kinetics, 1995), 42–49.

99 Claudia Pawlenka, 'The Idea of Fairness: A General Ethical Concept or One Particular to Sport Ethics', *Journal of the Philosophy of Sport* 32 (2005): 49–64.

100 Bruno Wischmann, *Die Fairness* (Frankfurt and M. Wien: Limpert, 1962), 41

101 Ludwig Siep, 'Arten und Kriterien der Fairneß im Sport', in *Fairness und Fair play*, 2nd ed., eds., Volker Gerhardt and Manfred Lämmer (St Augustin: Academia, 1995), 87–102.

102 This can be clearly seen in the discussion carried out in the 1980s in the *Journal of the Philosophy of Sport* concerning the logical (and moral) incompatibility thesis between winning and cheating.

103 Claudia Pawlenka, *Ethik, Natur und Doping* (Paderborn: Mentis, 2010), 21.

104 See Loland and McNamee, 'Fair Play and the Ethos of Sports: An Eclectical Philosophical Framework', and Hans Lenk, 'Wettkampf-Fairness, assoziative Moral und strukturelle Dilemma-Situationen', in *Sportethik. Regeln-Fairneß-Doping*, ed., Claudia Pawlenka (Paderborn: mentis, 2004), 119–132.

105 John Rawls, 'Justice as Fairness', *The Philosophical Review* 67 (1958): 80.

106 Ibid.

107 See Bernard Suits, 'Games and Paradox', *Philosophy of Science* 36 (1969): 316–21.

108 See Hartmut Gabler, 'Fairness/Fair play', 150–2 in *Lexikon der Ethik im Sport*, eds., Ommo Grupe and Dietmar Mieth (Schorndorf: Hofmann, 1998a), 26.

109 Ibid., 152.

Further reading

Frans De Wachter, 'Spielregeln und ethische Problematik', in *Aktuelle Probleme der Sportphilosophie*, ed., Hans Lenk (Schorndorf: Karl Hofmann, 1983), 278–294.

Claudia Pawlenka, *Ethik, Natur und Doping* (Paderborn: Mentis, 2010).

Formalism

110 Bernard Suits, 'The Elements of Sport', in *Philosophic Inquiry in Sport*, 2nd ed. eds., William J. Morgan and Klaus V. Meier (Champaign, IL: Human Kinetics, 1995), 8–15.

111 William J. Morgan, 'The Logical Incompatibility Thesis and Rules: A Reconsideration of Formalism as an Account of Games', in *Philosophic Inquiry in Sport*, 2nd ed, eds., William J. Morgan and Klaus V. Meier (Champaign, IL: Human Kinetics), 50–63. Another definition can be found in Fred D'Agostino, 'The Ethos of Games', *Journal of the Philosophy of Sport* 8 (1981): 7–18.

112 Graham McFee, *Sport, Rules, and Values: Philosophical Investigations into the Nature of Sport* (London: Routledge, 2004).

113 D'Agostino, 'The Ethos of Games'.

114 J.S. Russell, 'Are Rules All an Umpire Has to Work With?', *Journal of the Philosophy of Sport* 26 (1999): 27–49.

115 Robert L. Simon, 'Internalism and Internal Values in Sport', *Journal of the Philosophy of Sport* 27 (2000): 1–16.

116 Cesar R. Torres, 'What Counts as Part of a Game? A Look at Skills', *Journal of the Philosophy of Sport* 27 (2000): 81–92.

117 William J. Morgan, *Leftist Theories of Sport: A Critique and Reconstruction* (Chicago: University of Illinois Press, 1994).

Further reading

Graham McFee, 'Fairness, Epistemology, and Rules: A Prolegomenon to a Philosophy of Officiating?', *Journal of the Philosophy of Sport* 38 (2011): 229–53.

Mitchell N. Berman, 'On interpretivism and Formalism in Sports Officiating: From General to Particular Jurisprudence', *Journal of the Philosophy of Sport* 38 (2011): 177–96.

Games

118 Ludwig Wittgenstein, *Philosophical Investigations* (New York: Macmillan, 1953), 33e (section 66).

119 Bernard Suits, 'Words on Play', *Journal of the Philosophy of Sport* 4 (1977): 117.

120 Bernard Suits, *The Grasshopper: Games, Life, and Utopia* (Boston: David R. Godine, 1990), 41.

121 William J. Morgan, *Leftist Theories of Sport: A Critique and Reconstruction* (Urbana: University of Illinois Press, 1994), chap. 5.

122 Suits, *The Grasshopper: Games, Life, and Utopia*, 166–78.

Further reading

Bernard Suits, *The Grasshopper: Games, Life, and Utopia* (Boston: David R. Godine, 1990).

Scott Kretchmar, 'The Normative Heights and Depths of Play', *Journal of the Philosophy of Sport* 34 (2007): 1–12.

Scott Kretchmar, 'Why Do We Care So Much About Mere Games? (And Is This Ethically Defensible?)', *Quest* 57 (2005): 181–91.

Roger Caillois, *Man, Play and Games*, trans. Meyer Barash (Urbana: University of Illinois Press, 2001).

Klaus V. Meier, 'Triad Trickery: Playing with Sports and Games', *Journal of the Philosophy of Sport* 15 (1988): 11–30.

Gamesmanship

123 Stephen Potter, *The Theory and Art of Gamesmanship* (New York: Bantam, 1947), 4.

124 Leslie Howe, 'Gamesmanship', *Journal of the Philosophy of Sport* 31 (2004): 212.

125 Ibid., 213.

126 Potter, *The Theory and Art of Gamesmanship*, 18, 45 and 68.
127 Ibid., 70.
128 Howe, 'Gamesmanship', 214.
129 Ibid.
130 Ibid., 220.
131 Ibid., 221.
132 Ibid., 215.

Further reading

Nicholas Dixon, 'On Winning and Athletic Superiority', *Journal of the Philosophy of Sport* 26 (1999): 10–26.
Mark Hamilton, 'Coaching, Gamesmanship, and Intimidation', in *Ethics in Coaching Sports*, ed., Robert L. Simon (Boulder, CO: Westview Press, 2013), 137–149.
José Luis Pérez Triviño, 'Strategic Intentional Fouls, Spoiling the Game and Gamesmanship', *Sport, Ethics and Philosophy* 6 (2012): 67–77.

Internalism

133 Graham McFee, 'Normativity, Justification, and (MacIntyrean) Practices: Some Thoughts on Methodology for the Philosophy of Sport', *Journal of the Philosophy of Sport* 31 (2004): 15–33.
134 Robert L. Simon, 'Internalism and Internal Values in Sport', *Journal of the Philosophy of Sport* 27 (2000): 1–16.
135 Fred D'Agostino, 'The Ethos of Games', *Journal of the Philosophy of Sport* 8 (1981): 7–18.
136 William J. Morgan, 'Broad Internalism, Deep Conventions, Moral Entrepreneurs, and Sport', *Journal of the Philosophy of Sport* 39 (2012): 65–100.
137 Besides, it is the interpretation we make of the intrinsic features of sports that shows us the right way to both apply the constitutive rules of sports and to criticize and understand the ethos that governs them.
138 Cesar R. Torres has claimed that interpretivism's nature should be furthered by acknowledging the aesthetic dimension of sports. Cesar R. Torres, 'Furthering Interpretivism's Integrity: Bringing Together Ethics and Aesthetics', *Journal of the Philosophy of Sport* 39 (2012): 299–319.
139 Andy Miah, *Genetically Modified Athletes: Biomedical Ethics, Gene Doping and Sport* (London and New York: Routledge, 2004).
140 Scott Kretchmar, 'Competition, Redemption, and Hope', *Journal of the Philosophy of Sport* 39 (2012): 101–116.
141 J.S. Russell, 'Are Rules All an Umpire Has to Work With?', *Journal of the Philosophy of Sport* 26 (1999): 27–49.

Further reading

Nicholas Dixon, 'Canadian Figure Skaters, French Judges, and Realism in Sport', *Journal of the Philosophy of Sport* 30 (2003): 103–116.
Sigmund Loland, 'Normative Theories of Sport: A Critical Review', *Journal of the Philosophy of Sport* 31 (2004): 111–121.
William J. Morgan, 'Moral Antirealism, Internalism, and Sport', *Journal of the Philosophy of Sport* 31 (2004): 161–183.
J.S. Russell, 'Broad Internalism and the Moral Foundation of Sport', in *Ethics in Sport*, ed., William J. Morgan (Champaign, IL: Human Kinetics, 2007), 51–66.

Kinesiology

142 For a nice overview of the development of the separate sub-disciplines in the field, see Richard A. Swanson and John D. Massengale, *The History of Exercise and Sport Science* (Champaign, IL: Human Kinetics, 1996).

143 National Academy of Kinesiology, 'Doctoral Programs', n.d., <http://www.nationalacademyofkinesiology.org/doc toral-programs> (accessed 28 January, 2013). According to the National Academy of Kinesiology, seven out of the top 10 doctoral kinesiology programmes in the United States are called kinesiology or have kinesiology in their name (e.g. Department of Kinesiology and Health, etc.). For specific information on the ranking of kinesiology doctoral programmes see Waneen Spirduso and T. Gilmour Reeve, 'The National Academy of Kinesiology 2010 Review and Evaluation of Doctoral Programs in Kinesiology', *Quest* 63 (2011): 411–440.

144 It is worth noting that this is not only an academic argument. The dislocation of programmes and reorganization of departments is a pressing and contemporary problem. If, for example, sport management is a fundamental part of kinesiology then it is scandalous but nevertheless true that over 20 per cent of sport management programmes are housed in business schools. See Andrea N. Eagleman and Erin L. McNary, 'What are We Teaching our Students? A Descriptive Examination of the Current Status of Undergraduate Sport Management Curricula in the United States', *Sport Management Education Journal* 4 (2010): 1–17.

145 Gregg Twietmeyer, 'Kinesis and the Nature of the Human Person', *Quest* 62 (2010): 135–154.

146 Gregg Twietmeyer, 'What is Kinesiology? Historical and Philosophical Insights', *Quest* 64 (2012): 20.

147 Ibid.

148 Douglas Anderson, 'The Humanity of Movement or "It's not just a Gym Class"', *Quest* 54 (2002): 91.

149 The common materialistic move of denying meaning, or reducing it to the chemical interactions in the brain, is, of course, a *philosophic* move.

150 Gregg Twietmeyer, 'The Four Marks of Holistic Kinesiology', *Quest* 64 (2012): 240.

151 For a specific argument on what this might look like, see ibid., 229–248.

Further reading

Douglas Anderson, 'The Humanity of Movement or "It's not just a Gym Class"', *Quest* 54 (2002): 87–96.

Franklin Henry, 'Physical Education: An Academic Discipline', *Journal of Health, Physical Education, and Recreation* 37 (1964): 32–33, 69.

Scott Kretchmar, 'Jigsaw Puzzles and River Banks: Two Ways of Picturing our Future', *Quest* 57 (2005): 171–177.

Karl Newell, 'Physical Education in Higher Education: Chaos out of Order', *Quest* 42 (1990): 227–242.

Roberta J. Park, 'Of the Greatest Possible Worth: The Research Quarterly in Historical Contexts', *Research Quarterly for Exercise and Sport* 76 (2005): S5–S27.

Play

152 Johan Huizinga's opening chapter of *Homo Ludens: A Study of the Play Element in Culture* (Boston: Beacon Press, 1955) includes many of these contrasts, as does his summary definition. Bernard Suits' 'Words on Play' (*Journal of the Philosophy of Sport* 4 [1977]: 117–131) also includes several of these contrasts, most notably play is not serious and play is not instrumental because of the necessary reallocation of resources toward autotelic activities (121 and 124, respectively).

153 Mihály Csíkszentmihályi, 'Some Paradoxes in the Definition of Play', in *Play as Context: 1979 Proceedings of The Association for The Anthropological Study of Play*, ed., Alyce Taylor Cheska (West Point, NY: Leisure Press, 1981), 14–26.

154 One of the best discussions of this is Klaus V. Meier's clarification of Suits' stance in the former's 'Triad Trickery: Playing With Sports and Games' (*Journal of the Philosophy of Sport* 15 [1988]: 11–30). More recently, Chad Carlson examines the common conflation of play and games ('The "Playing" Field: Attitudes, Activities, and the Conflation of Play and Games', *Journal of the Philosophy of Sport* 38 [2011]: 74–87).

155 Huizinga, *Homo Ludens: A Study of the Play Element in Culture*, 13.

156 Suits, 'Words on Play', 117.

157 Huizinga, *Homo Ludens: A Study of the Play Element in Culture*, 18.

158 Roger Caillois, *Man, Play and Games* (New York: Free Press of Glencoe, 1961).

159 In 'Words on Play', Suits thinks autotelicity is necessary but not sufficient for the definition of play (119). In 'Triad Trickery: Playing with Sports and Games', Meier asserts that autotelicity is both necessary and sufficient for play (25).

160 Stephen E. Schmid, 'Reconsidering Autotelic Play', *Journal of the Philosophy of Sport* 36 (2009): 238–257.

161 Stephen E. Schmid, 'Beyond Autotelic Play', *Journal of the Philosophy of Sport* 38 (2011): 149–166.

162 Randolph Feezell, 'A Pluralist Conception of Play', *Journal of the Philosophy of Sport* 37 (2010): 147–165.

163 Brian Sutton-Smith, *The Ambiguity of Play* (Cambridge, MA: Harvard University Press, 1997).

Further reading

Mihály Csíkszentmihályi, 'Some Paradoxes in the Definition of Play', in *Play as Context: 1979 Proceedings of The Association for The Anthropological Study of Play*, ed., Alyce Taylor Cheska (West Point, NY: Leisure Press, 1981), 14–26.

Klaus V. Meier, 'Triad Trickery: Playing With Sports and Games', *Journal of the Philosophy of Sport*, 15 (1988): 11–30.

Stephen E. Schmid, 'Beyond Autotelic Play', *Journal of the Philosophy of Sport* 38 (2011): 149–166.

Bernard Suits, 'Words on Play', *Journal of the Philosophy of Sport* 4 (1977): 117–131.

Brian Sutton-Smith, *The Ambiguity of Play* (Cambridge, MA: Harvard University Press, 1997).

Rules

164 John R. Searle, *Speech Acts: An Essay in the Philosophy of Language* (London: Cambridge University Press, 1969).

165 Ibid., 35.

166 Bernard Suits, *The Grasshopper: Games, Life, and Utopia* (Peterborough, ON: Broadview Press, 2005).

167 Gordon Reddiford, 'Constitutions, Institutions, and Games', *Journal of the Philosophy of Sport* 12 (1985): 41–51.

168 Klaus V. Meier, 'Restless Sport', *Journal of the Philosophy of Sport* 12 (1985): 69.

169 William J. Morgan, 'The Logical Incompatibility Thesis and Rules: A Reconsideration of Formalism as an Account of Games', in *Philosophic Inquiry in Sport*, eds., William J. Morgan and Klaus V. Meier (Champaign, IL: Human Kinetics, 1998), 51.

170 Fred D'Agostino, 'The Ethos of Games', in *Philosophic Inquiry in Sport*, 2nd ed, eds., William J. Morgan and Klaus V. Meier (Champaign, IL: Human Kinetics, 1995), 45.

171 Chad Carlson and John Gleaves, 'Categorical Shortcomings: Suarez's Handball and Contextual Descriptions of Game Rules', *Journal of the Philosophy of Sport* 38 (2011): 197–211.

172 See Robert L. Simon. *Fair Play: The Ethics of Sport*, 3rd ed. (Boulder, CO: Westview Press, 2010); and Sigmund Loland, *Fair Play in Sport: A Moral Norm System* (London and New York: Routledge, 2002).

173 Cesar R. Torres, 'On Diving: Soccer's Integrity is at Stake', *Goal, The New York Times Soccer Blog*, 17 September, 2009 <http://goal.blogs.nytimes.com/2009/09/17/on-diving-soccers-integrity-is-at-stake/> (accessed 10 February, 2013).

174 Verner Møller, *The Ethics of Doping and Anti-Doping: Redeeming the Soul of Sport* (New York: Routledge, 2010).

175 Graham McFee, *Sport, Rules, and Values: Philosophical Investigations into the Nature of Sport* (London: Routledge, 2004).

Further Reading

Graham McFee, *Sport, Rules, and Values: Philosophical Investigations into the Nature of Sport* (London: Routledge, 2004).

William J. Morgan, 'The Logical Incompatibility Thesis and Rules: A Reconsideration of Formalism as an Account of Games', in *Philosophic Inquiry in Sport*, 2nd ed, eds., William J. Morgan and Klaus V. Meier (Champaign, IL: Human Kinetics, 1995), 50–63.

J.S. Russell, 'Are Rules All an Umpire Has to Work With?', *Journal of the Philosophy of Sport* 26 (1999): 27–49.

Skills

176 Bernard Suits, *The Grasshopper: Games, Life, and Utopia* (Boston: Godine, 1990). Though Suits writes of games, many philosophers conceive of sports as having this characteristic of games as artificial problems.

177 Cesar R. Torres, 'What Counts as Part of a Game? A Look at Skills', *Journal of the Philosophy of Sport* 27 (2000): 84.

178 Ibid.

179 Ibid., 84–89.

180 William J. Morgan, 'Chance, Skill, and Sport: A Critical Comment', *Journal of the Philosophy of Sport* 12 (1985): 62–63.

181 Daniel G. Campos, 'El buen juego y la mala suerte: habilidad, reacción y espontaneidad en el fútbol,' in ¿La pelota no dobla? Ensayos filosóficos en torno al fútbol, eds., Cesar R. Torres and Daniel Campos (Buenos Aires: Libros del Zorzal, 2006), 121–147.

182 Paul Davis, 'A Consideration of the Normative Status of Skill in the Purposive Sports', *Sport, Ethics and Philosophy* 1 (2007): 22–32.

183 Jens Birch, 'Skills and Knowledge – Nothing but Memory?', *Sport, Ethics and Philosophy* (2011): 362–378.

184 Jens Birch, 'A Phenomenal Case for Sport', *Sport, Ethics and Philosophy* 3 (2009): 30–48.

185 For Dewey's account of 'body-mind' see John Dewey, *The Later Works 1925–1953: Volume 1: 1925 Experience and Nature* (Carbondale, IL: Southern Illinois University Press, 1981), especially chapter 7, entitled 'Nature, Life and Body-Mind'.

186 Birch, 'A Phenomenal Case for Sport'.

187 See Jens Birch, 'Skills and Knowledge – Nothing but Memory?', Vegard Moe, 'Understanding the Background Conditions of Skilled Movement in Sport: A Study of Searle's "Background Capacities"', *Sport, Ethics and Philosophy* 1 (2007): 299–324; and Oyvind Standal and Vegard Moe, 'Merleau-Ponty Meets Kretchmar: Sweet Tensions of Embodied Learning', *Sport, Ethics and Philosophy* 5 (2011): 256–269.

188 'Skill', *Oxford Dictionaries* <http://oxforddictionaries.com/definition/english/skill?q=skill> (accessed 28 January, 2013).

189 Torres, 'What Counts as Part of a Game? A Look at Skills', 84. See Peter Arnold, 'Education, Movement, and the Rationality of Practical Knowledge', *Quest* 40 (1988): 115–125; Scott Kretchmar, 'Movement and Play on Higher Education's Contested Terrain', *Quest* 48 (1996): 433–441; and Scott Kretchmar, *Practical Philosophy of Sport* (Champaign, IL: Human Kinetics, 1994).

190 Peter Hopsicker, 'Polanyi's "From-To" Knowing and His Contribution to the Phenomenology of Skilled Motor Behavior'", *Journal of the Philosophy of Sport* 36 (2009): 76–87.

191 Ibid.

Further reading

Peter Hopsicker, 'Polanyi's "From-To" Knowing and His Contribution to the Phenomenology of Skilled Motor Behavior', *Journal of the Philosophy of Sport* 36 (2009): 76–87.

Cesar R. Torres, 'What Counts as Part of a Game? A Look at Skills', *Journal of the Philosophy of Sport* 27 (2000): 81–92.

Sport

192 See 'sport, n.1,' *Oxford English Dictionary Online* (Oxford University Press, March 2013) <http://www. oed.com/view/Entry/187476?rskey=g3F0bv&result=1> (accessed 20 March, 2013 and 'disport, n.' *Oxford English Dictionary Online* (Oxford University Press, March 2013) <http://www.oed.com/view/Entry/5510 1?rskey=9GSqkt&result=1> (accessed 20 March, 2013).

193 William J. Baker, *Sports in the Western World*, rev. ed. (Urbana and Chicago: University of Illinois Press, 1988), 3.

194 Allen Guttmann, 'The Development of Modern Sports', in *Handbook of Sports Studies*, eds. Jay Coakley and Eric Dunning (London, Thousand Oaks, New Delhi: Sage Publications, 2000), 248.

195 See Richard Holt, *Sport and the British: A Modern History* (Oxford: Clarendon Press/ Oxford University Press, 1992), chap. 2.

196 Bernard Suits, 'Tricky Triad: Games, Play, and Sport', *Journal of the Philosophy of Sport* 15 (1988): 1–9.

197 Bernard Suits, 'The Elements of Sport', in *The Philosophy of Sport: A Collection of Original Essays*, ed., Robert G. Osterhoudt (Springfield, IL: Charles C. Thomas, 1973), 55.

198 Suits, 'The Elements of Sport', 48–64.

199 Suits, 'Tricky Triad: Games, Play, and Sport', 1–9.

200 Klaus V. Meier, 'Triad Trickery: Playing With Sport and Games', *Journal of the Philosophy of Sport* 15 (1988): 11–30.

201 See Robert L. Simon. *Fair Play: The Ethics of Sport*, 3rd ed. (Boulder, CO: Westview Press, 2010), 43.

202 Linda L. Griffin, Stephen A. Mitchell and Judith L. Oslin, *Teaching Sport Concepts and Skills: A Tactical Games Approach* (Champaign, IL: Human Kinetics, 1997), 10.

203 Simon. *Fair Play: The Ethics of Sport*, especially chap. 3.

204 See William J. Morgan, *Why Sports Morally Matter* (New York: Routledge, 2006).

205 See Drew Hyland, 'Competition and Friendship', *Journal of the Philosophy of Sport* 5 (1978).

206 Simon, *Fair Play: The Ethics of* Sport, chap. 2.

207 Alfie Kohn, *No Contest: The Case Against Competition*, rev. ed. (Boston: Houghton Mifflin Company, 1986), especially chaps. 4 and 5.

208 Claudio M. Tamburrini, 'Sports, Fascism, and the Market', in *Philosophy of Sport: Critical Readings, Crucial Issues*, ed., M. Andrew Holowchak (Upper Saddle River, N.J.: Prentice Hall, 2002), 367.

209 See Charles S. Prebish, '"Heavenly Father, Divine Goalie": Sport and Religion', in *Sport and Religion*, ed., Shirl J. Hoffman (Champaign, IL: Human Kinetic, 1992), 43–53; and Michael Novak, 'The Natural Religion', in *Sport and Religion*, ed., Shirl J. Hoffman (Champaign, IL: Human Kinetic, 1992), 35–42.

210 Joan M. Chandler, 'Sport is Not Religion', in *Sport and Religion*, ed., Shirl J. Hoffman (Champaign, IL: Human Kinetic), 1992, 55–61. On the specific point about origins see 56–8.

Further Reading

John W. Loy, 'The Nature of Sport: A Definitional Effort', *Quest* 10 (1968): 1–15.

Spencer K. Wertz, 'Is Sport Unique? A Question of Definability', *Journal of the Philosophy of Sport* 22 (1995): 83–93.

Sportsmanship

211 James W. Keating, 'Sportsmanship as a Moral Category', *Ethics* 75 (1964): 25–35.

212 Loland, Sigmund, *Fair Play in Sport: A Moral Norm System* (New York: Routledge, 2002).

213 Keating, 'Sportsmanship as a Moral Category'; and idem, 'The Ethics of Competition and its Relation to Some Moral Problems in Athletics', *Philosophic Exchange* 1 (1973): 5–20.

214 Peter J. Arnold, 'Three Approaches Toward an Understanding of Sportsmanship', *Journal of the Philosophy of Sport* 10 (1983): 61–70.

215 William Lad Sessions, 'Sportsmanship as Honor', *Journal of the Philosophy of Sport* 31 (2004): 47–59.

216 Robert Butcher and Angela J. Schneider, 'Fair Play as Respect for the Game', *Journal of the Philosophy of Sport* 25 (1998): 1–22.

217 Randolph M. Feezell, 'Sportsmanship', *Journal of the Philosophy of Sport* 13 (1986): 1–13.

Further reading

Diana Abad, 'Sportsmanship', *Sport, Ethics and Philosophy* 4 (2010): 27–41.

Randolph M. Feezell, 'Sport: Pursuit of Bodily Excellence or Play? An Examination of Paul Weiss's Account of Sport', *Modern Schoolman* 58 (1981): 257–270.

Randolph M. Feezell, 'On the Wrongness of Cheating and Why Cheaters Can't Play the Game', *Journal of the Philosophy of Sport* 15 (1988): 57–68.

Leslie A. Howe, 'Gamesmanship', *Journal of the Philosophy of Sport* 31 (2004): 212–225.

Part VI

Resources and Careers

22 Resource Guide

Emily Ryall

This guide provides an indication of some of the key texts and resources available in the philosophy of sport. In addition to the bibliographic sections, which are thematically organized, this guide contains information on philosophy of sport associations, journals and different kinds of electronic resources. It is important to highlight that due to the extensive wealth of material available in the philosophy of sport, it is only possible to provide a snapshot of the literature available. Attention is given to the most cited and renowned books. It is also important to highlight that the texts and resources included here cover those published in English since the formal establishment of the discipline in the 1960s.[1]

Books

General Philosophy of Sport

Howard S. Slusher, *Man, Sport and Existence: A Critical Analysis* (Philadelphia: Lea & Febiger, 1967).

Paul Weiss, *Sport. A Philosophic Inquiry* (Carbondale: Southern Illinois University Press, 1969).

Ellen W. Gerber, ed., *Sport and the Body. A Philosophical Symposium* (Philadelphia: Lea & Febiger, 1972).

Robert G. Osterhoudt, ed., *The Philosophy of Sport. A Collection of Original Essays* (Springfield, IL: Thomas, 1973).

Ellen W. Gerber and William J. Morgan, eds., *Sport and the Body. A Philosophical Symposium* 2nd ed. (Philadelphia: Lea & Febiger, 1979).

Hans Lenk, ed., *Topical Problems of Sport* (Schorndorf: Verlag Karl Hofmann, 1983).

Carolyn E. Thomas, *Sport in a Philosophic Context* (Philadelphia: Lea & Febiger, 1983).

Harold J. Vander Zwaag, *Toward a Philosophy of Sport* (Fort Worth: University of Texas Press, 1985).

Pasquale J. Galasso, ed., *Philosophy of Sport and Physical Activity: Issues and Concepts* (Toronto: Canadian Scholars' Press, 1988).

William J. Morgan and Klaus V. Meier, eds., *Philosophic Inquiry in Sport* (Champaign, IL: Human Kinetics, 1988).

Drew A. Hyland, *Philosophy of Sport* (New York: Paragon House Publishers, 1990).

Robert G. Osterhoudt, *Philosophy of Sport: An Overview* (Champaign, IL: Stipes, 1991).

Robert Mechikoff and Steven Estes, *A History and Philosophy of Sport and Physical Education: From the Ancient Greeks to the Present* (Madison, WI: WCB Brown & Benchmark, 1993).

Scott Kretchmar, *Practical Philosophy of Sport* (Champaign, IL: Human Kinetics, 1994).

William J. Morgan and Klaus V. Meier, eds., *Philosophic Inquiry in Sport*, 2nd ed. (Champaign, IL: Human Kinetics, 1995).

Claudio M. Tamburrini, *The 'Hand of God': Essays in the Philosophy of Sports* (Gothenburg: University of Gothenburg Press, 2000).

M. Andrew Holowchak, ed., *Philosophy of Sport: Critical Readings, Crucial Issues* (Upper Saddle River, NJ: Prentice Hall, 2002).

Sheryle Bergmann-Drewe, *Why Sport? An Introduction to the Philosophy of Sport* (Toronto: Thompson Educational Publishing, 2003).

Verner Møller and John Nauright, eds., *The Essence of Sport* (Odense: University Press of Southern Denmark, 2003).

Scott Kretchmar, *Practical Philosophy of Sport and Physical Activity*, 2nd ed. (Champaign, IL: Human Kinetics, 2005).

Heather Sheridan, Leslie A. Howe and Keith Thompson, eds., *Sporting Reflections: Some Philosophical Perspectives* (Oxford: Meyer & Meyer Sport, 2006).

Robert G. Osterhoudt, *Sport as a Form of Human Fulfilment: An Organic Philosophy of Sport History* (Victoria, BC: Trafford, 2006).

Martin A. Bertman, *Philosophy of Sport: Rules and Competitive Action* (Penrith: Humanities EBooks, 2007).

Jim Parry, Simon Robinson, Nick J. Watson and Mark Nesti, eds., *Sport and Spirituality: An Introduction* (London: Routledge, 2007).

Jerzy Kosiewicz, *Sport and Philosophy: From Methodology to Ethics* (Warsaw: Wydawnictwo BK, 2010).

Steven Connor, *A Philosophy of Sport* (London: Reaktion Books, 2011).

Heather L. Reid, *Introduction to the Philosophy of Sport* (Lanham, MD: Rowman and Littlefield, 2012).

Mike J. McNamee and William J. Morgan, eds. *Routledge Handbook of the Philosophy of Sport*, forthcoming.

Emily Ryall, *An Introduction to the Philosophy of Sport*, forthcoming.

Ethics, Values and Fair Play

Fernand Landry and W.A.R. Orban, eds., *Philosophy, Theology and History of Sport and of Physical Activity* (Quebec: Symposia Specialists, 1978).

Peter McIntosh, *Fair Play: Ethics in Sport and Education* (London: Heinemann Educational, 1979).

Warren P. Fraleigh, *Right Actions in Sport: Ethics for Contestants* (Champaign, IL: Human Kinetics, 1984).

Robert L. Simon, *Sports and Social Values* (Englewood Cliffs, NJ: Prentice-Hall, 1985).

John W. Molloy Jr. and Richard C. Adams, eds., *The Spirit of Sport: Essays about Sport and Values* (Bristol, IN: Wyndham Hall Press, 1987).

Ommo Grupe, Christoph Hübenthal and Dietmar Mieth, *Lexikon der Ethik im Sport* (Schorndorf: Verlag Karl Hofmann: Schorndorf, 1988).

Robert L. Simon, *Fair Play: Sports, Values, and Society* (Boulder, CO: Westview Press, 1991).

Spencer K. Wertz, *Talking a Good Game: Inquiries into the Principles of Sport* (Dallas: Southern Methodist University Press, 1991).

Donald G. Jones and Elaine L. Daly, *Sports Ethics in America: A Bibliography, 1970– 1990* (New York: Greenwood Press, 1992).

Mike McNamee and Jim Parry, eds., *Ethics and Sport* (London: E & FN Spon, 1998).

Angela Lumpkin, Sharon Kay Stoll and Jennifer M. Beller, eds. *Sport Ethics: Applications for Fair Play*, 2nd ed. (Boston: WCB/McGraw-Hill, 1999).

Torbjörn Tännsjö and Claudio M. Tamburrini, eds., *Values in Sport: Elitism, Nationalism, Gender Equality and the Scientific Manufacture of Winners* (London: E & FN Spon, 2000).

Sigmund Loland, *Fair Play in Sport: A Moral Norm System* (London: Routledge, 2002).

Jan Boxill, ed., *Sport Ethics: An Anthology* (Oxford: Blackwell, 2003).

Mark Keech and Graham McFee, *Issues and Values in Sport and Leisure Cultures* (Aachen: Meyer and Meyer, 2003).

Robert L. Simon, *Fair Play: The Ethics of Sport*, 2nd ed. (Boulder, CO: Westview Press, 2004).

Graham McFee, *Sport, Rules and Values: Philosophical Investigations into the Nature of Sport* (London: Routledge, 2004).

Sigmund Loland, Berit Skirstad and Ivan Waddington, eds., *Pain and Injury in Sport: Social and Ethical Analysis* (London: Routledge, 2006).

William J. Morgan, *Why Sports Morally Matter* (London: Routledge, 2006).

Debra Shogan, *Sport Ethics in Context* (Toronto: Canadian Scholars' Press, 2007).

William J. Morgan, ed., *Ethics in Sport*, 2nd ed. (Champaign, IL: Human Kinetics, 2007).

Mike McNamee, *Sports, Virtues and Vices: Morality Plays* (London: Routledge, 2008).

Mike McNamee, ed., *Ethics in Sports: A Reader* (London: Routledge, 2010).

Jim Parry, Mark Nesti and Nick Watson, eds., *Theology, Ethics and Transcendence in Sports* (New York: Routledge, 2011).

Sport and Play

Johan Huizinga, *Homo Ludens: A Study of the Play-Element in Culture* (London: Routledge and Kegan Paul, 1949).

Roger Caillois, *Man, Play and Games*, trans. Meyer Barash (New York: Free Press of Glencoe, 1961).

Bernard Suits, *The Grasshopper: Games, Life, and Utopia* (Toronto: University of Toronto Press, 1978).

James W. Keating, *Competition and Playful Activities* (Washington: University Press of America, 1978).

James S. Hans, *The Play of the World* (Amherst, MA: University of Massachusetts Press, 1981).

Drew A. Hyland, *The Question of Play* (Lanham, MD: University Press of America, 1984).

Mihai I. Spariosu, *Dionysus Reborn: Play and the Aesthetic Dimension in Modern Philosophical and Scientific Discourse* (Ithaca, NY: Cornell University Press, 1989).

Randolf Feezell, *Sport, Play and Ethical Reflection* (Urbana, IL: University of Illinois Press, 2004).

Bernard Suits, *The Grasshopper: Games, Life, and Utopia*, with an introduction by Thomas Hurka (Toronto: Broadview, 2005).

Emily Ryall, Wendy Russell and Malcolm MacLean, eds., *The Philosophy of Play* (London: Routledge, 2013).

Sport and the Body²

Betsy C. Postow, ed., *Women, Philosophy and Sport: A Collection of New Essays* (Metuchen, NJ: Scarecrow Press, 1983).

Seymour Kleinman, ed., *Mind and Body: East Meets West* (Champaign: Human Kinetics, 1986).

Andy Miah and Simon B. Eassom, eds., *Sport Technology: History, Philosophy and Policy* (Amsterdam, Boston: JAI, 2002).

Ejgil Jespersen and Mike J. McNamee, eds. *Ethics, Dis/ability and Sports* (London: Routledge, 2009).

Paul Davis and Charlene Weaving, eds., *Philosophical Perspectives on Gender in Sport and Physical Activity* (London, New York: Routledge, 2010).

Henning Eichberg, ed., *Bodily Democracy: Towards a Philosophy of Sport for All* (London: Routledge, 2011).

Irena Martínková and Jim Parry, eds., *Phenomenological Approaches to Sport* (London: Routledge, 2012).

Doping, Genetic Technology and Sports Medicine

Andy Miah, *Genetically Modified Athletes: Biomedical Ethics, Gene Doping and Sport* (London: Routledge, 2004).

Claudio M. Tamburrini and Torbjörn Tännsjö, eds., *Genetic Technology and Sport: Ethical Questions* (London, New York: Routledge, 2005).

Claudio M. Tamburrini and Torbjörn Tännsjö, eds., *The Genetic Design of Winners* (London: Routledge, 2005).

Angela J. Schneider and Theodore Friedmann, eds., *Gene Doping in Sports: The Science and Ethics of Genetically Modified Athletes* (Amsterdam, Boston: Elsevier Academic Press, 2006).

Thomas H. Murray, Karen J. Maschke and Angela Wasunna, *Performance Enhancing Technologies in Sports: Ethical, Conceptual and Scientific Issues* (Baltimore: John Hopkins University Press, 2009).

Verner Møller, Mike McNamee and Paul Dimeo, eds., *Elite Sports, Doping and Public Health* (Odense: University of Southern Denmark Press, 2009).

Mike McNamee and Verner Møller, eds. *Doping and Anti-Doping Policy: Legal, Ethical and Policy Perspectives* (London: Routledge, 2011).

Claudio M. Tamburrini and Torbjörn Tännsjö, eds., *The Ethics of Sports Medicine* (London: Routledge, 2012).

Sport, Art and Aesthetics

Eleanor Metheny, *Connotations of Movement in Sport and Dance* (Dubuque, IA: W.C. Brown, 1965).

Eleanor Metheny, *Movement and Meaning* (New York: McGraw Hill, 1968).

H.T.A. Whiting and D.W. Masterson, ed., *Readings in the Aesthetics of Sport* (London: Lepus Books, 1974).

Benjamin Lowe, *The Beauty of Sport: A Cross-Disciplinary Inquiry* (Englewood Cliffs, NJ: Prentice-Hall, 1977).

David Best, *Philosophy and Human Movement* (London: George Allen & Unwin, 1978).

Hayden Ramsay, *Reclaiming Leisure: Art, Sport and Philosophy* (Basingstoke: Palgrave Macmillan, 2005).

Hans Ulrich Gumbrecht, *In Praise of Athletic Beauty* (Cambridge: Harvard University Press, 2006).

Stephen Mumford, *Watching Sport: Aesthetics, Ethics and Emotion* (Abingdon, Oxon; New York: Routledge, 2012).

Political Philosophy and Sport

John M. Hoberman, *Sport and Political Ideology* (Austin: University of Texas Press, 1984).

William J. Morgan, *Leftist Theories of Sport: A Critique and Reconstruction* (Urbana, IL: University of Illinois Press, 1994).

Adrian Walsh and Richard Giulianotti, eds., *Ethics, Money and Sport: This Sporting Mammon* (London: Routledge, 2007).

Philosophy of Sports, Coaching and Education

Elwood C. Davis and D.M. Miller, *The Philosophic Process in Physical Education*, 2nd ed. (Dubuque, IA: W.C. Brown, 1961).

Randolf W. Webster, *Philosophy of Physical Education* (Dubuque, IA: W.C. Brown, 1965).

Earle F. Zeigler, *Problems in the History and Philosophy of Physical Education and Sport* (Englewood Cliffs, NJ: Prentice-Hall, 1968).

Earle F. Zeigler, *Physical Education and Sport Philosophy* (Englewood Cliffs, NJ: Prentice-Hall, 1977).

Peter J. Arnold, *Meaning in Movement, Sport and Physical Education* (London: Pearson Education, 1977).

Peter C. McIntosh, *Fair Play: Ethics in Sport and Education* (London: Heinemann, 1978).

Robert G. Osterhoudt, *Introduction to the Philosophy of Physical Education and Sport* (Champaign, IL: Stripes, 1978).

Hans Lenk, *The Social Philosophy of Athletics: A Pluralistic and Practice-Orientated Philosophical Analysis of Top Level Amateur Sport* (Champaign, IL: Stipes, 1979).

Joseph C. Mihalich, *Sports and Athletics: Philosophy in Action* (Totowa, NJ: Rowman and Littlefield, 1982).

Earle F. Zeigler, *Ethics and Morality in Sport and Physical Education: an Experimental Approach* (Champaign, IL: Stipes, 1984).

Peter J. Arnold, *Sport, Ethics and Education* (London: Cassell, 1997).

Graham McFee, *Dance, Education and Philosophy* (Oxford: Meyer & Meyer Sport, 1999).

Paulo David, *Human Rights in Youth Sports: A Critical Review of Children's Rights in Competitive Sports* (London: Routledge, 2004).

Scott D. Wurdinger, *Philosophical Issues in Adventure Education*, 3rd ed. (Dubuque, IA: Kendall/Hunt, 1997).

Margaret Whitehead, ed., *Physical Literacy: Throughout the Lifecourse* (London; New York: Routledge, 2010).

Alun Hardman and Carwyn Jones, eds., *The Ethics of Sports Coaching* (London: Routledge, 2010).

Robert A. Mechikoff, *A History and Philosophy of Sport and Physical Education: From Ancient Civilizations to the Modern World*, 6th ed. (Dubuque, IA: McGraw-Hill, 2013).

Robert L. Simon, ed., *The Ethics of Coaching Sports: Moral, Social, and Legal Issues* (Boulder, CO: Westview Press, 2013).

The Olympic Games and Ancient Philosophy

Heather L. Reid, *The Philosophical Athlete* (Durham, NC: Carolina Academic Press, 2002).

John Bale and Mette Krogh Christensen, eds., *Post-Olympism: Questioning Sport in the Twenty-First Century* (Oxford: Berg, 2004).

Daniel A. Dombrowski, *Contemporary Athletics and Ancient Greek Ideals* (Chicago: University of Chicago Press, 2009).

Heather L. Reid and Mike W. Austin, eds., *The Olympics and Philosophy* (Lexington, KY: University Press of Kentucky, 2012).

Mike McNamee and Jim Parry, eds., *Olympic Ethics and Philosophy* (London: Routledge, 2012).

Heather L. Reid, *Athletics and Philosophy in the Ancient World: Contests of Virtue* (London: Routledge, 2012).

Epistemology, Critical Thinking and Research Ethics in Sport

Herbert Haag, *Theoretical Foundation of Sport Science as a Scientific Discipline: Contribution to a Philosophy (Meta-Theory) of Sport Science* (Schorndorf: Hofmann, 1994).

Mike McNamee, ed., *Philosophy and the Sciences of Exercise, Health and Sport: Critical Perspectives on Research Methods* (Abingdon, Oxon: Routledge, 2005).

Graham McFee, *Ethics, Knowledge and Truth in Sports Research: An Epistemology of Sport* (London: Routledge, 2010).

Emily Ryall, *Critical Thinking for Sports Students* (Exeter: Learning Matters, 2010).

Philosophy Applied to Specific Sports

Mike McNamee, ed., *Philosophy, Risk and Adventure Sports* (London: Routledge, 2007).

Jerry L. Walls and Gregory Bassham, eds. *Basketball and Philosophy: Thinking Outside the Paint* (Lexington, KY: University Press of Kentucky, 2007).

Michael W. Austin, ed., *Football and Philosophy: Going Deep* (Lexington, KY: University Press of Kentucky, 2008).

Carl Thomen, *Is It Cricket?: An Ethical Evaluation of Race Quotas in South African Sport* (Saarbrücken: LAP Lambert Academic Publishing, 2009).

Jesús Ilundáin-Agurruza and Michael W. Austin, eds., *Cycling: Philosophy for Everyone: A Philosophical Tour De Force* (Chichester; Malden, MA: Wiley-Blackwell, 2010).

Ted Richards, ed., *Soccer and Philosophy: Beautiful Thoughts on the Beautiful Game* (Chicago: Open Court Press, 2010).

Stephen E. Schmid, ed., *Climbing and Philosophy: Because It's There* (Chichester; Malden, MA: Wiley-Blackwell, 2010).

Andy Wible, ed., *Golf and Philosophy: Lessons from the Links* (Lexington, KY: University Press of Kentucky, 2010).

Patrick Goold, ed., *Sailing: Philosophy for Everyone: Catching the Drift of Why We Sail* (Chichester; Malden, MA: Wiley-Blackwell, 2012).

Journals in the Philosophy of Sport

Journal of the Philosophy of Sport (JPS)

The JPS provides a forum for discussion of philosophical issues – metaphysical, ethical, epistemological, aesthetic or otherwise – arising in sport, games, play, dance, embodiment and other motor-related activities. From 1973 to 2000 it published one issue per year; this increased to two issues per year from 2001 to 2013. From 2014 there will be three issues per year. It is the journal of the International Association for the Philosophy of Sport.

<http://www.tandfonline.com/toc/rjps20/current>

The LA84 Foundation holds free-to-access, electronic issues of the JPS from 1974 to 1976.

<http://www.la84foundation.org/5va/over_frmst.htm>

Sport, Ethics and Philosophy (SEP)

SEP is the journal of the British Philosophy of Sport Association. It publishes high-quality articles from a wide variety of philosophical traditions. The journal is particularly open to essays of applied philosophy that engage with issues or practice, policy and scholarship concerning the nature and values of sports. Fundamental essays in philosophy, as they inform our understanding of sport and related practices, are welcomed as are theoretical submissions from cognate disciplines.

<http://www.tandfonline.com/toc/rsep20/current>

Other Relevant Journals[3]

International Journal of Religion and Sport

The *International Journal of Religion and Sport* is a refereed print publication analysing the interchanges among world religions, religious practice, spirituality and global sport. It invites contributions that take seriously the study of religion

and sport as well as scholarship investigating notions of sport as religious or spiritual practice.
<http://www.glos.ac.uk/research/dse/cssr/Pages/irjs.aspx>

Journal of Sport and Social Issues
The *Journal of Sport and Social Issues* brings together the latest research, discussion and analysis on contemporary sport issues such as race, media, gender, economics, drugs, recruiting, injuries and youth sports. It presents discussion of the impact of sport on social issues from many perspectives, including sociology, economics, gender studies, political science, anthropology, history, media studies, psychology, cultural studies and ethnic studies.
<http://jss.sagepub.com/>

Kinesiology Review (KR)
KR is the official journal of the National Academy of Kinesiology and the American Kinesiology Association. It focuses on scholarly reviews from any and all of the kinesiology sub-disciplines. The review articles in *KR* address important issues and emerging research in all areas of the sport, movement and exercise sciences.
<http://journals.humankinetics.com/kr>

Olympika: The International Journal of Olympic Studies
Published annually, *Olympika: The International Journal of Olympic Studies* is the official peer-reviewed journal of the International Centre for Olympic Studies. It invites scholarly papers, research notes, review articles and other items relating to the historical, sociological, philosophical and anthropological dimensions of the Olympic Games and the Olympic Movement.
<http://www.uwo.ca/olympic/olympika.html>

Proceedings of the Aristotelian Society
Established in 1880, the Aristotelian Society aims to provide for a systematic study of philosophy, its methods and its problems. The proceedings from its public lectures are published three times per year in addition to a supplementary volume.
<http://www.aristoteliansociety.org.uk/the-proceedings/>

Quest
Quest is the official journal of the National Association for Kinesiology in Higher Education and the leading scholarly journal for professionals in kinesiology and physical education today. The journal does not publish original research reports but welcomes manuscripts that are based on, complement or review empirical research related to those professions.
<http://www.tandfonline.com/toc/uqst20/current>

Sport in Society
With 10 issues per year, *Sport in Society* is a multidisciplinary and interdisciplinary publication for academics to discuss the growing relationship of sport to

significant areas of modern life, such as economics, commerce, media and politics.
<http://www.tandfonline.com/toc/fcss20/current>

Philosophy Now
Ten years ago, *Philosophy Now* published a special issue (41, May/June 2003) on philosophy and sport that includes articles on cheating, competition, aesthetics and value.
<http://philosophynow.org/issues/41>

The Philosopher's Magazine
Recently, *The Philosopher's Magazine* published a special issue (58, 3rd Quarter 2012) on the philosophy of sport with articles from several leading scholars in the field.
<http://www.exacteditions.com/read/tpm/3rd-quarter-2012-31531/4/2/>

Philosophy of Sport Associations
International Association for the Philosophy of Sport (IAPS)
IAPS is committed to stimulating, encouraging and promoting research, scholarship and teaching in the philosophy of sport and related practices. To do so, IAPS organizes an annual conference and publishes a newsletter as well as the *Journal of the Philosophy of Sport*, which is widely acknowledged as the most respected medium for communicating contemporary philosophic thought with regard to sport. IAPS members are found all over the world and constitute a growing and vibrant international community of scholars and teachers.
<http://www.iaps.net>

British Philosophy of Sport Association (BPSA)
The BPSA aims to facilitate and promote the study of the philosophy of sport and its related areas, primarily but not exclusively for those living and working in the UK. It organizes an annual conference and is associated with the respected journal *Sport, Ethics and Philosophy*.
<http://www.philosophyofsport.org.uk>

European Association for the Philosophy of Sport (EAPS)
The aim of the EAPS is to promote and disseminate research and scholarship in the philosophy of sport, with respect for and development of different philosophical traditions, and for a variety of aspects of movement cultures (competitive sport, physical education, movement recreation, movement art, etc.). It works closely with the BPSA in order to facilitate conferences and academic scholarship.
<http://www.philosophyofsport.eu>

Other Related Associations
The International Centre for Olympic Studies (ICOS)
The ICOS, established at Western University (London, Ontario, Canada) in 1989, has as its primary mission the generation and dissemination of academic scholarship focused specifically on the sociocultural study of the Olympic Games

and the Olympic Movement. The centre produces *Olympika: The International Journal of Olympic Studies.*
<http://www.uwo.ca/olympic/index.html>

International Convention on Science, Education and Medicine in Sport (ICSEMIS)
The ICSEMIS is the associated Olympic Scientific convention that aims to celebrate sport sciences, exchange sport science, clinical and pedagogic information, promote education about science, education and medicine in sport, encourage multidisciplinary approaches, present cutting-edge research and developments and secure public engagement by young people and ordinary members of our communities. The International Council of Sport Science and Physical Education leads and coordinates, in cooperation with partners, the organization of ICSEMIS.

American Philosophical Association (APA)
The APA was founded in 1900 to promote the exchange of ideas among philosophers, to encourage creative and scholarly activity in philosophy, to facilitate the professional work and teaching of philosophers and to represent philosophy as a discipline. It consists of three Divisions, the Central, Eastern and Pacific, founded in 1900, 1901 and 1924, respectively.
<http://www.apaonline.org/>

The Royal Institute of Philosophy
The Royal Institute of Philosophy is a charity dedicated to the advancement of philosophy in all its branches through the organization and promotion of teaching, discussion and research of all things philosophical. It holds public lectures throughout the year, and publishes the journals *Philosophy* and *Think* in addition to books from specific lecture series.
<http://www.royalinstitutephilosophy.org/>

International Society for the History of Physical Education and Sport (ISHPES)
The ISHPES is the umbrella organization for sports historians all over the world. ISHPES promotes research and teaching in the area of physical education and sport. ISHPES organizes international congresses and seminars and provides information on sports history projects, publications and events through the ISHPES Bulletin.
<http://ishpes.org/home/>

International Association for Women Philosophers (IAPh)
The IAPh is a professional association and network that provides a forum for discussion, interaction and cooperation among women engaged in teaching and research in all aspects of philosophy, with a particular emphasis on feminist philosophy. The IAPh facilitates networking and collaboration for established and aspiring philosophers, in a stimulating atmosphere where participants present their research, with ample opportunity for discussion.
<http://www.iaph-philo.org/>

World Congress of Philosophy
The World Congresses of Philosophy are organized every five years by the International Federation of Philosophical Societies in collaboration with one of its member societies. The Congress aims to provide inquiry across philosophical traditions, reflect upon the tasks and functions of philosophy in the contemporary world, and to emphasize the importance of philosophical reflection for public discourse on global issues affecting humanity.
<http://www.fisp.org/>

Canadian Centre for Ethics in Sport (CCES)
The CCES aims to promote good sporting values in Canada.
<http://www.cces.ca>

Canadian Association for the Advancement of Women in Sport (CAAWS)
The CAAWS aims to provide leadership, education and equitable support, diverse opportunities and positive experiences for girls and women in sport and physical activity.
<http://www.caaws.ca>

World Anti-Doping Agency (WADA)
Established in 1999 as an international independent agency composed of and equally funded by the sport movements and governments of the world, WADA's activities include scientific research, education, development of anti-doping capacities and monitoring of the *World Anti-Doping Code*. WADA works towards a vision of a world where all athletes compete in a doping-free sporting environment.
<http://www.wada-ama.org/>

Electronic Resources

Although these electronic links were current and working at the time of writing, it is inevitable that some links in the near future will change or become obsolete. This is unfortunately one of the problems associated with the current pace of technological change.

Universities Offering Graduate Degrees in the Philosophy of Sport
<http://iaps.net/wp-content/uploads/2012/09/Philosophy-of-Sport-Graduate-Programs.pdf>

Higher Education Academy's Guide to the Philosophy of Sport
<http://www.heacademy.ac.uk/assets/hlst/documents/resources/philosophy_ethics_sport.pdf>

Scott Kretchmar's Introduction to the Philosophy of Sport
<http://iaps.net/wp-content/uploads/2009/01/R.-Scott-Kretchmar- Philosophy-of-Sport.pdf>

Archives at Penn State University
Approval for an archive of material relating to the philosophy of sport was given by the IAPS executive committee in 2012. The proposal moved to create a series of oral history interviews with IAPS pioneers, which is to be stored within the Penn State University Archives. An electronic link giving more information about the resources will be created on the IAPS website.

Email Lists

SPORTPHIL is the email list associated with the International Association for the Philosophy of Sport. It enables groups of academics and support staff to discuss relevant issues, ask questions and share information.
<https://www.jiscmail.ac.uk/cgi-bin/webadmin?A0=sportphil>

PHILSPORT is the email list associated with the British Philosophy of Sport Association. It enables groups of academics and support staff to discuss relevant issues, ask questions and share information.
<https://www.jiscmail.ac.uk/cgi-bin/webadmin?A0=philsport>

Blogs

Philosophy of Sport
The most comprehensive blog dedicated to the philosophy of sport with contributions by many established scholars working in the field.
<http://philosophyandsports.blogspot.co.uk/>

Dr. Ted's Sport and Pop Culture Blog
The blog of Professor Ted Butryn of San Jose State University, California.
<http://tedbutrynsportpopculture.blogspot.co.uk/>

The Sports Ethicist
Blog dedicated to ethical issues in sport, run by Dr Shawn E. Klein of Rockford University, Illinois.
<http://sportsethicist.com>

Sports Technology Ethics
Blog exploring ethical issues concerned with technology in sport run by Dr Rosemary Barnes, Coombes, New South Wales, Australia.
<http://sportstechethics.blogspot.co.uk/>

Virile Games
Blog exploring the links between football and philosophy, written by Simon Craft, a postgraduate of the University of East Anglia, Norwich, United Kingdom.
<http://virilegames.com/>

Dr Emily Ryall's Facebook Page
This facebook page contains information, discussion and links related to the
philosophy of sport and the academic work of Dr Emily Ryall, University of
Gloucestershire, United Kingdom.
<http://www.facebook.com/dremilyryall>

Fit, Feminist and (Almost) Fifty
Written by Tracey Isaacs and Sam Brennan, this blog is a conversational outlet
focusing on their three interests: philosophy, feminism and fitness.
<http://fitisafeministissue.wordpress.com/>

Practical Ethics – Sports
Although this blog by University of Oxford Professor Julian Savulescu covers a
wide range of applied ethical issues, there are many articles within it that are
specifically dedicated to sport.
<http://blog.practicalethics.ox.ac.uk/sports/>

You Kant Be Serious!
Written by Terence Davidson of Victoria University, Wellington, New Zealand,
this blog aims to provide philosophical analysis on controversial issues in sport.
<http://youkantbeserious.com>

Nordic Sports Science Forum – Making Sense of Sports
This website provides commentary and analysis on sports-related issues and
journal articles. It also provides notices of conferences and job vacancies.
<http://idrottsforum.org/>

Dr John Gleaves's Webpage
This is the professional website and blog of Dr John Gleaves, of California State
University Fullerton, who discusses a range of philosophical and sociocultural
issues on sport.
<http://www.johngleaves.com/>

Professor Andy Miah's Webpage – Sport
Professor Miah's website contains an interesting subsection on sport that
provides detailed comment and links on issues primarily concerned with
doping, genetic technology and other bodily enhancement.
<http://www.andymiah.net/category/sport/>

Talking Education and Sport
Dr Richard Bailey, sports sociologist and philosopher, discusses issues related to
sport and education.
<http://talkingeducationandsport.blogspot.co.uk/>

International Network of Humanistic Doping Research
Hosted by Aarhus University, Denmark, this website aims to provide a philosophical analysis of ethical and conceptual issues around doping in sport.
<http://www.doping.au.dk/>

YouTube Videos on Philosophical Issues in Sport
Doping Debate in Sports: Should Athletes Use Drugs?
Dr John Gleaves discusses the impact of doping and performance enhancement on the human condition.
<http://www.youtube.com/watch?v=dihP00AQa1o>

Drawing the Line on Doping in Sport
Professor Verner Møller, Professor Mike McNamee and Dr Alun Hardman discuss issues related to doping in sport.
<http://www.youtube.com/watch?v=mcIoUJ7mqMg>

The Philosophy of Sports Fans
Professor Stephen Mumford considers the philosophy of watching sport.
<http://www.youtube.com/watch?v=M58IEgvWSmA>

Enhancing Performance in Sport – Ethical Considerations
Created by VEA Australia – New Zealand, this short excerpt from a longer video that can be purchased indicates some of the ethical issues around enhancing performance in sport.
<http://www.youtube.com/watch?v=YIA_IAQNmXk>

Olympism: Ethics and Politics
Held at Gresham College, Professor Jim Parry gives a lecture on Olympism, and outlines the history of the Olympics and the ethical issues that it presents. These include: What are the core ideals and values behind a worldwide celebration of sport? Can an approach to life be derived from its values? What implications does this have for the Olympics touching on ethics and politics?
<http://www.youtube.com/watch?v=hiOKfDsy45I>

London 2012: The First Transhuman Games?
Sponsored by PODIUM as part of the London 2012 Olympic educational debate series, this three-part lecture by Professor Andy Miah explores the prospect of enhanced humans competing in elite sports competitions.
<http://www.youtube.com/playlist?list=PLC817D4BBB8E041C0>

Shawn Klein on Sports Ethics
Dr Shawn Klein briefly outlines some ethical issues within sport including performance-enhancing drugs, cheating, economics and the relationship between sport and wider society.
<http://www.youtube.com/watch?v=3_-Xg8aja8w>

Bending the Rules: Gamesmanship in Sport (and Life)
Hosted by Duke University, with panellists of Greg Dale (Professor of Sport Psychology and Ethics, Duke Athletics), Joe Heath (Associate Professor of Philosophy, University of Toronto) and Jan Boxill (Director, Parr Center for Ethics at the University of North Carolina), this filmed seminar examines the notion of gamesmanship.
<http://www.youtube.com/watch?v=eid262zmgic>

Sport: Giving the Red Card to Drugs?
Presented by the Voice of Russia Today, this discussion considers the place of drugs within modern sport. With Andy Parkinson (Chief Executive of Anti-Doping in the United Kingdom) and Julian Savulescu (Director of the Oxford Uehiro Centre for Practical Ethics).
<http://www.youtube.com/watch?v=TqXIRNm2WIA>

Expelled for Trying to Lose in the Olympics (in Chinese with English subtitles)
Commentary and analysis of the incident in the London 2012 Olympics in which four badminton players were expelled for not trying to compete.
<http://www.youtube.com/watch?v=PJI-TzWfhCs>

Ethics of Sport: Training Young Boxers
Commissioned by the University of Leeds and funded by the Welcome Trust, this short film explores some ethical questions surrounding the responsibilities that a father and a coach have towards a teenager who wishes to become an elite amateur boxer while still taking illegal drugs.
<http://www.youtube.com/watch?v=bsRHZ4piOdA>

Good Sportsmanship 1950 Coronet Instructional Films
A look back at a film from the 1950s that explores the concept of sportsmanship.
<http://www.youtube.com/watch?v=4JDS7gihsTU>

Should Surfers Starve?
Professor Steven Lecce (University of Manitoba) considers whether leisure time should be included in a theory of redistributive justice.
<http://www.youtube.com/watch?v=sOagxEZFF3o>

Inside Story Americas – Lance Armstrong: Villain or Hero?
A comprehensive discussion on the implications of the Lance Armstrong doping scandal for sport and whether doping should be legalized (recorded before Armstrong admitted to doping).
<http://www.youtube.com/watch?v=Ivp977a0oJQ>

Twitter (Associations and Sport Philosophers)
@Intphilofsport – International Association for the Philosophy of Sport.

@Britphilofsport – British Philosophy of Sport Association.

@SportsEthicist – The Sports Ethicist: The unexamined sport is not worth playing.

@virilegames – Virile Games: 'exploring the links between football and philosophy'.

@AndrewEdgar5 – Dr Andrew Edgar: Reader in Philosophy (Cardiff University), philosopher of sport and of medicine (among other things).

@andymiah – Professor Andy Miah: Director of Creative Futures Institute, Professor of Ethics and Emerging Technology.

@AskVest – Dr Ask Vest Christiansen: Researcher in issues related to doping in sport, Aarhus University, Denmark.

@Carwynjones9 – Dr Carwyn Jones: Reader in Sports Ethics, Cardiff Metropolitan University.

@CharlieBBoy – Charlie Barton: Teaches ethics and philosophy with an interest in sport.

@christianmunthe – Professor Christian Munthe: Philosophy Professor at Gothenberg University, bioethics researcher and blogger.

@davoh – Dr Dave O'Hara: Professor of Philosophy and Classics at Augustana College, South Dakota.

@doppioshawn – Dr Shawn Klein: Professor of Philosophy at Rockford College. Author of SportsEthicist blog.

@drbarissentuna – Dr Baris Sentuna: Assistant Professor, Balikesir University, Department of Sociology. Aikido instructor.

@DrDickB – Dr Richard Bailey: 'I write, research and talk about sport, learning, coaching, expertise, martial arts, science and anything else that gets my goat.' London, United Kingdom.

@DrDKilpatrick – Dr David Kilpatrick: Associate Professor of English and Philosophy, Mercy College (NY). Club Historian, New York Cosmos. Director of Coaching, Rivertowns United FC.

@DrTedsportcult – Dr Ted Butryn: 'research doping, cyborg sport, MMA/pro wrestling; ancient aliens sceptic'. Professor of Sport Sociology/Psychology at San Jose State University.

@emilyryall – Dr Emily Ryall: Senior Lecturer in Philosophy at the University of Gloucestershire and Director of Storm7rugby.

@joangforry – Dr Joan Forry: Visiting Assistant Professor of Philosophy at Linfield College, specializing in sports ethics, food politics and environmental philosophy.

@kennethkirkwood – Dr. Ken Kirkwood: Professor at the Western University, London, Ontario, Canada. Main areas of interest are health and drug-related ethics.

@michaelwaustin – Dr Mike Austin: Professor of Philosophy and Religion at Eastern Kentucky University. 'Mediocre footballer, cyclist and runner. Fan of The Arsenal.'

@ProfJohnGleaves – Dr John Gleaves: Assistant Professor at California State University Fullerton. Researches philosophy and history of sport.

@PamSailors – Dr Pam Sailors: Associate Dean, Missouri State University.

@SamJaneB – Dr Samantha Brennan: 'Philosopher, feminist, cyclist, ethicist, parent.' Professor at Western University, London, Ontario, Canada.

@SDMumford – Professor Stephen Mumford: Professor of Metaphysics and Dean of the Faculty of Arts at the University of Nottingham.

Philosophical Sport Films
There are many feature length films that contain philosophical issues in sport although most of these are a tacit and implicit exploration of the meaning and purpose of sports. A list of films that contain philosophical issues related to sport can be found at <http://iaps.net/resources/>.

Notes
1   All electronic references were correct at the time of writing (March 2013). The annotated bibliography in this volume expands on many of the books listed in this guide. In addition, the annotated bibliography includes numerous important articles on the philosophy of sport.
2   Includes sex, gender and (dis)ability.
3   These journals have published papers on philosophical issues in sport.

23 Careers

Charlene Weaving

The philosophy of sport involves and offers diverse and exciting career prospects. In this chapter on careers in the discipline, the following three components are outlined in order to provide insight into the opportunities available for those interested in this field: opportunities in the philosophy of sport, professional development in the philosophy of sport and examples of syllabuses and course descriptions for academic courses.

Opportunities in the Philosophy of Sport

This section includes information on potential careers available for those with a background in the philosophy of sport. As emphasized in the American Kinesiology Association's (AKA) text *Careers in Sport, Fitness, and Exercise*, the term 'career' is significantly different from the term 'job'.[1] A job, unlike a career, involves little intellectual capacity and creativity and is simply working in return for money. On the other hand, in a career, there is often a sense of personal meaning, and individuals believe they are making a valuable contribution in and through their work.

Philosophical training can be beneficial for numerous careers. Specifically, philosophy courses involve exercises in critical thinking, which is the ability to think clearly, independently and rationally. A critical thinker is able to understand the logical connections between ideas: identify, construct and evaluate arguments; detect inconsistencies and common mistakes in reasoning; solve problems systematically; identify the relevance and importance of ideas and reflect on the justification of one's own beliefs and values.[2] Such skills are necessary in pretty much every career. In a recent article published in *The New York Times* entitled 'Where the Smart Kids Are', Brian Leiter argues that 'What might help philosophy is the more widespread recognition that philosophy remains the only humanistic discipline that really teaches students to think critically and analytically'.[3] Another recent article featured in the *Guardian* lists 'famous individuals' with philosophy degrees as examples of the value of philosophy; the diverse list includes poet T.S. Eliot, film director Woody Allen, martial arts actor Bruce Lee and former United States President Bill Clinton.[4] Despite the obvious benefits of developing critical-thinking skills, a common question many students pose is: 'what can I do with a philosophy degree?' A similar question is often heard by students in kinesiology departments: 'what can I do with a degree in the philosophy of sport?' While philosophy departments typically list numerous careers as potential paths after graduation,[5] kinesiology departments do not delve into such potential paths for those interested in the philosophy of sport. So, outlined below are fields in which a background in the philosophy of sport would enhance one's career choice and also possible career opportunities and roles in the world of sport for individuals with a more focused interest in the philosophy of sport.

Professional

There are opportunities to utilize a background in sport philosophy for various professional careers. Many philosophy majors pursue a law graduate degree. Additionally, some students pursue medicine. The standardized testing for entrance into the above professions involves sections on logic and critical thinking. Individuals may also pursue a career in the realm of bioethics and examine the moral implications of cases related to the health-care system. A bioethicist can be part of the academic world and work in a university setting, or could be employed by various health-care organizations or hospitals.

Another career that fits well with experience in sport philosophy is education, specifically, teaching physical education at the preschool, primary and secondary school levels. Teachers are responsible for curriculum development, lesson planning and instruction. Many physical educators also choose to pursue coaching, and work in three possible settings: community, institutional and commercial. Coaches are often required to deal with numerous moral issues and a background in sport philosophy would prove useful. Additionally, coaching certification programmes in Canada, for example, entail a specific section on 'Ethics and Coaching'.[6] Pursuing refereeing and officiating at an elite level is a career where a background in the philosophy of sport would be beneficial. Officials oversee athletic games, maintain the flow and order of the game, call rule violations and impose penalties based on their interpretations of the rules and regulations of the sport.

Sports journalism requires the ability to write effectively and tell a story. Experience in critical thinking related to sport would be helpful, for example, when analysing doping scandals, instances of sexism and fair play in sport.

Students can also pursue careers in sport management or sport administration. Some career opportunities include: athletic director, general manager and director of community sport programmes. People and organizational skills are a must for such positions as well as knowledge of the inner workings of sport (for example, facilities management, budgeting skills and understanding governing bodies). Skills developed through the study of the philosophy of sport would undoubtedly be useful in sport management and administration careers.

Academic

A common path individuals with a background in the philosophy of sport pursue is research and teaching at college or university level. 'Academia' is the most frequent term used to describe the community of students, teachers and researchers engaged in higher education. *Akademia*, the original Greek word from which the current term was derived, indicates a town on the outskirts of Athens and 'was made famous by the Greek philosopher Plato, who acquired land there and established a place for teaching and learning'.[7] Interested individuals typically pursue a master's degree, often followed by a doctor of philosophy [known as PhD] degree. Each professor's career involves different tasks depending on the institution and the country, yet the crux remains fairly similar. A professor's responsibilities include teaching, researching and service work for the university, profession and the wider community. A passion for teaching and research is what attracts many academics to such a career. Generally, most professors who research in the philosophy of sport tend to work in kinesiology departments.[8] Others are based in philosophy departments and a few in religious studies departments. A philosophy of sport professor is characterized by studying the metaphysical, ethical, epistemological and political dimensions of sport as well as its sociocultural relevance. Within kinesiology departments, philosophers of sport tend to study sport from a variety of societal viewpoints and their topics of analysis include gender, racism, capitalism, violence, fair play and health. Hence, sport philosophers are often considered to approach sport from a broad 'sociocultural' perspective. There are a variety of different courses that one could teach related to sport philosophy at the undergraduate and graduate level. Becoming a professor involves many years of post-secondary education, yet it is a rewarding and exciting profession. According to the AKA:

> [...] a thick skin helps, as does a good sense of humour. An ability to relate to all types of people, an ability to adapt to change, an ability to multitask and an ability to function without sleep are all important. In addition, a professor must be able to write well, speak confidently and be fair, consistent and diplomatic.[9]

Although teaching assignments and loads vary across colleges and universities, it is not only a crucial aspect of professors' responsibilities but also one of the most challenging and demanding. Conceiving and developing courses could be an intimidating task, especially for a new faculty. For this reason, at the end of this essay there are a number of syllabuses that could be of help while thinking about new courses in the philosophy of sport.

Sport Organizations

In addition to pursuing careers in the academic and professional sectors, individuals with a background in sport philosophy could pursue employment at various national and international sport organizations. Some careers in these organizations may involve practical application of sport philosophy theory. For example, many organizations require research skills and the ability to examine sport-related issues and assist in the creation and implementation of policies. Although opportunities for sport philosophers in national and international sport organizations are relatively new and admittedly scarce, there seems to be a growing interest on behalf of these institutions in the skills and expertise of sport philosophers. Below is a list with a sample of relevant organizations (by country), including their websites. These represent the most well known, however, it should be noted that there could also be opportunities to pursue careers with local and regional sport organizations.

International
International Olympic Committee <www.olympic.org>
International Paralympic Committee <www.paralympic.org>
World Anti-Doping Agency <www.wada.org>

Australia
National Sport Information Centre <www.ausport.gov.au/nsic>

Canada
Canadian Association for the Advancement of Women <www.caaws.ca>
Canadian Centre for Ethics in Sport <www.cces.ca>
Sport Information Resource Centre <www.sirc.ca>

Germany
Institute of Applied Training Science <www.sponet.de>

United Kingdom
UK Sport <www.uksport.gov.uk>

United States
Amateur Athletic Foundation Los Angeles <www.aafla.org>
National Collegiate Athletic Association <http://www.ncaa.org>
Women's Sport Foundation <www.womenssportfoundation.org>

Professional Development in the Philosophy of Sport

This section includes opportunities for professional development in the philosophy of sport. It presents a number of professional organizations and their respective conferences, all of which provide both junior and senior scholars with opportunities to further their skills and expertise. Academic conferences are excellent opportunities to showcase research but also offer informal learning experiences. If one were to pursue graduate work in sport philosophy and a career in academics, participation at academic conferences would be expected. Detailed information is listed below for specific academic conferences, including their websites. This section also lists a number of grants and awards in the philosophy of sport that allow for professional development and recognize outstanding contributions and service to this field of study, respectively.

Academic Conferences
International Association for the Philosophy of Sport (IAPS) <http://iaps.net/conference/>
In the autumn of 2013, the IAPS hosted its 41st annual conference in Fullerton, California. The IAPS's annual conferences are relatively small and are very

student friendly. The annual conference's location changes each year and has been held around the world.

British Philosophy of Sport Association (BPSA) <http://www.philosophyofsport.org.uk/events.php>
In the spring of 2013, the BPSA hosted its 10th annual conference. Participants at the BPSA are generally from the UK and Europe. The conference is held every spring and is relatively small in size. Many IAPS members also present at the BPSA conference. It is a friendly conference for students to attend.

European Association for the Philosophy of Sport (EAPS) <http://www.philosophyofsport.eu/>
The EAPS works in conjunction with the BPSA and consists mainly of European IAPS and BPSA members. According to its constitution, the EAPS holds a conference every third year. Similar to the BPSA in size, the EAPS sets out to provide continental support for the IAPS, and it creates opportunities for European scholars to engage in sport philosophy discussions.

International Centre for Olympic Studies (ICOS) <http://www.uwo.ca/olympic/conference.html>
The ICOS was formed in 1989 and is housed at the Western University, London, Ontario, Canada. Each Olympic year, the ICOS organizes a symposium and publishes an edited collection of the conference papers. Many IAPS members as well as other scholars interested in the philosophy of sport present at this conference, and therefore there is a substantial presence of this area of study. The conference encourages student participation.

International Convention on Science, Education and Medicine in Sport (ICSEMIS) <http://www.icsemis2012.com>
The ICSEMIS is a scientific congress held before the Summer Olympic and Paralympic Games. Prior to the 2008 Beijing Olympics, the congress was called the 'Pre-Olympic Congress'. This large convention involves presentations from a variety of research fields related to sport studies. The IAPS typically hosts sessions during ICSEMIS.

American Philosophical Association (APA) <http://www.apaonline.org>
IAPS members organize sport philosophy sessions at the APA annual conferences. The APA meetings are divided by region. The Central Division meets in February/March, the Pacific in March/April and the Eastern in December/January.

World Congress of Philosophy <http://www.wcp2013.gr/en/universal/congress-filosofias.html>
The World Congress of Philosophy is held every five years and began in 1900. It is hosted by the *International Federation of Philosophical Societies*. The IAPS is a member of this organization, and occasionally the congress features sessions on the philosophy of sport.

International Association for Women Philosophers (IAPH) <http://www.iaph-philo.org>
The IAPH organizes a biennial international symposium attended by approximately 200 participants. IAPS members have presented at this conference in the past, and sport philosophy research was received well.

Grants and Awards in the Philosophy of Sport
There are extensive grants and awards available for philosophers of sport. Below is a list of the grants and awards, organized geographically, including websites.

International
International Association for the Philosophy of Sport (IAPS)
<http://iaps2012.fade.up.pt/index.php/en/r-scott-kretchmar-student-essay-award> and <http://iaps.net/honours/>
The IAPS honours distinguished member Professor Scott Kretchmar by organizing a student essay competition in conjunction with its annual conference. Student paper submissions undergo a blind review process, and each submission receives constructive and thorough feedback. The author of the winning essay is awarded the *Scott Kretchmar Student Essay Award* prize. The IAPS also honours members with the *IAPS Distinguished Scholar Award* and the *IAPS Distinguished Service Award*. Both award winners are selected by the membership. The recipient of the *IAPS Distinguished Scholar Award* is also honoured by delivering the *Warren P. Fraleigh Distinguished Scholar Lecture* at the IAPS annual conference.

International Olympic Academy (IOA) <http://www.ioa.org.gr/>
Since 1993, each summer, the IOA organizes in Olympia, Greece an *International Seminar on Olympic Studies for Postgraduate Students*. Invited participants travel from around the world to participate in Olympic research seminars. Many IAPS members have attended this seminar and some are regular instructors. Philosophy of sport is a main component of the programme. The IOA also organizes an *International Session for Young Participants*. It is a two-week annual session held in June or July. The programme is designed as an introduction to Olympism and the Olympic Movement. Research in the philosophy of sport plays a significant role in the session.

International Olympic Committee Olympic Studies Centre (OSC)
<http://www.olympic.org/content/the-olympic-studies-centre/categories-container/academic-activities-and-network/?subcat=129534>
The OSC offers two grants, the *PhD Students Research Grant Programme* and the *Advanced Olympic Research Grant Programme*. The first is intended for doctoral students engaged in scholarly research on the Olympic Movement, its history and ideals, and the impact of the Olympic Games on the various aspects of contemporary society and culture. The second is addressed to university professors, lecturers and research fellows; proposals should be directly linked to the priority fields of research identified in the grant programme.

Fédération Internationale de Football Association (FIFA)
<http://www.fifa.com/aboutfifa/footballdevelopment/education/cies/have langescholarship.html>
The FIFA encourages academic research in football through the *João Havelange Research Scholarship*. The scholarship is organized by the *International Centre for Sports Studies* in Neuchâtel, Switzerland. According to its criteria, the scholarship is awarded to researchers holding a university degree or equivalent in one of the following areas of study: law, economics, sociology, ethics, geography, history and medicine.

World Anti-Doping Agency (WADA)
<http://www.wada-ama.org/en/education-awareness/social-science/applying-for-research-grant/>
The WADA encourages research proposals in the social sciences to create effective doping prevention strategies through its *Social Science Research Grant*. Sport philosophy research proposals are encouraged and this grant provides opportunity for international collaborations. The WADA also awards a *Young Investigator Award* to master's degree-level students for outstanding and innovative research in anti-doping from a social science perspective.

Australia
Australian Institute of Sport (AIS) <http://www.ausport.gov.au/information/ais>
The AIS makes funding available through its Applied Research Centre for projects attached to the national sporting organizations and Australian universities. There are four main categories for projects: the big ideas fund, sport innovation fund, high-performance sport research fund and the clinical research fund.

Canada
International Centre for Olympic Studies (ICOS)
<http://www.uwo.ca/olympic/grad_paper_award.html>
In the autumn of 2012, in conjunction with its annual conference, the ICOS created the inaugural *Graduate Student Essay Competition*. Master's and PhD students are invited to submit their conference papers for this award. The winner receives an all-expenses-paid trip to attend the conference.

Social Science Research Council of Canada (SSHRC)
<http://www.sshrc-crsh.gc.ca/funding-financement/programs-programmes/sport_can-eng.aspx>
The SSHRC is the national granting agency for social science research in Canada, and has launched a *Sport Participant Research Initiative* in collaboration with Sport Canada. There are opportunities to apply to a variety of grants for research on sport from a philosophical perspective.

Sport Information Resource Centre (SIRC) <http://www.sirc.ca/research_awards/index.cfm>
Each year the SIRC awards the *SIRC Research Award*, which recognizes outstanding sport research that benefits the Canadian sporting community. There is a special category for sociocultural/humanities methodologies.

United Kingdom
Economic Social Research Council (ESRC)
<http://www.esrc.ac.uk/funding-and-guidance/funding-opportunities/index.aspx>
A variety of funding opportunities are available through the ESRC, and there is a specific category entitled 'health and well-being' where sport philosophy projects could fit well. Recently, there was an impact study funded by this group analysing the London 2012 Olympic Games.

Research Councils UK (RCUK) <http://www.rcuk.ac.uk/Pages/Home.aspx>
According to its website, the RCUK funds projects from a variety of disciplines: medical and biological sciences, astronomy, physics, chemistry and engineering, social sciences, economics, environmental sciences, and the arts and humanities. Sport philosophy projects would fall under the Arts and Humanities Research Council funding group.

United States
The Chronicle of Higher Education < http://chronicle.com/section/Home/5>
The Chronicle of Higher Education details information concerning jobs, advice, grant funding, forums and other pertinent material for individuals in higher education. There is a section reserved solely for research grant information.

Nike Foundation <http://nikeinc.com/pages/the-nike-foundation>
The Nike Foundation has funded sociocultural sport researchers in the past to examine various aspects of Nike from an academic perspective (for example, past projects involved gender construction analysis, racism in marketing, and empowering young girls through sport). This is a good example of how sometimes one can secure research funding in the most unlikely places. Most recently, the Nike Foundation has created the *Girl Effect* organization in conjunction with the United Nations Foundation and Coalition for Adolescent Girls to eradicate poverty among girls all over the world. There are opportunities for academics to get involved and receive funding.

Knight Commission on Intercollegiate Athletics
<http://www.knightcommission.org/resources/press-room/780-knight-commission-on-intercollegiate-athletics-2011-12-research-grants-initiative>
This organization was created in 1989 as a response to the numerous visible scandals in United States college sports. In 2012, it awarded $100,000 to projects examining different aspects of college sports. Projects involving ethical analysis in collegiate sport would fit well.

The Women's Sport Foundation (WSF) <http://www.womenssportsfoundation.org/home/research>
The WSF was founded in 1974 by American tennis legend Billie Jean King. The organization attempts to promote physical activity and sport for girls and women. Philosophy of sport research from a feminist perspective would fit well with this organization. The WSF partners with the SHARP Centre at the University of Michigan, and funding opportunities are available.

Examples of Syllabuses and Course Descriptions for Academic Courses in the Philosophy of Sport

In this section, samples of syllabuses are listed in order to provide examples of how sport philosophy professors design sport philosophy courses, which readings and theories are included as well as novel approaches for teaching a sport philosophy curriculum. The syllabuses highlight the objectives and readings for the courses as well as examples of assessment activities.

Undergraduate Courses in Sport Philosophy
Critical Thinking in Sport Sciences[10]

Objective: the purpose of the course is: 1) to introduce students to some of the basic tools and concepts that underlie effective critical thinking, and 2) to get students to apply these tools and concepts to selected debates in sport science. Part One of the course will consist of lectures in which the basic tools and concepts that underlie effective critical thinking will be introduced in more or less abstract form. Part Two will consist of group discussions in which students will be expected to apply these abstract tools to concrete issues and debates in sport science. In the tutorial sessions, special attention will be paid to the concepts of sport, game and play.

Text: Trudy Govier, *A Practical Study of Argument*, 6th ed. (New York: Wadsworth Publishing, 2010).

Assignment examples: mid-term and final exams. Commentaries presented in person at the beginning of each tutorial.

Metaphysical Foundations of Sport and Physical Activity[11]

Objective: this course represents an introductory philosophical inquiry into the essential nature, meaning and significance of sport and physical activity. Students will explore the branch of philosophy known as logic and the methods and principles used to distinguish good/correct reasoning from bad/incorrect reasoning. The purpose of this course is: 1) to introduce students to some of the basic tools and concepts that underlie effective critical thinking, and 2) students will then apply these tools to discuss, analyse and evaluate various philosophical arguments in the phenomena of sport and physical activity.

Texts: a course pack consisting of selected readings published in the *Journal of Philosophy of Sport* and previous sport philosophy anthologies (i.e. William J. Morgan and Klaus V. Meier, eds., *Philosophic Inquiry in Sport*, 2nd ed. (Champaign, IL: Human Kinetics, 1995).

Assignment examples: students will critique an article from the *Journal of Philosophy of Sport*. In a presentation component, students will make a case for removing one event from the Olympic Programme, and adding a new one. Claims must be backed up by the literature and thoroughly explained.

Philosophy of Physical Activity and Leisure[12]
Objective: issues in sport, physical education, recreation and leisure will be examined from a philosophical perspective. This course aims to enhance students' appreciation of the complexity of the philosophical dimensions of leisure, sport, games, play and physical activity. In doing so, the acquisition and refinement of critical-thinking skills will be emphasized. The course structure and content reflects the following objectives:

1. To analyse the nature of physical activity and leisure from a philosophical perspective.
2. To understand how past and present approaches to the body may trivialize and exclude people from undertaking physical activities.
3. To practise analysing assigned readings and writing critically on philosophical topics.
4. To learn to tolerate and appreciate views and arguments that differ from one's own in order to engage in academic discussions.

Text: Scott Kretchmar, *Practical Philosophy of Sport and Physical Activity*, 2nd ed. (Champaign, IL: Human Kinetics, 2005).
    Assignment examples: debates, critiques and reflections.

Introduction to the Philosophy of Sport[13]
Objective: the course will introduce students to the nature of philosophical inquiry and the activity of conceptual analysis. Philosophical skills such as the ability to construct and deconstruct logical arguments, and identify presuppositions and logical inferences, will be developed in relation to the analysis of key concepts such as sports, games and health. Consideration will be given to a range of philosophical and ethical issues in sport and exercise and will include: conceptual problems associated with the definition of sport; the nature and use of scientific and social scientific methods in the study of sport; the nature of rules in sport and games; and the concepts of fairness and fair play.
    Texts:
Emily Ryall, *Critical Thinking for Sport Students* (Exeter: Learning Matters, 2010).
Scott Kretchmar, *Practical Philosophy of Sport and Physical Activity*, 2nd ed. (Champaign, IL: Human Kinetics, 2005).
Jan Boxill, ed., *Sport Ethics. An Anthology* (Malden, MA: Blackwell, 2003).
Assignment examples: exams and portfolio (1000 words).

Ethics and Morality in Sport I and Ethics and Morality in Sport II[14]
Objective I: this module aims to build upon the student's awareness of the philosophy of sport and to think critically about key ethical issues in sports. In

particular, it will develop students' close reading and analytical skills on a range of topics such as cheating, doping, violence, equity, fair play and nationalism in sports. Focus will also be directed upon an analysis of key concepts involved in the arguments that underpin discrimination and the classification of success and failure in sport, such as 'sex', 'race' and 'disability'. The module will build upon the students' understanding of philosophical argument and will enable them to apply philosophical tools to the branch of ethics. While the module is issue driven it will also develop key critical-reasoning abilities that should extend to clear thinking about issues in sports generally.

Objective II: this module builds on the issue-driven Ethics and Morality in Sport I to develop an awareness of the theoretical bases that underpin ethics generally and the ethics of sport in particular. Through case studies in a variety of sports, students develop a sophisticated awareness of the importance of deontological, utilitarian and virtue theories and how they affect the perception and conduct of sports players, administrators, coaches/teachers and policymakers. Students apply ethical theory to key contemporary issues of their own choosing, in negotiation with the course tutor.

Texts:

Mike McNamee, ed., *The Ethics of Sport: A Reader* (London and New York: Routledge, 2010).

William J. Morgan, ed., *Ethics in Sport*, 2nd ed. (Champaign, IL: Human Kinetics, 2007).

Graham Gordon, *Eight Theories of Ethics* (London and New York: Routledge, 2004).

Graham McFee, *Sport, Rules and Value. Philosophical Investigations into the Nature of Sport* (London and New York: Routledge, 2004).

Assignment examples: essays (3000 words).

Gender, Sport and Physical Activity[15]
Objective: the course will explore the role of girls and women and boys and men in sport/physical activity/recreation from a historical, philosophical and social perspective. The course will focus on topics such as sexuality, homophobia, racism, politics of difference and identity, and the media from a predominately Canadian sociocultural approach.

The overall purpose/objective of the course is:

1. To understand the process of gender role socialization in sport.
2. To understand the history of gender in sport.
3. To recognize how the existing power structure trivializes, oppresses and excludes men and women from participating in sport.
4. To develop strategies for improving and enhancing gender-equitable practices.

Text: Paul Davis and Charlene Weaving, eds., *Philosophic Perspectives on Gender in Sport and Physical Activity* (London: Routledge, 2010).

Assignment examples: commentaries/reflections, article critique and presentations.

Modern Olympic Games[16]

Objective: over the past century, the Olympic Games have emerged as the most pervasive global sporting festival in the world. From the earliest efforts of Baron Pierre de Coubertin to solicit interest in establishing the games, to recent scandals – the awarding of the 2008 and 2010 games, the appointment of a new IOC president – this sporting festival has captivated modern audiences through conflict, celebration and spectacle. Called glorious and great by some and oppressive and fascist by others, the events, personalities and outcome of the Olympic Games are enmeshed in a fascinating history and important sociocultural examination. The cultural connection of the games and tertiary events are about power and privilege, social structures and negotiations, and a panorama of issues including class, gender, race, political economy, body culture, science and identity. The course is designed to provide opportunities for students, through lectures, seminars, films and research papers, to critically examine the Olympic Games and Olympic Movement as they have unfolded and culturally reproduced in the modern era. Students will examine the Modern Olympic Games from a sociocultural interdisciplinary approach and will be expected to reflect critically upon historical and current philosophical issues as they affect the world.

Texts:

Kevin Wamsley and Kevin Young, eds., *Global Olympics. Historical and Sociological Studies of the Modern Games* (Amsterdam: Elsevier, 2005) and additional readings (mainly from the *Journal of the Philosophy of Sport* special issue on Paralympic Sport and Olympism).

Assignment examples: commentaries, research paper outline discussions, major research paper and presentations.

Graduate Courses in Sport Philosophy

Philosophy of Sport[17]

Objective: philosophy is the art of wondering. The philosophy of sport, thus, ponders human involvement in sport. The investigation of sport from the perspectives of varying modern philosophic positions facilitates the clarification and understanding of the nature, purpose, significance and conduct of the activity. For this reason, selected, substantial philosophic analyses of, and discourses concerned with, sport will be read, discussed and evaluated.

Focus:

1. The ontology of sport, play and games
2. Sport and authentic existence

The particular focus of the course will be predominately twofold: first, a comprehensive study of the basic structure and nature of the phenomena of play, sport and games; and secondly, an extended investigation of the meaning and significance of sport as authentic existence as elucidated in, and derived from, the literature of existential philosophy and phenomenology.

Texts:

William J. Morgan and Klaus V. Meier, eds., *Philosophic Inquiry in Sport*, 2nd ed. (Champaign, IL: Human Kinetics, 1995).
Bernard Suits, *The Grasshopper: Games, Life, and Utopia* (Toronto: The University of Toronto Press, 1978).
Samuel Beckett, *Waiting for Godot* (New York: Grove Press, 1998).

Assignment examples: reaction paper and/or critique session, research paper and/or a philosophic project. In addition: any other philosophical creation or production approved in advance by the instructor as satisfying the course requirements. This option is to be exercised if a student feels that the previously delineated options are too limited and that a suitable critical, reasonably structured, alternative relevant to the philosophical analysis of sport, in accord with the course focus, is suggested as a project.

Seminar in the Ethics of Sport[18]
Objective: the course is designed to provide a review and critical analysis of readings in the ethics of sport. This will include both original sources and articles that are derived from them. Topics include an introduction to ethics, the nature of sport and the promotion of its values, fair play, violence and performance enhancement. The course permits students to select additional issues of personal or contemporary interest. An emphasis is placed on developing skills related to ethical reasoning.
    Texts:
William J. Morgan and Klaus V. Meier, eds., *Philosophic Inquiry in Sport*, 2nd ed. (Champaign, IL: Human Kinetics, 1995).
Michael Sandel, *The Case Against Perfection: Ethics in the Age of Genetic Engineering* (Cambridge: Harvard University Press, 2007).
Michael Sandel, *Justice: What's the Right Thing to Do?* (New York: Farrar, Straus and Giroux, 2009).
Selections From:
Ronald Dworkin, *Law's Empire* (Cambridge, MA: Harvard University Press, 1986).
John Searle, *Speech Acts: An Essay in the Philosophy of Language* (Cambridge: Cambridge University Press, 1969).
Alasdair MacIntyre, *After Virtue: A Study in Moral Theory* (Notre Dame, IN: University of Notre Dame, 1981/1984).
John Rawls, *A Theory of Justice* (Cambridge, MA: The Belknap Press of Harvard University Press, 1971).
Journal of the Philosophy of Sport
Sport, Ethics and Philosophy

Assignment examples: critical review of essays and a research project (oral presentation and written copy).

Human Intellect and Movement[19]

Objectives: this course aims to help students develop a clear understanding of the place of embodiment and movement in human intellectual capacities, to be able to articulate potential advantages of theories of holism over dualism and materialism (monism), to see complementary relationships between philosophic and empirical (measurement-based) inquiries into the mind, to understand the professional ramifications of holism for kinesiology and physical education and to improve research writing skills related to philosophy.

Learning outcomes:

1. The ability to articulate the foundations of mind-body dualism and materialism.
2. The ability to articulate the foundations of holism.
3. The ability to discuss and critique different notions of human intelligence.
4. The ability to identify benchmarks of intelligence in non-verbal acts.
5. The ability to describe the advantages of cross-disciplinary research among, for example, neuro-psychology, biology and philosophy.
6. The ability to argue persuasively for different interpretations of mind-body intimacy.
7. The ability to compose a research length paper on a topic of human intellect and movement suitable for publication or refereed presentation.

Texts:

Howard Gardner, *Frames of Mind: The Theory of Multiple Intelligences* (New York: Basic Books, 1985).

Michael Polanyi and Harry Prosch, *Meaning* (Chicago: University of Chicago, 1975).

Stuart Spicker, ed., *The Philosophy of the Body: Rejections of Cartesian Dualism* (Quadrangle Books: Chicago, 1970).

David Sudnow, *Ways of the Hand: The Organization of Improvised Conduct* (Cambridge, MA: MIT Press, 1978–1993).

Assignment examples: regular, careful and critical reading, three brief position papers and a major research paper on physical education and intelligence.

Theory of Games and Play[20]

Objective: to critically evaluate classical and contemporary philosophic literature on the nature and value of games and play. The course employs a seminar setting, regular dialogue and minimal lecture.

Texts:

Roger Caillois, *Man, Play, and Games*, trans. Meyer Barash (Urbana and Chicago: University of Illinois Press, 1958–2001).

Johan Huizinga, *Homo Ludens: A Study of the Play Element in Culture* (Boston: Beacon Press, 1950).

Bernard Suits, *The Grasshopper: Games, Life, and Utopia* (Toronto: The University of Toronto Press, 1978–2002).

Michael J. Ellis, *Why People Play* (New Jersey: Prentice-Hall, 1973).

William J. Morgan and Klaus V. Meier, eds., *Philosophic Inquiry in Sport*, 2nd ed. (Champaign, IL: Human Kinetics, 1995).

Assignment examples: critiques, lead responsibilities (each student designs and leads one class session), and an essay (which serves as a precursor to a presentation/publication).

Notes

1   Shirl J. Hoffman, *Careers in Sport, Fitness, and Exercise: American Kinesiology Association* (Champaign IL: Human Kinetics, 2011).
2   'What Is Critical Thinking?' Critical Thinking: Opencourseware on Critical Thinking, Logic and Creativity <http://philosophy.hku.hk/think/critical/ct.php> (accessed 10 April, 2013).
3   Brian Leiter, 'Where the Smart Kids Are', *New York Times, Room for Debate*, 23 August, 2010<http://www.nytimes.com/roomfordebate/2010/08/19/x-phis-new-take-on-old-problems/where-the-smart-students-are?scp=6&sq=philosophy&st=cse> (accessed 10 April, 2013).
4   Angela Foster, 'What Can You Do With a Degree in Philosophy?', the *Guardian*, 29 October, 2010 <http://ww w.guardian.co.uk/money/2010/oct/30/graduate-careers-philosophy> (accessed 10 April, 2013).
5   For examples, see Willamette University <http://www.willamette.edu/cla/philosophy/practical/>, University of Kent <http://www.kent.ac.uk/careers/Philosophy.htm>; and Cape Breton University <http://faculty.cbu.ca/rkeshen/front/why.html> (accessed 10 April, 2013).
6   See Alun Hardman and Carwyn Jones, eds., *The Ethics of Sports Coaching* (London: Rouledge, 2011). Coaching Association of Canada (CAC), 'Make Ethical Decisions', <http://www.coach.ca/workshop-s14169> (accessed 10 April, 2013).
7   Hoffman, *Careers in Sport, Fitness, and Exercise: American Kinesiology Association*, 140.
8   According to AKA, kinesiology 'is defined as the academic discipline that involves the study of physical activity and its impact on health, society and quality of life. Kinesiology draws on several sources of knowledge including knowledge gained through scholarly study and research, knowledge gained from professional practices centered in physical activity and knowledge gained from personal physical activity experiences.' See American Kinesiology Association, 'The Undergraduate Core in Kinesiology', <http://www.americankinesiology.org/the-undergraduate-core-in-kinesiology> (accessed 10 April, 2013). Kinesiology departments comprise a multidimensional approach to studing sport and physical activity. For example, undergraduate students take courses in the bioscience field (exercise physiology) as well as the humanities/sociocultural area (philosophy of sport).
9   Hoffman, *Careers in Sport, Fitness, and Exercise: American Kinesiology Association*, 150.
10 This course was created by Angela J. Schneider, Western University, Canada.
11 This course was created by Charlene Weaving, St Francis Xavier, Canada.
12 This course was created by Sarah Teetzel, University of Manitoba, Canada.
13 This course was created by Emily Ryall, University of Gloucestershire, United Kingdom.
14 This course was created by Emily Ryall, University of Gloucestershire, United Kingdom.
15 This course was created by Charlene Weaving, St Francis Xavier University, Canada.
16 This course was created by Charlene Weaving, St Francis Xavier University, Canada.

17   This course was created by Klaus V. Meier, Western University, Canada. See Klaus V. Meier, '"Time In": On Teaching Phenomenological Approaches to Sport and Meaning' in *Sport in the Classroom: Teaching Sport Related Courses in the Humanities*, ed., David L. Vanderwerken (Toronto: Associated University Press, 1990), 104–132.

18   This course was created by Scott Kretchmar, Pennsylvania State University, United States.

19   This course was created by Scott Kretchmar, Pennsylvania State University, United States.

20   This course was created by Scott Kretchmar, Pennsylvania State University, United States.

Part VII

The Literature

24 The Sport Philosophy Literature: Foundations, Evolutions and Annotations

Tim L. Elcombe, Douglas Hochstetler and Douglas W. McLaughlin

The title of a book published in 2006 by William J. Morgan encapsulates a project undertaken by many interested in sport from a philosophical perspective: to provide a rationale as to how and *Why Sports Morally Matter*.[1] Morgan's undertaking begins with the inference that sports do in fact matter to humans and their cultures. Based on the interest paid to global mega-events such as the World Cup and the Olympic Games, as well as the influence of sport in less organized, more local forms, Morgan's postulation appears valid.

Sports do matter. Sports matter because they demand our attention, for better or worse and for varying reasons, on a regular basis. Sports matter because they cut across tribal lines and form their own non-verbal languages. Sports matter because they reflect our cultural and personal values, beliefs and traditions. Sports matter because they sometimes challenge and sometimes reinforce our norms, our ideas and our expectations. Sports matter because within and through them we can explore our humanity, seek excellence and solve artificial yet meaningful problems.

Consequently sport clearly demands academic scrutiny. As early as the writings of Homer, and later Plato, sport's place in the life of Western civilization has found inclusion in works of literature and been deemed worthy of philosophical consideration. Yet despite its cultural significance and long history of scholarly relevance, sport eluded sustained philosophical notice. Only rare, random lenses focused on sport until the mid 20th century.

By the 1960s, however, attention paid to philosophical inquiry into sport had begun to grow exponentially. The formation of the Philosophic Society for the Study of Sport (PSSS) in 1972 hastened the proliferation of academic philosophers inquiring into issues related to sport. The creation of the *Journal of the Philosophy of Sport* (JPS) by the PSSS in 1974 provided a coherent scholarly resource for philosophers to publish examinations of sport and a locus, along with annual meetings, for academic sport philosophy dialogue.

JPS continues to serve as one of several resources available to provide focused scholarly attention on philosophical issues related to sport. The introduction of

Sport, Ethics and Philosophy (SEP) in 2007 added an additional academic journal to the field, along with the continued publication of sport philosophy-related articles in scholarly periodicals such as *Journal of Sport and Social Issues*, *Quest* and *Sport in Society: Cultures, Commerce, Media, Politics*. Furthermore, books dedicated to sport philosophy of varying styles remain important contributions to extending the field's literature content.

This collection of annotated bibliographies attempts to offer not only individual summaries of samples from the literature but also an overview of the evolution of sport philosophy as an academic field. Presenting such an emerging body of philosophical works as a coherent whole creates challenges, particularly how to identify and organize appropriate examples. As such, the various books, chapters and journal articles presented do not necessarily represent the 'best of the best' of sport philosophy – although the articles selected reflect the quality of the field's research – but instead highlight significant issues, prevalent debates and interesting topics emerging in the English language sport philosophy scholarship over the past 85 years.

To organize the material, a chronological structure functions best to historicize the developments of sport philosophy, identify trends within the literature and reflect both durable and particularized topics of interest to sport philosophers. Alternative approaches considered to arrange the annotations fell short of providing a full account of the literature. Many of the works selected resist clear classification under rubrics defined by traditional philosophical branches including metaphysics, ethics, aesthetics and epistemology. Some examples emphasize conceptual metaphilosophical inquiry, while others focus on more practical issues; yet virtually all of the selected works integrate both theory and application to some degree. The applied contexts under consideration similarly evade reductive clarity, with topics of inquiry regularly blending into one another. And simply dividing by the type of publication (books, journal articles, chapters) clouds the integrated influence works of varying stripes have on sport philosophy's scholarly advancement.

Enhancing the significance of the chronological structure, examples of books, chapters and articles are subdivided into five separate time periods: 1930–1973, 1974–1988, 1989–1999, 2000–2006 and 2007–2012. Although (once again) alternative frames were considered (e.g. by decade), significant milestones in the field and real issues arising beyond the walls of academia offered five coherent, although not independent, epochs. Prior to the presentation of the works selected for each time period, a summary of the field and related issues will serve to frame their rationale. To further highlight the comprehensiveness and coherence of the field's development, other exemplar works relevant to the material summarized will be identified and referenced in a separate bibliography at the conclusion of the chapter.

1930–1973

In 1940, Charles McCloy presented a collection of essays originally published between 1924 and 1938 in a book entitled *Philosophical Basis for Physical Education*. McCloy's articles represented a growing philosophical interest within academe of physical education, play and movement. Johan Huizinga's influential work *Homo Ludens: A Study of the Play-Element in Culture* further thrust issues related to play into the English-speaking scholarly culture following its translation in 1949. McCloy and Huizinga's work in the first half of the 20th century, however, reflected the isolated philosophical interest in human movement to that point. It wasn't until the late 1960s that philosophical inquiry into sport and movement became more prevalent. Books published by Howard S. Slusher, Eleanor Metheny and Paul Weiss from 1967 to 1969 drew the attention of other philosophers and scholars interested in sport. Spearheaded by Warren P. Fraleigh from the State University of New York College at Brockport, a group of scholars including P.J. Galasso, Ellen W. Gerber, James W. Keating, Seymour Kleinman, Hans Lenk, Robert Osterhoudt, Weiss and Richard Zaner eventually formed PSSS in 1972 to provide a channel for sport philosophy to develop. With the renowned American philosopher Weiss serving as the first president of PSSS, the group began meeting annually as a small but committed collective interested in and appreciative of the significance of sport philosophy inquiry.

Representative Works

Jesse Feiring Williams, 'Education through the physical', *The Journal of Higher Education* 1 (1930): 279–282.

Williams's essay examines the role of physical education in higher education, distinguishing 'education of the physical', which has a much narrower focus of the aims and purpose of physical education, from 'education through the physical'. While 'education of the physical' is concerned with physical health, posture and strength, 'education through the physical' develops skills, habits and knowledges that 'make for fine living'. He argues that attention must be given not only to the physical outcomes of physical education but also to people's motives and interests. When physical education is understood as a valued component of a liberal education, universities must provide adequate resources so that students may fully develop.

Charles H. McCloy, *Philosophical Basis for Physical Education* (New York: Appleton-Century-Crofts, 1940).

Published in 1940, this monograph includes various essays written by McCloy in publications such as the *Journal of Health, Physical Education and Recreation, Physical Training*; and the *Journal of Physical Education*. The essays, originally written between 1924 and 1938, examine a variety of philosophical topics in a manner written for practitioners of physical education. Drawing from the writings of John Dewey and William James, among others, McCloy argues for the place of physical education in modern democratic institutions. Of special note is McCloy's argument for 'education of the physical', which emphasized the physical and biological nature of the discipline. In Part I, titled 'Philosophical Considerations', McCloy outlines objectives important for the physical education discipline, in addition to practical matters such as selecting teaching material. Part II includes essays regarding physical education as it concerns the psychology of teaching and the development of character. McCloy concludes his work with a projection of how the discipline might change and grow in the coming decade.

Johan Huizinga, *Homo Ludens: A Study of the Play-Element in Culture* (London: Routledge & Kegan Paul, 1949).
Another influential tome appeared with Huizinga's *Homo Ludens: A Study of the Play-Element in Culture* (originally published in Dutch in 1938). From his perspective as an anthropologist, Huizinga articulates the extent to which play permeates human culture and is a cultural phenomenon. Huizinga begins by examining the nature and significance of play as a social occurrence wherein he argues that play holds a significant function for humans, a function that goes beyond the physiological or basic reflex. Huizinga defines play as 'a free activity standing quite consciously outside "ordinary" life as being "not serious", but at the same time absorbing the player intensely and utterly' (p. 13). In subsequent chapters, Huizinga examines the role of play across many fronts – as this phenomenon has been expressed in various languages: the role of play and contest in the evolution of civilization, and the relationship between play and various domains such as law, war, poetry, philosophy and art. Huizinga concludes this important work, translated into English in 1949, by examining the role of play in contemporary culture and civilization.

James W. Keating, 'Sportsmanship as a Moral Category', *Ethics* 75 (1964): 25–35.
Although ignored by philosophers, Keating identifies the moral relevance of sportsmanship by citing its usage by famous writers, former US presidents, university presidents and even a pope. Keating is concerned that the usage of sportsmanship is not particularly illuminating because it ranges from an all-inclusive concept undifferentiated from other moral concepts to a minimal standard that equates sportsmanship to anything that is not criminal in sport. To clarify sportsmanship, Keating offers a distinction between primarily co-operative sport and centrally competitive athletics. Applied to sport, sportsmanship involves magnanimity and generosity, thus, Keating proposes: 'Always conduct yourself in such a manner that you will increase rather than detract from the pleasure to be found in the activity, both for your own and that of your fellow participants' (pp. 29–30). Applied to athletics, with honourable victory rather than cooperation as the goal, sportsmanship involves a legal interpretation of the rules, acting with fairness in the contest and being modest in victory or composed in defeat.

Bernard Suits, 'What is a Game?', *Philosophy of Science* 34 (1967): 148–156.
In 'What is a Game?' Suits formulates a definition of games that remains central to the philosophy of sport literature today. By working through a series of hypotheses, Suits identifies the necessary and sufficient conditions of games. The first hypothesis, that game playing involves the selection of inefficient means, is rejected because game players use the most efficient means available to them. The second hypothesis, that in games the rules and ends are inseparable, is necessary but not sufficient to distinguish games from such things as morality.

Suits rejects the third hypothesis, which questions whether the rules of games, unlike moral rules, are not ultimately binding. The fourth hypothesis identifies a crucial limitation: the means are non-ultimate in that the rules restrict the means available to accomplish the goal. The fifth hypothesis identifies a further clarification in relation to why rules that limit means are accepted. While the limitation of means by rules in other activities is for external reasons, in games it is for the internal reason of making that activity possible. The final hypothesis identifies three distinct possible ends and argues that 'winning is not the end with respect to which the rules limit means' (p. 155). This article constructs the definition of games that becomes the keystone of Suits' *The Grasshopper: Games, Life, and Utopia* (1978).[2]

Howard S. Slusher, *Man, Sport and Existence: A Critical Analysis* (Philadelphia: Lea & Febiger, 1967).
With hopes that his book would serve as a 'representative of a "Model-T" of things to come' (p. xv), Slusher anticipated a development in the scholarly study of sport philosophy. *Man, Sport and Existence* thus helped publicize the disciplinary field once relegated to logic, metaphysics and ethics. Written from an existential perspective, Slusher examines themes of being, authenticity, freedom, meaning and truth. The book is organized into five distinct sections. The first section examines sport and being, delving into the realms of being with respect to sport and the place of truth. In the second section, Slusher takes up sport and purpose, exploring the characteristics of sport and sport 'as it is'. Section three focuses on issues of meaning related to sport. Here Slusher explores how sport impacts on human existence at the personal level. Section four looks at sport with respect to the religious or mystical elements of human existence. Along the way, Slusher examines the nature of sport rituals and sport itself as a religious symbol. Finally, the book closes with a section geared towards sport in relation to existence and decision. The author examines themes such as perfection, freedom, anxiety and death.

Eleanor Metheny, *Movement and Meaning* (New York: McGraw-Hill, 1968).
In the preface, Metheny explains that the text contributes to the 'growing body of literature that deals with nonverbal forms of human understanding' (p. x) of sport, exercise and dance. She draws from the concept of forms as proposed by Ernst Cassirer, considering examples of symbolic forms and their related connotation. Metheny examines human-made movement forms and the extent to which such activities provide meaning both to the performer and spectator. During the course of three chapters the author outlines the nature and meaning of three specific forms – dance, sport and exercise. Metheny concludes with a section devoted to the educational process; that is, how one learns to move and the development of this discovery. An appendix for educators includes strategies for using *Movement and Meaning* as part of the teaching and learning project.

Paul Weiss, *Sport: A Philosophic Inquiry* (Carbondale, IL: Southern Illinois University Press, 1969).
In 1969, pre-eminent American philosopher Weiss, following an established list of publications focused on more traditional philosophical topics, turned his attention to sport. Weiss clarifies his purpose in that the book 'is a work in philosophy, and not in sport. It is a work in philosophy just as a philosophy of history or a philosophy of art is a work in philosophy and not in history or in art' (p. viii). Drawing from scholars such as Aristotle and Plato, Thorstein Veblen, Roger Callois and others, Weiss examines a host of philosophic issues related to sport. He begins with a discussion of excellence followed by the attraction of athletic competition in general. In a comprehensive manner, Weiss covers the bodily nature of humans, the requisite dedication that sport excellence demands, the variety of athletic skills and proficiencies (from speed to endurance to coordination), and the nature of play, sport and games. He also examines such topics as amateurs and professionals as well as gender and sport.

Kathleen M. Pearson, 'Deception, Sportsmanship, and Ethics', *Quest* 19 (1973): 115–118.
In this oft-cited article, Pearson answers whether it is ethical or not to deceive one's opponent in sport. Asserting that the purpose of sport is to determine who is more skilful, she analyses how this informs the ethical implications of two types of deception. Strategic deception, such as utilizing misdirection, is ethical because it depends on the skilful execution of actions central to determining relative abilities. Definitional deception occurs when participants end up engaging in an activity different from the one they originally contracted to participate in. Examples of definitional deception not considered ethically problematic include when a player accidentally and without intention commits a foul and accepts the corresponding penalty, thereby restoring the game's ability to reveal skill discrepancies. But when acts are unsportsmanlike or fouls labelled unethical, the ability to determine who is more skilful is compromised. Therefore, such acts of intentional and unsporting definitional deception are unethical because they undermine the very purpose of athletic games.

1974–1988

As with other emerging contextualized forms of philosophy (including education, science, art and language), formalizing the field by creating an association such as the PSSS helped sport philosophy gain a foothold in academe. The introduction of JPS by the PSSS in 1974 marked the next step in the evolution of the field. With Robert Osterhoudt serving as the first editor, a small group of scholars began publishing for the first time in a single forum articles dedicated to the philosophy of sport. The list of contributors to JPS and participants in its annual meetings began to slowly widen, reaching beyond North America to include European scholars interested in philosophic inquiry into sport. The first sport philosophy anthology, edited by Ellen W. Gerber and William J. Morgan, published in 1979, exemplified the extension of the literature. Another anthology, edited by Morgan and Klaus V. Meier at the end of this period in 1988 reflected the growing influence of JPS, with many of the essays coming from the journal. Two topical books also left a lasting impact on the field: Bernard Suits' *The Grasshopper: Games, Life and Utopia* (published in 1978) and Warren P. Fraleigh's *Right Actions in Sports: Ethics for Contestants* (published in 1984).[3] Each elevated the scholarly dialogue regarding the metaphysics of games and sport ethics, respectively, to new heights. Suits' ontological conceptions of games (and eventually play and sports) defined terms and generated debate that continues to influence sport philosophy. Fraleigh's exploration of ethical issues in sport similarly set the groundwork for lasting discourse. Other topics explored with regularity during this period include concepts related to rule following, debates over the relationship between sport and art, issues related to cheating and sportsmanship, discussions regarding the values associated with sport, and the emergence of a topic of great future interest: doping in sport.

Representative Works

Robert Osterhoudt, 'Introduction', *Journal of the Philosophy of Sport* 1 (1974): 1–5.
'The philosophy of sport has developed in recent years toward a progressively greater association with philosophy proper. This development has served to significantly enhance our refined understanding of, and sensitivity for sport. Moreover, it is only under the influence of such development that the philosophy of sport may be plausibly expected to develop full-blown and to take its rightful place beside the other so-termed departmental philosophies' (p. 1). With this introductory paragraph, Osterhoudt launched the first issue of JPS. Volume 1 included essays on aesthetics (Paul Kuntz, Carolyn Thomas, Paul Ziff) and art (Geoffrey Gaskin and D.W. Masterson) relative to sport, a paper on embodiment (John O'Neill), and four articles pertaining to methods of inquiry in sport philosophy (Drew Hyland, Scott Kretchmar, Kathleen M. Pearson and Osterhoudt).

David Best, 'Aesthetic in Sport', *The British Journal of Aesthetics* 14 (1974): 197–213.
In 'Aesthetic in Sport,' Best outlines the relationship between sport and the aesthetic. For Best, the aesthetic is not a constituent feature of an object or activity but rather a way of perceiving that object or activity. Best distinguishes sport from art because the aesthetic is incidental in sport since it is not how a goal is scored but rather that a goal is scored that is of central importance to sport. Best's distinction between purposive and aesthetic sports, in particular, remains part of the field's canon. While it is possible, it is not necessary to engage with purposive sport from an aesthetic point of view. For aesthetic sport, where the end cannot be identified independent of the means, connections to art and the aesthetic are more central to the project. Best argues that while aesthetic feelings may be concurrent with the movement itself, those feelings should not be the basis of aesthetic criteria. Also, the aesthetic pleasure derived from watching or performing sport is not itself central to the project but aligned with idealized actions. Finally, Best concludes by arguing that even aesthetic sports are not art because of the different means-end relationship that exists between sport and art.

William Harper, 'Philosophy of Physical Education and Sport', *Exercise and Sport Sciences Reviews* 2 (1974): 239–264.

In this review of literature, Harper identifies a twofold philosophical awakening of physical education. The first awakening pertains to the philosophical process in physical education that manifests itself in three distinct ways. First, it relies on utilizing the same process and methods that philosophers use. Second, it attempts to build a coherent personal philosophy of physical education. Third, it attempts to build a comprehensible philosophy of physical education. Much of this awakening can be traced through the early volumes of *Quest* and often relies heavily on the philosophy of education. The second awakening pertains to identifying physical education as a discipline as opposed to a technical profession. Disciplinary boundaries require identification of the subject matter, body of knowledge and mode of inquiry. Harper recognizes the distinction between empirical and philosophical methodologies and how they battle to shape the discipline. Harper's final comments are on how most of the philosophical writing has been focused on sport, particularly the nature and significance of sport. While his review is confined to North American literature, it does conclude with a long list of additional references.

Scott Kretchmar, 'From Test to Contest: An Analysis of Two Kinds of Counterpoint in Sport', *Journal of the Philosophy of Sport* 2 (1975): 23–30.

A key to understanding games, Kretchmar argues in the second issue of JPS, lies in clarifying distinctions between tests and contests. Tests simultaneously challenge participants to face their vulnerability (possibility of successfully completing the test) and their impregnability (possibility of failing at the test). This opposition by cut (can/cannot) requires a delicate balance to create genuine tests. Tests made too easy or too hard dissolve the cut line and render the activities disinteresting. Contests, Kretchmar contends, are parasitic to tests: they require two or more participants or groups to engage in the same test for the purpose of comparing results. Consequently contests seek to determine distinctions relative to valid test takers by degree: scoring 82 is better than 80 assuming higher values represent a superior test score. Kretchmar's test/contest distinctions continue to influence the field, particularly the notion that a contest's main function is the determination of relative ability in completing some clearly defined testing condition.

Bernard Suits, 'Words on Play', *Journal of the Philosophy of Sport* 4 (1977): 117–131.

True to his published work in later issues of JPS and *The Grasshopper: Games, Life, and Utopia* (1978), Suits presents a serious and detailed definition of play using humourous dialogues, including conversations between Humpty Dumpty and Alice in Wonderland, Abraham Lincoln and a heckler, and Sergeant Salvatorius and Private Gluteus Maximus. Suits' first argument in the paper focuses on the need to clearly define terms like 'play' to overcome the problems often associated with uncritical, ordinary uses of the concept. He then seeks to delimit the use of the term to actual instances of play rather than 'anything can be play' notions commonly accepted. For example, Suits contends that not all 'game playing' is, in fact, playing. Play must be freely chosen, valued as an end in itself; his full definition of play is presented as 'x is playing if and only if x has made a temporary reallocation to autotelic activities of resources primarily committed to instrumental purposes' (p. 124). This essay, combined with *The Grasshopper* and other papers examining the relationship between the tricky triad (play, games and sport), gives a full account of Suits' definitional demarcation and continues to influence the field's scholarship.

Bernard Suits, *The Grasshopper: Games, Life, and Utopia* (Toronto: University of Toronto Press, 1978).
Suits uses the grasshopper from *Aesop's Fables* to formulate a philosophical theory on games in human life. The author's intent is to develop a definition of games and examine the role of game playing in contemporary culture. In Aesop's treatment, the grasshopper is typically portrayed as enjoying leisure activities over work, while the ant is lauded for a Puritan work ethic. Suits, however, points toward the grasshopper as an exemplar with regards to how one should live one's life. In the course of his book, Suits uses wit and humour to both define and examine such game-related topics as competition, make-believe, espionage, professional sport and Utopia. Suits poses a definition of game playing as 'the voluntary attempt to overcome unnecessary obstacles' (p. 41). In addition, he outlines various tenets crucial to his definition, such as the prelusory goal, lusory means, constitutive rules and lusory attitude. Throughout *The Grasshopper*, Suits contends that game playing, far from a trifling activity, actually holds 'clues to the future. And their serious cultivation now is perhaps our only salvation' (p. 176).

Jane English, 'Sex Equality in Sports', *Philosophy & Public Affairs* 7 (1978): 269–277.
This article answers the question: what constitutes equal opportunity for women in sports? Because the major positions of philosophers focus on fields known to or assumed to offer equal potentialities, it is important to understand how they apply to sport in which relevant differences exist. English argues that non-discrimination, or sex blindness, would not provide equal opportunity. Equal chances may be too strong, unless it refers to basic benefits such that everyone ought to have an equal right to, for example, health, self-respect and fun. Equal achievements for the 'major social groups' requires proportional attainments and may be more applicable to scarce benefits such as appearances on television. In attempting to determine a fair way to treat groups that are physiologically disadvantaged, English identifies the challenges of competition classes based on either clear-cut physical characteristics or ability levels. But the right to self-respect of women demands equal coverage and prize money for women's sport. Furthermore, recreational leagues should be provided for all levels of skill and made available to all ages, sexes, incomes and abilities. English provocatively concludes that a variety of sports should be developed to allow for the demonstration of women's specific traits and natural advantages.

Ellen W. Gerber and William J. Morgan, eds., *Sport and the Body. A Philosophical Symposium* (Philadelphia: Lea & Febiger, 1979).

Gerber and Morgan published an early anthology dedicated to philosophical issues and sport. The editors included essays organised into six particular sections – the nature of sport, sport and metaphysical speculations, the body and being, sport as a meaningful experience, sport and value-oriented concerns, and sport and aesthetics. The section on the nature of sport includes pieces by Bernard Suits, Johan Huizinga and Roger Callois along with sport philosophers such as Robert Osterhoudt and John Loy. The second section contains reflections on the nature of play, freedom, identity and friendship. Section three includes essays by Jean-Paul Sartre and Gabriel Marcel alongside a phenomenological essay by Seymour Kleinman. Numerous essays on play, meaning and symbolism comprise the bulk of section four. In section five, the editors include essays from notable scholars such as Herbert Spencer, Josiah Royce and John Rawls. Finally, section six examines the aesthetic element of sport, with essays from Friedrich Schiller and Terence J. Roberts, among others.

Fred D'Agostino, 'The Ethos of Games', *Journal of the Philosophy of Sport* 8 (1981): 7–18.

Reacting to formalistic accounts of games presented in the literature, D'Agostino (as well as Craig K. Lehman in the same JPS issue[4]) defends an alternative way to view games and sports. Referring to his anti-formalist account as 'conventionalism', D'Agostino argues that a game's social ethos overrides its formal properties. D'Agostino accuses formalists such as Bernard Suits of adopting either an unempirical Platonic vision of games or, to avoid charges of Platonism, an untenable dichotomization thesis separating rules into constitutive and regulative forms. Distinguishing kinds of rules, D'Agostino argues, is both an arbitrary and non-intuitive process. He uses examples from basketball to support this critique of the limits of formalism to address issues related to penalties. Appreciating the efficacy of unofficial conventions, in contrast, provides a clearer picture of how games work best in concrete situations. Formalists only distinguish between permissible and impermissible acts; conventionalism importantly creates a third category of behaviours: impermissible but accepted in light of a game's ethos. D'Agostino concludes by defending conventionalism as an intuitive and empirically sound alternative to rigid, non-concrete formalistic accounts of games.

Warren P. Fraleigh, 'Why the Good Foul Is Not Good', *Journal of Physical Education, Recreation and Dance* 53 (1982): 41–42.

In this short article, Fraleigh presents a compelling argument against the strategic foul. Rules, he contends, operate in order for contests to exist and, when athletes adhere to the letter and spirit of the rules, to ensure good contests. Inadvertent and unintentional rule violations are not problematic; however, intentional rule violations for the sake of gaining an advantage and avoiding a penalty are considered cheating and universally condemned. But Fraleigh is concerned with intentional rule violations for the sake of gaining an advantage while fully expecting and accepting a penalty. Such actions, or 'good fouls', are not good because they detract from the prescribed skills and tactics of a good sports contest.

Peter J. Arnold, 'Three Approaches Toward an Understanding of Sportsmanship', *Journal of the Philosophy of Sport* 10 (1983): 61–70.

Neglected in discussions about how to conceptualize sport and its ethical quandaries, Arnold contends, is the behaviour of the athletes themselves within a sporting context. To rectify this oversight, Arnold presents three different, although interrelated, views of sportsmanship. The first approach emphasizes sportsmanship from a 'social union' perspective. From this perspective, how one plays the game is equally important as any outcome realized. By genuinely committing to the values of sport grounded in the ethos of 19th-century English public school sport, Arnold contends, athletes meaningfully unite in a form of 'brotherhood'. A second approach, sketched out in the literature by James W. Keating, presents sportsmanship as a portal to personal satisfaction.[5] While Arnold critiques Keating's view of sportsmanship as overly dismissive of competition, he agrees that a spirit of play and compassion elicits value. Finally, Arnold describes the third approach of sportsmanship as grounded in altruism. True sportsmen, in this view, go beyond expected ideals of duty and justice to embody a genuine concern for the welfare of other participants. Randolph Feezell[6] similarly attempts to illuminate the concept of sportsmanship from a virtue ethics perspective.

W. Miller Brown, 'Paternalism, Drugs, and the Nature of Sports', *Journal of the Philosophy of Sport* 11 (1984): 14–22.

Reacting to the emergence of performance-enhancing substance (PES) debates in the literature (i.e. Robert L. Simon[7]), and anticipating the groundswell of attention yet to come, Brown examines the justificatory power of PES prohibitions in sporting contexts. Brown rejects the reasonableness of hard paternalism (based on voluntary, informed, competent and measured decisions) when considering PES use by adult athletes. In defence of this position, Brown rejects ignorance as an acceptable rationale for imposing PES bans on adult performers, argues for the acceptability of adopting extrinsic motivations in free societies, concludes fears of health risks lack empirical evidence, and points to the acceptance of other high-risk sporting behaviours to declare PES bans on paternalistic grounds hypocritical. Brown also challenges the notion that PES use runs counter to the nature of sport, arguing that a priori notions of sport ignore the ongoing evolution of athletic competitions. Brown justifies high-risk enhancement prohibitions, however, in youth sport. Unlike adults, children are at risk of falling prey to soft paternalism and participating in non-voluntary enhancement behaviours. Brown argues that children should be protected from unnecessary risk for health reasons while also promoting the need for youth sport to emphasize intrinsic goals and personal development.

Warren P. Fraleigh, *Right Actions in Sports: Ethics for Contestants* (Champaign, IL: Human Kinetics, 1984).

Pointing beyond metaphysical questions, Fraleigh published an early work focused specifically on the moral nature of sport, what he terms a 'systematic, comprehensive normative ethic' (p. ix). He begins with several problematic and illustrative cases (e.g. the case of the intentional foul) and then moves towards ways to answer such dilemmas and the rationale for a moral basis overall. Fraleigh develops a structural framework to discern right actions and provides a description of 'one good sports contest' as a helpful starting point. In chapters 3 to 7, he examines right actions with respect to winning and losing, rules, the relationship between opponents and values of a sports contest. Part three provides guidelines for making ethical decisions, from effective preparation to mutual respect to prudent withdrawal. Fraleigh acknowledges the difficulty of applying normative guides in specific situations. He concludes with observations on moral maturity as it regards sport contests.

David L. Vanderwerken and Spencer Wertz, eds., *Sport Inside Out: Readings in Literature and Philosophy* (Fort Worth, TX: Texas Christian University Press, 1985). In this anthology, Vanderwerken and Wertz examine philosophical themes through a wide range of written form – fiction and poetry as well as more traditional philosophical essays. The book begins with subjective experience as the focus – the participant, spectator and community. The second part includes essays geared towards societal themes such as competition and the American dream. The editors exhibit essays on the meaning of sport next, organizing essays around themes such as religion, myth and the aesthetic. Finally, part four provides a look at sporting language, humour and death. The editors include works by novelists such as Ernest Hemingway ('Fifty Grand') and John Updike ('Hub Fans Bid Kid Adieu'), sports writers like Frank Deford ('Religion in Sport'), scholars such as Allen Guttman ('The Sacred and the Secular') and Hans Lenk ('Herculean "Myth" Aspects of Athletics') and even a former president in Gerald R. Ford ('In Defense of the Competitive Urge').

Spencer Wertz, 'Representation and Expression in Sport and Art', *Journal of the Philosophy of Sport* 12 (1985): 8–24.
One of the most hotly debated sport philosophy topics in the 1970s and 1980s was David Best's claim, originally presented in a 1974 journal article[8] as well as in his book *Philosophy and Human Movement* (1978),[9] that no sport is art. It served as a lightning rod for later responses. Best[10] reaffirmed his conclusion in a JPS issue featuring articles related to aesthetics and art by Peter J. Arnold[11] as well as Wertz. Wertz, in particular, challenged Best's 19th-century depiction of art as well as his narrow conceptions of both representation and expression – functions of art Best believes sport fails to perform. Wertz argues for a more contemporary understanding of art, as well as for sports' potential to be both representational and expressive, using examples from tennis in particular to defend his counterclaims. Other participants in the sport/art debate included Jan M. Boxill,[12] Christopher Cordner,[13] Joseph Kupfer[14] and Terence J. Roberts.[15]

William J. Morgan, 'The Logical Incompatibility Thesis and Rules: A Reconsideration of Formalism as an Account of Games', *Journal of the Philosophy of Sport* 14 (1987): 1–20.
In his partial defence of formalism, Morgan counters critiques launched by conventionalists against the logical incompatibility thesis – the idea that rule-

breakers cannot be considered game players since rules define games. While Morgan acknowledges some acceptance of the ethos as important to games, he attempts to incorporate it into a revised formalistic account. To do so, Morgan turns to Alasdair MacIntyre's conceptions of social practices and social institutions. Practices, MacIntyre famously argues, are socially created activities that make certain, context-specific internal goods possible. Institutions govern practices (e.g. FIFA organizes international football) and tend to focus on external goods – goods such as money available in any number of human practices. Morgan contends that by considering sports first and foremost as social practices, internal goods can be realized. Sporting practices must therefore hold true to an internal logic by which excellence can be defined and protected from the corrupting influence of institutions. A sport's ethos thus flows from its distinctive rationale and 'internal point of view of the game' (p. 18). Morgan's use of MacIntyre's practice/institution concepts, as well as the promotion of an internal perspective when addressing sport issues, deeply influenced the field.

Joy T. DeSensi, 'PSSS Bibliography of the Philosophy of Sport – 1987', *Journal of the Philosophy of Sport* 14 (1987): 86–134.
DeSensi presents a bibliography of over 1100 published philosophical or socio-political works focusing (to a significant degree) on sport, play and games (but not physical education and pedagogy). In previous JPS issues, DeSensi[16] provided updated references to a list first constructed in 1984 and subsequently distributed to PSSS members. DeSensi added a further update in 1991.[17] In addition to DeSensi's bibliographies, Klaus V. Meier provided a reference index to all articles printed in JPS on the occasion of the journal's 10th (1983) and 20th (1993) anniversaries.[18]

Klaus V. Meier, 'Triad Trickery: Playing With Sport and Games', *Journal of the Philosophy of Sport* 15 (1988), 11–30.
Continuing an ongoing debate, Meier challenges Bernard Suits' updated definitional demarcations of the 'tricky triad': play, games and sport.[19] Suits presents play, games and sport as distinct overlapping circles in a Venn diagram, revealing seven possible combinations including sport as game but not play, sport as play only, sport as neither play nor game and so on. Meier redraws the diagram to fully enclose sport within the games sphere to represent his claim that all sports are games (but not all games are sports). Play, then, intersects with games and a small portion of sports. This, Meier contends, highlights the premise that only some games and some sports are also play. Despite their differences, Suits and Meier agree on the importance of rigorously demarcating play, games and sports to provide philosophical clarity, as well as to avoid applying inappropriate definitions to arrive at faulty conclusions. The Suits/Meier debate in this JPS issue also highlights key terms and ideas including four features of games ('prelusory goals', 'lusory means', 'constitutive rules' and 'lusory attitudes') as well as the central feature of play ('autotelicity').

William J. Morgan and Klaus V. Meier, eds., *Philosophic Inquiry in Sport* (Champaign, IL: Human Kinetics, 1988).
Morgan and Meier compiled a collection of essays related to the field of sport philosophy aimed at an undergraduate and graduate student level. The editors organized content into six parts: the nature of sport, play and games; sport and embodiment; sport, play and metaphysics; sport and ethics; sport and social-political philosophy; and sport and aesthetics. Furthermore, the sport and ethics part includes three subsections focused on: competition, sportsmanship, cheating and failure; drugs and sport; and women and sport. The anthology includes classic philosophic treatises such as Plato ('The Separation of Body and Soul'), René Descartes ('The Real Distinction between the Mind and Body of Man') and Jean-Paul Sartre ('The Body') as well as reprints from sport philosophers such as Jane English ('Sex Equality in Sports'), Warren P. Fraleigh ('Why the Good Foul is Not Good') and Drew Hyland ('Competition and Friendship'). In 1995, the editors published a second edition with numerous changes. Of particular note in the later edition, they devote more space to ethical issues and include a stand-alone section on the morality of hunting and animal liberation.

1989–1999

By 1988, the PSSS had established a strong foundation and the range of contributors to both JPS and the annual meetings continued to widen. Scholarship from Western Europe, Scandinavian countries and Japan became more prevalent within the sport philosophy literature. Combined with sprinter Ben Johnson's positive test for a banned performance-enhancing substance (PES) at the 1988 Seoul Olympic Games, global interest in scholarly issues related to sport ethics rose to new levels. Furthermore, ethical issues in sport became more prevalent in non-academic conversations globally. Thus the field continued to grow, with new contributors and emerging issues explored in books and JPS. Several scholars tackled the PES debate in the wake of the Seoul Olympic Games; discussions arose regarding ethical issues including blowing out opponents; philosophers explored issues including gender inequality, the purpose of sport, the sanctioning of violence in athletic contests and questions regarding character in sporting contexts. The socio-political philosophy espoused by Alasdair MacIntyre's *After Virtue* widely influenced the sport philosophy literature, while others employed neo-pragmatic ideas originated by Richard Rorty to challenge traditional conceptions of sports and athletic morality. The decade ended with the introduction and rapid adoption by many sport philosophers of a methodological approach termed 'interpretivism'.

Representative Works
Roger Gardner, 'On Performance-Enhancing Substances and the Unfair Advantage Argument', *Journal of the Philosophy of Sport* 16 (1989): 59–73.
The first article published in JPS following Ben Johnson's high-profile Olympic steroid scandal, Gardner challenges a central justification for the ban of performance-enhancing substances (PES): the unfair advantage argument.

Gardner posits four interrelated challenges to ban justifications based on unfair advantage claims. First, he contends that objections to PES use lie not in the creation of some imbalance among competitors, but in the methods used to gain said advantages. Second, Gardner dismisses claims that advantages always create unfairness; instead, he argues, ethical issues arise only in cases of unfairly gained advantages. Third, Gardner asserts that athletes routinely seek out advantages without facing ethical reproach, and attempts to find ways to overcome obstacles inherent to sport are a key feature of athletic competition. Finally, Gardner argues that sport depends on the creation of inequality, rendering unfair advantage critiques of PES use moot. Gardner's examination of the PES issue continued the debate initiated by Robert L. Simon,[20] W. Miller Brown[21] and Michael Lavin,[22] among others, and preceded examinations by philosophers including Angela J. Schneider and Robert R. Butcher,[23] Michael D. Burke[24] and Claudio M. Tamburrini.[25]

Robert L. Simon, *Fair Play: Sports, Values, and Society* (Boulder CO: Westview Press, 1991).
Following on Warren P. Fraleigh's work, Simon published an additional work focused on ethical issues in sport. He begins by emphasizing the appropriateness of making normative claims overall, and the extent to which moral reasoning is rationally justified. Simon examines the very nature of competition, if the concept is morally defensible and how important the pursuit of victory should be in healthy competitive activities. Simon contends that competition, at its best, means to be 'engaged in voluntarily as part of a mutual quest for excellence' (p. 23). This notion of competition invariably brings up issues of sportsmanship and fairness, concepts explored in connection to cheating and violence. Chapter 4 examines performance enhancement and Simon systematically explores various arguments against drug use in sport. He continues by analysing equality and excellence in sport with regards to justice and individual rights and in another chapter examines more specifically what equality means with regards to gender. Simon concludes by considering the place of intercollegiate sport as part of educational institutions, and finally with a look at how sport values might impact on the broader societal climate.

Jan M. Boxill, 'Title IX and Gender Equity', *Journal of the Philosophy of Sport* 20 (1993): 23–31.
Boxill presents a critical examination of American education legislation enacted in 1972 to address issues related to gender inequality. Intercollegiate sport in the United States, in particular, was affected by a significant number of changes implemented to increase participation rates and resource allocations to female student athletes. Boxill acknowledges the positive influence Title IX had on women's sport in general (even beyond intercollegiate athletics); however, she also points to some challenges and limitations women face in sporting contexts. For instance, Boxill highlights the male-oriented emphasis on game construction and competitive ideals, exceptions to legislation to protect male sports such as American football, the lack of available options to women to participate in certain

sports with other women, increased percentages of male administrators and coaches of women's sport, and recurring challenges related to homophobia. Boxill also discusses gender issues in JPS articles published in 1984 and 2006;[26] other articles in JPS related to gender include Betsy C. Postow,[27] Joy T. DeSensi,[28] Robert L. Simon,[29] Leslie P. Francis[30] and Melina Constantine Bell.[31]

Peter J. Arnold, 'Sport and Moral Education', *Journal of Moral Education* 23 (1994): 75–89.
The relationship between sport and a moral life is an ongoing debate in sport philosophy literature. Does sport have a positive, negative or neutral relationship to moral values? Arnold argues for a positive relationship with the important expectation of moral education as part and parcel of education in sport. Drawing on John Rawls's *A Theory of Justice*, Arnold argues that freedom and equality are moral components of sport. Sport pedagogy must be concerned not only with rules, skill and excellence but also with the virtues of sport. Judging, caring and acting are three interlocking moral dimensions of sport. The teacher must initiate sport as a valued practice, provide enlightened leadership, care and counselling on the values of sport, and represent a commitment to those values. The development of moral character is evident through students' commitment to the internal goals and standards of sport. In this sense, sport is not used for moral purposes, 'but rather as a valued practice in which the virtues have a necessary and vital part to play' (p. 87).

William J. Morgan, *Leftist Theories of Sport: A Critique and Reconstruction* (Urbana, IL: University of Illinois Press, 1994).
Many writers have attempted reform efforts for contemporary sport, most notably intercollegiate sport through professional and world-class competition. In particular, authors from a so-called leftist perspective (e.g. the New Left and hegemony theory) have taken aim, although, Morgan argues, with failed results. With the intent of developing a critical theory of sport, Morgan draws from social theory as well as philosophy, contending that both areas of scholarly inquiry connect in meaningful ways. This project involves exploring means, both theoretically and practically, to improve the social ethos of contemporary sport. He provides a critique of these leftist theories and proceeds to develop and defend a reconstructed theory of contemporary sport, one in the framework of a social practice outlined by MacIntyre. Morgan contends that the joint efforts of scholars (sports studies and political theorists) and sport enthusiasts may provide the necessary change required.

Terence J. Roberts, 'Sport and Strong Poetry', *Journal of the Philosophy of Sport* 22 (1995): 94–107.
Roberts' 1994 PSSS presidential address calls for philosophers to consider adopting new language forms to help see and understand sport in novel, more meaningful ways. Appropriating Richard Rorty's notions of truth, language and metaphor, Roberts concludes that sport desperately requires constant 're-redescription' to circumvent powerful, yet tired and limiting, athletic

vocabularies. Sport, Roberts contends, ultimately needs to cultivate 'strong poets' to remake sport in new and creative ways. Furthermore, the encouragement of athletes to adopt the life of a strong poet affords individuals opportunities to 'give birth to oneself' and to 'make anew' rather than conform to the strict, impoverished language gripping sport. A radical departure at the time from the emphasis in the literature on the sanctity of MacIntyrean-inspired allegiance to practices, Roberts' neo-pragmatic use of Rorty offers an emphasis on idiosyncrasy, creativity and contingency.

Alun Hardman, Luanne Fox, Doug McLaughlin and Kurt Zimmerman, 'On Sportsmanship and "Running Up the Score": Issues of Incompetence and Humiliation', *Journal of the Philosophy of Sport* 23 (1996): 58–69.
Reacting to Nicholas Dixon's ethical defence of blowing out opponents Hardman et al. construct a justification for the 'anti-blowout' (AB) thesis originated by Randolph Feezell.[32] Dixon's rejection of the AB thesis follows from his influential claim that the 'determination of athletic superiority' stands as the central purpose of competitive sport.[33] Consequently, Dixon contends that losers of lopsided contests should not feel strongly humiliated (moral shame) since the score simply reveals information about relative ability. Dixon acknowledges that blown-out participants may justifiably feel weakly humiliated (non-moral failings), but superior individuals and teams should not refrain from full-out efforts. Hardman et al. take issue with Dixon's conclusion, presenting counterarguments including the negative psychological realities of blowout losses, the cultural significance of athletic success and the limited validity of imbalanced contests. Dixon responded to Hardman et al., reaffirming his position that lopsided scores are not the cause of strong humiliation.[34]

Michael D. Burke, 'Drugs in Sport: Have They Practiced Too Hard? A Response to Schneider and Butcher', *Journal of the Philosophy of Sport* 24 (1997): 47–66.
Applying Richard Rorty's neo-pragmatic emphasis on contingency and language, Burke challenges Angela J. Schneider and Robert R. Butcher's MacIntyrean-based position against the use of drugs in Olympic competitions.[35] Burke contends that the main arguments presented by Schneider and Butcher are flawed. For instance, contra Butcher and Schneider, he makes a case for athletes focusing on the internal goods of sport while justifying drug use, challenges their claim that doping does not advance sport skill, and disagrees with their position that drug use is merely a means to secure external goods. Burke ultimately argues that Schneider and Butcher's position is a statement of social consensus rather than a rational argument – and one in need of further conversation. The joy of sports, Burke concludes, ultimately rests on a sense of private achievement. Applications of MacIntyre to sport, however, disregard subjective experience at the expense of privileging social institutions. Burke calls for a dissolution of the internal-external good distinction and the need for increased discussion on the doping issue grounded in the ideas of contingency and social solidarity rather than pure logic.

Robert R. Butcher and Angela J. Schneider, 'Fair Play as Respect for the Game', *Journal of the Philosophy of Sport* 25 (98): 1–22.
Extending on an earlier treatment of the doping issue and embodying the influence of Alasdair MacIntyre's *After Virtue* on the sport philosophy field, Butcher and Schneider turn to the concept of sports as social practices to reach a conclusion to the question 'why should athletes play fair?'[36] Butcher and Schneider begin with a survey of five traditional justifications for expecting athletes to play fair: to demonstrate virtuous behaviour, to maintain the playful character of games, to uphold implicit agreements to test relative abilities in a contest, to logically play the game by following binding rules, and to adhere to the agreed-upon conventions of a sport. Ultimately, Butcher and Schneider find these five philosophical treatments of fair play unsatisfying, instead positing the view of sports as social practices to offer a more reasoned justification for fair play expectations. Butcher and Schneider contend that athletes must place the best interests of the practice (sport) above all else to logically secure the internal goods made possible by the activity. Only by respecting the game through the adoption of intrinsic motivations, Butcher and Schneider conclude, can participants become members of the practice community and thus gain access to sport's richness.

Mike McNamee and Jim Parry, eds., *Ethics and Sport* (London: E & FN Spon, 1998).
The final years of the 20th century also served as a starting point for a prevalence of anthologies and collected readings focused on ethics in sport, starting with McNamee and Parry's edited volume *Ethics and Sport*. McNamee and Parry's anthology included sections dedicated to the place of philosophy, fair play, physical education and coaching, and contemporary ethical issues in sport. In 2001, William J. Morgan, Klaus V. Meier and Angela J. Schneider published *Ethics in Sport*.[37] This collection of articles examined fair play and sportsmanship, performance enhancement, gender identity and equity, animals and sport, and finally ethical issues regarding the social context of sport. Jan M. Boxill published an additional reader on sport ethics in 2003 with topics ranging from sport and education, sportspersonship and competition to gender and athletes as role models.[38] Subsequent readers focused on more specific ethical issues. For example, Claudio M. Tamburrini and Torbjörn Tännsjö edited *Genetic Technology and Sport: Ethical Questions*[39] and Alun Hardman and Carwyn Jones edited *The Ethics of Sports Coaching*.[40]

Nicholas Dixon, 'On Winning and Athletic Superiority', *Journal of the Philosophy of Sport* 26 (1999): 10–26.
Appealing to his claim that sport centrally exists to determine athletic superiority, Dixon considers the efficacy of game outcomes to reveal accurate measures of relative ability. The best athletes or teams, Dixon reinforces, often fail to win. Reasons explored to explain why this occurs include ill-timed refereeing errors, cheating and gamesmanship tactics employed by inferior participants, simple bad luck, sub-par performances by superior athletes, an overemphasis on psychological

traits and moral luck. Dixon describes contests won by lesser teams or athletes as inevitable but 'failed' in realizing sport's central purpose. He concludes by promoting less emphasis on sporting outcomes (winning) and reasserts his earlier argument against the anti-blowout thesis that focusing on winning (by any means) creates problems when viewed as the central feature of sport.

David Carr, 'Where's the Merit if the Best Man Wins?', *Journal of the Philosophy of Sport* 26 (1999): 1–9.
Carr challenges the commonly held notion that successful sport participants should be lauded for athletic accomplishments. Ultimately, he argues, we cannot take credit for athletic success since the ability to perform athletic skills and the capacity to learn these skills as well as relevant sporting knowledge all comes down to a biological lottery. Carr's materialistic view of human performance suggests taking credit for simply possessing genetic characteristics well suited to athletic competition is nonsensical; individuals can only take responsibility when they fail to perform up to predetermined levels. In this view, any celebration of personal endowment is grounded in extrinsic sensibilities; Carr instead calls for a redirected focus on the intrinsic, aesthetically satisfying, elements of competitive sport. His promotion of a disinterested, detached attitude toward personal achievement echoes, albeit from a very different perspective, Nicholas Dixon's criticism of the value in placing emphasis on sporting outcomes. In later essays, Scott Kretchmar[41] and Kretchmar and Tim L. Elcombe[42] challenge Dixon[43] and Carr's respective critiques of the value of competition (and emphasis on winning).

Sharon Kay Stoll, 'Should Character Be Measured? A Reply to Professor Gough and the Reductionist Argument', *Journal of the Philosophy of Sport* 26 (1999): 95–104.
Responding to critiques, particularly ones levied by Russell W. Gough,[44] Stoll defends her research group's creation of empirical tools to measure character among sport participants on the occasion of her 1998 PSSS presidential address. Stoll challenges philosophers to start adopting empirical and applied research methodologies found in fields such as sociology and psychology to provide a fuller account of ethical behaviour and moral development in sporting contexts. Countering Gough's 'post-positivist' charges that she inappropriately reduces moral character to a series of measureable standards, Stoll argues that universal morals do exist, can be learned, and subsequently quantified using appropriate research methodology. Stoll contends that most philosophers fail to adequately understand empirical research, thus she provides overviews of experimental moral development research, the process of creating and delimiting research projects and the formation of evaluation tools. By better understanding the definitive features of morality, and the subsequent ability to measure an individual's character, Stoll believes moral education can be greatly enhanced. M. Andrew Holowchak responded, expressing concerns with Stoll's clarity in her defence of empirical moral character research and failure to address Gough's critiques directly.[45]

J.S. Russell, 'Are Rules All An Umpire Has to Work With?', *Journal of the Philosophy of Sport* 26 (1999): 27–49.

An oft-cited exemplar of the emerging broad internalist or interpretivist methodology, Russell considers how baseball umpires can justly render decisions in situations not addressed by the formal rules. Applying Ronald Dworkin's 'interpretivist' approach to legal issues, Russell argues that principles and theories leading to the best interpretation of a game serve as the foundation for adjudicating sport actions. For instance, to deal with the dilemma faced by umpires making calls in indeterminate circumstances, Russell posits four 'principles of adjudication in sport'. First, Russell contends that 'rules should be interpreted in such a manner that the excellences embodied in achieving the lusory goal of the game are not undermined but are maintained and fostered' (p. 35). Second, 'rules should be interpreted to achieve an appropriate competitive balance' (p. 35). A third principle outlined states 'rules should be interpreted according to principles of fair play and sportsmanship'. Finally, Russell asserts that 'rules should be interpreted to preserve the good conduct of games' (p. 36). Russell elevates the first of the aforementioned principles to the status of 'the first principle of games adjudication'. By this Russell means the remaining three principles flow from the more central principle that officials should interpret the rules to 'create a context that allows for the realization of [the game's] obstacles and the related excellences ... that are available to overcome them' (p. 35).

2000–2006

To better reflect the emerging international character of the sport philosophy field, the Philosophic Society for the Study of Sport changed its name to the International Association for the Philosophy of Sport (IAPS) in 1999. In 2001, JPS added a second annual issue to reflect the expansion of scholarly work conducted in sport philosophy. The growth of the field in Europe precipitated the formation of the British Philosophy of Sport Association (BPSA) in 2004, with scholars from Great Britain, Scandinavia, Eastern and Western Europe as well as North America attending the annual meetings. The increasing range of issues explored, from conceptions about rules and debates regarding sportsmanship and gamesmanship to phenomenological analyses, represented the field's growth. PES debates widened to include related questions about technology and genetic doping. Special sections in JPS issues included topics such as the Olympic Games and ethical issues in disability and sport, as well as epistemology and movement. Another special topics section in JPS explored the central methodological discussion of the period: the shift from disagreements amongst interpretivists, formalists and conventionalists to debates pitting realist versus antirealist accounts of sport.

Representative Works
Jeffrey P. Fry, 'Coaching a Kingdom of Ends', *Journal of the Philosophy of Sport* 27 (2000): 51–62.

Fry uses a Kantian framework to address the world of high school and college sport coaching. In the first section, Fry delineates the 'kingdom of ends', Kant's conception of an exemplary moral community where people treat others as ends in themselves rather than means to an end. He explores what the coaching world might look like should coaches employ such an ends-focused approach. To treat others (and self) in such a way means placing value on them as persons. The second part of the essay describes several coaching scenarios, with intent to compare the coaching actions to the Kantian pattern of acceptability. Fry notes the complexity of coaching in that the task requires the ability to negotiate multiple potential ends or purposes that may at times conflict. In the end, Fry argues for the treatment of persons as ends over and above values placed on impersonal goals.

Cesar R. Torres, 'What Counts as Part of a Game? A Look at Skills', *Journal of the Philosophy of Sport* 27 (2000): 81–92.
Extending the influence of John Searle's conception of constitutive and regulative rules of language to sport philosophy, Torres argues for the need to shift the debate over the nature of sport from rules to skills. Torres begins by outlining the role of constitutive and regulative rules in sports: constitutive rules serve as indicators of prelusory goals and lusory means making games possible; regulative rules, in contrast, importantly enable the continuation of games when constitutive rules are broken. It is possible, Torres points out, that games can be played without violations, rendering regulative rules secondary. Thus when Torres shifts the attention from rules to skills, he argues that skills generated by restorative rules (e.g. free throws in basketball and penalty kicks in football) are secondary to skills required to overcome constitutively defined game barriers (e.g. dribbling in basketball and passing in football). Constitutive skills, Torres continues, attract us to games, whereas regulative skills parasitically exist merely for functional, restorative purposes. Torres concludes that emphasizing distinctions between constitutive and restorative skills helps us better appreciate good games (predominantly featuring constitutive skills) relative to flawed games (in which restorative skills are centrally featured).

Sigmund Loland, *Fair Play in Sport: A Moral Norm System* (London: Routledge, 2002).
This work by Loland appears as part of an Ethics and Sport series edited by Mike McNamee and Jim Parry. In concert with other titles related to ethics, *Fair Play in Sport* provides a critical examination of the concept of fair play and its relationship to human flourishing. Loland begins by examining the nature of sport competitions, both from a historical perspective and also from a current understanding (including informal and formal conceptions of fair play). He examines criteria such as 'a moral point of view' and develops his framework based on two concepts: utility and justice. During the course of his argument, Loland recognizes the nature of competition as a social contract. The conception of justice relates to fair play with respect to external conditions (e.g. equipment and training methods) as well as personal ones (e.g. age and sex). In addition, fair play may be compromised to varying degrees by the competitors' internal goals. Loland argues that competitors should indeed play to win when involved in a

just sporting ethos. In his final chapter, Loland attempts to balance the 'sweet tension' between fairness and play and contends that when competitors match wits in 'fair and good competition' the potential for human flourishing becomes possible.

Scott Kretchmar, 'A Functionalist Analysis of Game Acts: Revisiting Searle', *Journal of the Philosophy of Sport* 28 (2001): 160–172.
Like Cesar R. Torres, Kretchmar returns to Searle's ideas about rules and conventions to better understand sport. In particular, Kretchmar seeks to re-examine how, using Searle's language, rule changes and violations affect how conventions (such as games) function. Kretchmar considers how formalistic appropriations of Searle's constitutive/regulative rule distinctions lead to logical quandaries (embodied by the logical incompatibility thesis). Rather than view constitutive and regulative rules from this formalistic perspective, Kretchmar instead promotes a pragmatic understanding. For instance, Kretchmar argues that any rule that helps a convention realize its purpose is constitutive, with some constitutive rules considered more central than others. Consequently, these violations are penalized more harshly than violations of rules with less effect on the convention's degree of functionality. Kretchmar also places a greater emphasis on the role of regulative rules – which he contends establish the boundaries for good games, including aesthetics, ethics, culture, society and logic – all of which are 'baked into the lusory project' (p. 169) and play a central role in both the formation of games and their evolution.

Andy Miah, 'Genetic Technologies and Sport: The New Ethical Issue', *Journal of the Philosophy of Sport* 28 (2001): 32–52.
Considered a great looming ethical challenge, Miah examines issues related to genetic technologies and their possible effect on sport. Some of the conclusions regarding genetic manipulation offered by Miah include growing evidence that it would be possible that specialized training and commitment would still be required for athletic success, that even small enhancements would influence sport, that individuals could not be held responsible for the actions of their parents, and that naturally advantaged athletes are not excluded from athletic participation. Miah's conclusions centre on arguments that genetic engineering does not provide performance enhancements not already accepted in sport and is no worse than drug use.

Douglas Hochstetler and Tim L. Elcombe, 'Sportphilosophie: A Summary of Selected Research (2001–2002)', *International Journal of Physical Education* 39 (2002): 4–20.
Every other year, the *International Journal of Physical Education* publishes a review of the sport philosophy literature. Providing a thorough summary of the publications in the philosophy of sport over the past two years, the reviews are a useful resource to follow the trajectory of the field. Subsequent reviews have been compiled by Hochstetler and Elcombe (2004), Peter Hopsicker and Ivo Jirásek (2006 and 2008), Hopsicker and Emanuel Hurych (2010) and Hurych and Jim Parry (2012).[46]

M. Andrew Holowchak, 'Ergogenic Aids and the Limits of Human Performance in Sport: Ethical Issues, Aesthetic Considerations', *Journal of the Philosophy of Sport* 29 (2002): 75–86.

Holowchak introduces the concept of ergogenic aids to examine the ethical use of any 'substances, techniques, or materials' (p. 76) that might enhance performance in sport contexts. Classifying substances such as steroids or amphetamines as merely one type of ergogenic aid – pharmacological – Holowchak widens the ongoing debate regarding doping to include mechanical (e.g. materials and physical techniques), psychological (e.g. mental techniques), physiological (e.g. altitude training or lean body mass) and nutritional (e.g. diet) aids. In addition to identifying five categories of ergogenic aids, Holowchak also distinguishes between direct (potential to improve performance) and indirect (potential to prevent decrease in performance) applications. Rejecting both the unnatural and unfair arguments often levied against ergogenic aids, Holowchak introduces a Strong Principle of Harm, a Principle of Aretic Respect, a modified Principle of Enhancement of Skill and an Aesthetic Principle to help distinguish between permissible and regulated usage.

David Morris, 'Touching Intelligence', *Journal of the Philosophy of Sport* 29 (2002): 149–162.

Published in a special JPS issue on epistemology and movement (guest edited by Maxine Sheets-Johnstone), Morris considers how one comes to know through touch in a sporting context. Focusing on the 'wielding' of a tennis racquet, Morris examines how the experience of extending our bodies by fusing with things like sporting equipment transforms our exploration of the world around us. Materials become part of us, extending our reach and enhancing our sense of touch through objects. Morris' analysis considers phenomenological concepts such as wielding, the toucher and touched, reverberation and resonance, and the melodies of touch. Conclusions offered challenge dualistic conceptions of human existence, instead highlighting the holistic, fully integrated lived experience of moving bodies and the worlds they exist within.

Douglas R. Anderson, 'The Humanity of Movement or "It's Not Just a Gym Class"', *Quest* 54 (2002): 87–96.

The push for respectability for the field of kinesiology has resulted in a marginalization of human movement itself, Anderson argues. The drive toward a scientific focus to defend the academic and intellectual merit of the field and demonstrate its utility is marked by a reductive approach to movement inattentive to the features of embodied experience so important to developing personal and social meanings. Anderson further argues that the humanities must complement the sciences in order to discover the richness of meaningful movement experiences. Expressing through participation and skill, striving towards excellence, encountering limits and failures and developing knowledge of acquaintance are part of the holistic and meaningful encounter with physical activity. The purpose of kinesiology thus goes beyond being a purveyor of health and fitness to reawakening people to the potent meanings in the experiences of movement.

Nicholas Dixon, 'Canadian Figure Skaters, French Judges, and Realism in Sport', *Journal of the Philosophy of Sport* 30 (2003): 103–116.

Dixon uses the context of the figure skating controversy at the 2002 Salt Lake City Winter Olympic Games whereby judges, by all accounts, inappropriately awarded a Russian couple the gold medal over a more deserving Canadian pair, to test the efficacy of rival approaches to ethical deliberation. Following outlines of the key features of formalism (adherence to central rules), conventionalism (community assent) and interpretivism (appeal to broad principles defining the nature of a practice), Dixon concludes all three would rightfully find the decision problematic. However, when the example is tweaked, Dixon concludes that interpretivism, presented most clearly in earlier JPS articles by J.S. Russell[47] and Robert L. Simon,[48] stands as the lone method capable of rendering just conclusions by challenging the status quo. Dixon goes further, however, suggesting Simon's formalist, conventionalist and interpretivist classifications collapse into moral realist and antirealist camps.[49] Dixon champions a realist approach, whereby a general nature of truth about the purposes of sport can help reasonably address ethical dilemmas.

William J. Morgan, 'Moral Antirealism, Internalism, and Sport', *Journal of the Philosophy of Sport* 31 (2004): 161–183.

Reacting to Nicholas Dixon's[50] contention that moral realism offers a rationally superior approach to addressing sport ethics issues, Morgan conversely presents a case for an antirealist account as more normatively powerful. Morgan begins the essay, included in a special section in JPS examining moral realism and antirealism, by supporting Dixon's claim that interpretivism is normatively superior to formalism, conventionalism and subjectivism (a fourth methodological camp added by Morgan). He also points out that Dixon's collapsing of the methods into realist and antirealist typologies is invaluable to understanding how to best adjudicate ethical quandaries. However, he disagrees with Dixon's view that moral realism trumps antirealism. Morgan argues for an antirealist view that emphasizes the historical and social context of social practices such as sport – going as far as to suggest that Dixon's position is grounded in an antirealist, historical and contextual stance. Morgan challenges the viability of abstract, ahistorical, non-contextual deliberation associated with realist accounts, while also defending antirealism against charges of subjectivism or nihilism.

Leslie A. Howe, 'Gamesmanship,' *Journal of the Philosophy of Sport* 31 (2004): 212–225.

Howe begins her examination of the ethics of 'gamesmanship' by asking the question 'what are you prepared to do to win?' The answer one gives, Howe believes, reveals not only character within a sport context but also a person's wider moral character. Howe describes gamesmanship as the attempt to manipulate rules or opponents' psyche to gain a competitive advantage. In the first section, Howe defends gamesmanship against charges of unfairness or lacking athletic value. However, when considered against what Howe takes to be the point of sport – not winning, but the pursuit of victory – gamesmanship loses its ethical footing. The process of attempting to win, she contends, provides opportunities for 'self-revelation' (p. 218). Athletes are tested physically, psychologically and morally when engaged in pressure-filled competitive scenarios. Employing strategies that circumvent the risk, Howe suggests, is tantamount to cowardice. Consequently, Howe accepts that 'weak' forms of gamesmanship might enhance the test of self, however 'strong' gamesmanship ought to be rejected as it limits the challenge one is willing to accept – and thus runs counter to the value and purpose of sport competitions.

Carwyn Jones and P. David Howe, 'The Conceptual Boundaries of Sport for the Disabled: Classification and Athletic Performance', *Journal of the Philosophy of Sport* 32 (2005): 133–146.
Along with submissions by Leslie P. Francis[51] and Stanislav Pinter, Tjasa Filipcic, Ales Solar and Maja Smrdu,[52] Jones and Howe consider ethical issues related to sport for the disabled in a special section of JPS. In particular, Jones and Howe examine philosophical challenges in classifying disabled sport performers. Paralympic Games organizers, gatekeepers of the highest level of sport for the disabled, must decide how to establish parameters to create fair and equitable competitive categories. Considering the multitude and variance among potential participants in terms of their disabilities, Jones and Howe contend that governing bodies must find a balance between creating sufficient categories to ensure relatively fair and meaningful competitions and addressing logistical and commercial interests. Too many categories render the staging and marketing of sports for the disabled unfeasible, while too few categorical distinctions create unequal playing fields for athletes with widely varying disabilities.

Claudio M. Tamburrini, 'Are Doping Sanctions Justified? A Moral Relativistic View', *Sport in Society* 9 (2006): 199–211.
This issue of *Sport in Society* includes several articles on the topic of doping in sport from a philosophical perspective. Sarah Teetzel[53] analyses how arguments for unfair advantages related to participation of transgendered athletes are substantially different to advantages from doping. William J. Morgan[54] questions the changes in the standard of proof and the grounds of basic fairness in current anti-doping efforts that in the end compound the very doping issues they are meant to resolve. Tamburrini disputes the three main justifications offered for doping bans and is critical of the IOC and WADA's efforts to enforce those bans. Having previously critiqued the harm argument, Tamburrini[55] here challenges the arguments pertaining to fairness and the spirit of sport. Rather than being contrary to the spirit of sport, he contends that doping is compatible with 'today's crudely competitive, highly technified sports world' (p. 203). As for fairness, Tamburrini presents a moral relativistic approach to doping that accounts for the cultural context such as the social and economic factors that lead to doping. Although he does not support the doping bans, Tamburrini further argues that the IOC and WADA are better served with punishments that are neither generalized nor fixed – punishments that are unpredictable because they are determined on a case-by-case basis prevent athletes from making rational calculations about doping based on cost-benefit analysis.

2007–2012

In 2007, concurrent with the growth of the BPSA, a second journal dedicated to scholarly inquiry into sport philosophy was launched: *Sport, Ethics and Philosophy* (SEP). SEP began publishing three issues annually, adding a fourth in 2011. Special issues include topics such as the ethics of sports medicine, ethical issues related to dis/ability and sport, articles exploring phenomenology in a sport context and Olympic ethics. Another special issue comprised a series of articles exploring sport philosophy in relation to ancient Greece and Rome. JPS continued to publish two issues annually, adding a third in 2014, with one regularly dedicating space to special topics, including children and sport, Bernard Suits' influence on the field, sport philosophy in non-English-speaking regions, officiating and aesthetics. The range of contributors and topics explored in JPS continued to widen, with philosophical inquiry into issues related to spectators, violence, religion and performance enhancement to name but a few. Numerous books exploring, in most instances, topics related to sport ethics aimed at both scholarly and general populations continue to extend the sport philosophy literature.

Representative Works

Paul Davis, 'A Consideration of the Normative Status of Skill in the Purposive Sports', *Sport, Ethics and Philosophy* 1 (2007): 22–32.

In the first pages of the inaugural issue of SEP, editor Mike McNamee[56] provides readers with a concise history of the sport philosophy field (including the development of both IAPS and the BPSA), as well as a justification for the addition to the literature of a new academic journal exploring philosophical issues related to sport (widely conceived). In his contribution to the first SEP issue, Davis argues against the normative claim deeming purposive sport contests failures if the most skilled does not win. Davis, prior to defending his claim, outlines several platitudes relevant to skill: that skill does not necessarily translate to competitive success, that non-skill performance-relative qualities (i.e. courage and persistence) exist, that these non-skill performance-relative qualities may contribute to competitive success, and that more skilled performers can respond more skilfully in context-particular situations. The ideological commitment to the normative claim that *the* goal of sport is to reward more skilful performance, Davis continues, emerges in part from a disciplinary obsession with connecting sport to art or with the aesthetic in order for sport to warrant cultural prestige – a disposition Davis rejects outright. However, he contends, a widened view of what one considers skill in a sporting contest – particularly a de-emphasis on discrete exhibitions by gifted individuals – helps reorient the place of skill from *the* goal of sport to, more appropriately, *a* goal of sport.

Heather L. Reid, 'Sport and Moral Education in Plato's Republic', *Journal of the Philosophy of Sport* 34 (2007): 160–175.

Reid presents ideas about sport (*gymanstikê*) formulated by Plato in *The Republic* as a means to enhance the role sport plays in children's moral education. In the article's first section, Reid offers a historical guide to appreciating Plato as the originator of the view expounding that sport holds the potential to build character. Simply stated, Plato believed physical activity and healthy bodies were necessary for guardians of the city to live harmoniously and to prepare for the rigours and demands of public service. Reid then further develops Plato's view of the body's role in training the soul – in particular the cultivation of *arete*. In the paper's final sections, Reid considers how the ideas of Plato can translate to children's moral development through sport. Athletics, Reid argues by way of Plato, cultivates virtues and prepares youth to engage in foundational citizenship behaviours. Furthermore, athletics, Reid contends, prepares young people to engage in the strenuousness required for philosophical contemplation. Finally, Reid considers how athletics connects children with the social environment they are immersed within. The article, one in a series dedicated to exploring issues related to sport and children in a special JPS section, concludes with considerations related to modern sport, including several implications for education.

J.S. Russell, 'Broad Internalism and the Moral Foundations of Sport', in *Ethics in Sport*, 2nd ed., ed., William J. Morgan (Champaign, IL: Human Kinetics, 2007): 51–66. Russell argues in favour of the 'continuity thesis' over the 'separation thesis' in regard to moral reasoning in sport. In many ways the separation thesis, which posits a fundamental separation of moral values between sport and the rest of the world, seems to align with broad internalism. But, Russell argues upon further inspection, the moral principles central to a broad internalist account of sport are not unique to sport but rather reflect the basic moral values beyond the sporting realm. The pursuit of winning provides a clear example of how a value is internal to but not distinct to sport. Other forms of competitive achievement share the same features and are guided by the same moral principles. The continuity thesis argues that sport is a human institution continuous with our basic moral ideals. This is important for recognizing the deep relation between sport and morality and understanding why sport is a morally instructive institution. The continuity thesis explains how addressing important moral issues in sport engages participants in broader moral discourse.

Scott Kretchmar and Tim L. Elcombe, 'In Defense of Competition and Winning: Revising Athletic Tests and Contents', in *Ethics in Sport*, 2nd ed., ed., William J. Morgan (Champaign, IL: Human Kinetics, 2007): 181–194.
Kretchmar and Elcombe shift the discussion of tests and contests from an analytic account of the constitutive features of sport to an anthropological and phenomenological analysis supporting the role of competition in promoting human flourishing. Recognizing that people need challenges for meaning and that sport provides persons with durable challenges, they identify the interpersonal role that contesting plays in determining that meaning. Furthermore, contests, which require social collaboration, provide a more dynamic and complex foundation for meaning than tests do. Contests also expand the types of excellence available to all participants compared to tests alone and thus allow for more meaningful practices. Most importantly for a

defence of competition, contests create more responsible sporting practices that cultivate and expand the virtues. Given the public nature and the structure of contests, Kretchmar and Elcombe argue, an athlete's virtue is on display and additional dramatic opportunities to display virtue are created (such as contesting demands to play to the end). The defence of competition is found in the pragmatic move from testing to contesting that creates the possibility of narrating stories most worth telling.

Drew A. Hyland, 'Paidia and Paideia: The Educational Power of Athletics', *Journal of Intercollegiate Sport* 1 (2008): 66–71.
Several philosophers contributed to the inaugural edition of the *Journal of Intercollegiate Sport*. Robert L. Simon,[57] for instance, presents an overview of philosophical considerations pertaining to collegiate athletics including issues, controversies and misperceptions. Recognizing the role of sport in culture, he argues this worthy pursuit demonstrates that philosophy contributes much to the analysis of conceptual and ethical issues. William J. Morgan's[58] article expresses concern with two questions raised within Simon's analysis. The first asks whether a conception of intercollegiate athletics as morally and educationally defensible exists. The second asks about the defensibility of the reigning conception of intercollegiate sports. While Morgan does not take issue with the former, he does with the latter. Hyland presents a stronger claim than Simon about the relation between athletics and education. It is not a matter of athletics lacking educational potential, but rather that the potential is woefully neglected. In addition to the paradigmatic lessons of sport related to teamwork, winning and losing and health benefits, Hyland presents three additional educational opportunities afforded through sport: experiencing integration in the face of racism, deep commitment to a practice and self-knowledge. Hyland argues the problem is not that athletics undermines academics, but that 'the educational power of *athletics itself* is being undermined' (p. 70). By calling attention to the educational lessons of athletics, faculty liaisons, he contends, serve as one example of how to restore athletics to its proper educational place. Not only do these articles reach an audience extending beyond sport philosophers, they also demonstrate to readers the potential role of philosophy in addressing current issues.

Mike McNamee, 'Whose Prometheus? Transhumanism, Biotechnology and the Moral Topography of Sports Medicine', *Sport, Ethics and Philosophy* 1 (2007): 181–194.
Joining the growing debate about future biotechnologies transforming or even transcending current notions of human existence, McNamee problematizes possible applications of these looming scientific technologies within future sports medicine contexts. McNamee begins the paper by considering the telos of medicine to master or overcome human nature, and the views of medical technologies as either morally neutral or, more darkly, as tools fundamentally to control (either weakly or strongly) human existence – including sport performance contexts. The paper's focus then turns to pro and con arguments related to

transhumanism: pros considered include improved human life, an appreciation of individual autonomy and the opportunity to direct, rather than leave to chance, human evolution; cons emphasize the creation of distinct and divisive human classes, negative implications relative to human invulnerability and immortality, and the elevation of biotechnology experts to roles akin to gods. McNamee then offers two different interpretations of the myth of Prometheus: one whereby Prometheus' hubris expressed by challenging the gods leads to never-ending suffering; the other in which Prometheus' stealing of fire from the gods saves humankind and creates opportunities for flourishing. To best address the issue, McNamee continues, the establishment of a moral topography through dialogue featuring those on both sides of the divide would serve to inform and assist in critical assessments of the future of biotechnology. The article concludes with McNamee siding with those calling for biotechnological caution, highlighting the necessity of limits to human existence as a key reason for taking this position.

Scott Kretchmar, 'Gaming Up Life: Considerations for Game Expansions', *Journal of the Philosophy of Sport* 35 (2008): 142–155.
As part of a special issue celebrating the contributions of Bernard Suits to sport philosophy, Kretchmar's article highlights the centrality of the lusory attitude, most readily available to game players, to living the good life. Kretchmar argues, however, that Suits fails to 'fully appreciate how we "game up life"' (p. 142). Kretchmar's point of difference begins with a wider sense of what counts as a game. Suits considered games to be, metaphorically, like a journey. Kretchmar believes that while this metaphor is valuable, he misses a second metaphor that widens the inclusivity of games – that sometimes games are like exercises whereby the 'difficulty is homogenized into the activity' (p. 147). Kretchmar also takes issue with Suits' exclusion of games of chance, arguing these activities make life more interesting despite a lack of human effort required. In his conclusion, Kretchmar argues for the central need to create interesting artificial problems to overcome the tediousness of everyday life.

Leon Culbertson, 'Genetic Enhancement in the Dark', *Journal of the Philosophy of Sport* 36 (2009): 140–151.
In a special JPS section dedicated to sport and technology, articles by Culbertson and W. Miller Brown[59] focus on the issue of genetic doping. Brown argues in favour of supporting biotechnological manipulation in the future, remaining open to the possibility that such techniques may improve sporting performance and human life more generally. In particular, Brown challenges status quo biases privileging current, dominant ideals. Culbertson, in contrast, argues that genetic manipulation ought to be avoided in a sporting context. He arrives at this conclusion after considering a range of arguments (and types of argument) both in favour of and in opposition to genetic transfer technology. Culbertson and Brown both emphasize the unknown possibilities of genetic manipulation and its potential influence on sport to defend their positions: Culbertson arguing the unknown renders support for genetic transfer technology problematic; Brown

contending a lack of knowledge of how things will change in the future constitutes a reason to continue pushing forward with biotechnology research in relation to sport. Also included in the special issue is William J. Morgan's article[60] arguing for a historicized athletic ideal to inform our normative judgements about performance-enhancing drug bans – particularly in drawing distinctions between uses of performance-enhancing substances (PES) as treatments (acceptable) and uses for enhancement (unacceptable). In a subsequent JPS issue, John Gleaves[61] challenges Morgan's failure to fully strip his argument of essentialist features, but takes Morgan's notion of 'testing relevance' to construct a position on PES regulations.

Nicholas Dixon, 'A Critique of Violent Retaliation in Sport', *Journal of the Philosophy of Sport* 37 (2010): 1–10.
The rationalization of violence in sport remains a vexing issue for philosophers. Dixon wades in to the fray, focusing his attention on justifications offered for the implicit use of violence as a means of retaliation in sport. Dixon identifies other issues related to sporting violence in the opening paragraphs, including the condemnation of intentional attempts to injure by violating rules as well as within the rules, and the existence of sanctioned violence such as mixed martial arts and boxing. In terms of retaliatory violence, Dixon challenges claims presented by Sean McAleer's[62] defence of pitchers intentionally throwing at batters in baseball. Dixon's rejection of McAleer's points focus on examples from baseball as well as ice hockey – two sports where retaliatory violence are embedded in their ethos. McAleer supports acts of retaliation in situations to punish those engaged in unethical acts, as a form of deterrent for future wrongs, and to enhance team unity (assuming retaliatory acts do not cause great harm). In contrast, Dixon uses 'reality checks' from beyond sport to identify retaliatory violence as unacceptable, unfair, unnecessary and even barbaric. Dixon's conclusion emphasizes the needs to challenge an attitude of sporting exceptionalism that renders sport immune from moral scrutiny applied to other social contexts.

Takayuki Hata and Masami Sekine, 'Philosophy of Sport and Physical Education in Japan: Its History, Characteristics and Prospects', *Journal of the Philosophy of Sport* 37 (2010): 215–224.
Hata and Sekine provide an overview of sport philosophy in Japan as part of a JPS special issue dedicated to examining the field in non-English-speaking regions. In addition to providing an overview of the history of sport and physical education in Japanese culture, Hata and Sekine also highlight the annual activities of the Japan Society for the Philosophy of Sport and Physical Education, formed in 1978. Themes emphasized in the Japanese sport philosophy literature include theories of the body and consciousness, doping, gender and ethical issues related to the Olympic Games. Other contributors to the JPS special issue include Gunnar Breivik (Nordic countries), Ivo van Hilvoorde, Jan Vorstenbosch and Ignaas Devisch (Belgium and the Netherlands), Leo Hsu (Chinese-speaking regions), Ivo Jirásek and Peter Hopsicker (Slavonic countries), Claudia Pawlenka (Germany), and Cesar R. Torres and Daniel G. Campos (Latin America).

Jesús Ilundáin-Agurruza and Michael W. Austin, eds., *Cycling-Philosophy For Everyone: A Philosophical Tour De Force* (Malden, MA: Wiley-Blackwell, 2010).
In 2000, Open Court launched a series titled the Popular Culture and Philosophy Series, with the aim of making high-quality philosophy accessible to the general reader through connections with mainstream popular culture. Starting with two television series topics, *Seinfeld and Philosophy* and *The Simpsons and Philosophy*, the series soon extended to other topics, including sport. Since that time, Open Court has published works on *Baseball and Philosophy* (2004), *The Red Sox and Philosophy* (2010) and *Soccer and Philosophy* (2010). Other publishers followed suit. Blackwell-Wiley published *Philosophy For Everyone* volumes including Ilundáin-Agurruza and Austin's edited volume on cycling (2010) as well as works exploring running (2007), climbing (2010) and sailing (2012). Additionally, the University Press of Kentucky published *Football and Philosophy* (2008), *Basketball and Philosophy* (2008), *Golf and Philosophy* (2010), *Tennis and Philosophy* (2010) and most recently *The Olympics and Philosophy* (2012).

Gunnar Breivik, 'Dangerous Play with the Elements: Towards a Phenomenology of Risk Sports', *Sport, Ethics and Philosophy* 5 (2011): 314–330.
Breivik, in this special SEP issue featuring phenomenological studies of sport, explores sporting uses of the body in interaction with the natural features of the world. In particular, Breivik's interest lies with considering how a phenomenological account of humans engaging in potentially dangerous outdoor physical activities helps us better understand participants' being-in-the-world through sport in nature as well as sport more widely. Appropriating the work of Martin Heidegger, Maurice Merleau-Ponty and Samuel Todes, Breivik's essay first introduces key concepts from continental phenomenological approaches – focusing on the methodological middle ground phenomenology carves between objective and subjective views. Breivik concludes the paper by offering quick phenomenological accounts of being-in-specific-worlds related to dangerous, nature-based sports, including rock climbing, skydiving and white-water kayaking.

Graham McFee, 'Fairness, Epistemology, and Rules: A Prolegomenon to a Philosophy of Officiating?', *Journal of the Philosophy of Sport* 38 (2011): 229–253.
Included with other papers in a special JPS section dedicated to philosophical issues related to officiating, McFee considers whether a 'philosophy of officiating' is conceivable. To begin, McFee challenges formalistic accounts that idealize sporting rules. He then lends support to J.S. Russell's[63] use of a Dworkian-inspired principled approach to discount rule formalism as capable of addressing officiating challenges. McFee, however, parts ways with Russell's implicit conclusion that a general philosophy of officiating based on abstract principles was possible. Instead, McFee contends that principled accounts used to adjudicate in sport must be particularized and contextualized. McFee's paper extends content published in two books: *Sport, Rules and Values* (2004) and *Ethics, Knowledge and Truth in Sports Research* (2010).[64] Other contributors to the sport officiating symposium include Mitch Berman, Chad Carlson and John Gleaves, Mark Hamilton (guest editor) and Russell.

Stephen Mumford, 'Emotions and Aesthetics: An Inevitable Trade-off?', *Journal of the Philosophy of Sport* 39 (2012): 267–279.

Using a distinction drawn by Nicholas Dixon[65] between partisan and purist spectators, Mumford considers the interplay and conflict arising between emotional connections to and appreciation for the aesthetics of sport. Mumford first explores the trade-off thesis: how partisan fans, interested solely in the outcome, miss the beauty of sport available to puritans; conversely, puritans trade the emotional depth afforded to partisans by distancing themselves to objectively appreciate a game's aesthetic aspects. Yet Mumford also highlights ways in which emotions can enhance the aesthetic qualities of sport, and how recognition of beauty can stir the emotional connection one establishes with a game. Consequently, Mumford promotes a complex, mixed view whereby emotions and aesthetics sometimes enhance and detract from one another. The article picks up arguments developed in Mumford's book *Watching Sport: Aesthetics, Ethics and Emotion* (2011)[66] and is part of a special JPS issue dedicated to aesthetics and sport with contributions by Victor Andrade de Melo, Andrew Edgar, Tim L. Elcombe, Lev Kreft, Teresa Lacerda (guest editor), Heather L. Reid and Cesar R. Torres.

Jim Parry, 'The Youth Olympic Games – Some Ethical Issues', *Sport, Ethics and Philosophy* 6 (2012): 138–154.

As part of a collection of papers in a special SEP issue exploring philosophical matters related to the Olympics, Parry's entry focuses on ethical challenges facing the newly formed Youth Olympic Games (YOG). Parry begins the paper by overviewing the development and aims of the first YOG held in Singapore in 2010 for athletes aged 14 to 18. Following his concise historical reconstruction, Parry considers some ethical issues arising from the formulation of the YOG, including the selection of sports and their appropriateness for youth participants (i.e. boxing), the inclusiveness of the activities selected, the degree of equality of opportunity afforded by the YOG programme, the fairness of the age groupings, and concerns related to the Games' competitive design and nationalistic bent. Parry examines several examples of ethical dilemmas emerging from the inaugural YOG in Singapore, including alleged age falsification by players from Bolivia's gold medal football team and the forfeit by an Iranian participant scheduled to wrestle against an Israeli competitor due to a suspect injury claim. In the article, Parry also highlights innovations and changes employed at the 2010 YOG in contrast to the traditional Olympic Games competitive programme.

Warren P. Fraleigh, 'IAPS – Past to Future', *Journal of the Philosophy of Sport* 39 (2012): 1–10.

Fraleigh, one of the founders of IAPS and most important contributors to the development of sport philosophy, presents an oral history of the field's evolution over the past 40 years. Fraleigh's essay, first delivered at the 2011 IAPS conference, also offers suggestions for sport philosophy's future, particularly in relation to the IAPS organization. Throughout the article Fraleigh presents personal anecdotes of influential PSSS/IAPS members and original works of poetry written to celebrate sport and the moving body.

Notes

1   William J. Morgan, *Why Sports Morally Matter* (London: Routledge, 2006).
2   Bernard Suits, *The Grasshopper: Games, Life, and Utopia* (Toronto: University of Toronto Press, 1978).
3   Warren P. Fraleigh, *Right Actions in Sports: Ethics for Contestants* (Champaign, IL: Human Kinetics, 1984).
4   Craig K. Lehman, 'Can Cheaters Play the Game?', *Journal of the Philosophy of Sport* 8 (1981): 41–6.
5   James W. Keating, 'Sportsmanship as a Moral Category', *Ethics* 75 (1964): 25–35.
6   Randolph Feezell, 'Sportsmanship', *Journal of the Philosophy of Sport* 12 (1986): 1–13.
7   Robert L. Simon, 'Good Competition and Drug-Enhanced Performance', *Journal of the Philosophy of Sport* 11 (1984): 6–13.
8   David Best, 'The Aesthetic in Sport', *The British Journal of Aesthetics* 14 (1974): 197–213.
9   David Best, *Philosophy and Human Movement* (London: Allen & Unwin, 1978).
10 David Best, 'Sport Is Not Art', *Journal of the Philosophy of Sport* 12 (1985): 25–40.
11 Peter Arnold, 'Aesthetic Aspects of Being in Sport: The Performer's Perspective in Contrast to That of the Spectator', *Journal of the Philosophy of Sport* 12 (1985): 1–7.
12 Jan M. Boxill, 'Beauty, Sport, and Gender', *Journal of the Philosophy of Sport* 11 (1984): 36–47.
13 Christopher Cordner, 'Differences Between Sport and Art', *Journal of the Philosophy of Sport* 15 (1988): 31–47.
14 Joseph Kupfer, 'Commentary on Jan Boxill's "Beauty, Sport, and Gender"', *Journal of the Philosophy of Sport* 11 (1984): 48–51.
15 Terence J. Roberts, 'Sport, Art, and Particularity: The Best Equivocation', *Journal of the Philosophy of Sport* 13 (1986): 49–63.
16 Joy T. DeSensi, 'PSSS Bibliography for Sport Philosophy – An Update', *Journal of the Philosophy of Sport* 12 (1985): 101–7; and idem., 'PSSS Bibliography of Sport Philosophy – Update II', *Journal of the Philosophy of Sport* 13 (1986): 109–17.
17 Joy T. DeSensi, 'PSSS Bibliography of the Philosophy of Sport – 1991', *Journal of the Philosophy of Sport* 18 (1991): 97.
18 Klaus V. Meier, 'A Ten Year Index to the Journal of the Philosophy of Sport', *Journal of the Philosophy of Sport* 10 (1983): 119–25; and idem., 'A Twenty Year Retrospective Index for the Journal of the Philosophy of Sport', *Journal of the Philosophy of Sport* 20 (1993): 125–45.
19 Bernard Suits, 'Tricky Triad: Games, Play, and Sport', *Journal of the Philosophy of Sport* 15 (1988): 1–9.
20 Simon, 'Good Competition and Drug-Enhanced Performance'.
21 W. Miller Brown, 'Paternalism, Drugs, and the Nature of Sports', *Journal of the Philosophy of Sport* 11 (1984): 14–22.
22 Michael Lavin, 'Sports and Drugs: Are the Current Bans Justified?', *Journal of the Philosophy of Sport* 14 (1987): 34–43.
23 Angela J. Schneider and Robert R. Butcher, 'Why Olympic Athletes Should Avoid the Use and Seek the Elimination of Performance-Enhancing Substances and Practices From the Olympic Games', *Journal of the Philosophy of Sport* 20 (1993): 64–81.
24 Michael D. Burke, 'Drugs in Sport: Have They Practiced Too Hard? A Response to Schneider and Butcher', *Journal of the Philosophy of Sport* 24 (1997): 47–66.
25 Claudio M. Tamburrini, 'Are Doping Sanctions Justified? A Moral Relativistic View', *Sport in Society* 9 (2006): 199–211.
26 Boxill, 'Beauty, Sport, and Gender'; and idem, 'Football and Feminism', *Journal of the Philosophy of Sport* 33 (2006): 115–24.
27 Betsy C. Postow, 'Sport, Art, and Gender', *Journal of the Philosophy of Sport* 11 (1984): 52–5.

28 Joy T. DeSensi, 'Feminism in the Wake of Philosophy', *Journal of the Philosophy of Sport* 19 (1992): 79–93.

29 Robert L. Simon, 'Gender Equity and Inequity in Athletics', *Journal of the Philosophy of Sport* 20 (1993): 6–22.

30 Leslie P. Francis, 'Title IX: Equality for Women's Sports?', *Journal of the Philosophy of Sport* 20 (1993): 32–47.

31 Melina Constantine Bell, 'Strength in Muscle and Beauty in Integrity: Building a Body for Her', *Journal of the Philosophy of Sport* 35 (2008): 43–62.

32 Nicholas Dixon, 'On Sportsmanship and "Running Up the Score"', *Journal of the Philosophy of Sport* 19 (1992), 1–13; and Feezell, 'Sportsmanship'.

33 Dixon, 'On Sportsmanship and "Running Up the Score"', 3.

34 Nicholas Dixon, 'Why Losing By a Wide Margin is Not in Itself a Disgrace: Response to Hardman, Fox, McLaughlin and Zimmerman', *Journal of the Philosophy of Sport* 25 (1998): 61–70.

35 Schneider and Butcher, 'Why Olympic Athletes Should Avoid the Use and Seek the Elimination of Performance-Enhancing Substances and Practices From the Olympic Games', 64–81.

36 Ibid.

37 William J. Morgan, Klaus V. Meier and Angela J. Schneider, eds., *Ethics in Sport* (Champaign, IL: Human Kinetics, 2001).

38 Jan M. Boxill, *Sport Ethics: An Anthology* (Hoboken, NJ: Wiley-Blackwell, 2002).

39 Claudio M. Tamburrini and Torbjörn Tännsjö, eds., *Genetic Technology and Sport: Ethical Questions* (London: Routledge, 2005).

40 Alun Hardman and Carwyn Jones, eds., *The Ethics of Sports Coaching* (London: Routledge, 2011).

41 Scott Kretchmar, 'In Defense of Winning', in *Sports Ethics: An Anthology*, ed., Jan Boxill (Malden, MA: Blackwell, 2002): 130–5.

42 Scott Kretchmar and Tim L. Elcombe, 'In Defense of Competition and Winning: Revising Athletic Tests and Contents', in *Ethics in Sport*, 2nd ed., ed., William J. Morgan (Champaign, IL: Human Kinetics, 2007): 181–94.

43 Nicholas Dixon, 'On Winning and Athletic Superiority', *Journal of the Philosophy of Sport* 26 (1999): 10–26.

44 Russell W. Gough, 'Reaching First Base With a "Science" of Moral Development in Sport: Problems With Scientific Objectivity and Reductivism', *Journal of the Philosophy of Sport* 22 (1995): 11–25.

45 M. Andrew Holowchak, 'Can Character Be Measured? A Reply to Stoll's Reply to Gough', *Journal of the Philosophy of Sport* 28 (2001): 103–6.

46 Douglas Hochstetler and Tim L. Elcombe, 'A Summary of Selected Research In North America & Western Europe (2003–2004)', *International Journal of Physical Education* 41 (2004): 144–59; Peter Hopsicker and Ivo Jirásek, 'Selected Philosophy of Sport/Movement Culture Texts in English and Slavonic (2005–2006)', *International Journal of Physical Education* 43 (2006): 140–55; Peter Hopsicker and Ivo Jirásek, 'Selected Philosophy of Sport/Movement Culture Texts in English and Slavonic (2007–2008)', *International Journal of Physical Education* 45 (2008): 162–76; Peter Hopsicker and Emanuel Hurych, 'Selected Philosophy of Sport/Movement Culture Texts in English and Slavonic (2009–2010)', *International Journal of Physical Education* 47 (2010): 2–16; and Emanuel Hurych and Jim Parry, 'A Review of Selected Philosophy of Sports Texts in English and Slavonic (2011–2012)', *International Journal of Physical Education* 49 (2012): 2–16.

47 J.S. Russell, 'The Concept of a Call in Baseball', *Journal of the Philosophy of Sport* 27 (1997): 21–37 and idem, 'Are Rules All An Umpire Has to Work With?', *Journal of the Philosophy of Sport* 26 (1999): 27–49.

48   Robert L. Simon, 'Internalism and Internal Values in Sport', *Journal of the Philosophy of Sport* 27 (2000): 1–16.

49   Ibid.

50   Nicholas Dixon, 'Canadian Figure Skaters, French Judges, and Realism in Sport', *Journal of the Philosophy of Sport* 30 (2003): 103–16

51   Leslie P. Francis, 'Competitive Sorts, Disability, and Problems of Justice in Sport', *Journal of the Philosophy of Sport* 32 (2005): 127–32.

52   Stanislav Pinter, Tjasa Filipcic, Ales Solar and Maja Smrdu, 'Integrating Children With Physical Impairments Into Sports Activities: A "Golden Sun for All Children?" *Journal of the Philosophy of Sport* 32 (2005): 147–54.

53   Sarah Teetzel, 'On Transgendered Athletes, Fairness and Doping: An International Challenge', *Sport in Society* 9 (2006): 227–51.

54   William J. Morgan, 'Fair is fair, or is it?: A Moral Consideration of the Doping Wars in American Sport', *Sport in Society* 9 (2006): 177–98.

55   Claudio M. Tamburrini, 'What's Wrong with Doping?', in *Values in Sport – Elitism, Nationalism, Gender, Equality and the Scientific Manufacture of Winners,* eds. Claudio M. Tamburrini and Torbjörn Tännsjö (London and New York: E & FN Spon, 2000): 200–16.

56   Mike McNamee, 'Sport, Ethics and Philosophy; Context, History, Prospects,' *Sport, Ethics and Philosophy* 1 (2007): 1–6.

57   Robert L. Simon, 'Does Athletics Undermine Academics? Examining Some Issues', *Journal of Intercollegiate Sport* 1 (2008): 40–58.

58   William J. Morgan, 'Markets and Intercollegiate Sports: An Unholy Alliance?', *Journal of Intercollegiate Sport* 1 (2008): 59–65.

59   W. Miller Brown, 'The Chase for Perfection', *Journal of the Philosophy of Sport* 36 (2009): 127–39.

60   William J. Morgan, 'Athletic Perfection, Performance-Enhancing Drugs, and the Treatment-Enhancement Distinction', *Journal of the Philosophy of Sport* 36 (2009): 162–81.

61   John Gleaves, 'A New Conceptual Gloss that Still Lacks Luster: Critiquing Morgan's Treatment-Enhancement Distinction', *Journal of the Philosophy of Sport* 38 (2011): 103–12.

62   Sean McAleer, 'The Ethics of Pitcher Retaliation in Baseball', *Journal of the Philosophy of Sport* 36 (2009): 50–65.

63   Russell, 'The Concept of a Call in Baseball'; and idem, 'Are Rules All An Umpire Has to Work With?'

64   Graham McFee, *Sport, Rules and Values* (London: Routledge, 2004); and idem, *Ethics, Knowledge and Truth in Sports Research: An Epistemology of Sport* (London: Routledge, 2010).

65   Nicholas Dixon, 'The Ethics of Supporting Sports Teams', *Journal of Applied Philosophy* 18 (2001): 149–58.

66   Stephen Mumford, *Watching Sport: Aesthetics, Ethics and Emotion* (London: Routledge, 2011).

Index